The Psychology of Schizophrenia

The Psychology of Schizophrenia

John Cutting MD MPhil MRCP MRCPsych
Consultant Psychiatrist, Bethlem
and Maudsley Hospitals, London

CHURCHILL LIVINGSTONE
EDINBURGH LONDON MELBOURNE AND NEW YORK 1985

CHURCHILL LIVINGSTONE
Medical Division of Longman Group Limited

Distributed in the United States of America by Churchill Livingstone Inc., 1560 Broadway, New York, N.Y. 10036, and by associated companies, branches and representatives throughout the world.

First published 1985

ISBN 0 443 026637

British Library Cataloging in Publication Data

Cutting, John C.
The psychology of schizophrenia.
1. Schizophrenia
I. Title
616.89′82 RC514

Library of Congress Cataloguing in Publication Data

Cutting, John C.
The psychology of schizophrenia.

Bibliography: p.
Includes index.
1. Schizophrenia. 2. Brain — Localization of functions. 3. Brain — Diseases. I. Title. [DNLM: 1. Schizophrenia. 2. Schizophrenic Psychology. WM 203 C991p]
RC514.C88 1984 616.89′82 84–15578

Printed in Great Britain at The Pitman Press, Bath

Preface

When I first read Eugen Bleuler's account of schizophrenia I was enthralled. He had brought together under one heading a host of previously unconnected facts and theories. He had no explanation for the origin of the condition, but his description of it left me in no doubt that it existed, and that it had the characteristics which he laid down. This was in my first few months as a psychiatrist. After I had seen a number of 'schizophrenics', however, I began to wonder whether he was right. Few of the 'schizophrenics' whom I saw had any of Bleuler's four fundamental symptoms — loosening of associations, disturbance of affect, autism or ambivalence. They merely had unusual beliefs or heard voices. Other clinical and psychological accounts which I then read initially seemed to offer a truer picture, but it was soon apparent that they also were inaccurate, for a different reason. They were too general, and their authors seemed unaware that, if true, a large part of the population, if not the majority, would be schizophrenic.

This book arose out of my conviction that Bleuler was right to search for a specific and unifying psychological dysfunction, but wrong in his choice of the precise model. He was wrong, moreover, not through poor judgement, but because he did not have available our present considerable knowledge about the effect of localised brain dysfunction on mental functions. If he had known what we now know about neuropsychology, I think his model would have been very different.

The present book is my attempt to link what is known about the psychology of schizophrenia with what is known about the psychology of localised brain disease. In doing so, I hope to convince the reader that many otherwise unaccountable facts about schizophrenia become clearer.

I am deeply grateful to a number of teachers, friends and colleagues for the inspiration to write the book, and for their criticisms of the first draft.

From Professor Michael Shepherd I learned most about the nature of psychosis, to Professor Alwyn Lishman I owe my knowledge of neuropsychiatry, and Dr Roger Lindsay taught me all I know about psychology. I am particularly grateful to the following psychiatrists and psychologists who read parts of the first draft: Professor Ian Brockington, Professor Robert Cawley, Ms Susan Gessler, Dr Robin Jacoby, Dr Channi Kumar, Dr Roger

Lindsay, Professor Alwyn Lishman, Dr Robin Murray, Dr Rachel Rosser, Dr Andrew Smith, Dr Eric Taylor, Dr Brian Toone, Dr Tony Wainwright, Dr Fraser Watts, Dr John Weinman and Dr Maria Wyke.

I am particularly grateful to Dr Ralph Emery who translated an article by Schmidt reviewing German psychiatric opinion on schizophrenia in the 1920s and 1930s.

Finally, I should like to thank Anne Charlish for her advice and support during the preparation of the manuscript.

London 1985 J. C.

Contents

1

Notions of insanity before 1900

INTRODUCTION

The term schizophrenia was first coined in 1908 by Bleuler. It was based on the concept of dementia praecox, introduced by Kraepelin in 1896. This in its turn owed much to Kahlbaum's description of catatonia in 1874 and Hecker's account of hebephrenia in 1871. A discussion of the psychology of schizophrenia, therefore, should strictly begin with the year 1908, and at the very earliest the 1870s.

I propose, however, to devote this chapter to psychological notions of insanity before this period in order to trace the ideas which Kraepelin and Bleuler drew upon. Some writers on schizophrenia believe that the condition has only existed since the mid-19th century. Hare (1983), for example, attributes its emergence to a mutant virus which swept across Europe at this time. If Hare is right the present chapter is largely irrelevant to the theme of the book. Most commentators, however, are uncommitted on this issue or take the view that schizophrenia has always existed under different names and with different clinical pictures appropriate to contemporary social conditions. If this latter opinion is correct, a knowledge of earlier classifications and theories of insanity is clearly relevant.

ANCIENT TIMES

One of the earliest references to insanity is the biblical record of King Saul in the First Book of Samuel. He reigned from 1020 to 1000 B.C. and his condition is described therein as follows:

> 'But the Spirit of the Lord departed from Saul and an evil spirit of the Lord troubled him . . . Then Saul fell straightway all along on the earth . . . and there was no strength in him.

He believed 'that all of you have conspired against me . . . and there is none of you that is sorry for me.'

Nebuchadnezzar, King of Babylon from 605–562 B.C., is considered to have suffered from lycanthropy—looking and behaving like a wild animal. His condition is mentioned in the Bible in the Book of Daniel:

> And he was driven from men and did eat grass as oxen and his body was wet with the dew of heaven till his hairs were grown like eagles' feathers and his nails like birds' claws.

By 500 B.C., judging from the Talmud, which contains oral traditions of law stretching back to this period, quite sophisticated notions of mental disorder were in existence. An objective criterion was the occurrence of impulsive, uncontrolled and unreasonable behaviour. It was appreciated that one could not define mental disorder in purely behavioural terms—wandering about alone at night, spending the night in a cemetery, tearing one's garments—because people might do the same things for entirely sound reasons. They might spend the night in a cemetery to practise magic or tear their garments to show contempt for material things.

GREEK AND ROMAN PERIOD

The Greeks held sophisticated notions of mental disorder from at least the time of the historian Herodotus (484–425 B.C.). He gave a vivid account of the madness of Cleomenes, King of Sparta in 500 B.C. Cleomenes had bribed the priestess at Delphi to make a statement unfavourable to his rival. He then panicked, however, and, fearing a public outcry, fled to another country. He was later allowed to return, but by that time he was 'mentally deranged'. He began striking any Spartan whom he met and his relatives put him in the stocks to restrain him. He then managed to persuade an attendant to give him a knife, whereupon he gashed open his abdomen and died. What is interesting is the range of explanations for Cleomenes' madness which Herodotus discusses. Some saw it as a god-sent punishment for corrupting the Delphic priestess. Some thought that the King had never been of sound mind, and had always verged on madness. Some attributed the derangement to his heavy drinking of wine undiluted with water. Herodotus himself regarded it as a 'judgement on him for wronging' his rival. These possible explanations—supernatural, constitutional, organic and moral—have not changed much to this day.

Supernatural explanations, even then, were more common amongst the uneducated. Greek physicians, beginning with Hippocrates (460–377 B.C.), had rejected them in favour of physiological explanations. Mental abnormality was for them a disease of the brain, caused, as was bodily disease, by an excess of one of the four humours—blood, phlegm, yellow bile and black bile. Melancholia was a particular form of madness caused by an excess of black bile. Although Hippocrates rejected supernatural forces as a cause of madness, he accepted that they might influence its content:

> If the patient imitate a goat, if he roar, or suffer convulsions in the right side, they say that the Mother of the Gods is to blame. If he utter a piercing and loud cry, they liken him to a horse and blame Poseidon. If he foam at the mouth and kick, Ares has the blame.
>
> (Hippocrates, quoted by Rosen, 1968)

The criterion of madness was, as in the Talmud, some form of inexplicable action or belief. Hippocrates recognised three forms—phrenitis (the consequence of febrile illness), mania and melancholia.

Socrates (470–399 B.C.) regarded madness as the name that most men:

> . . . give to errors in matters of common knowledge. For instance, if a man imagines himself to be so strong as to try to lift houses or to perform any other feat that everybody knows to be impossible they say he's mad. They don't think a slight error implies madness, but just as they call strong desire love, so they name a great delusion madness.
>
> (Socrates, quoted by Rosen, 1968)

Plato reintroduced a mystical component. He regarded the soul as composed of a divine rational part and a more earthly irrational part. The rational soul resided in the brain while the irrational was distributed among various bodily organs. Madness could result, first, from a severing of the union of the irrational with the rational soul, the precise form depending on which humour was affected. A second form was divine, revelatory madness, where the rational soul itself was infected by one of the Gods.

Aristotle had a profound influence on philosophy until the time of Descartes. He believed that sensation was the process by which the form of an object minus its matter was taken from the external world into the heart, where the soul was situated. Here a 'common sense' worked upon sensations to turn them into images. These images then produced movements of the soul—emotions. The whole process was believed to be physiological, with the brain playing only a minor role. Reason itself was different from all this, and was independent of man. Madness was, therefore, invariably a physical or physiological disorder, as the psychological component of the mind was immune to disruption.

By Roman times opinions on the classification, phenomena, cause and treatment of madness had become more settled.

Asclepiades, an Epicurean philosopher and physician in the 1st century B.C., appreciated that the term insanity was too popular for use by professionals. He differentiated delirium from mental disease proper and distinguished acute and chronic forms of the latter. Celsus (c. 20 B.C.–40 A.D.) recognised six types of insanity. The first was phrenitis, a term used by most authorities for the delirium which accompanied febrile illness. The second was melancholia. The third was a form of delirium caused by fear. (Whitwell, 1936, suggested that this was equivalent to the modern term hysteria.) The fourth was called 'lethargus', its main feature being stupor, and the fifth was epilepsy. The sixth type corresponds most closely to schizophrenia. It had two subtypes: in one, the mind was deceived by false images but the intellect was intact; in the other, the intellect itself was disturbed. Aretaeus (30–90 A.D.) distinguished mania, melancholia, senile disorders and a type of insanity in which the patient appeared:

> stupid, absent, musing, with a stupefaction of the senses of reason and other faculties of the mind.
>
> (Aretaeus, quoted by Rosen, 1968)

Zilboorg (1941), in his *History of Medical Psychology* considered that Aretaeus's fourth type corresponded to schizophrenia.

False beliefs and false perceptions were distinguished at this time. Soranus (c. 50–100 A.D.) gave examples of the former—refusal to urinate for fear of causing a new deluge and various types of mistaken identity (sparrow, cock, earthen vessel, brick, god, orator, a piece of straw and a grain of mustard). Asclepiades defined false perceptions as a state of mind in which a subject 'hears or feels things although there is nothing near to hear or feel'.

Concerning the cause of insanity there was less agreement. Asclepiades regarded all forms of 'mental disease proper' as due to emotional disturbance. Cicero (106–43 B.C.), the Stoic philosopher, also held this view. He believed that mental disorder was a disease of the mind and that melancholia was ill-named because *physical* agents, such as black bile, could not be direct causes of abnormal *mental* phenomena. He identified the cause in strong emotions—anger, fear, pain—but not milder ones such as envy or pity. Aretaeus, however, believed that insanity was 'an impairment of reason resulting from bodily disease or indisposition', and could be caused by organic insults (head injury, exposure to strong sunlight, excessive consumption of wine, digestive ailments), temperamental differences or psychological factors (superstition, too much love of philosophy, search for glory, avarice). Galen (130–200 A.D.), famous as the chronicler of Greco-Roman medicine, believed that most forms of insanity had a physical cause in the brain.

Treatment varied according to the physician's theoretical notions. Celsus recommended vigorous psychological regimes—fright, oscillation and total darkness. Soranus practised milder therapies, for example gradual mental exercises. Galen advocated pharmacological treatments to redress the imbalance of humours.

MIDDLE AGES

How the concept of insanity and the insane themselves fared from the decline of the Roman Empire until the end of the 16th century is disputed by historians. Zilboorg (1941) paints a grim picture of a world gripped by demonology, reaching a climax with the publication in 1489 of the *Malleus Maleficarum* (The Hammer of the Witches). This manual of how to identify and prosecute witches was the work of Kraemer and Sprenger, the chief inquisitors for Germany at the time. According to Zilboorg the insane bore the brunt of its venom, and hundreds of thousands were tortured and killed. According to Galdston (1967), Mora (1967) and Rosen (1968), it was not the insane who were burnt but neurotics and social misfits. The attitude towards the insane was more complex.

It seems that for most of the Middle Ages they were largely integrated into common life. A few asylums were set up, in London (Bedlam), Jerusalem and some Arab cities. Local authorities were obliged at least to clothe them and, in the case of strangers, to pay for the return to their native town. They may have been the butt of vicious jokes and were often whipped, but their condition was probably not regarded as extraordinary. Mora claims that the mad served some social or at least symbolic function during the late medieval period. The Narrenschiff (ship of fools), the tradition of letting mad people wander down the rivers of Central Europe in boats, he argues, was a living example of human frailty and the biblical fall of man. According to Kroll & Bachrach (1982) people at that time who reported voices would not have been regarded as mentally ill. The 'folk criteria' for insanity at that time, according to these authors, were various types of irrational behaviour, not odd beliefs or the report of strange experiences.

Theories about insanity suffered the same fate as any other intellectual inquiry started by the Greeks. They were stultified or monopolised by the Church for its own purpose. Certainly, no new conceptual framework of madness was ever elaborated. Arab medicine and institutions stand out as the most sophisticated system of thought and practice. Avicenna (980–1037) was the most eminent physician. His list of mental disorders is longer than the Greeks', running to 12 items—phrenitis, lethargus, delirium, amentia, disorders of memory, disorders of imagination, mania, melancholia, lycanthropy, the insane form of love, incubus (nightmare) and 'pathic disorder' (the forerunner of psychopathy).

By the end of this period the humanists began to question the dogma and brutal practices of the witch-hunters. Paracelsus (1493–1541) took an aggressive stand in practice, but his theories were obscure even by medieval standards. Johan Weyer (1515–1588) is regarded by some as the father of psychiatry. Not only did he formulate the clearest indictment of witch-hunting but he tried to free the practice of dealing with the insane from philosophy as well as theology. He was a compassionate man, a skilled clinician and, unusual for that period, paid considerable attention to individual characteristics of his patients and less to their position in the world order.

The formulation of madness during the Renaissance still derived from Aristotle's beliefs. The only change was the greater role given to the brain. Imagination resided in the cerebral ventricles; emotion, the effect of imagination on the soul, remained in the heart. Imagination was the crucial factor in the cause of insanity. The spirits which it set in motion interacted with the humours to affect the soul within the heart.

SEVENTEENTH CENTURY

The 17th century saw startling changes in virtually every field of knowledge. This was particularly true of philosophy and medicine, the two disciplines closest to the field of mental disorder at the time. Contemporary philosophers—Descartes, Spinoza, Leibniz—took little direct interest in insanity. But Descartes, the greatest of the three, had a profound influence on its subsequent theoretical development. His dualism of mind and matter, and his method of critically doubting everything but his own existence, were his main contributions. In medicine, basic knowledge of anatomy and physiology advanced considerably. However, a physician such as Thomas Willis, despite making brilliant observations on cerebral anatomy, remained naive, superstitious and brutal in his opinions on mental ailments. The prevailing view amongst the growing bourgeoisie was that madness was shameful, that reason should prevail and that some attempt should be made to 'open madness to the gentle constraint of reason' (Foucault 1965). Mental disorder became the province of the minor philosopher and lawmaker, and this led to what the German psychiatric historian Doerner has called the 'sequestration of unreason'. In practice this meant the establishment of institutions—the private madhouse and workhouse in Britain, hôpital général in France, and prison or penitentiary in Germany. The insane were not the only ones in these institutions, but were part of a motley collection of:

> beggars, vagabonds, those without property, criminals, political gadflies, heretics, prostitutes, libertines, syphilitics, alcoholics, idiots, eccentrics, rejected wives, deflowered daughters and spendthrift sons.
>
> (Doerner 1981)

The insane were treated like beasts because they were regarded as beasts:

> because insanity was conceived as a derangement of those very faculties which were widely assumed to be unique to man.
>
> (Bynum 1981)

The general public paid money to visit them as one now visits the zoo.

Some philosophers attempted an analysis of their unreason. Locke, for example, suggested that:

> mad men join ideas together wrongly and so make wrong propositions, but argue rightly from these, whereas idiots make few or no propositions and argue and reason scarce at all.
>
> (Locke, 1690)

EIGHTEENTH CENTURY

General trends

In the 18th century there was the beginning of a more enlightened approach to insanity. Developments in Britain, France and Germany moved at different speeds but the same trends and debates can be identified throughout Europe and in America. Prominent philosophers, such as Kant, took a direct interest in the issue. Social theorists, like Rousseau, contributed to the discussion, and physicians began to specialise in the care of the insane. The number of institutions continued to grow, and this brought the matter increasingly to the attention of local and state authorities. Laws were needed to establish who should control and finance them. There were three issues under debate. First, to what extent should the insane be restrained in custody? Secondly, what degree of moral responsibility should be attributed to the insane? Thirdly, was insanity a disorder of the mind or a disease of the body?

If one can identify a general pattern, it is in the form of a change from the rationalist to the moral approach. Madness was no longer 'unreason' but a failure to control the passions. These changes were particularly evident towards the end of the century.

Britain

In Britain the main protagonists in these debates were Monro and Battie. John Monro, physician at Bedlam, was the spokesman for the laissez-faire, traditional school. In 1758 he wrote:

> Madness is a distemper of such nature that very little of real use can be said concerning it; the immediate causes will for ever disappoint our search, and the care of that disorder depends on management as much as medicine.
>
> (Monro 1758)

When pressed to state his theoretical orientation he admitted to being a rationalist, with the belief that insanity stemmed from 'vitiated judgement'.

William Battie was, by contrast, a different man, energetic and with broad interests. He was an eminent physician in physical as well as mental illness. As a governor of Bedlam he was appalled at the abuses he witnessed and so set up his own hospital for the insane. His *Treatise on Madness*, also written in 1758, defined it as:

> deluded imagination . . . where man is unalterably persuaded of the existence or of the appearance of any thing which does not exist or does not actually appear to him and who behaves according to such erroneous persuasion . . . madness or false perception being then a praeternatural state or disorder of sensation.
>
> (Battie 1758)

In contrast to Monro and the rationalist tradition, Battie regarded madness not as a disorder of reason but of sensation, perception and imagination. He distinguished 'original madness . . . internal disorder of the nervous substance, without assignable cause' from 'consequential madness' (secondary insanity, with cure if the determining cause was promptly removed). The cause of the latter could be 'mechanical' (e.g. opium, venereal disease) or 'moral' (e.g. indolence, gluttony). If these were allowed to remain active the 'consequential' form became 'original'. He insisted that some forms of madness could be 'cured' and that moral causes could be tackled by means of moral therapy.

A theoretical basis for this was developed by John Brown, a pupil of the Scottish physician William Cullen. Cullen had formulated a neurophysiological theory of nervous energy; Brown transformed this into a psychological theory of total vital energy, the extent to which one was aroused by stimuli. Mania was caused by overexcitement of the passions, melancholia by underexcitement.

Thomas Arnold, one of the more enlightened private madhouse owners, saw moral deviation, moral insanity and medical insanity as differing in degree only. An:

> empire of passions . . . love, superstition, avarice, misanthropy, nostalgia . . . could give rise to pathetic insanity.
>
> (Arnold 1782)

The pathogenic and curative effect of the passions were the dominant themes by the end of the century.

France

In France, Mesmer and Rousseau had undermined the doctrine that pure reason governed human affairs. Mesmer had done this by showing that whole audiences could lose control of themselves under the spell of 'animal magnetism'. Rousseau had written of how the contemporary human condition was man at variance with his true nature. Insanity was, for Rousseau, not loss of control, but a form of alienation. Both men demonstrated the ease with which reason could be overruled, and how it was merely a veneer on the surface of more powerful forces.

The Revolution of 1789 was an example of how these forces could convulse a nation as well as an individual mind. It also created an atmosphere which allowed Pinel to unchain the inmates of the Bicêtre hospital in Paris in 1793 and so begin humanitarian psychiatry in France. This dramatic gesture is rightly regarded as a brave one. Soon after, one of the freed inmates had to act as Pinel's bodyguard to avert a lynching by the frightened populace.

Germany

In Germany ideas about insanity were stagnant throughout the century. Part of the reason for this was lack of opportunity to study the insane, German states being slower to set up special institutions. The social, political and economic changes which were affecting Britain and France came later in Germany. In fact, the clearest statement of the rationalist position is contained in a book by Kant, *Anthropology from a Pragmatic Point of View*, published at the very end of the century. Kant is generally regarded as the greatest modern philosopher and his remarks on madness are therefore of considerable interest:

> The only general characteristic of insanity is the loss of sense for ideas that are common to all and its replacement with a sense for ideas peculiar to ourselves.
>
> (Kant 1798)

He regarded 'unreason as an essential and incurable disorder'. He believed that one should only admit those who are a danger to the community, and that, except for a small number of cases of 'ranting combined with fever', insanity was not the province of physicians but of philosophers. The only cause acceptable to him was heredity. Insanity was attributed to a disorder of the faculty of cognition, which produced not just a departure from the laws of reason, but 'fancies to comprehend the incomprehensible'. The result was:

> positive unreason, a different rule, a totally dissimilar standpoint, into which the soul is transported . . . but . . . the thinking faculty does not remain idle, even though it is employed not objectively in the true cognition of things.
>
> (Kant 1798)

Kant criticised the moral school, which was growing up in Britain and France:

> love, pride, economic speculation or studying too hard were not cause but result of derangement . . . for example, a merchant who overextends himself draws up his plan like a fool from the beginning.
>
> (Kant 1798)

Kant's position on the issues of restraint, responsibility and the psychological component in madness was already out of step, even with contemporary German views. New ideas were coming from poets and writers, who took an interest in madness in the last decade of the 18th century. Maimon, one of the editors of a Romantic magazine, *Sturm und Drang*, encouraged articles on dreams, passions and insanity, and regarded insanity as a derangement of lesser mental powers, imagination and memory, similar to alcoholic intoxication or dreams. Its therapy, according to him, should be an awakening. Novalis, the poet, helped promote similar ideas of insanity. In his view, imprudence in any form was a sufficient cause.

NINETEENTH CENTURY

General trends

From Galen until Pinel nothing new had been suggested about the classification of insanity. The 19th century, however, was to be a period of intense speculation on the matter and numerous systems were drawn up. It was also a time when the psychological components were discussed with some sophistication. The main topic of discussion in all accounts of insanity during this period, however, was its cause, and in particular the relative importance of psychological and organic factors. Treatment, as now, was a controversial subject and evoked strong emotions in all concerned.

Classification

Symptom-based

Pinel, sometimes called the father of psychiatry because of his humanitarian gesture in unchaining the inmates of Bicêtre, published a classification of insanity in 1801 which differed little from the Roman ones. It comprised five types. First there was melancholia:

> symptoms are taciturnity, a thoughtful, pensive air, gloomy suspicions and a love of solitude.

Secondly, there was mania without a delusional state:

> no sensible change in the functions of the understanding but perversion of the active faculties marked by abstract and sanguinary fury with a blind propensity to acts of violence.

Thirdly, he distinguished mania with delusions:

> continued or intermittent lesion of one or more of the functions of understanding accompanied by emotions of gaiety.

Fourthly came dementia:

> the dementia of which we are treating is generally accompanied by a turbulent and ungovernable mobility, by a rapid and unconnected succession of ideas . . . uninterrupted alternation of insulated ideas and evanescent and unconnected emotions, continually repeated acts of extravagance, complete forgetfulness of every previous state, diminished sensibility to external impressions, abolition of the faculty of judgement, and perpetual activity.

The fifth type was idiocy, with:

> total or partial obliteration of the intellectual powers and affections, universal torpor, detachment, half-articulated sounds or entire absence of speech from want of ideas.
>
> (Pinel, 1801)

Pinel's system was entirely based on symptoms. None of the five types had a characteristic cause. Even idiocy, a term which was later restricted to impairment of intelligence of congenital or perinatal origin, could occur, according to Pinel, following psychological trauma on the battlefield.

Causally-based

Spurzheim, a pupil of Gall the phrenologist, was one of the first to criticise the way in which insanity had hitherto been classified. In 1817 he wrote:

> the only practical division of insanity, I repeat, is that which is founded on the causes. The most useless, though the most common, is that according to the symptoms, such as into mania and melancholia.
>
> (Spurzheim 1817)

He considered that there were two main causes of insanity—'corporeal' (constitutional or genetic) and 'brain dysfunction' (organic)—and hence two forms of insanity corresponding to these. Spurzheim's suggestion was largely ignored for nearly a century, but then formed the basis for the contrasting terms functional and organic or endogenous and exogenous.

The usual way in which cause was incorporated into 19th century classifications is illustrated by the recommendations of Bucknill and Tuke, two British psychiatrists, in their *Manual of Psychological Medicine* in 1879:

> it is best we believe to adopt in a manual as our basis an orderly arrangement of morbid psychological phenomena and to place side by side with these a classification which recognises their aetiological and pathogenetic relations and by so doing embraces such forms of mental disease as general paralysis.
>
> (Bucknill & Tuke 1879)

They recognised six groups of organic factors (epilepsy, paralysis, senility, idiocy, miscellaneous organic disorders and cretinism) and various psychological and hereditary factors. All these could either predispose to mental illness (e.g. hereditary, delicate mental organism, unbalanced mind) or precipitate it (e.g. brain injury, intemperance, disappointed affections).

Pattern of psychological dysfunction

Heinroth, a German physician, proposed yet another type of classification in his *Textbook of the Disturbances of Mental Life* published in 1818. In it there were nine types of mental disorder (insanity, dementia, rage, melancholia, idiocy, apathy, insane melancholia, confusion and timidity), each with its own pattern of psychological impairment affecting one or more of the following functions: will, comprehension, decision-making, perception and thinking. Insanity itself was:

> an unfree disposition with exaltation of sensations and of the imagination, being beside oneself and daydreaming.
>
> (Heinroth 1818)

Although Heinroth was not the first to discuss the pattern of psychological impairment in insanity, his use of it in classification was a new and far-sighted development. He is rightly regarded by several historians of psychiatry as one of the first physicians to appreciate the psychological complexity of mental disorder.

Phenomena of insanity

Esquirol was the favourite pupil of Pinel and is probably the most eminent of all French psychiatrists. In 1838 he tried to integrate his master's traditional classification with contemporary ideas on psychological functioning. The result was a compromise between Pinel's symptom-based system and Heinroth's proposals based on psychological dysfunction. Esquirol was particularly interested in what he called the 'elements' of insanity. These included delusions and hallucinations, of which Esquirol gave one of the first detailed accounts. We would call these the major phenomena of insanity and so his classification can be considered to be based on phenomena.

He recognised five main types of mental disorder. The first, as usual, was:

> the melancholy of the ancients . . . a delusional state with respect to one or a small number of objects, with predominance of a sorrowful and depressing passion.

The second was a new invention on his part:

> monomania, in which the delusional state is limited to one or a small number of objects, with excitement and predominance of a gay and expansive passion.

There were three subtypes of monomania—intellectual, affective and instinctive—which arose respectively from partial impairment of intelligence, affect or will. The first subtype is the most important because it represented a significant departure from the traditional classification:

> the patients seize upon a false principle, which they pursue without deviating from logical reasonings, and from which they deduce legitimate consequences . . . aside from this they think, reason and act like other men.
>
> (Esquirol 1838)

Esquirol's third, fourth and fifth main types of insanity were mania, dementia and imbecility.

The intellectual subtype of monomania is the most relevant of these to the theme of this book because it is the first detailed description of a form of insanity not based on a simple disorder of emotions (like mania or melancholia) nor on a general impairment of intelligence or thinking (like dementia or idiocy). If one ignores the unconvincing descriptions in the Roman literature, Esquirol deserves the credit for being the first to appreciate that a major type of insanity (and he believed that intellectual monomania was relatively common) took the form of a delusional state which could not be explained simply as a disorder of emotion or intelligence. This, as I shall show, broadly corresponds to what is currently understood by the term schizophrenia.

Insanity as a single entity

William Griesinger is yet another candidate for the title of father of psychiatry. Although Pinel symbolises humane treatment and Esquirol revolutionised diagnostic ideas, Griesinger was the first to grasp the complex interplay in mental disorder between psychological and organic factors, between form and content and between reaction and disease. He was a German physician who published his influential book *Mental Pathology and Therapeutics* in 1845 when he was only 28 years old. His views on the classification of insanity are an attempt to integrate all the systems which I have just considered—traditional symptom-based, Spurzheim's plea to have it based on causes, Heinroth's elaborate system of psychological dysfunction and Esquirol's division into complete and partial disorders of intellect and emotion. Griesinger was an organic psychiatrist in his beliefs about the cause of mental disorder, but his eclectic approach to classification led him to conclude that insanity should not be subdivided. Instead of proposing several different types as his predecessors had done, he maintained that there was only one type. This suggestion is known as the 'Einheitspsychose' theory (unitary psychosis theory). Differences in the clinical picture between individuals were to him different stages of the same process:

> A classification of mental diseases according to their nature—that is according to the anatomical changes of the brain which lie at their foundation—is, at the present time, impossible. But, as the whole classification of mental diseases is merely a symptomatological one we must adopt the functional, the physiological, and this is also a psychological basis. Insanity is therefore to be divided according to the form and nature of the psychical anomalies . . . The analysis of observations leads to the conclusion that there are two grand groups or fundamental states of mental anomalies, which represent the two most essential varieties of insanity. In the one, the insanity consists in the morbid production, governing and persistence of emotions and emotional states, under the influence of which the whole mental life suffers according to their nature and form. In the other, the insanity consists in disorders of the intellect and will, which do not any longer proceed from a ruling emotional state, but exhibit, without profound emotional excitement, an independent, tranquil, false mode of thought and of will . . . Observations show further, that in the great majority of cases, those conditions which form the first leading group precede those of the second group; that the latter generally appear only as consequences and terminations of the first, when the cerebral affection has not been cured. There is moreover again presented within the first group a certain definite succession of the various forms of emotional states whence there results a method of viewing insanity which recognises in the different forms, different stages of one morbid process.
>
> (Griesinger 1845)

Course

Griesinger's proposal of one universal type of insanity with different manifestations at different stages of its course was not accepted by most psychiatrists. They were attracted, however, by his emphasis on the *course* of insanity, and used it not to explain the fundamental identity of all forms of insanity but to argue for their difference, the complete opposite of what Griesinger had intended.

Two French psychiatrists, Falret and Baillarger, in their respective descriptions of *folie circulaire* and *folie à double forme*, noted the fact that emotional insanity tended to run an intermittent course:

> there was a regular sequence of maniacal state, melancholic state and lucid interval of varying duration.
>
> (Falret 1854)

More important, Falret proposed that: 'a collection of characteristics . . . a group of constant physical, intellectual and affective or total behavioural symptoms . . . related together and following a definite course' was evidence of a disease. This was the psychiatric equivalent of Virchow's celebrated definition of a medical disease: 'diseases represent the course and appearance of life under changed conditions' (Virchow 1847). This definition was now applied to other associations between phenomena and course, a procedure which led to the isolation of catatonia, hebephrenia, paranoia and finally dementia praecox as disease entities.

Catatonia

After affective insanity (or manic depressive psychosis as it was later called) catatonia was then described, by Kahlbaum in 1874:

> Most cases of mental disease begin with a dejected mood . . . this turns into mania . . . confusion follows . . . ending with dementia . . . Whereas somatic diseases take their course in a brief period of time, usually in days or weeks, mental diseases continue through much longer periods of time, months and even years . . . The course of catatonia can be readily discussed in conjunction with this scheme. In this disease form we could establish an initial dejection . . . then however follows a succession of abnormalities in feeling and in thought which may be of striking severity and which finally turn into the other conditions . . . In a certain number of cases a definitely manic condition of short duration follows, and only after that does the clinical picture appear which has led to the term atonic melancholy . . . The cyclical nature of the whole disease process will have to be regarded as the unifying characteristic of catatonia . . . the chief symptom of the state of atony is the taciturnity . . . There is probably no case of catatonia in which the symptom of the tendency to negation is not present to some degree, sometimes more actively, sometimes more passively.
>
> (Kahlbaum 1874)

The importance of Kahlbaum's description is that both symptoms and course had equal weight as diagnostic criteria and he rejected both the old symptom-based approach and Griesinger's unitary psychosis theory.

Hebephrenia

Hebephrenia, vividly described by Hecker in 1871, was identified in the same way:

> Hebephrenia is a disease which invariably erupts following puberty . . . Under normal conditions this is the time when the psychologic renewal and transformation of the 'I' takes place. This psychological process, which is accompanied by a number of especially pronounced symptoms becomes pathological and permanent in the case of hebephrenia . . . In most cases the disease apparently begins as a sequel to a profound alteration in emotions with decidedly melancholic symptoms . . . A marked shallowness of affect soon appears in conjunction with the melancholia whose clinical picture is therefore quite different from the abject misery seen, for example, in genuine dysthymia

> . . . At the same time a heightened and frequently bizarre drive to action asserts itself . . . This drive expresses itself most frequently in aimless, purposeless silly actions and in a tendency to vagrancy and tramping . . . Definite delusions can only seldom be proven. There are all kinds of bizarre ideas. But these are transient and have the quality of being purposely affected, thereby differing from true delusions. Our patient, for example, said that he had been married for fifty years . . . of special importance are the disturbances of form which come to light in the speech of hebephrenics . . . The disturbance of form can be basically characterised as follows: first there is a peculiar deviation from logical sentence formation . . . This way of writing basically differs from that of other demented patients, e.g. dementia paralytica, in that significant disturbances and intervals in association and thought processes can be proven only exceptionally . . . Despite the differences among individual cases the always demonstrable peculiarity of the course and before all else the early appearance of the unmistakable silly dementia provide a definite delimitation of the total form of the disease.
>
> (Hecker 1871)

Again, it was the presence of a certain course of critical symptoms which allowed one to recognise the disease.

Paranoia

This term had been loosely employed in the context of insanity ever since the ancient Greeks. Heinroth used it for a type of mental disorder which predominantly affected the understanding. In the second half of the 19th century it was given a variety of meanings (Lewis 1970), but by 1890 it generally referred to persistent delusions of influence, persecution or grandeur usually associated with hallucinations.

Dementia praecox

Dementia had generally been considered the sequel to all forms of insanity. Maudsley (1899) expressed the traditional view:

> All such cases of wreck of mind consequent upon some other form of insanity are grouped together under the name of dementia.
>
> (Maudsley 1899)

Morel is credited with the first mention of the term 'démence précoce' in 1860, but he did not regard it as a nosological entity. He used it as a descriptive term for the mental state of a man whose illness had begun at the age of 14:

> The young patient progressively forgot everything he had learned; his brilliant intellectual faculties underwent in time a very distressing arrest. A kind of torpor akin to hebetude replaced the earlier activity, and when I saw him I concluded that the fatal transition to the state of démence précoce was about to take place . . . Such is in many cases the sad termination of hereditary insanity. A sudden paralysis of the faculties, a démence précoce indicate that the patient has reached the end of his intellectual life that he can control.
>
> (Morel 1860)

Kraepelin then used the term dementia praecox in the 5th edition of his *Textbook* in 1896 to cover three distinct diseases: Hecker's hebephrenia, Kahlbaum's catatonia and dementia paranoides. The last of these comprised cases of paranoia whose personality had deteriorated. Hebephrenia was the central one of these three. In the 6th edition of his *Textbook* in 1899 he no longer considered them distinct diseases, and in the 8th edition in 1913 he had incorporated a fourth variety, simple dementia. This was first described by Pick (1891) and then Diem (1903) and referred to patients who simply became apathetic and impoverished in their thinking without any fluctuations in mood or bizarre thinking as was customary in hebephrenia.

Schizophrenia

The schizophrenia of Bleuler developed out of these 19th century notions. It was in essence a subgroup of insanity distinct from mania, melancholia, idiocy or senile dementia, and was characterised by a certain course and a certain group of symptoms (negativism, bizarre ideas, disturbed form of speech, shallowness of affect and delusions with personality deterioration).

The development of the concept during the 20th century will be dealt with in the next chapter.

Psychological dysfunction

Ideas about psychological dysfunction in insanity also changed during the 19th century.

Emotional disorder

Pinel rejected the rationalist argument that insanity was a disorder of reason, and took the view, held by many Roman physicians, that it was an emotional disorder. He drew an analogy with the breakdown of law and order during the French Revolution which allowed uncontrollable forces to erupt. In the case of an individual, the effect of a breakdown in will was to unleash emotions which could not be tamed.

Phrenology

The next development was the application of phrenology, devised by Gall, a Viennese physician. He believed that mental functions or 'faculties' were localised within the brain in the form of 'organs'. He arrived at this conclusion after noting that his boyhood friends had different patterns of interests and capabilities, *and* differently shaped skulls. His linking of the two sets of observations became known as phrenology. Most of his ideas were nonsense and were ridiculed even at the time, but the principle of localisation is now seen as farsighted and revolutionary. He regarded insanity (Gall

1818) as the loss of control over an individual 'organ' of the brain because of its independent heightened activity or irritability. Gall had a profound influence on European psychiatry in the mid-19th century, mainly through the efforts of his followers, Spurzheim and Combe, who were better at communicating his ideas than he was himself. It was a convenient solution to the mind–body problem which preoccupied philosophers and physicians during the century.

Metaphysical formulation

Schelling, a successor to Kant as the chief philosopher of his day, believed that insanity resulted from an imbalance between soul (the highest level of an individual, in rapport with God) and spirit (an intermediate level containing will and intellect). This imbalance allowed the lowest level of an individual—mind, containing the emotions, and normally unconscious—to become manifest. Schelling regarded this as a fall from grace.

Heinroth was also a 'theological psychiatrist'. Although he classified mental disorder according to the type of psychological dysfunction which predominated, the pattern of this merely reflected energy disruption amongst Schelling's three levels—soul, spirit and mind.

Functional analysis

Reil, a German anatomist and physician, made the first systematic functional evaluation of insanity in his book *Rhapsodien*, published in 1803. As its title suggests, some of his notions were rather poetic. For example, he writes at one point, with reference to organic causes:

> one fibre in the brain slackens and the divine spark within us turns into a fairy tale.
>
> (Reil 1803)

However, he did show remarkable insight into the psychological dysfunction in insanity. He considered that there were three main ways in which mental disorder could be produced. First, there could be a disruption of the general mental, integrative operations of the brain. Secondly, there could be derangement of a sense organ which could give rise to false perceptions. Thirdly, excess physical stimuli from some part of the body could alter the balance of sensory input and lead to false ideas about the world.

These three mechanisms provide the central elements of some current psychological theories of schizophrenia. The first is fundamental to theories implicating thought disorder or general cognitive dysfunction. The second underlies theories of primary perceptual dysfunction. The third corresponds to proposals which emphasise a disorder of the amount or pattern of sensory input.

Moral degeneration

In the early part of the century the distinction between immoral acts and insanity was not always made. Esquirol noted, for example, that:

> this son would sacrifice his life for his father, but will do nothing at all in response to his commands from the moment he is deluded. This moral alienation is so constant that it would appear to me to be an essential characteristic of mental alienation.
>
> (Esquirol 1838)

Moral insanity had, however, been separated from insanity proper by Prichard, a British psychiatrist, in 1835. According to Prichard it was a:

> morbid perversion of the natural feelings, affections, inclinations, tempers, habits, moral dispositions, and natural impulses, without any remarkable disorder or defect of the intellect or knowing or reasoning faculties and particularly without any insane illusion or hallucination.
>
> (Prichard 1835)

In the second half of the century Prichard's views prevailed, and it was generally recognised that immoral behaviour was not an essential component of insanity proper.

Personality deterioration

By the second half of the century it had become apparent that neither emotional disorder nor moral deterioration were characteristic of all forms of insanity, and that metaphysical and phrenological explanations were inadequate. Functional analysis, as advocated by Reil, had not proved attractive either, and it was left to Griesinger to provide the most compelling psychological formulation. His original contribution was his appreciation that insanity brought about an entire change in personality, and this remains a key concept to this day. It became one of the central features of Kraepelin's and to a lesser extent Bleuler's ideas about schizophrenia. Griesinger believed that there was an:

> essential change in a man, an alienation from the former self . . . a state of indisposition, anxiety, suffering, pain . . . moral, intellectual or cerebral . . . the earliest states generally consist in an aimless feeling of ill-humour, discomfort, oppression and anxiety, owing to the fact that the new groups of ideas and instincts are usually at first exceedingly obscure. On this account the disturbances of the normal processes of thought and will and the new mental states obtruding on the 'I' are first felt as vague modifications of the sentiment and disposition. The diminished power and energy of the 'I,' the contraction of its sphere of ideas, produces an indefinite state of mental pain, and, from its vagueness, great irritation of the feelings. The new morbid perceptions and instincts produce divisions of the mind, a feeling of division of the personality, and of imminent annihilation of the 'I' . . . Everything appears strange to him because he acts strangely towards every mental impression . . . and he feels a strong inclination to ascribe his condition

> sometimes to the direct influence of the outer world—to believe that he is pursued, influenced, governed.
>
> (Griesinger 1845)

The 'I' was a set of ideas which acted, like our concept of personality or Freud's notion of the ego, to favour or impede the progress of other ideas into consciousness and action. Delusions and hallucinations were, according to Griesinger, the attempts by the sufferer to explain the alienation.

Causes of insanity

Throughout the 19th century there was a continual debate about whether insanity had an organic or a psychological cause.

Psychological causes

French psychiatrists generally favoured a psychological or moral cause for insanity. Pinel regarded it as a disturbance of self-command or self-control. Esquirol recognised both moral and physical causes, a combination of the two being more usual than either acting alone. Moral causes were more likely, according to him, in the rich, physical in the poor. He wrote:

> Of all moral causes, those which most frequently produce insanity are pride, fear, fright, ambition, reversal of fortune and domestic trouble.

More specifically he mentioned:

> one-sided training of the imagination in poets . . . a dependence on chance in officers . . . and idleness in court dignitaries.
>
> (Esquirol 1838)

Morel introduced the notion of degeneration:

> a maladaptive deviation from a primitive type . . . a congenital tendency for maladaptive temperament.
>
> (Morel 1857)

In this way he relegated the psychological component to a congenital predisposition towards a certain personality. Magnan (1893), the last of the great 19th century French psychiatrists, then incorporated the psychological element into a genetic frame-work:

> all conditions under the name of insanity are merely psychological stigmata of hereditary insanity.
>
> (Magnan 1893)

In Britain, more attention was paid to the role of adverse social conditions affecting groups of people rather than to individual psychological causes. Burrows (1828), the owner of a private asylum, believed that insanity was due to environmental factors, such as economic, political and religious crises, affecting an individual's constitution. Conolly, famous as the first asylum superintendent in Britain to abolish all forms of restraint, moral as well as mechanical, believed that poor health and poor education could be a cause.

In Germany there was the greatest polarisation between the advocates of a psychological cause of insanity (the 'Psychiker') and those who believed that it had an organic basis (the 'Somatiker'). The most celebrated 'Psychiker' was Ideler, a psychiatrist in Berlin, but as a group they contributed few original ideas.

Organic causes

The most striking development during the 19th century was the identification of a succession of unequivocal organic causes of insanity. Delirium tremens, from alcohol abuse, was described by Sutton in 1813. Dementia paralytica or general paralysis of the insane was first recognised by Bayle in 1822, and, although its syphilitic origin was not proved conclusively until 1912, the associated paralysis was clear evidence of an organic cause.

In addition to such positive associations between disease or dysfunction of the nervous system and insanity, the intelligent physician of the late 19th century must have been equally or even more impressed by the fact that most diseases of the nervous system did *not* produce insanity. James Parkinson described paralysis agitans in 1817, the first pathological account of disseminated sclerosis was given in 1835 and progressive muscular atrophy (or motor neurone disease) was recognised by Duchenne in 1847. In the latter half of the century the list of diseases of the nervous system grew rapidly. Some physicians acquired an expertise in this field and became known as neurologists. They established the fact that most diseases of the nervous system, including some with observable pathology in the brain, not only did not produce insanity but had no effect on mental function at all.

The next step was the realisation that even when mental disorder did result from brain disease, its form bore little resemblance to the ordinary conception of insanity. For example, Broca in 1861 demonstrated that a lesion in the left frontal lobe produced a specific disorder of language, not insanity. Other noninsane disorders of mental function were soon described in association with brain damage, for example asymbolia, an inability to recognise and use objects, by Finkelnburg in 1870.

The period between 1890 and 1910 was probably the most fertile for defining the boundaries between neurology and psychiatry and for clarifying psychological and organic issues. In 1890 Korsakoff's account of amnesia appeared in the German literature. In 1891 Freud separated agnosia from Finkelnburg's asymbolia. In 1900 Liepmann incorporated the remaining elements of asymbolia into the concept of apraxia. Pick in 1892 and Alzheimer in 1907 formulated the pathological criteria of presenile dementia, and in 1893 Möbius introduced the clinical concept of an exogenous psychosis which Bonhoeffer formalised in 1909.

By the end of the century, therefore, the rules for identifying organic causes of insanity were much clearer. One could no longer be a 'Somatiker' (organic psychiatrist) or 'Psychiker' (psychodynamically-orientated psyciatrist) in every case of mental disorder. For it was generally accepted that disorders of perception, movement, intellect and memory were nearly always organic in origin, and noninsane mental disorder ('neurosis') was the result of adverse life circumstances in conjunction with a certain personality. There *was* still controversy, however, about whether insanity without a patent organic lesion at postmortem was organically or psychologically determined. This form of insanity became known as functional psychosis and to this day the debate about the relative contribution of organic and psychogenic factors continues. Schizophrenia, as one of only two varieties of a functional psychosis (the other being manic-depressive psychosis), became the main focus of the Somatiker-Psychiker debate as it was pursued under different labels (e.g. psychiatry-antipsychiatry, organic-social) through the present century.

Treatment

Psychological treatment of insanity was popular at the beginning of the 19th century, particularly in France and Germany. Pinel advocated moral therapy to suit the specific moral cause that he had identified. If, for example, a patient believed that he had no head, he would be made to wear a heavy leaden cap until he capitulated. If he believed that there was a snake in his stomach he was given an emetic and a snake surreptitiously introduced into the vomit. If he claimed to be a king he would be told that his neighbour held the same belief yet he was powerless and the butt of jokes. Reil devised a number of fanciful treatments to fit the supposed cause. Some of the less barbaric were submersion in a tub of live eels, being made to walk across a flimsy bridge and being left to float in a leaky boat.

In some instances, moral treatments of this kind were administered with such zeal that the insane were worse off than when they had been chained. For example, Horn, professor of psychiatry in Berlin, was dismissed from his post in 1818 after an inmate died during treatment in 'Horn's bag', a hideous contraption in which patients were trussed up and lowered down a well.

The most enlightened approach was practised by Samuel Tuke in The Retreat, a model asylum set up in York in 1792, and by Conolly in the Hanwell asylum outside London. The principles governing these approaches were the limited use of restraint of all kinds and due attention to education, diet and general physical health.

SUMMARY

The first descriptions of insanity can be found in the Bible. The ancient Greeks made the first attempts to define it and the Romans then proposed a systematic way of classifying it and considering its causes. During the Middle Ages insanity was less of a medical concern, and more part of the religious and social ferment of the times. In the 17th and early 18th centuries insanity was regarded as a disorder of reason and, as this was what distinguished man from beast, the insane were considered and treated as subhuman. By the end of the 18th century the rationalist position had been undermined and insanity was regarded as a disorder of emotion.

It was during the 19th century that the notion of schizophrenia gradually emerged. The symptom-based classification of insanity which had remained since Roman times was criticised on three main counts: it had no place for cause; it did not take into account psychological dysfunction; and it did not include the course of insanity. Kraepelin, in formulating the concept of dementia praecox, drew on the insight of French psychiatrists like Esquirol and Falret, and German psychiatrists like Griesinger, Kahlbaum and Hecker. From Esquirol came the notion of a subtype characterised by a partial disorder of intellect. Griesinger drew attention to the importance of the course of insanity and stressed the frequency of personality deterioration. Falret identified what became known as manic-depressive psychosis, and Kahlbaum and Hecker described respectively catatonia and hebephrenia. In modelling schizophrenia on dementia praecox, therefore, Bleuler took over the following key concepts: a form of insanity characterised by a partial disorder of intellect, a particular course, personality deterioration, catatonic and hebephrenic phenomena and an overall clinical picture distinct from manic-depressive psychosis.

2

Development of ideas during the 20th century

1900s

The two major figures in this decade are Kraepelin and Bleuler. Freud and Jung were an important influence on Bleuler, and a handful of other figures contributed ideas.

Kraepelin

Kraepelin was professor of psychiatry in Munich for most of his professional lifetime. In 1896 he had grouped catatonia, hebephrenia and dementia paranoides (paranoia with personality deterioration) under the heading of dementia praecox and in 1899 had merged them into one disease. He believed that it was an organic disease, but the only evidence at that time was the presence in the brain at postmortem of microscopic changes of uncertain significance:

> In roughest outlines, therefore, clinical experience and anatomical findings in dementia praecox may with certain pre-suppositions be brought into agreement to some extent.
>
> (Kraepelin 1913)

He believed that psychological dysfunction was secondary to these organic changes and its characteristics were:

> weakening or annihilation of the influence which general conception, higher emotion and the trend of volition have on thought, feeling and acting . . . a weakening of those emotional activities which form the mainspring of volition . . . and a loss of inner unity of intellect, emotion and volition, in themselves and among one another . . . [in summary] an orchestra without a conductor.
>
> (Kraepelin 1913)

Bleuler

Eugen Bleuler was professor of psychiatry in Zurich. He first suggested the term schizophrenia as a replacement for dementia praecox in an article in

1908. In 1911 his major work *Dementia Praecox or the Group of Schizophrenias* appeared. He believed that schizophrenia was probably an organic disease, but was less convinced about this than Kraepelin:

> As yet we cannot answer the question whether there are psychic causes for schizophrenia. However, it is probably to be answered in the negative . . . Psychic events and experiences may release the symptoms but not the disease . . . It is conceivable that the entire symptomatology may be psychically determined . . . However the pathological anatomical findings exist and even though the nature of their relation to the psychosis remains enigmatic . . . complete justice to all these factors can only be done by a concept of the disease which assumes the presence of anatomic or chemical disturbances of the brain.
>
> (Bleuler 1911)

He devotes most of the book to the psychological mechanism by which symptoms develop. He believed that the primary problem was a loosening of associations:

> We do not know with certainty the primary symptoms of the schizophrenic cerebral disease. In all probability we also ought to include in these same primary symptoms a number of similar manifestations, above all a part of the disturbances of association.
>
> (Bleuler 1911)

This disturbance of association was the substrate for a second psychological mechanism which was then responsible for secondary symptoms such as delusions and hallucinations:

> The secondary symptoms are a direct consequence of the loosening of associations . . . Sometimes the anomalies of association may manifest themselves in blocking or in splitting of ideas; at other times in different schizophrenic symptoms . . . The splitting is the prerequisite condition of most of the disease. It is the splitting which gives the peculiar stamp to the entire symptomatology.
>
> (Bleuler 1911)

To explain how the secondary symptoms arose, he relied on Freud's account of the origin of psychosis (see below).

In summary, Bleuler believed that entirely psychic causes were not possible and that there were two stages in the disease, each with a different psychological mechanism. The first, which could exist by itself, had both organic and psychological components. The organic part was the cerebral substrate of the disease process and the psychological part was the disturbance in association. The second stage, which could only develop out of the first, was purely psychological, and was an elaborate version of Freud's ideas on the origin of the defence neuropsychoses.

Freud

In 1894 Freud published an article entitled *The neuropsychoses of defence*. It was subtitled: *An attempt at a psychological theory of acquired hysteria, of many phobias and obsessions and of certain hallucinatory psychoses*. There were three types of hysteria—hypnoid, defence and retention. Defence hysteria is the only one which is relevant to the current theme because it could lead to 'hysteria or an obsession or a hallucinatory psychosis'. There was a:

> splitting of the content of consciousness as a result of an act of will on the part of the patient. [Such patients] had enjoyed good mental health up to the moment at which an occurrence of incompatibility took place in their ideational life—that is to say until their ego was faced with an experience, an idea or a feeling which aroused such a distressing affect that the subject decided to forget about it because he had no confidence in his power to resolve the contradiction between that incompatible idea and his ego by means of thought-activity.
>
> (Freud 1894)

He explained the difference between hysteria, obsessions and psychosis in the following way:

> In *hysteria* the incompatible idea is rendered innocuous by its sum of excitation being transformed into something somatic—conversion . . . If someone . . . in order to fend off an incompatible idea . . . sets about separating it from its affect . . . the affect which has become free attaches itself to other ideas . . . and thanks to this false connection these ideas turn into *obsessional* ideas . . . In both the instances considered so far defence against the incompatible idea was effected by separating it from its affect; the idea itself remained in consciousness, even though weakened and isolated. There is however a much more energetic and successful kind of defence. Here, the ego rejects the incompatible idea together with its affect and behaves as if the idea had never occurred to the ego at all. But from the moment at which this has been successfully done the subject is in a *psychosis*, which can only be classified as hallucinatory confusion . . . the ego has fended off the incompatible idea through a flight into psychosis.
>
> (Freud 1894)

In a second article on *The neuropsychoses of defence* in 1896 he elaborated on this whilst discussing his analysis of a case of 'dementia paranoides' (part of Kraepelin's dementia praecox):

> . . . the self-reproach (at sexual experiences) is repressed in a manner which may be described as projection . . . other symptoms . . . are the return of the repressed . . . and bear the traces of the compromise which alone allows them to enter consciousness. Such are, for instance, my patient's delusional idea of being watched while she was undressing, her visual hallucinations, her hallucinations of sensation and her hearing of voices.
>
> (Freud 1896)

Jung

Jung was a student of Bleuler at this period and, at the latter's suggestion, carried out a study of word association in schizophrenia, which he published in 1907. Jung was largely responsible for the compromise which Bleuler made between the organic approach of Kraepelin and the purely psychodynamic approach of Freud. Jung believed that the:

> mechanisms of Freud are not comprehensive enough to explain why dementia praecox arises and not hysteria.

Instead, he proposed that an:

> intoxication . . . due primarily to somatic causes might seize upon the last complex (Jung's term for Freud's incompatible ideas) which happened to be there and pathologically transform it . . . cause the final fixation of the complex and injure the psychic functions as a whole.
>
> (Jung 1907)

In this way Jung suggested the two-stage model which Bleuler used: cerebral dysfunction causing primary thought disorder which then caused secondary impairment of all mental functions, the precise content of the delusions and hallucinations being determined by current emotional preoccupations.

In later years Jung (1939) was less convinced of this formulation and tried to account for the condition entirely on psychodynamic principles. At the time, however, his main contribution was his account of how organic and psychological causes could be integrated in a logical sequence.

General influences on Bleuler

Manfred Bleuler, Eugen Bleuler's son, had this to say about his father in a personal communication to me:

> The main influence on my father's choice to become a psychiatrist and his psychiatric research work originated from the opinion and the ideals of the simple country people among whom he was brought up . . . The first academic psychiatrists in Zurich were Germans who spoke a language foreign to the inborn population. The simple people felt that they were much too distant from the patients, that they did not speak with them and could not speak with them while their main interests concerned brain anatomy and pathology. During the youth of my father he was constantly confronted with a deep desire of the whole population around him: one of us should be the doctor of our mental patients; he would speak with them; he would understand their hopes and fears; he would help them better than the foreign academic professors. From this attitude came also the most important impetus for his research: he tried to understand what patients meant with their dissociated speech and what they felt in their hearts.
>
> The psychiatrists who influenced him most were Charcot in Paris and Forel in Zurich. My father became acquainted with Freud long before Freud went into psychotherapy. My father defended Freud against Wernicke's ideas in regard to aphasia. My father was also much attached to Emil Kraepelin. The lively discussions with Jung and Freud much influenced his ideas. Later on he was very much interested in Adolf Meyer's teachings.
>
> (Manfred Bleuler, personal communication)

Other contributions

Weygandt

Weygandt was a German psychiatrist who worked chiefly in Würzburg. He considered (Weygandt 1907) that the mental function most affected in dementia praecox was 'apperception.' This was a term introduced by Wundt, the founder of modern experimental psychology, for 'the single process by which any psychic content is brought to clear comprehension . . . the subjective side of attention . . . the accompanying feelings and sensations' (Wundt 1911). Weygandt was one of the first to appreciate that a disorder of apprehension or attention could provide a plausible and comprehensive explanation of schizophrenia.

Gross

Gross was an Austrian psychiatrist, who worked mainly in Graz. In 1904 he suggested that dementia praecox was a disorder of consciousness. He adapted the ideas of sejunction (or disintegration) of consciousness from the neurologist, Wernicke, and dissociation or lowering of consciousness from the French psychologist, Janet. Gross proposed renaming dementia praecox 'dementia sejunctiva', and was one of several psychiatrists at this period to emphasise a disorder of consciousness.

Stransky

Stransky was a Viennese psychiatrist who regarded a dissociation between various functions as more characteristic of dementia praecox than an impairment of any single function, such as thinking (Bleuler) or attention (Weygandt). He based his notion on Schopenhauer's division of the mind into intellect (noöpsyche) and will (thymopsyche). He (Stransky 1904) considered dementia praecox as an imbalance between these, which he termed 'intrapsychic ataxia'.

Chaslin

Chaslin was a French psychiatrist who worked at the Salpetrière in Paris. He published a textbook of psychiatry in 1912, one year after Bleuler's monograph appeared. His ideas were similar to Bleuler's and they belong to this decade, before the term schizophrenia was generally accepted. His suggested name for dementia praecox was 'la folie discordante', because, like Stransky, he considered that the chief characteristic was a discordance between mental functions. He likened the mind under these conditions to 'une machine sans combustible' (a machine without fuel).

Meyer

Adolph Meyer was Swiss by origin and had studied under Forel, Bleuler's predecessor as professor of psychiatry in Zurich. He emigrated to North America in 1892 and became the dominant figure in American psychiatry for 50 years. His ideas on psychiatry were based on what he called 'psychobiology'. This was his answer to the mind-body problem. He had a distaste for the European brand of academic philosophy and psychology, and a preference for 'common sense psychology'. Psychobiology was essentially an attempt to do away with Cartesian dualism and replace it with:

> one broad world of actuality, a world in which there are variously organised structures and their functions . . . which we strive to group in our symbolisations and test by our performances.
>
> (Meyer 1957)

He had a 'psychogenic conception' of dementia praecox:

> with dementia praecox essentially unlike general paralysis and more likely the inevitable outcome of conflicts of instincts, and, more concretely put, conflicts of complexes of experience and incapacity for a harmless constructive adjustment.
>
> (Meyer 1910)

Summary

The 1900s were a decade when Kraepelin's concept of dementia praecox was generally accepted by European and North American psychiatrists. (In France, the reception was not so enthusiastic.) It was generally agreed that the condition was primarily organic in nature, although most psychiatrists entertained doubts about this. Some (e.g. Freud, Meyer) believed it was entirely psychogenic in origin, arising from the mind's attempt to deal with unwelcome ideas, unpleasant emotions and conflicting experiences. There was most disagreement on the nature of the psychological dysfunction and on the appropriate name for the condition. Bleuler's opinions on both prevailed because he wrote most clearly about the condition and, helped by Jung, achieved the best compromise between organic and psychodynamic approaches.

1910s

Jaspers

The major event of the decade most relevant to our theme was the appearence of Karl Jaspers' *General Psychopathology* in 1913. It was not translated into English until 1963 and its influence even now is more by reputation than through any widespread awareness of its content. It is in fact a work of genius in approach, content, structure and style. It was a statement of the rules which should guide the investigator of mental disorder, biological or psychological. Jaspers later devoted himself to philosophy, but even in 1913 his approach to psychopathology was that of a philosopher. From this stance he was able to take a dispassionate look at the relatively new discipline of psychiatry. This is why he concerned himself with rules and methods. His philosophy derived from the phenomenology of Brentano and

Husserl and merged into the existentialism of Heidegger and Sartre. This is why he emphasised the idea of psychic life, however it might manifest itself and however it might be studied.

He championed what is now regarded as the phenomenological approach to schizophrenia. His ideas on this are best expressed in the following extract:

> The most profound distinction in psychic life seems to be that between what is meaningful and *allows empathy* and what in its particular way is *ununderstandable*, mad in the literal sense, schizophrenic psychic life, even though there may be no delusions. Pathological psychic life of the first kind we can comprehend vividly enough as an exaggeration or diminution of known phenomena and as an appearance of such phenomena without the usual causes or motives. Pathological psychic life of the second kind we cannot adequately comprehend in this way. Instead we find changes of the most general kind for which we have no empathy but which in some way we try to make comprehensible from an external point of view. Language has always distinguished *affective illness* from *madness* proper. For lay persons madness means senseless raving, affectless confusion, delusion, incongrouous affects, a crazy personality, and they think this all the more sensible and orientated the individual remains. Should this not be so the lay person rightly tends not to count these states of clouded consciousness as madness proper. Affective illness he indeed calls unmotivated but profound emotional disturbances, for which after their own fashion one can have empathy, as for instance those of melancholia. Holding these views the lay person has hit upon a basic difference within morbid psychic life which even today we cannot formulate clearly and precisely but which remains one of the most interesting problems . . . The theory, which so far seems the aptest, explains the various features of this ununderstandable psychic life in terms of a split in the psychic life; accordingly Bleuler decided to call it schizophrenic which we may also use as a mere descriptive term without necessarily accepting the theory . . . when we trace back behaviour, activities and the general conduct of life in an individual and try to understand all this psychologically and with empathy we always come up against certain limits but with schizophrenic psychic life we reach limits . . . earlier . . . and find ununderstandable what strikes the patients as . . . quite well founded . . . Among all this ununderstandable material search has been made for *a central factor*. All the unexpected impulses, incomprehensible affects and lack of affect, the sudden pauses in conversation, the unmotivated ideas, the behaviour so reminiscent of distraction and all the other phenomena which we can only describe negatively and indirectly ought to have some common base. Theoretically we talk of incoherence, dissociation, fragmenting of consciousness, intrapsychic ataxia, weakness of apperception, insufficiency of psychic activity and disturbance of association etc. We call the behaviour crazy or silly but all these words simply imply in the end that there is a common element of the ununderstandable.

This last extract contains the kernel of the phenomenological approach. Schizophrenia, according to Jaspers, was qualitatively different from normal, incomprehensible in terms of personality and life experiences and inexplicable by any known psychological principle or dysfunction. The key word in the passage is 'ununderstandable', as Jaspers, in different parts of his book, also rejects three other explanations: organic brain disease, emotional disorder and what came to be regarded as the existential approach.

On the question of organic brain disease he is least sure:

> The somatic findings are in favour of its organic somatic character so are the obviously severe, morbid somatic states which appear in metabolic catastrophes and febrile episodes, the similarity of many symptoms found in mescalin intoxication with those in acute schizophrenic states and the general prejudice that all illnesses must in the last resort be somatic. *Against this* we may note the profound psychopathological difference between, for example, general paralysis and schizophrenia, between the crude organic destruction—machinery smashed up—and the distraction of mind, the cessation of organic phenomena as the process advances, the absence of somatic findings in many cases and the unlikelihood that paranoia, for instance, should be based on the same principle as catatonic illness with acute febrile episodes.

He is certain that schizophrenia is not due to emotional disorder:

> Attempts have been made to make feelings the explanation for all abnormal phenomena. If we use the term feeling to denote everything for which common usage permits us to use the word, there is always some truth in this, but it then comes to very little if we go on to derive delusions, for instance, from feelings. Ideas of senselessness, sinfulness, impoverishment, can be understandably said to arise from depressive affects and it was generally supposed that the depressed patient concluded there must be something which made him so miserable. People also wanted to explain delusions of persecution by the effect of distrust, and delusions of grandeur by euphoric moods, but they did not realise that though one may understand ordinary mistakes and overvalued ideas in this way, one can never do this with delusions. Frightening hallucinations in sleep, during fever or a psychosis have been attributed to some kind of anxiety, otherwise conditioned. In all these cases we can, it is true, find meaningful connections, and they teach us something about the new relationship of delusional content and previous experiences but nothing at all of how the delusions, false perceptions, etc., could have come about in the first place.

Thirdly he had this to say about subsequent attempts to regard schizophrenia as a form of existential despair or an effort on the part of alienated individuals to describe their plight:

> The formal changes in experience and function never by themselves define the nature of the schizophrenic psychic life satisfactorily. Rather it is an established fact that schizophrenics are not surrounded by a single, schizophrenic world, but by a number of such worlds. If there was a single, uniform world-formation, schizophrenics would understand each other and form their own community. But we find just the opposite. They hardly ever understand each other; if anything, a healthy person understands them better . . . For the time being the question stays open: why is schizophrenia in its initial stages so often a process of cosmic, religious or metaphysical revelation? It is an extremely impressive fact: this exhibition of fine and subtle understanding, this impossible, shattering piano-performance, this masterly creativity, these peculiar experiences of the end of the world or the creation of fresh ones, these spiritual revelations and this grim daily struggle in the transitional periods between health and collapse. Such experiences cannot be grasped simply in terms of the psychosis which is sweeping the victim out of his familiar world, an objective symbol as it were of the radical, destructive event attacking him. Even if we speak of existence or the psyche as disintegrating, we are still only using

analogies. We observe that a new world has come into being and so far that is the only fact we have.

(Jaspers 1913)

Summary

Jaspers' influence on notions about schizophrenia was enormous. He inspired an existential school of psychiatry (p. 352), although he himself was wary of travelling that path. He cautioned against enthusiasm for any causal theory, organic or psychological, and emphasised instead the importance of describing as clearly as possible what the patient was experiencing or believing. This encouraged an interest in descriptive psychopathology and subjective experiences, but had a generally unfavourable influence on the search for causes and appropriate treatment. Most important of all, he had a direct influence on current diagnostic criteria, as Kurt Schneider became professor of psychiatry in Heidelberg where Jaspers had worked, and systematised Jaspers' notion of 'ununderstandability' in the form of first rank symptoms. These are still the most widely used diagnostic criteria in many parts of the world.

His immediate effect was to pose a dilemma for those seeking the cause of schizophrenia. If the condition was not due to understandable combinations of personality and life experience (psychodynamic and social formulations) or disturbed psychological functioning (cognitive and psychophysiological explanations) and did not resemble the clinical picture in any known type of organic brain disease (neuropsychological and organic theories), this virtually exhausted all possible explanations. It left only existential accounts (in terms of alienation and despair) which, as even Jaspers appreciated, are not plausible.

1920s

One solution to the dilemma posed by Jaspers was to attribute schizophrenia to a *complex* psychological dysfunction—subtle emotional disorder, personality change or thought disorder of a most unusual type. This would be a reasonable response to his demand that a simple disorder of feeling of the kind seen in mania, melancholia or anxiety could not be the critical factor, and yet avoid the pessimistic conclusion reached by him that no form of psychological dysfunction underlay it. Several psychiatrists made suggestions of this kind during the decade. Together they are sometimes referred to as 'existentio-analytic' (Schmidt 1940),because they analysed the way a subject experienced his existence without seeing in this existence the cause of his abnormal experiences. They were all German, with the exception of Minkowski who was French, and they belonged probably to the finest period of German psychiatry, before the initiative in such matters passed to North America and elsewhere. The main contributors were Kretschmer, Schilder, Minkowski, Zutt and Wetzel.

Kretschmer

Kretschmer worked in Marburg. He is now remembered for pointing out the link between body build and personality, for describing the schizoid personality and for giving one of the best accounts of a psychogenic psychosis (sensitiver Beziehungswahn—a nonschizophrenic delusional state largely comprehensible in terms of life events and personality traits).

His views on the psychology of schizophrenia are contained in his textbook of *Medical Psychology*, first published in 1922. He believed that the essential feature was a regression of thought processes to a form more typical of primitive man:

> What the schizophrenic describes here as an individual experience is something which like a red thread runs through the age-long cultural history of mankind. We can see the fraternisation of religion and erotism, in quite naive and unveiled form . . . In schizophrenia, a condition which brings so many phylogenetic mechanisms of importance to the surface, we can often observe . . . the sublimation of erotism into intense religious experience occurring before our eyes.
>
> (Kretschmer 1922)

Kretschmer had a tendency to speculate in a poetic and metaphysical way in the other subjects which he studied. His proposal of phylogenetic thought regression provoked strong criticism from later writers on thought disorder.

Schilder

Schilder mainly worked in Vienna before emigrating to North America in the 1930s. He also carried out important studies on body image disorders and pain perception. He was a great integrator and in his textbook, published in 1924 and like Kretschmer's called *Medical Psychology*, he hoped to 'unify in one framework phenomenology, psychoanalysis, experimental psychology and brain pathology'.

His views on the psychology of schizophrenia derived from the Wurzburg school of experimental psychology of whom Külpe was the leader and Bühler the most important member. Bühler had studied his own thought processes by the method of introspection and had concluded that they had originated with imageless and nonsensory thoughts, a radical statement in 1907. Schilder appreciated its importance and proposed that in schizophrenia there was some maldevelopment in the progression from unformed, imageless thoughts to their fully fledged form:

> There are two kinds of undeveloped concepts. The first . . . is incomplete as regards form as well as content: the many individual meaning experiences remain unconnectedly side by side . . . This lack of completion we see in normals in the course of thinking before they have reached their goal . . . and is seen particularly clearly in acute phases of schizophrenia . . . The second type is complete as regards form, but its content is dominated by symbol-like

> images and lack of directedness towards reality. Such are the errors and prejudices of normals and the consolidated delusions of schizophrenics.
>
> (Schilder 1924)

Schilder not only appreciated, and was the first to write about, the distinction between form and content in schizophrenic thought, but showed how thought disorder could derive from arrested development of otherwise normal thinking. This form of regression was more plausible than Kretschmer's phylogenetic variety and largely fulfilled Jaspers' criteria for schizophrenic psychic life—ununderstandable in terms of life events and personality, non-organic, and not attributable to a simple functional deficit. Why the normal goal-directed thinking should be subverted, however, was not clear in Schilder's account.

Minkowski

Minkowski was a Parisian psychiatrist much influenced both by Bergson, the French philosopher, and by Jaspers. His theory of schizophrenia is contained in his book *La Schizophrenie*, published in 1927. It is surprising that his work has never been translated into English. Perhaps his later reputation as an existentialist is responsible for this. English-speaking countries have never taken much notice of existentialism.

He first surveyed the major psychological theories and found a common theme. The 'discordance' and 'machine without fuel' of Chaslin, the 'loss of inner unity' and 'orchestra without conductor' or Kraepelin, the 'intrapsychic ataxia' of Stransky, and the 'schizophrenia' of Bleuler all expressed, in his view, the same idea:

> that the disorder is not to be found in this or that function, but in their overall cohesion . . . in, to use a metaphor . . . the interstitial space.
>
> (Minkowski 1927)

Minkowski then described four ways in which this was manifest. All are original, but rather slippery. The first was 'la perte du contact vital avec la réalité' (loss of vital contact with reality). This idea can only be understood if it is appreciated that the reality which he refers to is not the man-in-the-street's reality; that would be trivial. It is Bergson's reality. Bergson based his philosophy on a study of time, time as we think about it and time as we experience it. In reality, Bergson argued, time, space and consciousness flow, but we gain a false impression because our intellect chops them up into manageable portions. Minkowski took from this the idea that 'a whole side of our life, and not the least important, entirely escapes discursive thought'. It was this reality, according to Minkowski, and not the reality which our intellect demonstrates to us, which was faulty in schizophrenia.

His second contribution was the notion of 'morbid rationalisation', in particular a 'géométrisme morbide' (precoccupation with geometrical or spatial aspects of things). This was how he conceived the essential quality of schizophrenic thought. He illustrated his meaning with the following examples. A schizophrenic's son is shaving in front of him. This makes the patient think of all the soldiers in the local barracks who might be shaving and then the whole army. A metro ticket makes him think of all the train, bus and tram tickets which have ever been issued. Minkowski commented: 'thought flies away into infinite space without any limits'. Another way he conveyed his meaning was through a series of opposing modes or objects of thought. The first of each pair was 'atrophied', the second 'hypertorphied' in schizophrenia. These are shown in Table 2.1.

Table 2.1 Minkowski's opposing modes/objects of thought

Atrophied	Hypertrophied
Life	Plan
Instinct	Brain
Feeling	Thought
Synthetic ability	Analytic ability
Reliance on impressions	Demand for proof
Movement	Immobility
People and events	Objects
Realisation	Representation
Time	Space
Succession	Extension
Goal	Base

His third notion was the idea of a disorder in 'temps vécu' (experienced time), a central feature of Bergson's philosophy. It was, he says later (at a conference on delusions in 1950), his first psychotic patient who alerted him to this. For eight days he had been trying to convince the man that he was not about to die. Finally he said to him: 'You see, I'm right. Nothing's happened to you.' The patient replied: 'I agree. So far you're right. But what proof is there that you will still be right tomorrow?' He regarded this as evidence for some selective fault in thinking about or envisaging a future existence.

Finally, he suggested a solution to the issue of dementia. He rejected intellectual impairment, analogies with dreams and any explanation which stressed a primary emotional disturbance. He approved of Bleuler's term 'autistic' thinking but suggested, in his view, a better one: 'affaiblissement pragmatique' (pragmatic impairment). By this he meant that the dementia was most if not only evident when the schizophrenic was required to translate thought into action. The schizophrenic might excel in declarative knowledge—knowing *that* such and such—but would fail completely in procedural knowledge—knowing *how* such and such works.

Zutt

Zutt worked in Würzburg. He explained the features of schizophrenia in terms of a personality change of which the subject was unaware (Zutt 1929).

He supposed that the first event was an alteration in the beliefs, feelings and habits that make up a personality. The fact that this had happened, however, was unknown to the subject. When people in his environment, therefore, behaved differently towards him because they noticed the change and when objects and people looked different to him because they were perceived through the eyes of the new self he could only conclude that it was the environment which had changed. His experiences and ideas on his new world were then recorded by psychiatrists as hallucinations and delusions. Zutt gave an analogy of an actor who, at the end of the play, stepped out into the real world with his stage personality but did not realise this. The comments of friends and his 'stage personality's' view of the world would be interpreted as changes in those friends and that world.

Wetzel

Wetzel, who worked mainly in Heidelberg, proposed an emotional basis for schizophrenia. He took note of Jaspers' criticisms of simplistic emotional formulations and therefore studied the feelings accompanying complex beliefs such as the idea that the world was about to end. He concluded that an emotion of some kind had preceded the abnormal belief and that this emotion or delusional mood was responsible for the belief. As in the case of the primary personality change proposed by Zutt, the altered mood itself was not recognised by the subject, whereas the perceptual and ideational consequences (e.g. grim faces, impending doom for all) was immediately apparent.

Summary

Analysis of schizophrenic thinking, personality and mood by German and French psychiatrists during this period suggested mechanisms whereby a subject could develop delusions and hallucinations in the absence of adverse life events, pre-existing personality disorder or simple psychological dysfunction. Some of the suggestions were implausible (e.g. Kretschmer's phylogenetic regression), but most were intriguing and, in retrospect, far-sighted and unfairly neglected by subsequent writers on the issue.

1930s

The main development in this decade was the emergence of a North American concept of schizophrenia. Its characteristics were a loose application of psychoanalysis, a preoccupation with thought disorder and an attempt to incorporate social elements as recommended by Adolph Meyer. The new ideas circulating were those of Sullivan, Vygotsky, Cameron, Goldstein and Pavlov.

Sullivan

Sullivan was a psychoanalyst who set up an inpatient psychotherapy unit at Chestnut Lodge in Maryland. In contrast to Freud, who recommended that 'we must renounce the idea of trying our plan of cure upon psychotics' (Freud 1938), Sullivan believed that schizophrenics would respond to modified psychoanalysis. He wrote:

> In conclusion, it may be restated that, at least in the case of the male, fairly young schizophrenic patients whose divorcement from fairly conventional behaviour and thought has been rather abrupt, when received into care before they have progressed either into hebephrenic dilapidation or durable paranoid maladjustments, are to be regarded as of good outlook for recovery and improvement of personality, if they can be treated firstly to the end of socialisation, and thereafter by more fundamental reorganisation of personality.
>
> (Sullivan, 1931)

He had already formulated his views on the nature of schizophrenia in rather turgid prose:

> There is no profit from pondering on an organic substratum which cannot now or in the next many years be demonstrated ... There are attempts by regression to genetically older thought processes to infantile or even prenatal mental functions successfully to reintegrate masses of life experiences which had failed structuralisation into a functional unity and finally lead by that very lack of structuralisation to multiple dissociations in the field of relationship of the individual not only to external reality including the social milieu but to his personal reality.
>
> (Sullivan 1924)

His loose concept incorporated Kretschmer's ideas of regression, Freud's later views on psychological deficit (p. 357) and a social component. It was to remain the standard model in North American psychiatry until the 1970s. He trained other psychiatrists in his therapeutic technique, chief amongst whom was Frieda Fromm-Reichmann, who argued in a paper published in 1939 that schizophrenics could develop transference.

Vygotsky

Vygotsky was a Russian psychologist who died young. In 1934 an article of his entitled *Thought in schizophrenia* was translated in the *Archives of Neurology and Psychiatry*, and had considerable influence. His aim was to look anew at 'the old attempt to connect the psychology of adolescence with certain symptoms of schizophrenia' and his method was to 'offer patients a situation which required the formation of artificial concepts'.

He asked schizophrenics and adolescents to associate a meaningless syllable with a definite concept (e.g. bik = large and broad, loc = large and thin). He found that both groups of subjects tended to think less maturely than adults. For example, they grouped items according to personal preference or chance factors (e.g. those with dirt on) and failed to note formal similarities such as large or small. He called this 'complex thinking' in contrast to true conceptual thinking. He believed that:

> the psychology of adolescence gives a key for the understanding of schizophrenia . . . that each one of us carries schizophrenia in a latent form . . . and that in schizophrenia there is a destruction of the psychologic systems which lie at the basis of concepts.
>
> (Vygotsky 1934)

Cameron

Cameron was a professor of both psychology and psychiatry at the University of Wisconsin. In 1938 he published a monograph entitled *Reasoning, regression and communication in schizophrenics*. In it were the results of the first properly controlled experiment on the psychology of schizophrenia. His aim was to test Vygotsky's regression hypothesis and he did it by first defining what he meant by regression—schizophrenics should reason like a six-year-old—and then defining what he meant by reasoning—the type of response to a question requiring a causal explanation of some event. He consulted Piaget and found that the responses of six-year-old children fell into three classes: cause and effect (e.g. he fell down because he stumbled), logical justification (e.g. the animal is not dead because it is moving) and psychological motivation (e.g. the boy threw the stone because he wanted to hit me).

Table 2.2 Cameron's analysis of childhood and schizophrenic reasoning in terms of types of explanation given.

Response type	Subjects	
%	6-yr-olds	Schizophrenics
Cause and effect	8	45
Logical justification	9	23
Psychological motivation	83	32

His results (Table 2.2) indicate clearly that schizophrenics gave an entirely different pattern of responses from six-year-olds. The former preferred cause and effect explanations, whereas the children nearly always gave a psychological motive. He concluded:

> there is not simply a return to the infantile but a functional disintegration of a remarkable, mature organism . . . far from duplicating those of puerile reasoning their responses remain in many respects quite unique and together account for the more or less specific character of schizophrenic thinking disorder.
>
> (Cameron 1938)

With this simple experiment he had neatly refuted Vygotsky's regression hypothesis.

His second main contribution was his introduction of the term 'overinclusion', which became a central concept in various formulations of schizophrenic thought disorder. It was first mentioned in an article published in 1939 called *Schizophrenic thinking in a problem-solving situation*. He had asked subjects to group wooden blocks inscribed with symbols, and concluded:

> The inability to select and to restrict and to eliminate the less closely related elements from the conceptual structure means that the psychological boundaries are functionally insufficient. The result of this situation is overinclusion.
>
> (Cameron 1939)

His final contribution was an emphasis on a social formulation of schizophrenia:

> It is obviously a short step from Bleuler's Freudian interpretations and Meyer's formulation to the conclusion that schizophrenia is a disorganisation of the biosocial reaction systems that define personality . . . and their replacement by behaviour dominated or determined by private fantasy . . . The schizophrenic patient, because of his lost social skills, is a daydreamer who cannot completely return.
>
> (Cameron 1944)

Goldstein

Kurt Goldstein was a German neurologist who had gained his experience of psychological dysfunction studying brain-damaged soldiers in the First World War. He had written extensively on aphasia and agnosia, and conceived the notion that there was a single principle underlying the varied types of behaviour after brain damage. He called this an impairment of the abstract attitude. His ideas on the matter are not easily grasped. They are contained in a series of articles, all of which need to be consulted to gain a true picture of his meaning (Goldstein 1936, Bolles & Goldstein 1938, Goldstein 1939, Goldstein & Scheerer 1941, Goldstein 1944, Goldstein 1959). He is clearer on the meaning of a concrete attitude:

> . . . governed to an abnormal degree by outer-world stimuli and by images, ideas and thoughts which act upon us at the moment . . . action determined by momentary sense impressions . . . more realistic . . . performance influenced more by external factors . . . blurring of sharp boundaries between figure and ground.
>
> (Bolles & Goldstein 1938)

In his 1941 paper, in collaboration with Scheerer, he described eight aspects of the abstract attitude:

> . . . detaching ego from outer world or inner experience, assuming a mental set, accounting for acts to oneself or others, shifting from one aspect to another, holding several aspects in mind at the same time, grasping essential of whole, deriving common properties amongst items, and planning ahead.
>
> (Goldstein &Scheerer 1941)

It looks as if the term abstraction is more heterogeneous than the behaviour it was meant to simplify. Goldstein was much influenced by the Gestalt school of psychology whose members—Wertheimer, Koffka and Köhler—believed that the mind had an inherent tendency to organise the world according to a few simple principles. The two main principles were an ability to distinguish between 'figure' and 'ground' (how a part of the environment is separated from the whole field) and a preference for 'good', symmetrical forms over chaotic or ragged. It was the normal application of these principles which Goldstein believed was impaired following brain damage.

He formulated his views on schizophrenia after he emigrated to the United States. They were the same as his views on the effect of brain damage. Essentially he believed that schizophrenics adopted a concrete attitude in their perception, thinking and behaviour:

> A schizophrenic does not consider an object as part of an ordered outer world separated from himself as the normal person does . . . A word when used by a schizophrenic appears as part of an object or situation and not as representative of it . . . The reactions of schizophrenics are to a high degree determined by physiognomic concreteness.
>
> (Goldstein 1939)

His ideas had enormous influence on psychological formulations of schizophrenia despite their slipperiness and despite his failure to distinguish organic and schizophrenic patterns.

Pavlov

Pavlov was primarily a neurophysiologist, but his stature was so great in Russia that he became an authority on a wide variety of topics, including schizophrenia. Translations of his work appeared in American journals during the 1930s.

Pavlov had been struck by the behaviour of his dogs during and after the Leningrad flood of 1924. The psychological shock of nearly drowning had dissipated nearly all their conditioned reflexes. This aroused his interest in the relationship between psychological and physiological states. He would have been intrigued with Kraepelin's observation that long-standing catatonics had sprung to life during a fire in their hospital, behaved normally till the danger was over, and then resumed their abnormal postures and behaviour. He visited the Leningrad mental hospital at the invitation of its chief psychiatrist. He was told the characteristic symptoms of schizophrenia were apathy, dullness, stupor, stereotypes, facetiousness and silliness, and that the catatonic form made the best recovery. He noted:

> Usually the patient is considered apathetic and dull because he does not reply to the psychiatrist's questions. It is considered that his emotional life is impaired. But if one asks the same question quietly in a pleasant informal way one often gets a reply. This is a striking phenomenon to which little attention is paid.
>
> (Pavlov 1932)

He concluded that schizophrenia was a form of chronic hypnosis:

> In my opinion this symptom (referring to his observation above) is one of the most definite evidences of a beginning *hypnosis* . . . What causes the chronic hypnosis is a weak nervous system with special weakness of the cortical cells . . . We can look on schizophrenia as an inhibitory state of the cortex protecting the nerve cells from further exhaustion.
>
> (Pavlov 1932)

Summary

During the 1930s the concept of schizophrenia became looser. Its links with the original organic formulation and phenomenological description became tenuous and in the writings of some North American commentators completely ignored. It had acquired a strong social component and was being compared with such diverse conditions as adolescent thought, generalised brain damage and chronic hypnosis.

1940s

The fragmentation of the concept of schizophrenia continued during the 1940s. National trends and prejudices in diagnosis, the incompatibility of diverse schools of thought and the polarisation of different disciplines all combined to undermine the concept. Bleuler's integration of *diagnosis, psychological dysfunction, cause* and *treatment* no longer seemed tenable. Because of this it is necessary to trace the progress of ideas under these separate headings.

Diagnosis

North America

In North America the position at the time is best illustrated by the conclusions of Bellak, a New York psychiatrist, who reviewed the previous decade's literature (3200 references) in 1948:

> Schizophrenia or dementia praecox is not a disease entity but a syndrome or a reaction type associated with a large variety of aetiological factors. The best common denominator which we can find for the syndrome is what we may call a *deficit reaction* . . . typical of a human organism incapable at the time of adequate social functioning . . . One can conceive of all the cases actually occurring as being on some points of a continuum from a hypothetical locale of complete psychogenicity to a hypothetical locale of complete organicity of the syndrome.
>
> (Bellak 1948)

Schizophrenia had become a universal reaction with unlimited causes and no definite psychopathological diagnostic criteria.

The aim in diagnosis was to find evidence of this *deficit* in psychological functioning, and a number of 'psychodiagnostic' tests soon became available. The most widely used were projective tests such as that devised by Rorschach, a Swiss psychiatrist, who died young in 1922. He had published his 'form interpretation test' in 1921, but it was not translated into English until 1942. Another popular way of identifying the psychological deficit was by noting any inadequacy in proverb interpretation. Benjamin, a North American psychologist, suggested this in 1944 and administration and scoring were soon standardised. Goldstein (Goldstein & Scheerer 1941) proposed yet another psychodiagnostic test—object sorting—and this was standardised and promoted by Rapaport in 1945.

Germany

In Germany psychiatrists generally followed the recommendations of Kraepelin, Bleuler and Jaspers. This involved the identification of personality deterioration, the clinical recognition of thought disorder and emotional blunting, and the elucidation of subjective experiences. There were, however, three additional trends.

First, because most German psychiatrists still believed that schizophrenia was an organic disease, some claimed to have found physiological and biochemical criteria. In one of these, the Lehmann-Facius method, brain extract was shaken with the patient's cerebrospinal fluid for 15 minutes. If a coarse flocculation appeared it was positive, if only a fine one it was negative. The test was abandoned when it became clear that the coarseness of the flocculation depended on how hard one shook the test-tube! Another was the Klingman test—positive if the radial artery on palpation felt like a thick-walled rubber tube!

Another diagnostic approach came from a school of psychiatry which had never accepted the opinions of Kraepelin and Bleuler from the beginning. Its originators were Meynert and Wernicke, neurologists, who were more organically-minded even than Kraepelin. Its chief exponent at this period was Kleist who promoted a neuropsychological approach to classification. In his system (Kleist 1928) psychoses were distinguished according to the sphere of mental activity which they disturbed (which he divided into five types in rather arbitrary fashion), the site of the brain which he believed was dysfunctional and whether they were typical or not. This led to a bewildering array of terms (e.g. confusional psychosis, motility psychosis), some of which remained as names for psychoses which are now regarded as non-schizophrenic or atypical in some way (p. 92).

The third trend was the attempt by Kurt Schneider, professor of psychiatry in Heidelberg, to systematise Jaspers' notions on schizophrenic psychic life in a way which could be used for diagnostic purposes. He picked out the features of the mental life of a schizophrenic which possessed, in high degree, the qualities of incomprehensibility, irrationality and groundlessness which Jaspers had emphasised. The fullest account of what he called 'first rank symptoms' is found in the chapter 'Cyclothymia and schizophrenia' in his book *Clinical Psychopathology*, translated into English in 1959:

> The value of these symptoms is only related to diagnosis; they have no particular contribution to make to the theory of schizophrenia, as Bleuler's basic and accessory symptoms have, or the primary and secondary symptoms which he and other writers favour . . . Following the order in which we have reviewed them, they are: audible thoughts; voices heard arguing; voices heard commenting on one's actions; the experience of influences playing on the body—somatic passivity experiences; thought withdrawal and other interferences with thought; diffusion of thought; delusional perception; and all feelings, impulses and volitional acts that are experienced by the patient as the work or influence of others.
>
> (Schneider 1959)

Schneider's first rank symptoms were to have more influence in other countries, particularly Britain, than in Germany itself.

France

French psychiatry had taken a particularly independent course. In the first two-thirds of the 19th century it had formed European opinion. After this, when German-speaking countries began to dominate the world of ideas, France remained loyal to its own philosophers, psychologists and psychiatrists. Bergson more than Husserl, Janet as much as Freud, Morel and Magnan as well as Kraepelin influenced their 20th century psychiatrists. Dementia praecox and schizophrenia were accepted, but were restricted in meaning. They generally only referred to cases of hebephrenia. The acute schizophrenia of other countries was called 'bouffée délirante' after Magnan (literally 'a puff of madness'), or 'psychose délirante aigue' by Henri Ey (acute delusional psychosis). Chronic paranoid schizophrenia was rarely diagnosed. The equivalent clinical picture would be called chronic hallucinatory psychosis if hallucinations were prominent or one of several types of 'délires' (delusional states) if there were delusions. The word 'délire' is often misunderstood in translation. What it does *not* mean is delirium. Its meaning is somewhere between 'delusion' and 'delusional state'. The three main types of 'délires' acknowledged were those *of interpretation* (Sérieux and Capgras, 1909, corresponding to typical paranoia with delusions of reference and persecution); *of imagination* (Dupré & Logre 1911, characterised by fantastic delusions); and *of passion* ('délire passionnel') (de Clérambault 1942).

Psychological dysfunction

The only new idea on this aspect of schizophrenia was the notion of 'psychological deficit'. Because North American psychiatrists did not regard schizophrenia as an organic disease they were puzzled by the undoubted deterioration that some patients showed. They could not call it dementia because that had organic connotations. The term psychological deficit was, however, ideal for their purpose.

Two similar accounts of it were written during the decade, one by Hunt and Cofer in 1944, entitled *Psychological deficit*, and one by Shakow in 1946, called *The nature of deterioration in schizophrenic conditions*. All were psychologists and were influenced by the empirical tradition in North American psychology, particularly the attempts to measure intelligence over the previous three decades, and a study by Harriet Babcock in 1933 showing that the most striking feature of schizophrenics' performance on any task was slowness.

Hunt and Cofer stressed that, although schizophrenics might perform as badly on some tasks as patients with definite organic brain damage, the reasons in each case were different:

> Although the patterns in functional and organic disorders show many similarities there are some interesting differences when experiments are designed to bring out motivation and other factors controlling performance . . . The deficit in schizophrenia we conceive as an extinction of standards for performance and of thought skills that have been socially rewarded. The deficit is also complicated by conflicts between response tendencies and by distraction from idiosyncratic preoccupations which arise as substitutes for the socially rewarded skills and response.
>
> (Hunt & Cofer 1944)

The deficit in schizophrenia was therefore variable, and dependent on motivation, distraction, the extent of the social component and individual preoccupations.

Shakow believed that schizophrenics were not intrinsically incapable of doing any task, but that under normal conditions they always performed below their capacity. The discrepancy between competence and actual performance accounted for their apparent deterioration:

> The disturbance in psychological function . . . emerges especially in new situations where an adaptive difficulty is strikingly in evidence . . . Part of this may be accounted for perhaps by the schizophrenic patient's inability to keep an effective set, even . . . for longer than a few seconds. This may also account for his greater intraindividual variation . . . Fundamentally, within the limits of the kinds of psychological functions discussed here it is doubtful whether the schizophrenic patient is essentially abnormal, in the sense of a physiological limit . . . The problem is vulnerability of psychological functions to the deteriorative process . . . the greatest vulnerability seems to be found in a general characteristic, the ability to function quickly at one's own level of efficiency.
>
> (Shakow 1946)

Cause

In North America it was now incorrect to talk about the cause of schizophrenia. In Bellak's view it was a 'deficit reaction' which should be:

> considered on the following four dimensional schemes: somatic predisposition, sociopsychological predisposition, psychological precipitating causes, somatic precipitating causes . . . each of these factors should be expressed on a three-point, five-point or even seven-point scale.
>
> (Bellak 1948)

It was possible, according to him, to have 'relatively completely psychogenic causes' or 'completely organic aetiology'.

Genetic factors had been largely ignored in North America till now, although considerable research had already been done in Germany on families and twins of schizophrenics. It had been a rather disreputable subject in the 1930s and early 1940s because of the uses to which it had been put by the Nazis. But by the late 1940s twin studies by Slater, a British psychiatrist, and family and twin studies by Kallmann, who had emigrated to New York from Germany, had drawn the attention of English-speaking psychiatrists to the potential value of genetic studies.

Treatment

It was in the 1940s that specific treatment for schizophrenia was first administered on any wide scale. Four types of somatic therapy had been introduced in the 1930s—insulin by Sakel in Vienna in 1933, metrazol (a convulsant) by Meduna in Budapest in 1934, prefrontal leucotomy by Moniz in Portugal in 1937 and electroconvulsive therapy by Cerletti and Bini in Italy in 1938. Even though not one of them turned out to be beneficial they were hailed at the time as a significant advance.

At the same time, Sullivan's followers in North America were encouraging the use of psychoanalysis, against the advice of Freud and Jung.

Summary

No original ideas about schizophrenia came to the fore during the 1940s. What did happen was a regrouping of ideas to produce the separation of organic and psychological factors, and causal, phenomenological, diagnostic and therapeutic considerations that we see today. The actual ideas expressed on most of these topics were barren. The somatic therapies were later exposed as worthless, if not harmful. The diagnostic tests (Rorschach, proverbs) fell into disuse. The first attempts at a behavioural formulation of the psychological dysfunction gave way to more precise models, and the attempt to modify psychoanalytic therapy did not achieve popularity even amongst psychoanalysts.

1950s

Ideas on schizophrenia in the 1950s were dominated by two developments, both in the organic sphere. The first was the realisation that organic substances such as mescaline, LSD and amphetamine could mimic the symptoms of schizophrenia. The second was the introduction of neuroleptics in the treatment of the disorder and the rapid appreciation that they were more effective than any of the other somatic therapies. The psychological dysfunction was formulated in strict behavioural terms, and there was an interest, for the first time, in perceptual phenomena.

Diagnosis

The diagnostic trends of the 1940s were accentuated. The North Americans continued to diagnose the condition in a very loose way, relying on psychoanalytical notions and social considerations. The Germans followed the recommendations of Kraepelin and Bleuler. The French maintained their national prejudices, and the British began to employ Schneider's first rank symptoms.

Psychological dysfunction

Behaviourist models

For the first time, orthodox behaviourism was applied to schizophrenia. Launched in 1913 by Watson with an article entitled *Psychology as the behaviourist sees it*, it had undergone a number of changes by the 1950s. The model which was now applied was that of Hull and Spence, where anxiety, motivation, reward or drive accounted for the link between stimulus and response. Some commentators emphasised a disorder at the stimulus end of the chain, some a disorganisation of responses, and some, the majority, a disturbance of motivation or drive which interfered with the conjunction of the two.

Payne, a New Zealander working in Britain, put forward a stimulus disorder model. In a joint paper (Payne et al 1959) he applied Cameron's notion of overinclusion to perception as well as thinking. He pointed out that normal people learned the meaning of something new by 'stimulus discrimination', whereby the extraneous elements in the array of information were inhibited through lack of their reinforcement until the single correct association was made. Schizophrenia, he suggested, might consist of a failure to inhibit these extraneous elements which would leave the subject in a continuous state of stimulus generalisation. Mednick, a North American psychologist, had already reported an experiment in 1955 which showed that schizophrenics did indeed overgeneralise stimuli. Subjects had to release a button whenever the central light in a panel of 11 in front of them came on. They were told not to release the button if any of the other peripheral 10 came on. Schizophrenics were slightly more likely than normals to respond to the peripheral lights, evidence, Mednick claimed, of stimulus generalisation.

Chapman (1958), a North American psychologist, believed at this time that response disorder was the best explanation of the psychological dysfunction. With his wife he later wrote the best account of the behaviourist approach to schizophrenia in a book entitled *Disordered Thought in Schizophrenia* (Chapman & Chapman 1973). He came to his conclusion by chance. He had designed an experiment to test the two main theories of thought disorder at the time—Goldstein's and Cameron's. He handed a subject four cards, each with a word on. The first one might be horse (main item). The second might be mule (member of same class). The third might be shoe (associated with the first item but of a different conceptual class). The fourth might be bottle (irrelevant distractor). The subject's task was to pick from the last three the one which belonged to the same class as the first. (The conceptual similarity between first and second words, and associative strength of first and third words were varied). The results (Table 2.3) did not support Goldstein's position because, according to him, only schizophrenics should make more errors on hard concepts. Nor did it support Cameron's overinclusion theory because he would have predicted that only schizophrenics should make more errors on highly associated distractors.

Table 2.3 Errors on recognising conceptual similarity (Chapman 1958)

	Normals	Schizophrenics
Low associative strength		
Easy concepts	0.1	1.6
Hard concepts	0.8	3.4
High associative strength		
Easy concepts	0.7	4.0
Hard concepts	3.1	11.4

What it did suggest to Chapman was that whenever normals found one task harder than another, schizophrenics showed the same trend but more so. He called this principle 'accentuation of normal bias', 'excessive yielding to normal bias' and in later studies of language he called it 'choice of preferred meaning bias'.

Most investigators favoured a disturbance of drive or motivation which disrupted the link between stimulus and response. Mednick's (1958) account is the most plausible. (The other main behavioural models are described on page 366. In summary, Rodnick & Garmezy, 1957, emphasised a schizophrenic's differential vulnerability to social censure. Cavanaugh, 1958, stressed a motivation defect. McReynolds, 1960, believed that undue anxiety impeded the assimilation of percepts. Broen & Storms, 1961, claimed that unusually high drive would lead to what they called a 'collapse of response hierarchies', saying or doing ridiculous things because the normal probabilities of a stimulus evoking a certain response had been disrupted.) Mednick began his account by pointing out that lack of anxiety or flat affect is commonly observed in chronic schizophrenics, but that acute patients often show extreme anxiety. He then drew on Hull's theory to predict that high anxiety or drive may generalise from one stimulus (e.g. boss) to a new one (e.g. barman), without the subject being aware of this. So for example, following an incident at work, an habitually anxious man goes for his usual afternoon beer which previously calmed him. That day, however, the incident has made him more anxious than usual and he is not calmed by it. He rationalises this fact, not by admitting that he is more anxious than usual, but by blaming the barman, or the FBI, etc. This is Mednick's argument for delusions. His explanation for catatonia is that maintenance of a body position for long periods reduces this anxiety. For clang associations, he again turns to Hull, who said that high drive increases the likelihood that a distant response (previously of low associative strength) will be produced. Finally, he offers an explanation for the apathy, low anxiety, bizarre thinking and delusions of chronic schizophrenics. He supposes that in the acute stage the patient learns that whenever he touches on a thought which is irrelevant to his present condition (tangential thinking) or blames his mental state on something in his immediate environment (paranoid delusions, e.g. radiators are poisoning the air), he experiences a senses of calm. Hence, this 'behaviour'—bizarre thinking and delusional elaboration—is reinforced.

Mednick's account bears a remarkable resemblance to the existential description discussed on page 35. It is, furthermore, the first to attempt a plausible explanation for the entire range of psychotic phenomena without bringing in organic dysfunction. For Mednick, a psychophysiological abnormality is sufficient, though why most anxious people do *not* develop delusions is not explained.

Perceptual phenomena

Studies of perception in schizophrenia had been discouraged until now by Kraepelin's statement that he could find no abnormality in dementia praecox when he applied Wundt's tests. Under the influence of the Gestalt school of psychology, however, perception had become the wider concept of apperception, obeying the same rules as thinking, and therefore of potential significance in schizophrenia. Another development which encouraged interest in the issue was the increasing number of reports of illusions and hallucinations in normal subjects under unusual physiological and psychological conditions (e.g. sleep and sensory deprivation). Such 'anomalous experiences' were regarded by some as analogous to schizophrenia, and gave rise to speculations that the latter condition might itself be the result of the same physiological or psychological disturbance in accentuated form.

Weckowicz, a North American psychologist, suggested that perceptual disorder might be a critical determinant of many of the schizophrenic phenomena:

> Constancy of perception is one of the basic mechanisms of adjustment to the environment . . . Schizophrenia is a severe mental illness which leads to a

> profound disorganisation of behaviour, thought processes and perception—illusions and hallucinations. The latter occur in spite of the fact that the function of the sensory organs is normal and it has to be attributed to the disorder of some higher central processes . . . Whatever the interpretation—physiological or psychological—it is possible that in schizophrenia constancy of perception breaks down and this leads to the perplexity, feeling of change and strangeness of the world which they experience, particularly in the early phases of their illness.
>
> (Weckowicz 1957)

He began a series of experiments on size constancy. In a typical one, a subject had to adjust a rod in front of them until it appeared the same size as a rod which the experimenter had just altered 15 yards away. Schizophrenics generally performed this task poorly: their adjustments, unlike those of normals, did not bear a neat linear relationship to those of the experimenter. Weckowicz interpreted this as impaired size constancy. The idea became rather devalued in the 1960s when the same basic experiment was used to test hypotheses in areas for which it was not designed, such as attention and social psychology.

Abnormal perceptual experiences had recently been reported in unusual physiological and psychological states and these were now compared with the phenomena of schizophrenia. Kleitman, a physiologist from Chicago, had noted in 1939 that sleep-deprived subjects tended to hallucinate under these conditions. Tyler, a psychiatrist in Puerto Rico, then reported on experiments conducted on volunteer soldiers during the war. He claimed that 70% of 350 men who had gone without at least 40 hours of sleep developed illusions, hallucinations and delusions:

> The most common . . . was to see a girl or female relative . . . next common were hallucinations involving animals . . . hearing dogs barking or roosters crowing . . . visual hallucinations of animals were reported by a number of subjects . . . four men experienced true hallucinations, one insisted his mother and girlfriend were watching him in the testing room.
>
> (Tyler 1955)

Delusions as well as hallucinations could occur. Brauchi & West (1959) described the effect on two men of staying awake for 168 hours. They were both contestants in a competition to see who could stay awake the longest. One was challenging the other for his title and 500 dollars. The judge had to stop the competition because of psychotic developments in both. One believed his girlfriend, who was really there to give him support, was conducting an affair with one of the invigilators. Each man became convinced that he and his adversary were members of a secret club of nonsleepers, an example of folie-a-deux partly based on reality. Bliss & colleagues (1959) then put forward a convincing argument as to how sleep deprivation could produce a psychotic condition resembling schizophrenia in all its aspects.

A similar set of reports alerted those interested in schizophrenia to the pathogenic effect of sensory deprivation. The first experiments were carried out in Hebb's laboratory in Montreal. The idea was inspired by reports of its use as torture during the Korean War. Heron, one of Hebb's team, published the main findings on volunteer students under the title *The pathology of boredom*. Sensory deprivation was induced by the use of:

> translucent plastic visors which transmitted diffuse light but prevented pattern vision ... cotton gloves and cardboard cuffs restricted perception by touch ... auditory perception was limited by a U-shaped foam rubber pillow on which their heads lay and by a continuous hum of air-conditioning equipment which masked small sounds ... They were unable to think clearly about anything for any length of time ... They felt experimenters were against them and were trying to make things exceptionally hard for them ... The most striking result of the experiment ... was when they began to see images. One man repeatedly saw a vision of a rock shaded by a tree. Another kept on seeing pictures of babies. Hallucinations usually began with simple forms ... then the visions became more complex ... such as rows of little yellow men with black caps on and their mouth open ... Finally there were integrated scenes ... prehistoric animals walking about in a jungle.
>
> (Heron 1957)

Rosenzweig (1959) was convinced of its relevance to the problem of schizophrenia:

> We now have an experimental model of the schizophrenic syndrome superior to the model psychoses induced with mescaline or LSD. Not only will perceptual interference reproduce more closely the primary symptoms of schizophrenia but these disturbances are caused entirely by external manipulation without the confusion of a toxic psychosis . . . One cannot help noting that throughout these report—clinical, autobiographical (lone sailors and explorers), experimental—there appear again and again Bleuler's cardinal symptoms.
>
> (Rosenzweig 1959)

Rosenzweig's optimism was not shared by subsequent investigators but studies of anomalous experiences of this nature continued to stimulate research into perceptual phenomena in schizophrenia itself.

Cause

The resemblance noted between some drug-induced psychoses and schizophrenia was the main advance in causal notions during the decade. By the end of the 1950s three drugs were considered capable of mimicking schizophrenia—mescaline, LSD and amphetamine.

Mescaline had been known about the longest. Its effects, brought about by eating the peyote cactus in Mexico, had been well described by Havelock Ellis. Osmond and Smythies, two British doctors, first suggested that the mescaline-induced mental state was comparable to schizophrenia. They believed that in schizophrenia some endogenous mescaline-like compound arose from a fault in the final stage of synthesis of adrenaline from noradrenaline. The only difference in the chemical structure of mescaline and adrenaline is the position of a methyl group and the fact that it might become attached in the wrong place became known as the 'transmethylation hypothesis'.

The hallucinogenic properties of LSD were first noticed in 1943 by Hofmann, a Swiss chemist. He had manufactured the substance several years previously, but it was only when he ingested some by accident that he realised its effect. It began as he rode home on his bicycle. Later, he described his experience as 'wonderful, with fantastic images, kaleidoscopic details, the most extraordinary plasticity of surroundings and a feeling of intoxication' (Hofmann, quoted by Rinkel et al 1952). Stoll, a Swiss psychiatrist, investigated its effect more systematically. He claimed that it produced 'disturbances in perception, acceleration of thinking and slight dimming of consciousness' (Stoll 1947). A good account is given in a paper by Rinkel and colleagues in 1952. They were one of the first American groups to study its effects. They gave it to normal volunteers, chronic schizophrenics and acute depressives. The psychiatric groups became much worse; the normals developed:

> predominantly schizophrenia-like symptoms, manifest in disturbance of thought and speech, changes in affect and mood, hallucinations and delusions, but with basic intelligence not reduced.
>
> (Rinkel et al 1952)

Like Osmond and Smythies, they concluded that 'the mechanism of origin of natural and experimental psychotic phenomena is a similar one'. In 1957 Woolley and Shaw reported to the New York Academy of Sciences that the mechanism involved serotonin—later established as one of the few definite neurotransmitters. According to them, LSD usurped the role of serotonin, and 'fitted its receptors as a key fits a lock'.

The third substance in the list is amphetamine. It was first marketed as a cure for narcolepsy in the 1930s, but its stimulant properties soon became widely known. Soldiers used it in the Second World War, and by the 1950s it was being abused on a vast scale. Connell, a British psychiatrist, is largely responsible for pointing out the similarity between some of its mental effects and schizophrenia. He published his findings in a monograph in 1958:

> This work was suggested to me after the admission to the Maudsley Hospital of a patient who had been ingesting the contents of methedrine inhalers (a derivative of amphetamine) for the previous eighteen months . . . His delusions of persecution and auditory and visual hallucinations were indistinguishable from those occurring in paranoid schizophrenia . . . The remarkably close resemblance between the mental symptoms in these patients and in those with paranoid schizophrenia suggested that errors of diagnosis might often occur.
>
> (Connell 1958)

In the 1960s it was realised that amphetamine stimulated dopamine, another definite neurotransmitter.

The subsequent history of biochemical research into schizophrenia has largely been an evaluation of which of these three neurotransmitters—noradrenaline, serotonin, dopamine—is most critically involved in schizophrenia.

Treatment

The popularity of the four types of somatic therapy introduced in the 1930s was waning by the end of the decade. The most widely acclaimed, insulin, was judged ineffective in one of the first-ever controlled trials of psychiatric treatment, carried out in London by Ackner in 1957. In 1952, however, Delay, professor of psychiatry in Paris, published the results of administering a drug called chlorpromazine (trade name Largactil, family name phenothiazine). He coined the term 'neuroleptic' to distinguish its mode of action from that of a tranquilliser, which he considered quite different. Psychiatrists were quickly convinced of its efficacy and most were astonished at its ability to induce remission in back ward patients who had been actively psychotic for over a decade.

Summary

The 1950s saw the introduction of neuroleptics as the first effective and possibly specific treatment. This encouraged a more organic view of the condition amongst European psychiatrists than at any time since Kraepelin, and this was fuelled by analogies with drug-induced psychoses. In North America psychiatrists continued the Meyer-Sullivan-Cameron tradition of regarding schizophrenia as a special kind of social dysfunction, and psychologists there offered behavioural explanations of the phenomena. The most enlightened psychological approach was an interest in perceptual disorder in schizophrenia and in abnormal perceptual experiences arising during unusual physiological and psychological conditions such as sleep and sensory deprivation.

1960s

The attitude to schizophrenia in the 1960s was dominated by social considerations. Social causes and social treatments were vigorously upheld, and some commentators tried to dispose of the condition entirely by making it an artefact of social forces to label deviants as mad. There was a consensus amongst psychologists that the psychological dysfunction was due to a disorder of attention, and there was a concern with schizophrenia language.

Diagnosis

The official criteria were as in the previous two decades: identification of psychosocial deficit in North America, reliance on Kraepelinian or Bleulerian features in most of Europe except France, and an increasing use of Schneider's first rank symptoms in Britain.

Many sociologists and a few maverick psychiatrists, however, introduced a new element into the discussion. They denied the very existence of schizophrenia. 'Patients', they argued, were linguistic or social artefacts, whose status could be accounted for entirely by analysing the rules of the doctor-patient relationship. This led to an antipsychiatry movement, whose slogan was 'people not psychiatry'. Its leaders were Laing, a British psychiatrist, Szasz, a New York psychoanalyst, and Scheff, a North American sociologist.

Laing

Laing wrote several books on the theme. The best is undoubtedly *The Divided Self*, published in 1959. At this period he did not dispute the existence of the condition but took an existential view of its development:

> No-one has schizophrenia, like having a cold. The patient has not got schizophrenia. He is schizophrenic ... We can now state more precisely the nature of our clinical enquiry. A man may have a sense of his presence in the world as a real, alive, whole, and, in a temporal sense, continuous person. As such, he can live out into the world and meet others; a world and others experienced as equally real, alive, whole and continuous. Such a basically *ontologically* secure person will encounter all the hazards of life, social, ethical, spiritual, biological, from a centrally firm sense of his own and other people's reality and identity . . . for the ontologically insecure person . . . the ordinary circumstances of everyday life constitute a continual and deadly threat. Only if this is realised is it possible to understand how certain psychoses can develop.
>
> (Laing 1959)

In his later books, however, he took a more radical stance. In *Sanity, Madness and the Family*, Volume 1 he wrote:

> We believe that we show that the experience and behaviour of schizophrenics is much more socially intelligible than has come to be supposed . . . we are interested in what might be called the family nexus, that multiplicity of persons drawn from the kinship group . . . We have tried to develop a method therefore that enables us to study at one and the same time (1) each person in the family, (2) the relations between persons in the family, (3) the family itself as a system.
>
> (Laing & Esterson 1964)

This book is a set of case studies with three pages of introduction. He never developed his theme, however, because the second volume, in which these cases were to be discussed, never appeared. By 1971 in *Politics of the family* he resorted to gnomic statements such as:

> Schizophrenia is the name for a condition that most psychiatrists ascribe to patients they call schizophrenics;

and:

> Instead of the pathological connotation around such terms as acute schizophrenic breakdown I shall for the moment simply designate the hypothesised sequence as X.
>
> (Laing 1971)

He appeared to believe that schizophrenia could be formulated as the response of one family member to a certain set of ambiguous communications within the family, and that this did not necessarily mean that the family member had an illness. It is probable that he appreciated the implausibility of this, and abandoned the attempt.

Szasz

Szasz presented an entirely different argument but with the same purpose. Like Laing, he published several books, but most of his originality can be found in his first, *The Myth of Mental Illness*, published in 1961. He was not primarily concerned with schizophrenia, but with hysteria. Nevertheless, he mentioned in several places that the same principles apply to schizophrenia. He derived his ideas from two sources. The first was the relatively new field of semiology—the science of signs—the brainchild of a French linguist, Ferdinand de Saussure, and a French writer, Roland Barthes. In Szasz's hands semiology extends into modern symbolic logic and Popper's philosophy of science. The second source was Charcot's concept of hysteria. Charcot had gained a rather unsavoury reputation in the minds of neurologists during the first half of this century. His interest in hysteria and hypnosis was too unorthodox. Szasz appreciated, however, that Charcot represented, albeit in extreme form, the tendency of all doctors to conceptualise certain forms of manipulative behaviour as illness.

Szasz's argument was that there are different ways of communicating distress and that the recipient of a distress signal may misunderstand its nature and purpose. From his readings in semiology he knew that there was a difference between words—part of *symbolic language*—and body signs—which he called lower language or *protolanguage*. Either of these, according to him, could be used in three ways: *informative*, to impart information about one's distress; *affective*, to evoke feelings in others; and *promotive*, to make the recipient of the message perform certain actions. Szasz maintained that the terms hysteria and schizophrenia had arisen because neurologists and psychiatrists had mistaken which one of these uses was intended:

> La grande hystérie seen at the Salpètriere (Charcot's hospital) or the flamboyant schizophrenic bodily feeling encountered today . . . their aim is to suggest and induce mood rather than convey cognitive information . . . The masquerading of promotive assertions in the guise of indicative sentences is of great practical significance . . . Statements concerning psychosis or insanity . . . for example, the statement 'John Doe is psychotic' is ostensibly indicative and informative. Usually however it is promotive rather than informative and may be translated as . . . 'Mrs John Doe does not like the way her husband is acting', or 'Dr James Smith believes that men preoccupied by jealousy are crazy and potentially dangerous' . . . Clearly the indicative sentences do not have nearly the same promotive impact as does the much shorter assertion that 'John Doe is psychotic' . . . From the viewpoint of our present analysis the entire change in renaming certain illnesslike forms of behaviour, from malingering to hysteria and mental illness, can be understood as nothing but a

> linguistic change employed for the purpose of achieving a new type of action-orientation. This verbal change as first advocated by Charcot served to command those charged with dealing with hysterics to abandon their rejecting attitudes towards them and to adopt instead a benevolent attitude.
>
> (Szasz 1961)

Scheff

Scheff's thesis was first presented in his book *Being Mentally Ill* published in 1966. He is regarded as an exponent of 'labelling theory' because he claimed that once certain behaviour acquires a name it develops a spurious validity as a disease concept:

> Concepts of mental illness in general and schizophrenia in particular . . . reify and legitimate the prevailing public order . . . Every society provides its members with a set of explicit norms . . . Offences against these have conventional names . . . against property—theft, against sexual rules—perversion. However the public order also is made up of countless unnamed understandings. Everyone knows for example that during a conversation one looks at the other's eyes or mouth but not at his ear. For the convenience of the society, offences against these unnamed *residual understandings* are lumped together . . . In earlier societies the residual category was witchcraft, spirit possession or possession by the devil; today it is mental illness. The symptoms of mental illness are therefore violation of residual rules.
>
> (Scheff 1966)

Each of these commentators tried to undermine the concept of schizophrenia by showing how certain messages could be misunderstood. They believed that there was meaning in madness, and when this meaning was fully elucidated there was no madness.

Cause

Few psychiatrists went as far as Laing, Szasz or Scheff. A more moderate position was to accept that the condition existed but to regard it as largely psychosocial in origin, arising from exposure to adverse life experience. A number of such pathogenic experiences or circumstances were investigated at this period.

First, there was evidence that the pattern of mental illness differed between countries. Kraepelin himself had visited Java and concluded that dementia praecox was as common there as in Europe and that:

> not one of the symptoms common among Europeans was missing, but they were all much less florid.
>
> (Kraepelin 1904)

In the 1950s, however, a number of 'culture-bound psychoses' were identified with no counterpart in developed societies. For example, in South East Asia there is a condition called koro, where the subject believes that his penis is withdrawing into his abdomen. Leff (1981) regards this and several other sorts of mental disorders as neuroses, not psychoses, but at that time many thought that schizophrenia was merely the culture-bound psychosis of developed countries. This idea was only discredited in the 1970s when the results of the International Pilot Study on Schizophrenia (WHO 1973) were published. It showed that Schneider's first rank symptoms could be identified in roughly the same proportion of Nigerian, Colombian, Indian or Taiwanese psychotics as in English, Russian, Czech, North American or Danish psychotics.

A second source of evidence in favour of a social origin for schizophrenia was the existence of differential prevalence rates within a country. The simplest measure of social status within a country is class, and Hollingshead, professor of sociology, and Redlich, professor of psychiatry at Yale, obtained convincing differences in psychosis rates between higher and lower social classes (Hollingshead & Redlich 1958). As can be seen in Table 2.4,

Table 2.4 Incidence and prevalence rates per 100 000 of mental illness in New Haven

Incidence Class	Neurosis	Psychosis	Schizophrenia	Affective psychosis	Organic psychosis
I/II	69	28	6		
III	78	36	8		
IV	52	37	10		
V	66	73	20		
Prevalence					
I/II	349	188	111	40	9
III	250	291	168	41	24
IV	114	518	300	68	46
V	97	1505	895	105	254

the incidence of neurosis is the same across classes while the incidence of psychosis is highest in social class 5. (The differences in prevalence are, in fact, more striking than differences in incidence and are greater for some nonschizophrenic psychoses than for schizophrenia itself. This implies that social factors contribute more to the build up or poor recovery of cases than to the development of the condition.) Faris and Dunham carried out the other major study on within-country differences. They compared the incidence of psychosis in the centre of Chicago with that in the suburbs. They found a higher rate of schizophrenia but not affective psychosis in the centre. At that time they concluded that the poor social conditions which prevailed in the inner city slums were a causal factor. When he repeated the study in Detroit, however, Dunham (1965) came to the opposite conclusion. Rather, poor social conditions were a consequence not a cause of schizophrenia. Schizophrenics drifted to the slums. Hare, a British psychiatrist, came to the same conclusion in the case of Bristol (Hare 1956). Despite these later disclaimers, the causal significance of subcultural factors such as poverty was accepted as reality by many at the time.

A third focus of interest was the impact of personal misfortune on an individual. George Brown, a British sociologist, was the architect of some careful work on this topic (Brown & Birley 1968). He enquired into the nature and timing of any life event which had occurred in the 13 weeks prior to the onset of a schizophrenic episode. Fifty patients, where the date of onset was accurately known, were selected for the study. A life event had to be independent of the illness (e.g. youngest brother charged by police) or possibly independent (e.g. new girl friend). The rate of life events in local factory and office workers provided a normal control. The results are shown in Table 2.5. It shows a marked increase in both independent and possibly independent life events in, but only in, the three weeks prior to onset.

Table 2.5 Percentage of subjects with at least one life event in 12-week period prior to onset (schizophrenics) or interview (normals)

	0–3 weeks before	3–6 weeks before	6–9 weeks before	9–12 weeks before
Independent events				
Schizophrenics	46	14	8	14
Normals	14	14	15	15
Possibly independent events				
Schizophrenics	22	6	10	16
Normals	5	5	5	6

Fourthly, there were studies of a patient's family background. Frieda Fromm-Reichmann, a pupil of Sullivan, had coined the term schizophrenogenic mother in 1948:

> The schizophrenic is painfully distrustful and resentful of other people, because of the severe early warp and rejection that he has encountered in important people of his infancy and childhood, as a rule mainly in a schizophrenogenic mother.
>
> (Fromm-Reichmann 1948)

Then in the 1950s several authors reported exceptionally high rates of psychiatric disorder and marital dysharmony in the parents of schizophrenics. Lidz, a psychiatrist at Yale, found that only 5 out of the 50 schizophrenics whom he studied had had a stable home life (Lidz & Lidz 1949). The remainder had experienced one and usually several of five misfourtunes—death or separation of a parent before they reached the age of 19, chronic instability of the parents' marriage, chronic hostility between the parents, serious deviation from cultural norms in their upbringing or mental illness in a close relative. Lidz then concentrated on the quality of the parents' marriage in 14 cases (Lidz et al 1957). All were disordered in one of two ways. There could be 'marital schism'. This meant chronic disruption, with, for example, constant threats of separation and serious undercutting of one partner by another. The other he called 'marital skew'. Here one partner had abdicated parental and domestic authority to the other, who, although more dominant, had 'serious psychopathology'. Wynne and colleagues in Bethesda, Maryland (Wynne et al 1958) described another way in which the parental marriage could be abnormal. This pattern, which they called 'pseudo-mutuality', was characterised by a 'predominant but illusory absorption in fitting together'. The parents, according to Wynne, had made a single-minded effort to hold together a shaky marriage at all costs. (It should be said that the description of a normal marriage with which this is contrasted sounds idealistic in the extreme.) Alanen, a Dane, was the other main contributor in the field. In the second of his two studies on 30 schizophrenics (Alanen, 1966) he found only *1* normal parent out of 57 traced.

The results of this last group of studies, demonstrating that psychiatric morbidity or marital discord was almost universal in the parents, encouraged several family-based formulations of the origin of schizophrenia. The three main ones are those of Bateson, Wynne and Lidz.

Bateson, from Stanford in California, devised what is known as the double-bind theory. With co-workers Jackson, Haley and Weakland he first outlined this in an article in 1956. His inspiration was Bertrand Russell and his theory of logical types. This states that most philosophical and logical muddles can be put down to not realising that statements of the type 'I am lying' are different from statements such as 'I am eating'. The former is more complex because it refers to the truth value of other statements; the latter is a simple description of behaviour. It is interesting that Szasz used an almost identical argument to prove a different point. Szasz said that schizophrenia arose through a misunderstanding on the part of the *psychiatrist* as to the logical status of statements made by the *patient*. Bateson said that the *patient* becomes schizophrenic because he misunderstands the logical status of statements made by a key *relative*. The double-bind occurs when this key relative gives conflicting messages in different modes. One is usually a verbal command forbidding the child from doing something. The second is expressed in a different mode (e.g. smile—nonverbal) and on a more abstract level (smile means that the child is not to regard the verbal reprimand as punishment). A third component, inability of the victim to escape from the field, is also necessary for the first two to work. He gives examples, one from Zen Buddhism and one actual:

> Zen master holds a stick over his pupil and says, 'If you say this stick is real I will strike you with it. If you say this stick is not real I will strike you with it. If you don't say anything I will strike you with it'. A child's mother becomes anxious and withdraws if the child responds to her as a loving mother. But feelings of anxiety and hostility to the child are not acceptable to her. There is no strong insightful father to provide relief.
>
> (Bateson et al 1956)

Wynne, having identified 'pseudomutual marriages' as common amongst schizophrenic parents, then described their pathogenic effect:

> In the families of potential schizophrenics the intensity and duration of pseudomutuality has led to the development of a particular variety of shared family

> mechanisms by which deviations from the family role structure are excluded from recognition or are delusionally reinterpreted. These shared mechanisms act at a primitive level in preventing the articulation and selection of any meanings that might enable the individual family member to differentiate his personal identity either within or outside of the family role structure.

There was a:

> rubber fence . . . a continuous but elastic boundary . . . which obscures the idea of a family boundary . . . The fragmentation of experience, the identity diffusion, the disturbed modes of perception and communication . . . are to a significant extent derived by processes of internalisation from characteristics of the family social organisation.
>
> (Wynne et al 1958)

Lidz offered a similar theory in which the schizophrenic was:

> more prone to withdraw through distortion of his symbolisation of reality than other patients because his foundation in reality testing is precarious, having been raised amidst irrationality, and chronically exposed to intrafamilial communications that distort and deny what should be the obvious interpretation of the environment.
>
> (Lidz et al 1958)

These family-based explanations for schizophrenia seemed plausible at the time and continued to appeal to clinicians till the end of the 1970s. A critical study by Hirsch & Leff (1975), two British psychiatrists, was partly responsible for their abandonment by mainstream psychiatrists.

Psychological dysfunction

Attention

Both Kraepelin and Bleuler had remarked on the impairment of attention in the condition, but both had attributed it to some other more primary psychological dysfunction. Kraepelin believed it was secondary to a disorder of will, Bleuler to the affective disturbance. It then disappeared completely from formulations of schizophrenia until the early 1960s. The main reason for this was its neglect by psychologists in general. William James and Wundt had promoted the concept at the turn of the century, but the idea of some internal control over perception was unacceptable to behaviourists who dominated North American psychological thinking between 1920 and 1960. The resurrection of the idea was largely due to the publication in 1958 of a book called *Perception and Communication* by Broadbent, a British psychologist. In it he dealt with vigilance, selective listening and shifting attention, mechanisms involved when one is trying to do two things at once. His enquiry led him to the conclusion that normal people could filter out irrelevant information, a fact which indicates that there is some relatively central control mechanism—attention or filter. This dealt a major blow to behaviourism. Broadbent's model is shown in Figure 2.1. It was subsequently modified by other psychologists to account for the fact that normal

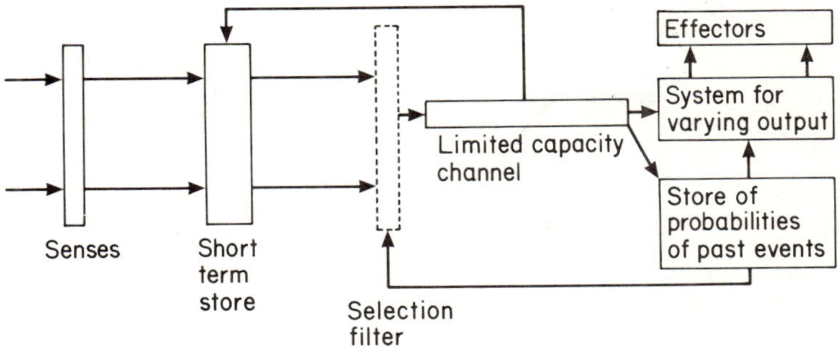

Fig. 2.1 Broadbent's filter theory.

people would respond to their name and other meaningful information if it were presented via the channel which they were not attending to. This sensitivity to meaning, prior to encoding the physical characteristics of a stimulus, implied the workings of an even more central mechanism than Broadbent had suggested. During the 1960s and early 1970s, however, Broadbent's filter was the accepted model of attention and the idea that an incompetent filter might underlie the psychological dysfunction in schizophrenia was soon appreciated. The main proponents of an attentional deficit in schizophrenia were Shakow, the North American psychologist discussed earlier for his views on the question of dementia, McGhie and Chapman, two British psychologists, Venables, another British psychologist, and Silverman, an American psychologist.

Shakow worked at the Worcester State Hospital in Massachusetts and spent most of his professional life studying reaction time in schizophrenics. His usual experiment was to ask a patient to press a button when he heard a bell and release it when he saw a light. The period between bell and light was called preparatory interval, and it had a curious effect on reaction time (how long it took the patient to release the button after the light came on). Two aspects of this preparatory interval (usually abbreviated to P I) affected performance. One was its length; the other was the effect of presenting runs of the same length (regular P I) or randomly varied lengths (irregular P I). Shakow discovered that schizophrenics were slower than normals under all conditions, but the pattern varied in the two groups (Figure 2.2). Whereas normals were consistently faster with regular than with irregular P I s, schizophrenics were faster with regular P I s of up to six seconds, but beyond this they were faster with irregular P Is. This 'crossover effect' intrigued Shakow. He regarded it as an inability to maintain a 'major set'. What he meant by this was that schizophrenics could not keep themselves in a state of readiness to receive incoming stimuli:

> A schizophrenic reacts to old situations as if new, and to new as if old; overresponds to small changes and underresponds to large changes ... There is a weakening of a control centre that provides major sets . . . a preoccupation

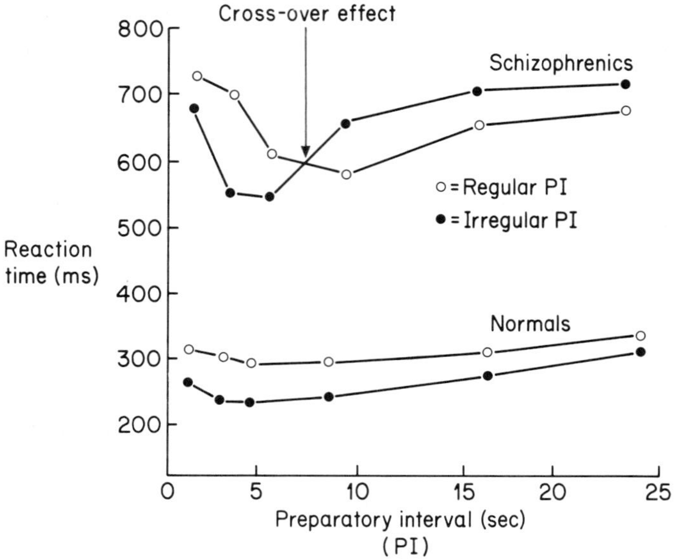

Fig. 2.2 The crossover effect in reaction time.

> with ordinarily unconscious bodily processes and mechanisms of processes rather than ends . . . an interest in details.
>
> (Shakow 1963)

McGhie and Chapman recorded exactly what schizophrenics said about the functioning of their mind during the early stages of their condition, and from these accounts produced a convincing argument for a primary disturbance in attention. Their patients reported experiences such as, 'I let all the sounds come in that are there' or, 'I see things more than what they really are' or, 'I have to do everything step by step, I am aware of my every movement' or, 'There are too many things coming into my head at once'. McGhie and Chapman concluded:

> The earliest reported symptoms of a schizophrenic illness indicate that a primary disorder is that of a decrease in the selective and inhibitory functions of attention . . . leading to . . . a gradual tendency for perception to become global . . . a heightened awareness of bodily functions and volitional impulses which are normally outside of the range of conscious awareness . . . and a decrease in concentration and progressive thought disorder.
>
> (McGhie & Chapman 1961)

Venables reviewed a number of experiments and theories in 1964, which supported, in his view, the existence of 'input dysfunction'. He meant by this a disorder of attention. His main contribution, however, was to relate it to a disturbance in arousal, and, for the first time since Bleuler, the psychological dysfunction was linked to some cerebral dysfunction, reflected in this instance by a psychophysiological disturbance. The main measure of this disturbance was skin conductance or galvanic skin resistance (GSR), the electrical potential between two electrodes on the hand, representing the amount of sweating and hence arousal. Venables claimed that acute schizophrenics were underaroused and had a broader attention span; chronic schizophrenics were, according to him, overaroused with restricted attention. Even though his conclusions were at variance with most psychiatrists' clinical impressions, and he himself (Venables 1977a) later corrected them, his general approach heralded a new era and paved the way for a return to the broadly neuropsychological theories of Bleuler and Kraepelin.

Silverman had the broadest concept of attentional disorder. He regarded attention as a 'cognitive control principle' by which 'percepts, ideas, memories and sensations were organised' (Silverman 1964). In schizophrenia, he believed, these cognitive controls were inefficient and, in particular, there was a deficit of 'sensory input processing—ideational gating', a very broad application of Broadbent's filter theory.

Silverman's views are an illustration of what happened to the attention theory of schizophrenia during the decade. Like many good ideas it was ruined by its own success, and became too general to be of any value. In the 1970s attempts were made to refine it again, by distinguishing various aspects of attention—selectivity, distractibility—and by seeking specific links with other functions—language, memory, perception. There was little experimental support for these modifications, and attention deficits were eventually given only a minor role in more general theories of cognitive dysfunction.

Language

Schizophrenic language had not been entirely neglected till now. Word association had been intensively studied by Jung (1907) in Switzerland and Kent & Rosanoff (1910) in North America. Neologisms (new words) had been of interest to Kleist (1914), who regarded their presence in both schizophrenia and aphasia as support for his neuropsychological theory of the former. To Carl Schneider (1930) they had a symbolic significance within an existential framework. In the 1940s the first experimental investigations were carried out by Whitehorn & Zipf (1943). Zipf had developed what became known as the Zipf curve, in which one took a large sample of language and plotted the frequency of each word (e.g. man might appear once every 250 words) against the rank order of frequency (e.g. man might be the 15th after the, and, he, etc.). If one used double logarithmic paper, one obtained a striaght line. This is illustrated in Figure 2.3. Whitehorn and he found that schizophrenics had a steeper curve than normals, indicating that they used fewer words. By the 1960s, a number of measures of language were available, and language itself had become of interest to experimental psychologists through Chomsky's insistence that grammar and not meaning

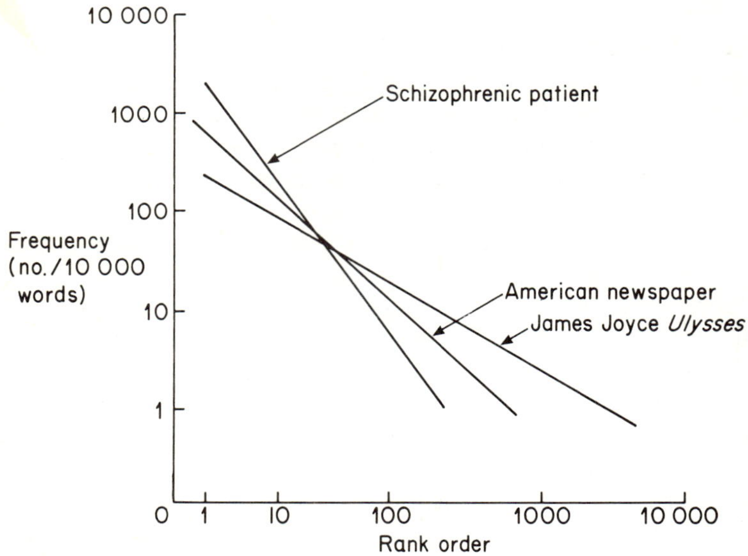

Fig. 2.3 Zipf curve for normal and schizophrenic language.

was the clue to its understanding. The publication of Chomsky's book *Syntactic Structures* in 1957 had generated an entirely new branch of psychology—psycholinguistics.

The commonest measurement was the Cloze procedure, devised by Taylor, a journalist, in 1953 to quantify readability in newspapers. Every fourth or fifth word from a real passage would be obliterated and subjects were invited to guess which word had been deleted. The Cloze score was then the ratio of correct guesses to the total number of words deleted. Several investigators found that schizophrenic speech, after transcription, deletions and rating by normals, had lower Cloze scores than that of normals (i.e. less predictable). This finding was then used to support several different theories of the psychological dysfunction. The most widely promoted was the 'immediacy hypothesis' of Salzinger and his colleagues from New York (Salzinger et al 1964). They found that the Cloze score of the first half of a 200 word sample of schizophrenic speech was higher (more predictable) than the second half, suggesting that schizophrenics were unduly influenced by the immediate stimuli in their environment.

Another measure of language was obtained by the method of contextual constraint, devised by Miller and Selfridge, North American psychologists, in 1950. Subjects are asked to remember sentences which vary systematically in their grammatical correctness (approximation to English) regardless of semantic meaning. This is illustrated in Figure 2.4, which portrays the results of an experiment on chronic schizophrenics by Truscott (1970), a North American psychologist. Normal subjects were much better at remembering normal sentences than were schizophrenics but this difference disappeared with the removal of semantic (anomalous sentences in Fig. 2.4)

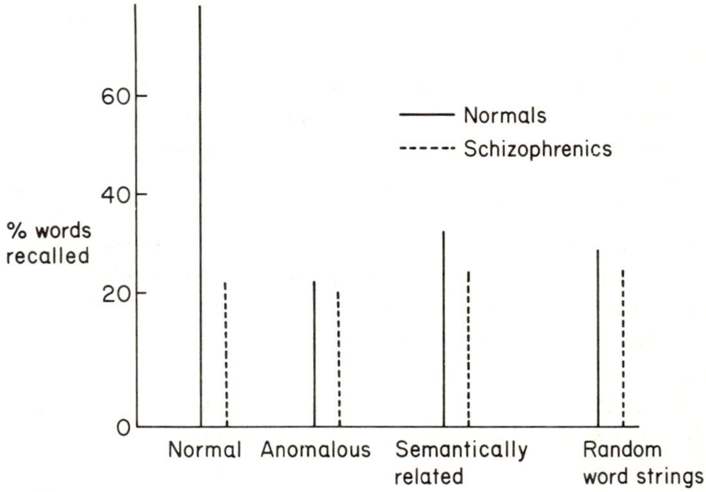

Fig. 2.4 Recall of sentences varying in contextual constraint. Normal: e.g. snug rings bind chubby fingers; anomalous: e.g. snug olives spread splintered subdivision; semantically-related: e.g. rings snug fingers chubby bind.

or grammatical constraints (semantically-related sentences and random word strings in Fig. 2.4). These findings were also attributed, like the low Cloze scores, to a variety of psychological deficits. By the mid 1970s, however, the findings themselves were disputed or considered of marginal significance in a few chronic schizophrenics, and their theoretical basis, therefore, of no further interest.

A third measure was content analysis. This also had its origin in journalism, and was a method for detecting the frequency of certain specified themes in a passage. It was hoped that this might throw some light on a schizophrenic's preoccupations or formal thought patterns. The two main studies, by Maher & colleagues (1966) and by Gottschalk & Gleser (1969), all North American psychologists, proved disappointing. In the latter study, for example, the investigators transcribed a segment of schizophrenic speech and then categorised the main themes found. The main conclusion was that schizophrenics were more likely to give mumbled inaudible phrases and make illogical bizarre remarks, and less likely to admit that others were helpful or friendly or that they themselves felt kindly disposed to others. This means little more than the fact that the schizophrenics had moderate clinical thought disorder and were suspicious, or frankly paranoid.

The yield of these experiments was meagre, but their value was the development of an experimental method which allowed the problem of communication disorder to be tackled in the 1970s.

Treatment

Of the various somatic therapies, all but neuroleptics had been abandoned by the end of the decade. Neuroleptics, however, were increasingly confirmed as the treatment of choice. Their effectiveness in shortening and abolishing the symptoms of the acute episode was convincingly demonstrated in a collaborative study organised by the National Institute of Mental Health (Cole et al 1964). Three hundred and forty-four schizophrenics completed a six-week trial in which they were randomly assigned to receive one of three neuroleptics or a placebo. Of those who received the active drug, 75% improved compared with 23% receiving placebo. Their effectiveness as a prophylactic, preventing recurrence of further episodes, was also demonstrated in several studies towards the end of the decade. Leff & Wing (1971), for example, assigned 35 schizophrenics recently recovered from an acute episode to placebo or neuroleptic. At the end of a year 80% on placebo had relapsed compared with 35% on the active drug.

The newest innovation in treatment, however, was the active attempt to manipulate the social environment of a schizophrenic. In Britain this was pursued under the broad regime of community psychiatry, which also included the deinstitutionalisation and rehabilitation of patients. The malign influence of institutions had been recognised since Bleuler's time. Indeed one of his pupils, Klaesi, had made a special study of the matter and recommended work and leisure activities to counteract it. Most mental hospitals were untouched by this or by the therapeutic community and group therapy movement started by Maxwell Jones, a British psychiatrist, in 1952.

Two events had some influence in initiating the change in emphasis from hospital to community care. The first was the publication in 1961 of a fiercely argued book *Asylums* by Goffman, a sociologist at Berkeley in California. It was a vivid account of all aspects of institutional life, based on his experience of mental hospitals but making frequent comparisons with prison and concentration camp. The second was a book by Wing, a social psychiatrist at the Maudsley Hospital, and Brown, mentioned above, entitled *Institutionalism and Schizophrenia* (Wing & Brown 1970). In it they reported their study of three large mental hospitals around London, whose superintendents had different attitudes towards the social welfare of their inmates and hence provided different standards of amenities. They analysed the different sorts of disability which they found, some premorbid or primary and due to the condition, some secondary and largely iatrogenic. They found a high correlation between the clinical poverty syndrome (withdrawal, flatness of affect and poverty of speech) and environmental poverty (e.g. few personal possessions). They pondered which came first, but were lucky enough to have a ready-made experiment, when the superintendent of one of the hospitals was replaced by someone less interested in providing social amenities. This intensified the clinical poverty syndrome in the patients in that hospital.

Two rules then began to determine the psychosocial management of schizophrenia. The first came from the appreciation of the malign influence of institutions. The rule was simply that one should do all one can to achieve as normal a life as possible for the patient. This included encouraging job searching, help with accommodation and promoting social and leisure activities. The second rule was that one should be prepared to manipulate the patient's environment to reduce exposure to the expression of pathogenic emotions and overinvolvement in his immediate family circle. This rule developed partly out of the ideas of Bateson, Wynne and Lidz, and partly out of definite evidence (Brown et al 1962) that returning to interpersonal situations rated high in emotional expression increased the risk of relapse.

Summary

Three themes dominated psychological formulations of schizophrenia in the 1960s. The first of these was the social dimension. Epidemiological evidence, observations on the families of schizoprenics and appreciation of the nature of institutional life alerted psychiatrists and psychologists to its importance. Some sociologists and a few radical psychiatrists responded by denying the very existence of schizophrenia. Psychoanalysts treated the family pathology as a psychogenic influence. Mainstream psychiatrists and psychologists incorporated the social evidence into their particular model of schizophrenia.

There was a surprising consensus that attentional deficits underlay the psychological dysfunction. This notion had only recently been resurrected as an acceptable concept in experimental psychology and it soon became a popular explanation for thought disorder, perceptual failure and peculiarities of language. In fact it became too widely used and lost its original appeal.

Finally, language attracted the interest of psychologists. Most studied was grammar, which Chomsky had identified as a central component. Little of intrinsic value emerged, but the experimental methods which were learned and the issues which were tackled all contributed to the sophistication in psychological approach which was to mark the 1970s.

1970s

Psychological notions of schizophrenia drew upon three sets of ideas during the 1970s. The first was information processing theory, the replacement for behaviourism as the mainstream psychologist's model of the mind. It gave a prominent role to memory and consciousness, both of which were then studied in schizophrenia. The second set of ideas broadly concerned communication and its breakdown. This combined two preoccupations of the 1960s: the suspicion that there was something wrong with schizophrenic language but the absence of any gross abnormality such as aphasia, and the overwhelming evidence that the schizophrenic condition was most apparent in social interactions. The third set of ideas were neuropsychological and drew upon the newly discovered differences between the hemispheres. This led to the realisation that schizophrenia might yet be an organic brain disease causing an imbalance of functions entirely unknown to Kraepelin, Bleuler and Jaspers.

Diagnosis

This was the decade of standardisation in psychiatry. Interviews, evaluation of mood and social functioning, and diagnostic criteria were all measured, and recommendations made for improving their reliability. By the end of the decade there were about a dozen 'operational definitions' in existence in addition to the clinical descriptions of Kraepelin, Bleuler, Jaspers and Schneider, and the various national and theoretical schools. The aim of the operational definitions had been to improve communication between various groups of research workers, so that if one group reported, for example, a low level of platelet monoamine oxidase in 'Spitzer schizophrenia' others would know what they meant. In fact, by the end of the decade there were so many definitions to choose from that it became necessary to retain only the best. They differed considerably in their degree of strictness (what proportion of psychotic subjects they designated as schizophrenic), their inter-rater reliability (the extent to which two operators came to the same conclusion on the same patient), their concordance rates (how closely they agreed with other definitions) and their predictive validity (how well they predicted outcome). The best in terms of all these measures (moderately strict, fairly reliable, concordant with most other definitions and better than most at predicting outcome) were the Research Diagnostic Criteria of Spitzer and his colleagues in New York (Spitzer et al 1975). Spitzer's criteria required two weeks of delusions and hallucinations which were neither explicable in terms of mood nor, in the case of delusions, purely persecutory. They were later incorporated into the official diagnostic recommendations of the American Psychiatric Association—DSM-III (APA, 1980) but with the additional proviso that they be present for six months.

Psychological dysfunction

Information processing models

Since the decline of behaviourism, cognitive psychology had been the ruling theory of those interested in the normal mind. One branch of this, more concerned with processes than structure, was known as information processing theory. It borrowed freely from computer terminology and saw the mind essentially as a channel through which information passed and was acted upon. There was some dispute about the stage at which meaning was processed (early? or late?) and about the extent to which serial (conscious, controlled) or parallel (subconscious, automatic) processing went on. Otherwise the model was straightforward.

The efficient workings of the peripheral stages were systematically tested in schizophrenics during the decade, more because of the existence of a ready-made experimental paradign than because of any clinical relevance. Attention, basic memory processes and the early stages of visual perception were all evaluated in well-designed experiments. The results indicated that these functions were intact in acute schizophrenics, if one took into account their preoccupation with delusional themes. Chronic schizophrenics on the other hand did show marked impairment of these functions, but it had become clear by the end of the decade, with the introduction of the CT scan, that they tended to have radiological evidence of generalised brain disease and their psychological status was not therefore comparable with that of acute schizophrenics. There was some evidence that acute schizophrenia was characterised by a deficit in 'selective attention' or vulnerability to distraction, a proposal championed by Oltmanns & Neale (1978), two North American psychologists. Another claim, by Koh (1978), from Chicago, was that their strategies for organising information to be memorised were particularly inefficient. Neither of these deficits appeared to be either specific to the condition or a central determinant of the clinical phenomena. The two most comprehensive theories of the psychological dysfunction during the decade, proposed by British psychologists Hemsley (1977) and Frith (1979), denied any primary importance to a disorder of perception, attention or memory.

Hemsley brought together several ideas from the previous two decades: Broen and Storms' notion of response disorganisation, Payne's version of stimulus overinclusion and McGhie and Chapman's suggestion of information overload. His own contribution was to explain more clinical phenomena than any of these authors had done, and without bringing in the concept of attentional disorder. He designed his theory around the response end of the information processing chain, the central problem, according to him, being one of the inappropriate 'pigeon-holing'. He gave psychological correlates for five different clinical phenomena, shown in simplified form

Table 2.6 Hemsley's information processing theory of schizophrenia

Clinical phenomenon	Psychological mechanism
Incoherence of speech	Intrusion of associated responses
Flatness of affect	Raised threshold for response
Delusions	Undifferentiated responding
Catatonia	Reduction of exploratory responses
Retardation	Delayed responding

in Table 2.6. Each of these was a form of adaptation to information overload, the precise pattern being determined by the severity of the overload, the quality of the environment and the premorbid personality.

Frith believed that:

> the symptoms of schizophrenia can be interpreted as the result of a defect in the mechanism that controls and limits the contents of consciousness. This defect can be understood as excessive self-awareness. Normally most of the complex information processing which is continuously required by even simple acts of perception, language and thought goes on below the level of awareness; whereas in schizophrenic patients some of this processing, or the results of this processing, not in themselves abnormal, become conscious.
>
> (Frith 1979)

Hallucinations, particularly the first rank symptoms of hearing one's thoughts spoken aloud, were due to the appearance in consciousness of incorrect interpretations of real sounds in the environment. Frith assumed that when one hears a sound, one makes, preconsciously, a number of interpretations. Normally, these 'guesses' and 'checks' do not reach our conscious awareness, but in schizophrenia they do. Delusions were due neither to a primary disorder of thought nor perceptual deficit but were:

> attempts to explain and understand, using entirely normal principles of reasoning and experience, the basic misperceptions we have already discussed . . . it is quite impossible for a percept to arrive in consciousness abnormally . . . The abnormality lies in the fact that normally we would not bother to interpret such an event. The very arrival of the percept in awareness means that it is important and therefore needs to be explained. This hyperawareness, noting and remembering, for example, the colours of the ties of all the guests at a party, is frequently observed in deluded patients.
>
> (Frith 1979)

Thought disorder, according to Frith, resulted from the premature entry into consciousness of normally discarded alternative meanings, and catatonia from a preoccupation with normally automatic motor sequences.

Communication breakdown

The unusual utterances of schizophrenics had always puzzled investigators. The received opinion from Bleuler's time until the 1950s was that the fault originated in the sphere of *thought* and that the processes of language encoding and emission of speech efficiently transmitted ideas which were already abnormal. Behaviourists in the 1950s and 1960s had considered that the problem lay with the selection of the correct *speech* response but the proposed mechanism had been inadequately described. In the 1970s, three novel suggestions were made. Chaika (1974), a linguist, considered that there was an actual breakdown in basic *language* competence. Rochester & Martin (1979), psychologists, found that the main abnormality only appeared in longer segments of speech, *speech discourse*, and that this was due to the use of poor links between clauses. Cohen (1978), a psychologist, believed that the most characteristic feature was an impaired ability to edit the final utterance with the result that it failed to convey the intended message; he called this a '*referent communication disturbance*'.

Chaika based her proposal on an intensive study of one patient whom she claimed had six specific linguistic deficits. The first was:

> sporadic disruption in the ability to match semantic features with sound strings comprising actual lexical items in the language ... e.g. I have distemper just like cats do 'cause that's what we all are, felines.

The second was:

> preoccupation with too many of the semantic features of a word in discourse . . . e.g. My mother's name was Bill and coo. St Valentine's Day is the official startin' of the breedin' season of the birds. All buzzards can coo. I like to see buzzards pronounced right. They work hard. So do parakeets.

The third was:

> inappropriate noting of phonological features of words in discourse . . . e.g. I had a little goldfish too like a clown. Happy Halloween down;

and the fourth:

> a disruption in the ability to apply rules of syntax and discourse . . . e.g. In a month I've been upstairs they're taking my brains out a piece at a time or all together.
>
> (Chaika 1974)

The fifth was a combination of the second and third, and the sixth was a 'failure to self-monitor'. Her paper provoked considerable discussion amongst linguists, most of whom pointed out that all her 'specific' characteristics could occur in normals. Her descriptions and examples, however, particularly the second and third, were in my view full of insight on the use of language in schizophrenia.

Rochester and Martin carried out a detailed analysis of the structure of clauses taken from speech samples of 10 clinically thought disordered schizophrenics, 10 schizophrenics without thought disorder and 10 normals. They presented their findings in a book entitled *Crazy Talk*. The speech samples were obtained during interview, whilst the patients were telling a story and whilst they were describing a cartoon. The authors noted the quality of the links which subjects made between one clause and the next and the complexity of the clauses. They evaluated the quality of the links by counting the number of 'cohesive ties'. For example, in the sentence 'John got a new bicycle; I got a used one', the word 'one' is a cohesive tie linking the second clause with the first. In the sentence 'John loves dogs; he has a collie', the word 'collie' is a lexical cohesive tie. They found that both thought-disordered and nonthought-disordered schizophrenics made significantly fewer cohesive ties than normals. The exact number varied according to the source of the speech sample. They assessed the complexity of a clause by counting the number of nominal groupings it contained. The clause, 'The house is red' contains only one nominal group; the clause 'The house on the hill by the water is old' contains several. They found that both groups of schizophrenics had fewer nominal groupings per clause than normals. In addition, whereas normals produced more complex clauses (more nominal groupings) when describing cartoons than when being interviewed, this increase was less marked in schizophrenics without thought disorder, and there was no increase at all in those with thought disorder. The authors concluded that schizophrenics, particularly those with clinical thought disorder, created fewer referential ties than normals. They attributed the deficit to short-term memory failure, an information processing explanation, but this is less interesting than their careful evaluation of the language itself.

Cohen carried out a number of experiments on what he called 'referent communication disturbances in schizophrenia', best summarised in a chapter in 1978. His basic method was to present two words similar in meaning, and ask a subject to give a clue which would distinguish them for a listener. For example, if the two words were freedom and liberty, and the instructions were to direct the listener to freedom (the 'referent' in his scheme), then academic was a helpful cue, judged by the accuracy of a panel of listeners. He also designed a nonverbal task, in which one of two similar hues of the same basic colour had to be communicated to a listener. A helpful cue in this case might be 'the greener of the two blues'. Schizophrenics and normals were paired in four ways so that the adequacy of a schizophrenic as speaker or listener could be evaluated. The results indicated that *schizophrenic speakers* but not schizophrenic listeners were responsible for the impaired communication. He showed that a schizophrenic's speech was just as incomprehensible to himself as to others, by taping his performance on the task and playing it back to him. He also found that schizophrenics were relatively less accurate than normals on very similar words or hues despite pausing longer before transmitting the message and using more words. This suggested to him that they were actually trying hard but kept sampling the same inadequate response which they could not edit out. He called this the 'perseverative chaining model' of the self-editing deficit.

These attempts to describe the use of language by schizophrenics were a considerable advance on the proposals of previous decades which had been restricted to unqualified statements such as thought disorder or speech disorder.

Cause

The two most significant advances in understanding the cause of schizophrenia during the decade were both organic. The first was the application of discoveries in the field of neuropsychology. The specific role of the right hemisphere in nonverbal processes had been identified in the 1950s and the functions of the corpus callosum discovered in the 1960s. Clinical, pathological, psychophysiological and psychological evidence of hemisphere imbalance were now found in schizophrenia. The second pointer to an organic cause of schizophrenia emerged when CT scanning was invented. It was the first noninvasive radiological technique to give a picture of the brain, and initial reports indicated that many chronic schizophrenics had generalised cerebral atrophy.

Hemisphere imbalance

In 1969 Flor-Henry, a Canadian psychiatrist working at that time in Britain, reported a series of patients who had both temporal lobe epilepsy and psychosis. When he analysed the type of psychosis and the side of the lesion responsible for the epilepsy, he found a statistical association between left-sided lesions and schizophrenia. In the same year, Davison and Bagley, two British psychiatrists, published a review of the literature on what they called a 'schizophrenia-like psychosis associated with organic disorders of the central nervous system'. They studied 15 different physical conditions which could cause cerebral dysfunction (e.g. epilepsy, head injury, Huntington's chorea) and defined schizophrenia as the presence of thought disorder, incongruous affect, hallucinations or delusions without evidence of depression, mania, amnesia, delirium or dementia. They then found an 'association of left cerebral hemisphere and particularly temporal lobe lesions with primary delusions'.

Lishman, a British psychiatrist (Lishman & McMeekan, 1976), then suggested that schizophrenics might have an abnormal pattern of handedness, indirect evidence of abnormal hemispheric balance. Because there were only 26 schizophrenics in the sample of patients whom he studied, he was only confident about the pattern in psychiatric patients in general. These patients were significantly more likely to be left handed than the normal population. An analysis of the diagnostic categories, however, revealed that it was only psychotic patients, particularly young, male and deluded, who accounted for the increased number of left handers.

Rosenthal & Bigelow (1972) measured the width of the corpus callosum in the brains of 10 chronic schizophrenics. It was 6 millimetres wide, 1 millimetre wider on average than control brains. This finding served to attract attention to a possible disorder of interhemispheric transfer in schizophrenia.

Gruzelier (1973), a British psychologist, measured skin conductance in each hand of 60 chronic and subacute male schizophrenics. He presented a series of sounds at the same time, in order to obtain an orienting response, a change in the electrical activity of the skin brought about by a new stimulus. Only half of the patients produced an orienting response and the overall difference between the magnitude of the right and the left hand responses was not significant. However, of the 15 subacute schizophrenics who responded, 10 showed higher right hand amplitudes, 3 had higher left hand amplitudes and 2 had equal responses. He attributed this lateralisation of orienting response to left-sided temporal lobe dysfunction, because some animal work conducted by Luria, a Russian neuropsychologist (Luria & Homaskaya, 1963) had suggested that frontotemporal lesions produce a reduction in skin conductance reactivity on the same side. Measurement of cortical evoked responses, the electrical activity evoked by a sensory stimulus in the tactile, visual or auditory modality, also provided neurophysiological support for a left-sided dysfunction in schizophrenia. Shagass & colleagues (1979), for example, demonstrated that the electrical activity to visual and auditory stimuli recorded over the left hemisphere was more unstable than that recorded over the right. Another question was whether one could demonstrate a physiological abnormality of the corpus callosum. This might be manifest as an alteration in the time it took for information to pass from one hemisphere to the other. Tress et al (1979) reported that the normal two millisecond delay between the tactile evoked potential contralateral to a stimulus and the ipsilateral potential was absent in schizophrenia. This suggested that the corpus callosum was not functioning, as in normals the ipsilateral potential was transmitted through these fibres. It was possible, therefore, that in schizophrenia some anomalous pathways had been set up.

Psychological tests designed to be sensitive to unilateral hemisphere dysfunction or defective interhemispheric cooperation were also applied in an attempt to identify some abnormality. They included standard intelligence tests such as the Wechsler Adult Intelligence Scale (WAIS) where the pattern of subtests could be related to hemispheric dysfunction. Tactile, visual and auditory tasks were also designed for the purpose of 'splitting the hemispheres'. The results of these were contradictory but, in conjunction with the clinical, pathological and neurophysiological evidence, served to attract the attention of investigators to a possible hemispheric imbalance in schizophrenia.

Generalised cerebral dysfunction

The invention of computerised tomography of the brain (C.T. scanning) allowed visualisation of the size of the ventricles and the width of the cortical sulci. The first study on schizophrenics was reported in 1976 by Johnstone, a British psychiatrist (Johnstone et al, 1976). She demonstrated enlarged ventricles and wide cortical sulci indicative of generalised cerebral atrophy in a small group of chronic schizophrenics. Further studies by other groups of workers confirmed this, but its significance and its relevance to acute schizophrenia had not been clarified by the end of the decade.

Treatment

There were no radical developments in this area during the decade. Neuroleptics were further confirmed as the treatment of choice, although their side-effects, particularly the type of abnormal movement known as tardive dyskinesia, became a topic of concern and limited their usefulness. The community psychiatry movement gathered momentum, but it was increasingly recognised that although institutions were a bad thing, exposure to the emotional pressures of family life was equally harmful for a schizophrenic. Family therapy, to educate relatives about the hazards of the way they dealt with a schizophrenic, or placement in a hostel, to remove the schizophrenic entirely from his family, were added to the repertoire of psychosocial treatment.

Summary

Three areas of psychological progress can be detected in the 1970s. Information processing theory, the chief model of the mind held by experimental psychologists, inspired the majority of studies. Many of these were descriptive rather than theoretical, investigators being content to evaluate visual perception, short-term memory or attention, without attempting an integration with clinical facts. The best effort incorporated ideas on the nature of consciousness and attributed the psychological dysfunction in schizophrenia to an increased awareness of the processes of the mind without these processes being in themselves abnormal.

Communication breakdown was a widely used term. It originated in the 1960s as a preoccupation with the social context of schizophrenia and found experimental backing in the early studies of language and attention. By the end of the decade the most interesting development was the appreciation that much of what used to be loosely called thought disorder or speech disorder could be better formulated as an abnormality in conveying the intended meaning of language.

The third topic was the application of neuropsychological knowledge to the condition. Clinical and psychophysiological findings suggested that schizophrenia might be associated with some kind of hemispheric imbalance. The most popular notion was of a left hemisphere dysfunction. The evidence was contradictory but the idea was attractive and brought notions of cause back full circle to the organic formulations of Kraepelin and Bleuler.

3

Diagnosis

INTRODUCTION

The diagnostic approach to schizophrenia has varied considerably from time to time and from place to place.

Kraepelin regarded dementia praecox as a disease of the brain, with a predilection for the function of the will. He therefore selected catatonic behaviour, particularly negativism, as the best diagnostic indicator.

Bleuler regarded an abnormality in thinking as the fundamental disorder. His diagnostic indicators were therefore those aspects of the mental state which best reflected the particular quality of thought disorder. A sample of speech or specimen of writing might serve this purpose. Alternatively, delusions and hallucinations of a particular kind or in a particular combination might also reveal the underlying disorder.

The third diagnostic trend was ushered in by Schneider who relied entirely on delusions and hallucinations. His first-rank symptoms, although based jointly on Bleuler's fundamental symptoms and on Jaspers' description of schizophrenic psychic life, were, according to Schneider, atheoretical and solely of diagnostic significance.

The current diagnostic climate is one of operational definitions devised by research workers and broad recommendations prepared by working parties of national psychiatric associations. Their common theme is the need to establish that a subject has held delusions or experienced hallucinations in the recent past, which have persisted for some time and which cannot be attributed to any recognised cause of brain dysfunction or pronounced elation or depression. Most weight is placed on evaluating the beliefs that a subject holds concerning the independence of his mind and body from outside influences.

In this chapter I shall give an account of the specific schemes which exist and then discuss them in the light of the general characteristics and purposes of a diagnostic instrument.

SPECIFIC DIAGNOSTIC SCHEMES

Kraepelin

Kraepelin based his diagnosis of dementia praecox on a combination of poor outcome and certain symptoms, particularly those which he believed derived from a disorder of will. With respect to the former he wrote:

> . . . the great majority of cases manifest a course leading to a psychic invalidity of varying severity.
>
> (Kraepelin 1913)

Of all the symptoms, the best for diagnostic purposes, in his view, were catatonic symptoms:

> Genuine negativism, instinctive purely passive resistance seems to me to possess the relatively greatest significance as an isolated symptom, and in no other disease do volitional disorders—automatic obedience, negativism, mannerisms, stereotypies, impulsive actions—come under observation in such extent and multiplicity.
>
> (Kraepelin 1913)

Bleuler

Bleuler was more definite than Kraepelin on the matter of diagnosis:

> The disturbance of associations and also probably the type of hallucinations are characteristic and sufficient for a positive diagnosis; in addition, a general flattening of affect may serve this purpose . . . the expression of sudden ideas, especially when they are at the same time senseless or in contradiction to the rest of the personality, is a fairly reliable sign . . . the phenomenon of thoughts being heard occurs only very rarely in other psychoses . . . the delusion that everyone already knows what the patient is thinking is almost pathognomonic . . . When a person continually produces entirely illogical ideas of persecution in a state of full clarity of consciousness he is nearly always a schizophrenic; if the characteristic hallucinations . . . preference for the auditory sphere and for body-sensations . . . are also present, the diagnosis is certain.
>
> (Bleuler 1911)

Schneider

In Mellor's (1970) account of Schneider's first rank symptoms there are 11: 3 types of auditory hallucinations, 7 types of delusions of influence or passivity experiences, and delusional perception (Table 3.1). According to Mellor, 72% of schizophrenics diagnosed by a typical British psychiatrist in the 1960s (probably on Bleulerian criteria) had at least 1 of these. The 4 commonest were: thought broadcasting—21% thought insertion—20%, voices arguing—13% and voices commenting—12%. The 4 rarest were: made impulse—3%, delusional perception—6%, made affect—6% and made volition—9%.

Table 3.1 Schneider's first rank symptoms (according to Mellor)

1. Audible thoughts	Voices speaking thoughts aloud. Echo de la pensée
2. Voices arguing	Two or more hallucinatory voices discussing the subject in the third person
3. Voices commenting on one's action	Voices describing subject's activities as they occur
4. Influence playing on the body-somatic passivity	Experience of bodily sensations imposed by external agency
5. Thought withdrawal	Thoughts cease and subject simultaneously experiences them as removed by external force
6. Thought insertion	Thoughts have quality of not being own, ascribed to external agency
7. Thought broadcasting	Thoughts escape into the outside world where they are experienced by others
8. Made feelings	Feelings do not seem to be own, attributed to external force
9. Made impulses	Drive or impulse seems to be alien and external
10. Made volitional acts	Actions and movements felt to be under outside control
11. Delusional perception	Normal perception has private and illogical meaning

ICD-9 (International Classification of Diseases)

The ninth and latest revision of the International Classification of Diseases was published in 1977. Its classification of psychiatric disorders is known as ICD-9. Schizophrenic psychoses are defined as:

> A group of psychoses in which there is a fundamental disturbance of personality, a characteristic distortion of thinking, often a sense of being controlled by alien forces, delusions which may be bizarre, disturbed perception, abnormal affect out of keeping with the real situation, and autism . . . The diagnosis should not be made unless there is, or has been . . . characteristic disturbance of thought, perception, mood, conduct, or personality, preferably in at least two of these areas.
>
> (WHO 1977)

RDC (Research Diagnostic Criteria)

Spitzer and colleagues in New York proposed criteria which later formed the phenomenological basis for the official DSM-III definition. Subjects had to have an illness lasting at least two weeks and not fulfil criteria for mania and depressive illness to 'such a degree that it was a prominent part of the illness'. For definite schizophrenia there had to be two of the following nine features, for probable schizophrenia only one:

1) thought broadcasting, insertion or withdrawal;
2) delusions of control, other bizarre delusions or multiple delusions;
3) delusions other than persecutory or jealousy lasting at least a week;

4) delusions of any type if accompanied by hallucinations of any type for at least a week;
5) auditory hallucinations in which either a voice keeps up a running commentary on the subject's behaviours or thoughts as they occur, or two or more voices converse with each other;
6) nonaffective verbal hallucinations spoken to the subject;
7) hallucinations of any type throughout the day for several days or intermittently for at least one month;
8) definite instances of formal thought disorder (illogicality, derailment, incoherence, poverty of content);
9) obvious catatonic motor behaviour.

(Spitzer et al 1975)

DSM-III (Diagnostic and Statistical Manual)

The third edition of the diagnostic recommendations of the American Psychiatric Association lists the essential features of schizophrenia as all six of the following:

1) The presence of certain psychotic features: at least one of—
   a) delusions of control,
   b) thought broadcasting,
   c) thought insertion,
   d) thought withdrawal,
   e) other bizarre delusions,
   f) delusions without persecutory or jealous content,
   g) delusions with persecutory or jealous content accompanied by hallucinations of any type,
   h) auditory hallucinations of running commentary or two or more voices conversing with each other,
   i) nonaffective auditory hallucinations on several occasions or
   j) incoherence, marked loosening of association, marked illogicality or marked poverty of content of speech if accompanied by blunted, flat or inappropriate affect, delusions, hallucinations or behaviour that is grossly disorganised or catatonic.
2) Duration of at least six months.
3) Deterioration from a previous level of functioning.
4) Onset before age 45.
5) The disturbance is not due to an affective disorder.
6) Absence of organic mental disorder.

(American Psychiatric Association 1980)

Feighner

Feighner and colleagues in St Louis were the first to propose an operational definition:

For a diagnosis of schizophrenia *A* through *C* are required.

A 1) A chronic illness with at least six months of symptoms prior to index evaluation without return to the premorbid level of psychosocial adjustment.

2) Absence of a period of depressive or manic symptoms sufficient to qualify for affective disorder or probable affective disorder.

B Either:
1) delusions or hallucinations without significant perplexity or disorientation; or
2) verbal production that makes communication difficult because of a lack of logical or understandable organisation.
C At least 3 of the following for a definite diagnosis and 2 for a probable diagnosis:
1) single;
2) poor premorbid social adjustment or work history;
3) family history of schizophrenia;
4) absence of alcoholism or drug abuse within one year of onset of psychosis;
5) onset of illness prior to age 40.

(Feighner et al 1972)

Catego

The first British operational definition was developed by Wing and colleagues. They designed a computer programme which allocated a diagnosis according to information fed into it from the Present State Examination. For a definite diagnosis of schizophrenia the subject had to have one of the following four symptoms:

1) thought intrusion, broadcasting or withdrawal;
2) delusions of control;
3) voices discussing the subject in the third person or commenting on thoughts and actions;
4) other nonaffective auditory hallucinations with other delusions.

(Wing et al 1974)

New Haven Index

Astrachan and colleagues at Yale in 1972 suggested a scheme whereby a diagnosis was arrived at on a points system. A subject had to score at least four points altogether and have delusions, hallucinations or any item of thought disorder. Points were awarded as follows:
1) delusions—2,
2) hallucinations—visual 1, auditory 1, other 1 (maximum 1),
3) thought disorder—bizarre thinking 2, autism 2, looseness of associations 2, blocking 1, concreteness 1, derealisation 1, depersonalisation 1, and
4) miscellaneous—inappropriate affect 1, confusion 1, suspiciousness 1, catatonia 1.

Carpenter's flexible system

Carpenter, from New York, was involved in the International Pilot Study on Schizophrenia and extracted the 12 PSE items (out of 415) which best discriminated schizophrenics (diagnosed by ICD criteria) from nonschizophrenics. The clinician can choose between 4 and 8 of the following as a diagnostic set:

> restricted affect, poor insight, thoughts heard aloud (audible thoughts), absence of early morning waking, poor rapport, absence of depressed facies, absence of elation, widespread delusions (involving more than one area of life), incoherent speech, bizarre delusions, nihilistic delusions, general rating of interview as unreliable.
>
> (Carpenter et al 1973)

Less widely used criteria

In addition to the criteria discussed above there are a number of other systems in restricted use, usually by research workers within the institute which designed them. These include the one of Taylor & Abrams (1975),which is very strict like Feighner's, and the Washington University criteria (Fowler et al 1980) which is similar to the RDC. A scheme which is sometimes mentioned is that of Langfeldt (1960). He was a Norwegian psychiatrist who suggested features which distinguished process or true schizophrenia from a schizophreniform psychosis (the kind which arose in the context of psychological distress or organic insult). He listed four 'diagnostic signs and symptoms of true schizophrenia':

1) a break up in the development of personality (emotional blunting which gives an experienced psychiatrist the 'praecox feeling');
2) catatonic stupor or excitement;
3) depersonalisation or derealisation (severe disturbance of perception and thought with loss of insight); and
4) primary delusions.

The interest of Langfeldt's scheme is that it is the only one which exactly incorporates Jaspers' view that schizophrenia induces a complete alteration in psychic life experienced by the *observer* as incomprehensible ('praecox feeling').

GENERAL CHARACTERISTICS OF THE DIAGNOSTIC SCHEMES

Categorical or dimensional

Psychiatrists prefer, and almost exclusively use, categorical diagnoses, even when considering personality. In the main, psychologists prefer dimensions, although in the case of schizophrenia most clinical psychologists now adopt a categorical approach.

The main proponent of a dimensional approach to psychosis was Eysenck. His opinion (Eysenck 1951) was based on the fact that correlations between test scores in normals were very similar to correlations between scores on the same tests in schizophrenic patients. The tests that he chose, however, for example how long it took to write the word YEAR, bore no relationship to the way psychiatrists usually diagnose schizophrenia (evaluating beliefs), and were not even representative of the sort of psychological functions thought to be affected in the condition. He later designed a personality scale of psychoticism, which is generally regarded as measuring callousness rather than any essential feature of madness. Criminals, for example, score just as highly on it as schizophrenics (Eysenck & Eysenck 1970). Even Cattell (1970), the other main advocate of a dimensional approach to personality, disagreed with Eysenck on the issue of a psychoticism scale. He admitted that psychosis was better regarded as a category.

The evidence for treating psychosis as a category is compelling in Kendell's (1975) view. He cites crosscultural data—psychosis exists in roughly the same form in different parts of the world; he claims statistical support—cluster analysis produces categories similar to clinically-derived ones; he is impressed by genetic evidence—some psychiatric disorders may be transmitted by a sex-linked gene, and are therefore qualitatively different from normal; and he notes the differential outcome and effect of treatment on psychotic subgroups. In fact, these arguments really apply to the validity of classifications within the broad category of psychosis, and do not justify a categorical split between normality or neurosis and psychosis. This issue is rarely discussed nowadays. It was, in my view, best formulated by Freud in his later writings (Freud 1924). More recently, Roth (1963) distinguished neurosis and psychosis in the following way. In neurosis some aspects of personality are unaffected, there is contact with reality, there is a degree of insight, behaviour is largely understandable, the response is initially relevant to the stress which existed, and there is a close relationship between the behaviour during the illness and premorbid personality. In psychosis the opposite of each of these propositions is true.

The issue rests on whether the diagnostic criterion chosen is normally distributed (e.g. psychomotor speed, selected by Eysenck) or all-or-nothing (e.g. belief that one's thoughts are being withdrawn by the KGB, a typical first rank symptom illustrating the usual psychiatric approach). Statistical, crosscultural, genetic and treatment considerations have not been systematically validated against each of these—dimensional and categorical—and so one cannot dismiss Eysenck's approach so easily. In fact, as Kendell admits, categorical and dimensional schemes are to some extent different aspects of the same process. In the former, similarities between one mad person and another are stressed; in the latter, the way in which madness resembles normality is emphasised. As Kendell points out, and I agree with him, Eysenck's approach was political and, as the particular battle that he was fighting is past, psychologists and psychiatrists can safely return to the categorical approach.

Axes

A diagnosis is a convenient way of describing the outstanding problem in a person's life at a given moment in time. Ideally one should present a vignette of a person, condensing their lives to the most salient features. In practice a diagnosis of schizophrenia is a poor way of conveying information about the complexity of human existence, and it is for this reason that diagnosis in general has been rejected by a number of psychiatrists and psychologists, as well as sociologists. One compromise is to devise a multiaxial diagnostic system, where phenomena, cause, severity, intelligence, personality and other selected factors can all be presented. Essen-Möller, a Swedish psychiatrist, has been campaigning for this for nearly 40 years (Essen-Möller & Wohlfahrt 1947).

Schizophrenia is the product of a uniaxial system, and has by itself to convey information about mental state, cause and duration.

Hierarchical levels

Psychiatric diagnosis is arranged hierarchically (Fig. 3.1). Conditions higher up the tree can supervene on conditions lower down (e.g. neurosis on personality disorder, schizophrenia on obsessional neurosis, drug-induced organic psychosis on schizophrenia). Conditions lower down the tree cannot begin de novo in the course of an active condition higher up (e.g. obsessional neurosis does not develop during acute schizophrenia, schizophrenia is not diagnosed in the presence of pre-existing organic psychosis).

The main controversy is about the position of schizophrenia with respect to affective psychosis. Kraepelin, Bleuler, Schneider, and most recently Wing et al (1971) in their Catego system, placed schizophrenia higher than affective psychosis. This means that in the presence of typical schizophrenic features (catatonia for Kraepelin, thought disorder for Bleuler, first-rank

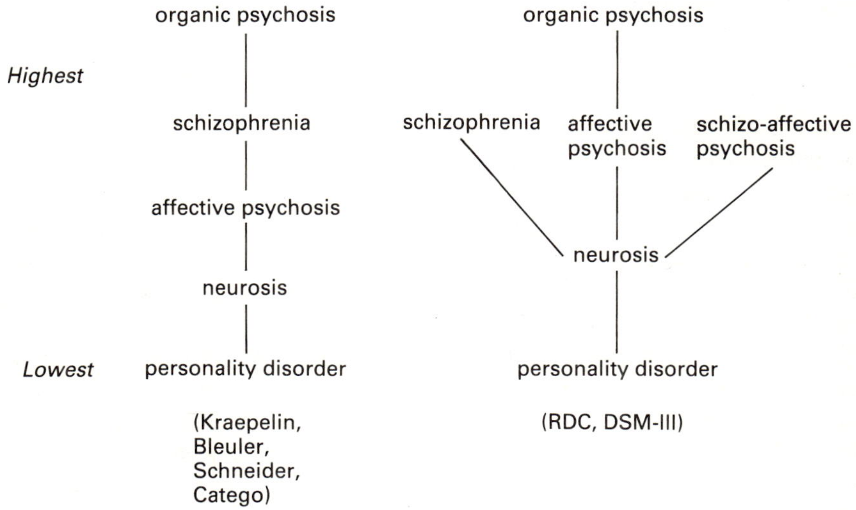

Fig. 3.1 Diagnostic hierarchies.

symptoms for Schneider and Catego) affective features have no diagnostic status. Spitzer et al (1975) in their Research Diagnostic Criteria (RDC), and the official recommendations of the American Psychiatric Association (A.P.A. 1980) in the third version of their Diagnostic and Statistical Manual (DSM-III), give equal weight to schizophrenic and affective features, and if both are present label the condition schizoaffective.

Foulds (1965), a British psychologist, regarded the hierarchical arrangement as more than just a convenient way of allocating different weights to diagnosis. He believed that it represented clusters of symptoms, corresponding to different degrees of psychic integration. The most severe condition was schizophrenia, a disintegrative psychosis. Less severe were paranoia and melancholia, which he regarded as integrative psychoses; less severe still were depressive and anxiety neurosis. What was special about Foulds' proposal was his claim that a disorder at any level necessarily contained as part of its clinical picture symptoms of the milder more integrated disorders lower down the hierarchy. His proposal is now mainly quoted as an explanation for the high incidence of depressive symptoms in otherwise typical schizophrenia, and constitutes an explanation for at least some of the cases which are diagnosed as schizoaffective psychosis.

Source of information

Interview

Psychiatrists mainly rely on an interview to establish a diagnosis of schizophrenia. Open-ended interviews, however, are notoriously unreliable in producing agreement between two observers on the presence or absence of a psychiatric symptom (46%—Kreitman et al 1961) or a diagnosis of schizophrenia (68%—Norris 1959).

Structured interview

Because of the unreliability of open-ended interviews, several groups of research workers developed their own standardised (structured or semistructured) interviews. Questions about salient aspects of the mental state over a specific period are asked, the wording of the questions is standardised and the severity of each symptom is rated. The two most widely used for the diagnosis of schizophrenia are the Present State Examination (PSE—Wing et al 1974) and the Schedule for Affective Disorders and Schizophrenia (SADS—Spitzer & Endicott 1978). Each provides the information for an operational definition of schizophrenia—Catego and RDC respectively. Each has been revised several times and has an established, satisfactory reliability. The PSE has been translated into several languages and was the basis of the International Pilot Study on Schizophrenia (IPSS—World Health Organisation 1973), a crosscultural study of the incidence of schizophrenia in nine countries. There are two versions of the SADS, a regular one covering the previous seven days, and a lifetime version to cover all previous mental ill-health. The latest standardised interview is the Diagnostic Interview Schedule, DIS (Robins et al 1981), which provides the basis for making a DSM III diagnosis of schizophrenia.

To illustrate these interviews, the following is an item from the lifetime version of the SADS:

> Did you ever feel that your thoughts were broadcast so that other people knew what you were thinking, or feel that thoughts were put into your head that were not your own, or that thoughts were taken away from you by some external force?

Case notes

A retrospective examination of case notes is even more unreliable than an open-ended interview for establishing a diagnosis of schizophrenia, unless the information has been collected in a standardised way. Anyone who has carried out a case notes study will testify to the unsatisfactory nature of the technique. Sometimes, however, there is no alternative, for example when a condition is so rare that it would take 20 to 30 years to collect a statistically viable sample. This was the case in a study I carried out on whether some of the psychoses induced by alcohol resembled schizophrenia (Cutting 1978a). There is a version of the PSE called the Syndrome Check List which is designed for this purpose.

Projective test

Rorschach's (1921) book *Psychodiagnostics* had enormous influence when it was translated in the 1940s. Several manuals recommending its use as a diagnostic aid in schizophrenia were then published. The usual method is to identify deviant responses, as suggested by Rapaport (1945). The person administering the test has to make an overall assessment of the appropriateness of a patient's remarks when shown the various patterns. It has never been properly evaluated for this purpose, and has been undermined by the current concern with abnormal beliefs and auditory hallucinations.

Questionnaire

The Minnesota Multiphasic Personality Inventory (MMPI—Hathaway & McKinley 1943) has a schizophrenia scale. It was used extensively in North America in the 1960s as a diagnostic instrument. Like the Rorschach it is virtually obsolete as a tool for diagnosing schizophrenia. Positive answers to the following questions contributed to a high schizophrenia score:

> I dislike having people about me; I often feel as if things were not real; I hear strange things when I am alone.

Objective measure of thought

In Britain during the 1940s and 1950s, and in North America from the 1940s till the 1970s, tests of thought disorder were major source of information for making a diagnosis of schizophrenia. Proverb interpretation, object sorting and abstract similarities or differences (e.g. what is the difference between a child and a dwarf?) were used. The introduction of Schneiderian and operational definitions in the last 20 years has made them redundant. Psychiatrists now regard abnormal performance on such tests as evidence of formal thought disorder, a phenomenon seen in a minority of schizophrenics, and not an essential part of the condition.

The diagnostic process

How the diagnosis is arrived at has been well researched and is well reviewed by Kendell (1975) in his book *The Role of Diagnosis in Psychiatry*. Psychiatrists tend to rely on what patients say rather than how they behave; they concentrate on the current mental state rather than the history; and they make their decision very quickly, usually in the first 2 minutes of a 30-minute interview.

Cantor et al (1980) examined how diagnostic categories are actually represented in the psychiatrist's mind. They concluded that categorisation proceeds in a naturalistic way. By this they meant that it was like deciding whether an object in the sky was a bird or an insect. People ask themselves in such situations whether it looks like a bird or an insect, not whether it fulfils bird-criteria better than insect-criteria. According to Cantor and colleagues, psychiatrists have an internal representation of a typical schizophrenic and cases are compared against this standard, rather than subjected to a logical analysis of defining features.

VALUE OF THE DIAGNOSTIC SCHEMES

General principles

The value of a diagnostic instrument can be judged in the same way as that of a psychological test. It should fulfil four criteria: *validity* (whether it measures what it is supposed to measure), *reliability* (whether it produces the same result at different times and in different hands), *sensitivity* (whether it identifies an acceptable proportion of the designated group) and *specificity* (whether it excludes an acceptable proportion of nondesignated groups, i.e. there are not too many false positives).

By way of illustrating these principles compare standing motionless for at least 1 minute (catatonic behaviour, typical Kraepelinian criterion), giving at least 10 unusual word associations amongst the responses to 50 common words (loosening of thought associations, typical Bleulerian criterion), believing that one's thoughts are known to the head of the KGB (thought

	Reliability	*Validity*	*Sensitivity*	*Specificity*
Standing motionless	High (easily measured)	Low (nothing to do with madness)	Low (few schizophrenics stand motionless)	Low (depressed people stand motionless)
Unusual word associations	Moderate (some problems in deciding cut-off of 'unusual')	Moderate (passes some validity tests)	Moderate (some schizophrenics tend to give unusual associations some of the time)	Low (manics, neurotics and eccentrics give unusual associations)
Belief in thought broadcasting	Moderate (fairly easy to establish this belief)	Moderate (conforms to lay view of madness)	Moderate (only ¼ of schizophrenics have this belief)	Moderate (manics have first rank symptoms)
Slow writing	High (easily measured)	Low (lots of reasons for slow writing)	Moderate (schizophrenics tend to write slowly)	Low (depressed, dyslexic and other people write slowly)

Fig. 3.2 Illustration of reliability, validity, sensitivity and specificity of diagnostic criteria.

broadcasting, a first-rank symptom of Schneider) and taking more than 30 seconds to write the word YEAR (psychomotor slowing, part of Eysenck's battery). These are presented in Figure 3.2. Each criterion has a different profile. All are highly or moderately reliable. The validity of standing motionless and writing the word YEAR slowly is low, however, because they have nothing essentially to do with madness; their sensitivity is also low because few schizophrenics diagnosed on other grounds will show these; their specificity is low because there are a host of reasons why normal or psychologically distressed people might stand still for unusually long periods or write slowly. Unusual word associations fares better on this rough assessment, but has low specificity because a number of other groups also give unusual word associations (p. 257). A belief in thought broadcasting is the best of these four because it captures the 'ununderstandability' of Jaspers, is relatively easy to rate, occurs in about one-quarter of schizophrenics diagnosed in other ways (being the commonest first-rank symptom) and is rare in other psychiatric disorders.

Reliability

In the 1960s the unreliability of the diagnosis was the chief concern. Observer agreement in one series of patients in Britain was only about 70% (Norris 1959). By standardising the interview and operationally defining the criteria observer agreement rose to over 90% (92% in a study by Wing et al 1967, using the PSE).

It was hoped that an improvement in reliability would lead to advances in fundamental research and hence to a validation of all or part of the schizophrenia concept against biological, social or psychological standards. This has not happened, and there is now a risk that reliability has been achieved at the expense of validity. As in the four examples above the most *reliable* measures of insanity may be the *least valid*. The danger in the present climate is that the formulation of insanity may stagnate as PSE—Catego schizophrenia, SADS—RDC schizophrenia or DIS—DSM III schizophrenia, whilst less reliable accounts concerned with the quality of psychic life, such as Jaspers, may be more valid.

Validity

Four types of validity are recognised in the context of psychological testing (Anastasi 1961): content validity, predictive validity, concurrent validity and construct validity. The issue of validity as it applies to diagnosis can also be discussed under these headings.

Content validity

This is a measure of whether the instrument covers a representative sample of the behaviour in question. In order to check this all the items or components of a diagnostic scheme must be analysed to establish that it covers all major areas and in the correct proportions. The single criteria, for example standing motionless for one minute, used as illustrations earlier in this chapter, are clearly low on content validity, but the operational criteria, covering delusions, hallucinations, thought disorder and in some cases catatonic behaviour as well, have a high content validity.

Predictive validity

Kraepelin, by his very use of the term dementia praecox, placed considerable emphasis on this measure. Like Kahlbaum in the case of catatonia, and Hecker in the case of hebephrenia, he distinguished dementia praecox from other types of insanity chiefly by its particular course and outcome. This approach has had enormous influence on diagnostic practice. One of the few certain facts about schizophrenia came to be its poor prognosis relative to other forms of insanity.

There are a number of problems with this approach, however. First, outcome depends on which particular diagnostic scheme is adopted. Feighner's criteria, which require at least six months' continuous symptoms, would be expected to predict a poor outcome, whereas Spitzer's, with only two weeks' illness, would predict relatively better outcome. The obvious fact that chronic illnesses continue to be chronic has very little to do with formal mental state. This was borne out by the International Pilot Study on Schizophrenia (IPSS—World Health Organisation 1979). Of 47 possible predictors of overall 2-year outcome, the 5 best were duration of episode prior to initial evaluation, history of past psychiatric treatment, marital status, social isolation and premorbid behaviour disturbance. Amongst the 47 were 29 relating to mental state, and not 1 of these was amongst the top 5.

The second problem concerns the way in which outcome is measured. In the IPSS it was a composite calculation based on three ratings—proportion of follow-up for which patient was psychotic, presence of social impairment and number of full remissions. Kendell et al (1979) examined the predictive ability of six diagnostic schemes (Spitzer's, Carpenter's, Langfeldt's, Catego, Schneider's and New Haven). Social impairment, whether unemployed or socially isolated, was not well predicted. Only Spitzer's and Carpenter's (five or six items) significantly discriminated the employment status of schizophrenics from other psychotic groups, and only Carpenter's (five items) predicted which patients would be socially isolated seven years later (in hospital, hostel or on their own). Turning to the IPSS again, the single outcome measure of social impairment was best predicted by the premorbid level of social functioning. Just as chronicity predicts chronicity, premorbid social impairment predicts postpsychotic social impairment almost independently of any psychopathological factors. More worrying, for the issue of predictive validity, is the fact that not all the schemes examined by Kendell et al could even predict *symptomatic* outcome better than chance.

Despite these discouraging findings the lack of any viable alternative still makes outcome the most widely used way of evaluating diagnostic schemes. Of the six which Kendell et al studied, Spitzer's, Carpenter's and Langfeldt's were the best at predicting the widest range of social and symptomatic outcomes. Spitzer's was the best of all. Catego, Schneider's and New Haven were very poor. This is particularly surprising in the case of Schneider's and Catego (based on Schneider's), since first-rank symptoms are held in such high esteem as a diagnostic tool in Britain.

Concurrent validity

This covers attempts to ensure that the diagnostic instrument is better in some pragmatic way—cheaper, quicker, more useful—than other available schemes. In the case of psychological tests the concurrent validity of a new intelligence test would be established by showing that it had the same power as a more traditional test, but was simpler to administer. It is not so clear what constitutes better concurrent validity amongst diagnostic schemes. One issue which falls roughly in this category concerns the range of psychotic patients which each diagnostic scheme classifies as schizophrenic. At least three studies have tackled this (Strauss & Gift 1977, Brockington et al 1978a, Endicott et al 1982). The consensus is that Spitzer's and Carpenter's are the best, in that they fall in the middle of the range. For example, in the study by Endicott and colleagues 168 psychiatric patients were initially identified. The criteria of Feighner, and Taylor and Abrams, were relatively strict, allocating a diagnosis of schizophrenia in only 11% and 5% patients respectively. The New Haven was relatively lax, identifying schizophrenia in 39%. However, 18% were schizophrenic by Spitzer's criteria and 19% by Carpenter's (5 items).

Construct validity

This is the most comprehensive concept of validity, and incorporates and extends the previous three types. Essentially, one is asking here what theoretical construct the diagnosis represents. It requires, for a satisfactory answer, the gradual accumulation of information from a variety of sources. In the case of diagnosis these could be statistical, therapeutic, genetic, social, psychological, physiological, biochemical and neuropathological.

What does a diagnosis of schizophrenia represent? For some psychiatrists it is an attempt to identify a disease. Scadding, a British chest physician who took a general interest in nosology, gave the sort of definition they would approve of:

> the sum of the abnormal phenomena displayed by a group of living organisms in association with a specified common characteristic or set of characteristics by which they differ from the norm for their species in such a way as to place them at a biological disadvantage.
>
> (Scadding 1967)

This is similar to Virchow's definition (p. 14) and what Kraepelin, Bleuler, Schneider and probably Jaspers believed.

Kräupl Taylor (1971), a British psychiatrist, and Linder (1965), a North American psychologist, felt that this was too strong a view of diagnosis and disease. Kraüpl Taylor suggested that the purpose of diagnosis was to identify 'whatever invites therapeutic concern' and Linder to produce 'a prescription for medical care'. According to this approach schizophrenia would probably be the residuum of insanity after organic psychosis and affective psychosis were removed, because the guidelines for treatment are more definite in these last two cases. Myxoedema madness and amphetamine psychosis for example, are simply managed, and antidperessants in depression or lithium in mania are probably more specific and more effective than neuroleptics in schizophrenia. In the Foulds hierarchy it would be *lower* down than affective psychosis for these reasons.

These issues are conveniently side-stepped by adopting operational definitions. In this way the term schizophrenia is defined in a circular fashion as only entailing what is involved in the diagnostic operation, with no biological, psychological or social reality outside of this. In my view this is a sensible first stage from which to test the constructive validity of each definition. But so far, the only systematic evaluation has been in terms of outcome, which, as already discussed, is misleading, because definitions which incorporate an element of chronicity (e.g. Feighner's, DSM-III) carry a spurious validity. Statistical approaches have also been unhelpful. Everitt et al (1971) cluster-analysed information from a series of psychotic patients. The first three clusters corresponded to mania, paranoid psychosis and endogenous depression, a result which, if anything, supports the notion of schizophrenia as a heterogeneous, residual category when the more homogeneous types have been extracted. Everitt's fourth cluster was chronic schizophrenia, but as I shall show in the chapter on classification this is unlike acute schizophrenia in many ways. Another statistical study by Kendell & Gourlay (1970) produced a unimodal distribution of psychotic patients, supporting the unitary psychosis theory, without even distinct affective categories.

The usual solution proposed is to intensify the search for biological markers. The problem with this approach is that it may be the wrong level to study. It may be too low in the hierarchy of reasons and causes (see p. 104) and what one should be seeking are psychosocial causes or the pattern of psychological dysfunction. This point is illustrated in a study by Caine & Shoulson (1983) of the psychiatric complications of 30 patients with Huntington's chorea. Each patient was carefully interviewed with the SADS and then given a DSM-III diagnosis. Twenty-four of the patients met criteria between them for no less than seven different DSM III diagnoses; one of them was schizophrenia (three patients). The authors pointed out that if a physical condition with 'a known unitary pathogenetic mechanism' could produce such 'clinical heterogeneity' this raised questions about the hope that any of these seven psychiatric conditions, including schizophrenia, would have an 'underlying biological unity'. I agree with these conclusions, and suggest that the best approach is to evaluate the validity of psychiatric conditions at levels closer to their phenomenological status—psychological and psychosocial. Leff (1983) recently suggested that a way of distinguishing depression from schizophrenia is in terms of their relationship to life events. Schizophrenia tends to be *precipitated* by a life event in the preceding *three weeks*, whilst depression tends to be *caused* by a life event a *year* or more before (see p. 125). Others (Wieck 1979) have tried to validate the functional psychoses against the pattern of psychological dysfunction. I approve of both these approaches, tentative though they may be.

SUMMARY

Diagnostic considerations are central to any real understanding of the psychology of schizophrenia. There are four phases identifiable during this century. Kraepelin relied on catatonic symptoms and poor outcome, which represented for him the neurological basis for the condition. Bleuler widened the criteria to include any manifestation of thought disorder, as he conceived it. Schneider introduced the idea of atheoretical symptoms. The fourth and current trend, emanating from research institutes, is for operational definitions, evaluated in terms of usefulness and predictive validity. The main ones in use are Spitzer's RDC criteria, the Catego system of Wing and colleagues, and DSM-III of the American Psychiatric Association. Each is based on information from a structured interview.

Diagnostic schemes have general characteristics and there are recognised ways for evaluating them. The present ones are highly reliable but of uncertain validity. Unfortunately the easiest ways of validating them—outcome, biochemical markers—have proved to be the least suitable. Outcome is largely determined by social and personality factors external to the condition itself, and such biochemical abnormalities as are known to affect the brain produce a range of psychiatric disorders or different disorders from schizophrenia. The solution, in my view, is to define the condition in terms of its psychological dysfunction and then look for nonbiochemical biological markers such as physiological or structural changes.

At the present time the diagnostic schemes which most correspond to the consensus of opinion during the century are Bleuler's, Langfeldt's, Schneider's and Catego as these incorporate the notion of "ununderstandability". Kraepelin's and DSM-III are too reliant on poor outcome, while Spitzer's is too broad. On the other hand DSM-III and Spitzer's are reliable, agree well with other definitions and predict outcome better than most of the others, and are probably the definitions of choice until valid markers, whether psychological or biological, are found.

4

Classification

INTRODUCTION

There are three issues of classification which have a bearing on the theme of this book. The first is the classification of psychosis in general, and the position of schizophrenia with respect to affective psychosis, paranoia and less well-established entities such as cycloid psychosis. The second is whether schizophrenia itself can with any justification be subdivided. Finally, can the symptoms or phenomena be classified in a logical way?

CLASSIFICATION OF PSYCHOSIS

'Typical' psychosis

The way in which schizophrenia and affective psychosis emerged during the 19th century as the two 'typical' psychoses was described in Chapter 1. During this century their nosological status, though frequently criticised, has not been substantially challenged.

'Atypical' psychosis

There are a welter of terms applied to psychoses which differ in some way from these typical varieties. Every national and theoretical school of psychiatry and every major shift in the way schizophrenia has been diagnosed has left behind another label. It is worth looking at the main themes, however, for the light which they throw on schizophrenia itself.

Definition

An atypical psychosis is one which either 1) fails to meet the diagnostic criteria for any of the typical psychoses, 2) meets criteria for more than one typical psychosis or 3) fits the description of one of the more well-defined atypical psychoses (e.g. psychogenic or cycloid psychosis).

Incidence

This depends on which criteria of a typical psychosis are used. There is surprising agreement, however, from various sources that about 10% of functional psychoses fall into each of the three definitions given above.

1) Pauleikhoff (1957) from Heidelberg, and therefore influenced by Jaspers and Schneider, found that only 6% of nonorganic psychoses were completely excluded from the typical categories. Fowler et al (1980), using Washington University criteria (similar to DSM-III), found that 8% of nonorganic psychoses met none of their criteria.

2) Brockington & Leff (1979) found that of 119 psychotic patients, 14 (12%) met 1 of 10 current criteria for schizophrenia *and* one of 9 current criteria for mania or depressive psychosis. Fowler et al (1980) also found that 12% of their patients met the Washington University criteria for more than 1 typical psychosis.

3) Amongst functional psychotics the incidence of cycloid psychosis (one of the better-defined categories) was estimated at 8% by Cutting et al (1978) and 12% by Brockington et al (1982a).

Types

Paranoia is the most well-established variety of atypical psychosis. Kraepelin kept it distinct from dementia praecox in all editions of his textbook. He meant by it an insidious development of delusions in an intact personality. It was psychogenic in cause, arising out of the stresses of life in someone of paranoid disposition. It has been called different things before and since (Lewis 1970). The latest synonym is 'delusional disorder' (Winokur 1977). The main subtypes are paraphrenia—a paranoid psychosis of the elderly, particularly common amongst deaf, solitary, unmarried women (Kay & Roth 1961); erotomania (De Clérambault 1942); querulant states (Baruk 1959); and monosymptomatic hypochondriacal psychosis (Munro 1980).

Schizoaffective psychosis is the most frequently diagnosed variety of atypical psychosis, although probably the least valid. The term was first introduced by Kasanin in 1933 as a description of nine patients where there was a blending of schizophrenic and affective symptoms. According to Brockington et al (1978b) the schizomanic subtype resembles mania more than schizophrenia in its course and response to treatment. Schizodepression is more heterogeneous (Brockington et al 1982b) and includes typical depressive psychosis with delusions, and typical schizophrenia with depression (whether drug-induced, reactive or an integral part of the condition, see p. 235).

Other varieties bearing the name of an unusually prominent phenomenon are mainly of historical interest, e.g. oneirophrenia (with marked perplexity), schizophasia (prominent language disorder) and chronic hallucinatory psychosis (a French term for a psychosis dominated by hallucinations).

Psychogenic or reactive psychosis is a potentially more valid entity. Jaspers (1913) laid down strict criteria for its diagnosis: the preceding event should be significant for the person, the psychosis should begin soon after, the content should have some comprehensible relationship to the event and the event should dictate the course and termination of the psychosis. However, even using lenient criteria—the regular association between relapse of a psychosis and an adverse life experience—two follow-up studies (Faergeman 1963, McCabe 1975) found that only a small minority of originally diagnosed psychogenic psychoses conformed to this pattern. Kretschmer's (1927) 'sensitiver Beziehungswahn' (delusional states of references in sensitive individuals) is a variety of psychogenic psychosis, occurring, according to him, in those of:

> delicate nature who not only feel their experiences deeply but are consumed by them in a quiet manner . . . whose intense experiences they are unable to assimilate so that they brood with compulsive ideas or develop delusions of reference . . . They harbour some shameful insufficiency in one area of life—sexuality, ambition—and if this becomes exposed . . . there is an ensuing psychosis.
>
> (Kretschmer 1927)

Psychoses with an unusual course have also been given special consideration. If there is an abrupt onset the French have called it 'bouffée délirante'. If the condition lasts less than six months the DSM-III schedule recommends it should be called schizophreniform (if less than two weeks 'brief reactive psychosis' if there is psychosocial stress, and 'atypical psychosis' if there is none). An unusually remittent course is characteristic of cycloid psychosis. Kleist introduced this term for psychoses which were marginal to the affective psychosis, but it was then given its own diagnostic criteria by Leonhard (1961) and Perris (1974). Cutting et al (1978) and Brockington et al (1982a) confirmed that psychoses with these criteria (fluctuations in mood, perplexity, anguish, ecstasy and a particular kind of movement disorder) did pursue a distinctive course giving the condition a predictive validity.

The nature of 'atypical' psychosis

Without valid or even agreed definitions of the typical psychoses it might seem unprofitable to discuss the nature of atypical varieties. One opinion, however, is that their very existence undermines the status of typical psychoses such as schizophrenia and testifies to Griesinger's unitary psychosis theory (see p. 13). For this reason it is worth examining this and other opinions on the matter.

According to this first view, apparent differences between patients do not reflect the existence of distinct conditions, but merely the interplay of what are known as pathoplastic factors, giving individual content to a universal predisposition to psychosis. Birnbaum introduced the distinction between *pathogenic* and *pathoplastic* in his book *The Making of a Psychosis*:

> Pathogenic factors are those which refer to the actual cause of the illness, which endow it with a specific character, its quality of being 'thus and no other' . . . Pathoplastic factors are those which may be said to shape the disorder in that they give content, colouring and contour to individual illnesses whose basic form and character have already been biologically established.
>
> (Birnbaum 1923)

Although I accept the importance of pathoplastic factors, I do not support the notion of a unitary psychosis. I consider it highly improbable that psychosis is inherited in an all-or-nothing manner, or that there is only one psychological dysfunction which can give rise to delusions and hallucinations, or that there is only one biological pathway.

A second view is that some at least of the atypical psychoses represent independent nosological entities. Of those mentioned here the most well-defined in phenomenological terms are paranoia and cycloid psychosis, and the most plausible from a causal point of view are psychogenic psychosis and 'sensitiver Beziehungswahn'. In my view, all four have as much claim as schizophrenia itself to be regarded as valid entities, although each is rather rare. It is likely that there are a *handful* of relatively independent pathways (psychological and biological) by which a psychosis can develop, and that although schizophrenia, mania and depressive psychosis are the commonest and most well-described products, these do not exhaust the possibilities.

The majority view on the nature of atypical psychoses is to regard them as distortions of a typical psychosis by some pathoplastic factor. The four most commonly mentioned factors are personality, genotype, cerebral dysfunction and adverse life experience. These are of course potentially pathogenic as well, but, it is argued, if one of them is discordant with the actual pathogenic factor then an atypical clinical picture will ensue. For example, Kleist (1928) and Langfeldt (1939) believed that some atypical psychoses arose in individuals with a cyclothymic personality who had inherited a schizophrenic genotype. Two recent studies, however, failed to support this. Klein & Williamson (1981) found that Spitzer schizoaffectives were no differenct from Spitzer schizophrenics on the Phillips premorbid adjustment scale. We (Cutting et al 1978) found that cycloid psychotics were *less* likely than patients with typical depression to have an abnormal personality. The pathoplastic effects of cerebral dysfunction and adverse life experience are particularly hard to disentangle from their causative effect, and even the undoubted influence of age, sex, culture and intelligence on the clinical picture could be because of some associated pathogenic factor. For example, the atypical psychoses of the elderly (Kay & Roth 1961) could be psychogenic psychoses due to social isolation or deafness. Women tend to predominate in some varieties of atypical psychosis (e.g. cycloid—66 women : 7 men, Cutting et al 1978) but not others (e.g. paranoia—9 women: 20 men, Winokur 1977) which argues against a simple pathoplastic effect in this case. In my view, the importance of pathoplastic effects has been exaggerated. Commentators too readily assumed that any deviation from a typical psychosis was the influence of pathoplastic factors. They failed to see that some of these might be the effect of pathogenic factors, neither 'schizophrenogenic' nor 'affectogenic'.

CLASSIFICATION OF SCHIZOPHRENIA

Original clinical subtypes

Paranoid schizophrenia

In the fifth edition of his *Textbook* in 1896, Kraepelin proposed that dementia praecox should cover three distinct degenerative diseases: hebephrenia, catatonia and dementia paranoides. By the sixth edition in 1899, he had fused them to produce a single disease of dementia praecox. Dementia paranoides, later paranoid schizophrenia, was a subgroup. It is now the largest, comprising 40% of all schizophrenics in the International Pilot Study of Schizophrenia. It denotes a form of schizophrenia dominated by delusions or hallucinations of any type.

Hebephrenic schizophrenia

The hebephrenia of Hecker (p. 14) was the key concept in Kraepelin's dementia praecox. Its hallmarks, disturbances in emotion and thinking, became the fundamental symptoms of Bleuler. The current diagnostic emphasis on delusions and hallucinations has meant that the hebephrenic subgroup has been largely neglected in the last two decades. Only 11% of cases in the International Pilot Study of Schizophrenia were given this label.

Catatonic schizophrenia

Kahlbaum's catatonia (p. 14) became one of Kraepelin's three degenerative diseases which then became dementia praecox. It now denotes a subtype of schizophrenia dominated by a disorder of movement and posture. Of all the subtypes it has the most tenuous link with the core concept of schizophrenia. This is ironic, since it was one of the first of the components of dementia praecox to be identified. The main argument in favour of its exclusion is its increasing rarity despite a steady incidence of other forms of schizophrenia. As early as 1913, Kirby had noted a closer connection between catatonic symptoms and affective psychosis, and Magrinat et al (1983) suggest that the rarity of catatonia nowadays is due to the introduction of E.C.T. and antidepressants which prevent mild or moderate forms of depression from developing into severe catatonia. Mahendra (1981) has another explanation for its virtual disappearance. He believes that many of the original cases were a sequel to a form of encephalitis common at the turn of the century, but whose virulence has since diminished. Gjessing (1938) made the most radical suggestion of all. He believed that it was an independent nosological entity caused by nitrogen balance and cured by thyroxine, claims which have never been substantiated. In my view, most cases are better regarded as severe forms of affective psychosis.

Simple schizophrenia

Pick (1891) and Diem (1903) described the condition of simple dementia. Kraepelin incorporated it into dementia praecox in the eighth edition of his book (1913). Bleuler called it simple schizophrenia, defining it as:

> patients [who] simply become affectively and intellectually weaker; the will seems to lose its power; the capacity for work, for caring for themselves diminishes. They appear stupid and finally show the picture of severe dementia.
> (Bleuler 1911)

In ICD-9 it is defined as:

> a psychosis in which there is insidious development of oddities of conduct, inability to meet the demands of society, and decline in total performance ... With increasing social impoverishment vagrancy may ensue and the patient becomes self-absorbed, idle and aimless.
> (World Health Organisation 1977)

I have been unable to find any recent studies of this subtype. It is not diagnosed very frequently: only 4% of the schizophrenics in the International Pilot Study of Schizophrenia were given the label.

Other clinical subtypes

Latent schizophrenia

This is mentioned in ICD-9 and is defined there as:

> a condition of eccentric or inconsequent behaviour and anomalies of affect which give the impression of schizophrenia though no definite and characteristic schizophrenic anomalies, present or past, have been manifest.
> (World Health Organisation 1977)

It is not used much. Helmchen (1975) looked at the distribution of the subgroup diagnoses in his clinic in Berlin. Latent schizophrenia was the least used of all (0.9% of 432 schizophrenics). It is now regarded as equivalent to various North American terms (pseudoneurotic, borderline schizophrenia).

Residual schizophrenia

Also mentioned in ICD-9, residual schizophrenia means schizophrenic deterioration without any florid phenomena. In Helmchen's series, it was the second commonest subdiagnosis (14.1%) after paranoid schizophrenia.

Soviet subtypes

Soviet psychiatrists have a wider concept of schizophrenia than their counterparts in Western Europe. They also have a different classification. Sukhareva and Melekhov in the 1930s distinguished sluggish or continuous (early onset, poor prognosis), acute or periodic (late onset, good prognosis) and mixed or shiftlike (with manifestations of both). Snezhnevsky (1968), their most influential modern psychiatrist and head of the 'Moscow school', recognises nine types—asthenic, affective, pseudoneurotic, paranoid, hallucinatory, hallucinatory-paranoid, paraphrenic, catatonic and terminal.

North American subtypes

In the United States until recently, there was also a wider concept of schizophrenia than in Western Europe. This was mainly due to a reluctance to distinguish personality disorder and neurosis from psychosis. The excess cases were labelled pseudoneurotic (Hoch & Polatin 1949), abortive (Mayer 1950) or pseudopsychopathic (Bender 1959).

Borderline schizophrenia

This term was introduced by Rosenthal et al (1968) as a description of odd but nonpsychotic relatives of typical schizophrenics. It included 'paranoid states, borderline states, schizoid personality and inadequate personality'. Heston (1970) used it to cover 'eccentrics, recluses, women with incapacitating fear in social situations and men who carried out motiveless crimes'. The value of the term lies in the claims of Schulsinger and his colleagues (p. 112) that what is inherited will only manifest itself as true schizophrenia if there is an organic insult. Otherwise it will appear as a personality disorder. The two conditions—borderline schizophrenia (the personality disorder) and schizophrenia (the psychosis)—are jointly referred to as schizophrenia spectrum disorder in these schemes.

Clinical and theoretical dichotomies

Reactive-process

Suggested by Jaspers and Bleuler, this distinction was first systematised by Kantor et al in 1953. They examined over 200 case histories and noted that some schizophrenics had abnormalities in their premorbid development. They called these process schizophrenics. In their first five years they had 'early psychological trauma, physical illness and an odd member of the family'. From the age of five to adolescence they had experienced 'difficulties at school, family troubles, introverted behaviour, a breakdown of social or physical or mental functioning, pathological siblings, an overprotective or rejecting mother—momism—and a rejecting father'. During adolescence they had shown 'lack of heterosexuality, insidious onset to the psychosis, physical aggression, a poor treatment response and a lengthy stay in hospital'. As an adult they had exhibited 'massive paranoia, little capacity for alcohol, no manic-depressive component to their illness, failure under adversity, a discrepancy between ability and achievement, an awareness of change in self, somatic delusions, a clash between culture and environment and loss of decency'. Reactive schizophrenics were those who had none or few of these.

Garmezy (1970) reviewed the validity of the distinction. It is essentially a list of factors which are thought to affect prognosis. Process schizophrenics have a poor outcome, reactive a relatively good one.

Acute-chronic

When it was realised that not all schizophrenics had a chronic illness, the acute-chronic distinction became interesting in its own right. Wing and Venables, in the early 1960s, championed its theoretical importance. Wing (1961) devised a subclassification of chronic patients, based on the severity of speech disorder and affective disturbance. Venables (1964) linked this with psychological and psychophysiological dysfunction: acute patients had wide attention and were underaroused; chronic patients had narrow attention and were overaroused.

A period of six months is usually taken as the cut-off between acute and subacute, and over two years as a definition of chronic. Serban & Gidynski (1975) found no difference in mental state between patients in their first episode and those who had had numerous previous admissions, but the crucial point about chronicity, in psychological studies at least, is the length of the current episode, and not whether there have been previous episodes. When this is taken into consideration, large differences in the pattern of psychological dysfunction have been found.

Paranoid-nonparanoid

Contrasting paranoid with nonparanoid (hebephrenic, catatonic) schizophrenia is regarded as important by some psychologists. Magaro (1980), for example, goes as far as saying that psychological differences between paranoid and nonparanoid subtypes are greater than those between normals and schizophrenics. According to Magaro, paranoid patients have a distinct cognitive style, marked by a tendency to overgeneralise from one aspect of their environment to an entire conceptual system.

Berkowitz (1981), reviewing the issue, was less impressed by the value of the distinction. I am inclined to agree with her, because of the uncertain status of catatonic cases and the fact that delusional formation (p. 340) is not specific to schizophrenia. Magaro's claim that paranoid and nonparanoid schizophrenics have a different cognitive style may well be true but this may have nothing to do with the intrinsic psychological dysfunction of schizophrenia.

Good premorbid-poor premorbid

This distinction was first systematised by Phillips (1953). Like the reactive-process dimension, it is a list of factors which predict outcome, but unlike the former the factors used are few in number and all relate to social and sexual adjustment. They are: 1) recent sexual adjustment (0—stable heterosexual relation and marriage, 6—no sexual interest in either men or women); 2) social aspects of sexual life (0—married with children in a family unit, 6—single, occasional contact with same sex, no interest in opposite sex); 3) past history of personal relations (0—always had a number of close friends, 6—no desire to be with boys or girls); and 4) recent adjustment in personal relations (0—habitually mixed with others, 6—antisocial). Good premorbid schizophrenics obtain a low score, poor premorbid a high one.

The simplicity of the scale has made it popular amongst researchers, but it is a guide to prognosis rather than a categorisation of the condition itself.

Type I-Type II

Crow (1980) proposed a distinction based on the relative proportions of positive or negative symptoms. Type I schizophrenia is characterised by positive symptoms (delusions, hallucinations, florid thought disorder), dopaminergic abnormalities suggesting a biochemical cause, a good prognosis and a good response to phenothiazines. Type II schizophrenia has negative symptoms, cerebral atrophy, a possible viral cause, a poor prognosis and a poor response to treatment.

Organic-genetic

There is an increasing tendency to separate what is called 'familial' from 'sporadic' schizophrenia. A familial schizophrenia is someone who has a first degree relative with the condition. Kendler & Hays (1982a) showed that sporadic cases had a higher incidence of E.E.G. abnormalities, and Shur (1982) that they were more likely to have been born in the winter than familial cases. Both these findings suggest that sporadic cases have organic causes. Some investigators have gone further and designated particular organic subtypes: with minimal brain damage (Bellak 1979), LSD-induced (Vardy & Kay 1983), with enlarged ventricles (Golden et al 1982), with lateralised skin conductance responses (Gruzelier & Manchanda 1982) and with particular patterns of hemispheric imbalance (Magaro & Page 1983).

Value of the distinctions

It is difficult to evaluate these distinctions because they all reflect genuine differences between schizophrenics, and until some valid marker of schizophrenia itself is found, subtypes will continue to proliferate. In my view it is possible to identify four relatively homogeneous subtypes within the broad concept of DSM-III schizophrenia. There is undoubtedly considerable overlap between these, and contradictory evidence on each, and I shall list them in decreasing order of the strength of each case.

First, catatonia should probably be removed and placed with affective psychosis. The justification for this is its closer resemblance to the latter than to other subtypes of schizophrenia (Magrinat et al 1983). This is true for the associated clinical phenomena, the type of psychiatric disorder seen in relatives and the response to treatment.

Secondly, there is a group of patients who are poorly socialised prior to their first florid episode and use psychiatric services frequently thereafter. Some have generalised brain damage and most fit Kraepelin's concept of dementia praecox and the descriptions of process, poor premorbid, type II and chronic schizophrenia. They tend to have negative symptoms and organic causes. The evidence that these features cluster together comes from a number of sources, in particular the C.T. scan studies of Johnstone et al (1976) and Weinberger & Wyatt (1982). Klein (1982) also found, in a clinical study, that the poor premorbid and chronic subtypes contained the same patients.

The third and fourth subtypes are more speculative but together form the bulk of what might be called typical schizophrenia. I suggest that the third conforms roughly to hebephrenic and the fourth to paranoid schizophrenia. Either may be sporadic or familial, but hebephrenia tends to be familial (Winokur et al 1974, Kendler & Hays 1982a, Farmer et al 1983) and more homogeneous, whilst the paranoid subtype tends to be sporadic and more heterogeneous. Neither is directly attributable to generalised brain damage, although each may have its own particular pattern of hemispheric imbalance. Each probably has its own pattern of psychological dysfunction as well, but this is more likely to be true of the hebephrenic than the paranoid type. My reason for saying this is that whereas delusions and hallucinations, the hallmarks of paranoid schizophrenia, can probably arise from diverse psychological mechanisms, the emotional and thought disorder of a special kind, the characteristics of hebephrenic schizophrenia, are probably the product of a relatively unique psychological mechanism.

These four subtypes do not exhaust the possible list of non-affective, non-organic psychoses. Others, such as psychogenic or cycloid, have already been considered, but these do not usually fulfil current definitions of schizophrenia, particularly DSM-III.

CLASSIFICATION OF PHENOMENA

Fundamental-accessory

Bleuler (1911) distinguished fundamental symptoms, which were characteristic of schizophrenia, from accessory symptoms, which could also appear in other types of illness. The former comprised disturbances of association and affectivity, ambivalence and autism. The first two were more important than the latter. Accessory symptoms included hallucinations, delusions, alterations in personality, speech and writing disorders, and catatonic symptoms. They were meant as diagnostic aids only.

First rank-second rank

These were Schneider's diagnostic criteria. The first-rank symptoms are listed and discussed on pages 42 and 76.

Primary-secondary

Bleuler (1911) also introduced the idea of primary and secondary symptoms. Unlike the fundamental-accessory distinction, a diagnostic aid, the primary-secondary one was theoretical and represented his views on how the symptoms were caused (p. 24). The disturbance of association was the only primary symptom. All other symptoms were secondary and a direct consequence of the loosening of associations.

Schneider (1957) pointed out, however, that by the 1950s the terms primary and secondary were being used in five different ways. First, there was the temporal sense of Griesinger (p. 13). Some symptoms, for example depression, tended to appear first; some, for example dementia, came on later. Secondly, primary and secondary were sometimes used interchangeably for Bleuler's fundamental and accessory symptoms. Thirdly, the term primary was used to mean final and irreducible, as in the primary delusions of Gruhle. Next, primary and secondary sometimes meant pathogenic and pathoplastic, as defined by Birnbaum (p. 94). Finally, there was Bleuler's meaning, discussed above.

Positive-negative

Hughlings Jackson, the British neurologist, believed that some neurological symptoms arose from direct interference with a psychological function through brain damage. Others, according to him, came about indirectly by the release of functions in a neighbouring normal part of the brain previously inhibited by the now damaged part. The former he called negative symptoms, the latter positive.

Andreasen (1982a) and Crow (1980) consider that schizophrenic symptoms develop in a similar way. Bleuler's fundamental symptoms are the negative symptoms, of which Andreasen recognises five types: *affective flattening, attentional impairment, alogia* (poverty of speech), *avolition-apathy* (impoverishment of motivation) and *anhedonia-asociality* (inability to feel intimate). Hallucinations, delusions, bizarre behaviour or positive thought disorder (derailment, flight of ideas, illogicality) are the positive symptoms.

Andreasen & Olsen (1982) compared schizophrenics with only positive symptoms, those with only negative symptoms and those with both on 11 social, psychological and clinical measures. The 6 measures which were significantly associated with negative symptoms were a low Phillips premorbid adjustment score, a poor employment record, poor educational level, left-handedness, a high ventricular–brain ratio indicative of cerebral atrophy, and a low 'minimental state' score implying cognitive impairment. This suggested that negative symptoms were a function of both pre-existing personality disorder and generalised brain damage.

SUMMARY

The phenomena of schizophrenia, schizophrenia itself and psychosis in general have all been the subject of numerous classifications.

The phenomena have been divided up for diagnostic purposes (e.g. first rank and second rank) and for theoretical purposes (e.g. primary and secondary, positive and negative).

There are four traditional clinical subtypes of schizophrenia—paranoid, hebephrenic, catatonic and simple. There are then subtypes based on national prejudices (e.g. pseudoneurotic in North America, sluggish in the Soviet Union), and distinctions based on notions about psychological dysfunction and cause (reactive-process, paranoid-nonparanoid, good premorbid-poor premorbid, type I-type II, organic-genetic). One of the most useful of these is between acute and chronic, as this reflects many of the other distinctions: acute illnesses tend to be reactive to some event, occur in those of good premorbid personality and be dominated by positive phenomena. It is likely that schizophrenia as currently diagnosed is a heterogeneous collection of more discrete conditions. Catatonia is probably better excluded, and regarded as an affective disorder. Chronic schizophrenia resembles presenile dementia more than it does acute schizophrenia. Hebephrenia stands out because of the peculiar nature of the disorder of thought and emotion and its common familial basis.

A bewildering array of terms have been used to describe atypical psychoses. The most well defined and plausible varieties are paranoia, sensitiver Beziehungswahn, psychogenic psychosis and cycloid psychosis.

5

Cause

INTRODUCTION

The cause of schizophrenia is still uncertain. There are a few established facts but these are chiefly epidemiological and can be made to fit rival hypotheses. Even the cornerstone of the genetic argument, the huge difference between concordance rates in identical (about 50 times normal) and non-identical twins (about 15 times normal), has at times been attributed to psychological (identical twins are emotionally closer—Jackson 1960) or organic factors (identical twins are more likely to be physically closer and could transmit a virus more readily—Crow 1983).

In this chapter I shall discuss the evidence under three headings—genetic, psychosocial and organic—which between them cover all possible causes of schizophrenia. There may of course be *several causes* of schizophrenia, producing their effect in conjunction (e.g. organic superimposed on genetic) or separately. There may also be *several schizophrenias* (see p. 100) each with its own cause, a point recognised by Bleuler when he called his monograph *Dementia Praecox or the Group of Schizophrenias*.

The distinction between causal (pathogenic) and modifying (pathoplastic) factors has continually to be borne in mind (see p. 94), as must the possibility that an apparent cause of the condition can equally well be a consequence of it (e.g. mother's attitude to child).

A further distinction is between causal and meaningful connections. Jaspers (1913) gave this much thought. Meaningful connections were those which one arrived at through empathy and understanding. For example, knowing the background, personality and recent experiences of a person one can reach some conclusion about whether their behaviour is reasonable in the circumstances. A man might give up family, friends, job and home and go and live in Patagonia. Superficially this might seem crazy, but a more thorough acquaintance might tell one that he has had a life-long preoccupation with the flora and fauna of that region, which finally overruled all other considerations. (This example is an exaggerated form of the account in Chatwin's book *In Patagonia*.) According to Jaspers, meaningful connections were always unproven, biased and inadequate. He criticised Freud, for example, for having mistaken meaningful connections for causal. Causal connections of psychic life were, for Jaspers, the actual determinants of mental illness. Unlike meaningful connections they were, by nature, 'alien and not-understandable'. They were also, and this is the crucial point in his scheme, always biological.

This division between meaningful, understandable connections and causal, nonunderstandable connections has come under criticism more recently. Wittgenstein in 1948 and Ryle (1949) began this trend. In his *Last Writings on the Philosophy of Psychology* (vol. 1, note 907, published in 1982), Wittgenstein expressed the essence of the problem:

> Would it be correct to say that the language-game of stating someone's motive is the same as stating the cause, but not when the statement is made by the person who is confessing his motive.
>
> (Wittgenstein 1982)

If one substitutes motive for meaningful connections we have a tentative refutation of Jaspers' position, and the realisation that cause and motive are virtually indistinguishable to an outsider but not to the individual concerned. Ryle, in his *Concept of Mind*, attributed Jaspers' mistake to 'the dream of psychology as a counterpart to Newtonian science' and to the assumption that underlying our behaviour are forces or agencies of a biological nature. He points out that the terms 'cause' and 'causal explanations' are solemn expressions, which relegate, as Jaspers did, all psychological explanations to the level of trivia. It was quite clear to Ryle that psychological explanations were entirely adequate for most human behaviour:

> We know quite well why the heroine took one of her morning letters to read in solitude . . . The heroine recognised her lover's handwriting on the envelope.
>
> (Ryle 1949)

Hill (1982) and Bolton (1984) have examined the implications of this change of emphasis for psychiatric disorders. Hill points out that the difference between cause and reason is our tendency to use the latter when discussing social and psychological issues but to use cause when biological or physical considerations apply. Bolton considered that the term cause implied a *breakdown* in the functioning of a system while motive or reason were used when the mind was functioning normally. An analogy is the chess-playing computer. Its moves can be understood as originating at three levels—the physical (hardware), the design (software) or the intentional (assumption that the computer will make the best move relative to its goals). If everything is going well, only the last consideration is pertinent. If the computer makes a glaring mistake, however, this may be more than just a bad move, it may have arisen from a fault at one of the lower levels. The implications for mental illness are obvious. One is inclined to drop a level to the design stance (functional) or further to the physical stance (organic) when things go wrong, but there is no reason to regard these explanations as superior to the intentional.

This chapter is mainly concerned with essential causes, answers to questions such as, 'Would schizophrenia have developed in this person were it not for such and such?'. The bulk of the chapter is devoted to possible organic and psychosocial causes, because there is most controversy on whether either or both can act in this way. Genetic causes are generally accepted and the main issue is the extent of their interaction with organic and psychosocial factors.

GENETIC CAUSES

Evidence

Methods

Four main methods have been used to identify the genetic component of schizophrenia: calculations of the risk of schizophrenia in family members of a known schizophrenic; comparison of concordance rates in monozygotic with those in dizygotic twins; natural experiments in which the effects of nature and nurture have been separated by adoption of a child at birth; and long-term, prospective follow-up of children of schizophrenic mothers (high-risk studies).

Familial incidence

Rüdin (1916), who worked with Kraepelin in Munich, carried out the first competent study of the heritability of schizophrenia. He concentrated on the risk to the siblings of a known schizophrenic, which he estimated at 5% (five times the expected rate). Kallmann (1938), whilst in Berlin, studied the risk to the children. It was 8% if the parent had the paranoid form of schizophrenia, and 17% if they had the hebephrenic form.

Twin studies

Luxenburger (1928) was the first to investigate the concordance rate in twins (the chance that both will have the condition). He collected 19 monozygotic pairs, where the concordance rate was 58%, and 13 same sex dizygotic pairs, where the concordance rate was nil. Kallmann (1946), when in New York, did a more careful study. He had 691 twins at his disposal, he corrected his figures for age, and he established that the diagnosis was 'definite schizophrenia'. His concordance rates were 86% for monozygotic and 15% for dizygotic twins. Slater (1953), using the twin register at the Maudsley Hospital, obtained concordance rates of 65% for 37 monozygotic pairs and 14% for 58 same-sex dizygotic pairs.

Adoption studies

Heston (1966), in Oregon, traced 47 people with schizophrenic mothers who had been permanently separated from them in the first two weeks of life. He had a matched group of adoptees without schizophrenic mothers. They were born between 1915 and 1945, and by the middle 1960s (when most were in their 30s) five of the 47 (10%) with schizophrenic mothers but none of the 50 adoptees with normal mothers had developed schizophrenia. This was more powerful evidence that schizophrenia had an hereditary component.

Kety et al (1968) confirmed this with a different adoption study. In Denmark, where psychiatric records are easily available, there were 5 500 children adopted between 1924 and 1947. Of these, 507 had been admitted to psychiatric hospitals by 1968, of whom 33 were schizophrenic. They traced the biological relatives of these 33 schizophrenics, and then compared their psychiatric morbidity with that of the relatives of 33 control adoptees without psychiatric illness. Of 150 biological relatives of the 33 schizophrenics, 13 (9%) were schizophrenic; of 156 biological relatives of the 33 controls, 3 (2%) were schizophrenic.

High-risk studies

Mednick & Schulsinger (1968) designed the first prospective study. There were 207 children of chronic schizophrenic mothers (a high-risk group) and 104 controls (a low-risk group, children of normal mothers). They were born between 1941 and 1954 and were first examined in 1962. At this time they were given a psychiatric interview; they were globally assessed as to whether they had cognitive disturbance, evidence of 'negative contact' (e.g. being reserved) or evidence of 'positive contact' (e.g. being amiable); their school reports were examined; their parents were questioned; they were tested psychologically (the main item was a continual word association test, e.g. afraid—fear, yellow, sun . . .); and various psychophysiological recordings were made (the main item was the amplitude and speed of recovery of the galvanic skin response).

It is sometimes difficult in the published work of Mednick and Schulsinger to follow what happened to these children, because they introduced two idiosyncratic concepts. First, they designated a subgroup (20) of the 207 'sick' because they had had some sort of breakdown by 1967. Hardly any of these, by that time, were schizophrenic, and most were merely antisocial incidents. Secondly they followed Kety and Rosenthal in talking about 'schizophrenia spectrum disorders' (p. 97). Nevertheless, by 1980 (Parnas et al 1982a), when the children were now between the ages of 26 and 38, 13 of the high-risk group had Catego schizophrenia and 5 had committed suicide. In the low-risk group only 1 had developed Catego schizophrenia, and there were no suicides.

The interest of the study, however, is not confirmation of an increased risk to the children of schizophrenic mothers. That was established by Rüdin and Kallmann. What is important is whether anything in the original interview, school reports, parental remarks, psychological measures or psychophysiological recordings distinguished the ones who were now schizophrenic from those who were not. The significant predictors are shown in Table 5.1.

Table 5.1 Predictors of adult schizophrenia (Schulsinger study)

Psychiatric interview	
1 of 35 items	poor emotional rapport
Global assessment	
1 of 3 items	cognitive disturbance
School report	
7 of 30 items	isolated
	uneasy about criticism
	easily upset
	affect persists when upset
	disturbs class
	discipline problem
	poor prognosis
Parental observations	
3 of 13 items	passive baby
	short attention span in play
	impolite child
Psychophysiological measures	fast GSR recovery

The relationship between schizophrenia and borderline schizophrenia (p. 97) particularly interested them. They found that, in addition to the 13 with Catego schizophrenia, a further 29 had borderline schizophrenia, making 42 instances of schizophrenia spectrum disorders. Borderline schizophrenics differed from normals in having had cognitive impairment (incoherence, pathological associations) and poor emotional rapport (facial expression, global rating) in the childhood psychiatric interview. They were not much different from normals in their school and parental reports.

Parnas and colleagues concluded that schizophrenia and borderline schizophrenia were both characterised by 'premorbid defective emotional rapport and formal disturbance of cognition', and schizophrenia itself was further marked by 'poor affective control and attentional deficit'.

There are a number of high-risk studies in progress at the moment, but Mednick and Schulsinger's is the only one that has been running long enough to allow satisfactory statistical analyses.

Current estimates of familial risk and twin concordance rates

Gottesman & Shields (1982) estimated the life-time prevalence of schizophrenia in first-degree relatives of a known schizophrenic as 10% and in second-degree relatives as 3%. More details are shown in Table 5.2. They

Table 5.2 Current estimates of familial risk and twin concordance rates

Familial risk		
1st degree relatives	*Life time prevalence*	
Parents	6%	
Children	13%	
Siblings	10%	
	Mean 10%	
2nd degree relatives		
Half-siblings	4%	
Uncles, aunts, etc.	2.5%	
	Mean 3%	
Twin concordance rates	*Range*	*Mean*
Older studies (mean of 6)		
Monozygotic	58–69%	65%
Same sex dizygotic	0–15%	12%
Newer studies (mean of 5)		
Monozygotic	35–58%	46%
Same sex dizygotic	9–27%	14%

based these figures on the most competent family studies. They also pooled data from the better twin studies, six old and five new ones. In the newer studies the average concordance rate for monozygotic twins was 46% and for dizygotic twins 14%.

Summary of genetic knowledge

Gottesman & Shields (1982) end their book *Schizophrenia: The Epigenetic Puzzle* with 18 points which summarise current knowledge on the issue. I am in agreement with all but 2 of them. They are well formulated and I shall list them in abbreviated form, with my comments in brackets.

1) The life-time risk of developing schizophrenia is 1% by age 55.

2) The risk of schizophrenia increases with the degree of genetic relatedness to the proband.

3) The risk of schizophrenia is proportional to the severity of the proband's illness, and to the number of relatives affected. (This indicates that whatever is inherited should be quantifiable as well as recognisable.)

4) Gender is not important except for age of onset. (This excludes the possibility of a sex-linked gene.)

5) The monozygotic concordance rate is three times the dizygotic, and lies between 35 and 60 times that of the general population.

6) More than half the monozygotic pairs studied are discordant (proving that environmental causes must also exist).

7) Discordant monozygotic twins each transmit schizophrenia at the same high rate, proving that there is incomplete penetrance and expression of the genotype.

8) Identical twins reared apart have the same concordance rates as those reared together (invalidating theories which attribute the high monozygotic

concordance rate to pathological emotional closeness of the twins).

9) Children of schizophrenics adopted at birth develop schizophrenia at the same rate as those reared by their own parents (invalidating theories which *only* recognise organic or psychological causes and, for example, incriminate the behaviour of the mother rather than her genes).

10) Adoptive relatives of schizophrenics do not have a high rate of schizophrenia (making it unlikely that schizophrenia is contagious, either through organic—transmissable agent—or psychological means—appropriation of behaviour).

11) Children of normal parents fostered in a home where one of the adoptive parents later becomes schizophrenic, of which there are 21 examples (Wender et al 1974), do not have an increased rate of schizophrenia. (Negative instances are more powerful invalidators of a theory than positive, in Popper's view, and this fact undermines the claims of Lidz, Wynne and Bateson that schizophrenic or preschizophrenic parents communicate the disorder through their behaviour rather than transmit it through their genes.)

12) Probands with schizophrenia-like illnesses after head injury or epilepsy do not have an increased familial incidence of schizophrenia. (This suggests that what Gottesman and Shields call 'phenocopies or nongenetical schizophrenics' also exist, or, in simpler language, a genetic cause is not essential to the development of schizophrenia.)

13) No environmental cause will invariably or even with moderate probability produce genuine schizophrenia in people unrelated to a schizophrenic individual. (I disagree with this, which appears to contradict point 12. Their argument relies on evidence that organic causes will produce a psychosis which always differs from one due to nonorganic causes in some respect. This is not proven.)

14) Social class gradients for schizophrenia exist, most of which is due to downward drift of predisposed people.

15) Twins do not themselves have a higher incidence of schizophrenia than normal people. (This disarms critics who might argue that being a twin is psychologically stressful. It is also evidence against the view that obstetric complications increase the risk of developing schizophrenia, as twins, with a high perinatal morbidity, would be particularly at risk.)

16) Childhood psychosis (e.g. infantile autism) has nothing to do with schizophrenia.

17) Multifactorial polygenic inheritance fits the facts best.

18) Premorbid schizophrenia is not identifiable. (This is true at the moment.)

The nature of the genetic cause

The genotype. (What is inherited?)

Meehl (1962) gave one of the best accounts of the genotype and its transformation into schizophrenia. He called it *schizotaxy*, an 'integrative neural defect, the consequence of genetic mutation'. He believed that anyone who inherited this would develop *schizotypy*, a disorder of personality, made up of four 'core behaviours': anhedonia (p. 234), interpersonal aversiveness, ambivalence and cognitive slippage (loosening of associations). With a certain unfavourable upbringing (largely, according to him, the presence of a schizophrenogenic mother), a schizotype would 'decompensate' into *schizophrenia*.

Meehl's three stages—schizotaxy (the genotype), schizotypy (the abnormal personality) and schizophrenia (the illness)—is a common way in which the genetic model is formulated.

Mechanism of inheritance. (How is it inherited?)

There are three broad groups of genetic theories, according to Gottesman & Shields (1982): distinct heterogeneity, monogenic and multifactorial polygenic. Distinct heterogeneity assumes that schizophrenia is like blindness or mental retardation in being composed of separate disease entities. Some of these are genetically, some environmentally determined. Monogenic theories regard schizophrenia as the expression of one abnormal gene at the same locus, whose penetrance, in those who inherit it, is not high. Huntington's chorea is a condition which is inherited in this way although here the penetrance is high. Multifactorial polygenic theories, of which Meehl's is a simple example, acknowledge the combined effect of a number of genes and a number of environmental contributions.

Genetic markers. (How is the genotype reflected in the organism?)

The genotype is a hypothetical construct, but it might have a regular accompaniment in some biological or psychological constant. The ideal criteria for such a marker are that it should occur in all but the most atypical schizophrenics during their active illness, it should be detected in the same subjects both premorbidly and in remission, it should be apparent in a proportion of clinically unaffected relatives and it should be absent in normals.

No reliable *biological* marker has as yet been found. McGuffin et al (1978) found an alteration in the pattern of human leucocyte antigens (HLAs) in one study but not in a later (McGuffin et al 1983). Murphy & Wyatt (1972) suggested a biochemical marker, low monoamine oxidase in platelets, but despite numerous replications of the association (Wyatt et al 1980) it is too universal a biological substance for the marker to be of much value.

Both Asarnow & MacCrimmon (1978) and Holzman et al (1974) believed that they had found a *psychological* marker in a measure of attention. In the former case this was the pattern of mistakes on a continual performance test (identifying a certain digit, e.g. 7, every time it appeared on a screen). In Holzman's case it was an abnormal pattern to the saccadic movements of the eyes as a subject tracked a pendulum. In neither case was their initial optimism justified. McConaghy (1959) obtained abnormal scores on an object-sorting test in either the mother or the father of every 1 of 10 thought-disordered schizophrenics. He claimed that this was a marker of the schizoid personality, but as with the other markers subsequent investigation failed to replicate the claim.

The magnitude of the genetic contribution. How much of the variance of the cause of schizophrenia is inherited?

Rao et al (1981) estimated that the genetic contribution was as high as 70%, leaving only 30% to what they called 'environmentality', which in my scheme covers both organic and psychosocial factors. The figure is arrived at after a complex series of calculations and superficially appears far too high, since the concordance rate in identical twins, where 'environmentality' is at a minimum, is only 65%.

Relationship between genetic and other causes. (Is the cause of schizophrenia necessarily multifactorial?)

The three possibilities, according to the present scheme, are genetic acting alone, genetic-psychosocial or genetic-organic.

It is impossible to say whether *genetic factors by themselves* would be a sufficient cause of schizophrenia until one knows the critical psychosocial and organic determinants. It appears, however, that when one divides up cases into familial (those with first-degree relatives with schizophrenia) and sporadic (those without), the latter tend to have more evidence of generalised cerebral dysfunction (E.E.G. changes—Kendler & Hays, 1982a) and more indirect evidence of an environmental cause (more winter births, suggestive of viral infection—Shur 1982). This raises the possibility that organic factors might be pathogenic in the absence of a genetic predisposition and conversely that genetic factors can act alone. There is more evidence, however, in favour of an interaction, particularly a genetic-organic one.

Meehl's (1962) model, discussed above, was an example of a *genetic-psychosocial* interaction. The schizotaxy (the genotype) is expressed in life as the schizotypal personality, which is then transformed into schizophrenia if the individual is unfortunate enough to have a schizophrenogenic mother. Assuming that schizophrenogenic mothers are not universal, this model would predict the existence of more schizotypal individuals than actual schizophrenics in a pedigree. This is what Rosenthal et al (1968) found in the Danish adoptees. Of 5 500 adoptees, 69 had psychotic parents (56 schizophrenic and 13 affective). By 1968 3 of these 69 adoptees had become schizophrenic but 6 had borderline schizophrenia, 3 a schizoid personality and 1 a paranoid personality. According to Kringlen (1968), in a study of

55 monozygotic twins, 14 concordant and 41 discordant for schizophrenia, the eventual schizophrenic had been more submissive than the normal twin and more overprotected by the mother. This is slim evidence for a genetic-psychosocial interaction, but Wahl (1976), reviewing the issue, found agreement in several studies that the future schizophrenic twin had had a lower birth weight, more feeding problems and more physical illness than the other twin, features which might explain an abnormal parental attitude.

The most likely mechanism, however, in my view, is a *genetic-organic* interaction. This emerged in the high-risk studies of Mednick and Schulsinger and the twin studies of Murray and the Reveleys. Parnas et al (1982b), part of the Mednick-Schulsinger team, reported that the high-risk group who developed typical schizophrenia had suffered more obstetric complications than either normals or borderline schizophrenics. Even more striking was the fact that borderline schizophrenics (those with only a personality disorder) had sustained fewer obstetric complications than even the normals, suggesting that they remained free of psychosis only because they had been unusually lucky in having a nontraumatic birth. In another paper, the same research group (Machon et al 1983) reported another example of a genetic-organic interaction. They found that high-risk children who developed typical schizophrenia were also more likely to have been born in towns and in the winter months, conditions which favour the spread of a virus. (The rate of schizophrenia for high-risk subjects with urban-winter births was 23% compared with 9% for high-risk subjects overall and 6% for high-risk subjects born in the country in the summer.) Another approach is to look for actual evidence of brain damage in the twin who develops schizophrenia compared to the one who does not. Reveley et al (1982) did this by measuring the ventricular size (by C.T. scan) in 11 monozygotic normal twin pairs and 7 monozygotic twin pairs discordant for schizophrenia. They found that there was an extremely high correlation ($r = 0.98$) between the ventricular areas in the normal monozygotic twins but not so high ($r = 0.87$) in monozygotic twins discordant for schizophrenia. (The mean intrapair differences in ventricular area were six times greater in the latter than in the former, and the schizophrenic twin had bigger ventricles than the normal member of the pair.) They concluded that:

> some common environmental factor, possibly perinatal damage, may have led to the increase in ventricular size in schizophrenic-discordant pairs, with schizophrenia developing in the more severely affected twin.
>
> (Reveley et al 1982)

In a more recent study (Reveley et al 1984) they found that only twins without a family history of schizophrenia had the ventricular enlargement and the affected member *had* suffered a more traumatic birth than its partner. Finally Boklage et al (1979) found an unusual number of left handers amongst identical twin pairs discordant for schizophrenia: if both twins were schizophrenic there was only an 8% chance of one of them being left handed, but if only one of the twins was schizophrenic, there was a 75% chance of one of them being left handed. Left-handedness is indirect evidence of abnormal hemispheric lateralisation of function which, in the absence of a family history, is itself frequently the effect of brain damage. Like Reveley et al, therefore, they were suggesting that organic causes interacted with genetic, but unlike Reveley et al they believed that they could attenuate as well as potentiate the genetic risk.

Conclusion

Genetic causes of schizophrenia cannot be reasonably disputed. There is still doubt, however, about the extent of the genetic component and whether organic or psychosocial factors are needed in addition before a typical schizophrenic episode can develop. At the moment several lines of research point to the necessity of additional organic factors (perinatal complications, viral infection in the neonatal period) before the genotype is manifest as a phenotype. Several psychiatrists have expressed the *opinion* that psychological factors can also complement the genetic component in this way, but the evidence is less convincing.

PSYCHOSOCIAL CAUSES

In introducing this chapter I pointed out that with the change in philosophical thinking since the end of the Second World War it became acceptable to give mental causes the same weight as biological in discussions of human behaviour. The change is essentially a move away from Cartesian duality. Instead of searching for yet another solution to the mind-body problem, the problem itself is recognised as an artefact, an artefact of our linguistic use of the word mind. According to Ryle and Wittgenstein, philosophers and psychologists invent problems for themselves if they stray too far from the everyday use of psychological expressions. Of course this does not condone the uncritical acceptance of any old wives' tale or subjective opinion on the cause of one's own mental condition. As Bolton (1984) pointed out, there is always a danger that psychological explanations can lead one astray in the other direction. (The literary school of structuralism, where meaning is in the eye of the observer and the text largely irrelevant, is the ultimate in this.) The study of meaning in this sense is sometimes known as hermeneutics. Originally it meant the discovery of God's will through examination of biblical texts. Because there are no limits, hermeneutics is characterised by diversity and endlessness. For example: What was the cause of the First World War? The assassination of Archduke Ferdinand at Sarajevo? The military rivalry between Britain and Germany? The late unification of Germany and her search for Nationalism? The war-like spirit of the European nations, frustrated by the final colonisation of Africa and Asia and by the lack of major conflict since Napoleonic times? To avoid such train of thought one needs some rules, which strike a balance between, on the one hand, rigid biological explanations and, on the other, the listing of endless psychological trivia. What these rules are remains to be worked out.

Bolton suggests that acceptable psychological causes should at least have the following characteristics. They must be reasonable. (A schizophrenic cannot be designated as someone who is just avoiding work, although this may form part of the clinical picture.) They should have caused a breakdown in the hierarchical arrangement of the aims in life. (The man who went to Patagonia was normal in this respect, because his desire to go there was always near the top of his hierarchy. It should also be noted that what may superficially appear as a breakdown may in fact be a wise and far-sighted move. For example, a computer chess player who loses the queen may be sacrificing the piece for higher goals. A child who exhibits school phobia may be doing so to unite the family. Laing, at times, argued that a florid schizophrenic illness was a worthwhile experience because it led to subsequent personality maturation.) Thirdly, causal explanations should avoid too much internal explanation and should rely more on events which come before or after the 'breakdown'. (Bolton criticises Freud for having designed an elaborate system of symbolic processes without checking the validity of their development or outcome.)

These considerations at least allow the possibility that psychogenic causes of schizophrenia exist, even though, as I shall show, most of the suggestions this century have been unsatisfactory.

The term 'psychogenic' was introduced by Sommer in 1894 to describe 'morbid states which are evoked by ideas'. It was heavily criticised by Lewis (1972), but it is difficult to know what to replace it with, except 'psychosocial' as used here. The latter implies that a wide range of experiences, social conditions and feelings could also be causal in addition to 'ideas'. The two terms will be used interchangeably.

Three types of psychogenesis will be examined, corresponding roughly to adversity at three separate periods of life: abnormal rearing in early childhood, abnormal personality development in childhood and adolescence, and adverse life events in adulthood.

Abnormal rearing

Loss of a parent, living with odd parents, abnormal parent child relationships and being a participant in deviant family communications have all been blamed for the development of schizophrenia.

Loss of parents

Manfred Bleuler (1972) provides the best evidence on this point. He claims that broken homes (premature loss of parents through death, separation or divorce) are 'not much greater than normal if they exist at all', and are probably *less* common in the backgrounds of schizophrenics than in those of psychopathic and neurotic persons. Although Lidz & Lidz (1949) found a higher rate of parental loss than in depressives or normals, and Wahl (1956) a higher rate than in normals, it can be fairly safely concluded from the majority of studies that Bleuler was right to dismiss the causative influence of a broken home.

Odd parents. Odd marriage

There is much more evidence that schizophrenics were brought up with parents who were odd themselves or who related to one another in an odd way. Lidz & Lidz (1949) estimated that 61% of parents had been 'chronically unstable' and 48% were chronically hostile to one another. Lidz et al (1957) described the marriages as characterised by schism (each parent going their own way) or skew (one submitting to the other). Alanen (1958) found 84% of mothers were 'neurotic' and 63%, in addition, had 'more serious psychopathology than neuroticism'. In a later study (Alanen 1966), he found only 1 normal parent amongst the 44 that he interviewed, and only two 'well-integrated' marriages. Wynne at al (1958) introduced the concept of pseudomutuality' (holding the marriage together at all costs), which they claimed was pathogenic.

Hirsch & Leff (1975), reviewing these issues, concluded that schizophrenics *are* more likely than normals to have been brought up by parents who were abnormal in personality or whose marriage was marked by dysharmony. However, the extent of the personality and marital disorder, which ranged in these early studies from 60% to 95%, is almost certainly an overestimate. Stephens et al (1975) found that 18% of 146 parents of 73 schizophrenics had personality disorders compared with 7% of 100 parents of 50 neurotic and medical ill controls. (When psychoses, suicides, heavy drinking and neurosis were added, the respective figures were 52% and 25%.) Schofield & Balian (1959) found that marital relations between parents of a schizophrenic were abnormal in only 24% of cases, exactly the same figure as they found in parents of normal children.

Abnormal parent-child relationships

The first proposal of this nature was made by Kasanin et al (1934), who obtained accounts of the parent-child relationship in 45 schizophrenics. In 27 cases (60%) it was abnormal: in 25 instances (56%) the mother was overprotective and in 2 she was rejecting. (Kasanin and colleagues did not in fact believe that overprotection was causal. They considered it was a consequence of the condition, 'the biological inferiority of the schizophrenic child being easily detected by the parents'.)

Since that time *overprotection*, *rejection*, *domination*, '*symbiosis*', '*sacrifice*', *treating the 'child as mate'*, and *exclusion* have all been used as descriptions of the abnormal relationship, and in some cases this has been claimed as a cause, not a consequence. There are two broad patterns: overinvolvement (overprotection, symbiosis, treating the child as a mate) and underinvolvement (rejection, overdomination, sacrifice). This is an oversimplification of the matter, but the standard of the experimental data does not properly allow the sort of nuances which are claimed.

Overinvolvement has been a regular finding since the report of Kasanin and colleagues, though the proportion of schizophrenics with this is relatively small: overprotection in 13% of 178 schizophrenics and 0.7% of 150 medical inpatients (Schofield & Balian 1959); symbiosis in 38% of chronic schizophrenics, 13% of acute schizophrenics and 3% of controls (Ricks & Nameche 1966). It has been identified by questionnaire: mothers of schizophrenics were more likely to answer 'yes' to the question 'A devoted mother has no time for social life' than mothers of nonschizophrenics (Mark 1953). It has been observed in the interpretation of pictures in the Thematic Apperception Test (TAT): mothers of a schizophrenic (Summers & Walsh 1977) but not fathers (Summers & Walsh 1979) were more likely than parents of a nonschizophrenic to see symbiotic themes in the pictures (dependency, disapproval of other relationships, separation difficulties). In a study by Farina & Holzberg (1967) mothers and fathers of a schizophrenic child did not actually report significantly different attitudes towards childrearing than parents of a normal child, but the schizophrenic child itself rated its mother more overprotective and its father more dominant than normal children did. Treating the child as more grown up than is appropriate for its age is another form of overinvolvement. Walsh (1979) found that families of schizophrenics were more likely to regard the 'child as a mate' than were control families. They asked the family to interpret TAT pictures all together, and then observed the families' reaction when one member brought up the 'child as a mate' theme. According to Walsh, the theme found more ready acceptance in the schizophrenic's family than in the control's.

Underinvolvement in any form appears to be less characteristic. Rejection is unusual. Kasanin et al found it in only 4% of their cases, and Schofield & Balian (1959) in only 6% (the same incidence as in normals). Domination, particularly of a son by his father, is more common. Schofield and Balian identified it in 11% of the life histories of their schizophrenics (compared with 0.7% of normals). Wild et al (1977) noted it while they watched families play the game of 20 Questions. (The family had to guess which of 42 pictures of objects on a board the experimenter had selected.) Ricks & Nameche (1966) coined the term 'family sacrifice' for instances where the child was openly considered an outsider, for example, as a child of a first marriage threatening the stability of the second.

Deviant family communication

During the 1950s it was first suggested that deviant family communication might cause schizophrenia. There was the double-bind theory of Bateson et al (1956), the proposal of Lidz et al (1958) on how the parental marital schism and skew affected the child, and the ideas of Wynne et al (1958) on the effect of parental psuedomutuality. (All these were discussed in detail in ch. 2.)

In the 1960s Wynne and his colleague Margaret Singer carried out a series of experiments to test their ideas. They used the Rorschach and the TAT. First they discovered that virtually all the parents of schizophrenics gave abnormal responses. (On the Rorschach, 95% of both parents of 40 schizophrenics were abnormal—Singer and Wynne, 1963). Next they analysed the nature of these abnormalities and concluded that there was both *individual* and *family* thought disorder. The parents (Singer & Wynne 1963) considered 'people, events, feelings as global, abstract, overly general' and had attention which was 'fragmented and amorphous'. The schizophrenic child (Wynne & Singer 1963) showed more extreme fragmentation of thought ('disruption by ego-alien primary processes') or amorphous thought ('less bizarre, quieter abnormalities'). The family as a whole showed 'transactional thought disorder' (Wynne & Singer 1963). The following is an illustration:

> (Daughter) — Nobody will listen to me. Everybody is trying to still me.
> (Mother) — Nobody wants to kill you.
> (Father) — If you're going to associate with intellectual people you're going to have to remember that still is a noun and not a verb.
>
> (Wynne & Singer 1963)

They considered that the 'form or structure of these family transactions was comparable to that of individual schizophrenics' thought disorder'. By this, they meant that if the entire extract had come from only one person the loose connection between each contribution and the one before would fulfil criteria for derailment.

The next step (Singer & Wynne 1966) was to list and define the characteristics of individual and family thought disorder. They produced 41 items, each of which they illustrated. For example, the item 'contradictory information' was illustrated by: 'I've never seen a bat. Last summer a bat got in my hair.' The 41 items were classified into 3 groups: closure problems (e.g. responses in question form, 'if' responses, contradictory information), disruptive behaviour (e.g. extraneous remarks, interruptions) and peculiar verbalisations.

Finally (Wynne 1968), they reported that between 85% and 95% of families of schizophrenics could be correctly (and blindly) distinguished from the families of controls on the basis of their Rorschach responses alone.

Hirsch & Leff (1975) tried to replicate this work. They followed the same method as closely as possible, even to the extent of visiting Singer and

Wynne and discussing the ratings. Despite this, they obtained different results. The Rorschach responses of the parents of their 20 schizophrenics were overall more deviant than those of the parents of 20 neurotics. But the cut-off was not so striking as Singer and Wynne had reported, and the deviance could all be attributed to the father's contributions, and this effect became nonsignificant when his verbosity was taken into account. According to Hirsch and Leff, parental communication deviance, though a genuine finding in some families, was largely attributable to an overtalkative father. What this represented remained unclear.

Since the mid-60s, investigators have addressed themselves to four issues. Does communication deviance reliably discriminate between parents of schizophrenic and normal children? Is it apparent in tasks other than the TAT and the Rorschach? Is there any formal pattern to family interactions? And is it the cause or merely a consequence of having a schizophrenic child?

On the issue of reliable discrimination, Jones (1977) derived 6 factors from Wynne and Singer's 41 items. These were verbal productivity (long-windedness), misperceptions, evidence of anxiety, overpersonalised closure problems (e.g. statements ending in 'I hope'), faulty overintellectualisation, and 'failure to integrate closure' (e.g. saying that one aspect of the picture has nothing to do with the rest). Parents of schizophrenics were best distinguished from controls by factors 2 (misperception) and 6 (failure to integrate closure); and all parents of patients with schizophrenia spectrum disorders had at least 1 of the 6 factors. Wild et al (1975) scored only 4 variables on the Rorschach: quality of attention, ability to close (conclude), adequacy of problem solving and dominance patterns. The combination of a mother with 'amorphous attention' and a dominant father distinguished families of schizophrenics from controls.

The second issue, whether communication deviance was apparent in tasks other than the TAT and the Rorschach, was the subject of several ingenious experiments. In one, Solvberg & Blakar (1975) gave five sets of parents of schizophrenics and five sets of parents of normals the task of explaining to their partner a route through town using maps. They were not told, however, that the map given to the partner had an additional street marked on it. The task was to discover this. Only one out of five schizophrenics' parents but all the normals' parents achieved this goal. This and other work confirmed earlier notions that *many* forms of communication were abnormal in the parents.

The third issue, the search for particular patterns of interaction, was intensively studied by Mishler & Waxler (1975). They devised a complex scheme for rating who followed whom in family conversations. They found that in families containing a schizophrenic child the sequence of speakers was more predictable (e.g. father-mother-father) than in normal families (e.g. father-child-mother, mother-father-mother, etc.). Most other studies found a variable pattern, or dominant father-passive mother interactions.

Neither of these bore out Fromm-Reichmann's notion of a schizophrenogenic mother.

The fourth issue tackled was the 'direction of causality', as it is often called in this literature. It was also the subject of some ingenious experiments, but all with the same general conclusion that any parental communication deviance is *secondary* to living or associating with a schizophrenic child. In one of these (Liem 1974), artificial families were created by placing the parents of a normal person with a schizophrenic and the parents of a schizophrenic with a normal person. Each party took it in turns to decide what object, hidden behind a screen, the other party was describing. A normal person had no difficulty understanding the parents of a schizophrenic but a schizophrenic child did badly both as communicator and listener.

Conclusion

Studies on the early experience of schizophrenics are difficult to evaluate, because of the complexity of the issue and the problem of disentangling cause and effect. One is inclined to dismiss the whole issue as causally irrelevant, and regard the few consistent findings (maternal overprotection, paternal dominance, peculiar parents, deviant family communication of one kind or another) as secondary to bringing up a preschizophrenic child recognised as strange in some way or a consequence of the parents themselves being schizoid. These are the most likely explanations. There is still a possibility that one of these might be causative but the nonspecific form of the communication disorder, its mild nature and its inconsistent appearance amongst the parents of a schizophrenic makes this unlikely.

Abnormal personality development

Kretschmer's description of schizoid personality

According to Manfred Bleuler, the term schizoid was first used by students of Eugen Bleuler in the 1910s to refer to peculiar people who were not sufficiently odd to warrant the label schizophrenia. It became well known after the publication of Kretschmer's book *Physique and Character* in 1921. In it he gave a vivid, and at times poetic, account of the schizoid personality:

> Schizoid . . . are those abnormal personalities which fluctuate between sickness and health, which reflect the fundamental symptoms of the schizophrenic . . . Schizoid men have a surface and a depth. Cuttingly brutal, dull and sulky, bitingly sarcastic or timidly retiring like a mollusc without a shell—that is the surface. Or else the surface is just nothing; we see a man who stands in our way like a question mark . . . Behind . . . nothing but broken pieces, black rubbish heaps, yawning emotional emptiness or the cold breath of an arctic soullessness.
>
> (Kretschmer 1921)

The main traits were unsociability, reserve, seriousness, humourlessness and eccentricity. He believed that the majority of schizoid people were neither wholly oversensitive nor entirely cold but oversensitive and cold at the same time. He illustrated this with a quote from Strindberg's autobiography: 'I am as hard as ice and yet so full of feeling that I am almost sentimental'. Some people did fall at one or other end of what he called the 'psychaesthetic' dimension. 'Hyperaesthetic' types included the sensitive, the sentimental, the passionately violent, the quiet enthusiast and the sulky eccentric. At the 'anaesthetic' end were the affectively lame, the 'cold fish' and the totally indifferent.

Other descriptions of schizoid personality

Slater (1953) took as a criterion the words used by the relatives of schizophrenics to describe other nonschizophrenic relatives. He derived four groupings of traits: paranoid eccentricities (suspicious, difficult, pedantic, spiritualistic, opinionated); absence of feeling (passive, cruel, withdrawn); reserve (shy, serious, unsociable); and anergy (tired, slack, unreliable).

Heston (1970) included antisocial behaviour, eccentricity, suspiciousness, being a recluse, rigid thinking, blunted affect, and 'behavioural lapses warranting the term micropsychotic episodes'.

Wolff & Chick (1980) found that four 'core characteristics' of schizoid personality had persisted over 10 years, from childhood into early adulthood. These were solitariness (rare heterosexual relations, 'often prefers to be alone'); poor empathy ('not sensitive to what other people are feeling or thinking'); rigidity (single-minded pursuit of interests); and unusual styles of communication (overtalkative, odd forms of communication, unguarded communication).

Bleuler (1911) used his term autism to refer to a personality trait as well as a phenomenon:

> Undoubtedly many of the later schizophrenics were peculiar, withdrawn and autistic already in youth.
>
> (Bleuler 1911)

Hoch (1910) believed that a 'shut-in personality' (retiring, reticent, oversensitive, seclusive) was a 'constitutional factor in dementia praecox'.

Strauss et al (1979) regarded Piaget's concept of egocentrism ('cognitive difficulty in taking the other person's perspective') as both cognitive style and pathogenic personality trait. (They measured it by asking a child to select the one photo in a set of four which represented how the experimenter saw a certain arrangement of items. Amongst the three alternatives was a photo of how the child saw the arrangement. If that one was picked it was regarded as evidence of egocentrism.)

In DSM-III a distinction is drawn between schizoid and schizotypal personality disorder. (Borderline personality disorder is entirely different in this scheme and includes such traits as intolerance of being alone, intense anger, affective instability and impulsivity, all alien to schizoid people.) Schizoid personality disorder is less severe than schizotypal and is defined as:

> emotional coldness, aloofness and absence of warm, tender feelings for others; indifference to praise, criticism or feelings of others; and close friendship with no more than one or two people including family.
>
> (American Psychiatric Association 1980)

Schizotypal personality disorder is defined as the presence of at least four of the following:

1) magical thinking (superstitions, clairvoyance, telepathy, 6th sense);
2) ideas of reference;
3) social isolation (no close friends, social contacts limited to essential everyday needs);
4) recurrent illusions, depersonalisation or derealisation;
5) odd speech (digressive, vague, circumstantial);
6) inadequate rapport (noted in face to face contact);
7) suspicious or paranoid ideation; and
8) undue social anxiety or hypersensitivity to criticism. Siever and Gunderson (1983) believe that 'social isolation' and 'suspiciousness' are more characteristic than 'psychotic-like ideation or perceptual distortion'.

Frequency of premorbid personality in adults

Bond & Abbot (1912) carried out one of the earliest studies. Using Hoch's concept of shut-in personality they classified 16 of 34 (47%) dementia praecox patients as abnormal (10 shut-in, 6 unspecified) compared with 7 of 43 (16%) manic-depressives (2 shut-in, 5 unspecified). Gruhle (1924) divided 139 schizophrenics, 110 psychopaths, 79 organic patients and 31 manic-depressives into five types: capricious and odd (schizophrenics 27%), malicious and suspicious (schizophrenics 11%), thoughtless and rude (schizophrenics 4%), shy and solitary (schizophrenics 26%), and cheerful and sociable (schizophrenics 42%). Schizophrenics were more likely than any of the other groups to have been shy and solitary, and less likely to have been thought less and rude. Arnold (1955) categorised 26% of 500 schizophrenics as schizoid, 15% as otherwise abnormal, 26% as uncertain and only 32% as premorbidly normal. Johanson (1958) regarded 15 of 71 schizophrenics as schizoid and a further 4 abnormal. Manfred Bleuler (1972) considered 24% of 208 schizophrenics pathologically schizoid, another 28% schizoid but not pathological, 13% pathological but not schizoid, 4% 'aberrant' (neither schizoid nor pathological) and only 30% normal.

In summary, the average incidence of premorbid schizoid personality from these studies is 26% and of other abnormal personality 16%.

Assessment of premorbid personality in children

Robins (1966), following up attenders at a child guidance clinic, found that those who later became schizophrenic were overdependent, ruminative, depressed and tended to bite their nails. (None of these four features was either particularly specific or common.) Kringlen (1968), comparing the previous personalities of twins discordant for schizophrenia, noted that the schizophrenic member had been more obsessional, more dependent and more introverted than the healthy twin. Watt (1972), comparing school records of 23 schizophrenics with those of 69 normal children, found that 53% of the schizophrenics could be distinguished from normals by their emotional instability (boys and girls), anti-social behaviour (boys only) or introversion (girls only). The changes did not occur until adolescence. (This agrees with the social study of Goldberg & Morrison 1963, where future schizophrenics had reached the same level of academic achievement as their siblings at the age of 11, winning places to grammar school to the same extent, but deteriorated thereafter, ending up, unlike their siblings, in only skilled and semiskilled jobs. It does not agree with the study of Hanson et al 1976, where 33 children of 29 schizophrenic patients, when compared with 36 normal children, were manifesting schizoid behaviour at the ages of 4 and 7—withdrawal, distractibility, passivity, negativism, flatness.) Mednick and Schulsinger's data (John et al 1982) suggest that some personality traits (poor emotional rapport, preference for isolation, sensitivity to criticism) can be detected at an early age in future schizophrenics.

In summary, the most that one can say is that there is a degree of social withdrawal around puberty in a minority of future schizophrenics. A more precise categorisation of the components or reasons for this is not possible. (Is it lack of interest in others? Is it lack of understanding or empathy for others? Is it fear of their criticism?)

Nature of the link between schizoid (or related) personality and schizophrenia

Bleuler summed up the problem:

> At this time we cannot decide whether such behaviour is the expression of a disposition to the disease or the surreptitious beginnings of the disease itself.
> (Bleuler 1911)

Existential, behavioural and psychodynamically-oriented psychiatrists believe that the personality disorder does constitute a cause.

Wyrsch (1956), an existential psychiatrist, was critical of the overinclusiveness of the schizoid concept, but believed that personality disorder of some sort was important.

Claridge (1972) and Eysenck (1972) believed that schizophrenia was only an exaggeration of normally distributed cognitive and personality characteristics. To Claridge, schizophrenics were only 'nervous types'; to Eysenck, only individuals at one end of a dimension of psychoticism. These theories do not so much support the causal significance of personality as proclaim its inseparability from psychosis. Hartmann et al (1981) took the view that a certain personality might predispose to a range of behaviours and modes of thinking, of which schizophrenia was only one. Vivid nightmares and artistic talent are others which they grouped with schizophrenia as loose expressions of creativity.

Like the behaviourists, psychoanalysts use the term psychosis in a looser way than is usual. In addition, they regard schizoid personality as more widely distributed in the general population than the figures given earlier would suggest. Some indeed (Klein 1946) consider a 'schizoid position' as a normal stage of development. In view of these considerations it is difficult to treat psychoanalytic claims about the link as comparable to others. Arieti (1974), for example, who combined the psychobiological approach of Meyer with European psychoanalytic traditions, saw an understandable progression through four stages. In the first, in earliest childhood, the 'parents are experienced as grotesque inner images'. The second is the development of a schizoid personality 'because the early experiences have made the future patient awkward socially, clumsy in his activities and somewhat inadequate in coping with life'. In the third stage, which he calls prepsychotic panic, the 'patient comes to believe that the future has no hope, that the promise of life will not be fulfilled' and this precipitates the fourth stage, the psychosis, which arises because 'in most cases only one solution, one defence, is available to the psyche'. Kendler & Hays (1982b) take a more modest approach. Within a group of schizophrenics, they claim, there might be some in whom an abnormal personality is causally significant. They found that 31 of 122 DSM-III schizophrenics had had 'premorbid inferiority feelings' and a lower incidence of schizophrenia in their first-degree relatives (1.5%, the same as in the normal population) than the schizophrenics without this trait (9.1%). Further, the former group had experienced more stress in their life than the latter. This is similar to Kretschmer's (1927) suggestion of a sensitiver Beziehungswahn (p. 93), but Kendler and Hays claim that the form of the condition is no different from other subtypes of schizophrenia.

Genetically- and organically-minded investigators hold Bleuler's second point of view. Meehl (1962) believed that schizotypal personality was the expression of the genotype 'under all actually existing social learning regimes'. Rosenthal, Kety, Mednick and Heston, in promoting the idea of schizophrenic spectrum disorders, considered that schizoid personality was merely a forme fruste of schizophrenia. Weinberger et al (1980b) found that chronic schizophrenics with poor premorbid adjustment on Phillips' scale had larger ventricles on C.T. scan. They believed this to be evidence for a 'neuropathological process occurring early in development', the view held by Kraepelin.

Conclusion

A statistically abnormal personality appears more commonly than expected in the premorbid phase of a schizophrenic's life. Prominent traits include solitariness, insensitivity to the feelings and thoughts of others, rigid intellectual interests, suspiciousness and unusual styles of communication. This is known as the schizoid personality and is probably a genetically-determined cognitive and emotional pattern. It is a cause of schizophrenia in that the florid psychosis may supervene in someone with this personality when they encounter an event which they cannot adapt to (e.g. overintrusive and critical family). Were it not for their personality they might be able to accommodate this. In another sense, however, it is not a cause, because the personality and the florid psychosis share a similar pattern of psychological dysfunction. In addition, some apparently typical schizophrenics may have had a different personality altogether from the schizoid type. The prominent traits in these cases—shyness, self-consciousness, anxiety, feelings of inferiority—may have been causal, in the same way as Kretschmer's suggestion of sensitiver Beziehungswahn.

Adverse life events

General considerations

The opposing arguments on whether recent adverse life experience can cause schizophrenia are well put by Hudgens (1974) and Brown et al (1973).

> It does not seem to me that investigators have yet convincingly demonstrated that life stress can cause madness in a person previously sound of mind.
> (Hudgens 1974)
>
> We shall systematically examine the hypothesis that for schizophrenic patients most life events serve to trigger the florid onset of symptoms in those who are predisposed and are experiencing tense and difficult situations either at home or in some key relationship; but that for some, events may be sufficiently traumatic to bring about onset without the experience of such situations.
> (Brown et al 1973)

The following considerations need to be taken into account in the debate.

First, any effect which life experience might have on the pattern of the clinical picture or on outcome must be strictly excluded from discussions of cause. It might be that relapse is precipitated by the same factor or set of factors which determined the initial episode, but one cannot be sure of this.

Secondly, cause and effect are more inextricably linked than is the case with the other potential causes (genetic, organic, early life experience and personality). For this reason, Brown & Birley (1968) were at pains to distinguish between independent and possibly independent life events in their study. War provides an opportunity to study the effect of genuinely independent life events, as in peacetime only physical illness, death of friend or relative, or a rare natural catastrophe such as an earthquake can be considered independent with any degree of certainty.

Thirdly, even if one can establish that an event is potentially pathogenic rather than pathoplastic or an effect of schizophrenia, the crucial point is its significance for the individual. What to some might seem trivial could be for others a devastating blow. The loss of a pet to an old woman bereft of human contact could be equal in its effect to death of a parent in another person. Further, the pangs of desire, remorse or anger suffered alone can be no less overwhelming than fear and the threat of death shared with companions in the heat of battle. In the First World War, for example, British troops on the Western Front were taunted by propaganda leaflets from the Germans to the effect that wives and girlfriends back home were being unfaithful. According to some sources this was more demoralising than the constant artillery barrage. As Menninger (1967) pointed out in his account of psychiatric casualties in the Second World War: 'disturbing and arousing incidents can occur in the kitchen as well as in the front line trenches'.

Fourthly, early life experience, personality and recent life experience must of course interrelate and the last, except for natural calamities, will only acquire significance in the context of the former two.

Next, the time of life at which the individual undergoes the experience is probably critical. There are times when the individual is preoccupied with other matters, ill or recovering from some earlier life experience, and the psychological impact which an event might otherwise have had is considerably dampened or absent. Psychoanalysts give overriding importance to the first few years of life, which is why most psychogenic explanations of schizophrenia have concentrated on abnormal child-rearing practices and deviant family communication. There are other critical times in one's life, however, puberty and adolescence for example, which may require considerable mental effort to get through without mishap.

Mental life has its own time scale. An experience has an effect *over* a certain period (the time taken to consolidate it) and *within* a certain period (the time taken for it to affect the mind). Brown et al (1973) called the former 'causal period'. The latter they divided into short-term—if event is followed soon after by illness—and long-term—if it is delayed.

Next, it is possible that one disturbing life event can be accommodated, but that two or more are disproportionately disruptive. Dohrenwend & Egri (1981) suggested that a devastating triad in close proximity might be necessary before schizophrenia were induced: loss of a loved one, a life-threatening physical illness or injury and a move to a new community which upset social supports. They considered that this combination would recreate the conditions of a soldier in war-time, and the infrequency of such a combination in peacetime would explain the rarity of purely psychogenic determinants of schizophrenia. They also pointed out that one group of people who are particularly vulnerable to the triad are chronic schizophrenics released into the community. Estranged from their family, suffering the extrapyramidal side effects of their phenothiazines and trying to cope with an unfamiliar part of their city make up a formidable combination of handicaps. In this way Dohrenwend and Egri propose a common cause for relapse and original episode, although as discussed earlier, it is safer, for methodological purposes, to separate the two.

Finally, the general method of deciding if social conditions or life experience are causal is to compare the prevalence or incidence of schizophrenia under these circumstances with some standard. The two most used for this purpose are *life-time prevalence* (the chance of developing the condition at some period of one's life) and annual inception or 'first break' rate (the number of first-ever episodes in a given population in one year). The average life-time prevalence for schizophrenia is just under 1% and the annual inception rate 15/100 000. These figures are pooled from various studies in North America and Europe, and if adverse life experience were a significant cause of schizophrenia one would expect substantial differences from these figures under different social conditions.

Differences over time?

There has been no change in the prevalence during this century, although the position with regard to the 19th century and before is uncertain (see p. 1). Varga in Hungary, for example, found no changes in the admissions for schizophrenia between 1910 and 1960 (Jablensky & Sartorius 1975), and Goldhamer & Marshall (1953) in the United States no changes in the incidence of psychoses of early and middle life between 1885 and 1940.

Schizophrenics are more likely to have been born in the winter months than at other times of year (Hare 1975), and are more likely to have had their first psychiatric admission in the summer months (Hare & Walter 1978). This is usually taken as evidence of an organic cause in some cases, because the winter months, particularly in towns, are a time of increased transmission of viruses.

Differences between countries?

Three areas of the world have been found to have an abnormally high rate of schizophrenia: Southern Ireland (Kelleher et al 1974), Western Croatia in Yugoslavia (Murphy 1968) and Northern Sweden (Böök 1953). What is more remarkable is how similar the rates are throughout the world. Leff (1981), for example, concluded that although the incidence in developing countries is largely unknown, its prevalence is similar in nearly all parts of the world where it has been studied. Even the three exceptions just mentioned are not certain. Böök claimed that the prevalence in 9000 people in Northern Sweden was 3%, three times the expected, but his diagnostic criteria were idiosyncratic and anyway he favoured a genetic not a psychosocial explanation. The high rate, according to him, was the combined effect of inbreeding and a 'very mutable gene'. The Irish figures, although well-established, have been attributed to a variety of factors, not all of them psychosocial (e.g. selective emigration of the mentally healthy leaving behind a higher proportion of genetically disadvantaged individuals—genetic explanation; higher maternal age with a higher rate of obstetric complications—organic explanation). The Yugoslavian figures are not well established, and the explanation for them given by Murphy (1968) is highly implausible. He claimed that as Western Croatia is at the boundary of Western and Eastern Europe, this induces an unsettled attitude towards life which facilitates the development of mental illness.

Subcultural differences?

Social class is the most researched variable, beginning with the study of Hollingshead & Redlich (1958, see p. 55). Being in a lower social class can now be discounted as a cause of schizophrenia. Dunham, who had earlier believed in social causes (see p. 55), concluded in 1976 that:

> although schizophrenia is heavily concentrated in the lowest social class . . . selective social forces account for the distribution pattern . . . and social class is not an aetiological factor . . . nor has any social or psychological factor been conclusively demonstrated to play a role in the development of schizophrenia.
> (Dunham 1976)

Goodman et al (1983) carried out a competent epidemiological survey of first admission rates for schizophrenia, alcoholism and depression in different social classes and found no difference for schizophrenia but a significantly higher rate of depression and alcoholism in the lower social classes.

Torrey et al (1974) claimed that rural inhabitants of Papua New Guinea had a lower rate than urban, but used this to support a viral cause of the condition.

Pattison & Pattison (1981) demonstrated that schizophrenics had a different psychosocial network from other people. This is a measure of the number, type and whereabouts of the people with whom an individual maintains contact. Normal middle-class individuals in Western society maintain infrequent contact with many far-flung friends and to a lesser extent relatives. The members of the network are not themselves acquainted except through the individual in question. Normal lower-class people have frequent contact with a few close friends and relatives, who know one another for reasons other than their mutual acquaintance with the individual. Schizophrenics had a different pattern from either of these. Their network was the smallest of all (only 8 to 12 people); it included people with whom there was little possibility of a long-term relationship (e.g. fellow patient); it might completely exclude first-degree relatives (e.g. siblings); it was characterised by emotional ambivalence; and members of the network satisfied 'instrumental' (they were useful) or affective needs, but not, as in normals, both simultaneously. Lipton et al (1981), however, showed that these characteristics were not evident until after the first psychiatric admission and therefore of no causal significance.

Differences between races have not been conclusively demonstrated. Murphy (1968) claimed that Tamils, whether as students in Singapore or soldiers in the Indian army, had unduly high rates. He attributed this to their tendency to have 'difficulty with authority', a poor explanation because it is neither confined to Tamils nor of obvious causal significance in schizophrenia. Rin & Lin (1962) found higher rates amongst the Chinese in Taiwan than amongst the indigenous population, and Littlewood & Lipsedge (1981) higher rates amongst West Indians in London than the rest of the population. Their status as migrants (p. 130) is probably more relevant than their race.

Individual differences?

A particular *birth order* (e.g. last-born for males only, Granville-Grossman 1966) has occasionally been reported, but does not appear with any regularity. Nor is the *size of the family* (Hare & Price 1970) of any consequence.

The *age* at first admission was 34 for women and 27 for men, in a study by Zigler & Levine (1981). The 20s and 30s are therefore the critical decades for the first clinical manifestations of the psychosis. No-one has ever shown, however, that these particular decades are more stressful than others for developing schizophrenia, and it is generally held that the particular age incidence is part of the natural history of the disorder and not of causal significance.

The *sex* distribution is also curious: equal overall life time prevalence and inception rates but a delay of almost a decade between onset in males and females. Seeman (1982) suggested three explanations for this. Either, according to her, there are two *distinct forms* of the condition, one with early onset, mainly affecting men, and another with later onset, mainly affecting women. Or, some nonspecific stress impinges on men selectively and *causes* the condition to occur earlier. Or, women have some biological protection which *prevents* the condition from occurring earlier. In this last case the protection could be psychosocial or organic. Seeman favoured the latter and suggested bilateral representation of left hemisphere function and relative dopaminergic inhibition by oestrogen as possibilities.

Particular life experiences?

In contrast to such epidemiological approaches, one can examine whether adverse life experience is causal or not by direct study of the effect of an event.

1) Anecdotal accounts. There are a number of anecdotal accounts of the effects of particular life experiences. There is Jung's example of unrequited love:

> A young student experiences a great disappointment in a love-affair. He has a catatonic attack from which he recovers after several months. He then finishes his studies and becomes a successful professional man. After a number of years he returns to Zurich where he experienced his love-affair. Instantly he is seized by a new and very similar attack. He says that he believes he saw the girl somewhere. He recovers and avoids Zurich for several years. Then he returns and in a few days he is back in the clinic with a catatonic attack.
> (Jung 1939)

Boisen (1947) gave a vivid account of a man whose psychosis began after he heard a sermon, in which the parson said: 'Are there not many men who are willing to give their lives for others'. The same night, the man was awakened by a voice saying: 'You must be put to the test to see if you will really give up your life'. Benedetti (1975) mentioned a man brought up by a dominant father and then apprenticed to a brutal employer. A seduction by a callous man in later life acted, according to Benedetti, as 'the final straw' or trigger. Unfortunately, for advocates of the psychogenesis of schizophrenia, few of these accounts are recognisable as typical schizophrenia.

2) War and catastrophe. Paster (1948) discovered that one million United States soldiers were admitted to army hospitals for neuropsychiatric disorders between January 1942 and July 1945. Of these, 7% were psychotic. He compared 500 who became ill before posting overseas, 500 who became ill overseas but without combat experience and 500 in whom the psychosis was precipitated by battle. The proportion of schizophrenics, the familial rate of schizophrenia and the proportion of schizoid individuals are shown in Table 5.3. Those who became psychotic after combat had a higher genetic

Table 5.3 Psychosis in American soldiers in Second World War

	Nonpsychotic controls	Psychosis before going overseas	Psychosis overseas but before combat experience	Psychosis after combat
Proportion schizophrenic	0	71%	71%	79%
Family history of psychosis	5%	26%	20%	15%
Said to be shy and secretive	24%	48%	45%	22%

loading than normal but were no more likely to be schizoid. Wagner (1946) found 66 schizophrenics amongst 4865 neuropsychiatric casualties (1.5%) in one sector of the Normandy offensive in the summer of 1944. In both of these studies, the clinical picture was undoubtedly schizophrenic, but the course more short-lived than the writers were used to in their civilian practice. The most striking feature, however, of these and other studies is the low rate of schizophrenia relative to other forms of psychiatric morbidity.

Menninger (1967) described the typical battle casualty as showing disorganised behaviour (e.g. discarding belongings, aimless running about, babbling) and emotional changes (irritability, apprehension, uncontrollable sobbing), which he noted did 'not correspond either in its moderate or extreme form to any recognised or established psychiatric syndrome'.

Other catastrophes produce the same pattern of psychiatric disorder. There is a low or negligible incidence of schizophrenia and a high rate of personality and emotional problems. Jaspers (1913) mentions, for example, that an explosion in an armaments factory in Germany during the First World War killed 657 and injured 1977 of the 6000 workers, but not one case of psychosis ensued among the survivors. Eitinger (1965) assessed the effect of having been in a concentration camp during the Second World War. He examined the records of the 3800 inpatients in Israeli psychiatric hospitals on one day in 1961. Ten per cent had been in concentration camps, of whom 62 were schizophrenic. He excluded 9 with a family history of schizophrenia, a further 10 with schizoid personality and a further 2 with tuberculosis. This left only 42 whose condition, he claimed, could be attributed to their harrowing experience.

3) Migration. Odegaard (1932) found that the inception rate of schizophrenia amongst Norwegian immigrants in Minnesota was twice the rate of Norwegians in Norway (28 as opposed to 14/100 000/year). He concluded, however, that it was not an example of psychogenesis because the rates for affective psychosis were comparable, the age of onset was the same in the two groups, the psychosis had not begun in the first five years in America, few people gave migration as a cause and the psychosis was not coloured by the experience of immigration. Mezey (1960) found a high rate of schizophrenia amongst Hungarian refugees to Britain in the wake of the 1956 uprising but, like Odegaard, discounted migration as the cause of this because schizophrenics, unlike patients with other psychiatric disorders, gave nonpolitical reasons for having left and they had already migrated within Hungary before their departure. Littlewood & Lipsedge (1981) found that 20% of schizophrenics in a London psychiatric hospital were West Indian in origin compared with 9% amongst the local population and 6% were West African compared with 2% in the local population. They concluded, however, that there *was* a general increase in migration-induced classical schizophrenia, with an average interval of eight years between migration and illness.

It is now accepted (Murphy 1977) that the relationship between migration and psychiatric disorder is more complex than hitherto appreciated. In some cases it may act as a stressor (e.g. West Indians and West Africans in Britain), but in others it provides an opportunity for odd people to escape from their home environment (e.g. Norwegians in Minnesota). Sometimes, it is the more mentally healthy who migrate: Astrup & Odegaard (1960) found that migrants from town to countryside within Norway had a lower than expected rate of schizophrenia. It would appear therefore that higher rates of schizophrenia amongst migrants cannot necessarily be taken as evidence of psychosocial causes.

4) Individual life events. The best way of determining whether adverse life experience is causal or not is to establish whether typical schizophrenics have had a life event prior to their psychotic episode. Brown and Birley showed (see p. 56) that life events were more common in the three weeks before an episode (occurring in 46% of schizophrenics compared with 14% of normal controls), but most of the patients they questioned were in a relapse rather than entering their first episode. In a further study (Birley & Brown 1970) they examined whether life events were significant in precipitating the first episode. They collected a new group of 50 schizophrenics, 24 first admissions and 26 readmissions. The same proportion of each group had a significant life event in the previous three weeks—16 of the 24 admissions and 14 of the 26 readmissions. (In 12 of the first admissions it was definitely independent, and in 4 it was possibly independent.) Jacobs & Myers (1976) then compared 62 first admission schizophrenics with 62 normals and found that 25 schizophrenics (40%) and 18 normals (29%) reported an independent life event in the previous year. Although this difference was not significant, the mean number of life events (3.2 in schizophrenics, 2.1 in normals) was significantly different.

On the basis of these studies, Paykel (1978) calculated that a life event doubles the risk of schizophrenia occurring over the next six months, and Andrews & Tennant (1978) that it increases it by 50% over the next year.

Conclusion

The question tackled in this section was whether an adverse life experience can cause schizophrenia in someone, as Hudgens put it, 'previously of sound mind', or whether some genetic or organic substrate has to be present. The evidence, in my view, suggests that traumatic experience in adulthood is rarely a cause, by itself, of a schizophrenic episode. Virtually all cases require some predisposition, genetic or organic, for life events to take effect. The mechanism is probably the vulnerability induced by the pattern of psychological dysfunction (p. 387). However, I believe that in a *small minority* of cases (Brown et al estimated it at 16%) a 'markedly threatening event' (Brown et al 1973) can be *causal*, though whether the typical picture of schizophrenia is seen in these cases, or whether it resembles paranoia is uncertain. (I suspect that the latter is true and that these cases are essentially psychogenic in cause and paranoid in form and not schizophrenic at all.

ORGANIC CAUSES

Introduction

As with genetic and psychosocial factors, one must first distinguish between a pathogenic and a pathoplastic influence. Acquired cerebral dysfunction undoubtedly has a modifying effect on phenomena and course, but a causal effect is not universally accepted. Manfred Bleuler (1951), for example, stated that all cases of brain tumour which presented with depression or schizophrenia had an appropriate family history or a susceptible personality.

Secondly, one must also distinguish between cause and effect. Holzman et al (1976), for example, found an abnormality in the regulation of eye movements, and claimed that this reflected some underlying, physiological cause. It was soon apparent, however, that the same pattern was present in normal people when anxious (Brezinova & Kendell 1977) or distraced (Acker & Toone, 1978). It was more likely, therefore, to be an effect rather than a pointer to the cause of schizophrenia.

Thirdly, although a physical condition may be cause rather than modifier or consequence, its action may not be mediated by cerebral dysfunction, and therefore it cannot be considered organic in origin. This was the case in studies by Bender (1934) and Cutting (1980). Bender reported 13 cases of psychosis associated with physical illness, but considered that the mechanism was not its effect on the brain but its psychological impact. The illnesses were ones which distorted the body (e.g. Paget's disease) and she claimed that the 'mysteriousness and the thwarting of social drives' were the causal factors. I reported 100 cases in which a physical condition and a psychosis coexisted. In 10 of these, there was no cerebral dysfunction, but considerable evidence that the illness had disrupted the patient's psychological well-being. The younger patients amongst them had been moved from other parts of the country to face a risky operation; the elderly had been suddenly removed from their socially isolated but well-ordered life to face uncertainty. (In both studies the psychoses were paranoid rather than schizophrenic in form, but they serve to illustrate the point that psychosocial causes may be mistaken for organic.)

Despite occasional errors of this kind, one can generally be more certain of the existence of an organic than a genetic or psychosocial cause. The reason for this is that organic causes are measurable, and therefore their onset, duration and termination can be estimated with some confidence. Psychosocial causes can only be inferred from a regular association between a particular life experience and schizophrenia. And genetic causes are essentially hypothetical constructs, based on the exclusion or manipulation of environmental factors (as in adoption, twin and high-risk studies).

As a corollary of this, one can test a particular organic hypothesis in a more exact manner than is possible with genetic and psychosocial claims. In particular, one can usually obtain an answer to two crucial questions, 'Is the organic factor regularly found in a random sample of schizophrenics?' and, 'Is schizophrenia regularly seen in a random sample of patients with the particular organic factor?'. So, for example, if one is proposing that schizophrenia is caused by a virus, one has to show that the virus (or a reliable biological indicator of its presence) is consistently found in schizophrenics but not appropriate controls, and that infection by the virus consistently leads to schizophrenia. Such methodological precision is not possible in the case of psychosocial and genetic proposals. Its value to an investigator is, however, two-edged. It gives more weight to a theory, but leaves it more vulnerable to refutation by future investigators.

Any organic theory of schizophrenia has to survive another test. Cerebral dysfunction usually produces a mental state which is entirely different from that seen in schizophrenia. Clouding of consciousness, disorientation and amnesia are some of its characteristic features. Further, each site within the brain (e.g. frontal lobe, basal ganglia) and, to a much lesser extent, each physical condition (e.g. thyrotoxicosis, LSD) produces a predictable range of clinical pictures, none of which resembles schizophrenia. For this reason, the organic-functional dichotomy in psychiatry, as well as indicating cause (cerebral dysfunction-no cerebral dysfunction) was, until recently, believed to correspond fairly accurately with the respective mental state. 'Functional' causes (genetic, psychosocial) produced 'functional' mental states (schizophrenia, mania, depression, neurosis); organic causes (cerebral dysfunction) produced organic mental states (delirium, dementia, amnesia). It was appreciated by many that the relationship between organic cause and organic mental state was not an invariable one, but it was felt that the exceptions were not numerous enough to discard the rule. It is now officially recognised in DSM-111 that organic causes of 'functional mental states' do occur with sufficient frequency to warrant disbanding the notion that delirium, dementia and amnesia are the only organic syndromes. One of the factors which influenced the American Psychiatric Association to make these recommendations was evidence that cerebral dysfunction alone can produce a mental state indistinguishable from schizophrenia. Davison & Bagley (1969), on the basis of a literature search, claimed that eight physical conditions had a greater than chance association with schizophrenia. These were epilepsy, head injury, cerebral tumour, encephalitis lethargica, Sydenham's chorea, syphilis, basal ganglion disease (Wilson's disease and Huntington's chorea) and narcolepsy. Manfred Bleuler's (1951) claim that such cases either have a family history of schizophrenia or a schizoid personality is now considered incorrect. In my study (Cutting 1980) of 74 cases of cerebral dysfunction associated with psychosis, only 2 cases (3%) had first-rank symptoms of schizophrenia, and only 1 had these in the absence of clouding of consciousness, disorientation or marked amnesia. But a psychotic state with delusions and hallucinations in relatively clear consciousness was fairly common: 17 patients had a clinical picture which would fulfil Spitzer's criteria for schizophrenia. This indicates that an organic cause for some diagnostic varieties of schizophrenia is frequent, and much of the evidence presented in this section should be viewed in this light. The problem of organic causes of schizophrenia, therefore, cannot be considered without reference to diagnosis and classification and, as discussed on page 100, it supports a view of schizophrenia, in DSM-111 terms at least, as heterogeneous, one component of which being a predominantly organically-induced paranoid variety.

Organic causes will be evaluated under four main headings: level of cerebral dysfunction (anatomical, biochemical, physiological and neuropsychological); site of cerebral dysfunction (frontal, parietal, temporal, occipital, subcortical, callosal, acute generalised and chronic generalised); hemisphere imbalance; and physical conditions (infections, toxins, epilepsy, trauma, tumour, metabolic, vascular, inflammatory, nutritional, endocrine and degenerative).

Level of cerebral dysfunction: anatomical

Pathological evidence

From Kraepelin's time until the 1950s neuropathological changes were regularly reported in schizophrenia. Most psychiatrists felt obliged to take note of them even if they could not explain them. Then in the 1950s there was a wave of scepticism. Wolf & Cowen (1952) concluded:

> All the reported microscopic abnormalities have been challenged by a group of competent histologists and have been attributed to misjudgements of the limits of normal variation, misinterpretation of artefacts or the uncritical attribution of special significance to casual, coincidental findings.
>
> (Wolf & Cowen 1952)

In the last few years there has been a renewal of interest in the matter. The two potentially most significant findings are gliosis in the mid-brain and changes in the thickness of the corpus callosum.

Several investigators have reported glial proliferation (evidence of a previous inflammatory process) in the mid-brain, around the 'junctions and major pathways of the limbic system' (Stevens 1982).

Rosenthal & Bigelow (1972), Nasrallah (1982) and Bigelow et al (1983) reported that the corpus callosum was thicker than normal. They claimed that this hypertrophy might have come about from chronic overuse (increased interhemispheric transmission) from an early age.

It may be that the new set of findings will be discounted in the same way as those in the first half of the century were. Matthysse & Williams (1982) are sceptical of them, although they point out that new techniques of 'examining dendritic geometry of granule cells' might provide a more accurate answer in the future:

> Reliable neuropathological changes have yet to be found, but if there are abnormalities they may be at a finer structural level than can be examined using traditional methods.
>
> (Matthysse & Williams 1982)

Radiological evidence

Before Johnstone et al reported the first C.T. study in 1976, there had been over 50 pneumoencephalographic studies. Weinberger & Wyatt (1982) review them. Haug's (1962) is the best known. He found that 43 of 101 schizophrenics had definite and a further 21 possible enlargement of the ventricles; only 1 patient had surface cortical atrophy. Altogether 58% of chronic schizophrenics had abnormal brains.

The first C.T. study was that of Johnstone et al (1976), where 17 of 18 chronic schizophrenics had abnormal scans. Then Weinberger et al (1979a) reported that 53% of 58 chronic schizophrenics had ventricular enlargement at least two standard deviations outside that of controls, and 32% of 60 chronic schizophrenics (Weinberger et al 1979b) had one of three cortical abnormalities — wide Sylvian fissure, wide interhemispheric fissure or at least three visible cortical sulci.

Since the late 1970s, it has become apparent that those early figures were an overestimate of the true incidence of abnormalities. There is at least one good study (Jernigan et al 1982) demonstrating no abnormality whatsoever in chronic schizophrenics. And when Andreasen et al (1982a) scanned 52 DSM-111 schizophrenics, although the mean ventricular size was significantly larger than controls, only 6% of the schizophrenics fell outside two standard deviations of the control size. Another good study (Gross et al 1981) identified abnormalities in 28% of 117 schizophrenics.

There are several possible explanations for the positive findings. Weinberger's group have published numerous articles claiming that ventricular enlargement is associated with poor response to treatment (Weinberger et al 1980a), abnormal premorbid personality (Weinberger et al 1980b), neuropsychological impairment (Donnelly et al 1980) and is found in acute schizophrenics in their first admission (Weinberger et al 1981). They believe that ventricular enlargement and atrophy predate the onset of the psychosis, and ascribe a causal role to it. Weinberger & Wyatt (1982) summarise their views:

> Some patients with the diagnosis of chronic schizophrenia have subtle structural abnormalities of the brain. The most frequent finding is mild ventricular enlargement. Dilation of cortical sulci and fissures were less common. Together, these abnormalities probably represent brain atrophy. They may also correspond to developmental defects or dysplastic process . . . The findings do not appear to be a result of treatment, either institutional or somatic. The aetiology of the abnormalities is unknown. The results of a study of premorbid adjustment suggest that atrophy may predate the onset of the typical syndrome in late adolescence. Individuals with this finding are a more homogeneous population. They tend to have the following characteristics — negative symptoms, neuropsychological deficits, nonfocal neurological signs, disordered smooth-pursuit eye movements, less frequent E.E.G. abnormalities, poor premorbid adjustment, and poor response to drug treatment. These patients may comprise a group for whom dopaminergic hyperactivity is not an important pathogenic factor.

The evidence that these changes are causal rather than a consequence is not as strong as Weinberger suggests. Tanaka et al (1981) found no abnormalities in schizophrenics under the age of 40 and only mild changes in those over 40. Marsden (1976) suggested that the changes might be a side effect of phenothiazines, and Lyon et al (1981) demonstrated a correlation between C.T. scan abnormalities and lifetime consumption of phenothiazines. Crow & Johnstone's (1977) defence, that they had demonstrated the changes in patients who had never taken phenothiazines, is therefore unconvincing.

Even if they are not a consequence, it is possible that they are pathoplastic and not pathogenic. Gross et al (1981) found that only 3% of 35 schizophrenics with complete remission had any abnormality, whilst 69% of 36 with deterioration had some form of pathology. Andreasen et al (1982b) found a good correlation between enlarged ventricles and the presence of negative symptoms, an indication that chronic patients tend to have the cerebral atrophy.

If they do represent or reflect a cause it appears to be acquired rather than inherited. Weinberger et al (1981) found correlations in ventricular size between healthy but not schizophrenic siblings, and Reveley et al (1982) very high correlations between healthy monozygotic twins but much lower ones between twins discordant for schizophrenia.

It is probable, in my view, that the best explanation is Hill's (1976), that brain atrophy is a factor which is of causal significance in only a minority of schizophrenics, but as it also worsens prognosis, they are overrepresented amongst chronic inpatients.

Neurological evidence

A number of studies report a higher incidence of what are variously called 'neuromotor abnormalities', 'neurological soft signs', 'neurobiological impairment', 'minimal brain damage' or 'neurological deviations'. They all refer to minor abnormalities, without localising value, detected during neurological examination. Each study reports a different subset of the following — involuntary movements, unco-ordinated fine movements (as in piano playing or foot tapping), dysarthric speech (only apparent when attempting tongue twisters), mistakes in fine sensation (astereognosis, agraphaesthesia, impaired localisation), inability to maintain a posture for long (motor impersistence), hypotonic reflexes, and various so-called primitive reflexes thought to reflect cortical disinhibition (grasp, snout, sucking, rooting and palmomental). Sometimes these signs are combined with hemispheric lateralising signs, sometimes with evidence of psychological impairment (e.g. on continuous performance task) and sometimes with psychophysiological dysfunction.

The value of most of these studies is in my view very limited because of the heterogeneity of the abnormalities, the unreliability that must attend their assessment, and the variety of questions which they have been expected to answer.

In adults 50% of 26 schizophrenics had either one hard neurological sign (localising) or at least two soft signs compared with 41% of 27 cases of personality disorder (Rochford et al 1970). One (9%) of 11 acute, 9 (24%) of 37 subacute and 19 (53%) of 36 chronic RDC schizophrenics had at least one soft sign (Torrey 1980). Cox & Ludwig (1979) found no difference in the total number of abnormal signs between schizophrenic and depressed patients, but when they grouped them according to the lobe of the brain which was presumed to be responsible, frontal signs were significantly more common in schizophrenics. Walker (1981), on the other hand, obtained a different subset of significantly abnormal signs, largely reflecting parietal dysfunction.

The purpose of the preceding studies was to determine the extent and nature of cerebral dysfunction in adult schizophrenics. Another set of studies is directed at children at high risk for developing schizophrenia. Fish (1977) claimed that preschizophrenic children show 'pandevelopmental retardation' (which in addition to neurological signs includes delayed growth, impaired arousal and abnormal proprioception). She believed that this was the expression of the genotype, a 'marker in infancy for the inherited neurointegrative defect'. It occurred in children of schizophrenic mothers but was not related to obstetric complications. Unfortunately, her claim is not based on acceptable data, as none of her infants (born in the 1950s) has yet developed schizophrenia, diagnosed by conventional criteria. The same criticism applies to the work of Erlenmeyer-Kimling et al (1982) whose claims that neuromotor impairment predicts later schizophrenia are based on whether 'patients are in treatment' and not whether they fulfil criteria for schizophrenia.

Immunological evidence

There is indirect evidence for a structural abnormality of the brain in claims that schizophrenics have unusually high levels of antibrain antibodies (Pandey et al 1981) or abnormal immunological responses in general (Goldstein et al 1980). Such claims are intriguing but as yet unconfirmed.

Level of cerebral dysfunction: biochemical

General considerations

It was in the 1950s that the biochemical origins of schizophrenia were first investigated with any degree of scientific rigour. (The background is discussed in Ch. 2.) The abuse of drugs such as amphetamine and LSD, growing knowledge about neurotransmitters and the efficacy of phenothiazines influenced the early investigators.

Since the 1950s a number of theories have been proposed and then discarded, and a number of striking claims later shown to be false or artefact. In fact, of all the proposed causes of schizophrenia, biochemical ones have the shortest life-span.

Transmethylation hypothesis

In the 1950s the most promising proposal was the transmethylation hypothesis, the idea (Osmond & Smythies 1952) that an hallucinogenic compound could be produced by the body through an error in one stage of the synthesis of a normal neurotransmitter. Mescaline (a known hallucinogen) is a methylated derivative of dopamine (a known neurotransmitter), and dimethyl tryptamine (another known hallucinogen) is a methylated derivative of 5 hydroxy tryptamine or serotonin (another known neurotransmitter).

Dopamine hypothesis

In the 1960s and 1970s the field was dominated by the dopamine hypothesis, the idea that the neurotransmitter dopamine was either produced in too great a quantity or its brain receptors were too sensitive to normal amounts. Its factual base was the demonstration by Carlsson & Lindquist (1963) that chlorpromazine, the first phenothazine, blocked dopamine receptors. The hypothesis has had to be modified (Crow 1978) to explain several inconsistencies: no increase in breakdown products of dopamine can be detected in the C.S.F of schizophrenics; patients with Parkinson's disease (who have reduced dopamine) can develop schizophrenia; and prolactin, a pitutitary hormone whose secretion is inhibited by dopamine, is found in normal concentrations in the bodily fluids of schizophrenics. The modification in the theory has been the replacement of absolute over-secretion by either a supersensitivity to the effects of dopamine at the postsynaptic level, or a deficit in some system which normally acts in antagonism to dopamine. Henn, reviewing the topic in 1982, concluded:

> Dopamine is involved in a variety of psychotic symptoms regardless of their origin and little if any evidence directly links a disorder in the dopamine system of schizophrenic patients with the aetiology of their illness . . . It appears that the liberation of dopamine and its action on a variety of receptors modulates the expression of delusions and hallucinations rather than regulates the central features of any specific illness.

Current position

With the decline of the dopamine hypothesis, the 1980s have witnessed a bewildering proliferation of other biochemical hypotheses. There are those which propose an abnormality in one of the other four well-established neurotransmitters (noradrenaline, acetyl choline, serotonin and γ-amino butyric acid — GABA); those which propose the manufacture within the body of an hallucinogen or psychotomimetic which usurps the usual neurotransmitter or neuroregulator pathways (e.g. by transmethylation); and those which implicate a neuroregulator (e.g. prostaglandins, endorphins).

Drug-induced psychoses

A biochemical theory of schizophrenia is usually supported by claims that there is a psychotomimetic drug with a similar chemical structure to the proposed abnormality or to a stage in the aberrant process. Davison (1976) gave the most comprehensive review of clinical, and Kleinman et al (1977) the best review of autobiographical accounts.

Psychotomimetic refers to the consistent production of changes in thought, perception and mood without major disturbance of the autonomic system, intellectual impairment, amnesia, stupor or sleepiness (Davison 1976).

The main psychotomimetic drugs are mescaline, LSD, amphetamine and cannabis. Other drugs generally produce delirium, and even these four rarely cause a typical schizophrenic picture. Mescaline, for example, caused visual hallucinations in 9 of 13 subjects who ingested it and auditory hallucinations in only 5 subjects (Kleinman et al 1977). LSD tends to produce visual illusions (7 out of 16 subjects, Kleinman et al) rather than auditory hallucinations (2 out of 16 subjects, Kleinman et al); and when the picture is typically schizophrenic the proportion of relatives with schizophrenia is the same as in first episode, nondrug-induced schizophrenia (Vardy & Kay 1983). In Connell's (1958) study of amphetamine psychosis most of the 42 subjects had a paranoid psychosis and very few had first rank symptoms of schizophrenia. Thacore & Shukla (1976), comparing 25 cases of cannabis psychosis with 25 nondrug-induced paranoid schizophrenia, found that 22 of the former were panicky compared with none of the schizophrenics, and only 3 had thought disorder compared with 15 of the schizophrenics.

In my view, the drug-induced psychoses make poor analogies with typical schizophrenia, and their importance in this respect has, in my view, been exaggerated in the literature. There are some similarities with the paranoid subtype only, but this does not allow one to generalise about biochemical causes of the entire condition.

Level of cerebral dysfunction: physiological

Early opinions

In the early part of the century, there were a variety of claims that schizophrenics had disordered physiological or endocrine systems (e.g. labile vascular system, abnormal glucose metabolism).

E.E.G.

The development of the E.E.G. by Berger in the 1930s raised hopes that there might be some electrical abnormality. Berger himself in 1937, and Lemere, another E.E.G. pioneer, in 1936 (see Itil 1977), obtained abnormal recordings from schizophrenics. Their conclusions, that schizophrenics have a less well organised resting rhythm (poor alpha) and more low voltage faster activity (more beta waves), have not been substantially challenged (Itil 1977).

In the 1940s and 1950s E.E.G. techniques were refined and there were several reports of specific abnormalities in schizophrenia. The most striking claim was made by Heath (1954). He inserted electrodes into various parts of the brain of 20 schizophrenics. He claimed that in two parts of the limbic system, septal nuclei and hippocampus, but only there, he consistently recorded spikes, indicating a localised and specific abnormal electrical discharge. These claims have never been substantiated. Hill (1952) systematically investigated E.E.G. changes in a wide variety of psychiatric disorders. Of his 147 schizophrenics, a significant proportion had nonspecific abnormalities (e.g. immature waves usually only seen in children), and the only feature in any way specific was a 'fast spike and wave', and that was restricted to catatonics.

Recent reviews of the resting E.E.G. in schizophrenia have been rather dismissive of its value. According to Buchsbaum (1979) it is only abnormal in between 6% and 20% of schizophrenics, the rhythm is sometimes referred to as 'choppy' (increase in low voltage, high frequency activity), and in general the alpha rhythm (normally at 7–13 cycles per second) is slower and less prominent.

Arousal

In the 1960s interest shifted to measures of arousal. This coincided with the preoccupation with attention at the time. Venables was the chief investigator and skin conductance (galvanic skin response, GSR) the chief measure. This was the electrical potential between two electrodes on the palm, reflecting the amount of sweating. By the 1970s (Venables 1977b), schizophrenics were considered to have the following abnormalities in response to some orienting stimulus. First, a proportion simply fail to respond. (Frith et al 1982 found this in only 5% of unmedicated acute schizophrenics, but other groups have found a higher proportion of nonresponders.) Secondly, some schizophrenics have a GSR which recovers faster than in other types of patients. (Frith et al 1982 considered this the most specific feature of their unmedicated group, and Mednick and Schulsinger found it to occur in high-risk children who later developed typical schizophrenia.) Thirdly, some schizophrenics do not habituate to the stimulus at all. (Frith et al 1982, however, found this to be more common in patients with an anxiety neurosis than with schizophrenia.) Fourthly, there is some evidence of lateralised responses. (This has since been virtually discounted, p. 154.)

Evoked potentials

By the 1970s, it had become technically possible to measure evoked potentials, the cortical electrical activity following a discrete stimulus in the visual, auditory or somatosensory modalities. Shagass (1975) and Buchsbaum (1979) have been the main investigators. There are a number of components to each evoked potential—positive and negative waves which can be recorded up to several hundred milliseconds after the stimulus. The five most used measures are a positive wave at 100 milliseconds (P_{100}), a negative wave at 120 milliseconds (N_{120}), a positive wave at 200 milliseconds (P_{200}), a positive wave at 300 millisecond (P_{300}) and the contigent negative variation, a slow negative shift in potential during a warning period. Changes in all these measures have been reported. Connolly et al (1983) found that the P_{100} and N_{120} waves were reduced in amplitude and delayed in their appearance, but only in the left hemisphere. Buchsbaum (1979) found the P_{200} wave most abnormal, and Dongier et al (1977) demonstrated a delay in the contingent negative variation. Morstyn et al (1983) and Brecher & Begleiter (1983) found an abnormal P_{300}. In addition to changes in amplitude and latency, there is some evidence that schizophrenics show a progressive reduction in amplitude with repeated stimuli, known as a 'reducing response' (Buchsbaum 1975), and have an abnormal reactivity to stimuli, termed an 'ectropic brain state' (Koukkou 1982).

P.E.T. scan and cerebral blood flow

The most promising development in the 1980s has been the invention of positron emission tomography (P.E.T. scanning). This allows investigation of the cerebral distribution of specific substances, currently glucose (Buchsbaum et al 1982) and oxygen (Sheppard et al 1981), but potentially many more. It is an extension of early work by Kety et al in 1948 into cerebral blood flow in schizophrenia. This involved calculating the arteriovenous difference in the concentration of nitrous oxide between jugular vein and femoral artery while the subject was breathing nitrous oxide. Ingvar (1980) also developed a method of estimating cerebral blood flow, by injecting radioactive Xenon into the carotid artery and then measuring radioactivity at various points over the scalp. The studies of Kety and Ingvar, however, involved arterial puncture, which is potentially hazardous, whereas the P.E.T. studies only require venous puncture and are safe.

There is some agreement between all these studies that chronic schizophrenics have a low blood flow to both frontal lobes. Acute, unmedicated patients (Sheppard et al), however, showed no changes.

Sleep

Sleep disturbance has been implicated as a cause of psychosis in two ways. Sleep deprivation leads to the development of a psychosis resembling schizophrenia (Bliss et al 1959), and schizophrenics show sleep disturbance (Kupfer & Gordon Foster 1975). The most consistent feature is a failure to show a rebound increase in r.e.m. (rapid eye movement) sleep, after being deprived of it. Buchsbaum (1979) also gives weight to a reduction in the amount of stage IV sleep and a shortened r.e.m. sleep latency (r.e.m. sleep appearing sooner after going to sleep than normal). He even suggested that a 'short r.e.m. latency psychosis' might be a valid entity in its own right.

Level of cerebral dysfunction: neuropsychological

The presence of cerebral dysfunction may also be inferred from a subject's performance on certain psychological tests. The issue is complex and has already been mentioned in the book. Dementia, deterioration, defect state, psychological deficit and pseudodementia all refer to the fact that some schizophrenics are disorientated, inattentive, amnesic and intellectually impaired. In other circumstances one would have no hesitation in diagnosing an organic mental state and searching for the cause of the cerebral dysfunction. In the case of schizophrenia, however, these features cannot be relied upon to indicate cerebral dysfunction. The 'organicity' may be spurious and explained by one of three classes of factors. First it might be a consequence of a nonessential aspect of schizophrenia — preoccupation with psychotic experiences, autism, retardation, apathy or treatment. Secondly it might be an integral part of schizophrenia, a phenomenon, as discussed in Chapter 6. In this case it would not indicate cerebral dysfunction, as the term is normally used, but a psychological deficit which is specific to schizophrenia (Babcock 1933, Hunt & Cofer 1944, Shakow 1946). Thirdly, the 'organicity' might be a true reflection, in some patients at least, of cerebral dysfunction. This is the issue in question here.

The main neuropsychological evidence for cerebral dysfunction is the fact that some schizophrenics achieve scores on standardised neuropsychological tests which are indistinguishable from those of patients known to have brain damage. Using the Halstead battery, Tucker et al (1975) found that 12 out of 38 (32%) of consecutively admitted New Haven schizophrenics had moderate or severe impairment compared with 9 of 71 (13%) nonschizophrenic admissions. Using the WAIS, Abrams et al (1981) found that 17 chronic schizophrenics had a mean verbal IQ of 86 and performance of 85 compared to 81 and 83 in definite organic patients, 102 and 89 in manics, and 103 and 95 respectively in depressives. Moses & Golden (1980) compared 50 chronic schizophrenics with 50 definitely brain damaged patients on the Luria-Nebraska battery; 4 of the 14 scales failed to distinguish the two groups (receptive language, memory, intelligence and rhythm). Puente et al (1982) gave the Luria-Nebraska battery to 11 schizophrenics with C.T. scan evidence of brain damage and 15 schizophrenics with normal C.T. scans. Seven of the 14 scales significantly discriminated the two groups (motor, tactile, visual, writing, arithmetic, left hemisphere and right hemisphere) and 7 did not (rhythm, receptive speech, expressive speech, reading, intellectual processes, memory, and pathognomonic). Heaton et al (1978) analysed 34 published reports of neuropsychological comparisons between schizophrenics and organic patients. Taking all the reports together there was no difference between the two groups.

The most convincing evidence for cerebral dysfunction is the association between neuropsychological impairment and radiological evidence of cerebral atrophy in the same subjects (Johnstone et al 1976, Weinberger & Wyatt 1982, Golden et al 1982).

As with other organic factors it is easy to establish a significant association with schizophrenia, but much harder to ascertain the nature of the link. Johnstone et al claimed that it could not be preoccupation with psychotic experiences because the neuropsychological impairment was worse in patients with negative than in those with positive symptoms. They rejected the idea that it was an effect of institutionalisation because a control group with physical illness and the same length of hospitalisation did relatively well. They also discounted any effect of phenothiazines (Crow & Johnstone 1977), because the same degree of impairment was apparent in drug-free schizophrenics. Goldstein & Halperin (1977) cast doubt on these claims, as they found that length of institutionalisation was the most significant determinant of WAIS and Halstead scores in 140 schizophrenics.

In summary, neuropsychological impairment does exist in a substantial proportion of schizophrenics. In some of these, it probably reflects cerebral dysfunction, and in a further proportion of these it probably antedates the first breakdown and acts as a causal factor.

Site of cerebral dysfunction

General considerations

Each area of the brain has a different set of functions, and one might expect localised brain damage to produce a characteristic clinical and psychological pattern. However, clinicopathological correlations even for typical 'organic' phenomena — amnesia, disorientation, inattention — are not strong, and it is unlikely that 'functional' clinical syndromes will have a simple link with some site in the brain. Nevertheless some sites of brain damage have been implicated in schizophrenia, and a knowledge of the characteristic organic mental state resulting from each area of damage does allow one to conclude that some are more likely than others to be of significance in causing the condition.

For each site of brain damage, therefore, I shall provide a brief account of the typical mental state, mention any reported instances of psychosis resembling schizophrenia and note any evidence that typical schizophrenics show dysfunction (anatomical, biochemical, physiological or neuropsychological) in that area.

Frontal lobe

The frontal lobe syndrome comprises intellectual, emotional and volitional symptoms. The intellectual impairment is manifest as a failure to plan ahead, stereotyped thinking and limitation of the capacity to synthesise complex material. The emotional changes include euphoria, hostility, boasting and social disinhibition, apathy and depression. The volitional changes are apparent in a lack of initiative. Psychological impairment is manifest in tests involving the inhibition of the most obvious association (verbal fluency, Stroop test), shifting from one plan or category to another (e.g. Wisconsin card sorting) and problem solving.

There are very few reports of frontal lesions leading to a schizophrenia-like psychosis. Ramani (1981) described a single case due to frontal lobe sclerosis from Schilder's disease.

Cox & Ludwig (1979), in their study of neurological soft signs, reported a significant difference between schizophrenics and patients with depression, personality disorder or alcoholism on frontal signs (e.g. grasp reflex, visual perseverations, verbal recall) but not parietal, temporal or occipital signs. Ingvar (1980) reported reduced frontal blood flow in chronic schizophrenics, and Buchsbaum et al (1982) low glucose distribution in this region.

In conclusion, it would appear that acute psychotic states have no special link with frontal lobe damage. Chronic schizophrenia and negative symptoms do, however, resemble the frontal lobe syndrome.

Parietal lobe

The parietal lobe syndrome is characterised by a disorder in the appreciation of tactile stimuli (agraphaesthesia, astereognosis) in the presence of intact basic sensation (pinprick). Right parietal lesions, in addition, give rise to disorders of visuospatial perception (visuospatial agnosia, neglect of the left side of one's spatial environment, constructional apraxia), visual hallucinations, disorders of body image (hemiasomatognosia) and failure to acknowledge bodily disability (e.g. anosognosia for left hemiplegia). Left parietal lesions produce disorders in which perception and language are both involved — finger agnosia, dyscalculia, right-left disorientation and dysgraphia.

There are more reports of psychotic phenomena following parietal than following frontal lesions.

In most cases, the damage has been right-sided and has usually extended into the temporal region. Lance (1976) described a number of patients with well-formed visual hallucinations and lesions confined to the right parieto-occipital region. Mesulam et al (1976) described three patients with acute infarcts affecting the right inferior parietal lobule, who developed delirium. They claimed that the underlying cause was a disorder of attention. (Later,

Mesulam & Geschwind 1978 argued that the development of a psychosis in these patients was analogous to the development of schizophrenia.) Levine and Finklestein (1982) described 8 patients with a schizophrenia-like psychosis who had incurred right tempero-parietal lesions between 1 month and 11 years previously. In my study of psychosis and physical illness (Cutting 1980) 4 patients had a right middle cerebral artery infarct (the cause of the inferior parietal lesions in Mesulam and Geschwind's patients) and 1 of these was a Schneiderian schizophrenic. (There were only 2 Schneiderian schizophrenics in the entire group of 74 patients with cerebral dysfunction.)

Walker (1981) found a greater degree of astereognosis and right-left disorientation in schizophrenics compared with schizoaffectives or depressives. Erwin & Rosenbaum (1979) compared 15 chronic schizophrenics with 15 patients with parietal lesions on three tasks sensitive to parietal dysfunction (weight discrimination, finger gnosis, tactile size estimation and a body image questionnaire.) Schizophrenics resembled the parietally-damaged patients on weight discrimination; only schizophrenics reported disturbances of body image; only parietal patients were poor on finger gnosis; and neither was impaired on tactile size estimation.

In conclusion, parietal lesions, particularly right-sided, do have a tendency to produce some acute psychotic phenomena. The issue is further discussed on page 343.

Temporal lobe

The temporal lobe syndrome is best illustrated by the range of experiences reported by temporal lobe epileptics (Williams 1968). There are visual, auditory, gustatory and olfactory hallucinations; complex states of unreality — 'dreamy states'; distortions of the perception of self and environment (e.g. 'Things crowd in', 'I seem enormous'); changes in the experience of time (e.g. 'Time stands still', 'Everything rushes by'); disturbances of memory — fugue, déjâ vu; intense emotions, particularly fear; visceral experiences (e.g. butterflies in the stomach); and quasipurposive behaviour (e.g. lip smacking, fumbling in handbag).

Of all brain areas, the temporal lobe has been most often linked with schizophrenia. Gibbs (1951) demonstrated a highly significant association between temporal lobe epilepsy and psychosis. Of 163 patients with a focal seizure in the anterior temporal region, 17% were psychotic; this compared with none of 37 mid-temporal, 3% of 30 occipital, none of 19 frontal and none of 26 parietal lesions. Hill (1953) suggested a specific association between the usual phenomena of schizophrenia and temporal lobe epilepsy. This was later confirmed by Slater et al (1963), Bruens (1971), and Perez & Trimble (1980). Hillbom (1951) analysed the outcome of 1821 Finnish soldiers who had sustained a head injury during the Russo-Finnish war. Of the 81 who had become psychotic, 20 were schizophrenic, and 17 of these had some involvement of the temporal lobe. (In a later collaborative study, however, Achté et al 1969 had identified 317 post-traumatic psychoses, 76 of whom were schizophrenic and in this sample thetemporal link was insignificant.) Malamud (1967) reported the clinical picture during life of 9 cases in which a temporal tumour was found unexpectedly at autopsy: 4 had been schizophrenic. Himmelhoch et al (1970) gave case histories of 8 patients with autopsy-proven temporal encephalitis: 2 had been schizophrenics.

Whereas the parietal link, if it is genuine, appears to be with right-sided lesions, the critical temporal side has usually been the left (see p. 152). Parnas et al (1982c), however, cast doubt on both the laterality effect and the entire temporal association in a study of chronic epileptic psychosis diagnosed according to various definitions of schizophrenia. Only 5 of 29 epileptic psychoses met Bleuler's criteria, 2 met criteria for pseudoneurotic schizophrenia, 16 had what they called a paranoid-hallucinatory state, 5 had a paranoid psychosis and 1 had an affective psychosis. Only the paranoid-hallucinatory and paranoid psychoses were associated with left temporal pathology. In fact 4 of the 29 epileptic psychoses did not have temporal lobe epilepsy at all and 3 were amongst the 7 with Bleulerian or pseudoneurotic schizophrenia.

Anatomical studies (pathological, radiological, neurological) in typical schizophrenics have not confirmed the link with the temporal lobe, but there is some support from physiological and neuropsychological studies. Venables (1977b) found that a large proportion of schizophrenics did not show a GSR in response to noise. He regarded this as evidence for temporal dysfunction, because animals with temporal lesions also failed to respond. Flor-Henry & Yeudall (1979) obtained a frontotemporal pattern to the errors on a battery of neuropsychological tests, and Taylor et al (1979) a temporal pattern.

In conclusion, there is evidence from a number of sources that temporal lesions can give rise to a psychosis indistinguishable from DSM-111 schizophrenia, though possibly different from Bleulerian and Schneiderian schizophrenia.

Occipital lobe

The only psychiatric sequelae of occipital lesions are Anton's syndrome (denial of cortical blindness) and simple, unformed visual hallucinations and distortions. There have been no satisfactory reports of any link with schizophrenia.

Subcortical areas

The areas which have been linked with schizophrenia are the limbic system including the cingulate gyrus (the cerebral representation of emotion); the brain stem (concerned in part, through the reticular activating system, with attention); the basal ganglia (mainly of significance to the motor system, but containing some of the most important nuclei in the neurotransmitter systems); and the cerebellum (usually thought of as serving purely motor functions, but with a possible role in emotion).

The limbic system has been linked most strongly with schizophrenia. Nielsen (1958) considered that lesions in the following sites could 'regularly cause a psychosis: mammillary bodies, anterior and mesial thalamic nuclei, anterior cingulate gyri and hippocampi'. Malamud (1967) reported 18 autopsied cases of limbic tumours where 'an erroneous diagnosis of a functional disorder had been made during life'. Two were in the cingulum (both schizophrenic), nine in the temporal lobe (four schizophrenic) and seven around the third ventricle (four schizophrenic). Escobar & Chandel (1977) reported a case with 'nuclear symptoms of schizophrenia after cingulotomy'. Heath's E.E.G. work, Malamud's study of tumours and Taylor's (1975) analysis of temporal lobectomy specimens suggest that the hippocampal region of the limbic system rather than the rest of the temporal lobe is the most important area. Torrey & Peterson (1974) put forward the strongest argument for the link.

The brain stem has been implicated in some apparently functional psychotic states, but the descriptions suggest an affective rather than a schizophrenic picture.

The basal ganglia have been linked indirectly with schizophrenia because they are the source of dopamine. Lidsky et al (1979) put forward a theoretical argument for their role in the catatonic, affective and attentional features of schizophrenia. Francis (1979) reported a family whose members had calcification of the basal ganglia and schizophrenia. Physical conditions with a predilection for the basal ganglia have been linked with schizophrenia—Parkinsonism (Crow et al 1976), Wilson's disease (Beard 1959), postencephalitic brain damage (Fairweather 1947), and Huntington's chorea (Heathfield 1967).

The cerebellum must have the weakest link of all with schizophrenia. But physiologists are currently reappraising its function, and some allow a role in emotion and intellect. One large series of cerebellar tumours (Schlesinger, 1950) produced no case which mimicked a functional psychosis, but there are single case reports of cerebellar atrophy and psychosis, by myself (Cutting 1976) and Kutty & Prendes (1981), for example. Both patients had been psychiatrically ill since childhood, and my patient fulfilled criteria for chronic mania not schizophrenia.

In conclusion, there is some support in the literature for a link between limbic and possibly basal ganglion lesions and psychosis, although most of the subcortically-induced psychoses have a strong affective component, and in my view the subcortical link with schizophrenia has been overemphasised in the literature.

Corpus callosum

The corpus callosum is a band of fibres connecting the two hemispheres and is responsible for the integration of some of their functions. Akelaitis (1944), an American neurosurgeon, was the first person to carry out the operation of commissurotomy (surgical section of the corpus callosum and lesser cerebral commissures). Twelve patients were operated on in an attempt to relieve their intractable epilepsy, and subsequently tested by a psychologist. No obvious change in any cognitive activity could be detected, and the function of the corpus callosum continued to be a mystery. Then in 1962 Bogen and Vogel, both neurosurgeons in California, reintroduced the operation of commissurotomy. Nine patients were carefully tested by a number of psychologists over the next 15 years. The best accounts of the early work can be found in a book by Gazzaniga (1970) called *The Bisected Brain*. The chief surprise was the extent to which each hemisphere could function independently of the other. Casual observation revealed nothing remarkable about these split-brain patients. In this respect Akelaitis had been right. Under certain conditions, however, they behaved in a quite extraordinary way. In the immediate postoperative period, one patient had antagonistic movements of the two hands. With one hand he would attempt to put on his trousers, with the other he would pull them off. More striking, because it occurred in all patients, and persisted, was the response to contradictory messages to either hemisphere. If the right hemisphere received a visual stimulus of a triangle, the left hand could draw the outline of a triangle. If, however, while this was going on, the left hemisphere was presented with a circle, the right hand would begin drawing a circle. The most extraordinary behaviour of all was elicited when a stimulus was presented to the right hemisphere and the patient was asked to account for what had happened. For example, when a picture of a nude woman was flashed to the right hemisphere, one of the male patients grinned and chuckled. When he was asked why he had done this, he said, 'You guys really make me laugh'. He found an explanation in his environment for behaviour which really derived from his perception of the nude woman. This source of his amusement, however, was not available to the expressive speech centres of the left hemisphere.

Psychiatric complications of a recognised callosal lesion have been rarely reported in the literature, but this may be because the lesion until recently could only be identified at autopsy. Nasrallah & McChesney (1981) did find psychiatric symptoms in five cases of callosal tumour: three were demented and two had a functional-type psychosis. Callosal lesions, atrophy and cystic change can be picked up on C.T. scan now and with increasing use of these radiological techniques it is possible that pathological changes in the corpus callosum will be increasingly recognised as a cause of psychotic phenomena.

In typical schizophrenia, pathological, neurophysiological and neuropsychological evidence for callosal dysfunction have all been found.

The pathological evidence is the least convincing of these: Rosenthal &

Bigelow (1972), Nasrallah (1982) and Bigelow et al (1983) all found that the corpus callosum was thicker than normal at autopsy in chronic schizophrenics.

Tress et al (1979) and Jones & Miller (1981) studied its physiological functioning in schizophrenia. They found *synchronous* somatosensory evoked potentials in both hemispheres after unilateral stimulation of the median nerve in the hand. This was abnormal, because there should be a 2 millisecond delay. Gulman et al (1982) found nearly synchronous peaks if the signal were travelling from left hemisphere to right. In this study he too concluded that the callosal transfer time was shortened, suggesting some functional deficit and the presence of aberrant pathways. Tress et al (1983) obtained the same results on a new set of chronic patients, but Shagass et al (1983) failed to confirm these in their series of six chronic schizophrenics.

Neuropsychological studies provide conflicting evidence on the efficiency of the corpus callosum.

The first study (Beaumont & Dimond 1973) required subjects to compare letters, digits or abstract shapes within or across hemispheres (flashing them up on screens in one or both visual fields). The results indicated both a left hemisphere deficit (comparisons within the right visual field were poor) and a callosal deficit (comparisons across the visual fields were poor). Dimond (1979) later reported an experiment, in which he touched subjects on a finger of one hand and asked them to indicate with the same or the opposite hand the finger which had been touched. Unlike controls, who made no mistakes at all, schizophrenics made many more mistakes when indicating with the opposite hand. He also showed (Dimond et al 1979) that schizophrenics were worse at naming objects placed in their left hand than in their right. Both these experiments indicated to him that there was a callosal deficit, disrupting the passage of information about touch localisation (first experiment) or distinctive features of objects to the naming hemisphere (second experiment).

Carr (1980) also found defective interhemispheric transfer on a tactile task similar to the one in Dimond's 1979 experiment. All the tactile experiments are summarised in Table 5.6 on page 157.

Green (1978) obtained similar results in a shape-posting experiment: when required to transfer learned information to the opposite hand (involving callosal transfer) the error rate rose steeply, unlike controls where there was no change. He also (Green & Kotenko 1980) showed that comprehension of auditory information (stories) was worse in the left and in both ears than in the right ear alone, again consistent with a callosal deficit, because auditory information arriving in the left ear has to go to the right hemisphere and then cross the corpus callosum before it is fully decoded by the linguistically competent left hemisphere. (He then showed that plugging the left ear improved a subject's comprehension.)

Blau (1977) claimed that most people, when asked to draw a circle, did so in an anticlockwise direction. Drawing circles in a clockwise direction, which he called torque, was unusual, and, according to him, indicated a 'neural integrative defect in the corpus callosum'. He found that torque was relatively common in children referred to a child guidance clinic (52 out of 106) and amongst the 12 of those who later developed schizophrenia (diagnostic criteria uncertain) 11 had shown torque. Tolor (1981), however, found no significant difference in the incidence of torque between schizophrenics (42%) and a variety of other groups (institutionalised elderly—47%, medical inpatients—42%, normals—32%), a result which severely undermined Blau's claim.

In conclusion, there is, in my view, considerable evidence that a malfunction of the corpus callosum might be of significance in schizophrenia. The physiological and neuropsychological evidence is particularly striking, although (see p. 151) some of it contradicts other work on hemisphere imbalance.

Acute generalised dysfunction

Although rapidly developing cerebral dysfunction usually produces delirium, in which clouding of consciousness dominates the clinical picture, a small proportion of cases will show typical 'functional' phenomena. In my series of 74 patients with acute cerebral dysfunction, 28 had delusions or hallucinations without clouding of consciousness. Of these, only 1 had first-rank symptoms of schizophrenia. Wolff & Curran (1935) mentioned 3 patients with delusions of influence or thought interference amongst 106 cases of delirium. Stengel et al (1958) found 12 instances of 'schizophrenia' in 80 (15%) and Knox (1961) 9 in 36 (25%) consecutive postoperative psychoses. Both Bonhoeffer (1909) and Schneider (1959) recognised these facts, but avoided the issue of whether the cerebral dysfunction was causal or merely a precipitant in these cases. As argued on page 100, I believe it could be a cause in a significant minority of DSM-III-type schizophrenics.

Chronic generalised dysfunction

Chronic cerebral dysfunction may also produce apparent functional states rather than dementia. In a consecutive series of 230 referrals with dementia, Gaspar (1980) found 25 (11%) with a 'paraphrenia-like picture'.

Summary

The following areas, listed in *decreasing* order of significance, have been implicated as sites of cerebral dysfunction pathogenic for schizophrenia: corpus callosum, temporal lobe, parietal lobe, limbic system, basal ganglia, generalised dysfunction and frontal lobe.

Hemisphere imbalance

General considerations

There is now a large literature on the possible role of hemisphere imbalance in causing schizophrenia. For this reason it is necessary to give a brief account of what is known about normal hemisphere functions.

Broca's observation in 1861, that aphasia followed a lesion of the left hemisphere, led to the universal acceptance that language was situated in the left hemisphere. But nearly 100 years passed before a comparable role for the right hemisphere was found. Hughlings Jackson, the most insightful of the early British neurologists, had an inkling of the problem in 1932. In an article entitled *On the nature of the duality of the brain* he suggested that word processes were not of the same kind in each of half of the brain. The left hemisphere was the one that we speak with, the right the one by which we receive propositions. The left was involved in the voluntary reproduction of a word, the right in its automatic reproduction. The next step was the publication of an article by Paterson & Zangwill in 1944 entitled *Disorders of visual space perception associated with lesions of the right cerebral hemisphere.* They described two patients with right parieto-occipital lesions, who ignored objects in the left half of their field of vision, had disturbed form perception throughout their visual field, had poor oculomotor co-ordination and did particularly bad drawings. They concluded that the right hemisphere had a specific role in visual perception and manipulation of objects in space. By the early 1960s the respective roles of the two hemispheres seemed clear, although this was later shown to be an oversimplification. The left hemisphere was concerned with language, the right with nonverbal aspects of things. Milner (1958), a psychologist working with a neurosurgical team in Montreal, discovered that removal of the left temporal lobe led to impaired memory for stories; after right-sided operations patients failed to remember nonverbal sounds. Kimura (1963) showed that this distinction between verbal and nonverbal skills applied to perception as well as memory.

The most radical change in opinion about hemisphere specialisation since the early 1960s has been an emphasis on characteristic strategies rather than on a predilection for a particular type of information. The verbal-nonverbal distinction is still generally true, but it is regarded as a consequence of a more fundamental difference between the two hemispheres. This difference has been formulated in a number of ways, listed in Table 5.4 as a series of contrasting modes of thought. Current interest concerns the way in which the two separate strategies are co-ordinated in the normal brain. Gazzaniga & LeDoux (1978) gave one of the best accounts. One of the split-brain patients had been presented with a snow scene to his right hemisphere and a chicken claw to his left. He was then shown four cards. With his right hand (directed only by the left hemisphere) he picked a picture of a chicken, and with his left (directed only by the right hemisphere) a picture of a

Table 5.4 Formulation of hemispheric differences as contrasting modes of thought

Left hemisphere	Right hemisphere
Analysis	Synthesis
Serial processing	Parallel processing
Sequencing	Nonsequencing
Propositional	Appositional
Logical	Creative
Preoccupation with particular	Holistic approach
Ideation	Imagery
Concern with familiarity	Concern with novelty
Concern with similarity	Concern with difference

shovel. When asked what he had seen, he replied without hesitation: 'I saw a claw and picked a chicken and you have to clean out the chicken shed with a shovel'. The crucial point about the experiment was that he showed no surprise or hesitation when confronted by the behaviour of his left hand (right hemisphere), and found no paradox in having to incorporate the consequence of this (i.e. picking up the snow shovel) into the account of his behaviour. Gazzaniga and LeDoux regard this as a fundamental property of the mind, that the verbal self looks out and sees what the person is doing. Behaviour, according to them, is made up of several mental systems, each with its own impulses for action. They regard the mind as a *sociological* not a *psychological* entity.

Language, attention, perception, emotion and memory are all a joint effort of both hemispheres, each with a different approach.

These considerations led to a flood of articles in the 1970s on possible hemisphere imbalance in schizophrenia.

Clinical evidence

The first piece of evidence came from a study by Flor-Henry (1969), in which 19 of 50 patients with temporal lobe epilepsy and psychosis had a left-sided focus and nine a right-sided focus. In 50 temporal lobe epileptics without psychosis there were 13 with a focus on the left and 25 with one on the right. Toone et al (1982b) carried out almost an identical study with a new series of psychotic epileptics, 57 of whom had temporal lobe epilepsy and psychosis. They looked at the lateralisation of radiological abnormalities as these were the most reliably rated. Amongst the 57 psychotics, there were 20 schizophrenics, 9 of whom had abnormal C.T. scans. Four of these had *clearly* lateralised abnormalities, *all* left-sided. There were 20 patients with an affective psychosis: 10 of these had abnormal scans, 2 of whom had clearly lateralised abnormalities, all right-sided. The numbers were too small to achieve statistical significance, and when *predominantly* left or right-sided abnormalities were studied, 6 schizophrenics had left and 2 right-sided abnormalities; and 5 affectives had left and 2 right-sided. Sherwin (1981) investigated 61 cases of unilateral temporal lobectomy. Seven were schizophrenic, and of these 5 had left and 2 right-sided operations. Parnas et al (1982c) collected 29 patients with a chronic epileptic psychosis: 7 had Bleulerian or pseudoneurotic schizophrenia of whom 1 had a left-sided, 3 right-sided and 3 diffuse lesions; 16 had a 'paranoid-hallucinatory' state of whom 7 had left-sided, 2 right-sided, 6 bilateral and 1 a diffuse lesion; 5 had a paranoid psychosis of whom 4 had left-sided and 1 a right-sided lesion.

From these studies one can conclude that left-sided lesions are associated with some diagnostic varieties of schizophrenia more commonly than right-sided lesions, but this does not apply to typical Bleulerian schizophrenia (which if anything has an association with right-sided damage).

An abnormal pattern of handedness was another early pointer to hemisphere imbalance. Oddy & Lobstein (1972) reported that schizophrenics (particularly young and male) were less likely to show concordance between hand and eye dominance than normals. Lishman & McMeekan (1976) found that young, male psychotics were more likely to be left-handed, and Gur (1977) and Chaugule & Master (1981) found that this was true of schizophrenics of both sexes. In contrast, Fleminger et al (1977) found more right-handed female schizophrenics than expected, and Nasrallah et al (1982) an excess of left-handed, paranoid (33%) but not nonparanoid (11%) schizophrenics compared with controls (6%). Some of the discrepancies can be attributed to different measures of handedness being used. It is also likely, as demonstrated in Nasrallah et al's study, that an abnormal handedness pattern is seen in the paranoid but not the hebephrenic subtype, yet more evidence that acquired organic causes are appreciable in the former but negligible in the latter.

Radiological evidence

Two claims about hemisphere imbalance have been made on the basis of radiological studies. The first is *left hemisphere atrophy*. Golden et al (1981) and Takahashi et al (1981) found a left-sided reduction in density on C.T. scan, which they claimed was evidence of atrophy. The second is *reversed asymmetry*. In a normal brain the right frontal and left occipital poles are relatively larger than the left frontal and right occipital poles (Chang Chui & Damasio 1980). Luchins et al (1979) demonstrated on C.T. scan that schizophrenics tended to have the reverse pattern, so-called reversed asymmetry (relatively larger left frontal and right occipital lobes). They claimed that reversed asymmetry was confined to younger patients without brain atrophy and with a milder illness. They did not demonstrate it, however, in the brains of 12 schizophrenics at autopsy (Luchins et al 1981); and Andreasen et al (1982c) and Jernigan et al (1982) did not confirm their C.T. scan findings.

Physiological evidence

Skin conductance, E.E.G., evoked responses, direction of gaze and cerebral blood flow have all been examined for any trace of lateralisation.

Gruzelier (1973) measured skin conductance in each hand of 60 chronic and subacute male schizophrenics. He presented a series of sounds at the same time, in order to obtain an orienting response, a change in the electrical activity of the skin brought about by a new stimulus. Only half of the patients produced an orienting response and the overall difference between the magnitude of the right and the left hand responses was not significant. However, of the 15 subacute schizophrenics (in hospital for less than 5 years) who responded, 10 showed higher right-hand amplitudes, 3 had higher left-hand amplitudes and 2 had equal responses. He attributed this lateralisation of orienting response to left sided temporal lobe dysfunction. The logic of this last step is rather shaky. There is some animal work conducted by Luria, a Russian neuropsychologist (Luria & Homaskaya, 1963), suggesting that a frontotemporal lesion produces a reduction in skin conductance reactivity on the *ipsilateral* side. Gruzelier's results could then be interpreted as an abnormally low responsivity in the left hand, indicating a left frontotemporal lesion. However, Rippon (1979) did not obtain the same result in schizophrenics, Toone could find no consistent laterality effects either in patients with unilateral temporal lobectomy (Toone et al, 1979) or schizophrenia (Toone et al 1981), and Schneider (1983) has failed to find any lateralisation of GSR.

The claims concerning lateralisation of E.E.G. abnormalities are also contradictory. Flor-Henry et al (1979) demonstrated more energy in the faster frequencies over the left temporal lobe than over the right. Weller & Montagu (1979), on the other hand, reported higher power over the right parieto-occipital region than over the same area on the left. Schneider (1983) found no laterality effect.

The position with regard to evoked responses is very complex, because there are three modalities—visual, auditory and somatosensory—and two pathways to each hemisphere—direct and indirect via the corpus callosum. Buchsbaum (1979) demonstrated a different pattern of lateralisation with virtually every one of these six combinations. The most prominent abnormality was usually seen with the indirect pathway, supporting a callosal deficit. Shagass et al (1979) found a pure left hemisphere dysfunction and Connolly et al (1983) bilateral abnormalities (reduced P_{100} and N_{120} waves in the left hemisphere and an increase in amplitude of the same waves in the right hemisphere).

A fourth frequently used psychophysiological measure of hemisphere imbalance is the direction of gaze in response to spatial or verbal questions. This was an idea first put forward by Kinsbourne (1974a). He claimed that in normals the direction of the first lateral eye movement after a verbal question was to the right, and after a spatial question to the left. In several studies schizophrenics have shown more movements to the right than normals

Table 5.5 Proportion of eye movements to the right in response to different questions (Gur, 1978)

Subjects	48 schizophrenics 24 normals
Material	20 questions: a) 5 verbal emotional, e.g. What is the meaning of the word shame? b) 5 verbal neutral, e.g. What is the meaning of the word repair? c) 5 spatial emotional, e.g. Picture the last car accident that you have seen, in which direction were the cars going? d) 5 spatial neutral, e.g. Imagine Lincoln on a penny, to which direction does he face?
Method	Videotape recording of first lateral eye movement after each question, then rated by two judges.
Results	Proportion of eye movements to *right*:

%	*verbal emotional*	*verbal neutral*	*spatial emotional*	*spatial neutral*
Schizophrenics	69	70	65	68
Normals	60	56	50	55

(Gur 1978—Table 5.5, Schweitzer et al 1978), particularly when asked spatial questions (Schweitzer 1979) and particularly so in females (Schweitzer & Chacko 1980). Gur interpreted this as *left hemisphere overactivation* in schizophrenia. She has later admitted that it is consistent with right hemisphere dysfunction.

Mathew et al (1981), using Ingvar's technique for measuring cerebral blood flow, found reduced flow in the right hemisphere, but the few P.E.T. studies to date have shown no lateralised abnormalities.

Neuropsychological evidence

Four types of experiment—test batteries and specific tactile, visual or auditory tasks—have been carried out to determine whether hemisphere imbalance exists.

1) *Neurological test batteries*. Flor-Henry (1976) gave 27 subtests of various batteries (e.g. Wechsler Adult Intelligence Scale, Raven's Matrices, aphasia screening test) to 54 schizophrenic 13 depressive, 26 manic and 21 schizo-affective patients. He claimed that, relative to the other groups, schizophrenics did worse on tests which were sensitive to left hemisphere damage. Five of these significantly discriminated schizophrenics from the combined affective group—aphasia screening test, finger writing with the right hand, ideomotor praxis, identifying speech sounds and word fluency. Taylor et al (1979) gave the aphasia screening test only to schizophrenics, manics and depressives, and also found that schizophrenics were significantly worse than the affective groups. They interpreted this as support for Flor-Henry's position, but in a subsequent study (Taylor et al 1981), when they gave five specially selected left hemisphere-type tests (e.g. Benton sentence repetition) and five right hemisphere-type tests (e.g. Benton's visual retention

test), schizophrenics were impaired on both sets, suggesting bilateral dysfunction. Kolb & Whishaw (1983) also gave a huge battery of tests and found no evidence of a lateral bias.

2) *Tactile experiments.* The simplicity of design and the knowledge that all information will only reach the contralateral hemisphere make tactile discrimination ideal for evaluating hemisphere imbalance. Most of the experiments have been directed at callosal function (p. 148) and have demonstrated that when information has to be transferred from one hemisphere to another (as in localising touch on one hand with the *other* hand) schizophrenics' error rate increases over the error rate when the task is carried out with the same hand as was touched. The experiments are summarised in Table 5.6. Scarone et al's experiment was directed specifically at hemisphere function: 60 schizophrenics and 60 normals were touched simultaneously on both hands 60 times. Schizophrenics missed significantly more touches on the left hand than on the right, but this was also true of the controls. Over most of the other experiments, there was also a tendency for left-hand performance alone to be worse than right-hand performance. In conclusion, these experiments give some support to the idea of callosal dysfunction and very tentative support to the notion of right hemisphere dysfunction.

3) *Visual experiments.* Beaumont & Dimond (1973) carried out the first experiment on matching items visually within and across visual fields (p. 149). Their aim was principally to test callosal function, but they also found a left hemisphere-based matching impairment. Since that time there have been at least eight experiments testing hemisphere imbalance in schizophrenia with the use of a tachistoscope (Gur 1979, Colbourn & Lishman 1979, Connolly et al 1979, Eaton 1979, Hillsberg 1979, Tress et al 1979, Schweitzer 1982, Magaro & Page 1983). Bare arithmetic indicates a left hemisphere dysfunction in five of seven where it was sought, right hemisphere dysfunction in only one of six and a callosal deficit in none of five. Although these figures appear to give impressive support to the idea of left hemisphere dysfunction in schizophrenia, there are a host of variables (p. 306) involved in determining hemisphere dominance, and such a conclusion would be premature. Magaro & Chamrad (1983) claim, for example, that nonparanoid schizophrenics are poor on sequencing tasks carried out by the left hemisphere, whilst paranoid schizophrenics are poor on automatic tasks carried out by the right hemisphere.

4) *Auditory experiments.* Similar problems diminish the value of dichotic listening experiments, in which auditory stimuli can be directed to one or other hemisphere. The experiments, however, highlight a number of methodological and theoretical points of interest. First, laterality (Colbourn 1979) is a complex issue and cannot be simply measured by subtracting the errors at one ear from the errors at the other. Secondly, there is the effect of phenothiazines or other antipsychotic medication. Hammond & Gruzelier (1978) claimed that errors at the right ear (left hemisphere) in identifying

Table 5.6 Tactile experiments on hemisphere imbalance

Author	Experiment	Patients (all schizophrenics)	Errors *Schizophrenics* LL	RR	LR	RL	*Controls* LL	RR	LR	RL
Dimond 1979	Touch localisation	Chronic	6	3	40	30	0	0	0	0
Weller & Kugler 1979	Touch localisation	Acute	0.8	1.2	1.7	1.7	0.8	0.8	1.3	0.8
Weller & Kugler 1979	Reproduction of imposed finger pattern	Acute	—	—	1.9	1.9	—	—	1.1	1.0
Carr 1980	Object recognition	Chronic	1.9	1.7	2.5	2.3	0.4	0.4	0.4	0.4
Scarone et al 1982	Tactile extinction	Acute	35	10	—	—	19	9	—	—
Dimond et al 1979	Object naming	Chronic	34	15			0	0		
Weller & Kugler 1979	Identification of inscribed number	Acute & Chronic	1.7	1.4			0.4	0.2		
			1.6	1.2			0.6	1.2		
			Number of trials to learn *Schizophrenics*				*Controls*			
Green 1978	Object posting	Remitted	71	57	118	101	68	63	62	65

a long tone occurring amongst short tones *decreased* on chlorpromazine, suggesting a specific therapeutic action on the proposed left hemisphere dysfunction. Thirdly, apparent left hemisphere dysfunction may be an artefact of the close connection that exists between language and the left hemisphere. Caudrey & Kirk (1979), for example, demonstrated that speech perception was impaired in *both* hemispheres whilst the perception of musical chords was unimpaired in *both* hemispheres. Fourthly, Wexler & Heninger (1979) showed that, regardless of medication, there was a shift in laterality during resolution of a schizophrenic episode, and that whereas acutely disturbed schizophrenics were more likely to make errors in the perception of digits at their right ear, this became less marked as their clinical state improved.

5) *Summary of neuropsychological evidence in favour of particular theories.* Left hemisphere dysfunction has been demonstrated in the pattern of impairment on neuropsychological batteries (Flor-Henry & Yeudall 1979, Taylor et al 1979, Taylor et al 1981). It is also supported by a left visual field advantage in the tachistoscopic perception of dots and consonants (Gur 1978); numbers, letters and dots (Connolly et al 1979); letters (Kostandov 1980); and positions of arrows (Hillsberg 1979). There is a right ear disadvantage during dichotic listening for syllables and pitch (Colbourn & Lishman 1979) and tones (Hammond & Gruzelier 1978). After phenothiazines the right ear scores during dichotic listening improve (Hammond & Gruzelier 1978).

Right hemisphere dysfunction was evident in an experiment by Gur (1979), in which schizophrenics had to decide if two similar pictures, presented simultaneously or consecutively (after 20 seconds), were the same or different. Schizophrenics were slower than normal, depressed, or left temporal lobe damaged subjects on simultaneous presentation, and most like patients with right temporal damage. She interpreted this as evidence of 'left hemisphere overactivation'. Schweitzer (1982) found that schizophrenics were significantly worse in identifying shapes in the right hemisphere than normal subjects, and better than normals, but not significantly so, at identifying them in the left hemisphere. This suggested that a left hemisphere overactivation, if it did occur, was a compensation for a right hemisphere deficit. Johnson & Crockett (1982) gave schizophrenics, depressives and normals four tasks on three occasions. There were two tasks normally regarded as requiring an intact right hemisphere (dichotic listening for musical chords, identifying the orientation of man with a flag), and two requiring an intact left hemisphere (dichotic listening for words, verbal fluency). The two patient groups were tested when psychotic, when recovering and just prior to discharge. Both patient groups showed evidence of right hemisphere dysfunction (relative right ear advantage for chords, impaired on the flags) when psychotic, but, whereas this was transient in the depressives, it was still evident prior to discharge in the schizophrenics.

The evidence for callosal dysfunction was discussed on page 149.

There are several reasons for being quite sceptical about the above claims because of the complexity of the hemispheric component in psychological functions. In normal psychology the simple models of hemisphere differences of the 1950s and 1960s have given way to much more complex accounts, in which a subject's sex, handedness and preferred strategy interact with the experimenter's instructions, previous task and present task. It is not surprising, therefore, that investigations of hemispheric imbalance in schizophrenia have found a number of confounding variables which detract from or even override the possibility of hemispheric dysfunction. Some investigators have simply failed to find any hemispheric differences at all. Small et al (1972) found no lateralisation effects on a battery of neuropsychological test items designed to discriminate best between left and right hemisphere-type functions (e.g. finger tip writing with the left or right hand). Clooney & Murray (1977), in a same-different judgement task with items clustered to the right or left of the centre of the visual field, also found no lateralisation. Others have found confounding variables or particular groups with hemisphere imbalance. Lishman et al (1978) found differences in ear preference during dichotic listening in males only. Pic'l et al (1979) found differences in tachistoscopic perception of dots and letters between paranoid and nonparanoid patients, but no overall difference between schizophrenics and psychiatric controls. Eaton (1979), in a tachistoscopic matching task, attributed all the apparent hemispheric differences to a longstanding verbal deficit. She found verbal deficits in left *and* right hemispheres, whereas the schizophrenics perceived nonverbal stimuli as accurately as normals in the left hemisphere. Caudrey & Kirk (1979) came to the same conclusion using verbal (consonant–vowel–consonant triads) and nonverbal stimuli (musical chords) in a dichotic listening task. Finally, the stage of the illness is critical. Wexler & Heninger (1979) found no group differences between schizophrenics and controls in dichotic listening for digits when the patients were psychotic, but a small laterality effect in some schizophrenics as they moved from a severe to a mild condition.

Summary

The anatomical evidence for hemisphere imbalance in schizophrenia derives from three sources—reversed asymmetry on C.T. scan (now in doubt), left hemisphere atrophy on C.T. scan (unconfirmed) and an association between left temporal damage and schizophrenia (probable, but not universally accepted).

The physiological evidence includes lateralised orienting GSR responses (difficult to evaluate because of the large number of other factors involved), lateralised differences in resting E.E.G. (disputed), lateralisation effects in evoked responses (difficult to assess because of their complexity) and differences in the direction of lateralised eye movements (a procedure with a shaky theoretical foundation).

The neuropsychological evidence includes performance on test batteries which resemble those of patients with left temporal damage, tachistoscopic experiments in which schizophrenics show a different field advantage from normals, and dichotic listening procedures in which they have an abnormal ear advantage. Most of the data are consistent with several rival hypotheses. On balance left hemisphere dysfunction is the most convincing, but the complexity of many of the tasks and the numerous factors which determine the pattern of hemispheric participation in normals make evaluation of the data very difficult.

Physical conditions

General considerations

There is a higher incidence of physical illness than expected in a sample of typical schizophrenics. Maguire & Granville-Grossman (1968) examined 27 consecutive admissions and found 6 with what they called 'significant physical morbidity' (polymyositis, iron deficiency anaemia, inguinal hernia, leukoderma, chronic otitis media, mild acne). None of these physical conditions can be regarded as a cause of cerebral dysfunction. Hall et al (1980) estimated that a physical illness had 'caused or exacerbated symptoms' in 15 out of 38 (39%) consecutive admissions. This figure is almost certainly unrepresentative and largely incorrect as very few of the physical illnesses which they included are acceptable as causes of cerebral dysfunction (e.g. peptic ulcer, essential hypertension). Retterstol (1981) estimated that 12% of schizophrenics had 'a somatic illness of importance for the disorder'. This is probably a more accurate reflection of genuinely causal organic influences in a random series of typical schizophrenics.

Davison & Bagley (1969) and Baldwin (1979, 1980) have carried out the most comprehensive surveys on the association between physical illness and schizophrenia. The first authors conducted a literature search, running to 800 references. Baldwin made use of computer records of links between 2314 instances of schizophrenia and all admissions for physical illness in the counties of Oxfordshire and Berkshire between 1963 and 1970. Both sets of authors calculated any significant difference from a chance association in their data. The Oxford Record Linkage Study is more trustworthy than the literature search for obvious reasons, but cannot be relied upon for rare conditions such as Wilson's disease or systemic lupus erythematosus. Both studies will be referred to in the succeeding pages.

Infections

The only infectious agents which have been regularly linked with schizophrenia are a virus and the syphilitic organism. Other infections can probably be ruled out completely as specific pathogens. Davison and Bagley incriminated Sydenham's chorea, but its rarity nowadays makes this of historical interest only.

The viral hypothesis of schizophrenia is probably the most popular of current organic theories of schizophrenia. Crow (1983) presents the best argument. He points out some minor discrepancies in the genetic evidence from twin studies, which could conceivably be due to physical proximity rather than shared inheritance; he notes that other infectious diseases, such as tuberculosis, have a genetic component; and quotes a Russian study, in which 36 schizophrenics were found in a block of flats 25 years after a known schizophrenic had lived there, compared to 9 and 3 in two comparable blocks in which no primary case had been identified.

Crow's actual evidence is slim. Thirteen of 38 schizophrenics had C.S.F. which was cytopathic to certain cultured cells (Tyrrell et al 1979), but so was the C.S.F. of 8 of 11 miscellaneous neurologically ill patients. Eighteen of 47 schizophrenics actually contained a virus-like agent in their C.S.F. (Crow et al 1979), but no controls are reported.

If schizophrenia is caused by a virus, one would expect at least some epidemics and sporadic outbreaks of viral encephalitis to result in schizophrenia. Encephalitis lethargica, the most famous example, produced many psychiatric symptoms (Symonds 1921) but only rarely a schizophrenic picture (Menninger 1926). Rail et al (1981) found 6 new cases of sporadic encephalitis lethargica in their practice in the last 20 years, but the only psychiatric phenomena in these were derealisation, euphoria and apathy. There are several case studies of viral encephalopathy (Wilson 1976) or glandular fever (Rubin 1978) mimicking a functional psychosis, but mistakes of this nature are not common in the experience of most psychiatrists.

On balance, therefore, the viral hypothesis, although attractive, does not rest on strong evidence. A cynic might say that its attraction lies in the very difficulty in establishing the presence of a virus.

The relationship between schizophrenia (dementia praecox) and syphilitic disease of the brain (dementia paralytica) is important in a historical sense, as the former was largely modelled on the latter. There is some evidence, however, that syphilis can present, in the early stages at least, the typical picture of schizophrenia. Davison and Bagley included it amongst their eight definite associations. Dewhurst (1969) collected 91 patients between 1950 and 1965; schizophrenia was the initial diagnosis in 6. If it is a cause, it is not common, because the incidence of syphilitic disease of the brain has dropped dramatically during the century and is now very rare. (Luxon et al 1979 only managed to collect 17 cases of recently diagnosed neurosyphilis and none of these was schizophrenic. This should be set alongside the fact that the inception rate of schizophrenia has remained steady during this time.)

Toxins

The effect of drugs was discussed on page 139.

The relationship between alcoholism and schizophrenia has a number of facets: some typical schizophrenics become alcoholics; sometimes there appears to be a joint genetic predisposition to both conditions; but most instances of an association between the two indicate that high alcohol consumption has acted as a causal factor. This is well documented by Victor & Hope (1958), Benedetti (1952), May & Ebaugh (1953) and myself (Cutting 1978a). In these cases the diagnosis of alcohol hallucinosis has usually been made in preference to schizophrenia, because the clinical picture has lacked the phenomena of typical schizophrenia.

Epilepsy and sleep disorders

The link between schizophrenia and epilepsy is the strongest of any physical condition. It is also the most extensively studied, and probably for this reason the most complex.

Meduna (1937) and Landolt (1958) believed that the two were mutually antagonistic, and on the basis of this Meduna suggested electroconvulsive therapy in psychotic disorders. Landolt noted that when epileptics became psychotic, a previously abnormal interictal E.E.G. was much improved. He called this 'forced normalisation'.

It soon became clear, however, that there was a strong positive association between the two conditions. The reason for this is still far from clear (Toone 1981, Trimble 1982). Schizophrenia could be a manifestation of subictal electrical activity or 'kindling' (induction of distant brain damage by repeated fits). It could be an effect of brain damage, and nothing intrinsically to do with epilepsy, which would then be another independent consequence of brain damage. The two conditions might share the same neurotransmitter abnormality. The psychosis could even be psychologically rather than organically linked to the epilepsy. Pond (1957) suggested that repeated dreamy states, typical of temporal lobe seizures, might in some way induce a permanent disorder of cognition and affect. Finally, schizophrenia could conceivably be a consequence of anticonvulsant medication (Reynolds 1968), in which case Meduna and Landolt might still be right in their belief that there was a mutual antagonism between the two conditions.

Narcolepsy, an irresistible desire for sleep due to disruption of the control of sleep, particularly the balance and timing of r.e.m. and non-r.e.m. phases, was specifically linked to schizophrenia by Davison and Bagley. They found 18 case reports in the literature, 10 of them in a single study by Sours (1963) of 75 primary narcoleptics. The link is now disputed. Roy (1976) found only 1 schizophrenic amongst 20 cases, and suggested that the usual treatment with amphetamine might have led to a spurious association. Kales et al (1980) found no instances of schizophrenia amongst 50 narcoleptics. Some narcoleptics, and patients with the Kleine-Levin syndrome ('periodic hypersomnia and megaphagia in adolescent males', Critchley 1962a), describe dreamy states and disorders of thinking, and this might be another cause of the spurious association.

Trauma in adulthood

Baldwin, and Davison and Bagley, all stressed a link between head injury and schizophrenia. The strongest evidence comes from follow-up of war injuries. Achté et al (1969) found that 76 (2.1%) of 3552 brain-damaged Finnish soldiers had developed schizophrenia after 25 years. (However, of the entire group of 317 with some form of psychosis, 57% of those who had been injured under the age of 20 developed schizophrenia compared with only 11% of those over the age of 35 at the time of injury. Further, it was more common after mild than severe injuries. This suggested to them that constitutional factors were also important, because the younger men had still to pass through the main constitutional risk period.) Lishman (1968) found only 5 instances of psychosis in 670 soldiers injured in World War II.

Trauma at birth

McNeil and Kaij (1978) reviewed the relationship between obstetric complications and the risk of later developing schizophrenia. They found evidence for an increased risk from three sources of enquiry.

Adult schizophrenics are retrospectively found to have had a greater number of such complications (Woerner et al 1973). The schizophrenic of identical twins discordant for schizophrenia is more likely to have had a complicated birth (Stabenau & Pollin 1967). The high risk children of Mednick and Schulsinger who eventually became Catego schizophrenics were more likely to have had perinatal complications, particularly an abnormal foetal position (Parnas et al 1982b).

Bellak (1979) suggested that 'minimal brain damage' in childhood, from encephalitis as well as perinatal complications, was a recognisable cause of schizophrenia.

Tumour

Cerebral tumours increase the risk of a schizophrenia-like psychosis, according to Davison and Bagley's review. There is some evidence that they increase this independently of the risk attached to their site. Taylor (1975) analysed 88 cases of temporal lobectomy, 47 with a tumour and 41 with mesial sclerosis (thought to represent the effect of anoxia in childhood). Of patients with tumours 23% were psychotic, but of those with sclerosis only 5% were psychotic.

Metabolic conditions.

Liver and kidney disease, diabetes and cancer have occasionally been linked with schizophrenia.

Renal failure and hepatic encephalopathy are certainly potent causes of psychiatric disorder, including psychosis, but there are no clear links with a typically schizophrenic picture.

Diabetes has occasionally been linked *negatively* with schizophrenia. Baldwin (1980) did find fewer diabetics than expected in his population of schizophrenics, but regarded this as an artefact.

Cancer has been regarded as rare in schizophrenics. Baldwin (1980) investigated this thoroughly and could find 'no robust differences' for any forms of carcinoma.

Cerebrovascular disease.

Acute cerebrovascular accidents usually present with motor disorder (typically hemiplegia), language disorder (aphasia) or a disturbance in consciousness. A small minority present with a purely psychiatric disorder. I examined 100 patients in the first week of their hemiplegia (Cutting 1978b) and found an abnormal mental state, other than aphasia, disorientation for place or amnesia in 12. None of these had any characteristic features of schizophrenia. In my study of 74 psychoses associated with acute cerebral dysfunction, 8 were due to a cerebrovascular accident, and 1 of these had first-rank symptoms of schizophrenia.

Those who have investigated the chronic sequelae of strokes (60 cases—Ullman 1962) or subarachnoid haemorrhage (261 cases—Storey 1970) have not reported any instances of schizophrenia, but Davison and Bagley mentioned a possible link with late-onset schizophrenia and Levine & Finklestein (1982) reported 7 cases of psychosis bearing some resemblance to schizophrenia which developed after a vascular lesion in the right parietal region.

Inflammatory disease

Chronic inflammatory conditions of unknown cause, possibly autoimmune, such as rheumatoid arthritis and systemic lupus erythematosus (SLE), have been linked in different ways with schizophrenia.

Rheumatoid arthritis has the strongest claim to be linked *negatively*. Nissen & Spencer (1936) first suggested this, and Baldwin confirmed its low prevalence in his Oxford Record Linkage Study. (Of all the conditions which he included, it was the only one with an appreciably and significantly lower risk.)

SLE, on the other hand, has been frequently linked *positively* with schizophrenia. Rudin (1981) was so impressed with this that he proposed:

> SLE might provide a model for schizophrenia since SLE is strongly associated with schizophreniform psychoses and exhibits only a covert C.N.S. pathology revealed by immunofluorescent immune complex deposits in the choroid

> plexus . . . In this context both SLE and schizophrenia are viewed as expressions of combined transport dysfunction syndromes, resulting from polygenic-induced sensitivity to exogenous peptides or viruses.
>
> (Rudin 1981)

Rudin's enthusiasm is rather premature, as the link is not as strong as he supposes. Baldwin found only one instance of schizophrenia amongst 516 cases of SLE, and other large studies of the condition give a similarly low association with schizophrenia. In a study in which I was involved (Bresnihan et al 1979) 15 patients with definite cerebral involvement (brain antibodies or abnormal brain scans) were interviewed. Four of these had Catego schizophrenia.

Nutritional disorders (including vitamin deficiency)

Some investigators have placed great weight on a dietary cause of schizophrenia. This has led to the recommendation of certain dietary regimes and the practice of 'orthomolecular psychiatry'.

The starting point for much of this was the observation by Dohan (1966) that the admission rates for schizophrenia fell in some countries during the Second World War. Of the countries which he studied, the fall was most marked in Finland, less in Norway and Sweden, insignificant in Canada and Switzerland, and there was a rise in the United States. Dohan argued that psychological factors could not be held responsible because of the social differences involved. Instead, he suggested the changes were due to altered diet and concluded:

> There is enough circumstantial evidence to warrant investigation of the role of specific food substances in the pathogenesis of schizophrenia.
>
> (Dohan 1966)

It had been noted by others that patients with coeliac disease had also improved during the war, and a link was then made between gluten (the dietary substance pathogenic for coeliac disease) and schizophrenia. Singh & Kay (1976) reported deterioration in 14 schizophrenics, who had already been placed on a gluten-free diet, when gluten was reintroduced.

The gluten hypothesis has been severely undermined by the following evidence. Stevens et al (1977) found reticulin antibodies in only 26 of 380 chronic schizophrenics. (In coeliac disease they occur in 70% of cases). They carried out duodenal biopsy in 21 of these 26 and found no evidence of coeliac disease. Potkin et al (1981) obtained no improvement in a group of schizophrenics maintained on a gluten-free diet.

Other nutritional and digestive theories of schizophrenia are speculative. Baruk (1978) claimed that 'many cases of schizophrenia might be reactions to biological factors . . . very often digestive'. Buscaino (1978) attributed schizophrenia to toxic substances from the gut bacteria entering the circulation.

Deficiencies of vitamin B_1 (thiamine), B_2 (nicotinic acid), B_6 (pyridoxine), B_{12} and folic acid produce psychiatric symptoms. Only B_{12} and folic acid have been linked with schizophrenia, and neither link is convincing. Zucker et at (1981) reported a paranoid psychosis in conjunction with B_{12} deficiency and traced 12 similar reports of schizophrenia-like psychoses in the literature. Reynolds (1968) suggested that schizophrenia might be precipitated in epileptics whose folate level had fallen during anticonvulsant therapy.

Endocrine disease

There are reports that hypothyroidism (Tonks 1964), hyperthyroidism (Bursten 1961), hypopituitarism (Blau & Hinton 1960) and Addison's and Cushing's disease (Michael & Gibbons 1963) produce schizophrenic as well as typically organic pictures. The strongest link is probably with hypothyroidism, and this emerged in Baldwin's study.

Degenerative disease of the brain

Parkinson's disease, Huntington's chorea and Wilson's disease have all been strongly linked with schizophrenia.

In the case of Parkinson's disease the link is more theoretical than real. Schwab et al (1951) reported several 'paranoid psychoses' in their series, and Crow et al (1976) four typical schizophrenics. Baldwin confirmed the link, but it only applied to Parkinson's disease which supervened in an existing schizophrenic. The theoretical link is with dopamine metabolism.

Huntingson's chorea is a triad of dementia, choreiform movements and psychosis. Heathfield (1967) examined all known cases of Huntington's chorea in a population of over three million people. There were 96 cases; 26 were psychotic and 9 of these were schizophrenic. Caine & Shoulson (1983) assigned DSM-111 diagnoses to 30 patients with Huntington's chorea. Twenty-four of these had between them 7 different psychiatric conditions: 3 were schizophrenic. Therefore, although schizophrenia may be more likely in patients with Huntington's chorea than in normals, the most striking thing about this study is the heterogeneity of the psychiatric sequelae.

Wilson's disease presents with psychiatric symptoms in about one-quarter of cases (Lishman 1978), and sometimes the picture is one of schizophrenia. Beard (1959) thought the link with typical schizophrenia was coincidental, but Davison and Bagley traced 22 cases, 11 definite and 11 probable, and concluded that it was genuine.

SUMMARY

Prevalence

The life-time prevalence of schizophrenia is just under 1%. The annual inception rate for new cases is about 15/100 000. The prevalence has not changed much this century, although it may have been lower prior to 1800. A few parts of the world have relatively high rates, the cause of which is unclear. The rate is higher in low social classes and in the centre of big towns. There is no real difference amongst siblings within a family. The mean age on first admission is about 34 for women and 27 for men. Racial differences are not prominent.

Genetic causes

Established knowledge

The risk to a first-degree relative of a known schizophrenic is 10%, and to a second-degree relative 3%. The monozygotic twin concordance rate is about 45% and the dizygotic rate about 15%. The risk of developing schizophrenia is proportional to the severity of a relative's condition and to the number of relatives affected. Discordant monozygotic twins transmit the condition at the same rate. Identical twins reared apart have the same rates. Children of schizophrenic mothers adopted at birth have the same rates as those reared by their own parents.

Theories

Polygenic inheritance is the most likely mechanism. There are no reliable indices in a high-risk child (with a schizophrenic parent) which will allow one to predict the subsequent development of schizophrenia, but there is some evidence that perinatal birth complications, a labile autonomic system (measured by GSR), inattention and poor emotional rapport are extra risk factors. There is no reliable marker in nonschizophrenic relatives. (Immunological, biochemical and psychological markers are currently being investigated.) The heritability of schizophrenia has been estimated at 70%. There are interactions with psychological and organic factors.

Psychological causes

Theory

Purely psychological causes are theoretically possible, even if difficult to prove in practice.

Early life experiences

Loss or separation of parents is not significant. The parents of schizophrenics have a personality disorder, a neurotic illness or alcoholism more often than parents of normals or even neurotics. Their marriages may be unharmonious, but not to the extent that some investigators have claimed. A minority of schizophrenics (about 20%) have been overprotected as children. A smaller proportion have been dominated or rejected by their parents.

A large number of studies have been carried out on deviant communication in the families of schizophrenics. It is difficult to summarise the findings, but my general impression is that deviant family communication, although real and open to measurement, is not of causal significance. The most comprehensive study, that of Wynne and Singer, documents the often bizarre interchanges between family members but does not establish those as causal. The most recent studies have also demonstrated disordered communication between parents themselves and within the family as a whole. Father tends to dominate and exclude son, and mother tends to be less involved in decision-making, but these are probably effect not cause.

Personality

A schizoid personality—eccentric, withdrawn, suspicious, cold, nonempathic—is evident in about one-quarter of the premorbid histories of schizophrenics. A further 15% have other types of abnormal personality. Some authors believe that it is a forme fruste of schizophrenia, genetically determined, and part of a wider concept of inherited 'schizophrenia spectrum disorders'. The terms borderline schizophrenia and schizotypal personality (but not borderline personality) are related concepts.

Recent life experience

Wars, other harrowing experiences and migration should be expected to provide some clues to the effect of life experience on the development of schizophrenia. They have proved disappointing. Anecdotal accounts are impressive but untrustworthy. The best evidence is contained in a study by Brown and Birley which demonstrated a small but definite increase in independent life events in the three weeks prior to a schizophrenic episode.

Organic causes

Anatomical evidence

Neuropathological changes in schizophrenia were commonly reported in the first half of the century, were then discounted in the 1960s and 1970s, but are now undergoing a re-evaluation. The current interest is in gliosis in the brain stem, possibly representing some healed inflammatory process. Thickening of the corpus callosum and cerebellar atrophy have also been reported. There are numerous C.T. scan reports of ventricular enlargement and cortical atrophy, particularly in chronic schizophrenics. The cause of these findings is at present unclear, but they may reflect organic causes in a small minority of schizophrenics who then have a bad prognosis. Neurological soft signs are another indication of brain damage in some schizophrenics.

Biochemical evidence

A primary disorder of one of the five neurotransmitters—dopamine, noradrenaline, acetyl choline, serotonin, GABA—is believed by many to underlie schizophrenia. The evidence is contradictory. Others favour the presence of an endogenous psychotomimetic, on which the evidence is no clearer. A neuroregulator, such as one of the endorphins or prostaglandin, may be involved. Drug-induced psychoses, particularly those due to amphetamine, are often cited in support of a biochemical theory, but the model has its limitations.

Physiological evidence

The resting E.E.G. is not a helpful tool in promoting the understanding of schizophrenia. Evoked potentials, however, are more encouraging in this respect, and they can be used to evaluate lateralised differences and callosal functioning. Psychophysiological measures of arousal, such as GSR, are abnormal in schizophrenics, and possibly children at risk for schizophrenia. New techniques such as the P.E.T. scan, which measures the cerebral distribution of nominated substances, will undoubtedly be of value in the future.

Neuropsychological evidence

Neuropsychological impairment can be demonstrated with standardised test batteries. What it represents is unclear. It correlates highly with the cerebral dysfunction found in the minority of schizophrenics with C.T. scan changes.

Site of cerebral dysfunction

The temporal lobe, the limbic system and the corpus callosum have been most often implicated as sites of pathogenic cerebral dysfunction.

Hemisphere imbalance

The best anatomical evidence is the association between left temporal lobe damage and schizophrenia. Physiological evidence includes claims that there are lateralised differences in orienting GSR, resting E.E.G., evoked responses and the direction of eye movements. None of this presents a coherent picture, although left hemisphere and callosal dysfunction are the two most favoured proposals.

Physical conditions

The following conditions have a well-established, positive link with schizophrenia, in roughly descending order of significance: epilepsy (particularly temporal lobe), Huntington's chorea, virus infection (the current favourite), trauma at birth (the effect of perinatal birth complications), head injury in adulthood (its site being more important than its nature), alcohol, cerebral tumour (particularly in the limbic system), cerebrovascular accidents (possibly in the right parietal region), systemic lupus erythematosus, myxoedema, Parkinsonism and Wilson's disease.

6

Course of schizophrenia

OUTCOME

General outcome

There is a large literature on the course and outcome of schizophrenia. It is one of the most researched topics. There are about 10 main studies.

Kraepelin followed 1054 of his original patients over 10 years. Langfeldt (1937), in Norway, examined 100 'unmistakable' schizophrenics after 10 years. Harris et al (1956), at the Maudsley Hospital, followed up 125 schizophrenics admitted for insulin treatment for 5 years. Holmboe & Astrup (1957), in Norway, followed 255 first admission schizophrenics for 6 years. Brown et al (1966), in London, followed 339 schizophrenics, of whom one-third were first admissions, for 5 years. Manfred Bleuler (1972) personally looked after 208 schizophrenics for 20 years; 66 were first admissions. Bland & Orn (1978), in Canada, traced 45 first admission schizophrenics 13 years later. Brockington, in London, traced virtually all surviving patients of 134 consecutively admitted functional psychotics after 6½ years (Kendell et al 1979); he had interviewed them with the PSE initially and 57 had been given a clinical diagnosis of schizophrenia. The 2-year follow-up of the IPSS cohort in 9 different countries was published in detail by the WHO in 1979, and in summary by Sartorius et al (1977). Huber et al (1980), in Bonn, reported a 22-year follow-up of 502 out of an original 758 unspecified schizophrenics.

The most useful figures to emerge concern the extremes of good and bad outcome. These are defined differently from study to study. For the purposes of comparison (Table 6.1), good outcome will be defined as *discharge from hospital without readmission at any time*. Bad outcome comprises *continuous stay in hospital throughout follow-up or moderate to severe intellectual or social impairment at last follow-up*.

Two points emerge from the Table. First, there is a marked difference in outcome after a first admission compared with subsequent or unspecified admissions. The mean good outcome rate for first admissions in the four studies listed is 29%, and the bad outcome rate 30%. For unspecified admissions, the mean good outcome rate for the seven studies listed is 13%

Table 6.1 Outcome in schizophrenia: analysis of best follow-up studies

Investigator	Year	Length of follow-up	Number of patients	Outcome Good* %	Outcome Intermediate %	Outcome Bad* %
Unspecified admissions						
Kraepelin	1913	10 yr	1054	4	13	83
Langfeldt	1937	10 yr	100	17	23	60
Harris	1956	5 yr	123	14	43	43
Brown	1966	5 yr	339	17	42	41
Bleuler	1972	20 yr	208	10	61	29
IPSS	1979	2 yr	811	27	47	26
Huber	1980	22 yr	502	10	43	35
				Mean 13	42	45
First admissions						
Holmboe & Astrup	1957	6 yr	255	29	38	33
Brown	1966	5 yr	111	35	37	28
Bleuler	1972	20 yr	66	32	45	23
Bland & Orn	1978	13 yr	45	21	42	37
				Mean 29	41	30

*Good—no further readmissions; bad—continuous inpatient or severe or moderate social or intellectual impairment at last follow-up.

and the bad outcome rate 45%. (Brockington's study has been excluded because it does not provide these figures.) Secondly, it appears that there has been a slight overall improvement in outcome during the century. Kraepelin considered only 4% had recovered and 83% had progressed to dementia. Langfeldt, in the 1930s, estimated that 66% of his 100 were the same as on admission or worse. (Wing 1982 concluded from other studies that until the 1930s as many as 60% of first admissions never left hospital.) By the 1950s, even before the neuroleptic era, the proportion of continuous inpatients had dropped to 34%, by the 1960s to 8%, and in the 1970s only 1 of Bland and Orn's 45 patients had remained in hospital ever since admission. (Neuroleptics and changing discharge policies must account for some of this improvement; some authors, however, regard it as a sign that schizophrenia is becoming a milder condition.)

The course of the 50% or more who are neither completely recovered nor severely disabled can be assessed in various ways. The usual factors to be examined are the duration or number of admissions, the psychiatric state at follow-up interview, the extent of the psychological deficit and the level of social functioning. Their pattern in any patient determines the specific outcome.

Specific outcomes

Institutionalisation

Since the 1950s it has been general policy to keep as few patients as possible in hospital, with the result that institutionalisation is a specific outcome for only a tiny minority. (Day hospitals, hostels, and even home, however, can take on some of the characteristics of an institution.) Goffman (1961), and Wing & Brown (1970), described the adverse effect on the condition itself and on the quality of life of such conditions. Mann (1971) studied the factors which have led to prolonged stay since open-door or revolving-door policies were introduced (the new long-stay patient). These are mainly social (e.g. no relatives to maintain contact with outside world), but 'low drive' noted at interview also distinguished long-stay from short-stay patients.

Remitting course

Although few patients now remain permanently in hospital, about two-thirds of first admissions will be readmitted at some point in the future (80%—Bland and Orn over 13 years; 48%—Brown et al over 5 years; 68%—Bleuler over 20 years). Wing (1982) concludes:

> Approximately two-thirds alternate for decades between acute psychotic phases and phases of improvement or recovery.

In the IPSS, factors associated with this course were: being female, depression or elation during the original psychotic episode, high premorbid occupational achievement, neurotic traits and absence of stress.

A remitting course is also characteristic of some atypical psychoses, particularly cycloid psychosis. Vaillant (1964b) considered nearly all the atypical psychoses to be merely remitting schizophrenia. In our study of cycloid psychosis (Cutting et al 1978), we compared the course of 73 patients with the cycloid mental state (most of whom fulfilled Spitzer's and Schneider's criteria for schizophrenia) with 73 schizophrenics without cycloid phenomena. A similar number in each group were readmitted (48 and 46 respectively), but the mean annual admission rate for cycloid patients (0.28) was higher than for schizophrenics (0.20); and the mean annual time spent in hospital was less (0.86 months compared with 2.52 months for schizophrenics).

In some subsequent episodes the form of the psychosis may be different from the original. Ziskind et al (1971) reported 5 patients whose diagnosis was changed from schizophrenia to affective psychosis. Sheldrick et al (1977) reported 12 instances of this amongst Maudsley schizophrenics and 17% in the IPSS series. Mellor et al (1981) followed 57 Schneiderian schizophrenics for five years, during which time 7 were given other diagnoses, all patients in whom the original diagnosis was based on the isolated presence of 'voices discussing patient'. The presence of cycloid phenomena (perplexity, anguish, ecstasy, labile mood, movement disorder) does, however, predict a variable symptom pattern in subsequent episodes. Half (49%) of our cycloid patients were later diagnosed as affective psychosis on at least one readmission.

Psychiatric morbidity in the community

About 15% of discharged schizophrenics are deluded or hallucinated at any point in time (Cheadle et al 1978). About 30% show negative symptoms, particularly affective flattening. About 70% have neurotic symptoms (Cheadle et al 1978), the commonest being depression (25%—McGlashan and Carpenter 1976; 21%—Glazer et al 1981).

Psychological deficit

Virtually all institutionalised schizophrenics show psychological impairment. Owens & Johnstone (1980) found that 65% of 407 chronic inpatients were at least 2 standard deviations below normal controls on the Hinton and Withers cognitive battery (Hinton & Withers 1971).

In the community it is difficult to be sure of its prevalence, because there are so few studies. Johnstone et al (1981) tested 68 Feighner schizophrenics with the Hinton and Withers battery: 21% obtained a score at least 2 standard deviations below that of a group of normals.

Social impairment

In the study of Brown et al in the 1960s about one-third were socially impaired at follow-up. (37% of men were unemployed and 31% of women were not managing a household.) In the IPSS study 23% showed severe social impairment at 2 years, an outcome which was determined mainly by premorbid factors (unmarried state, social isolation). In Brockington's study 58% were socially isolated at the time of follow-up, but this is a very broad criterion of social impairment.

Death

There is a higher mortality amongst schizophrenics than in the general population. It was particularly high amongst institutionalised patients in the early part of the century, due to intercurrent infections such as tuberculosis. Now, the excess mortality is made up of ischaemic heart disease (Baldwin 1979) and unnatural deaths, mainly suicide (Tsuang et al 1980).

Pokorny (1964) estimated the suicide rate at 5 times the expected for the general population. Ciompi (1980) found a rate of 3% (compared with 11% in patients with a depressive illness, 7% for alcoholics, and 6% for those with personality disorders). Huber et al (1980) found a rate of 5%. Roy (1982), comparing 30 schizophrenics who had committed suicide with 30 who had not, found it was more common in younger men, if the condition took a remitting course and if depressed mood had been a prominent part of the clinical picture.

Recovery

Complete recovery, though doubted by Kraepelin, is by no means rare. Earlier investigators were inclined to change the diagnosis retrospectively when they found that a patient had recovered on follow-up. They were also inclined to doubt recovery if complete insight were not present (p. 183).

Factors influencing outcome

General considerations

A large number of factors have been reported to affect outcome. They can be divided into premorbid (sex, body build, family history, early life experiences, personality, recent life experiences, cerebral dysfunction, abnormal hemispheric lateralisation); previous psychiatric illness; nature of the episode under consideration (diagnostic criteria, particular phenomena, psychological aspects, mode of onset); and subsequent factors (culture, life situation, family atmosphere, treatment, personal attitude towards the condition).

The best evaluation is undoubtedly the IPSS, which ranks the factors according to how much of the variance they account for. Also, by placing factors in three main groups—sociodemographic, past history, current episode—it achieves a balanced perspective on their relative importance. (Some of the individual factors mentioned in smaller series, particularly certain phenomena, fade into insignificance in this way.) It also emphasises the point that different groups of variables predict different types of outcome. As one might expect, social variables predict social outcome, but less expectedly individual phenomena are poor predictors of any sort of outcome.

The 47 'predictor variables' examined in the IPSS accounted for 38% of the variance. Each of the three classes was roughly equal to the other two in its predictive power—sociodemographic (11%), past history (14%), current episode (13%). Within each class, a small group of variables dominated the others. Five sociodemographic variables explained 9% of the variance: social isolation, marital status, sex, occupation and educational level. Five past history variables explained 7%: family history, psychosexual adjustment, childhood behavioural symptoms (e.g. truancy, panic attacks, tantrums), unfavourable environment (e.g. migration, belonging to a minority religious sect) and history of past psychiatric treatment. Five features of the episode itself explained 10%: duration prior to evaluation, derealisation, type of onset, degree of cooperation at interview and presence of depression or elation. Finally, the five most powerful *overall* predictors were social isolation, long duration of episode, a history of past psychiatric treatment, marital status and a history of behavioural symptoms.

The following claims about individual factors should be viewed in the context of the IPSS findings.

Premorbid factors

1 General factors such as sex, and to a lesser extent body build (rarely studied nowadays), have been reported to influence outcome. Lewine et al (1981), reviewing sex differences in schizophrenia, found considerable evidence in the literature that women had a more remitting course than men. This is borne out by the IPSS and studies of cycloid psychosis, including our own. There is some evidence that men are more likely to be found amongst the bad outcome group: Christie Brown et al (1977) found that amongst 147 long-stay schizophrenics, 115 (78%) were men. A pyknic build emerged as a good prognostic factor in a comparison by Kant (1941) of deteriorated and recovered schizophrenics. It was also mentioned by Langfeldt.

2 Genetic factors such as family history of schizophrenia or affective psychosis are not consistently found to be influential. A family history of affective psychosis conferred a good prognosis in studies by Vaillant (1964a) and Fowler et al (1972), but a family history of schizophrenia does not appear to affect overall outcome either way (Baron et al 1982). There is some

evidence that family members share the same subtype of schizophrenia—hebephrenia (Farmer et al 1983), phasic variety (Bleuler 1972)—and this might affect outcome.

3 Psychological factors are influential. Family atmosphere and rearing patterns in early childhood are generally discounted, but a schizoid personality (Langfeldt 1937, Holmboe & Astrup 1957, Vaillant 1964a) or evidence of social and sexual maladjustment (Phillips 1953, Nameche et al 1964) have consistently been shown to exert a malign influence. Stress (Wallis 1972) or identifiable life events (Harder et al 1981) confer a good prognosis in most small series, although they did not emerge as particularly important in the IPSS.

4 The evidence concerning cerebral dysfunction is contradictory. On the one hand, chronic hospitalised patients have a higher rate of C.T. scan abnormalities than first admissions. On the other hand, schizophrenia precipitated by some physical conditions (e.g. the postinfluenzal cases of Menninger 1926) has a better prognosis than when constitutionally determined. It presumably depends on the site, nature and degree of cerebral dysfunction. Left-handed schizophrenics had a better prognosis than right handers in a study by Luchins et al (1980), who suggested that 'anomalous lateralisation' was responsible for a milder variety of schizophrenia.

Previous psychiatric illness

The IPSS placed this factor amongst the five best predictors of poor outcome. This should be set against the long-term studies of Bleuler and Huber et al, who showed that after about 5 years, schizophrenics do not deteriorate further. The implication of this is that a schizophrenic whose first episode was, for example, 15 years previously has the same prognosis, other things being equal, as one first diagnosed 5 years ago.

Form of episode

1 Diagnostic criteria predict outcome. This was discussed in Chapter 3. Spitzer's, Carpenter's and Langfeldt's schemes were the only successful predictors in the study by Kendell et al (1979), and these only for a few outcome measures. Schemes which incorporate six months duration as a criterion (Feighner, DSM-III) would be expected to predict worse outcomes than those such as Spitzer's which accept shorter periods of disability. Atypical psychoses, such as schizoaffective (though only schizomanic not schizodepressive according to Brockington et al 1978b) and cycloid, have a more favourable outcome than typical schizophrenia.

2 The phenomenon of affective flattening is a consistent pointer to a poor prognosis (Harris & Norris 1954, Carpenter et al 1978, Knight et al 1979). It also emerged as a reliable predictor of symptomatic but not social or general outcome in the IPSS. Depressed or elated mood is generally regarded

as a good predictor (Vaillant 1964a, IPSS). Derealisation is also a good predictor (IPSS, Hwu et al 1981). Other phenomena (confusion—Vaillant 1964a, delusions of personal identity—Yarden & Raps 1981) have been mentioned as favourable signs, but it is probable that, unless part of a more widespread cycloid or manic picture, they are not significant.

3 Psychological variables, independent of clinical phenomena, have rarely been studied. Zahn (1980) claimed that good prognosis schizophrenics had a faster reaction time than other patients. Frith et al (1979) showed that patients whose GSR habituated quickly to a noise had a better prognosis than nonhabituators. Memory impairment from the outset (Tsuang 1982) is a pointer to poor outcome.

4 Acute onset is universally agreed to confer a good prognosis.

Subsequent events

1 The culture in which one develops schizophrenia has a marked influence. In the IPSS the best outcomes were in Nigeria, India and Colombia; in Taiwan, England, the United States and Czechoslovakia it was intermediate; and in the Soviet Union and Denmark it was worst of all. The reason for this is not at all clear, but it may be due to a more tolerant attitude towards mental illness, particularly less overinvolvement on the part of relatives, in developing countries.

2 Life situation is another moderating variable. Life events precipitate relapse in a known schizophrenic (Birley & Brown 1970), even if their role in determining the original episode is less certain. A clue to the mechanism was identified by Stone & Eldred (1959), when they transferred some patients from long-stay to acute, research wards. Two of them became acutely psychotic, the cause of which, in the authors' view, was an increase in social stimulation. Whilst positive symptoms get worse, negative symptoms generally improve under more lively conditions. Wing & Brown (1970) elaborated this principle in their book *Institutionalism and Schizophrenia*.

3 Family life exerts its own independent effect. Following the study of Brown et al in 1962, three more studies on different groups of patients (Brown et al 1972, Vaughn & Leff 1976, Leff et al 1982) have all shown that a high degree of expressed emotion (high EE) by the relatives to whom a patient returns provokes relapse. In the four studies, the relapse rates amongst patients returning to a high EE household were 76%, 58%, 51% and 50%, compared with 28%, 12%, 13% and 14% respectively for low EE households. Emotional expression is rated by counting the number of critical comments and degree of overinvolvement by a key relative during a semi-structured interview. Both these factors exert an independent influence. Tarrier et al (1979) obtained psychophysiological confirmation that the relative was upsetting the patient, by showing an increase in spontaneous fluctuations in the GSR when the key relative entered the room while the recording was being made.

4 Treatment will be considered in Chapter 7.

5 A patient's attitude towards their illness influenced prognosis in a study by McGlashan & Carpenter (1981). They administered a 55-item questionnaire on this to 30 schizophrenics, and found, surprisingly, that both very negative attitudes (e.g. 'My happiest days are in the past') and very positive attitudes (e.g. 'In a way my illness helped me grow up') conferred a poor prognosis. A negative attitude had the worst effect of the two.

STAGES

Prodromal phase

Several authors noted nonspecific changes in mood, behaviour and thought in the days, weeks or even months before the florid episode. Anxiety, fatigue, a vague feeling of being watched and an altered sense of familiarity have all been mentioned. Varsamis & Adamson (1971), Herz & Melville (1980) and Conrad (1958) did the most objective studies. In the first, 44 schizophrenics (Langfeldt criteria) were asked about the prodromal phase. The features, in descending frequency, were general disturbance of drive (79%), anxiety (67%), school or work deterioration (64%), depression (63%), impaired flow of thought (58%), suspiciousness (48%) and withdrawal (48%). Herz and Melville interviewed 145 patients who had just relapsed. The first signs, corroborated by a relative in over half the cases, were tenseness. dysphoria, poor concentration, anorexia, insomnia and reduced visits to friends. Conrad called this phase 'the trema'. He studied 107 schizophrenics who had developed their condition while in the army. Often a senseless breach of military discipline had occurred, sometimes a sense of suspicion had affected all relationships and sometimes there was an inexplicable depression.

Docherty et al (1978) collected the main terms which had been used to characterise this phase. They comprised feelings of not fitting in, frustration, nervousness, anxiety, feelings of overstimulation and feelings of losing one's grip.

The following account by a recovered schizophrenic of mine gives the flavour of his subjective experiences:

> Things just slipped out of my grasp. It was unsteady relationships. I got worked up. All of a sudden things slipped out of my grasp. I couldn't hold my thoughts. Especially the reasoning processes. I saw everything in abstract terms, a void. But that was basically to do with unsteady relationships. And also, both times it was spurred on by other people. Always some kind of emotion, a shock experience to the system. I'd put my faith in a friend and I was then let down. Then things went out of my grasp. Then after that I couldn't keep hold of my thoughts. My mind was wandering all over the place. I couldn't keep it together.

Early stage

Of the 44 patients interviewed by Varsamis & Adamson (1971), 16 began their episode with a complex perceptual disturbance, which the authors labelled oneirophrenia. A further 8 began with voices, 8 with a primary delusion, 4 with delusional awareness, 4 could not recall their experiences properly, 1 had thought broadcasting, 1 was stuporose, 1 was excited and 1 was already deteriorated.

Freedman (1974) read 60 autobiographical accounts of schizophrenia in books or articles and extracted 25 separate early experiences. Six of these were clearly perceptual in nature (enhanced sensory awareness, muted sensory awareness, less acute vision, visual illusions, changes in depth perception and changes in perception of own voice). The remainder involved more complex mental functions (e.g. thought replaced by emotion, thinking in images, mistaking identities of other people, experiences of loss of meaning of objects and physical sensations in the brain). She also carried out an objective study, in which she compared the answers of 20 Spitzer schizophrenics to 46 questions about their subjective experience with those of nonpsychotic patients (Freedman & Chapman 1973). Only 8 out of the 46 possible subjective experiences significantly separated the two groups—thought block, mental fatigue, inability to focus attention, visual illusions, hyperacute auditory perception, misidentification of people, failure to comprehend others' language, and poor concentration due to preoccupation with other matters.

Table 6.2 Semistructured interview on early subjective experiences

Item	Sample response
1. I should like to ask you about the time when you first experienced a change in the way things were. What was it like?	Nasty . . . horrible
2. Did you see things differently?	
a) Colours?	Very vivid colours
b) People?	All distorted
c) People's faces?	Distorted, funny-looking
d) Their clothes?	No
e) The world around you?	Nasty, horrible. I didn't want to live in it
3. Did things sound differently?	
a) Things around you?	Everything seemed louder
b) Words and language?	Seemed a bit different
4. Did you feel different?	I must have felt different
a) Did your emotions change?	Must have been
b) Did you feel different in yourself?	
5. Did your mind seem to be functioning differently? What about concentration and attention?	Yes. My concentration was terrible
6. Did your awareness of your own body or movements change?	Things were odd
7. Were your thoughts affected?	Must have been
8. Was your memory affected?	It seemed like I was back in the past. Not today's time

McGhie & Chapman (1961) interviewed 24 schizophrenics at an early stage of their condition and obtained vivid accounts of changes in attention, perception, awareness of movement, thinking and emotion. One of their patients reported:

> It's not that I can't concentrate right, it's just that I can't concentrate on the major issues. I get fogged up with all the different bits and lose the important things in the picture. I find myself paying attention to all sorts of tiny things instead of getting on with things I should be doing. I have to concentrate on simple things like walking, pedalling my bike and even talking.
>
> (McGhie & Chapman 1961)

Conrad (1958) called this stage 'apophany'. He regarded it as the essence of the schizophrenic process. In the purest form of apophany, the world around took on a new meaning but the patient could not say what this was. The compulsion of significance (p. 350) overwhelmed the patient.

I interviewed 30 schizophrenics (15 remitted, 15 acute) and 15 depressives about their early subjective experience of the condition. The semistructured interview is shown in Table 6.2 along with one of the schizophrenic's replies. The features which characterised schizophrenia rather than depression (Table 6.3) were visual and auditory perceptual distortions, impaired understanding of language and qualitative distortions in memory.

The following account, given by one of my schizophrenics on the third day of a relapse while still psychotic, illustrates the prevailing atmosphere:

> Yesterday I thought it was the end of the world. Everlasting night. I thought the atom bomb was going to be dropped. Walking along I seemed to be walking on the spot. I didn't seem to be getting anywhere. Fog seemed to be thicker down roads where I shouldn't go than roads where I should go. Some weird thing was telling me I was Jesus Christ. I didn't want to be. I just wanted to be a whore. It's difficult to think. My thoughts seem to turn to stone. Are they stone or is it VD. I see innocence turn to evil in people's faces. My thoughts appear above my head in a bubble. Mick Jagger and Marianne Faithful are making love in an aeroplane. Listen there they go. I think they're making love in every aeroplane that flies over.
>
> (Acute schizophrenic)

Table 6.3 Comparison of schizophrenic with depressed subjects on subjective experience interview

Function	% subjects admitting abnormality	
	Schizophrenics (n=30)	*Depressives* (n=15)
Visual perception	50%	20%
Auditory perception	17%	7%
Emotion	50%	100%
Attention	40%	80%
Awareness of movements	33%	44%
Thinking	70%	67%
Memory	27%	7%
Language understanding	30%	7%

The next account was given in remission by another schizophrenic:

> There was a tremendous feeling of claustrophobia, of being trapped. Traffic was too loud. Too many people on the pavement. Walls were moving in on me. I'd panic when the house was getting too small. Then I'd go outside. But outside the noise was too great. Nowhere, nowhere I could cope. Not even safe in bed . . . All the bright colours frightened me most, orange and red . . . I recognised people everywhere . . . I had all these thoughts in my head but when I spoke it was just noise, just high-pitched noises came out. It had lost its meaning. I could understand other people's language but not my own.
>
> (Remitted schizophrenic)

By comparison, the next account is by a patient with a *depressive psychosis* of the early weeks of his illness:

> It was a dramatic realisation that it was so quiet and I had nowhere to go. It seemed like I was living in a desert. There were horrible trees in front of me full of rooks. People seemed terribly old, like old octogenarians. I got overcome by terrible bouts of sadness. My sense of humour went completely and I could only think what a bloody fool I'd been.
>
> (Depressed patient)

Established psychosis

It is in this phase that positive symptoms such as delusions, hallucinations and formal thought disorder dominate the picture. First-rank symptoms can be elicited in up to 80% of patients (Mellor 1970) and, in general, the typical phenomena of schizophrenia are most clearly recognisable during this stage. These are considered in the chapter dealing with the corresponding psychological dysfunction: delusions (Ch. 15), hallucinations (Ch. 14), formal thought disorder (Chs 11 & 15) and catatonic phenomena (Ch. 13).

Chronic phase

Negative symptoms such as flattening of affect, inattention, apathy and memory impairment dominate this phase. Five terms—dementia, deterioration, defect state, psychological deficit and pseudodementia—are used, more or less interchangeably, to describe it. Dementia praecox was Kraepelin's name for the entire condition, in which dementia was the outcome in all but 13% of cases. The terms deterioration and defect state were then substituted by psychiatrists after Bleuler rejected the name dementia praecox. Hunt & Cofer (1944) introduced the term psychological deficit, which they felt was more neutral than the others. It found favour with North American psychologists. Pseudodementia is the most recent addition. Caine (1981) defined it as 'intellectual impairment in patients with primary psychiatric disorders'. The term is favoured by neurologists and is better known through its depressive and hysterical varieties. It is being increasingly used, however, to refer to schizophrenic deterioration (Caine 1981, Bienenfeld & Hartford 1982).

Manfred Bleuler (1983) considered that about 45% of schizophrenics would develop chronic symptoms of some kind: 'single psychological signs' (e.g. passivity or delusions) in about 20%, mild deterioration in 15% and severe deterioration in 10%. Huber et al (1980) gave a figure of 35% for the proportion who developed the 'characteristic schizophrenic deficiency syndrome'. (However, they categorised another 43% who did not completely remit as having 'noncharacteristic symptoms' such as decreased initiative, reduced capacity for adaptation, inability to be pleased and sleep disturbance. This is almost certainly an overestimate of the extent of chronicity, although a large number of remitted schizophrenics do complain of neurotic symptoms—p. 174.)

Opinions are divided on the nature of schizophrenic deterioration. Crow (1983) believes that it is a subtype of schizophrenia, caused by generalised cerebral atrophy of viral origin. The development of this 'type II schizophrenia' rather than 'type I', the established psychosis in my scheme, he argues, is genetically determined. Subjects inherit a predisposition to whether the virus is localised to a neurotransmitter receptor (producing type I, established psychosis) or is spread more widely (producing type II, chronic phase). Wing & Brown (1970) regarded it as predominantly psychosocial in origin, the effect of the circumstances of a patient's life on the condition rather than the converse, as Crow argues. Ciompi (1983) takes an intermediate position, regarding it as a:

> multidetermined state . . . related to a diminution of energy potential . . . and in its aetiology psychosocial factors play at least an equal, and perhaps even a greater role than organic factors.

By a diminution of energy he was following the ideas of early German psychiatrists such as Gross and Weygandt (p. 27) and North American psychologists such as Hunt and Cofer (p. 43).

Apart from its puzzling nature, the most curious feature of deterioration is its tendency to plateau or even burn itself out after a number of years. In general there is a drop of about 10 IQ points between premorbid assessment and testing on admission (school→admission, Rappaport & Webb 1950, army→admission, Schwartzman & Douglas 1962). After admission some patients, particularly hebephrenics, drop further IQ points (Trapp & James 1937) but some, particularly paranoid schizophrenics, gain in IQ (Rabin 1944, Haywood & Moelis 1963). Manfred Bleuler (1983) believed that a plateau was reached after about 5 years, and Abrahamson (1983) that there was a trend towards improvement after 10 or so years.

Recovery

The mark of recovery has usually been the development of *insight* into the preceding months or years of psychotic phenomena. Insight is 'a correct attitude to a morbid change in oneself' (Lewis 1934).

Jaspers considered that complete insight was rare in schizophrenia:

> . . . we get a clear picture of complete insight in patients who recover from deliria, alcoholic hallucinosis or mania . . . in the schizophrenias subjectively honest judgements seem to show full insight, but when examined more closely it is clear they do not.
>
> (Jaspers 1913)

A number of studies have given support to this view. Of 68 schizophrenics in remission (Brooks et al 1968) 22 stoutly denied any previous mental illness at all. Lin et al (1979) gave 3 simple questions to 100 chronic schizophrenics (free of florid phenomena): Do you think you had to be in this hospital? Do you think you had to see a psychiatrist? Do you think you had to be in hospital? Only 31 answered 'yes' to even 1 of these. McEvoy et al (1981) gave 11 insight questions to 45 chronic DSM-III schizophrenics. Only 13% admitted that they had had a mental illness, and only 27% appreciated the need for their previous admission.

Table 6.4 Degree of insight in remitted schizophrenics (n=20)

Question 1. What do you think was the matter?		
Simple causal explanation	9	e.g. 'Overtired', 'Shock'
Don't know	4	
Rationalisation	3	e.g. 'I was drugged'
Description of psychotic ideas	2	e.g. 'I thought I was special'
Description of general state of mind	2	e.g. 'Horrible phase of my life'
Question 2. Do you think you had a breakdown?		
Yes	14	
No	3	
Don't know	3	
Question 3. Do you regard it as an illness?		
Yes	17	
No	3	
Question 4. What do you think was the cause?		
Simple psychosocial cause	9	e.g. 'Overwork', 'Dislocated shoulder'
Sophisticated explanation	6	e.g. 'Shy personality faced with stress', 'Partly genetic I suppose', 'Combination of social and psychological things', 'No one thing really'
Don't know	3	
Rationalisation	2	e.g. 'Drugged', 'Devil in me'

In my own study (Table 6.4) the degree of insight achieved was much greater than this. Virtually all 20 remitted schizophrenics admitted that they had had an illness or breakdown and even their causal explanation was often quite sophisticated. In my view, psychiatrists have often had unreasonable expectations about insight, and have been too ready to suspect lingering delusions. Patients almost certainly adopt various strategies for integrating their unusual experiences into the framework of their life. Denial, minimisation and joking are acceptable defence mechanisms in normal life and their use by schizophrenics does not necessarily imply continuing psychosis.

Some subjects become unduly preoccupied and introspective, others angry, yet others miserable and anxious. There is no reason to suppose that the repertoire of psychological responses to a psychiatric disorder is any different from those seen after a physical illness (Lloyd 1977). The only special consideration concerns the way in which patients alter their beliefs about the content of their delusions and hallucinations. This is much under-researched. Sacks et al (1974) pointed out that in moving from a delusional to a nondelusional state of mind the subject passes through an intermediate stage of double-awareness.

The following statements from different patients, all free of any psychotic phenomena at the time, illustrate the range of insight which occurs:

> I was paranoid about microphones. I don't feel that anymore. I push it to the back of my mind. It's not a major issue. It's not going on any more. It was governing my life. I wouldn't speak indoors because I thought the room was bugged. Now I can speak freely.

> I still think it was factual. I get the impression when I go into Tesco's [supermarket] that they empty the tills when I arrive as if someone's given them information that I'm not honest. So I still get the sort of feeling that I'm being watched. I don't know about the television. I don't get that feeling so much. I don't know if they can spy on you. I don't get any voices. That's one good thing.

> I just accept that I was ill and had a breakdown. Too much stress. The first time I was ill I was always delving into it, studying psychology. Now I'm just grateful that I'm well. It's God's grace. It was just a set of unfortunate circumstances. Bad luck, that's how I see it.

> I just think that I was really ill. I must have been, to do that. Yes, a real bad breakdown. [Cause?] Anything and everything. It's hard to say.

SUMMARY

The outcome of schizophrenia following a first admission is very good in one-quarter of patients (complete recovery), poor in another quarter (chronic social and intellectual impairment requiring frequent admissions and much community support), and moderately good in one-half (occasional subsequent admissions, some neurotic symptoms, some social impairment manifest as difficulty in interpersonal relationships).

The factors which predict a poor outcome are mainly social and personality deviance prior to the first psychotic episode. Schizoid personality, social isolation, poor sexual adjustment, behaviour disorder in childhood and unmarried status are the most powerful predictors. Women have a more remittent course, though this may not ensure a good overall prognosis. The form of the actual psychosis is not a reliable predictor of outcome, although the presence of depression or elation and the absence of flattened affect are generally favourable signs. Any history of previous psychiatric treatment, a prior schizophrenic episode or an insidious onset carry a bad prognosis.

Once the episode has remitted, life events and a critical or overinvolved family predispose to relapse. In underdeveloped countries schizophrenia appears to have a better outlook than in Western Europe and North America.

Several stages can be identified. The prodromal period is marked by nonspecific emotional and thinking disturbance. The early stage of the psychosis is usually a period of disordered perception, memory and thinking. During the established phase the typical phenomena—delusions, hallucinations, formal thought disorder—appear. A minority of subjects progress to a chronic phase where they appear demented. This state has been called various names, none of them very satisfactory, because the nature of the apparent intellectual decline is uncertain and many patients subsequently improve. Those subjects who do recover adopt a variety of ways of coping with their previous psychotic state. A substantial number have considerable insight into the nature and cause of their 'breakdown'.

7

Treatment

INTRODUCTION

Without knowing the cause or the precise psychological dysfunction in schizophrenia all treatment must be largely empirical. The most rational treatment is in fact family therapy because it is now firmly established that regular contact with an overinvolved and overcritical relative predisposes to relapse. Despite the theoretical uncertainties there has been, however, no shortage of practical suggestions of treatment. The poor prognosis associated with the condition in the first half of the century encouraged the search for and application of a large number of useless and in some cases harmful treatments. The three areas of concern are psychological, social and organic treatments.

PSYCHOLOGICAL TREATMENT

General considerations

Because schizophrenia has usually been regarded as a condition where mental life is incomprehensible, idiosyncratic and relatively impervious to outside influences, the role of psychological treatment has never been a central issue.

The large majority of psychiatrists believed in organic or genetic causes, and administered organic treatments. Psychoanalysts largely followed the advice of Freud and, although taking a theoretical interest, declined practical commitment.

Eugen Bleuler's belief that the phenomena, at least, had a psychological cause, led to his pupils trying to modify the course of the condition by psychological means. They devised therapeutic environments to maximise the chances of recovery. In America, however, a more ambitious attitude was adopted by some psychiatrists. Beginning with Sullivan and Fromm-Reichmann in the 1920s and 1930s, the belief grew that psychoanalysis, even the orthodox variety, might be beneficial. In the last decade, a decline in enthusiasm for psychoanalysis in general has led to its virtual abandonment in schizophrenia. This historical process, however, left behind a number of widely held opinions on psychological aspects of treatment. These are now jointly referred to as the psychotherapy of schizophrenia.

In the 1950s, behaviour therapy was introduced, initially in individual cases, and later in entire wards to counteract institutionalisation. By the 1970s individual therapy had been made virtually redundant by the efficacy of neuroleptics.

It then became apparent that even when no longer psychotic or under the malign influence of institutions, schizophrenics were still disabled relative to the rest of the population. They lacked the ability to cope with everyday aspects of life, such as making friends, putting on a good impression at job interviews and finding accommodation. These skills, which most people take for granted, became the new focus of behaviour therapists. Social skills training replaced individual programmes and token economies.

Lastly, the revival of cognitive psychology and the growth of information processing and cognitive theories of schizophrenia led, in the late 1970s, to a number of cognitive therapies, directed at hallucinations, delusions and thought disorder.

Psychotherapy

Psychoanalysis

Both Freud and Jung cautioned against psychoanalysis in schizophrenia. In Freud's case, the reason was theoretical. In Jung's case it was a concern for the mental health of the practitioner:

> Naturally only a few doctors, in a very limited number of cases, can undertake such a difficult task . . . provided one's own constitution holds out.
>
> (Jung 1958)

Sullivan (1931) disagreed, and set up a special unit in Maryland, where young, recent-onset schizophrenics were managed along psychoanalytic lines. The aim was to promote 'socialisation, and thereafter a more fundamental reorganisation of personality'.

The general aim of Sullivan and his pupils was to enforce reality by establishing transference and encouraging interpersonal contacts. Fromm-Reichmann (1939) wrote about the way in which transference could and should be developed. Federn (1943) advised pursuing several goals:

> . . . solving outer and inner conflicts, fortifying the ego by protection, transference, identification, and last but not least insight into the patient's terrors and inner turmoil.
>
> (Federn 1943)

Federn believed that the boundaries between the id and the ego, and the ego and the external world, were defective, and that unconscious material from the id broached the boundary into the ego and even passed through into the external world. Therapy, therefore, involved repressing the id. Fenichel (1945) believed that schizophrenia was a regression to a narcissistic stage before the ego had properly developed, a more profound regression than occurred in neurosis. He divided treatment into two stages. The first was to establish and preserve contact and 'make the psychosis . . . as nearly like a neurosis as possible'. The second stage was then the conventional analysis as if it were a neurosis. Wexler (1951) believed that the ego was weak, and strengthening it the best form of treatment.

A second group of psychoanalysts adopted the most radical approach of all. They were mostly followers of Melanie Klein, who believed that the schizoid position, or splitting between 'good' and 'bad' objects, was a normal stage of development, and that schizophrenia was the late consequence of not negotiating this stage properly. The principle of treatment proposed by these psychoanalysts was diametrically opposed to Sullivan's. They did not distinguish between neurosis and psychosis, and in schizophrenia, as in neurosis, they actively explored, participated in and encouraged the flow of unconscious material (in this case delusions, hallucinations and thought disorder). Rosen (1947), for example, talked to the patient:

> in the language of the unconscious . . . interpreted freely . . . [and believed that] each symptom must be untwisted clear down to its earliest ontogenetic and even phylogenetic roots in the unconscious. Only when the symptom is so clearly unmasked to the patient will it no longer serve its purpose and he will be able to relinquish it for a more sensible way of handling his instinctual drives.
>
> (Rosen 1947)

Segal (1950) described how she was prepared to 'bring into consciousness new unconscious material'. Sechehaye (1954) applied what she called the 'method of symbolic realisation', allowing a patient to 'relive the fundamental event of infancy which had frustrated them and thrown them into a psychosis'. This required using 'presymbolic, magical and concrete' words and behaviour during the treatment (e.g. offering apples as a symbolic representation of the mother's breasts). Rosenfeld (1976) also advocated the use of unconventional forms of communication.

Individual psychotherapy

Only a tiny minority of intrepid psychoanalysts would attempt Sullivan's and even fewer Klein's approach nowadays. A number, however, have incorporated the best and most sensible aspects into what is commonly referred to as individual psychotherapy for schizophrenia.

Arieti's (1976) approach is a good illustration:

> Psychotherapy aims at re-establishing the bond of human relatedness with the patient, attacking psychotic symptoms, understanding the psychodynamic history, and helping the patient unfold towards new nonpsychotic patterns of living . . . It is just as nourishing as it is interpretative.
>
> (Arieti 1976)

Benedetti (1980) discussed the ways in which psychotherapy with a schizophrenic differed from that with a neurotic patient. First, there are particular problems establishing a therapeutic relationship; then, the therapist has to be aware of the manifestations of countertransference (e.g. transformation of patient's autistic symbols into the language of the therapist); and thirdly, there are specific issues concerning the way one should interpret the therapeutic relationship (e.g. resistance is not the same as in neurosis). Lamb (1982) repeats earlier warnings about the risk of a transference psychosis and advises no more than one hour's treatment each week. He recommends strengthening ego control, giving advice, dealing with life's problems, introducing existential subjects (death, freedom, isolation and meaninglessness) and reducing guilt by 'taking sides against the superego'. Strauss (1983) suggests that therapy should be versatile and suit the individual's needs. He mentions 'reality-oriented individual therapy' as the most suitable for the majority.

Group therapy

This achieved greatest popularity in the years following the Second World War. Powdermaker & Frank (1953) give one of the fullest accounts of experience with schizophrenics. In a trial of two wards, one where group therapy was part of the milieu, the other where it was not, the first ward was generally less disturbed, but the discharge rate was no better.

Since that time it has become part of milieu treatment, but there is little evidence of its efficacy. Klein (1980), discussing a review by Mosher & Keith (1980), concluded that of 19 studies on its reputed efficacy published in the previous 10 years, only 1 (Shattan et al 1966) was acceptable. In this, 90 patients (86% of whom were schizophrenic) were followed up for 1 year. Half received monthly group therapy, the other half none. (Nearly all were on medication.) The patients receiving group therapy were less likely to be readmitted during the year, but did not achieve a better employment level, and spent overall the same amount of time in hospital.

Family therapy

This will be discussed under social treatments, although it has a large psychological component.

Psychotherapy as an adjunct to other treatments

A combination of individual psychotherapy and neuroleptics has occasionally been reported to be superior to neuroleptics alone in the treatment of an acute psychosis (Rogers et al 1967, Grinspoon et al 1972). Klein (1980) dismisses these claims, and it did not emerge in the best study, that of May (1968). There are no studies on the prophylactic effect of joint treatment (if one excludes those with a family component).

Some treatments which purport to be social have a large component of individual psychotherapy. For example, milieu therapy, considered later, is essentially hospital care with very limited use of neuroleptics. Gunderson (1983) attributes its reputed efficacy to six qualities—distribution of power in the ward, use of peers to emphasise correct interpersonal relations, a high sense of involvement, a high staff ratio, enthusiastic staff and a shared belief that psychosis is a time-limited experience from which learning can ensue. All these have a potential to modify an individual's mood, beliefs, behaviour or cognition.

Strauss (1983) makes the point that all treatments include nonspecific factors, some of which may be more important than any organic agent itself. Such nonspecific factors come under the heading of individual psychotherapy. (Ackner et al 1957, who discredited the specific value of insulin therapy, attributed its apparent efficacy to such nonspecific factors.)

Behaviour therapy

Individual behaviour therapy

Lindsley & Skinner (1954) were the first to test whether behaviourist principles applied in psychotic patients. They found that a simple motor response, such as pulling a lever, could be reinforced by the delivery at the right time of cigarettes, cards or pictures. Ayllon & Michael (1959) then demonstrated that a variety of unwanted behaviours—repeatedly entering the nursing office, violence, refusal to feed—could be abolished or reduced. They published this in an article entitled, *The psychiatric nurse as a behavioural engineer*. Three principles were applied: 'extinction, strengthening incompatible behaviour, and escape and avoidance conditioning'. In the first case, nurses were instructed to tally each entrance to the nursing office but give no reinforcement. In this way entrances were reduced from 16 a day to 2 a day by the seventh week of the extinction programme. In the case of a violent patient, the nurses encouraged some of his other behaviour, e.g. lying on the floor, which was incompatible with violence. Self-feeding was achieved by the nurses spilling the patient's food whenever he asked for help.

A variety of psychotic phenomena were then tackled in this way. Two patients who had been mute, one for 14 years, the other for 19 years, were successfully made to talk by means of simple rewards (Isaacs et al 1960). The psychologist noted that one of the patients had shown interest in a packet of fruit gums which had accidentally fallen out of the investigator's pocket, and, by using these as a reward, the patient eventually said 'gums' and later 'ping pong'. The frequency of auditory hallucinations was markedly reduced (Rutner & Bugle 1969) by making a patient record privately, then publicly on a ward chart, every time he heard voices. From 180 instances on the first day, they dropped to only 5 on the fifteenth. Incoherent talk also diminished (Ayllon & Michael 1959) when systematically ignored, and when normal talk was reinforced.

Token economies

It was soon appreciated that one had to ensure compliance from all members of staff who were involved with the patient. In the last example, Ayllon and Michael discovered that what they called 'bootleg reinforcement from a visiting social worker' was responsible for a recurrence in incoherent talk at one point in the programme. For this reason, Ayllon and Azrin (1965) introduced programmes for an entire ward. Metal tokens could be earned for completing tasks on and off the ward, and then exchanged for privacy, leave, recreation and interaction with selected staff. They described their initial success in a book entitled *The Token Economy* (Ayllon & Azrin 1968).

By the middle 1970s there was a large literature on token economies (Kazdin 1977). Liberman (1970) summarised the features which led to the best results: clear definition and measurement of goals, attachment of clear positive and negative consequences to adaptive and maladaptive behaviour, reinforcement for making small steps, and the use of instructions and prompts to elicit the desired behaviour. Gripp & Magaro (1974) reviewed the large number of variables which had been reported to affect the outcome. These comprised the behaviours themselves, the way they were rated, the characteristics of the patients, the staff involved, the way the programme was carried out, and the value and nature of the tokens used. Jones (1978) reported a typical programme. Seven male schizophrenics were observed for six weeks, then allowed to work for three weeks without tokens, then given tokens freely during their work, and finally given tokens contingent on their performance or standard of self-care. He noticed an improvement in dressing and initiative even before the contingent phase, but this was at the expense of an increase in socially embarrassing behaviour.

By the latter part of the 1970s, many were sceptical of the effectiveness of token economies (Hersen 1976). The chief drawback was their failure to generalise to community settings, once patients were discharged. For this reason, along with the run-down of the long-stay population and the demonstrated superiority of neuroleptics in eliminating psychotic phenomena, behaviourally-minded clinical psychologists turned their attention to social skills training.

Social skills training

Wolpe (1969) had introduced assertive training as a treatment for patients:

> who in interpersonal contexts have unadaptive anxiety responses that prevent them from saying or doing what is reasonable and right.
>
> (Wolpe 1969)

Goldstein et al (1973) videotaped 54 chronic schizophrenics before and after being exposed to an audiotape of an assertive interaction (modelling), being given advice on being assertive (instructions) or both (modelling and instructions). They found some improvement in the assertiveness of the patients in all three conditions. Hersen et al (1975) attempted a more sophisticated programme for a young, withdrawn chronic schizophrenic. They used instructions, rehearsal, feedback and in vivo modelling on three behaviours—poor eye contact, slowness to respond and absence of spontaneous talk. All three diminished, and this led to an increase in overall assertiveness.

The potential for social skills training is still being explored. Hersen & Bellack (1976), in an early review of the more orthodox behavioural approaches, were optimistic. The scope has since been enlarged to cover:

> the ability to express feelings or to communicate needs and desires to others . . . and the ability to influence the environment sufficiently to obtain basic personal goals.
>
> (Wallace et al 1980)

This may be overenthusiastic as it incorporates the very features of schizophrenia which many regard as the core deficit. Some of the impetus for social skills training came from labelling theorists such as Scheff (p. 54), who believed that any social impairment was secondary to the loss of self-esteem and practice which came about in an institution. However, Lindsay (1982) demonstrated that schizophrenics were rated lower on social skills than normal subjects even when the blind raters were told that the schizophrenics were normal subjects. Labelling was much less important than diagnostic status. Despite this rebuff to Scheff's theories, some of the social gaucheness, whether intrinsic, extrinsic or an interaction of the two (Wing 1978), might still be amenable to social skills training.

Cognitive therapy

Background

The most radical treatment approach in recent years has been the attempt to modify delusions, diminish hallucinations and improve thought disorder by cognitive methods. This was commonplace in the 19th century. Some of the moral treatments recommended by Pinel, for example (p. 21), were more cognitive than moral. The influence of Jaspers on the definition of a delusion (a belief held with extraordinary conviction and impervious to experience or counterargument) then discouraged attempts at psychological modification. This attitude was maintained by the development of effective drugs for schizophrenia, and the behavioural ethos of mainstream psychology. In the past decade, the cognitive revolution in psychology and the realisation that some schizophrenics' illnesses are uninfluenced by neuroleptics (Gelder & Kolakowska 1979) have altered the climate of opinion.

Cognitive therapy for depression is a well-established procedure, and from the middle 1970s there have been a trickle of reports on belief modification, and to a lesser extent manipulation of hallucinations, in schizophrenics.

Modification of delusions

Watts et al (1973) first reported the results of belief modification, in three male schizophrenics, all of whom believed that they looked odd in some way. (The characteristic schizophrenic delusions had abated at the time of the study.) They followed four rules in treatment: they began with the most weakly held beliefs, they avoided direct confrontation, they discussed the evidence for the belief rather than the belief itself, and they encouraged the subject to bring up counterarguments. At the end of several sessions each patient rated their beliefs as less strong.

Milton et al (1978) reported a study of 16 schizophrenics, all with bizarre delusions (e.g.'Dr B. gives me a hundred E.C.T. every night', 'I have a chalice in one eye and a star in the other'). They compared the effect of confrontation with the approach of Watts et al. Both procedures led to a lower rating on belief intensity, but the effect was less marked in those treated by confrontation. Rudden et al (1982) claimed some reduction in delusional intensity in three patients when their beliefs were systematically discussed and alternative explanations given. (None was schizophrenic, however.) Colby et al (1979) suggested how paranoid beliefs might be modified, but did not report any clinical examples. Hartman & Cushman (1983) tried to modify delusions in three patients by following Beck's approach for depression. They encouraged the patient to imagine the threatening situation or even search it out in reality (e.g. visit a gay bar in the case of a man who believed others thought he was a homosexual). Their results were not impressive, but they pointed out the complex interaction between feelings and thoughts, which future cognitive therapists might take into account.

Manipulation of hallucinations

Slade (1972) noted that auditory hallucinations were more frequent in one patient whenever he was aroused or had a low level of environmental stimulation. This suggested an effective treatment: relaxation, and physical or mental activity. Green & Preston (1981) replicated a finding by Gould (1949) that subvocal whispers and auditory hallucinations had the same content. They suggested that treatment might be to encourage the patient to talk aloud and thus diminish the hallucinations. Feder (1982) was successful in eliminating auditory hallucinations in one man by playing music over radio headphones.

Improvement of thought disorder

Adams et al (1981) reported a schizophrenic who complained of 'crazy thoughts' and thoughts which 'wandered to completely unrelated ideas'. He improved subjectively when they taught him to attend to appropriate external and internal stimuli (e.g. to recognise crazy thoughts), and to avoid the interpersonal events which precipitated his thought disorder. Meichenbaum & Cameron (1973) had earlier taught a small group of chronic schizophrenics to emit 'healthy talk' by getting them to talk to themselves and monitor what they were doing, e.g. 'What is it I have to do? I'm supposed to fill in these forms'.

Conclusion

Of the various psychological treatments tried over the decades, the most successful so far has been ward-based behaviour therapy for chronic schizophrenics. Paul & Lentz (1977), for example, regard it as much more effective than milieu treatment or psychotherapy. Trials of psychotherapy have not produced much evidence in favour of its efficacy. (This conclusion is supported by a recent study by Denford et al 1983, where 10 of 13 neurotic patients improved with inpatient psychotherapy, but only 2 of 7 borderline schizophrenics improved.) Social skills training and cognitive therapy are more promising, but have been introduced too recently for them to be properly assessed.

SOCIAL TREATMENT

General considerations

Social care, rather than specific treatment, has usually been the more pressing consideration in the management of schizophrenia. Moreover, madhouses, lunatic asylums and, from the 19th century onwards, mental hospitals were more for the protection of the community than for the benefit of the insane. In the late 1950s in Britain, even before the benefits of neuroleptics had been widely accepted, a move was made towards flexibility in the care of schizophrenics. This accelerated in the 1960s and 1970s and it became known as the community psychiatry movement.

It was evident inside and outside the mental hospitals. Initially, it took the form of a more lenient discharge policy. New admissions were discharged sooner than before, and efforts were made to rehabilitate as many long-stay patients as possible in preparation for discharge. The admission procedure for newly psychotic patients used to be a 28-day stay in an observation ward close to their home, and if they failed to recover in that time, transfer to a mental hospital outside the city. This system was replaced by small psychiatric units of two to three wards attached to a general hospital in the centres of populations. These units tried to provide a comprehensive service for their catchment area. The large mental hospitals were expected to act as acute psychiatric units for their catchment area while running down the long-stay population which had built up under the former regime.

The role of the mental hospital in providing long-term care was transferred to day hospitals attached to the acute psychiatric units, where patients went during the day, and hostels or community homes where they spent the rest of the time. Families were required to provide more support than hitherto. As schizophrenics formed the bulk of the young and middle-aged mental hospital population in the first half of this century, they now provide the core of the day hospitals, hostels and community homes.

Unlike social causes, which can be reduced to their psychological, genetic or organic components, social treatments have an independent status. The current social treatments of schizophrenia can be considered under three headings: the milieu of the acute psychiatric unit in which the acute psychotic stage is treated; efforts to prevent relapse by modifying the behaviour of key relatives; and the provision of care, support and rehabilitation after discharge.

Milieu treatment

Milieu treatment is a good example of social treatment in which the psychological component is restricted to nonintensive psychotherapy. On the widest level it means the provision of a ward atmosphere conducive to recovery of the acute stage. It is usually taken to mean a form of management in which drugs and specific psychological treatment (behaviour and cognitive therapy) are excluded or kept to a minimum.

Therapeutic communities, which flourished in the 1950s and 1960s, promoted by Jones (1952), were an example of intensive milieu treatment.

Milieu treatment was used in the 1960s as a control against which to evaluate the effect of neuroleptics. May (1968), in this way, convincingly demonstrated the superiority of the latter.

There is currently a reappraisal of milieu therapy in American. Mosher & Menn (1976), Carpenter et al (1977) and Rappaport et al (1978) all claimed success for their experiment. Mosher and Menn compared 30 schizophrenics treated with milieu therapy and 30 schizophrenics treated conventionally. The former required an admission of 167 days compared with only 21 days for the conventional approach, 17% of them had to be given drugs at some stage, and there was no difference in outcome at 2 years. Carpenter et al (1977) claimed that their milieu regime was actually superior to conventional ones. They defined it as 'sharply limited use of medication', and after discharge the 49 patients had a better social and employment record and less depression than 73 patients treated conventionally. Rappaport et al (1978) assigned acute schizophrenics to either neuroleptics or placebo. The medicated were better than the placebo patients on discharge, but the latter were said to be functioning better socially at 3 years. (The follow-up, however, was inadequate.)

Gunderson (1980), reviewing the issue, notes that the three regimes shared a high patient-staff ratio, distribution of responsibility amongst staff (one of the components of a therapeutic community), a view of psychosis as a process to be lived through and understood, and iconoclastic zeal.

It is probable that economic considerations (high staff ratio, longer admission) will limit the enthusiasm for such experiments.

Family therapy

Family therapy is another example of what Gunderson (1983) called an 'outside-in strategy' (providing a social context which makes symptomatic relapse less likely) rather than an 'inside-out strategy' (traditional psychoanalytic approach of altering the personality to allow a successful adaptation to the endless vicissitudes of life). The impetus came from the demonstration by Brown et al (1962) and their successors that selective aspects of family life, particularly criticism of and overinvolvement with the schizophrenic, led to relapse.

Anderson et al (1980) outlined the goals and strategies. The goals are increased understanding of the illness by the family, reduction of family stress, enhancement of social networks, and diminution of long-term issues contributing to family stress. They described four phases in the treatment: connection with the family (being the family ombudsman, mobilising the family's concern, eliciting reactions to the condition, treatment contract); teaching survival skills for living with a schizophrenic (information, communication skills); monitoring the application of these skills; and continued treatment or disengagement.

There are now several evaluations of the effectiveness of family therapy in preventing relapse (Goldstein et al 1978, Hogarty et al 1979, Leff et al 1982, Falloon et al 1982). Two earlier studies (Langsley et al 1969, Hogarty et al 1974) are not comparable but are worth noting for the points which they raise. Langsley et al assigned 50 schizophrenics and 50 nonschizophrenic psychiatric patients to either hospital care or outpatient family crisis treatment. They then rated the number of crises (life events) and, more importantly, the family management of a crisis. (They give a family argument as an example of a crisis, and jailing the instigator as an extreme, maladaptive way in which it could be managed.) The crisis and its management were each rated separately. After six months the schizophrenics' families were no better at managing crises, whether treated or not, while families with nonschizophrenic patients (mainly personality disorders) did improve (e.g. seeking help from psychiatric or lay services at the time of a crisis). Hogarty et al (1974) assigned remitted schizophrenics to either placebo or neuroleptics, and either what they called major role therapy (part family, part individual) or not. The relapse rate after two years was 80% in the placebo and 48%

in the neuroleptic group, and major role therapy had no effect with or without neuroleptics.

The points made by these two studies are that families of schizophrenics remain bad managers of their lives despite training (which contradicts the positive claims for family therapy reported by some investigators), and that social manipulation, even if effective, gives minimal protection compared with neuroleptics.

In the four evaluations of family therapy as a prophylactic, all patients were on neuroleptics. Goldstein et al (1978) assigned 104 acute schizophrenics to high or low dose neuroleptics *and* family therapy or not. Relapse at six months was greatest in the low dose-no therapy group (48%), next in the low dose-family therapy group (22%), next in the high dose-no therapy group (18%), and lowest in the high dose-family therapy group (0%). Hogarty et al (1979) assigned schizophrenics to oral or intramuscular neuroleptics *and* 'social therapy' (intensive individual and family casework). The relapse rates after two years for the four conditions were: intramuscular neuroleptics plus social therapy—23%, intramuscular neuroleptics alone—50%, oral neuroleptics alone—55%, and oral neuroleptics plus social therapy—66%. It is not clear why social therapy was effective when joined with intramuscular neuroleptics, but ineffective with oral preparations. Leff et al (1982) selected 24 schizophrenics on neuroleptics living with relatives rated high on expressed emotion. Half were assigned to routine outpatient care, and half to a 'package of social intervention'. Only 1 in 12 of the latter relapsed after 9 months compared with 6 receiving routine care. Falloon et al (1982) assigned 36 schizophrenics on neuroleptics to either individual or family therapy. At 9 months 1 of the latter (6%) compared with 8 of the former (44%) had relapsed.

Provision of care and rehabilitation

Pattern of care

There is now a large literature on what is loosely called community psychiatry. Most of it is descriptive or prescriptive rather than evaluative, and much of it dependent on local financial or administrative considerations. In addition, it is not always easy to identify any specific proposals for schizophrenia. Bennett (1978) gives a good account of the general issues involved, including the political and emotional arguments which are frequently heard. Mosher & Keith (1980) describe the range of 'community support systems' in North America—training in community living, family crisis intervention, visiting nurses, enablers, family foster care, community lodges and day care centres. In Britain, the best account is given by Wing (1982), who summarises 30 years of experience in studying the provision of care.

Chronic schizophrenics are found outside the official psychiatric services (prison, lodging houses, home) as well as within them (mental hospital, day hospital, outpatients, supervised hostel, visits by community psychiatric nurse). In each of these situations, specific problems may arise. The commonest life situation is with a relative (85%—Brown et al 1966, 42%—Kendell et al 1979), but this is stressful for the relative as well as patient. They may have frequent access to social and psychiatric services, in the form of attendance at day hospital or day centre, and regular visits to outpatients or visits from a community nurse. Other patients may make contact at times of relapse, but disappear in between.

If one can choose amongst facilities one should try and match these with the individual needs, weighing up factors which might increase the risk of relapse (e.g. family atmosphere) against factors which might lead to social impoverishment (e.g. isolated bed-sitter).

Specific problems

Employment, recreation, everyday living and interpersonal contact are legitimate targets for social treatment. Most attention in the past was focussed on employment, although with the steady rise in general unemployment in the past decade the prospects for schizophrenics now look bleak. Wansborough (1981) gives a practical guide to the current facilities in Britain. Recreational activities, competence in day-to-day living and interpersonal contact can be fostered by official services (day centres) or self-help groups (e.g. National Schizophrenia Fellowship).

Rehabilitation

Lehman et al (1982) analysed the quality of life of 278 'chronic mental patients' in North America. They were worse off than normal subjects in 5 of 8 areas of life—family relationships, social relations, work, finance and safety (fear of attack or robbery) but adequate in their living situation (all were in hostels), leisure activities and physical health. Rehabilitation is aimed at improving a schizophrenic's social functioning in all these areas.

The first stage is to identify an individual's mental and physical disability, to discover potential talents that could be developed, to specific goals, to seek the co-operation of relatives and the help of professionals, and to monitor progress (Wing & Morris 1981). These are achieved by assessing individuals in a setting in which they can be observed under conditions which test their motivation. In Britain this is usually a day hospital with a range of available activities and professional helpers. Psychological assessment has a key role in this. If the patient is a chronic schizophrenic with many years of institutionalisation behind him, the assessment will probably be directed at rating the residual psychological deficit. In less disabled cases the main issues may be premorbid shyness, unassertiveness or unsatisfactory employment status. Social skills training, group therapy or vocational guidance may be recommended in these latter cases, whereas in more disabled patients simple procedures such as supervision with basic activities—washing, dressing, travelling—may be required (Griffiths 1981). The psychological principles of rehabilitation are well set out in a recent book by Watts & Bennett (1984).

ORGANIC TREATMENT

Miscellaneous treatments

From Kraepelin's time onwards a host of organic treatments have been tried and then rejected. The initial enthusiasm for leucotomy, E.C.T. and insulin was discussed in Chapter 2. Of these, leucotomy and insulin have now been discarded, although as late as the 1970s one can find psychiatrists and neurosurgeons still recommending leucotomy for schizophrenics. (The long term side-effects of leucotomy may not be as bad as was once supposed. On attention tasks, Stuss et al 1981 found that a group of leucotomised schizophrenics did better than a group of nonleucotomised schizophrenics. It is possible, of course, that the operation was carried out on a subgroup with a better prognosis anyway.) E.C.T. is still recommended by some psychiatrists. Occasional small studies (e.g. Taylor & Fleminger 1980) have found some benefit, but Hirsch (1982), reviewing the issue, was distinctly sceptical.

In addition to neuroleptics, which will be covered next, only lithium, propranolol, naloxone and endorphin derivatives are currently in use, and only by a small number of psychiatrists or in clinical trials. Antidepressants and anticholinergics are frequently prescribed, the former as an adjunct to neuroleptics, the latter to alleviate some of their extrapyramidal side-effects. (There is some evidence that anticholinergics reduce the efficacy of neuroleptics, Johnstone et al 1983, and produce impaired memory, Tune et al 1982.)

Neuroleptics

Clinical effect

Efficacy in acute psychosis. Followong the initial report by Delay and Deniker in 1952, the ability of chlorpromazine to abolish the acute phenomena of schizophrenia was satisfactorily established by the mid-1960s. A National Institute of Mental Health (NIMH) collaborative study (Cole et al 1964) provided the firmest proof. Out of 463 schizophrenics 344 completed a 6-week trial in which they were randomly assigned to receive 1 of 4 treatments—chlorpromazine, fluphenazine, thioridazine or placebo. The mean overall clinical assessment at the end of the trial was significantly higher in the three neuroleptic groups than in the placebo group (2.0 against 3.1 on a scale running from 1 — very much improved, to 7—very much worse). Moreover, 75% of the patients who received drugs were markedly or moderately improved compared with 23% of the placebo group. By 1978 (Davis & Garver, 1978), there had been 66 well-designed double-blind trials of chlorpromazine against placebo. In 83% of these the neuroleptic was more effective than placebo; in 17% the reverse was true.

Effect in acute psychosis. In the NIMH study, Goldberg et al (1965) reported that drug treatment led to significant improvement in all aspects of psychopathology, including signs of deterioration such as indifference, poor self-care, 'hebephrenic symptoms' and slowness. On placebo, however, there was some improvement in auditory and other hallucinations, poor memory and unreality feelings. The authors concluded that neuroleptics had a specific action on Bleuler's fundamental symptoms, and a lesser effect on the accessory symptoms. Johnstone et al (1978) came to the opposite conclusion. In their study, negative symptoms, such as flattening of affect, retardation and poverty of speech, did not change; whereas hallucinations, incoherence and delusions—positive symptoms—did. The issue is not resolved.

Efficacy as prophylactic. By the early 1970s it was further satisfactorily established that neuroleptics had a second clinical property, that of preventing relapse of acute psychotic phenomena in patients in remission from an earlier episode.

One of the trials which established the prophylactic effect was that of Leff & Wing (1971). They started with 116 schizophrenics who had recently recovered from an acute episode. Thirty-five entered a double-blind placebo against phenothiazine (chlorpromazine or trifluoperazine) trial. (The remainder were either considered not to need drugs, were too precarious to risk not having drugs, had stopped their drugs before the trial began, or were on different drugs.) At the end of a year 80% on placebo had relapsed compared with 35% on active drug.

Davis et al (1980) analysed the results of 29 controlled trials of maintenance therapy with neuroleptics, covering 3519 patients. The mean relapse rate on placebo was 55%, and on active drug 19%. Every study showed at least a 10% superiority of drug over placebo.

Effect as prophylactic. The clinical mechanism by which neuroleptics exert this convincing prophylactic effect is suggested in the studies by Birley & Brown (1970) on life events, and Vaughn and Leff (1976) on expressed emotion.

Birley and Brown found that amongst 50 recently admitted schizophrenics, 13 had stopped or reduced their medication, 32 had had no medication in the previous year, and 5 were still taking their medication. Of those still taking their neuroleptics when they relapsed, all 5 had recently experienced a life event, 3 in the specified three weeks before admission, and 2 in the previous 2 months. Amongst the 13 who had stopped their neuroleptics, life events occurred in only 4. Birley and Brown concluded that whatever the

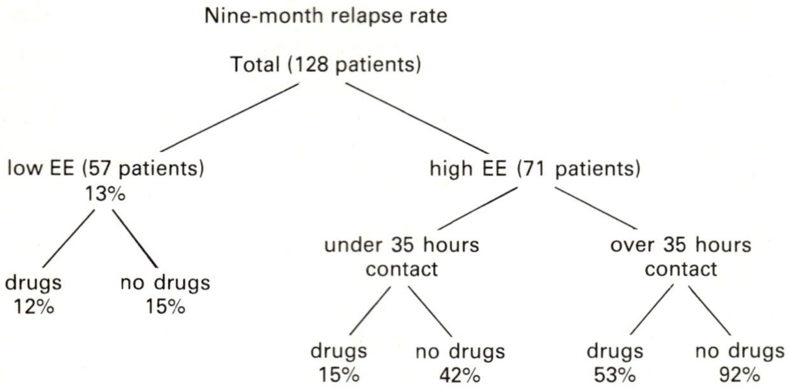

Fig. 7.1 Interaction between expressed emotion, neuroleptics and face-to-face contact.

effect of neuroleptics it did not appear to give protection against the malign effect of life events.

Vaughn and Leff provide a positive suggestion in their diagram (Fig. 7.1) showing the interaction between expressed emotion, neuroleptics and emotional overinvolvement. It appears that neuroleptics protect against the effect of expressed emotion in a key relative. Leff has since argued (Leff 1983) (in contradiction to Birley and Brown) that neuroleptics protect against life events as well as expressed emotion, but not when both are present at the same time. He regards (Fig. 7.2) the predisposition to acute symptoms to be linear, and believes that neuroleptics raise the threshold required for their appearance whether due to life events or exposure to expressed emotion.

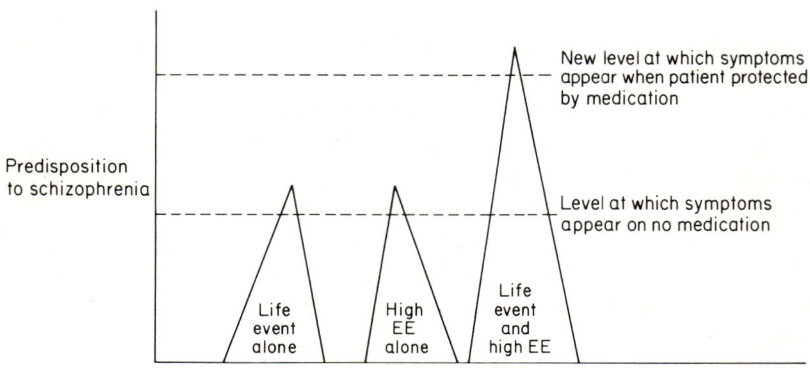

Fig. 7.2 Predisposition to schizophrenia from life events and expressed emotion in patients on neuroleptics or not.

Psychological effect

Remarkably little has been written specifically about the psychological effects of neuroleptics. In the 1950s, soon after their introduction, Anton-Stephens (1954) wrote:

> psychic indifference . . . this is perhaps the characteristic response to chlorpromazine. Patients responding well to the drug have developed an attitude of indifference both to their surroundings and their symptoms best summarised by the current phrase 'couldn't care less'.
>
> (Anton-Stephens 1954)

Porteus (Porteus 1957, Porteus & Barclay 1957) carried out some of the first experiments on this using the maze test which bears his name. (This is a pencil and paper test in which the subject has to trace the correct path along a maze from entry to exit.) Schizophrenics on chlorpromazine did worse than those on placebo. He considered that they resemble leucotomised schizophrenics in performance.

Since then, there have been a handful of studies comparing the effect of neuroleptics on attention with the effect on thought. Orzack et al (1967) found improved performance by medicated schizophrenics on the continuous performance task (CPT—a measure of attention) but not on the digit symbol substitution task (a measure of general cognition). Spohn et al (1977) demonstrated a drug-induced improvement in attention (digit span, CPT) and arousal (skin conductance, heart rate), but not general cognition (proverbs, digit symbol subtest of the WAIS). Kay & Singh (1979) also showed some improvement in attention (digit span) and arousal (sleep pattern) but not thought (right-left orientation on self or others, preference for colour or form). In other studies an improvement in attention has been demonstrated, but as this was the only function measured the results are less impressive (e.g. reduced error rate on dichotic listening, Maloney et al 1976).

Some investigators have shown an improvement in thought disorder, but this is less often reported than improvement in attention. (Fewer patients produced abnormal sortings on Payne's object classification test, Namyslowska 1975; fewer patients made overinclusion errors, e.g. apple = vegetable, on a category inclusion test, Chapman & Knowles 1964).

Rappaport et al (1972) investigated the effect on auditory perception. They analysed the results using signal detection theory, and found a complex interaction between type of patient (paranoid – nonparanoid), dose of drug, and response measures (sensitivity—d'—or response bias—B). Hammond & Gruzelier (1978) attempted an equally complex analysis in which laterality was incorporated as an additional variable. They claimed that perception at the right ear (left hemisphere function) improved differentially.

The most consistent finding in a rather poorly researched field is a differential improvement in attention, whilst on phenothiazines, relative to measures of thinking.

Organic effect

There is a large literature on the anatomical, biochemical and physiological effects of neuroleptics. I shall only mention this, and point out that the psychological component in much of this research is neglected.

Practical considerations

According to Hirsch (1982) the effective daily dose is between 400 and 800 mg of chlorpromazine or its equivalent in another neuroleptic. Below this, there is less or possibly no therapeutic effect. Above this, the efficacy is not enhanced, but the risk of side-effects increases proportionately.

The drug does not take effect until the third week of its administration. (Sedation will begin straight away, however.)

There are no established differences in efficacy between any of the neuroleptics.

Long-acting preparations which can be injected at weekly, fortnightly or monthly intervals do not have any specific advantage over oral preparations, except by improving compliance.

There is still no agreed policy on the length of time that patients should remain on neuroleptics. It is generally recognised that after whatever period relapse on withdrawal is common. Whether this is an artificially-induced relapse (withdrawal syndrome) rather than a natural relapse, previously only delayed by the drug, has not been established.

It is still uncertain which patients will benefit from phenothiazines. The psychological literature on the issue is scanty. Schneider (1982) found that a diminished GSR during a four-week drug-free period predicted poor response on restarting neuroleptics. Hogan et al (1983) showed that if a subject experiences unpleasant side effects they are less likely to comply with recommended medication. Buckley (1982) speculated that, whereas 'traditional signs and symptoms' were poor predictors of outcome, a schizophrenic's subjective experience might be more useful in this respect, and recommended that 'those patients who are free of both a negative attitude toward their illness and a romantic idealisation of the psychotic experience' might do better without medication.

Side-effects

Physical. Extrapyramidal effects—dystonia, akinesis, Parkinsonism, tardive dyskinesia—are common (Marsden & Jenner 1980). Anticholinergics are effective against the first three, but not the last—involuntary movements of tongue, lips and lower face. It is a troublesome and treatment-resistant consequence, and a major drawback to neuroleptics (Berger & Rexroth 1980).

Psychological. Less often reported are psychological consequences. These include depression (Galdi 1983), akathisia (a subjective feeling of restlessness and unease, often mistaken for anxiety, Shen 1981), disturbed behaviour if very high doses are given (Barnes & Bridges 1980), and neuropsychological impairment (Lidsky et al 1981, Struve & Willner 1983).

It should be pointed out that there is considerable doubt whether neuroleptics cause depression (see p. 235) and the evidence that they cause neuropsychological impairment (implying cerebral dysfunction) is scanty.

SUMMARY

The most effective organic treatment is the administration of neuroleptics. In recommended doses they not only abolish the acute psychotic phenomena (delusions, hallucinations, positive thought disorder) in most schizophrenics, but significantly reduce the risk of relapse in about 40% of patients.

Psychological treatments comprise psychotherapy, behaviour therapy and cognitive therapy. Psychoanalysis was never a serious proposition, but non-intensive, reality-oriented individual psychotherapy has a place alongside other treatments. Behaviour therapy was first practised on an individual basis, was then applied to whole wards in the form of token economies to counteract institutionalisation, and is now being explored as a means of improving social skills in remitted schizophrenics. Cognitive therapy, particularly belief modification, is a new experimental addition to the repertoire.

Social care and social treatments have always been the mainstay of psychiatric practice. Despite the undoubted efficacy of neuroleptics, they are still the chief consideration in management. The milieu of the ward in which the acute stage is treated, attempts to influence the behaviour of key relatives, and the provision of aftercare and rehabilitaion are the main concerns.

8

Attention

INTRODUCTION

Kraepelin had remarked on the quality of attention in dementia praecox. He considered it to be abnormal, but secondary to a disturbance in will. According to him:

> the disorder (of attention) was nearly related to behaviour . . . it represents a partial manifestation of volitional disturbance.
>
> (Kraepelin 1913)

Bleuler also recognised a disorder of attention but, as he believed that attention was 'nothing more than a special form of affectivity' (Bleuler 1906), he considered any abnormality secondary to a disorder of affect. Some contemporary German psychiatrists (e.g. Weygandt 1907, see p. 26, Berze 1914) gave it a more crucial role in the psychological dysfunction.

Attention then disappeared from formulations of schizophrenia until the late 1950s. This was mainly due to its neglect by experimental psychologists, who were rejecting the introspective methods of the founders of their discipline. Wundt (1911) and William James (1891) had both promoted the concept, but the behaviourists who followed them had no use for it. Broadbent's (1958) reintroduction of the idea of a 'filter' (see p. 58) led to a reappraisal of attentional deficit in schizophrenia.

By the 1960s, deficient attention had become the most popular explanation of the psychological dysfunction. Shakow, McGhie and Chapman, Venables and Silverman were the main figures in this movement. Their theories are described on pages 59–61.

During the 1970s, enthusiasm for these theories waned, partly because experimental psychologists had demonstrated that attention was not such a simple process as Broadbent had believed, partly because the various measures of attention intercorrelated poorly and it had become necessary to separate at least four components, and partly because the search for attention deficits in schizophrenia had produced conflicting results.

In the 1980s the importance of attentional deficits has declined further with the publication of several negative studies using careful methods and recommended diagnostic criteria. It is nevertheless appropriate to devote a chapter to attention because most schizophrenics do have a problem with attention and it is still not clear what this represents.

CLINICAL CONSIDERATIONS

General disorders of attention

In normal subjects, Posner & Boies (1971) identified three main properties or components of attention. It could be *maintained* (alertness, vigilance), it was *selective*, and it had a *limited processing capacity* (attention or apprehension span). Zubin (1975) added a fourth, the ability to stop heeding one source of information and *shift* to a new one. Most of the terms used in clinical practice to refer to disordered attention can be considered as a deficit in one of these components.

Poor concentration, *apathy* and *sluggishness* refer chiefly to a failure in the maintenance of attention. *Low arousal* emphasises the physiological element in this and *low drive* the constitutional and emotional aspects. *Distractibility* denotes an impairment in the selection of information from one source rather than another, and *neglect* or *sensory extinction* a consistent tendency to ignore one set of information. *Reduced attention span* and *widened attention span* are a contraction or enlargement of the limited processing capacity. *Perseveration* is the inappropriate repetition of a previous response to a new stimulus due to a failure to disattend.

These phenomena occur in a variety of psychiatric disorders, functional and organic, as well as schizophrenia. Impaired maintenance of attention, for example, has been reported in dementia (McGhie 1969), frontal lesions (Rylander 1939), callosal section (Trevarthen 1974), the somnolent form of akinetic mutism from occlusion of the mesencephalic artery (Segarra 1970) and depression (McGhie 1969). Distractibility occurs in delirium, frontal lesions (Luria & Homaskaya 1963), the hyperkinetic syndrome of children (Taylor 1980), mania (Andreasen 1979a) and bilateral temporal damage—the Klüver-Bucy syndrome (Terzian & Ore 1955). Perseveration is characteristic of frontal lesions, reduced attention span is typical of acute and chronic organic reactions, and a widened attention span occurs in drug-induced and mystical states.

Any claim concerning attentional disorder in schizophrenia, therefore, should be viewed in the context of the varieties which exist and the range of other psychiatric disorders in which they occur.

Typical schizophrenic phenomena

Claims that there was a specific disorder of attention in schizophrenia were always the result of psychological or psychophysiological experiments. Clinicians never recognised any typical phenomena of attention in acute schizophrenics, and the inclusion of inattention as one of five typical negative symptoms of chronic schizophrenics (Andreasen 1982a) is a recent proposal.

Subjective experience

Three studies of acute schizophrenics indicate that many subjects have a subjective awareness of disordered attention. McGhie & Chapman (1961) obtained accounts such as the following:

> Everything seems to grip my attention although I am not particularly interested in anything. I am speaking to you just now, but I can hear noises going on next door. I find it difficult to shut these out, and it makes it more difficult to concentrate on what I am saying to you.
>
> (McGhie & Chapman 1961)

Freedman & Chapman (1973) asked 20 acute Spitzer schizophrenics and 20 neurotics 46 questions about their subjective experiences. Only 8 answers distinguished the 2 sets of subjects, 4 of which concerned attention: mental fatigue, inability to focus attention, more acute auditory perception and attribution of impairment of concentration to preoccupation. Freedman (1974) derived 25 categories of subjective experiences from reading 60 autobiographical accounts of schizophrenia. Amongst these, she regarded 7 as disturbances of attention: enhanced sensory awareness, muted sensory awareness, less acute vision, heightened mental efficiency, mental exhaustion, deficient focusing of attention, and confusion. In my study (p. 181), however, a subjective awareness of impaired concentration was more common in the early stages of depression than of schizophrenia.

EXPERIMENTAL EVIDENCE

It is convenient to consider claims about attentional disturbance in schizophrenia in terms of the four components discussed earlier — maintenance, selectivity, span and shifting. The measures themselves are often complex, and will be described first.

Measurement of attention

A large number of tests have been used to measure attention. At first sight they appear a heterogeneous assortment, more concerned with language, perception or thinking than with attention. They can be roughly grouped as follows: reaction time, continuous performance, digit span or span of apprehension, measures of the maintenance of attention by the quality of performance on certain tests, measures of the selectivity of attention by the quality of performance under conditions of distraction, and psychophysiological measures.

Reaction time

Shakow's (1963) method was to ask a subject to press a button when a bell rang and to release it when a light came on. In addition to recording the

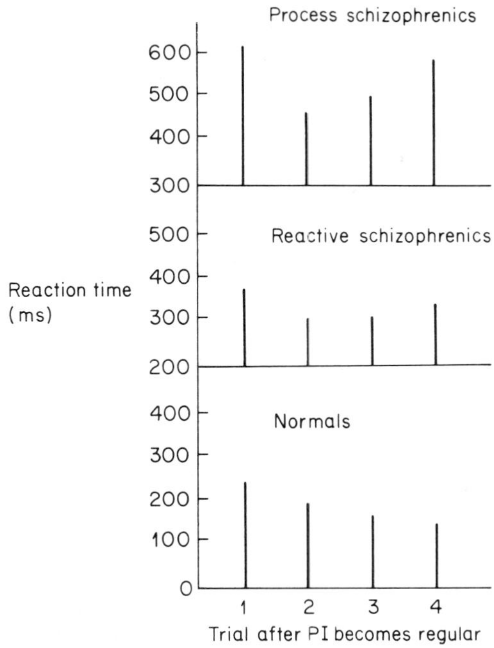

Fig. 8.1 Redundancy-associated deficit (for PIs of one second).

speed of the reaction (from light to release of button), he examined the effect of altering the preparatory interval (PI—time between bell and light). This gave rise to four measures of reaction time. The first is simple latency—overall speed of reaction. The second is known as the 'crossover effect' (p. 59), the claim that schizophrenics, unlike normals, have faster reaction times with irregularly spaced PIs above six seconds than with regular PIs. The third is the 'set index', an equation derived from seven different mean reaction times under different conditions, which is claimed to provide the best discrimination between schizophrenics and normals (Rodnick & Shakow, 1940). The fourth is known as the 'redundancy-associated deficit' (Bellissimo & Steffy 1972), and is the claim that schizophrenics initially benefit when the preparatory interval becomes regular, but then lose this advantage (Fig. 8.1). The authors called it redundancy-associated deficit because they believed that process schizophrenics were differentially affected by the extra (redundant) information provided by too many regular PIs.

Continuous performance test (CPT)

Rosvold et al (1956) introduced this as a test of brain damage, and it was later (Orzack & Kornetsky 1966) used as a test of attentional dysfunction in schizophrenia. Subjects sit in front of a revolving drum with letters on, and have to press a button when a specified letter is displayed. According to Kornetsky & Orzack (1978), normals rarely make 2 omission errors in 50 presentations, whereas 45% of testable schizophrenics make 3 or more errors (Garmezy 1978).

Digit span. Span of apprehension

Digit span, the number of digits which can be repeated immediately after hearing them, is a popular test of cerebral dysfunction. The normal digit span is 7 + or − 2. Hinton & Withers (1971) and myself (Cutting 1980) found that it was reduced in schizophrenia as well in organic conditions.

Neale et al (1969a) presented tachistoscopically a matrix of letters (between 1 and 8). The task was to report the number present, and this was called span of apprehension. Saccuzzo et al (1974) presented a letter T or an A singly or mixed with other letters, and then masked it after a variable exposure time. The shorter the exposure time at which the letter was correctly identified, the better the attention, according to the authors.

Maintenance of attention by quality of performance on some task

Although the continuous performance test, and to a lesser extent reaction time, are measures of the maintenance of attention, it is sometimes instructive to give a standardised test of another function and note any variability in performance over time.

Fishkin et al (1979) gave the Whitaker index of schizophrenic thinking to 36 schizophrenics and observed 2 patterns of overall performance. One group performed randomly throughout the test, suggesting a persistent degree of inattention. Another group they labelled 'streakers', because they achieved an error-free performance for a while, but then suddenly deteriorated. The pattern suggested an episodic imbalance of attention.

Holzman and colleagues' (1978) test of 'smooth pursuit eye movements' can be regarded as a motor task to highlight impaired maintenance of attention. Holzman claimed, following some early work by Diefendorf & Dodge (1908), that normal subjects, when asked to track a moving pendulum, showed smooth pursuit eye movements when they got into the rhythm of the task. Before this the movements were jerky or 'saccadic'. Schizophrenics, Holzman claimed, differed in two ways. Their eye movements continued to be saccadic when tracking the pendulum, a pattern which to Holzman suggested that they had not changed from 'voluntary' to 'involuntary' attention. They also showed 'spikey movements', not seen in normals (most recent review, Lipton et al 1983).

Selectivity of attention measured by undue sensitivity to distraction

Although any task could be used for this purpose, the favourites have been dichotic listening and card sorting. An example of the former is an experiment by Schneider (1976) (see below), where a patient had to shadow a specified passage in one ear, whilst in the other they received one of six sorts of distraction (nothing, soft noise, loud noise, someone reading a physics book, someone recounting the history of the hospital or someone discussing the patient's own delusions). Hemsley's (1976) experiment is a good example of card sorting with or without distraction. Patients had to sort decks of cards displaying different shapes in one of several colours. In some decks, a symbol in the corner provided the distraction.

Psychophysiological measures

The two main physiological measures are galvanic skin resistance (GSR) and contingent negative variation (CNV). The first is a peripheral measure of arousal (p. 61), which relies on the assumption that attention and arousal are linked by the inverse Yerkes-Dodson U-shaped curve. The other is the pattern of the E.E.G. in between a warning that a stimulus to be received and the record of its reception in the cortex. A slow negative cortical potential shift is observed in the E.E.G. during the warning period. This is known as a contingent negative variation. Several investigators have claimed that this is a measure of attention, and that abnormalities in it reflect attentional disorder (Dongier et al 1974).

Intertest correlations

Despite the ingenuity which has gone into designing these tests, there is some doubt as to whether they are measuring the same thing. Kopstein & Neale (1972) gave reaction time, size estimation, proverbs, object sorting and auditory vigilance to 60 schizophrenics and 60 nonschizophrenic patients. There was little common variance between any of the tests in schizophrenics or nonschizophrenics. Van den Bosch (1982) compared reaction time, continuous performance, smooth pursuit eye movements and contingent negative variation in 20 DSM-III schizophrenics, 20 patients with other functional psychoses, 20 neurotics, 20 patients with a schizotypal personality and 20 normals. There was some correlation between a slow reaction time, omission errors on the CPT, inadequate smooth pursuit eye movements and one phase of the CNV, but the redundancy-associated deficit and other phases of the CNV were not part of the common variance.

Deficit in maintenance of attention?

All studies of the CPT in psychotic schizophrenics have demonstrated impaired performance relative to normal subjects (e.g. Asarnow & MacCrimmon 1978, Walker 1981). The same is true of reaction time and smooth pursuit eye movements. However, not all psychotic schizophrenics show this: only 40% have an abnormal CPT (Garmezy 1978); acute paranoid schizophrenics are not impaired on reaction time (Scherer & Storms 1981);

and only 65% of psychotic schizophrenics show the smooth pursuit eye movements deficit (Holzman et al 1978). Further, a variety of other groups of subjects also perform badly on these tasks. Nonschizophrenic (DSM-III) psychotics are no different from DSM-III schizophrenics on the CPT, reaction time and smooth pursuit eye movements (van den Bosch 1982). In fact all three measures were a better guide to the level of psychiatric disturbance than to specific diagnostic entities in this study. Normals under pressure show the same abnormality in smooth pursuit eye movements as do schizophrenics (Brezinova & Kendell 1977, Acker & Toone 1978).

Despite these last studies showing that none of the test results is either particularly sensitive or specific to psychotic schizophrenics several investigators have claimed that impaired maintenance of attention represents a 'core schizophrenic process' (Asarnow & MacCrimmon, 1978). They support their claim with evidence that the deficit also occurs in drug-free remitted schizophrenics (CPT—Wohlberg & Kornetsky 1973) and children of schizophrenics (vigilance task—Nuechterlein 1983, smooth pursuit eye movements—Holzman et al 1978). Van den Bosch (1982) found that subjects with a schizotypal personality also had impaired attention on the CPT, reaction time and smooth pursuit eye movements.

Against an intrinsic abnormality of attention is the fact that the deficit is more responsive to neuroleptics than are other types of psychological dysfunction (Orzack et al 1967, Spohn et al 1977, Kay & Singh 1979, see p. 203). This suggests that impaired attention may accompany or even contribute causally to the florid psychosis but is nothing to do with the background psychological dysfunction out of which the psychosis develops. Another possibility is that attentional disturbance is pathoplastic, determining course but not acting as a cause. Zahn (1980) reported, for example, that schizophrenics with a good prognosis had a faster reaction time than those with a poor prognosis.

Deficit in selective attention?

This was a popular notion in the early 1970s, when it became clear that a general deficiency in attention was not likely. Schizophrenics, according to Oltmanns & Neale (1978), were not inattentive all the time, but were especially vulnerable to distraction.

The weight of evidence is now against any deficit of selective attention in schizophrenia. Blum et al (1969), using a memory task, Maloney et al (1976), in a dichotic listening experiment, and Oltmanns (1978), with digit span, all found that distractors did impair performance, but there was no evidence that this was restricted to schizophrenics. Cavanaugh (1958) in a test of conceptual thinking, and Hirt et al (1977) in a card-sorting task, found that schizophrenics actually improved under distracting conditions. Schneider (1976), Korboot & Damiani (1976) and Straube & Germer (1979), using dichotic listening, and Hemsley (1976) in a card-sorting task, all found no significant effect of distraction, except, in Schneider's case, when the distractor was the delusional material itself. Schneider's is one of the best designed experiments in the area. Appropriately diagnosed schizophrenics had to follow a passage read in one ear while exposed to one of six distracting conditions in the other ear. These conditions were: (1) no distraction. (2) quiet noise, (3) loud noise, (4) someone reading a passage about physics, (5) someone describing the history of the hospital and (6) someone talking about the precise content of the patient's delusions. Only in condition (6) did their performance deteriorate indicating that attention failure was secondary to preoccupation with their delusions and not an intrinsic deficit. Allen (1982) undermined the selective attention deficit theory in a different way. He presented a series of words to two groups of chronic schizophrenics, with positive or negative symptoms, and to normals. If the words 'dog' or 'lion' appeared, subjects were asked to press a button. He designed the experiment so that these words would either appear in the same ear, which he considered would test focussed attention, or in either ear, a test of divided attention. If psychosis were a consequence of a selective attention deficit, he argued, schizophrenics with positive symptoms should find the focussed and divided conditions equally difficult, whereas normals and schizophrenics with negative symptoms should find the divided condition harder. All subjects found focussed easier than divided attention, a result which went against the selective attention deficit theory. Baribeau-Braun et al (1983) also found that acute schizophrenics were worse on a divided attention task than on a focussed task.

Deficit in span of attention?

There is conflicting evidence on whether attention span is intact in psychotic schizophrenics. Spohn et al (1970) reported a reduced span of apprehension and Saccuzzo et al (1974) a slower processing of a visual display. Cegalis et al (1977), however, found a wider visual span in acute schizophrenics and Neale et al (1969a) a normal visual span in chronic schizophrenics except when distracted. In view of these conflicting findings, the radical claim of Asarnow & MacCrimmon (1981), that remitted schizophrenics have a reduced span of apprehension, is particularly doubtful.

Deficit in ability to shift attention?

Zubin (1975), in one of the most reasoned discussions of the whole topic of attention and schizophrenia, concluded that neither maintenance nor selectivity nor span were intrinsically at fault. Instead, he favoured a deficit of shifting attention. Heilbrun (1977) also favoured impaired 'disattentional strategies'., though, like Zubin, produced no experimental evidence. Davies–Osterkamp et al (1977) provided the most compelling evidence. They asked 16 chronic nonparanoid schizophrenics to attend either to two lights, two sounds or a combination of one light and one sound. The schizophrenics were the same as normals in their button-pressing speed when there was a change within the same modality (light or sound going off or on), but when they had to carry out 'intermodal shifting' (combinations of light *and* sound involved) their reactions were markedly slower than normals. Further support comes from a study by Fonseca et al (1978). Schizophrenics were presented either a yellow or red light on a panel of buttons; if the yellow was showing they were not given an electric shock, if the red they were shocked if they failed to depress one of three buttons. Normals moved rapidly to depress a button when they say the red light, but not if they saw the yellow. Schizophrenics behaved in the same way under either condition. Fey (1951) had earlier shown that perseveration on the Wisconsin card-sorting test was typical of chronic schizophrenics.

CONCLUSIONS

Is there a deficit of attention in schizophrenia?

The answer is yes, in about 50% of acutely psychotic and chronic schizophrenics, and in about 25% of remitted schizophrenics, nonpsychotic relatives or subjects with a schizotypal personality.

What is the nature of the deficit?

Selective attention and attention span are not critically involved, although a wide attention span may occur in the acute stage and narrowed attention, as in dementia, in the chronic stage. There may be problems in shifting attention from one source of information to another. This means that the immediate effects of a stimulus would persist longer than in normal subjects. (This would fit in with Salzinger's immediacy hypothesis, p. 62, and Shakow's belief that schizophrenics are more affected by the physical qualities of things and cannot maintain a set, p. 59). The most striking abnormality, however, is a *deficit in the maintenance of attention.*

What is the cause of the attention deficit?

Theories in this area can be divided into three types. There are those which regard attentional disturbance as the chief psychological dysfunction in schizophrenia, from which all other dysfunctions and phenomena derive. Then there are theories which acknowledge its existence in schizophrenia but consider it of secondary importance. Another set of theories gives attentional deficit an important role in causing psychosis of any kind in someone already predisposed. My own view is different from all of these. I believe that attentional disorder is neither of primary significance, nor an artefact of preoccupation with disturbing beliefs or experiences, nor a precipitant of psychosis in a predisposed individual, but is part of a more fundamental disturbance in hemisphere balance which gives it pathogenic or pathoplastic significance depending on the individual concerned.

Attentional deficit as a primary cause of the psychological dysfunction?

Berze (1914) believed that 'insufficient attention' underlay all the clinical phenomena. Shakow (1963) attributed schizophrenia to 'a weakening of a control centre that provides major sets'. McGhie & Chapman (1961) considered that 'a primary disorder is that of a decrease in the selective and inhibitory functions of attention' leading to all other types of dysfunction.

These early theories did not explain how the attentional deficit itself arose. In later accounts this was remedied with one of two sets of suggestions. One made the prime cause a defect in arousal, the other attributed it to cerebral dysfunction in one of the brain sites with a role in attention.

Venables (1964) first suggested that an arousal defect might underlie the attentional disorder. Kornetsky & Orzack (1978) were of the same opinion. They believed that under resting conditions schizophrenics were already highly aroused and could not respond to the demands of a task by raising the level any higher. Hence they would make mistakes on a continuous performance task. Gjerde (1983) is the latest to suggest an arousal deficit. His version is similar to that of Kornetsky. He believes that as schizophrenics are already overaroused they cannot 'mobilise or allocate sufficient attentional resources'. The problem with these theories is that they do not explain how the arousal deficit comes about, nor why the vast majority of anxious people do not become schizophrenic.

The most plausible of this group of theories, in my view, are those which attribute the attentional deficit to localised cerebral dysfunction in an area of the brain known to play a part in attention. The main areas concerned are the reticular formation in the brain stem, the limbic system, the frontal lobe and the parietal lobe. (There is some doubt about whether the basal ganglia are involved.)

Holzman et al (1978) considered that the eye-tracking abnormalities were evidence of brainstem dysfunction. Mesulam & Geschwind (1978) noted that attention was impaired in both schizophrenia and in acute confusional states following right parietal infarction. They suggested that schizophrenia might also arise from a disturbance in the right parietal lobe's contribution to attention. Torrey & Peterson (1974) nominated the limbic system as the site of the attentional deficit, and Walker & Green (1982), noting a correlation between poor CPT performance and poor motor proficiency, suggested the basal ganglia as the site for a general 'neuromotor deficit'. One criticism of this group of theories is that the experimental evidence, reviewed in this chapter, does not support the view that attentional deficit is either invariable in or specific to schizophrenia.

Attentional deficit as secondary to some other cause?

This was the view of Kraepelin, Bleuler and most psychiatrists and psychologists until the 1960s. There is now a return to this standpoint. Zubin (1975), for example, believes that most of the observed attentional deficit can be attributed to a preoccupation with disturbing delusions and hallucinations. (Schneider's 1976 experiment, p. 213, supports this.) Any remaining deficit, he claims, can be attributed to 'the culture of a schizophrenic, making him classify his environmental stimuli with a system uniquely his own'. This approach dismisses all the experimental results and theories of attention as virtually worthless. This is too extreme a view, in my opinion, and a more plausible way of explaining the considerable experimental evidence is outlined in the next two sections.

Attentional deficit as a contributory factor?

The most balanced opinions on the role of attention in schizophrenia are those of Parnas et al (1982a), reporting the outcome of the high-risk children studied by Mednick and Schulsinger (see p. 106), and van den Bosch (1982), who has carried out the most comprehensive and rigorous study so far of attention in adult psychiatric patients.

Parnas et al (1982a) base their argument on the fact that borderline schizophrenia (schizotypal personality) and true Catego schizophrenia share some psychological dysfunctions (thought disorder, disturbed emotional contact) but not others (attentional deficit, affective dyscontrol). Only true schizophrenics, according to them, have the disorder in attention, but it is only a cause of psychotic symptoms if the appropriate background psychological dysfunction (thought disorder, disturbed emotional contact) is also there. The authors believe that that attentional deficit is acquired (perinatal complications, viral infection) while the background psychological dysfunction is inherited.

Van den Bosch (1982) found that psychotic patients who did not fulfil DSM-III criteria for schizophrenia had the same degree of attentional deficit as DSM-III schizophrenics, and suggested that attentional disorder predisposed to psychiatric disturbance in general but was not specific to schizophrenia. His claim is surprising because he found that subjects with a schizotypal personality had more attentional disorder than neurotics despite having the same or even less 'psychiatric disturbance'. In general, though, his claim is similar to the Schulsinger group, in proposing that attentional disorder, though not specific to schizophrenia, is significant in determining whether the inherited psychological dysfunction remains latent in the form of personality disorder or becomes manifest as a florid psychosis.

Attentional deficit as part of hemisphere imbalance?

Another possibility is that attentional disorder is part of a more fundamental psychological dysfunction which affects all mental functions to a greater or lesser extent. Individual differences will determine the extent to which attention is affected and this will then determine the pattern and course of the entire condition—schizoid personality, several episodes of a florid psychosis or a chronic unremittent illness. In some ways this view is similar to those of Parnas et al and van den Bosch. But they treat attentional disorder as an additional factor unrelated to the fundamental psychological dysfunction. In my proposal, attentional disorder is part of the same fundamental dysfunction. The general dysfunction itself, I believe, is a consequence of hemisphere imbalance, and so my theory is a neuropsychological one.

My argument is based on two pieces of evidence.

The first is neuropsychological data suggesting that each hemisphere has a different style of attention. Dimond, on the basis of tachistoscopic experiments in normals (Dimond & Beaumont 1973) and split-brain patients (Dimond 1976), believed that the left was better than the right hemisphere in maintaining attention in the short-term, but tired easily. The procedure he chose was similar to what is demanded of a radar operator. Faint signals appeared in random sequence over a stretch of time. The operator had to identify as many as possible, but not at the expense of too many false positives (saying a signal exists when it does not). Dimond found that the left hemisphere was more accurate than the right for short periods, but tired easily. The error rate then became worse than that of the right, which all the time was producing a constant but moderate number of errors without tiring. Dimond concluded:

> The right hemisphere appears therefore to provide a skeleton service capable of maintaining performance after decrement occurs at the left hemisphere.
> (Dimond & Beaumont 1974)

The two strategies were complementary and there was no conflict. Kinsbourne (1974b) believed that the left hemisphere was superior than the right in focusing on some specific aspect of a situation (selectivity), whereas the right excelled at 'preattentive focusing' (arousal).

The second piece of evidence is a study by Niwa et al (1983). They asked schizophrenics to carry out a dichotic auditory vigilance task. The schizophrenics' errors fluctuated substantially over time, omission errors at the right ear being mainly responsible for this. The authors concluded that the 'left hemisphere response set' was at fault. They were unaware of the work of Dimond and Kinsbourne, but their results would fit the notion that in schizophrenia left hemisphere functions are exaggerated (greater fluctuation in vigilance than normal) while right hemisphere functions are reduced (no 'skeleton service' to cover the left hemisphere's lapses).

This explanation of attentional deficit in schizophrenia has the following merits. It explains theories such as Shakow's of a 'weakening of a control centre that provides major sets' and his data suggesting that 'a schizophrenic reacts to old situations as if new, and to new as if old'. If the balance between the right hemisphere's steady low level vigilance and the left hemisphere's bursts of high-level focussing is disrupted there would be no overall control and a subject would vacillate between the novel and the familiar in his environment. It would also explain Salzinger's immediacy hypothesis, because the bursts of left hemisphere focussing would be more extreme and each intense effort would leave a stronger trace on a subject's mind. It also accounts for the main finding in this field, impaired maintenance of attention, and the observation by Fishkin et al (1979) of intermittent lapses in attention or 'streaking'.

Some of the attentional deficit in schizophrenia may well be secondary to a preoccupation with the content of the psychosis (Zubin, Schneider), but some, I would suggest, is a reflection of hemispheric imbalance. What determines the florid psychosis rather than a schizoid personality may be, as Parnas et al and van den Bosch suggest, the extent of the attentional deficit in any individual, but not in the form of additional organic cerebral dysfunction as they suggest, but as an integral part of the disorder.

SUMMARY

Normal attention is a control function which ensures that cognitive processing is directed towards significant features of one's environment or content of mind. It has several properties. It can be maintained (concentration, vigilance, arousal, drive). It can be selective. It has a limited span. And it can shift from one topic to another. Several parts of the brain are involved in its functioning. The most important are the reticular formation in the brain stem and the limbic system, but the parietal and frontal lobes, and each hemisphere, make a contribution. The most frequently used measures of attention are reaction time, the number of mistakes on a continuous performance test of vigilance, digit span or span of apprehension, application to any psychological test, and the decrement in performance on any psychological test when distraction is introduced.

Disorders of attention include poor maintenance of attention (impaired concentration, apathy), distractibility, perseveration, episodic attention disorder, altered attention span, and 'confusion'. Most organic and functional psychiatric disorders are accompanied by one or more of these disorders.

In acute schizophrenia subjects are commonly aware of a disorder of attention. Chronic schizophrenics are regularly rated as inattentive and apathetic. There are some reports that remitted schizophrenics and high-risk subjects have a disorder of the maintenance of attention. The main issue is whether psychotic schizophrenics have one of the following four disorders — poor maintenance, distractibility (poor selectivity), altered span and inability to shift attention (or disattend). The weight of evidence suggests that deficits of selective attention or span of attention are not primary or specific to schizophrenia. There is more evidence incriminating impaired maintenance of attention and an impaired ability to disattend.

The cause of the attentional deficit has been the subject of much controversy. Some authors believe that it is a primary and specific feature of schizophrenia, related to a disturbance in arousal or the result of focal cerebral dysfunction in a region of the brain subserving attention. Others believe that it can be dismissed as the effect of preoccupation with disturbing experiences. Yet others regard attentional dissorder as a nonspecific precipitant of psychosis but not part of the specific psychological dysfunction of schizophrenia. A fourth possibility, which I suggest, is that a disorder of attention is one manifestation of hemisphere imbalance and one which frequently determines the form and course of schizophrenia, particularly the likelihood of florid relapses.

9

Consciousness

INTRODUCTION

At the beginning of the century a disturbance of consciousness was a popular explanation for all kinds of psychiatric disorder. The influence of Freud, Janet and Hughlings Jackson was then at its height. Wernicke (1900) suggested that a splitting or 'sejunction' of consciousness was the main psychological dysfunction in psychosis. Gross (1904) believed that it was a disintegration of consciousness. Freud (1894), himself, regarded 'hallucinatory psychoses' (see p. 25) as a consequence of the dissociation of one set of contents of consciousness from another. The dissociated set was so unacceptable that its relationship to the individual was denied and projected as the psychosis.

During the behaviourist era, the idea of consciousness was anathema to experimental psychologists, and in the English-speaking world it is only within the last 10 years that schizophrenia has again been linked with a disorder of consciousness.

French psychiatrists, however, always out of line with their German and English-speaking colleagues, maintained an interest in the psychopathology of consciousness throughout the century, and most of their explanations of psychosis were based on this. Dupré's (1913) 'coenestopathic states' and De Clérambault's (1942) 'automatisms' were both aspects of mental life which had become split off from the foreground of consciousness and, as such, were treated as foreign by the individual. Dupré's version was peripheral and sensory in form, whilst De Clérambault's was a central cluster of memories, emotions and attitudes. Psychosis was a:

> reaction of that part of the mind and emotions that are still healthy to an automatism which arises spontaneously, and takes the patient by surprise at a time when he is quite calm both emotionally and mentally . . . This process, the prime mover of the psychosis, chooses amongst the subconscious certain memories or attitudes to disengage or exhume. It hypertrophies and deforms them.
>
> (De Clérambault 1942)

Delay, professor of psychiatry in Paris after the Second World War, and famous for his discovery of the action of neuroleptics, gave the model a neuropsychological stamp. He linked together consciousness, the mid-brain and schizophrenia. Ey (1950) turned to Hughlings Jackson for inspiration and suggested that schizophrenia was due to the freeing of subcortical modes of functioning from cortical inhibition. Hence subjects experienced the world at a lower, more primitive level of consciousness, akin to dreaming. Guiraud (1950) combined De Clérambault's notion of mental automatisms with Ey and Delay's neuropsychological notions, arguing that subcortical dysfunction disrupted one's recognition of self and the outside world and caused everything to be tainted with a sense of foreignness.

In recent years cognitive and neuropsychological models have been revived by British and North American psychologists and psychiatrists, in particular by Frith and Nasrallah.

CLINICAL CONSIDERATIONS

General disorders of consciousness

There are a number of definitions of consciousness and a number of clinical phenomena generally considered to be disorders of consciousness.

Some of these definitions are presented below to illustrate the different aspects to its meaning.

> Consciousness is the selector input to the dominant action system.
>
> (Shallice 1972)
>
> Consciousness is a cause rather than a correlate . . . and it is strictly a property of brain circuits.
>
> (Sperry 1976)
>
> Consciousness is a representative mode . . . things can be talked about . . . this contrasts with expressive functions.
>
> (Savodnik 1976)
>
> Consciousness is a holographic construction by the brain of the world.
>
> (Pribram 1976)
>
> Consciousness is . . . not a copy of experience, not necessary for concepts, not necessary for learning, not necessary for thinking, not necessary for reason . . . it is an operation rather than a thing, repository or function . . . it operates by way of analogy . . . there is nothing in consciousness that is not an analogue of something that was in behaviour first.
>
> (Jaynes 1976)
>
> Consciousness . . . is awareness at . . . any of four levels . . . sensorimotor . . . limbic . . . neocortical . . . symbolic . . . the affective state is the consciousness experience at any of these four cognitive levels.
>
> (Brown 1977)

There is some common agreement that consciousness is not a function, like memory, thinking or perception, but on a different level and more a representation or analogue of other functions.

A disorder of consciousness is implied or predominates in the following terms: confusion, clouding of consciousness, stupor, perplexity, oneiroid states, depersonalisation, derealisation and dissociative states.

Confusion (Verwirrtheit in German) is the loosest term. It is defined by Lishman (1978) as: 'an inability to think with customary clarity and coherence', in the context of an acute organic reaction. It is often used to cover any state with a disturbance of consciousness.

Clouding of consciousness denotes a lowering of the level of awareness of surroundings. It is inferred from drowsiness and lapses in concentration in mild forms and stupor fluctuating with excited behaviour in more severe forms. It is a composite impairment, reflecting disturbances in sleep function, attention and perception.

Stupor is sometimes classified as a catatonic disorder and sometimes as a disorder of consciousness. It was defined by Joyston-Bechal (1966) as a triad of akinesis (lack of movement), mutism (lack of speech) and relative preservation of consciousness.

Perplexity is:

> the uneasy awareness of an inability to weigh up the external or internal world to such an extent that one begins to be uncertain about the very nature of experience itself.
>
> (Störring 1939)

According to Hoch & Kirby (1919), it is characterised by the following: statements of the type, 'I don't know what's going on', a puzzled facial appearance, bewilderment about the environment rather than the self, and apparent disorientation on initial questioning but correct orientation present when carefully enquired about.

Oneiroid states or oneirophrenia (Mayer-Gross 1924, Meduna 1950) are those in which the prominent feature is a dream-like quality to experience.

Depersonalisation is:

> a state in which the individual finds himself changed throughout in comparison with his former state; this change extends to both the self and the outer world and leads to the individual not acknowledging himself as a personality; his actions seem automatic; he observes his actions like a spectator.
>
> (Schilder 1935)
>
> It is a subjective feeling of internal and/or external change . . . there is an unpleasant or even highly distressing quality to the experience: there is the retention of insight . . . and an affective disturbance characterised by the complaint of loss of affective responsiveness.
>
> (Ackner 1954)

Derealisation is a qualitative alteration in the appearance of the external world, such that objects look unreal, two-dimensional and lustreless compared with previously.

Dissociative states are hysterical, hypnotic or self-induced meditative states in which a subject allows or denies entry into consciousness of events or aspects of the environment which are not normally amenable to such manipulation.

Other disturbances of self-consciousness, not covered by the above terms, also occur. Jaspers, as an existentialist, placed considerable emphasis on involvement of the self in all morbid phenomena. He devoted a whole section in his book to disorders of awareness of self, of which he listed six involving activity of the self, unity of the self, identity of the self, awareness of the self as distinct from the outside world, awareness of one's personality and awareness of the possibility of multiple personalities. Fish (1967) condensed these to four: disturbance of awareness of self-activity (equivalent to depersonalisation), of self-unity (belief that one is two people), of continuity of self (belief that one is now a different person from before) and of the boundaries of the self (manifest as delusions of control).

These disorders of consciousness occur in a wide variety of normal and pathological states. In general, however, confusion, clouding of consciousness and stupor are characteristic of organic disorders; perplexity and oneiroid states are features of functional psychosis, particularly the atypical varieties (p. 92); whilst depersonalisation, derealisation and dissociative states are chiefly seen in neurosis, although may be part of a psychotic condition.

Typical schizophrenic phenomena

Opinions differ on whether any of these or a particular variety of these is typical of schizophrenia. Langfeldt (1960), for example, regarded depersonalisation as a critical diagnostic feature (p. 79), but his definition was wider than those given above:

> a special type of disturbance of volition and the self, without insight, originating, in the patient's opinion, outside of himself, and characterised by passivity feelings and ideas of reference.

Similarly, existential psychiatrists such as Binswanger (1944) and Laing (1959) considered the 'emptying of the personality' and 'the divided self' as central to schizophrenia. Psychoanalysts (e.g. Lewis 1949) used to regard all instances of depersonalisation as schizophrenic, although modern psychoanalysts would be content with a diagnosis of schizoid, narcissistic or borderline personality. Scharfetter (1980) considered all the phenomena of schizophrenia as disorders of 'ego-consciousness' and Schneider (1959), although reluctant to give his first-rank symptoms any theoretical status, referred to them tentatively as the effect of 'lowering of the barrier between the self and the surrounding world'.

In contrast, very few studies using reliable, standardised interviews have found that any of these is either common in or typical of current definitions of schizophrenia. In the IPSS about 10% of all patients had 'distortions of self-perception' (the closest phenomenon to depersonalisation in that study). Mayer-Gross (1935) regarded only 6 out of 26 patients with depersonalisation as schizophrenic (diagnosed using Bleulerian criteria) and Ackner (1954) none of 54 cases. Derealisation occurred in 42% of 85 Catego schizophrenics (Hwu et al 1981).

Oneirophrenia and perplexity are more common, but are not regarded as typical. In fact, some psychiatrists include them amongst the defining criteria of nonschizophrenic functional psychoses such as cycloid psychosis (Perris 1974) or oneirophrenia (Meduna 1950). Varsamis & Adamson (1971) reported that an oneiroid state was the commonest presenting feature of a schizophrenic episode, occuring in 16 out of 44 Langfeldt schizophrenics. Cutting et al (1978) and Brockington et al (1982a) found perplexity in a substantial minority of functional psychotics, and when it was present it conferred a particular course on the condition.

In summary, it would appear that carefully defined clinical disorders of consciousness are not part of the mainstream concept of schizophrenia and are not included in the majority of current diagnostic criteria. In the case of depersonalisation, I would agree with most of the comments of a recent reviewer (Nuller 1982) who concluded that it was a nonspecific phenomenon, occurring in normal, neurotic and psychotic people and that it was often preceded by emotional stress. He believed that in psychosis it occurred at the peak of psychotic 'anxiety or vital depression'. I disagree with this and believe that it occurs in the convalescent or postpsychotic phase as a form of accommodation between the individual's partly resolved mental condition and the outside world which, for the first time for several months, he is taking notice of. In the case of perplexity and oneiroid states I suspect that these are also nonspecific and represent a response to a rapidly occurring change in the quality of perception. The reason that they are linked with nonschizophrenic functional psychosis probably reflects the rapidity of onset of these conditions. This does not entirely explain their existence because one would expect perplexity, by this argument, to be less prominent in subsequent episodes of psychosis, a fact which in our study (Cutting et al 1978) did not appear to be true. Also it does not explain the distinct tendency for perplexity to be more common in women psychotics (Mentzos et al 1971, Cutting et al 1978).

The following are illustrative accounts by schizophrenic patients in my care of some of these phenomena.

Perplexity:

> Something funny is going on. I think that someone is trying to test me out. I might by dying. I think that I am being harmed, drugs pumped through the window. Someone is trying to harm her next door. Listen. Can't you hear it . . . [What day it it?] I don't know [It's Friday] Impossible. I don't believe you. [Why don't you believe me?] I just know it's not Friday. It's June 26th 1977 [correct], but it's not Friday. I can tell you that.
>
> (Acute schizophrenic)

Depersonalisation:

> My right side feels empty. My personality has shifted to my left shoulder. I am the same as that person opposite. I am a fraud. I have no sensation down my left side.
>
> (Acute schizopherenic)

Multiple personality:

1) A young Italian woman, whose name was Maria, believed that she was a man called Bruno and came from Copenhagen; she talked like a man and only responded when addressed as Bruno.

2) A young Irish woman believed that she was her own mother and would talk to herself in one voice and reply, often in the third person (e.g. 'she's being a good girl'), in another voice.

Subjective experience

McGhie & Chapman (1961) gave some verbatim accounts of their subjects' altered consciousness. They were particularly conscious of their movements:

> I am not sure of my own movements any more . . . It's not so much thinking out what to do, it's the doing of it that sticks me . . . If I am going to sit down, for example, I have got to think of myself and almost see myself sitting down before I do it.
>
> When I have been rushing about I have to stop and be still for a minute. It's like watching a miniature railway. There is split-second timing. One train misses the other by a split second . . . My mind is always taking in little things at the side.
>
> (McGhie & Chapman 1961)

EXPERIMENTAL EVIDENCE

As consciousness is not a function but a representation of all functions no objective measure can be taken. It is probably true to say, therefore, that there is no experimental evidence for a disorder of consciousness in schizophrenia. Introspective accounts, such as those of McGhie and Chapman, however, do provide some measure of the pattern of changes in the content of consciousness.

CONCLUSIONS

Is there a disorder of consciousness in schizophrenia?

Yes, but consciousness is a broad concept and this bare statement has little meaning.

What is the nature of the disorder of consciousness?

There are good grounds for believing that acute schizophrenics are aware of mental functions which normally occur subconsciously. Frith (1979), for example, proposed that:

> The symptoms of schizophrenia can be interpreted as the result of a defect in the mechanism that controls and limits the contents of consciousness. This

> defect can be understood as excessive self-awareness. Normally most of the complex information processing which is continuously required by even simple acts of perception, language and thought goes on below the level of awareness; whereas in schizophrenic patients some of this processing, or the results of this processing, not in themselves abnormal, become conscious.
>
> (Frith 1979)

Nasrallah (1982) suggested that this overawareness applied to a particular set of functions, sited in a part of the brain normally silent with respect to awareness of its functions:

> Schizophrenic symptoms are due to weakened inhibitory mechanisms that mediate left hemisphere dominance for consciousness. This may result in awareness by the left hemisphere consciousness of another right hemisphere consciousness which communicates with and intrudes on it, leading to Schneider-type delusions to explain the external influence.
>
> (Nasrallah 1982)

Frith's suggestion is probably correct, and has some basis in the subjective experience studies of McGhie and Chapman. Nasrallah's proposal is more speculative as the only experimental evidence for this are the reports by Rosenthal & Bigelow (1972) and himself (Nasrallah 1982) that schizophrenics have an unusually thick corpus callosum.

In contrast, Jaynes (1976) has suggested that schizophrenics have an unusually restricted consciousness, similar, in his view to that of primitive man, where behaviour is determined by or attributed to God's wishes without the mediation of the individual's consciousness. To Jaynes, auditory hallucinations are a reversion to the sort of commands which God gave to the characters in early Jewish history. Jaynes' view, in my opinion, is out of line with the others and shows that his knowledge of schizophrenia is at least less than his knowledge of history. Even in chronic schizophrenia, where the outside world may go unnoticed for years, self-consciousness is not diminished, as is shown by the writings and drawings of such people. One could regard autism as an example of this, but again there is no restriction of consciousness, only a neglect of one source of information (the outside world) in favour of another (contents of mind). According to Bleuler, autism occurs in:

> the most severe schizophrenics, who have no more contact with the outside world [and] live in a world of their own. They have encased themselves with their desires and wishes or occupy themselves with the trials and tribulations of their persecutory ideas . . . this detachment from reality, together with the relative and absolute predominance of the inner life we term autism.
>
> (Bleuler 1911)

Other clinical varieties of altered consciousness—depersonalisation, perplexity, oneirophrenia—are probably reactions to altered perception and are not specific to schizophrenia.

What is the cause of the disorder of consciousness?

Different schools of psychiatry have their own view on this and a review of these would cover the same ground as Chapter 16. Existentialists regard it as the prime cause of schizophrenia, in that schizophrenia develops *because* the individual becomes aware of certain fundamental truths about life. Some psychoanalysts regard the dissociation of certain emotionally-laden ideas from the rest of consciousness as the main cause of schizophrenia. There are psychophysiological explanations such as that of Dussik (1968):

> ... hallucinations and delusions are due to the persistence or emergence of dreamlike patterns which contaminate the wake state . . . in psychosis arousal from sleep and snapping out from dreams and accepting oneiric experiences as real do not coincide.
>
> (Dussik 1968)

There are cognitive explanations such as Frith's, and neuropsychological accounts such as Nasrallah's, both discussed above.

My own preference is for a neuropsychological explanation, along the lines suggested by Nasrallah. There is considerable evidence from experiments on split-brain patients (p. 151) that each hemisphere does subserve a different style of cognition from its fellow. Sperry went as far as saying that:

> Each hemisphere seems to have its own conscious sphere for sensation, perception, ideation and other mental activities and the whole realm of gnostic activity of the one is cut off from the corresponding experiences of the other hemisphere.
>
> (Sperry 1976)

Eccles (1977) argued that trying to attribute consciousness to the right hemisphere was like trying to decide whether animals were conscious, because in neither case could one rely on language. An interview with a split-brain patient conducted by Gazzaniga & LeDoux (1978), however, produced convincing proof for Sperry's position. If the right hemisphere had conscious properties, they argued, it should have a sense of self, a sense of who and what it likes, a sense of the future, and goals and aspirations. They evaluated all these properties in a teenager who had undergone commissurotomy at the age of 15. His right hemisphere was addressed by questions presented in the left half of his visual field, and allowed to communicate by spelling the answers with the left hand. The conversation ran as follows:

> Who are you? Paul.
> What is your favourite hobby? Cars.
> Who's your favourite girl? Liz.
> What will you do when you grow up? Car racing.
> What day is it tomorrow? Wednesday [correct].

Paul's right hemisphere fulfilled all the criteria for conscious properties. When he had been asked directly what he would like to be when he grew up he (i.e. his left hemisphere) had answered that he wanted to be a draughtsman. In addition to supporting Sperry's position, this demonstrated that the aspirations of each hemisphere conformed to their characteristic modes of thought—sensation-seeking by the right hemisphere, analytic problem-solving by the left.

Such dissociation is not just a rare curiosity confined to split brains, but occurs in normals. Landis et al (1981), for example, produced what they called 'dissociated awareness of manual performance' in normal people. Subjects were presented with stylised drawings of common objects (e.g. corkscrew) or faces (e.g. happy face). This was done tachistoscopically. They were then given a photograph of an object or a face and asked to press a button if the stylised drawing that they had seen matched the photograph. They were asked after each presentation if they thought that their response was correct or not. There was no difference in *actual* error rates between faces and objects (faces—74% accurate, objects—76% accurate), but there was a sizeable difference in the *subjective* estimates of correct performance (faces—58% accurate, objects—93% accurate). The authors concluded that whilst actual performance on faces reflected right hemisphere functioning, the discrepancy between actual and estimated facial matching indicated that the speaking left hemisphere was entirely unaware of its partner's performance.

It is not inconceivable, as Nasrallah suggests, that the flow of information between the left and right hemispheres could increase, and the left hemisphere, because it still maintains complete ignorance of the right hemisphere's role in mental processes (see p. 148), would then produce a plausible explanation of the new stream of information by projecting the cause on to the outside world (e.g. thought insertion, auditory hallucinations). This explanation would also fit the general neuropsychological theory espoused in this book, namely of exaggerated left hemisphere functions (in this case overawareness) and reduced right hemisphere functions (inapplicable in this case because the right hemisphere has no conscious awareness under normal circumstances).

SUMMARY

Schizophrenia has been attributed to a disturbance of consciousness by the early neurologically-orientated psychiatrists, by psychoanalysts, by existential psychiatrists, by French eclectic psychiatrists and most recently by cognitive psychologists and neuropsychiatrists. A variety of the clinical phenomena seen in schizophrenia are to do with disordered consciousness, but none of these is central to the typical concept or crucial to its diagnosis. These phenomena include perplexity, depersonalisation and an oneiroid state. In the early stages of an episode, schizophrenics are often subjectively more aware of the world around them and of the workings of their body and mind.

The disorder of consciousness in schizophrenia appears to be a non-specific increase in awareness. There are some grounds for believing that it might represent increased awareness by the left hemisphere of the workings of the right hemisphere, but unawareness by the left hemisphere of the origin of this.

10

Emotion

INTRODUCTION

Freud considered a disorder of emotion the primary cause of all forms of psychosis:

> . . . the ego rejects the incompatible idea together with its affect . . . through a flight into psychosis.
>
> (Freud 1894)

This has remained the view of most psychoanalysts since. Shapiro (1981), for example, believes that:

> a schizophrenic episode is precipitated by an unassimilable incident that paralyses the schizophrenic with anxiety.
>
> (Shapiro 1981)

The early German existential psychiatrists (e.g. Wetzel 1922, see p. 35) attributed schizophrenia to an altered emotional state which a person was not aware of, but which led to a change in their world view. Subsequent existentialists (e.g. Binswanger 1963, see p. 353) then gave primary importance to the change in world view, which through its emotional consequences led to schizophrenia. Janet, though primarily interested, like Freud, in neurosis and the unconscious, offered an existential view of psychosis in 1932 when he was in his 70s. He regarded all delusional states as a consequence of morbid emotions. Two of these, 'sentiment du vide' (a feeling of emptiness) and 'sentiment d'une action humaine extérieure et intentionelle' (a feeling of social alienation and malign intentions on the part of others), were, according to him, particularly significant. Behaviourists also gave abnormal emotion a crucial role, either in the form of high anxiety (Mednick 1958), excess drive (Broen & Storms 1961, Epstein & Coleman 1970), overarousal (Venables 1964), 'divergence among arousal systems which were formerly in equilibrium' (Lapidus & Schmolling 1975) or undue sensitivity to criticism (Rodnick & Garmezy 1957).

The view of most European psychiatrists until the 1960s was that a disorder of emotion, although not causative, was one of the most characteristic symptoms of the condition. Kraepelin (1913) believed that emotion was especially vulnerable to the effects of the disease process. There was a 'weakening of those emotional activities which form the mainspring of volition'. Bleuler (1911) placed a disturbance of affectivity second only to a weakening of associations in importance, and regarded it as determining the content of all the secondary symptoms such as delusions and hallucinations. A flattening, blunting or incongruity of affect (affect being Bleuler's preferred term for emotion) came to be the hallmark of typical schizophrenia.

In the 1960s and 1970s there was a tendency, particularly in Britain, to give the disorder of emotion less prominence. This was due to an increased reliance on Schneider's first-rank symptoms when making the diagnosis (all of which are either delusions or hallucinations) and the influence of the social psychiatrists, who regarded much of the emotional disorder as secondary to institutionalisation and not intrinsic to the condition. Flattening of affect came to be associated with chronic schizophrenia, a poor prognosis and bad management. Some of the empirical definitions of schizophrenia suggested during the 1970s (see Ch. 3) gave hardly any weight at all to emotional disorder.

In recent years there has been renewed interest in the subject, for a number of reasons. First, it was demonstrated in the International Pilot Study of Schizophrenia conducted by the World Health Organisation (1973) that flattening of affect was one of the few symptomatic predictors of outcome. Secondly, it emerged from studying children genetically at risk for schizophrenia (Parnas et al 1982a) that poor emotional rapport in childhood is one of the few predictors of adult schizophrenia. Thirdly, it was appreciated that flattening of affect is not the only form of emotional disorder which is seen. Depression is particularly common, and there has been considerable debate about how it arises—whether intrinsic to the condition, an effect of drug treatment or a natural consequence of the insight which accompanies recovery. Finally, there have been several studies of how schizophrenics themselves experience emotion as well as how others rate their ability to communicate emotion; these have indicated a difference from normals in the way they judge facial expression or intonation in speech. These considerations have rekindled interest in the nature of emotion in schizophrenia.

The theme of this chapter will be that, despite the complex nature of emotion, there is evidence that schizophrenics do have in common a disturbance in the way they experience and communicate emotion.

Before embarking on this it is necessary to mention the topic of 'will'. The term has virtually disappeared from psychological and psychiatric vocabularies, but Kraepelin, Bleuler and Jaspers devoted considerable space to it in their textbooks. I am including it as an aspect of emotion (see below), although some of the disorders of will mentioned by these authorities are dealt with in the chapters on movement (negativism, catalepsy) and thinking (delusion of influence, ambivalence).

CLINICAL CONSIDERATIONS

General disorders of emotion

There are as many definitions and classifications of emotion as there have been major philosophers and psychologists. In this century those of Wittgenstein, Ryle, Jaspers and Izard can serve as some basis for discussing disordered emotion.

> Emotions are experiences . . . an emotion has duration; it has no place; it has characteristic . . . thoughts; it has a characteristic expression which one would use in miming it.
>
> (Wittgenstein 1980)

> Emotion is used to designate at least three or four different kinds of things, which I shall call inclinations or motives, moods, agitations and feelings.
>
> (Ryle 1949)

> *Emotion* . . . comprises feelings—individual unique and radical commotions of the psyche . . . *affect*—a momentary and complex emotional process of great intensity with conspicuous bodily accompaniments and sequelae . . . and *mood*—states of feeling or frames of mind that come about with prolonged emotion.
>
> (Jaspers 1913)

> Emotions are complex motivational phenomena with characteristic neurophysiological, expressive and experiential components.
>
> (Izard & Buechler 1980)

There is a consensus on the fact that emotion is an experience and some agreement that it also refers to motivation. The experience can be classified according to intensity and duration (feelings, affect, mood—as Jaspers above) or according to the type of emotion. (Ekman et al 1969 suggested six fundamental emotions—happiness, surprise, fear, anger, disgust and sadness—based on correspondence across cultures in recognising facial expressions.) Emotions can be expressed in face, speech, or gesture. (Some authorities, such as Darwin, regarded these as the most basic aspect of emotion, more so than the experience. Others, such as James 1891, claimed that the experience followed the neurophysiological expression.)

Following this scheme, disorders of emotion can be classified into abnormal experiences, abnormal motivation and abnormal expression of emotion. Abnormal experiences can be further divided into abnormal feelings, affect or mood, and into different types (e.g. elation, anxiety, depression). Emotion in others can be misperceived or emotive topics poorly remembered, although these are not of course emotions themselves.

These disorders occur in a variety of normal, psychiatric and neurological conditions. Some such as depression are themselves the central feature of a psychiatric condition, whilst some have a link with certain sites of brain damage (e.g. impaired ability to express emotion in speech and right hemisphere damage—Tucker et al 1977).

Typical schizophrenic phenomena

The most typical schizophrenic phenomena, according to various authorities, are blunting or flattening of affect, inappropriate affect, anhedonia and apathy. Other disorders of emotion do occur but are either uncommon or nonspecific: they include heightening of feelings, depersonalisation, depression, elation, anxiety and dread.

Blunting of affect

This is a judgement by an observer that a subject shows lack of emotional expression in gesture, facial expression and tone of voice. Some authors include speech content as well (Dixon 1968), and others include inappropriate affect under the same heading. Both Abrams & Taylor (1978) and Andreasen (1979b) devised rating scales for it, the former with 16 items, the latter with 9 (unchanging facial expression, decreased spontaneous movement, paucity of expressive gestures, poor eye contact, affective nonresponsivity, inappropriate affect, lack of vocal inflections, slow speech and increased latency of response—each rated 0–4). Boeringa & Castellani (1982) showed that a single item of the SADS standardised interview (see p. 82) was as reliable as Abrams and Taylor's 16- item scale, but blunting of affect is generally regarded as harder to rate than most other typical schizophrenic phenomena (WHO 1973).

Andreasen (1979b) made a global rating of blunting in 63% of 30 schizophrenics, but also in 53% of 20 depressives. When the 9 components of her scale were looked at individually, only affective nonresponsivity (schizophrenics 30%, depressives 5%, manics 0%) and inappropriate affect (schizophrenics 20%, depressives 5%, manics 0%) characterised schizophrenia. Both items, however, were in the bottom 3 for unreliability of rating. Harris & Metcalfe (1956) found evidence of marked blunting in only 6% of 413 case notes. In the International Pilot Study of Schizophrenia, blunting was the sixth most commonly occurring item (after lack of insight, inadequate description, suspiciousness, unwillingness to co-operate, and ideas of reference). Boeringa & Castellani (1982) found that 46% of 64 schizophrenics had blunting as measured by either Taylor and Abrams' scale or the item from the SADS. Only 23% of the schizophrenics, however, had a score which distinguished them from 9 depressives, and this score did not separate them from small groups of patients with mental retardation and organic brain damage. Andreasen (1982a) included it amongst her 5 negative symptoms.

Inappropriate affect

Bleuler (1911) gave the fullest account of this. He mentioned several components—incongruity between facial expression, speech and activity; parathymia (opposite emotion expressed from that expected, e.g. laughing on hearing unpleasant news); paramimia (showing emotion on one part of the face only); and 'a different adjustment of the zero-point' (anhedonia). They are a heterogeneous collection of items and have been largely (and unfairly in my view) ignored by subsequent investigators.

Anhedonia

This term was introduced by Rado et al (1956) and Meehl (1962) and denotes a loss of the ability to feel pleasure. Physical and social anhedonia are distinguished. In the former, a wide variety of pleasures are affected (e.g. admiring the beauty of a sunset, eating, drinking, being massaged). In social anhedonia, pleasures derived from having friends or being with other people are disturbed. Meehl (1975) summed it up picturesquely: 'Some people are just born three drinks behind'.

Chapman et al (1980) devised a questionnaire covering the two types and Harrow et al (1977) rated it at interview (on a 1 to 7 scale running from 'pleasure in accordance with external events' to 'constant sadness or boredom').

Using Chapman's questionnaire Watson et al (1979) found that 45% of 312 schizophrenics fell outside the 90th percentile of alcoholic controls. In a subsequent study (Watson & Jacobs 1980) they found that social, not physical, anhedonia was characteristic: 'joys of successful achievement and pride' were lacking. Cook & Simukonda (1981), also using Chapman's questionnaire, found that only 18 of 52 schizophrenics fell outside 1 standard deviation of 106 nurses and only 4 outside 2 standard deviations. They also found that social anhedonia was responsible for this. Harrow et al (1977), using their own interview, found that chronic, but not acute, schizophrenics were significantly anhedonic. Andreasen (1982a) included 'anhedonia-asociality' amongst her 5 negative symptoms.

Apathy

This has been given various names. Kraepelin and Bleuler referred to weakening of volitional impulses, including this amongst other disturbances of will. Jaspers considered that inhibition of will and loss of will could both occur in schizophrenia. Schneider mentioned lack of drive but regarded it as nonspecific. Andreasen (1982a) included 'avolition-apathy' amongst her five negative symptoms. She rated it as present if any of the following were prominent: physical anergia, impersistence at work, or marked disregard of personal appearance. I would regard it as a disorder of the motivational component of emotion as identified by Ryle.

It is regarded as an integral part of schizophrenia by organic psychiatrists such as Crow (1980) but as an effect of institutionalisation by social psychiatrists (e.g. Wing & Brown 1970).

Nonspecific phenomena

Some schizophrenics experience an intensification of feelings in the early stages of their condition. A patient of McGhie & Chapman (1961) recalled:

> You have no idea what it's like doctor. You would have to experience it yourself. When you feel yourself going into a sort of coma you get really scared. It's like waiting on a landing craft going into D-day. You tremble and panic. It's like no other fear on earth.

Strauss & Carpenter (1981) singled out the feelings of isolation and terror that subjects experienced in these early stages. Jaspers discussed whether the development of schizophrenia promoted or degraded the creative spirit:

> Why is schizophrenia in its initial stages so often a process of cosmic, religious or metaphysical revelation? It is an extremely impressive fact: this exhibition of fine and subtle understanding, this impossible shattering piano performance, this masterly creativity [van Gogh, Hölderlin].
>
> (Jaspers 1913)

The existential psychiatrists laid great emphasis on the experience of new feelings. Loathing and nausea, for example, could, according to them, herald an episode.

Depersonalisation, the experience that a person no longer feels about things as before, is an emotion. It was discussed on page 222, as it is also an aspect of consciousness. It is nonspecific but occurs in a minority of schizophrenics.

Depressed mood is common. Knights & Hirsch (1981) found that a pathological degree of depression (PSE—neurotic depression) occurred in 70% of 27 acute Catego schizophrenics. Donlon et al (1976) found that 60% of 40 acute schizophrenics scored above the cut-off point on four items of the Hamilton scale: sleep disturbance, somatisation, apathy and observed anxiety-depression. Significant depression above the Hamilton cut-off also occurs in about one-third of remitted and chronic schizophrenics (Johnson 1981). There are several explanations for the high rate of depression. Hirsch (1982) believes that depression and schizophrenia both arise from a 'shared pathophysiological mechanism', and that the depression is 'revealed' as an integral part of schizophrenia in line with Foulds' hierarchy of psychiatric symptoms (see p. 82). Galdi (1983) believes that it is mainly neuroleptic-induced. Another suggestion is that it is reactive to the disturbing nature of the psychotic state when insight returns during the restitution of normal psychic life—postpsychotic depression (McGlashan & Carpenter 1976). It is also frequently misdiagnosed for drug-induced Parkinsonism (van Putten & May 1978) or blunted affect (McGlashan 1982).

Other disturbances of mood—ecstasy, elation, anxiety and dread—are more common in mania or atypical psychoses (Anderson 1938, Cutting et al 1978).

Subjective experience of emotional disorder

McGhie & Chapman (1961) obtained the following accounts from their patients:

> At times I can't even control what I want to think about. I am starting to feel pretty numb about everything because I am becoming an object and objects don't have feelings.
>
> I think so deep that I almost get out of this world. Then you get frightened that you are going to get into a jam and lose yourself. That's when I get worried and excited.
>
> It must look queer to people when I laugh about something that has got nothing to do with what I am talking about, but they don't know what's going on inside and how much of it is running round in my head.

One of my patients gave the following account:

> At the beginning I was suffering inwardly. I felt I was being turned inwards against reality. A sense of despair, almost amounting to terror came on. Later this was replaced by flattening . . . A woman would become a name, she would then become a symbol for all my sexual feelings. Some of these names would become overdetermined, charged with emotion. Whereas I would respond to people very flatly, the name would be very emotional.
>
> (Chronic schizophrenic)

EXPERIMENTAL EVIDENCE

There is a very small experimental literature on the expression of emotion by schizophrenics. There is considerably more on how schizophrenics perceive emotion in others or remember emotional topics, but as these are not emotions themselves they will only be summarised here, and the main evidence presented in the appropriate chapters. There are a few poorly designed experiments on the sensitivity of schizophrenics to emotive topics; as these have a bearing on the clinical observation that schizophrenics relapse more readily under conditions of high emotional expression by their families, they are worth discussing.

Expression of emotion

Gottheil et al (1976, 1979) carried out two studies on the expression of emotion in schizophrenia. In the first, 16 schizophrenics and 16 normals were asked to pose as happy, sad, fearful, surprised or angry. They were then photographed, and the photos were rated by normals, first, on the same emotions, regardless of which emotion was supposed to be portrayed, and secondly, as to whether the pose did correspond to the request. Overall, schizophrenics showed significantly less sadness and surprise, but they were as proficient as normals in making their pose correspond with the request. In the second study, 10 normals and 10 schizophrenics were filmed describing three personal experiences, which had made them either happy, sad or angry. Normal raters were significantly better at identifying the requested emotion in normals, indicating that schizophrenics expressed their feelings in a way which made it difficult for others to recognise them. Andreasen et al (1981) found a correlation between ratings of flattened affect and reduced variability and amplitude of schizophrenic speech, measured on a spectrograph. Leff & Abberton (1981) also found an association between blunted affect and a particular voice spectrograph. Brown (1981) reported that a schizophrenic's *own* subjective rating of their pleasure at some event was higher than an observer's rating of it based on their facial expression or gesture. This 'dissociation', she claimed, was not so marked in normals or depressives.

Perception and memory of emotion

Neither of these topics has been extensively studied. Most work has been done on the ability of schizophrenics to perceive emotion in the facial expression of others (see p. 295). These studies have indicated that schizophrenics are less proficient than normals at this. The perception of emotion in another person's speech (see p. 254) is also abnormal. Emotive subjects, particularly happy ones, do not appear to facilitate memory in schizophrenics as they do in normals (see p. 270). This is claimed to be evidence of anhedonic memory.

Sensitivity to emotive topics

Feffer (1961) claimed that schizophrenics were unduly sensitive to emotive words, as judged by their impaired perception of neutral words in the centre of a tachistoscopic presentation card when emotive rather than neutral words were displayed simultaneously in the periphery. On the same theme, Dixon & Lear (1962) demonstrated a lower tachistoscopic threshold than in normals or depressives for the perception of emotionally-charged words than for neutral. Dunn (1954) presented four types of pictures for one second—displaying either a scolding, whipping, feeding or neutral theme. Subjects were then shown a picture with the same theme and asked to say if it were the same or different. Chronic schizophrenics were worse than normals at recognising the scolding theme, but not the others. Turbiner (1961) showed three types of pictures in pairs, to say whether they had the same or a different theme. They had either positive (woman and child showing affection), neutral (geometrical patterns) or negative content (reprimand). Schizophrenics were worse than normals in both the emotional conditions but not the neutral. Chapman (1961) asked chronic schizophrenics to add up emotive items (e.g. If Al kisses five aunts and three cousins . . .) and neutral items (e.g. If a highway passes six barns and three houses . . .). Brodsky (1963) asked acute and chronic schizophrenics and appropriate controls to sort cards displaying neutral or aggressive themes. In both experiments schizophrenics did worse with emotive material. Feldstein (1962) noted that schizophrenic speech became more disturbed when the subject was describing emotive rather than neutral pictures, and Deering (1963) that word associations were more idiosyncratic in response to emotive words.

None of these studies is methodologically very sound, but together they suggest that schizophrenics may be oversensitive to some emotional themes. If this is so it appears to contradict the idea of anhedonia, that schizophrenics experience emotions less than normal. Vaughn & Leff's (1976) study, showing that schizophrenics are more likely to relapse if they remain in close contact with a relative who expresses a lot of emotion (see p. 178), is also against the notion of anhedonia. When one of these key relatives entered a room while a schizophrenic was having their GSR measured there was a marked increase in arousal, also indicating that the subject was experiencing emotion at this point.

CONCLUSIONS

Do schizophrenics have a disorder of emotion?

There is overwhelming evidence that some schizophrenics have an emotional disorder. Some diagnostic schemes give it more prominence than others: schizophrenics diagnosed according to Bleulerian criteria will show more than those diagnosed according to Catego, Schneiderian or RDC criteria. Some subtypes of schizophrenia have more emotional disorder than others: chronic, hebephrenic and familial types show more affective flattening than acute, paranoid or sporadic forms. (For example, Slater et al 1963 found that schizophrenia-like psychoses of epilepsy—acute, paranoid and sporadic—had less flattening of affect than nonorganically induced schizophrenia.)

What is the nature of the emotional disorder?

The characteristic disorder *is not the experience of intense feelings or mood*, although in the acute stage all feelings may be intensified and depressed mood is common. The most characteristic disorder *is a reduction in the capacity to experience and communicate emotion*. To an observer this appears as blunting or flattening of affect and on questioning subjects often report what is known as anhedonia—experiencing no pleasure, particularly in social intercourse. An additional feature, virtually confined to the chronic stage, is apathy, a state of reduced motivation, akin to the 19th century concept of impaired will. Associated with these disorders there is deficient perception of emotion in other people's speech and facial expression, and possibly a selective impairment, relative to normals, in remembering pleasurable material.

It is probable that the emotional disorder precedes the florid psychosis in some cases, as it has been identified in children of schizophrenic parents long before they eventually develop a diagnosable schizophrenic episode themselves. It may also remain as part of a personality disorder in schizoid (or schizotypal) individuals who inherit the schizophrenic genotype but never develop a psychotic episode.

It may seem paradoxical that, despite this anhedonia, some schizophrenics are unduly sensitive to interpersonal contact. They may relapse into psychosis, for example, when living with a critical and overinvolved relative. The reason for this is not clear at the present time, but there are several possible explanations. In the first place, not all schizophrenics have anhedonia and flattened affect. Most studies have found them to be present in only about half of any group of schizophrenics and in only about a quarter is it significantly more common than in groups of depressive patients. It might be therefore that only schizophrenics free of anhedonia (blunting) are sensitive to interpersonal contact. Secondly, in the early stages of schizophrenia feelings are often intensified rather than blunted and it might be that during remission schizophrenics remain in a moderately aroused state rendering them vulnerable to domestic strife, whereas the anhedonia/blunting only occurs in nonremitted cases. Thirdly, there is some evidence that anhedonia/blunting is not a universal phenomenon for all forms of environmental stimuli. The patient whose subjective account was quoted earlier noticed that, although he experienced little emotion in response to his surroundings, words would arouse more emotion even than before. It is possible therefore that anhedonia may occur with objects and events whereas undue sensitivity may occur in response to language. I shall take up this theme in the next section, as it has a possible basis in the neuropsychology of the condition.

What is the cause of the emotional disorder?

Some authorities, as discussed in the introduction, considered that emotional disorder was itself the cause of schizophrenia. Psychoanalysts, existentialists and behaviourists all offered suggestions along these lines. For them, the cause of the emotional disorder was psychic conflict, existential despair or a labile autonomic system, which then produced the entire schizophrenic picture. Most authorities, however, have regarded emotional disorder as only one aspect of schizophrenia and attributed it to some other dysfunction. To Kraepelin it was secondary to a disorder of will, to Bleuler a disorder of mental associations. More recent suggestions are a disorder of response selection (Hemsley 1977): a raised threshold for responding would appear to an observer as a blank face—flattened affect—whenever the subject was asked a question. To Alpert & Martz (1977) flattening of affect was the endpoint of a tendency to invest symbols with feelings—part of a wider semantic language deficit.

In my view, none of these proposals captures the essence of the disorder. If emotional disorder were itself the primary cause of schizophrenia, one would expect a uniform pattern in all cases, and, more important, one would expect that individuals who went through psychic conflict or existential despair or who had anxious personalities would always develop schizophrenia. None of this is the case. As for the suggestions of Kraepelin, Bleuler, Hemsley, and Alpert and Martz, they may be true but they are not specific enough to have any heuristic use.

In line with the rest of my thesis I believe that a neuropsychological explanation involving hemispheric imbalance is the most plausible explanation. The neuropsychology of emotion is still the subject of much debate but there is sufficient evidence to support my claim that right hemisphere dysfunction coupled with exaggerated left hemisphere functioning might give rise to the pattern of emotional disorder outlined in this chapter.

The main evidence for this is the large literature implicating the right rather than the left hemisphere in nearly all aspects of emotion. Normal people express emotion more intensely on the left side of the face than the right (as judged by other normals rating the intensity of emotion in photographs in which each side of the face is made into separate, composite photographs—Sackeim & Gur 1978). The right hemisphere in normals is also more proficient in perceiving the emotional expression in another face (as judged by left visual field superiority on this task—Ley & Bryden 1979). Normals have a left-ear advantage for identifying the emotional tone in spoken sentences (Bryden et al 1982) and in nonverbal stimuli (e.g. laughing, crying—Carmon & Nachson 1973). A greater right hemisphere involvement in the processing of other emotional stimuli is also evident—storage of emotional words (Suberi & McKeever 1977), associating drawings of faces with emotional labels (Landis et al 1979) and rating the intensity of the emotion in films directed to one or other hemisphere by specially constructed contact lenses (Dimond et al 1976). Investigation of brain-damaged subjects supports these findings. Right hemisphere lesions disrupt the following abilities more than do left—recall of emotional stories (Wechsler 1973), perception of mood in a tape-recorded message (Heilman et al 1975), expression of emotion in speech (Ross & Mesulam 1979), and recognition of emotion in other faces (Dekosky et al 1980) and pictures (Cicone et al 1980).

The right hemisphere cannot have a complete monopoly of emotion, because patients with left hemisphere lesions score more highly than those with right-sided on the MMPI (Black 1975), exhibit catastrophic reactions (Gainotti 1972) and are more likely to show pathological crying (Sackeim et al 1982). The respective contributions of each hemisphere have been formulated in several ways. Ley & Bryden (1981) proposed that the right hemisphere was more sensitive to emotional information, particularly negative information, and that the recorded cases of depression following left hemisphere lesions arose because the influence of the intact right hemisphere was then unimpeded. Bear (1979) suggested that the right hemisphere was mainly concerned in 'nonverbal behavioural reactions—emotive, impulsive and dispositional', whereas the left contained 'a logical, verbal representation of affect as reflected in cosmological or religious conceptualisations'. Ross & Rush (1981) agreed that both hemispheres were intimately concerned with emotion and reported cases of depression arising from damage to either hemisphere. The issue under discussion, however, is not whether right hemisphere dysfunction is responsible for all forms of emotional disorder, but whether it could account for the pattern seen in schizophrenia. (Damage to the limbic system, both temporal lobes or both frontal lobes also gives rise to emotional disorder.)

From the evidence outlined above the flattening of affect and the impaired perception and memory of emotional themes in schizophrenia are all consistent with right hemisphere dysfunction. Apathy is also more characteristic of right than left hemisphere dysfunction. Anhedonia, as discussed earlier, is a heterogeneous phenomenon, but it can occur following brain damage involving the right hemisphere. Bauer (1982) reported a man with a bilateral occipitotemporal haematoma which had produced prosopagnosia, topographical amnesia (a typical right hemisphere symptom) and what he called 'visual hypoemotionality'. This last term referred to the man's report that 'all natural scenery seemed the same', for which reason he had given up hiking, and his report that he derived no emotional reaction on seeing an attractive woman, for which reason he had cancelled his subscription to Playboy magazine. (In this case the hypoemotionality was confined to the visual modality as he derived normal emotion from listening to music or from touching delicate fabrics.) Sensitivity to the critical language of a relative and my patient's report of intensified emotions to words but not the world around him could be explained by assuming that the left hemisphere's contribution to emotion in language, following Bear's hypothesis, was exaggerated. Finally, incongruity of affect could also be accounted for in terms of hemisphere imbalance. After section of the corpus callosum Bogen (1979) noticed that there was sometimes 'a disparity between facial expression and verbalisation of emotion'. Bleuler's paramimia—showing emotion on one part of the face only—could also be a consequence of a disturbance in the right hemisphere's control of the left side of the face. It would also explain Brown's (1981) observation that a schizophrenic's own report of pleasure tended to be higher than an observer's judgement of it based on their facial expression and gesture.

SUMMARY

Emotion has a broad meaning. It covers how the significance of a perception or thought is experienced, the motivation to carry out a certain course of action and the way these interact with other mental functions. The crucial brain areas are the limbic system and its connections with frontal, parietal and temporal lobes. The right hemisphere is more concerned than the left.

Disorders of emotion include disturbances in how it is experienced (depression, elation, anxiety, anhedonia), in how it is expressed (flattening of affect), in general motivation (apathy) and in how it is perceived and remembered.

Emotional disorder is frequent in the prodromal period of schizophrenia (disturbance of drive), in the acute phase (fear, depression, numbness) and in subsequent stages (inappropriate or flattened affect). Some schizophrenics are anhedonic, in that they report a diminution of emotional experiences. There is also evidence that schizophrenics are impaired in their ability to express emotion in their face and speech, to perceive emotion in the faces and speech of others and to remember emotive material.

Some authorities have attributed the entire clinical picture to a disorder of emotion, stemming from intrapsychic conflict, existential despair or a labile autonomic nervous system. These accounts are unsatisfactory. Others, such as Kraepelin and Bleuler, have regarded a disorder of emotion as a consequence of the underlying brain disease. In this chapter I have outlined the evidence for a right hemisphere dysfunction as the chief determinant of many of the characteristic features.

11

Language

INTRODUCTION

Kraepelin and Bleuler described the unusual use of language in dementia praecox and schizophrenia but ascribed no primary importance to it. For them it was a manifestation of abnormalities in will and thought. Word association was systematically investigated by Jung (1907) in Switzerland, and Kent & Rosanoff (1910) in America, but with the object of measuring thought disorder. The neurological school of psychiatry took a special interest in language, however, because they believed that schizophrenic language resembled organic aphasia and this provided a clue to the organic basis of schizophrenia. Kleist (1914), for example, gave an account of neologisms, new words, some of which he believed were the same as the errors made by aphasics.

In the 1940s there were several attempts to measure the language disorder. The first, by Whitehorn & Zipf (1943), was a frequency analysis of different types of words (p. 61). This indicated that schizophrenics used a smaller repertoire of words. Fairbanks (1944) applied another frequency measure, the type-token ratio. This was the ratio of different words (types) to total words (tokens). A low ratio also meant that there was a smaller repertoire or functional vocabulary. She found this to be true of schizophrenia. Their language, according to her, was 'less highly differentiated in structure'. Mann (1944) came to the same conclusion using the type-token ratio and then looked at the frequency of different grammatical classes—nouns, verbs, adjectives, etc. She found that schizophrenics used fewer adjectives per noun and fewer adverbs per verb. She interpreted this to mean that schizophrenics did not adequately:

> define, modify and restrict their language in such a way as to make it more accurately representative of the actualities which they are attempting to symbolise.
>
> (Mann 1944)

It was during the 1960s, however, that schizophrenic language was first extensively studied. Inspired by Chomsky and his book *Syntactic Structures*, published in 1957, psychologists realised that language could be studied by psychological methods. Hitherto it had been regarded as the province of philosophers, linguists and neurologists. This generated a new branch of psychology, psycholinguistics, whose methods were now applied to schizophrenic language.

At first, general measures of coherence and grammatical structure were the focus of interest. Chomsky in his early work had put grammar (syntax) before meaning (semantics) and this approach was followed in the study of abnormal language. The two most widely used methods at the time were the Cloze procedure and contextual constraint. The Cloze procedure was a way of measuring readability in language, devised by Taylor (1953), a journalist. He had suggested obliterating every fifth word in a passage, and asking normal people to guess which word had been deleted. The Cloze score was then the ratio of correct guesses to the number of words deleted. A number of investigators then showed that samples of schizophrenic speech, transcribed and rated by normals in this way, had lower Cloze scores (were less predictable) than samples taken from normals. Miller & Selfridge (1950) suggested a way of assessing how normal people were influenced by the grammar of a sentence independently of its meaning. The extent to which the sentence was grammatically correct was known as the degree of contextual constraint. They asked people to remember a set of sentences which varied systematically in their grammatical correctness, regardless of semantics. For example, 'Was he went to the newspaper is in deep and' is low in contextual constraint, in other words low in approximation to English. Lawson & colleagues (1964), British psychologists, and Truscott (1970), an American psychologist, claimed that schizophrenics did not benefit from contextual constraint. Unlike normals, their memory for grammatical sentences was no better than for ungrammatical (p. 62). These investigators attributed the peculiarities of schizophrenic language to a failure in 'perceiving the organisation inherent in normal speech' (Lawson et al) or 'a lack of memory facilitation due to syntactic constraint' (Truscott). These findings were later shown to be incorrect, or at best to apply only to chronic schizophrenics (Levy & Maxwell 1968, Straube et al 1979), but at the time they were regarded as a significant contribution to the psychology of schizophrenia.

There were also attempts in the 1960s to analyse the semantic aspects of schizophrenic language. Maher et al (1966) and Gottschalk & Gleser (1969) approached this using the method of 'content analysis'. This, like the type-token ratio, also originated with the needs of journalists. A long passage of written language or transcribed speech was analysed by computer for certain themes (e.g. death, illness, religion) or references (e.g. to self, to others being unfriendly). Little of value emerged from these analyses. Another method was to study the use of metaphor. Chapman (1960) and Eliseo (1968) devised sentences with multiple choice answers, for example, 'David turned yellow when he faced the enemy, means: a) David is cowardly (metaphoric meaning), b) hungry (irrelevant distractor) or c) discoloured (literal meaning)'. Chapman found that schizophrenics did tend to select the real rather than the metaphorical alternative, whereas Eliseo did not get a significant result, and the topic attracted little further interest.

By the 1970s there were several distinct opinions on the nature of schizophrenic language. The first was the traditional opinion of Bleuler, that there was nothing intrinsically wrong with language or its translation into speech, and that the fault lay with thought disorder. Brown (1973), a linguist, gave the clearest exposition of this. He first distinguished language as being those systems that have so far been characterised in terms of rules. These rules are phonological (matching ideas with the correct sounds) and grammatical. There are some semantic rules (e.g. 'John astonished the rock' is semantically wrong), but he believed that the vast part of semantics consisted of knowledge of the world, which he did not regard as part of language. He argued that it was this knowledge of the world which was faulty in schizophrenia, and that this was best considered as thought disorder. He quoted the example of a schizophrenic who was contemplating going to Scotland from America to try for a star part in the film *Fiddler on the Roof*. His knowledge of the world was faulty, according to Brown, because he did not appreciate that Scotland was an unlikely location for shooting the film, that he was the wrong age and that the film had already been made. He suggested some rules which might be contravened in such a case, but regarded them as outside language because they had not been evaluated in normals. They were rules:

> of rationality on which we operate . . . psychological implication, principles of affective consistency, principles of attribution, common logic and evaluation of evidence. All of these seem to be efforts to describe rules we really use rather than rules we ought to use, and it seems chiefly to be the rules we use that cause propositions to be considered delusional.
>
> (Brown 1973)

LeCours & Vanier-Clément (1976), linguists, expressed this more succinctly:

> Ordinary speakers think and talk standard, most jargonaphasic speakers think standard but talk deviant, and schizophasic speakers think quaint and talk accordingly.
>
> (LeCours & Vanier-Clément 1976)

The second opinion was that the deficit was nothing to do with thought or language, but was a speech or communication disorder. Chapman et al (1977), for example, believed that 'the most likely explanation is that schizophrenics fail to screen their own potential responses for appropriateness'. Silverman (1973) found that schizophrenics tended to pause less between clauses than normals and that this correlated with a low type token ratio and low Cloze score, both measures of comprehensibility. He produced evidence from normal psycholinguistic studies that the length of a pause was related to the conciseness of a subsequent proposition, and suggested that schizophrenics were not allocating enough time to plan an utterance. Cohen

(1978) demonstrated in a series of elegant experiments that schizophrenics were poor at communicating the exact content of a message. If they were asked to indicate to a listener which of two similar words (e.g. liberty, freedom) the experimenter had asked them to pass on, the listener had great difficulty in identifying the one which had been selected (p. 70). Cohen believed that this came about because schizophrenics failed to edit their message, despite putting sufficient thought and effort into the task and despite a competent linguistic system. Rochester & Martin (1979), in a book entitled *Crazy Talk*, put forward a similar proposal. They analysed clausal structure and clausal links in schizophrenic and normal speech. They found that schizophrenics produced only simple clauses when the situation required a more complex description (e.g. describing a picture as, 'A house on a hill' instead of, as normals did, 'The red house with a pretty garden beside a mountain stream'). Schizophrenics also failed to link clauses together in a way which gave a listener a coherent story (e.g. instead of saying, 'John got a new bike but Jim got a used *one*' they would omit the last word referring back to the previous clause). These studies were a significant advance in the understanding of schizophrenic language.

A third opinion, not widely shared, was that language itself was disturbed. Chaika (1974) advocated this most strongly in a paper entitled *A linguist looks at schizophrenic language*. She claimed that there were six characteristics (see p. 69), for example:

> . . . the production of sentences according to phonological and semantic features of previously uttered words rather than to a topic . . . e.g. All buzzards can coo. I like to see buzzards pronounced right. They work hard. So do parakeets.
>
> (Chaika 1974)

Her paper provoked considerable discussion amongst linguists. Fromkin (1975) claimed that all six characteristics could be found in normals and Lecours &Vanier-Clément (1976) claimed that all but one of these—a preoccupation with semantic features of a word—could be found in patients with Wernicke's aphasia. It also inspired a number of studies comparing aphasics with schizophrenics (e.g. Gerver et al 1976).

The theme of this chapter is the debate between these schools of thought. Are the peculiar things schizophrenics say the expression of abnormal thought? abnormal speech? or abnormal language?

CLINICAL CONSIDERATIONS

General disorders of language

> A natural language is based on a system of rules. The system of rules is the grammar of the language. The function of the grammar of a language is to enable us to map meanings onto sequences of sounds or to put what we think into words. Grammar is the essential link in communication between meaning and sound or meaning and symbol . . . Once meaning has been mapped onto

> a sentence that sentence has some semantic interpretation. It says something . . . When meaning is made manifest in language it may be said to be semantics.'
>
> (Deese 1970)

Language has these three basic components—sounds (phonemes), grammar (syntax) and meaning (semantics). Phonemes have inherent distinctive features which give them their uniqueness (e.g. 'p' rather than 'b'). They also have a prosodic quality (pitch, rhythm and stress) which allows emotion to be expressed or perceived in language. A fourth component, pragmatics, has recently been suggested. This is a subdivision of meaning whereby the intended meaning of something (pragmatics) is separated from its formal meaning (semantics). For example, the sentence, 'This room is very cold' has one formal meaning but several possible intended meanings (e.g. statement of fact, a hopeful request for someone to close the window or a promise to bring round an electric fire, etc.). I believe that the separation of the semantic and pragmatic aspects of meaning is of considerable importance in understanding schizophrenic language, whose peculiarities are pragmatic in nature rather than semantic. This theme will be developed in the chapter.

Disorders of the phonemic, syntactic and semantic aspects of language are generally referred to as aphasia and result from lesions to the 'language areas' of the left hemisphere. There are other types of language disorder variously referred to as 'nonaphasic disorders of speech' (Geschwind 1964) or 'neurogenic communication problems' (Halpern et al 1973). These, too, affect the sound, grammar and meaning of language but not in the same way as in classical aphasia.

Whereas the phonemic abnormalities in aphasia are of the inherent quality of distinctive features leading to phonetic disintegration, in nonaphasic disorders the prosodic quality is generally disrupted. An inability to convey or comprehend emotion—aprosody (Ross 1981)—and a speeding up of speech—logorrhoea (Frey & Hambert 1972)—are examples of phonemic, nonaphasic disorders and are common with right hemisphere lesions.

A disturbance of syntax, agrammatism, is characteristic of aphasia from anterior left hemisphere lesions, and is rare in other conditions. (Exceptions are incoherence in some schizophrenics, ungrammatical sentences in some manics, Durbin & Martin 1977, and hypnagogic states and sleep-talking, e.g. 'And find that all with syphilis is immediately', Froeschels 1946.)

A disturbance of formal meaning is characteristic of posterior aphasia, but can occur in other conditions. The aphasic form is illustrated by one of Brown's (1977) patients, a doctor, who when asked if he were a doctor replied, 'Me. Yes sir. I'm a male demaploze on my own. I still know my tubaboys'. Nonaphasic disorders of meaning have been given various names: neologisms and nonaphasic misnaming (Weinstein & Kahn 1952) are the most widely used. In both cases, the implication is that new words are invented or old words wrongly applied for reasons other than a breakdown in formal semantic competence. Weinstein and Kahn described patients with generalised or right hemisphere brain damage who would misname objects, persons or places connected with their illness, in order, as the authors claimed, to express their feelings on the matter (e.g. Dr Wiseman for Dr Weinstein).

A disorder of the intended meaning of language with preservation of the formal aspects is not characteristic of aphasia. By contrast most neologisms and Weinstein and Kahn's nonaphasic misnaming do affect the intended meaning rather than the formal meaning of language. This is also true of a number of other examples of peculiar language or a loss of richness in conversation reported in various psychiatric and neurological conditions. Tow (1955) noted that patients after frontal leucotomy were 'pedantic . . . introspective . . . used unnecessary punctuation . . . used alliteration . . . and were lazy'. One patient defined a lecture as, 'a talk generally given by doctors to enable other men to get on in the world'. Tow regarded this definition as 'off centre'. Petrie (1952) wrote about postleucotomy language being 'out of focus . . . hitting the periphery . . . and emanating from a decreased critical attitude'. Both authors noted the resemblance between this and the utterance of schizophrenics. In dementia, Stengel (1964) noted 'improvisation . . . disregard of language as communication . . . use of clichés . . . not finishing sentences'. Obler (1981), reviewing a book by Irigary (1973) *Le Langage des Dements*, regarded most of the abnormalities such as muteness, perseveration, echolalia and empty speech as evidence of a disordered pragmatic component. In right hemisphere lesions, Eisenson (1961) drew attention to an 'impairment in the richness and depth of concepts . . . and a difficulty in adjusting to the linguistic formulations of another person'. Critchley (1962b) reported that creative literary work was affected in professional writers who had suffered right hemisphere lesions. Winner & Gardner (1977) noted an impairment in the appreciation of metaphor with right hemisphere damage. In one patient with congenital absence of the corpus callosum, Dennis (1981) found an impairment in pragmatic language. Her patient was poor in judging the intended meaning of certain verb phrases. For example, given the sentence, 'Jill managed to win the race', the patient found it difficult to decide if Jill had won the race or not. Presented with the sentence, 'Jim knows that the dinner is ready', the patient could not decide if dinner was ready or not.

I believe that these nonaphasic disorders of language, particularly those involving prosody and pragmatics, closely resemble the peculiarities of schizophrenic language.

Typical schizophrenic phenomena

Andreasen (1979a) believed that peculiarities in language in schizophrenia could arise from either abnormal thought, speech *or* language. She collected all the terms ever used to refer to these peculiarities and called them 'thought, language and communication disorders'. She narrowed them

Table 11.1 Andreasen's 18 thought, language and communication disorders

1. Poverty of speech (poverty of thought)	Restriction in amount of spontaneous speech
2. Poverty of content of speech (poverty of thought, empty speech)	Speech is adequate in length, but conveys little information
3. Pressure of speech	Increase in amount of spontaneous speech
4. Distractible speech	Repeatedly stopping during speech in response to nearby stimulus
5. Tangentiality	Replying to a question in an oblique, irrelevant manner
6. Derailment (loose association, flight of ideas)	Spontaneous speech in which ideas slip off track on to another that is nearly related
7. Incoherence (word salad, schizophasia)	Incomprehensible speech
8. Illogicality	Conclusions reached that do not follow logically
9. Clanging	Sounds rather than meanings govern word choice
10. Neologisms	New word formation
11. Word approximations (paraphasia, metonym)	Old words used in new, unconventional manner
12. Circumstantiality	Speech which is indirect and long-winded in reaching its goal
13. Loss of goal	Failure to follow a chain of thought to its conclusion
14. Perseveration	Persistent repetition of words, ideas or subjects
15. Echolalia	Echoing of interviewer's words
16. Blocking	Interruption of a train of speech
17. Stilted speech	Excessively formal and pompous speech
18. Self-reference	Continual return to talking about oneself

down to 18 mutually exclusive terms and then defined them. They are shown in Table 11.1. Some of them need no further explanation, but poverty of content of speech, tangentiality, derailment, incoherence, illogicality and neologisms do require illustration.

Poverty of content of speech is difficult to rate, but is recognised by loss of richness, circumlocution and general 'padding'. This example is taken from Andreasen's article. The patient was asked what sort of person he was:

> Ah one hell of an odd thing to say perhaps in these particular circumstances. I happen to be quite pleased with who I am or how I am and many of the problems that I have and have been working on are difficult for me to handle or to work on because I am not aware of them as problems which upset me personally.
>
> (Andreasen 1979a)

Tangentiality and *derailment* are Andreasen's terms for what most authorities regard as the most typical characteristic of schizophrenic language. In Andreasen's scheme derailment and tangentiality have the same form, but she uses the former term if the abnormality is evident in spontaneous speech, and the latter if it appears in response to a question. The term derailment is apt, because it suggests a train gradually slipping off the rails with the rear carriages becoming more and more displaced from the line of the engine. Knight's move thinking and loosening of ideas are other metaphors for the same phenomenon. The following answer by a patient of mine when asked how things were at home illustrates this:

> What I'm saying is my mother is too ill. No money. It all comes out of her pocket. My flat's leaking. It's ruined my mattress. It's Lambeth Council. I'd like to know what the caption in the motto under their coat of arms is. It's in Latin. It must mean that you've got semen in you, the spunk to do something. The other thing I'm telling you is my birth certificate. Do you remember when I was in that hospital; I was on my knees. Well I was frightened of those nurses. Well they were stealing. Well I burnt all my papers. Look at this now. It is a coin, from Jersey. That's where all the criminals go, Jersey. I'm telling you all this because my wife wants British nationality.
>
> (Chronic schizophrenic)

Incoherence is by definition difficult to transcribe other than phonetically because there is loss of grammar as well as meaning. The following is an unpunctuated answer by a young woman when asked how she was feeling:

> Yes I mean er I mean are you from London I mean do you like London particular of London I think that London is wild buses wild buses in London and wild trains underground is wild in London bus I mean it is Lebanon bus of London and Lebanon train of London so we are the chancellor if it is the underground.
>
> (Acute schizophrenic)

Illogicality is more obviously a disorder of thought and will be considered in detail on page 313. The following brief examples give some idea of its nature:

> I lost my head and mind and eyes. Once my eyes were like fishes' eyes, then I lost them and I found them again and I was all right.
>
> (Chronic schizophrenic)
>
> (How long have you been in this hospital?) 29 years. (What is the matter with you?) Pneumonia. (That's a long time to have had pneumonia?) I caught it from a thermometer at Guy's Hospital. The thermometer said that everyone of the age of 20 would get either 'flu or pneumonia and I got pneumonia. (In my view thermometers only measure temperature. They don't actually specify what illnesses people have.) Well you better go back and look up your medical books. (Chronic schizophrenic)

Neologisms are invented words which do not exist in the dictionary. The following examples are taken from patients under my care:

'When I get the *sticks* I can't think' (chronic schizophrenic, sticks = hallucinations).

'My *sidevoices* are bad today' (acute schizophrenic, sidevoices = hallucinations).

'What I want to tell you is *compliateaeconyts*' (acute schizophrenic, who explained that the word meant, 'I sympathise with all the people laughing at me').

'I have been studying *recepts*. They are sense impressions, contemplations of society, types of plutarchy, capitalism, gynarchy, kakistocracy' (acute schizophrenic whose neologism covered various sorts of government).

Various classifications of neologisms exist, all rather arbitrary. Kleist (1914) distinguished three sorts of true neologisms: those which resembled the paraphasic errors of aphasics, those which were an attempt to express some delusional experience (e.g. compliateaeconyts above) and those which were a repetition of an auditory hallucination. Carl Schneider (1930) classified them according to their grammatical form (e.g. those with suffixes—*camerist* for someone who goes in front of a camera). Vetter (1969) distinguished between true neologisms (entirely new words) and other inventions—portmanteau words (e.g. 'cageweather juice'), a change in grammatical class (e.g. 'real-estated') and words made to sound foreign (e.g. 'thiefus' for thief). Forrest (1969) listed 20 types, all of which he claimed corresponded to the way new words appeared in normal language (e.g. use of proper names, as in sandwich from the Earl of Sandwich's habit of snatching a quick meal in between his gambling sessions).

Clinical significance of language phenomena

Andreasen (1979a) assessed the frequency and discriminating power of each of her 18 phenomena in manics, depressives and schizophrenics. Some (clanging, neologisms, word approximations, echolalia, stilted speech, blocking, circumstantiality and distractible speech) did not appear or were very infrequent in schizophrenics. Most of the others, although frequent (derailment 56%, loss of goal 44%, tangentiality 36%, illogicality 27%), did not distinguish schizophrenics from manics. Only poverty of content of speech (40% schizophrenics, 19% manics) did so in association with distractibility (2% schizophrenics, 31% manics) and pressure of speech (27% schizophrenics, 72% manics).

Diagnostic schemes vary in how much weight they give to these phenomena. For example, Spitzer's recognises only five readily identifiable, non-mutually exclusive forms of disturbance of speech which in certain contexts strongly suggest schizophrenia—incoherence, loosening of associations (Andreasen's derailment and tangentiality), illogical thinking, poverty of content of speech and delusions involving von Domarus's principle (a special type of illogicality, see p. 329). Catego gives no weight to them, whereas the New Haven Index gives the most weight.

Some psychiatrists distinguished subtypes of schizophrenia on the basis of prominent language disorder—schizophasia (Kleist 1928) and circumstantial schizophrenia (Peck 1962). Many psychologists (e.g. Rochester & Martin 1979) distinguish between clinically thought disordered and non-thought disordered schizophrenics, but there is no real evidence that the distinction is superior to the paranoid-hebephrenic one (p. 98).

Subjective experience of abnormal appreciation of language

McGhie & Chapman (1961) gave several examples of a subjective awareness of language disorder:

> When people are talking I have to think what the words mean.
>
> When people are talking I just get scraps of it.
>
> When people are talking the words are going on and on and I don't understand them.
>
> (McGhie & Chapman 1961)

A difficulty in understanding language emerged as one of eight subjective experiences which distinguished schizophrenics from nonschizophrenics (Freedman & Chapman 1973). A loss of the meaning of words, confusion of their literal and figurative meanings and recurrent intrusions of meaningless words into mind and speech were common in Freedman's (1974) survey of autobiographical accounts. Awareness of language disorder was one of the few characteristic features of the early experiences of schizophrenia in my study (p. 181). The following accounts illustrate this:

> I used to get the sudden thing that I couldn't understand what people said. Like it was a foreign language. My mind went blank.
>
> (Remitted schizophrenic)
>
> I thought my language was wrong. I believed that no-one could understand what I said. I couldn't understand what I said. Just high-pitched noises came. I could understand other people's language, not mine.
>
> (Remitted schizophrenic)

EXPERIMENTAL EVIDENCE

General abnormalities

Some investigators have merely attempted to measure the abnormality in schizophrenic language, either to test some general theory of schizophrenia (e.g. attentional deficit, Salzinger's immediacy hypothesis, p. 62) or to compare schizophrenics with another group of abnormal subjects (e.g. typical aphasics).

The most widely used measure has been the Cloze technique. The standard procedure is to take a transcript of schizophrenic speech, delete every fourth or fifth word and ask a normal person to guess the deletions. The Cloze score is the proportion of correct guesses, and the lower the score the more abnormal or unpredictable is the speech. Salzinger et al (1964) reported that segments of schizophrenic speech were more unpredictable than segments of normal speech. Rutter et al (1975) confirmed this if the deletions were every fifth word, but not if they were every fourth. Manschreck et al (1979) also confirmed this, but only for clinically thought-disordered (Spitzer criteria, p. 251) subjects. A variation of the technique is to ask schizophrenics themselves to guess the deletions in speech transcripts of other schizophrenics or normals. Under these circumstances schizophrenics are considerably worse than normals (Rutter et al 1975, de Silva & Hemsley 1977).

Other measures of predictability give similar results. Rutter (1979) obtained 10 consecutive sentences from the speech of schizophrenics and normals, and then gave them to normal raters in jumbled order. The raters found it harder to reconstruct correct sequences of 3 or more sentences from the schizophrenic samples than from the normal.

Silverman (1973), Rutter (1977) and Clemmer (1980) looked for an abnormality in the time spent in pauses. Silverman found that schizophrenics spent less time pausing than normals, Rutter that there was no difference, and Clemmer that schizophrenics paused more. The issue is clearly unresolved.

The Zipf curve (p. 61) and the type-token ratio (p. 243) are both measures of the diversity of language: whether subjects use a wide vocabulary or not. There is some disagreement on this issue. Whitehorn & Zipf (1943), Silverman (1973) and Manschreck et al (1981b) demonstrated a smaller repertoire of words in schizophrenia. Feldstein & Jaffe (1962), however, found no difference between schizophrenics and normals, and Pavy et al (1969) found that a restricted repertoire was confined to chronic schizophrenics.

Several investigators have given language tests taken from aphasia batteries, or looked for similarities between schizophrenia and aphasia. Chaika (1974, p. 69) studied one patient intensively, and concluded that this patient did resemble jargon aphasics in showing phonemic, syntactic and semantic abnormalities. (Fromkin 1975 and Lecours & Vanier-Clément 1976 disagreed on theoretical grounds, but produced no new evidence of their own.) Gerson et al (1977) compared the speech of schizophrenics with that of 'posterior aphasics' on a number of dimensions (e.g. fluency, awareness of communication problem, word finding problem) and found marked differences. Strohner et al (1978) compared the number of semantic and acoustic errors produced by Broca's aphasics, Wernicke's aphasics and chronic schizophrenics on a sound–picture matching task. There were no significant differences on this single task. Faber & Reichstein (1981) gave eight subtests of the Boston aphasia scale, the token test and the Peabody picture vocabulary to thought-disordered and nonthought-disordered schizophrenics, manics and depressives. Only thought-disordered schizophrenics were impaired relative to the affective groups, and only on 2 of the 10 tests—phrase repetition and token test. Silverberg-Shalev et al (1981) gave acute, subacute and chronic schizophrenics 42 neuropsychological tests, including 6 language tests (mainly naming different types of things). Chronic schizophrenics were only significantly impaired relative to normal controls on 7 of these, including all 6 language tests. Acute and subacute patients were relatively normal.

In summary, schizophrenic speech is less predictable than that of normals and schizophrenics have difficulty in predicting the speech of others. It is not clear if they use a smaller repertoire of words or pause in an unusual fashion. Differences from aphasics are more striking than any similarity, although chronic schizophrenics do perform badly on some of the tests designed to be sensitive to aphasia.

Phonemic abnormalities

There are some reports that schizophrenics misperceive words (Moon et al 1968, Bull & Venables 1974, Mefferd 1979) and tones (Gruzelier & Hammond 1979), implying that their perception of the inherent quality of phonemes is faulty. It is doubtful if this plays a significant part in any language disorder. Silverstein & Harrow (1980), for example, found no difference in the number of unusual associations when words were presented aurally rather than visually.

There is more evidence that the ability to perceive the prosodic quality of speech is impaired. A group of Russian investigators (Bazhin et al 1978) reported that paranoid (but not nonparanoid) schizophrenics were poor judges of whether a sentence was spoken in a fearful, anxious, apathetic or elated mood. Turner (1964) instructed a professional actor to read out 36 nonsense sentences in an emotive fashion and then asked 6 different people to read them in a neutral fashion. Schizophrenics and normals listened to these and then pointed to 1 of 6 cards (sad, happy, angry, surprised, frightened, neutral) in the case of the emotive sentences and nominated 1 of the 6 people in the case of the neutral sentences. The two groups were equally proficient in identifying the speaker of a neutral sentence but schizophrenics, particularly paranoid subjects, were significantly inferior in recognising the intended emotion. Jonsson & Sjöstedt (1973) asked acute schizophrenics and neurotics to identify three types of intonation (friendly, threatening, neutral) in spoken words. They were then tested for perception of duration, loudness and pitch. Schizophrenics were significantly worse on all four measures, but the deficit in intonation perception still remained significant when the other three were taken into account.

Prosodic expression is also abnormal. Todt & Howell (1980) found that normal raters could reliably distinguish taped schizophrenic speech from that of other types of patients, and that the critical cues were less inflection and poor enunciation. Leff & Abberton (1981) analysed voice pitch using a microphone over the throat. Schizophrenics with blunted affect had a characteristic pattern.

The only other reported phonemic abnormality is Chaika's (1974) claim (see p. 69) that her schizophrenic had:

> sporadic disruption in the ability to match semantic features with sound strings . . . inappropriate noting of phonological features of words . . . and the production of sentences according to phonological features of previously uttered words.

This claim is disputed by other linguists.

In summary, phonemic abnormalities are not marked in schizophrenic speech, but there is some experimental evidence of a change in the perception or expression of the prosodic quality of phonemes.

Syntactic abnormalities

There have been two main approaches to this problem. First, the relative frequency of different grammatical classes (noun, verb, adjective, etc.) has been examined in spontaneous speech. Secondly, perception or memory for sentences differing in grammatical complexity has been studied.

Fairbanks (1944), Mann (1944), Lorenz & Cobb (1954), Giliarovsky (1957), Pylyshyn (1970) and myself (Cutting & Ryan 1982) all looked for any change in the distribution of the main grammatical classes. Taking all these studies together, there is no real evidence of an abnormal or characteristic pattern. In my study, for example, there was a nonsignificant excess of adjectives at the expense of nouns in acute schizophrenics compared with depressives and normals. Only the Russian study of Giliarovsky lent any support to this.

The other approach, looking for a failure to appreciate (remember or understand) grammatical complexity, has also proved sterile. Most of the experiments are reported under the heading of *contextual constraint*. This has already been discussed (p. 62). Chronic schizophrenics, it was claimed, did not show the same memory superiority as normals for grammatically correct (e.g. The boy ran across the road) as opposed to grammatically anomalous sentences (e.g. The boy across the ran road). Lawson et al (1964), Truscott (1970) and Gerver (1967) all reported this finding. Later investigators, in better designed experiments (Levy & Maxwell 1968, Raeburn & Tony 1968, Straube et al 1979), failed to confirm it.

Several related approaches have been tried. One is known as the click test (Fodor & Bever 1965). If, while a sentence is read out, a tone is sounded at some point in the sentence, normal subjects subsequently report it closer to syntactical (clausal) boundaries than it actually occurred. Carpenter (1976) and Andreasen (1982b) found the same effect in schizophrenics, another indication that their ability to manipulate syntax was normal. Another approach has been to give a series of increasingly complex sentences (e.g. It is true that the dots are red. It is not true that the dots are blue). This is then followed by a picture showing dots of a particular colour, and the subject has to judge the truth of the statement. Neufeld (1978) found that schizophrenics could answer the more complex sentences, although they took longer than normals. In yet another approach, Miller & Phelan (1980) presented sentences which violated syntactic rules (e.g. The stone thought it could climb the stairs). Subjects had to decide if the sentences were acceptable or not. Schizophrenics were no different from normals in this, and although some of the anomalies were semantic rather than syntactic, this was yet more evidence for an intact syntactic component. In a final approach, Rausch et al (1980) gave 20 sentences with 10 different levels of complexity (e.g. simple declarative, passive embedded). They were presented in scrambled order and the subject had to order them correctly. Schizophrenics were as quick as normals and only made errors on 1 of the 10 grammatical types.

In summary, a considereable amount of ingenuity has gone into testing the syntactic component in schizophrenic speech. With the exception of a small minority of chronic or incoherent patients, one can say with confidence that syntax in schizophrenics is intact.

Semantic abnormalities

There are a large number of studies inquiring into the integrity of the semantic component. The commonest approach has been to look for a consistent underuse or overuse of one class of words (e.g. abstract, figurative, superordinate). Some investigators have been more concerned with how the content of speech reflects the dominant themes of thought. Others, particularly the Chapmans (see p. 46), have used language experiments as a means of testing general cognitive theories of schizophrenia.

The first issue is whether schizophrenics are impaired in their general understanding of the meaning of sentences. The best procedure is known as the gist test (Bransford & Franks 1971). Subjects are presented with sentences containing one idea (e.g. The ants are in the kitchen), two ideas (e.g. The ants in the kitchen came from under the sink) or three ideas (e.g. The ants in the kitchen ate the jelly on the table). Later, they are given sentences containing four ideas (e.g. The ants in the kitchen came from under the sink and ate the jelly on the table), and are asked if they have heard this last type before. Normals typically report that they *have* heard the four-idea sentences. Andreasen (1982b) found the same pattern in schizophrenics, indicating that they too had understood the gist of the series. Knight & Sims-Knight (1979) also showed that this held for acute schizophrenics in a similar experiment.

The next issue is whether words carry the same associations in schizophrenics as in normals. This has been extensively investigated by means of word association studies, beginning with Jung (1907) and Kent & Rosanoff (1910). Most subsequent studies have shown a small increase in idiosyncratic responses, but when compared with appropriate controls (depressives, Murphy 1923, institutionalised tuberculosis patients, O'Brian & Weingartner 1970) the differences have been nonsignificant. In an unpublished study of my own (Fig. 11.1), using 50 of the Kent-Rosanoff words, idiosyncratic responses were more common in thought-disordered schizophrenics (Andreasen's scale, p. 249) but not nonthought-disordered schizophrenics. Responses were deemed idiosyncratic if they were not amongst the 90% most common responses in the student norms published by Jenkins (1970).

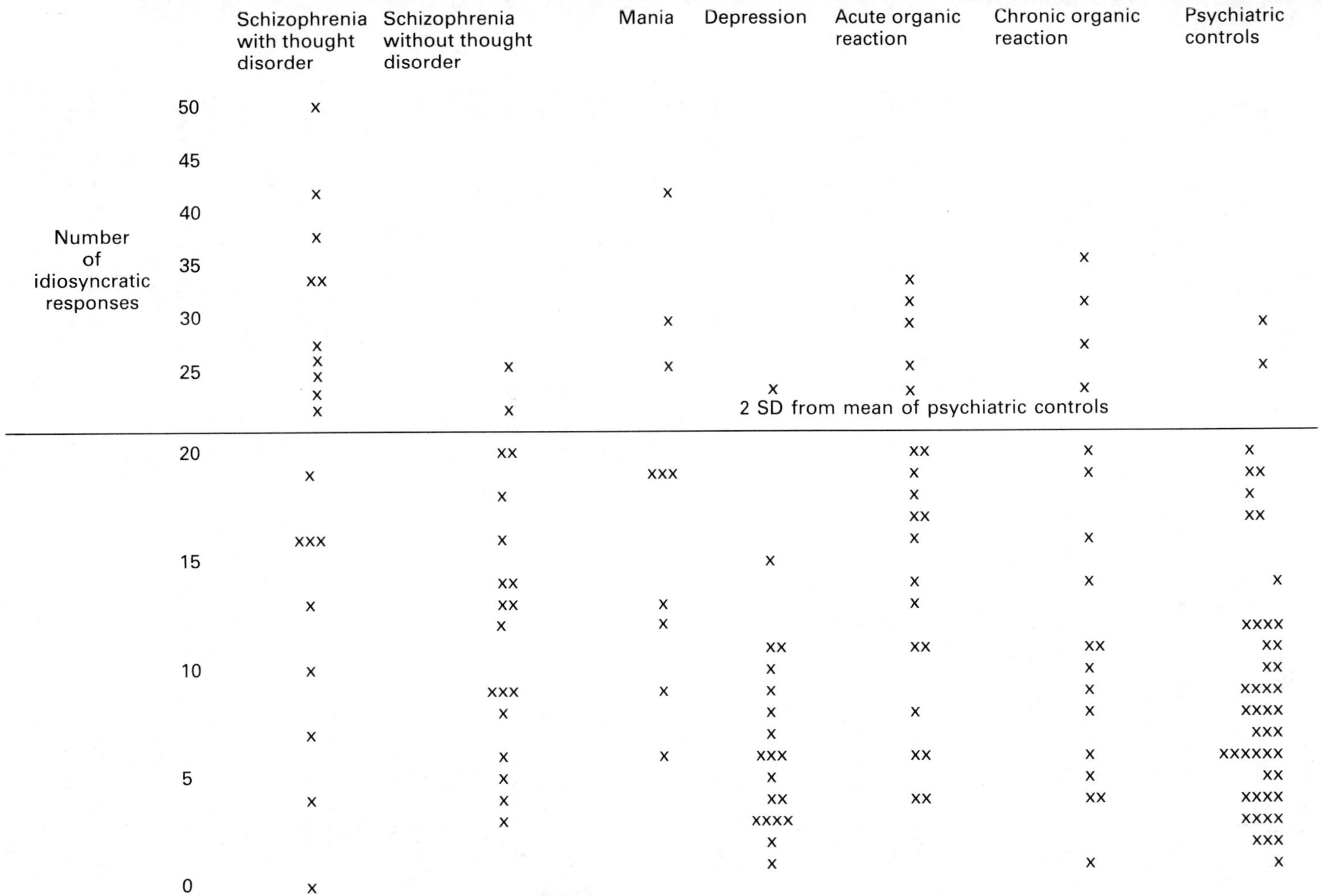

Fig. 11.1 Plot of the number of idiosyncratic responses in every patient

The third issue is whether schizophrenics use certain classes of words more or less than other people. It has been claimed that they are more likely to select the following classes of words in a multiple choice task—concrete rather than abstract (Rabin et al 1955, Milgram 1959), literal rather than figurative (Chapman 1960), homonym rather than synonym (Hogben & Jacobs 1972), and primary or dominant rather than secondary meaning (e.g. staff as group of people rather than stick) despite contextual cues suggesting the secondary meaning (Chapman 1958). None of these claims is well supported, as in each case there are several reports to the contrary.

In the case of concreteness (the most extensively investigated claim) although schizophrenics are less likely to choose an abstract alternative, this is because they tend to make more errors on any cognitive task and are not specifically liable to select concrete rather than other types of words (Chodorkoff & Mussen 1952, Benjamin & Watt 1969). In a different approach to the issue, I studied the imagery value (one aspect of concreteness) of the words produced in a verbal fluency task (Cutting & Ryan 1982). Acute schizophrenics were more likely to give words *low* in imagery (*more* abstract) than controls, though not significantly so.

The next most investigated claim is that of Chapman (Chapman 1958, Chapman et al 1977) that schizophrenics are biased towards selecting the dominant (most common) meaning of a word, regardless of context. Neither Neuringer et al (1969), Blaney (1974) nor Miller (1974) could replicate these findings; Williams et al (1976) found that it only affected chronic schizophrenics; and Kritskaia (1971), a Russian investigator, found the reverse: that schizophrenics tended to choose improbable words regardless of context (e.g. Under the tree lay a raft, rather than, Under the tree lay a fruit).

The final issue is whether certain themes rather than classes of words appear more frequently than normal. The main studies of what is called *content analysis* were carried out by Gottschalk & Gleser (1964), Laffal (1965) and Maher et al (1966). The usual procedure is to take a written or transcribed speech segment and classify the words into a number of categories. Gottschalk and Gleser chose nine in their 1964 article (self unfriendly to others, others unfriendly to self, unsure, denial of feelings, bizarre statements, inaudible words, questions to interviewer, references to religion, and others avoiding self). It is apparent that this is a heterogeneous collection of items covering emotion, beliefs, preoccupations and verbal behaviour. Later (Gottschalk & Gleser 1969) they increased the number of categories to 83, and tried to identify a characteristic pattern. Laffal had 114 categories which he applied to the autobiography of Freud's patient, Schreber. Maher et al collected 53 documents from 50 schizophrenics and subjected them to a computer programme called The General Inquirer, originally developed for classifying themes in newspaper articles. As one might expect from such wide ranging examinations, there were some significant findings (more self-reference, more incoherent statements, preoccupation with others being unfriendly), but these are predictable from the common sorts of delusions and the inclusion of the occasional patient with clinical thought disorder. Subsequent investigations of this topic have contributed little. 'Self immersion' and 'inability to follow own train of thought' emerged in a study by Reilly et al (1973); frequent reference to death, medical themes and cognitive processes, and infrequent reference to pleasant interpersonal connections were evident in a General Inquirer analysis by Rosenberg & Tucker (1979); 'social alienation and personal disorganisation' were the dominant themes in a study by Angermeyer & Timpe (1980).

In summary, the semantic component of schizophrenic language is not obviously deranged in the large majority of patients. (This statement requires some qualification. It may not apply to some patients with neologisms, including Chaika's patient who was 'preoccupied with too many of the semantic features of a word . . . had sporadic disruption in the ability to match semantic features with sound strings . . . and produced sentences according to . . . semantic features of previously uttered words'. It may not apply to some chronic schizophrenics, but phonemic and syntactic abnormalities have been reported in them as well, and the presence of brain damage may render them atypical. It is only true if the semantic component is defined strictly, and not if it covers pragmatic language and thought content.)

Pragmatic abnormalities

Searle, in his book *Speech Acts* (1969), alerted linguists to the importance of the pragmatic aspect of language. Searle believed that 'speech acts, not sentences . . . are the basic or minimal units of linguistic communication'. Two important types of speech acts, according to him, were: illocutionary—communicating information about oneself (e.g. stating, requesting, promising), and perlocutionary—trying to influence others (e.g. warning, persuading). The intended meaning of these was usually ambiguous in everyday discourse and could only be understood from the context. For example, the question, 'Has everyone had enough?' could have been asked to draw attention to a scanty helping of dinner. The term pragmatics had been used intermittently throughout the century by philosophers (e.g. Carnap 1964) and linguists, but it was not until the late 1970s that it was officially adopted as the fourth component of language. It covers more than just the ambiguity of illocutionary acts. It includes the need to relate new information to old. (For example, the question, 'Did John go to Oxford or did he fail his exam?' presupposes prior knowledge about John by the listener.) It assumes that there are rules of conversation. (For example, the request, 'You must have some of this cake' can be followed at a party by, 'I don't mind if I do' but not, 'Must I', except in jest.) It also embraces what is known as deixis, a linguistic device which anchors the utterance to the context in person, place or time. Failure of deixis is a frequent basis for jokes. (For example, 'I hate to think of life at 40', 'Why what happened then?' relies for its humour on misunderstanding temporal deixis.)

Many of the terms used to describe schizophrenic language point to a derangement in the pragmatic function of language: failure to benefit from contextual constraint, unpredictability (using the Cloze technique), 'failure to use the context to judge the appropriateness of the interpretation' (Chapman et al 1977) and 'referent communication disturbances' (Cohen 1978). The main evidence for a disorder of pragmatics comes from four sources.

First, when meaning as well as grammar was systematically varied in the standard procedures such as the Cloze technique it became apparent that schizophrenics were only impaired under the semantic conditions. They could guess the correct grammatical form of a word but not its meaning. Blaney (1974), for example, gave Chapman's lexical ambiguity test (p. 244) and the Cloze technique to chronic schizophrenics, depressives and normals. He designed two versions of each of these—semantic and grammatical. For instance, 'The farmer led his sheep to the pen ? writing instrument ? enclosed space?' was semantically ambiguous. 'The package was left by the man in the green sweater not by the boy' was grammatically ambiguous. In the Cloze technique subjects either had to guess the exact word (semantic form) or only the grammatical form of the deletions. Blaney found that the schizophrenics were only significantly worse on the two semantic versions. This indicated that they were only impaired when required to derive the intended meaning from context. The word-in-context test (Werner & Kaplan 1963, Salmon et al 1967), where subjects have to guess the meaning of a rare word in context (e.g. The painter used a *corplum* to mix his paints) is also poorly carried out by schizophrenics.

The second piece of evidence comes from the studies of Cohen (1978), fully described on page 70. The essential finding is that schizophrenics fail to give an adequate enough description of two similar things (related words or similar colours) for someone listening to select the intended item. Smith (1970) conducted a similar experiment with the same results.

Thirdly, there is the work of Rochester (Rochester 1978, Rochester & Martin 1979), described earlier (p. 69). Here, the main finding was inadequate cohesion between clauses, so that anyone listening found it difficult to follow what was being referred to. A subsidiary finding was the failure to produce more complex nominal groupings when the task demanded it: patients would say, 'The house is on the hill', instead of, 'The green house with the blue curtains and pretty roof is on the hill'.

Finally, most linguists have concluded that schizophrenic language is not formally disturbed, and most investigators of its content have found that irrelevance rather than incompetence is the most characteristic feature. For example, Brown (1973) suggested that what is abnormal is 'knowledge of the world . . . psychological implication . . . affective consistency . . . principles of attribution . . . and poor evaluation of evidence'. Cohen et al (1976) found that in a verbal fluency task (naming as many yellow things as possible in five minutes) schizophrenics gave acceptable but not entirely adequate responses (e.g. blouse). The same tendency was emphasised by Gerver et al (1976) in proverb interpretation, and by di Simoni et al (1977) in the scores on an aphasia test battery.

CONCLUSIONS

Is there a language disorder in schizophrenia?

Language use in schizophrenia is often peculiar but, depending on one's definition of language, this could be due to a disturbance in other functions. If one defines language in a way which includes the intended meaning of speech as well as its formal meaning, grammar and sounds, then language is disordered in a significant proportion of schizophrenics.

What is the nature of the language disorder?

The most outstanding feature of schizophrenics' language is a reduced ability to convey their intended meaning. This has come to be known as a disorder of the pragmatic function of language. The other abnormal feature is an impairment in expressing and perceiving the prosodic quality of sounds. The inherent quality of phonemes, grammar and formal meaning of language are generally unaffected.

The pragmatic disorder, as presented here, has been referred to in a number of ways, but most of the differences can be attributed to alternative definitions of language or differing theoretical orientations.

Bär (1976) preferred the term, 'semantic dissociation . . . loosening of ties which link a sign to its referential and emotive infrastructure'. The mildest form of this was 'semantic fluctuation', in which the range of signs could be larger or smaller than normal, e.g. An artist is someone who expresses feelings (restricted) or, All medicines are purges (overextended). Another was 'semantic distortion', where new signs were fabricated or borrowed from those which previously signified something else, e.g. gruesor from gruesome, water now meaning poison. Bär was using the term semantic in a wider sense than usual, encroaching on what is regarded here as the pragmatic component of language. Chaika's claim (p. 69) that there are semantic, grammatical and phonemic disorders can also be criticised on these grounds, as her examples indicate her broad definition of these terms. Brown's proposal (p. 245) that schizophrenics have thought disorder not language disorder suffers by contrast from too narrow a definition of language.

Chapman et al (1977) described the peculiarity of schizophrenic language as:

> a failure to use the context to judge the appropriateness of the interpretation . . . it is a screening deficit . . . related to other aspects of cognition.
> (Chapman et al 1977)

Dawson et al (1980) proposed:

> an inability to encode the characteristics of others, particularly those that require active continuous monitoring.
>
> (Dawson et al 1980)

Both these reflect the authors' orientations as cognitive psychologists rather than any difference in opinion on the nature of the disorder.

What is the cause of these disorders?

Some authors have attributed the peculiarities in language to a primary disorder of some other function. In the 1940s and 1950s emotional disorder was a common explanation. Sullivan (1944), for example, believed that:

> schizophrenic language behaviour arises from his extreme need of personal security . . . the fact that he has given up any hope of satisfaction . . . and therefore uses autistic speech.
>
> (Sullivan 1944)

Stengel (1964) suggested that schizophrenic speech, and neologisms in particular, were an attempt to express new feelings, for which everyday language had no words. In the 1960s and early 1970s attentional disorder was the most frequently used explanation. Maher (1972), for example, believed that the best interpretation of the literature at that time was in terms of a 'combination of associative intrusion and attentional deficit'. In the late 1970s a general cognitive disorder involving memory was suggested by several authors. Hemsley (1977) proposed intrusion of associated responses. Rochester (1978) entertained several hypotheses for the failure to provide adequate cohesive ties between one clause and the next. One of her suggestions was that schizophrenics had a short-term memory deficit, and simply forgot what they had said previously. Andreasen & Grove (1979) also considered that amnesia might play a part:

> One has the impression that the speaker is scanning his memory bank, is unable to find the word which he is seeking, and so inserts one which comes to mind instead.
>
> (Andreasen & Grove 1979)

In my view none of these explanations is adequate to explain the pattern of the disorder. If emotion, attention or memory were the underlying deficit, one would expect all aspects of language to be affected more or less equally. This is not the case and one has to search for explanations which are consistent with the selective impairment of prosodic and pragmatic aspects. (There may of course be a variety of causes. Raven 1958 listed eight reasons why a person might use words in an unusual way: missed opportunities, lack of interest, poor recall, apathy, rigidity of ideas, poor attention, poor comprehension and ambivalence between two objectives. Some of these, he argued, were not intrinsic to the condition. Missed opportunities, lack of interest and apathy might be the effect of institutionalisation;

rigidity of ideas and ambivalence about the purpose of language could conceivably be a personality trait.)

The most plausible explanation, in my view, is a neuropsychological one, in which the primary cause is dysfunction of the parts of the brain which subserve those aspects of language which are selectively disturbed. Neuropsychological explanations are not new. Kleist (1960) believed that schizophrenic speech was a form of aphasia, originating in some disturbance of the left temporal lobe. This view has been revived by Shimkunas (1978) and Flor-Henry (1979) in the light of recent suggestions that schizophrenia is a consequence of left hemisphere dysfunction. Andreasen and Grove (1979) proposed a general neurophysiological deficit of:

> the brain's electronic circuitry which monitors ongoing development of language . . . and when the feedback loop somehow misfires the speaker is unable to plan appropriately for the next phrase.
>
> (Andreasen & Grove 1979)

Neither a general nor a left hemisphere dysfunction is a satisfactory explanation, in my view, because it does not explain the specific pattern of the disorder. If left hemisphere dysfunction were the cause of the problem one would expect the disorder to reflect the contribution which that hemisphere makes to language. According to Levy (1978), 'the left hemisphere constructs spoken language by the generation of phoneme-elicited articulemes properly ordered in time', and according to Zaidel (1978) it 'possesses an innate and highly specialised linguistic mechanism whose paradigmatic functions are phonetic and syntactic encoding and analysis'. As phonemes and syntax are largely undisturbed in schizophrenia it is highly unlikely that left hemisphere dysfunction plays much part in producing the peculiar language.

Right hemisphere dysfunction is, however, a plausible explanation. The importance of the right hemisphere's role in language has only become apparent in the last two decades. According to Zaidel (1978) it 'represents the limited linguistic competence that can be acquired by a more general purpose nonlinguistic-cognitive apparatus through repeated exposure to experience and the formation of associations'. Its main contributions are to the phonemic and pragmatic aspects of language, less to formal semantics and not at all to syntax. It is involved in the perception of the inherent quality of phonemes and in particular their prosodic quality (Weintraub et al 1981). Patients with right hemisphere lesions have a disorder of pragmatic language: they fail to understand jokes and 'the underlying intention of a question or comment . . . and . . . the plausibility of a particular fact within an adventure story or a fairy tale' (Wapner et al 1981). The semantic capacity or competence is still uncertain because the main evidence has come from cases of left hemispherectomy or callosal section, where there was preexisting brain damage and therefore possible atypical cerebral dominance. Gazzaniga (1970) claimed that the isolated right hemisphere in split-brain patients could appreciate nouns and adjectives but not verbs.

These right hemisphere contributions—to prosody and pragmatics—are the very aspects of language which are affected in schizophrenia, and right hemisphere dysfunction is, in my view, a very attractive explanation for the schizophrenic's peculiar use of language. Further, hemispheric imbalance, in which right hemisphere dysfunction is combined with exaggerated left hemisphere functions, is an even more attractive possibility. It would explain, for example, Chaika's claim that schizophrenics are *preoccupied* with the phonemic and semantic aspects of a word, the propensity to invent neologisms and a tendency to be overabstract (see p. 335) in their choice of words.

SUMMARY

Normal language has four components—phonemic, syntactic, semantic and pragmatic. Phonemes are made up of distinctive features representing certain positions of the vocal apparatus and their corresponding acoustic energy; they have prosodic and inherent qualities. Syntax is grammar, and semantics is the way meaning is mapped on to phonemes and syntax. Pragmatics is the intended rather than the formal meaning of speech.

The neuropsychology of language is the study of the cerebral substrate of each of these components. The phonemic, syntactic and a large part of the semantic components are represented in a few, discrete areas in the left hemisphere, whilst other parts of the brain, including the right hemisphere, contribute to the pragmatic and to a lesser extent the semantic components.

Clinical considerations include the subjective experience of loss of comprehension in the early stages of schizophrenia, the descriptive phenomena (e.g. incoherence, perseveration, echolalia), claims that schizophrenics with marked language disorder form a separate subtype (e.g. schizophasia), and the nature of neologisms.

Experimental studies on schizophrenic language are of five types. First, schizophrenic speech is *generally* unpredictable, if regular deletions are made and normals asked to guess the missing words (Cloze procedure). In addition, some schizophrenics use a restricted vocabulary and some do badly on aphasia test batteries. Secondly, there are some reports of a *phonemic* abnormality, mainly affecting prosody. Although under-researched, this is probably not the major determinant of any speech disorder. Thirdly, the *syntactic* component, a relatively over-researched topic, is almost certainly normal, except in a few atypical patients. Fourthly, schizophrenics show no striking abnormalities either in their understanding of the *semantic* component of language, in the structure of their lexicon (from word association tests) or in their predilection for using certain classes of words (e.g. abstract-concrete, figurative-literal). Finally, their abnormal speech is best described as a *pragmatic* disorder. They fail to understand the meaning of words in context, cannot communicate their intended meaning to others, produce insufficient internal cohesion in their own speech, do not cater for the listener's needs and talk irrelevantly rather than incompetently.

There are numerous theories of the cause of the peculiar use of language. It has been attributed to a disorder of thought, attention, memory, emotion and general cognition. It has been regarded as an artefact of hospitalisation. The most plausible explanation, in my view, is a disorder of language itself, primarily affecting the pragmatic component and possibly related to right hemisphere dysfunction.

12

Memory

INTRODUCTION

It had generally been accepted as one of the few psychological truths about schizophrenia that their memory was unimpaired. In fact, as Bleuler pointed out, some schizophrenics appeared to have a remarkably good memory, what he called 'hypermnesia', for incidents bearing on their delusions.

In the 1970s, however, as part of the information processing approach to schizophrenia (p. 66), some psychologists began to study memory in schizophrenia because it held such a central position in information processing theory. A second reason was the introduction of C.T. scanning and the realisation that those chronic schizophrenics with cerebral atrophy performed poorly on simple tests of memory.

CLINICAL CONSIDERATIONS

General disorders of memory

Memory impairment or amnesia is the commonest disorder of memory. Different stores of information can be affected (iconic, short-term or long-term), different types of information can be selectively forgotten (e.g. retrograde, verbal, nonverbal or emotional) and different processes may be selectively disrupted (encoding, consolidation or retrieval). In addition to these simple types of amnesia, some subjects have particular difficulty with what is known as memory strategies or 'metamemory'. These include imagery, cueing and mnemonics. Hirst (1982) found, for example, that, when asked how they might remember a friend's birthday, Korsakoff patients had a smaller repertoire of strategies than normals. Warrington & Weiskrantz (1982) now regard such a defect as central to the understanding of Korsakoff's syndrome, previously considered the most pure form of amnesia. Koh (1978), as I shall show, presents a convincing case for a similar problem existing in schizophrenia.

Qualitative disorders of memory also occur: déjâ vu—an increased sense of familiarity, jamais vu—a sense of unfamiliarity, confabulation—'the momentary displacement of true memories with false, often fantastic memories'

(Berlyne 1972), and paramnesia or reduplicative paramnesia—'a transformation of successive occurrences of the same event into manifold occurrences of that event' (Pick 1903, temporal repetition becoming spatial reduplication, e.g. the same doctor seen twice becoming two different doctors living in different places).

Amnesia of some sort is characteristic of organic brain damage, focal or generalised. Qualitative disorders of memory have a closer link with focal damage (déjâ and jamais vu with temporal lobe damage, Cole & Zangwill 1963; confabulation and paramnesia with right frontal damage, Kapur & Coughlan 1980).

Typical schizophrenic phenomena

There are scattered references to pseudomemories (Kraepelin 1913), confabulation, delusional memories (e.g. I came down from the moon on a rocket last week) and sudden loss of memory for personal identity (Wilson et al 1950, Kennedy & Neville 1957) in the acute stage of schizophrenia. Amnesia, sometimes in the form of age disorientation (Crow & Mitchell 1975)—a consistent tendency to underestimate age—occurs in the chronic stage. None of these is confined to schizophrenia.

Subjective experience

An altered awareness of memory processes was not referred to by McGhie & Chapman (1961) in their comprehensive investigation of subjective experiences in schizophrenics. In my study several subjects reported a change in the way they viewed the past while psychotic. In fact it was one of the few discriminators between schizophrenia and depression. I obtained the following accounts:

> Time seemed to be infinity. I thought I was controlling time. I thought I was here and in a different dimension at the same time.
>
> (Remitted schizophrenic)
>
> Well you know Dr Who (TV character) has got a Tardis (space ship) and can go back to the same time again and again. I was like that. I kept going back to the same thing. It all seemed a waste of time. I kept going back for proof of things.
>
> (Remitted schizophrenic)
>
> Time is somewhat changed. It isn't supposed to be the way it is. I don't know in what way.
>
> (Acute schizophrenic)
>
> It's just as if I've visited a place for the first time . . . Time is sequential but just what happens around one affects the memory of it.
>
> (Acute schizophrenic)

EXPERIMENTAL EVIDENCE

Despite these meagre clinical hints, a number of psychologists, from the 1960s onwards, considered the subject worthy of experimental study.

Are the different stores intact?

Iconic memory

Iconic memory, the very short-term retinal store, is intact. Knight et al (1978) presented different patterns tachistoscopically in each visual field. Singly they were meaningless, but combined together they formed a recognisable object. The authors argued that if there was a fault in iconic memory, bilateral integration would not take place, and the patterns would remain unrecognisable. Schizophrenics were as good as controls in their recognition score. In an earlier paper (Knight et al 1977) the authors found that 11 of 31 New Haven schizophrenics were impaired on a visual display test, but these subjects were the more chronic, who showed underinclusion on Payne's (see p. 331) test of thought disorder. Royer and Friedman (1973) found that acute schizophrenics were actually faster than normals in identifying if a letter was an F or a T in a visual display. Braff et al (1977) reported a 'very short memory dysfunction' in 10 schizophrenics, on the basis of a delay in their auditory evoked potentials, but there was no psychological correlate of this.

Short-term memory

Short-term memory, however, has been found to be impaired in several studies. In one experiment (Smith 1969) 4 chronic schizophrenics were worse than 4 chronic nonschizophrenic psychiatric controls at remembering the sequence of pictures presented to them. Bauman (1971a) found that 24 subacute schizophrenics were impaired relative to normals at remembering lists of trigrams (e.g. ARP). In a second experiment (Bauman 1971b), acute and subacute schizophrenics were worse than normals at remembering lists of 7 letters, half random, half pronounceable (e.g. BADANAF). Bauman &Kolisnyk (1976) then showed that 24 MMPI diagnosed schizophrenics were worse than normals on immediate repetition of 7-digit strings, and that they were differentially impaired when a delay was introduced. Rieger & Friedman (1970) found that acute schizophrenics were worse than normals when asked to repeat strings of letters beyond their normal span (8–12 items).

Although these results look impressive, none of the experiments on acute patients employed the appropriate psychiatric controls.

Long-term memory

Long-term memory in chronic, institutionalised schizophrenics is almost invariably impaired (Jonstone et al 1981, Cutting 1979). In acute schizophrenics long-term memory is normal under some conditions and abnormal under others. Even when abnormal, it is probably no worse than that of depressives. When tested by recognition, virtually all investigators agree that it is normal, relative to appropriate controls (memory for public events, Johnson et al 1977; words, Bauman & Murray 1968; words, Nachmani & Cohen 1969; pictures, Sims-Knight & Petchers-Cassell 1977; patterns, Cutting 1979). There is some dispute about verbal recall, but when one looks at the studies which have reported abnormalities, there are a number of flaws. Most either fail to mention the stage of the illness, use unconventional diagnostic criteria or employ normal rather than psychiatric controls. Six studies which took these factors into account (Lewinsohn & Elwood 1961, Levy & Maxwell 1968, Russell & Beekhuis 1976, Straube et al 1979, Cutting 1979, Pogue-Geile & Oltmanns 1980) all found that acute schizophrenics were as good as, and in three reports actually better than, depressed subjects.

Is there memory impairment for specific information?

Verbal and semantic information

The issue of a verbal deficit has already been touched upon. It is doubtful if acute schizophrenics have a memory impairment for all verbal material under all conditions. Chronic schizophrenics do have impaired verbal memory, but also impaired nonverbal memory (Cutting 1979). There have been a number of studies purporting to show that certain types of verbal information—grammar or meaning—are selectively poorly memorised. Yet other studies have demonstrated that verbal memory is sensitive to distraction (though not always selectively so).

Lawson et al (1964), Gerver (1967) and Truscott (1970) reported that schizophrenics were worse than normals at remembering sentences, and that their performance, unlike that of normals, did not improve when the sentences were grammatically correct (see p. 62). All the subjects were chronic patients, and when the experiments were repeated with acute schizophrenics and appropriate controls, the overall impairment and the effect of grammatical correctness both disappeared (Levy & Maxwell 1968, Straube et al 1979). Even chronic schizophrenics, who are poor overall, have now been shown to remember English sentences better than meaningless word strings or ungrammatical sentences (Straube et al 1979, Maher et al 1980).

The issue of whether schizophrenics have a specific impairment in remembering meaningful as opposed to meaningless words, or certain types of meaningful words as opposed to others, will be fully discussed in the next section, on processes. Here it should be noted that, although the issue is complex, it appears, from Koh's (1978) work, that there is no absolute failure in this, but rather a tendency to use inappropriate strategies in organising the material. The problem, according to Koh, is one of control, not an intrinsic deficit. (Sattler & Normark 1971 did show that chronic schizophrenics remembered evaluative words, from Osgood's scheme, better than potency or activity words, but in the case of acute subjects the majority opinion is with Koh.)

In addition to syntax and semantics there is the question of whether verbal memory is subject to a specific distractibility. The general issue of distractibility was discussed in Chapter 8. Pogue-Geile & Oltmanns (1980), however, claimed that although acute schizophrenics were no worse than depressives, manics or normals in immediately reporting what they heard on one channel while being distracted on the other (normal selective attention), their subsequent recall of the material was markedly impaired, unlike all three control groups. This suggests a specific effect of distraction on verbal memory. Berg & Leventhal (1977) did not find this effect in chronic schizophrenics, but Watson & Plemel (1981) confirmed a small but significant effect in acute schizophrenics.

Nonverbal and visual information

Whitman (1969) found that schizophrenics were no different from neurotics in remembering the position of a dot within a grid. Knight & Sims-Knight (1980) found that both acute and chronic schizophrenics could remember the spatial configuration of designs, made up of dots and lines. Long-term picture (Sims-Knight & Petchers-Cassell 1977) and pattern recognition memory (Cutting 1979) appear to be normal.

Emotional information

Koh et al (1976) reported that borderline schizophrenics (see p. 97) did not show the Polyanna effect. (This is the normal tendency to remember pleasant words better than unpleasant.) He later (Koh et al 1981) confirmed this in a new experiment in a group of DSM-III schizophrenics. In this second paper he included a further experiment, in which faces were paired with five types of description, ranging from nice or likeable to unlikeable or cruel. Whereas normals remembered more likeable than unlikeable faces, this was not true of schizophrenics, an effect which the authors claimed was evidence of anhedonia (p. 234).

Appreciation of time

Rabin (1957) reported that schizophrenics tended to underestimate, relative to normals, a 2-hour period. Orme (1966) also found that schizophrenics tended to underestimate, relative to normals, personality disorders and manics, but not depressives, a 30-minute period. Crain et al (1975) reported that acute schizophrenics were no different from neurotics in estimating the duration of 1 second or in judging whether 2 periods of about 2-seconds were equal or not. Wahl & Sieg (1980) found that schizophrenics tended to overestimate periods of up to 1 minute, but were no different from normals in judging periods of about 1 hour. It is apparent from these reports that the issue is unresolved.

Are any specific processes affected?

Encoding

The issue is whether schizophrenics are selectively impaired in encoding certain aspects of a stimulus. The general opinion is that they have no selective deficit. Russell et al (1975) found that highly associated word pairs (e.g. man-woman) were better remembered than pairs with low associative strength. Traupmann (1975) showed that acute, but not chronic, schizophrenics remembered high imagery better than low imagery nouns, and highly categorised better than poorly categorised lists. Traupmann et al (1976) then showed that chronic schizophrenics also demonstrated release from proactive inhibition (Figure 12.1) on changing categories. In this procedure three words from the same category (e.g. all animals) are presented one after the other. There is then a period of distraction (e.g. reading numbers), and the subject is asked to recall all three. After several trials of triads from the same category, recall deteriorates due to the build-up of proactive inhibition. If, however, the category is changed (e.g. from animals to colours), recall for the new category improves. This is illustrated in Figure 12.1. This release from proactive inhibition, Wickens argued, is evidence of intact categorisation. Traupmann showed that schizophrenics had the

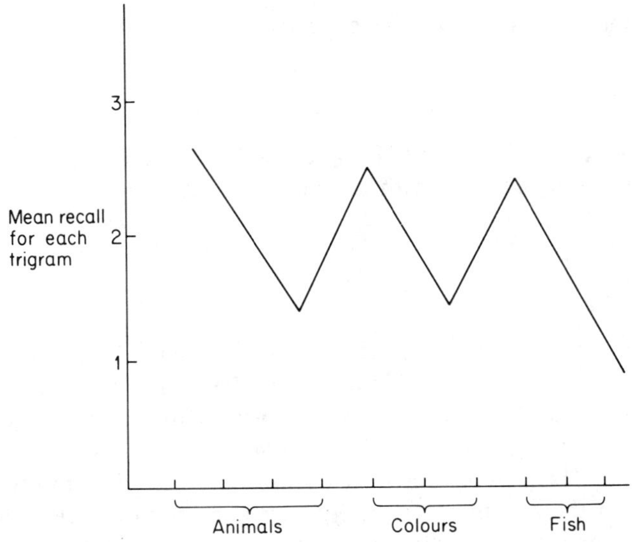

Fig. 12.1 Application of Wicken's release from proactive inhibition paradigm as a test of categorisation.

same amount of release as normals, and therefore intact categorisation. Larsen & Fromholt (1976) then showed that, although schizophrenics took longer to sort words into categories, once this was done their memory for them was the same as that of normals. Russell & Beekhuis (1976) also showed that their recall after sorting was not significantly different from that of normals, whereas a group of depressives was significantly inferior to normals.

Traupmann (1980) claimed that schizophrenics encoded less elaborately than normals but accepted that his subjects were 'not insensitive to conceptual attributes of an item'. This is tantamount to saying that their memory is poor but that there is no particular pattern to this. A study by Kay (1982), however, did reveal a striking encoding deficit for emotional words. He used the release from proactive inhibition paradigm, and gave three types of word triads: physical, conceptual and affective. After three similar triads of each he changed to a different kind, still within the same type. For example, the sequence of conceptual triads might be horse, elephant, pig; cat, tiger, dog; lion, cow, deer; and then Italy, France, England. An affective sequence was church, kiss, God; love, excellent, rest; sweet, family, unity; and then terrible, hurt, burn. He claimed that in chronic schizophrenics, mean recall for the fourth, different triad improved in the conceptual and physical sequences but not in the affective sequences. In nonschizophrenic psychotic controls, release from proactive inhibition occurred in all three types of sequence.

Consolidation

This has not been specifically investigated.

Retrieval

Bauman & Murray (1968) and Nachmani & Cohen (1969) demonstrated impaired recall in association with normal recognition, and claimed that this implicated a retrieval deficit.

Mnemonic strategies

This is the area about which there is most agreement. Even those who propose an encoding deficit (e.g. Traupmann 1980) or a retrieval deficit (e.g. Bauman & Murray 1968) attach more importance to a failure to benefit from cues, imagery, organisation or other mnemonic strategies.

Bauman (1971a) demonstrated that schizophrenics failed to show any improvement in their memory for a sequence of trigrams (ARP, BAN, CRA, DIR) even when it was pointed out to them that the next in sequence began with the next letter of the alphabet (Fig. 12.2). Yu & Johnson (1979) reported that acute schizophrenics did not benefit from imagery. Larsen &

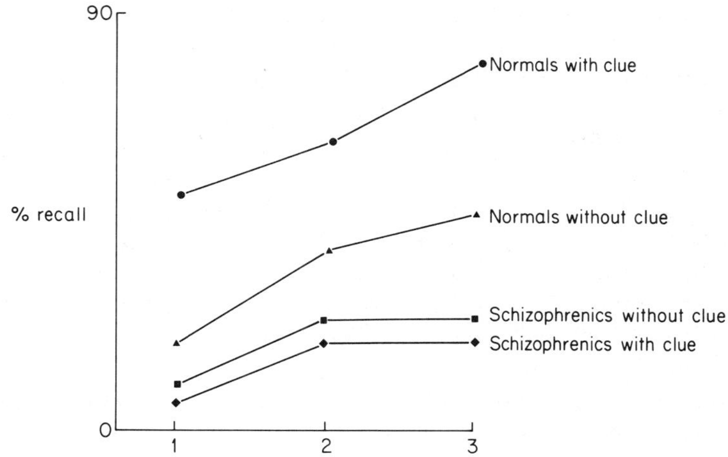

Fig. 12.2 Evidence of impaired subjective memory organisation.

Fromholt (1976) and Russell & Beekhuis (1976) attributed the inferior memory not to a failure of encoding or retrieval but to an 'inability to completely use perceived structuring of list during recall' (Russell & Beekhuis) or to 'poor organisation and difficulty in maintaining stable categories . . . a mnemonic organisation deficiency' (Larsen & Fromholt).

There can be no general failure to profit from mnemonic strategies, because Bauman (1971b) found that acute schizophrenics improved their performance when asked to voice the words, and Cutting & Ryan (1982) found that acute schizophrenics did profit from imagery in a verbal recognition test with highly and poorly imageable nouns. In my study, however, chronic schizophrenics did not benefit from the imagery component.

The best evidence on the issue comes from a series of studies by Koh and his colleagues. Unfortunately, they used unconventionally diagnosed, nonpsychotic schizophrenics, and their results may not generalise to acute subjects. In the first study (Koh et al 1973), recall of categorised and uncategorised lists of words was examined with reference to Bousfield and Bousfield's 'stimulus category repetition', the degree to which subjects use the conceptual categories provided by the experimenter. The second was Mandler and Dean's 'intertrial repetition', the extent to which subjects recall pairs of words in contiguity on two successive recall trials. The second measure can be used on uncategorised lists and indicates the adequacy of a subject's own strategies, whereas the first measure assesses whether a subject can benefit from the experimenter's suggested strategy (i.e. categorisation). The investigators found that whereas schizophrenic recall correlated well with Bousfield and Bousfield's measure (schizophrenics 0.79, normals 0.67, nonschizophrenic controls 0.28), it did not correlate well with Mandler and Dean's subjective measure (schizophrenics 0.35, normals 0.63, nonschizophrenic controls 0.66). These results suggested to them that 'strategies for employing subjective organisational strategies in recall' were deficient.

In a second study, Koh & Kayton (1974) examined whether nonsemantic strategies were also faulty. They tested recall of lists of 12 words immediately after hearing them and after a 10-second delay, counting backwards to prevent rehearsal. They then examined subjective organisation by employing Mandler and Dean's measure on input-output concordance (whether subjects maintained the order of presentation in their recall sequence). In schizophrenics, the input-output concordance was significantly lower than in normals, and did not correlate at all with the recall score, whereas it did in normals. Again they interpreted their results as indicating impaired utilisation of mnemonic strategies.

This conclusion is supported by the findings of Lutz & Marsh (1981) in a similar experiment to Koh's first one. It should also be viewed in the light of another experiment by Koh and colleagues demonstrating that clustering strategies themselves, as opposed to their incompetent application, are normal (Koh et al 1974).

CONCLUSIONS

Is there a disorder of memory in schizophrenia?

In acute schizophrenia memory is superficially intact, although certain psychological tests may reveal subtle difficulties with memory strategies and certain types of information, particularly with an emotional content. In chronic schizophrenia there is often marked amnesia, associated with C.T. scan changes of cerebral atrophy.

What is the nature of the memory disorder?

In acute schizophrenia the disorder affects what is known as metamemory or memory strategies rather than memory itself. Subjects have difficulty in organising material so that it can be memorised and in taking advantage of memory aids that normal people find useful—cues and categorisation. Koh (1978) sums this up:

> the basic difficulty of schizophrenics in the remembering of verbal materials is largely attributable to their inefficiency in the executive control that regulates the flow of information through the structural components. This . . . is not obvious in the short-term memory processing that requires little high-level organisation . . . it emerges when the processes involved require high-order stimulus elaboration and mnemonic strategies.

They also appear to have a selective deficit in remembering emotional items.

In chronic schizophrenia amnesia is common and is probably the same form as is seen in presenile dementia of definite organic origin.

What is the cause of the memory disorder?

In chronic schizophrenia it is mainly the effect of generalised brain damage. In acute schizophrenia, the cause of the two deficits—impaired strategies and hedonic amnesia—is uncertain. In my view the evidence points again to a disorder of hemisphere balance. Studies of brain-damaged subjects demonstrate that the hemispheres impose their characteristic cognitive styles on memory. Lesions of the left temporal lobe produce an impairment in verbal (Milner 1958), semantic nonverbal (Zaidel & Rausch 1981) and abstract memory (Jones-Gotman 1979). Right temporal lesions impair nonverbal meaningless (De Renzi 1968) and imagery-mediated memory (Jones-Gotman & Milner 1978). Commissurotomy produces a mild amnesia (Zaidel & Sperry 1974), indicating that interhemispheric connections have some role. Right-sided lesions are also known to selectively impair the processing of emotional information (see p. 240) and to disrupt what Coughlan & Warrington (1978), in the case of language, called general control strategies rather than language itself. Impaired verbal memory strategies and hedonic amnesia, the only two established memory deficits in acute schizophrenia, are therefore quite consistent with the idea of exaggerated left and depleted right hemisphere functions.

SUMMARY

Normal memory, although extensively investigated, still lacks a generally accepted theoretical framework. For this reason, the various disorders of memory encountered in clinical practice lack any clear psychological categorisation. Disorders of a particular store or phase of memory (short-term, long-term) are distinguished. Disorders affecting specific types of information are also recognised (verbal, nonverbal, retrograde, emotional, temporal, personal). Most controversy surrounds the way in which certain processes might be selectively impaired (encoding, storage, retrieval, mnemonic strategy).

In schizophrenia, there are few clinical indications of a disorder of memory, except in the chronic stage, where it forms part of deterioration. Psychological investigations into the adequacy of the stores and the efficiency of intrinsic processes in acute schizophrenics have not revealed any convincing deficit. There is some evidence, however, that the ability to use mnemonic strategies (metamemory) might be impaired, and this might account for some of the reports of mild memory impairment (poor supraspan short-term memory, impaired verbal recall under certain conditions). There is also evidence that acute schizophrenics are selectively impaired in remembering items with an emotional content. Both these deficits are consistent with a diminution of the right hemisphere's contribution to memory.

13

Movement

INTRODUCTION

Catatonia was one of the first subtypes of dementia praecox to be described, and Kraepelin gave movement disorder the highest diagnostic significance of any functional deficit. Bleuler included it as a major subtype but gave it less diagnostic importance, and from then on it became more and more alien to the generally held concept of schizophrenia. There were two reasons for this. First, severe movement disorder as described by Kraepelin became increasingly rare. Secondly, there was a change in theoretical and diagnostic emphasis in the concept of schizophrenia. It became less widely believed that schizophrenia was a disease with a poor outcome, and more accepted that it was a 'deficit reaction' (in North America) or an empirically derived cluster of certain sorts of delusions and hallucinations (in Britain) so there was less place for movement disorder with its neurological connotations.

The link between movement disorder and schizophrenia has become further weakened in the last decade with the realisation that many cases of acute catatonia resemble depression more than they do other subtypes of schizophrenia and that most of the movement disorder seen in chronic cases can be attributed either to neuroleptics or to recognisable forms of acquired brain damage. The main question concerning movement disorder at the present time is whether Kraepelin was misled by the severity of catatonia into classifying it alongside other severe forms of insanity, such as hebephrenia.

CLINICAL CONSIDERATIONS

General disorders of movement

Excluding disorders of power, tone and co-ordination, most movement disorders fall roughly into three types—dyspraxia, involuntary movements and catatonia.

Involuntary movement disorders include tremor, tics, chorea, athetosis, ballismus and general disturbance in the speed (e.g. bradykinesia) or smooth flow of movement (dyskinesia). They occur primarily in neurological conditions whose pathology lies in the basal ganglia, e.g. Parkinson's disease and Huntington's chorea. They may be neuroleptic-induced, e.g. tardive dyskinesia, and are therefore common in treated schizophrenics.

There are several kinds of dyspraxia or apraxia. The chief varieties are ideomotor, ideational and constructional. In ideomotor apraxia there is failure to carry out single gestures (e.g. cannot wave goodbye). Ideational apraxia consists of a disruption in the logical and harmonious succession of separate elements of a complex gesture (e.g. lighting a cigarette), although each element itself is correctly executed. Constructional apraxia is a disturbance in the ability to manipulate objects in their spatial context. They are not part of the schizophrenic picture.

Catatonia is the generic name for about 8 separate disorders of movement and posture, which have in common a tendency to be intermittent, to defy classification as disorders of power, tone, co-ordination, praxis or involuntary movement, and in a general sense to involve the surrender of the affected person's will. Five authorities on the subject—Kraepelin (1913), Bleuler (1911), Ey (1950), Spitzer et al (1975) and Abrams & Taylor (1976)—each list between 5 and 8 different items out of a pool of 17. I have suggested in Table 13.1 a reduction to 8 mutually exclusive items.

Table 13.1 Catatonic phenomena listed by five authorities

	Kraepelin	Bleuler	Ey	Spitzer et al	Abrams & Taylor
Stupor	mutism	√	psychomotor inertia	√	mutism
Negativism	√	√	√	catatonic rigidity	√
Stereotypies	√	√	√		√
Catalepsy		√	√	waxy flexibility	√
Automatism	automatic obedience	command automatism	√		√
Mannerisms	√	√	√	posturing	posturing
Excitement	√	impulsiveness hyperkinesis		√	
Echopraxia			mimicry		√

Stupor is a triad of akinesis (lack of movement), mutism (lack of speech) and relative preservation of consciousness (Joyston-Bechal 1966).

Negativism is 'an apparently motiveless resistance to all interference . . . an accentuation of opposition' (Fish 1967). Kraepelin used to demonstrate this by asking a patient to put out their tongue, and then prick it, a sequence which could be continued indefinitely.

Mannerisms, which include grimacing and posturing, are defined and illustrated by Fish as:

> unusual repeated performances of a goal-directed motor action or the maintainence of an unusual modification of an adaptive posture . . . e.g. unusual

> hand movements while shaking hands . . . peculiarities of dress, hair style and writing . . . strange use of words, high-flown expressions and postures which are out of keeping with the total situation.
>
> (Fish 1967)

They are 'strikingly unnatural distortions of common activities' (Kraepelin 1913).

Catatonic excitement or hyperkinesis is restless overactivity without adequate psychological explanation in terms of life event, mood or content of ideas or experiences.

Echopraxia 'is the automatic repetition of visually perceived actions of others' (Stengel 1947, Chapman & McGhie 1964). It is associated with echolalia (repetition of the words of others). (Perseveration, the repetition of one's own words and actions, is usually omitted from lists of catatonic phenomena. According to Allison & Hurwitz, 1967, it is 'the continuation of an experience or activity without an appropriate exciting stimulus'.)

Stereotypies are 'repetitive nongoal-directed actions carried out in a uniform way' (Fish 1967).

They are:

> movements which are combined into rhythmic or complex sequences of obscure purpose and which have attained a level of functional autonomy.
>
> (Ridley & Baker 1982)

They may be verbal (e.g. 'We dig nurse. We do digging' endlessly repeated as the sole utterance) or motor (e.g. A woman spent six hours one day alternately rocking back and forth on the floor and walking heel to toe across the room.)

Catalepsy is the maintenance of an uncomfortable posture for an abnormally long time. It is conventionally elicited by casually lifting the patient's arm up, leaving it in an odd position, and noticing whether it stays like that, or is moved to a more comfortable position. Fish (1967) tried to distinguish between a number of related phenomena—waxy flexibility (flexibilitas cerea, the tendency to maintain whatever postures were imposed), Mitmachen (the fact that there was no resistance to these impositions), and Mitgehen (the most extreme co-operation of all, in which slight pressure on a limb would induce movement which would continue until the pressure stopped). The rarity of these phenomena, the dearth of studies on the reliability of observer ratings and the absence of any plausible theoretical explanation make such distinctions rather academic.

In *automatism* (command automatism or automatic obedience) the patient carries out every instruction regardless of the consequences.

A few movement disorders cannot be classified as involuntary, dyspraxic or catatonic. These include '*disorders of motility*', a doubtful category introduced by the neurological school of psychiatry. According to Leonhard (1957) they are finer, more varied and more purposive than catatonic phenomena. The *psychomotor retardation* of depression is a disorder of movement, the same in kind but less severe than stupor (Greden & Carroll 1981).

Clumsiness, is characteristic of Asperger's syndrome (p. 316), a personality type linked with both schizoid personality and infantile autism (Wing 1981). *Motor impersistence* (Fisher 1956) denotes impaired maintenance of posture (e.g. difficulty in keeping eyes closed, inability to hold breath). It is thought to be due to failure of sensory feedback and is characteristic of right hemisphere lesions. The '*alien hand sign*' (Brion & Jedynak 1972, Goldberg et al 1981) or '*auto-criticism*' (Bogen 1979) are spontaneous movements by one hand which a subject senses as strange and reacts to with amazement as if they (the subject) are not responsible. One hand may reach out and touch a door knob, pick up a pencil, start scribbling or even interfere with the action of the other hand, whereupon the subject will react with dismay, say, for example, 'Let go of my hand, you stop me dressing' or experience the feeling that their hand does not belong to them. The phenomenon is indicative of a callosal transfer deficit.

In general ideomotor and ideational dyspraxia occur with left temporal and parietal lesions, involuntary movements with basal ganglion dysfunction, and catatonic phenomena have been reported in a variety of organic states (Gelenberg 1976), depression (Kirby 1913) and mania (Abrams & Taylor 1976) as well as schizophrenia.

Typical schizophrenic phenomena

The most striking thing about catatonic schizophrenia is how rarely it is diagnosed now, compared with formerly. Whereas they made up 20% of Kraepelin's 1000 cases of dementia praecox, they accounted for only 54 of 811 schizophrenics of all types in the IPSS. Even more striking, 48 of these 54 cases came from the four centres in Asia, Africa and South America (India, Taiwan, Nigeria and Colombia), leaving only 6 out of 403 (1.5%) in Europe and North America. Other estimates (Morrison 1973, Guggenheim & Barbigian 1974) put the relative incidence at between 5% and 10%. It is difficult to say whether any of the catatonic phenomena are typical of schizophrenia, partly because they are so rare, partly because the recent diagnostic criteria have in general ignored them and partly because of their increasingly recognised link with affective disorder.

Of the individual phenomena, regardless of their relationship to schizophrenia, mannerisms are the commonest according to Abrams & Taylor (1976), followed in decreasing order of frequency by stereotypies, stupor, negativism, automatism and echopraxia. Each phenomenon may of course be heterogeneous and include one type which may be more characteristic of schizophrenia. Jones (1965) showed that schizophrenic stereotypies, for example, had a variety of causes: some were based on delusions and some, he claimed, were a protection against fear.

In addition to catatonic phenomena, some clinicians have claimed that other types of movement disorder, if not typical, are at least common and an integral part of the condition. These include involuntary movements, disturbances of voluntary motor behaviour, abnormal perceptuomotor co-ordination and perseveration. As these claims rest on experimental ratings they will be dealt with in the section on experimental evidence.

Subjective experience

McGhie & Chapman (1961) obtained several accounts of an increased awareness of movements during the early stage of the condition:

> I am not sure of my own movements any more. It's very hard to describe this but at times I am not sure about even simple actions like sitting down. It's not so much thinking out what to do, it's the doing of it that sticks me. People just do things but I have to watch first to see how you do things. I have to do everything step by step, nothing is automatic now. Everything has to be considered.
>
> (McGhie & Chapman 1961)

EXPERIMENTAL EVIDENCE

Involuntary movements?

Using the Abnormal Involuntary Movement Scale (NIMH 1974) Cunningham Owens et al (1982), all members of Crow's team, found that about 50% of 411 chronic schizophrenics in a large mental hospital had significant involuntary movements. They also found involuntary movements in the same proportion of 47 chronic schizophrenics who, according to the authors, had never received neuroleptics. For this reason, they proposed that involuntary movements were intrinsic to schizophrenia and not iatrogenic, as most psychiatrists believe. This claim is hard to substantiate, becaue small doses of phenothiazines can have a very long half-life, drug administration is not always recorded and some non-neuroleptics such as the antiemetic metaclopropamide (Maxolon) can produce dyskinesia.

Disturbances of voluntary motor behaviour?

Manschreck and colleagues reported a number of movement disorders in medicated schizophrenics, which they claimed were due to intrinsic 'disturbances of voluntary motor behaviour' (Manschreck et al 1982). They first tested the smoothness with which subjects shook their head, opened and closed their eyes and walked (Manschreck et al 1981a), and then tested 'motor synchrony' (tapping in time with an auditory stimulus, Manschreck et al 1981b). In each case, schizophrenics carried out these tasks less fluently than patients with depression, a result which the authors claimed could not be attributed to neuroleptics because the depressed patients were on the same dose.

Other investigators have also found deficient performance by schizophrenics on similar tasks (e.g. poor articulation of tongue twisters, impaired 'piano playing movements', jerky pronation—supination sequences, Quitkin et al 1976). The abnormalities are often regarded as 'neurological soft signs' (see p. 136), indicative of underlying cerebral dysfunction.

It is difficult to be certain that so-called voluntary movement disturbance is not due to either medication or coexistent brain damage and, even if genuine, it may still be a nonspecific accompaniment rather than a critical feature of schizophrenia.

Abnormal perceptuomotor co-ordination?

Holzman et al (1974), as well as stressing the link with attentional deficit (p. 210), also referred to abnormal smooth pursuit eye movements as 'an incapacity to maintain stable centring of perceptual activity . . . (partly due to) neuromuscular dysfunction'. Walker & Green (1982) demonstrated a reduction of motor proficiency (e.g. speed of cutting out a circle from paper, foot tapping) which correlated with impairment on the continuous performance test of attention. Malenka et al (1982) claimed that schizophrenics were impaired at following a target on a screen because they were poor at 'monitoring ongoing motor behaviour on the basis of internal cues'.

In my view, these abnormalities have been underemphasised, but are probably more perceptual than motor in nature, and may relate to a deficiency in size estimation, a disorder of spatial perception (p. 299).

Perseveration?

Some investigators have claimed that failure to disattend is a characteristic feature of schizophrenia (Zubin 1975). Perseveration, the clinical expression of this, one would therefore expect to be relatively common. Although it does occur in schizophrenia, it is not common and is usually seen in chronic cases who may have underlying generalised cerebral dysfunction. Further, an impairment in switching attention does not appear to be the critical element. For example, Freeman & Gathercole (1966) administered 16 tasks to bring out perseveration in chronic schizophrenics and dements. They identified three types: compulsive repetition (e.g. repeatedly protruding tongue), impairment of switching (e.g. repeating a previous response to a new stimulus) and ideational perseveration (e.g. spontaneous recurrence of words or phrases). Both sets of patients showed all three types of perseveration, but compulsive repetition was more common in schizophrenics and impaired switching more common in dements.

In my view, perseveration is more likely to be an effect of frontal cerebral dysfunction and not a pointer to the essential nature of the psychological or movement dysfunction.

CONCLUSIONS

Do schizophrenics have a disorder of movement?

A small minority of typical, untreated acute schizophrenics and the majority of chronic schizophrenics have a disorder of movement.

What is the nature of this disorder?

In untreated, acute schizophrenics it is more like a disorder of will, motivation, drive, inclination or desire than a disorder of motor function, because there is no disturbance in power, tone, co-ordination, praxis or smooth execution of movement, and it is intermittent. This is what is meant by catatonia. In chronic schizophrenics, who nowadays will almost certainly have been given phenothiazines, the disorder is probably different in nature and origin. Involuntary movements, impaired planning and fluency of voluntary movements, perceptuomotor inco-ordination and perseveration are all, in these patients, part of a more complex and heterogeneous picture.

What is the cause of the movement disorder?

In chronic schizophrenia it is easy to dismiss the movement disorder as a combined effect of neuroleptics and generalised cerebral dysfunction, and nothing intrinsically to do with the typical underlying psychological dysfunction.

In acute, unmedicated schizophrenia it is not so easy to dismiss the movement disorder. Some cases, particularly where catatonic phenomena are the only criterion of psychosis, are better regarded as affective disorders (Maginat et al 1983). Some may be examples of a viral encephalitis, as suggested by Mahendra (1981), but some authorities (e.g. Crow 1983) believe that all subtypes of schizophrenia are viral in origin, and Mahendra's argument is not therefore very useful.

There are still cases, however, who cannot be redistributed amongst affective or typically organic categories in this way. They either fluctuate between catatonia and other subtypes of schizophrenia, or show the full range of phenomena during a single episode. In my view one has to admit that in such cases *conation* as well as cognition is affected. The separation of these two aspects of the mind is not as complete as some psychologists used to believe and there has been a recent revival of interest in the psychology of conation (pragmatics, planning, doing)—'knowing how'. This coincides with a reduced emphasis on cognition (perception, memory, thinking)—'knowing that'. Norman's (1981) model of motor function is a good example of current trends. He assumes a hierarchy of action schemata, each one triggered by a certain range of events and each characterised by a degree of autonomy from consciousness. For example, one might be so accustomed to driving home in one's car that putting on one's coat at work triggers an entire 'going home' schema and frees the mind for other things, e.g. day-dreaming. (This explains, amongst other things, action slips, such as the absent-minded professor who, when sent upstairs to fetch something from the bedroom, undressed and got into bed. His 'getting into bed' schema was triggered by entering the bedroom.)

It is possible that conation of this kind as well as cognition is affected in schizophrenia, and this gives rise to catatonia. Behaviourally-oriented clinical psychologists never had any difficulty in explaining catatonia. Hemsley (1977), for example, believed that all schizophrenic phenomena were the result of a disturbance in response selection (p. 67). Catatonia was one form of faulty responding. Neuropsychologists such as Brown (1977) and psychiatrists such as Ey (1950) have also tried to close the gap between cognitive and conative disturbances. They assume that thought, perception and action have a common origin in undifferentiated cognition-conation in their earliest development. If a fault occurs at this stage, therefore, it could just as easily give rise to 'troubles in the motor sphere . . . as to thought disorder' (Ey).

A neuropsychological model in terms of hemispheric imbalance, however, explains the association of cognitive and conative disturbances even more plausibly, in my view, because it demonstrates their joint origin rather than explaining one in terms of the other. The left hemisphere, according to Kimura (1977), is dominant for higher order motor skills:

> The left hemisphere contains a system specialised particularly for producing the correct limb posture (or, in the case of speech, articulatory posture), and consequently also for controlling the transition from one position to another . . . and its complex verbal and praxic functions are derived from such control.
>
> (Kimura 1977)

Right hemisphere damage impairs the ability to use kinaesthetic feedback (Carmon 1970), i.e. information about muscular position. In addition, whereas left hemisphere lesions disrupt bilateral motor performance, right hemisphere lesions only affect the left side of the body (Wyke 1971). If the left hemisphere were overactive and the right underactive it is possible that gestures and movements would be exaggerated, perceptuomotor feedback impaired and control of movement disturbed. All these are characteristics of catatonic phenomena, and indicate that hemispheric imbalance is at least consistent with their development.

SUMMARY

Motor function has not been a central preoccupation of psychologists in recent years, except during the behavioural era. It has been extensively studied, however, by neurologists and neuropsychologists. Currently, there is renewed interest in action and pragmatics. It is usually measured during a neurological examination, but there are some standardised rating scales of involuntary movements and some well-established tests of complex voluntary movement.

Movement disorder normally falls within the province of the neurologist and neuropsychologist, but catatonia, perseveration, involuntary movements and disturbed voluntary movements have all been linked with schizophrenia. It is not clear how these relate to the commoner and more well-established phenomena and psychological dysfunctions of schizophrenia. Some have tried to dismiss them altogether as faulty diagnosis or neuroleptic side-effect. This is probably true of some of the movement disorders seen in chronic schizophrenia. In acute schizophrenia, catatonic phenomena cannot be so easily dismissed. Some cases are better grouped with affective illness, but a minority may well represent a disorder of conation (action, planning, pragmatics) which originates along with the more typical cognitive disorders from hemispheric imbalance.

14

Perception

INTRODUCTION

None of the early writers on schizophrenia laid much emphasis on a disorder of perception. Kraepelin (1913) commented that perception 'was not unusually lessened'. Bleuler (1911) wrote:

> Sensory response to external stimulus is quite normal. To be sure, the patients will complain that everything appears to be different . . . However, this strangeness is usually attributable to a deficit in customary associations and particularly to an alteration of emotional emphasis.
>
> (Bleuler 1911)

Jaspers (1913) gave an exhaustive account of hallucinations and other abnormal experiences in the condition, but did not consider that a perceptual deficit was responsible. Gruhle (1915, see p. 350) in his analysis of 'delusional perception' was emphatic that the abnormality concerned the significance of the object perceived rather than perception itself, and this view was adopted by the early existential psychiatrists (see p. 35) and Kurt Schneider.

Under the influence of Gestalt psychology, however, perception came to be regarded as a more active process, involving a wider set of mental functions and only distinguished from thinking by the conviction of reality which attached to the image. For this reason, from the late 1950s onwards, some investigators began to regard schizophrenic symptoms, and not just hallucinations, as a consequence of a complex perceptual disorder. Conrad (1952) was one of the first to analyse psychotic experiences and beliefs from this standpoint. He believed that in schizophrenia the 'gestalt structure disintegrated' and this caused the subject to give more weight to 'physiognomy' (details) in the world around him. This led to false judgements and eventually to fixed delusions. Weckowicz (1957) came to a similar conclusion:

> In schizophrenia the constancy of perception breaks down and this leads to perplexity, feelings of change and strangeness of the world.
>
> (Weckowicz 1957)

In the 1960s perceptual deficit continued as an attractive hypothesis, but it was regarded as secondary to a disorder of attention. McGhie & Chapman (1961), for example, concluded:

> a primary disorder is that of a decrease in the selective and inhibitory functions of attention . . . leading to . . . a gradual tendency for perception to become global, undifferentiated and lacking in spatio-temporal constancy.
>
> (McGhie & Chapman 1961)

In the 1970s, for the first time, perception itself was studied. Visual perception, auditory perception, proprioception and the factors predisposing to auditory hallucinations were all the focus of extensive investigation, and at the present time there is compelling evidence that a perceptual disorder does exist in schizophrenia.

The purpose of this chapter is to present this evidence systematically, to analyse the cause of the disorder and to examine its significance in causing other aspects of the schizophrenic condition.

CLINICAL CONSIDERATIONS

General disorders of perception

There are a large number of perceptual disorders, but most of these are a feature of focal or generalised brain damage and are not characteristic of schizophrenia. It is appropriate, however, to survey the entire range of perceptual disorders in order to emphasise the particular pattern which does occur in schizophrenia, considered in the next section.

In the visual modality these include *blindness* and *impaired sight*. *Distortions of form* can occur: with brain damage, particularly in the right parietal region, objects may appear distorted in size or shape: 'inclined like in a rolling boat . . . two halves of unequal size . . . one object passing into another' (de Morsier 1938). *Visual object agnosia* is a disorder in which the subject can no longer appreciate the meaning of an object (neither demonstrate its use nor name it) in the presence of preserved lower-order sensation. *Prosopagnosia* is a difficulty in 'recognition and identification of well-known and intimate faces in conscious, nonconfused patients without aphasia and with ability to see objects well with normal orientation and memory' (Bornstein 1963). *Simultanagnosia* is an inability to perceive two or more items simultaneously but not when the same items are presented singly. It is usually identified when subjects fail to appreciate the full meaning of a picture but can recognise individual segments. *Visuospatial agnosia* covers a variety of disorders of space perception—impaired visual searching, poor position discrimination, constructional apraxia and disturbed judgements of distance. *Disturbed colour perception* may follow localised brain damage: colours may appear in a monotone or take on a particular hue. *Visual perseveration* or palinopsia denotes a condition in which the image of a perceived object recurs with all the characteristics of the original experience (i.e. reality) after the stimulus has been removed. A patient of Critchley's (1951) noticed a cat in the street and then re-experienced the same event several times over the next few days. *Disorders of the emotional experience* accompanying perception can occur, particularly with parietal or thalamic damage. Objects may appear unduly menacing or friendly, become imbued with an intense personal significance, or seem to have a significance which is elusive or nearly achieved ('presque vu', Critchley 1953). *Visual hallucinations* are usually classified according to their complexity, the sense of reality attached to them, their form and their cause. (De Morsier 1938, Bender 1963, Brown 1977, give the best general accounts). Bender divided true hallucinations into simple, e.g. flashes, zigzags; and complex, e.g. cinematographic, Pick's visions ('ability' to see through ceilings and walls). De Morsier distinguished true hallucinations from 'normal phenomena'—photopsia, after-images, eidetic images, hypnagogic phenomena and sound-induced photisms. I would add pseudohallucinations, 'out-of-body experiences', 'near-death experiences' and other anomalous experiences which occur in extreme states (sleep and sensory deprivation) and which fall short of hallucinations. Pseudohallucinations are morbid experiences which are less than true hallucinations in some way. (Jaspers, 1913, regarded them as a special form of imagery; Hare, 1973, as morbid experiences with preserved insight; Mullen, 1979, as 'the patient's own thoughts with a feeling of responsibility for them . . . but not under voluntary control'; Kräupl-Taylor, 1981, as experiences without the quality of reality.) Lilliputian hallucinations (Lewis 1961) are true hallucinations where the object seen is smaller than the corresponding real object. Autoscopic hallucinations (Lukianowicz 1958) are hallucinations of the self but are difficult to separate phenomenologically from other morbid experiences or beliefs about the self such as the double (Thompson 1982) or 'out-of-body experiences' (Gabbard et al 1981). Finally organic and functional hallucinations can be distinguished. The former differ according to the site of the lesion: brain stem (usually called peduncular from their origin in lesions alongside the cerebellar peduncles), occipital, parietal and temporal. They can also be considered according to the underlying pathology: epileptic, migrainous, infective and drug-induced. Functional types include those occurring in functional psychosis, sleep deprivation and sensory deprivation.

In the auditory modality disorders include *deafness* and *impaired hearing*, *distortions of sound* (clearer, closer, louder, more friendly or the opposite of these) *auditory agnosia* (inability to appreciate the meaning of sounds such as keys rattling with preserved basic perception) and *auditory hallucinations*. Auditory hallucinations can be nonverbal (e.g. music, barking, clicking) or verbal (voices calling name, talking to, or talking about the subject). They occur in temporal lobe epilepsy (Bingley 1958), during electrical stimulation of the temporal lobe (when they are much rarer than visual hallucinations, Horowitz & Adams, 1970), in acute organic reactions (Cutting 1980) rarely in LSD intoxication (Malitz & Kanzler 1970), commonly in amphetamine addicts (Connell 1958), commonly in the alcohol withdrawal syndrome and delirium tremens (Parker & Schilder, 1935), in the hypnagogic state (simple calling of name, Oswald 1962), in depressive psychosis (the best example of pseudohallucinations), during grief reactions (Rees 1971) and in schizophrenia.

Tactile and kinaesthetic disorders include *impaired tactile sensation* (anaesthesia—loss of sensation, dysaesthesia—unpleasant sensation, loss of vibration or postural sense, astereognosis—inability to recognise objects by touch, agraphaesthesia—inability to recognise numbers inscribed on the skin, impaired two-point discrimination and failure to distinguish between two weights). Subjects may *neglect* one side of the body or manifest *sensory inattention* or extinction (ignoring a stimulus when it is paired with another, but recognising it by itself). Amputees may report a *phantom limb*, and *pain* may be enhanced or diminished (congenital indifference, acquired asymbolia for pain). *Distortions and hallucinations* of bodily sensation can occur, most characteristically in epilepsy, migraine, mescaline and cocaine intoxication and right parietal lesions.

Olfactory, *gustatory*, *visceral* and *vestibular* hallucinations also appear in both organic and functional conditions.

Synaesthesia, 'the imagery of one sense mode aroused by sensations of a different sense mode' (Simpson & McKellar 1955), is a perceptual disorder which crosses modalities. (A tap in the field of vision was experienced as a drip on the cheek by a patient with hepatic encephalopathy, Summerskill et al 1956. 'I seemed to be travelling through a thick ocean of air, and felt and saw the pressure of this' was reported during intoxication with mescaline, Simpson & McKellar 1955.)

Typical schizophrenic phenomena

Auditory hallucinations

Of all the perceptual disorders listed above, verbal auditory hallucinations are most typical of schizophrenia. Characteristically they tend to be true hallucinations (as opposed to pseudohallucinations), to be neutral in emotional content (unlike those seen in depressive psychosis or mania), to contain more than one word and to be in the third person (e.g. 'He's a lunatic and should be in an asylum' or 'She's a simple girl'). Schneider was even more specific in his selection of three first-rank symptoms—voices commenting, thoughts heard spoken aloud and two or more voices arguing. They are illustrated in the following case histories of two patients in my care.

> A man of 37 began hearing a man's voice, unrecognisable, probably outside his head and far away, and certainly not his own voice. The voice would repeat his own thoughts as he thought them. For example it would say, 'He's getting things the wrong way' while he was thinking that himself. It would comment on his own activities and those of others around him. Whilst the interviewer was making notes, the patient heard a voice saying, 'He's writing it down'.

On another occasion the voice said, 'He's not moving', when the patient was sitting quietly. Sometimes he heard two voices, one male, one female, discussing him. The male voice said, 'I can't get anything out of him', the female, 'He can actually hear us'.

The second patient was a woman of 27 who heard two sets of voices which she termed 'the bad people' and 'the humanoids'. The first set had said on occasions, 'You're not going to smoke the cigarette the way you want to but the way we want you to' or 'You have to cook shepherd's pie today'. They tended, in her words, to 'confuse actions, tell me about myself, where I came from and where I'm going'. The humanoids were less insistent and acted as an 'antidote' to the others. She could not remember what they said.

The frequency of auditory hallucinations in schizophrenia varies according to the diagnostic scheme followed, but was around 50% in each of three studies (Catego—WHO 1973, Spitzer—Cutting 1980, hospital diagnosis—Malitz et al 1962). This compares with much lower figures in other conditions (e.g. 15% in acute organic reactions, Cutting 1980). Alcoholic psychosis is the most likely other condition to give rise to auditory hallucinations and even here there are differences in form. According to Parker & Schilder (1935) schizophrenic auditory hallucinations have a less marked sensory quality and a greater symbolic component than the alcoholic variety. Alpert & Silvers (1970) also found that schizophrenic hallucinations were periodic rather than continuous, were rarely of music, were localised inside the body or in the sky but not in an object or person, were exacerbated by social isolation but not arousal, had an intelligible message and incorporated a substantial emotional element. Taylor & Fleminger (1981) demonstrated lateralisation of schizophrenic auditory hallucinations: of 76 schizophrenics studied, 11 had lateralised auditory hallucinations—6 to the left, 2 to the right and 3 to both sides. Most investigators have found, however, that it is difficult to identify such physical characteristics, and some (Strauss 1969, Chapman & Chapman 1980) even regard the distinction between hallucinations and delusions as difficult to make. Strauss argued that hallucinations and delusions lay along on a continuum running from definite hallucinations with clear physical qualities to definite beliefs at the other end. In between there were phenomena which had both the qualities of abnormal percept and abnormal belief. Maack & Mullen (1983) gave an example of this in a schizophrenic patient who reported a Doppelgänger which was part belief in a double and yet had auditory, tactile and visual qualities. Sakai (1983) attributed such instances of phenomenological ambiguity to the unconventional use by subjects of words such as ear, head and hear.

Visual hallucinations

In general visual hallucinations are more characteristic of organic conditions. In my study comparing acute organic reactions with functional psychoses (mainly schizophrenic), 30% of the former had visual hallucination compared with 15% of the latter. In the study of Malitz et al (1962) the incidence in schizophrenia was 9% and in the IPSS (WHO 1973) 10%. However, there are some characteristics of the visual hallucinations which help one to distinguish them from those occurring in other conditions. In organic states they are generally of animals, brightly coloured and moving. (A patient of mine with delirium tremens saw chicken livers dripping blood coming down the stairs.) In depression they are often formless and horrible. (A depressed woman kept seeing black holes, 'blobby-like things' and faceless men.) In schizophrenia they are mainly complex scenes which are difficult to distinguish from ideas. They usually complement the delusions. (A schizophrenic woman saw a figure of God or Jesus out of the corner of her eye. This figure was reassuring, spoke with her voice and was occasionally involved in trying to empty her mind. It lasted about half an hour.) Feinberg (1962) obtained the following characteristics from questionnaires given to a large number of schizophrenics: they are related to delusions; brief episodes (seconds) characterised the acute and brief glimpses of familiar persons the chronic stage; there was often a withdrawal to a delusional world peopled by friendly relatives; usually only a single aspect of the environment would change (e.g. a huge eye in a normal face); or the environment remained the same but something was added to it (e.g. an angel on a wall). He concluded that the visual hallucinations were sudden, accompanied by emotional disturbance and were superimposed on a normal environment. In his comparison group, LSD takers, the visual hallucinations were patterns rather than objects, there was no emotional change and the environment underwent a complete alteration. In a study by Frieske & Wilson (1966) schizophrenic visual hallucinations differed from delirious and depressive types in rarely appearing at night, being less often experienced as moving and always being accompanied by hallucinations in some other modality.

Other hallucinations

Olfactory (Rubert et al 1961), gustatory (de Morsier 1938) and tactile hallucinations (Lukianowicz 1967) have been described in schizophrenia, but there are no studies on whether these have specific characteristics distinguishing them from those in other conditions (e.g. temporal lobe epilepsy).

Other perceptual disorders

In the early stages of a schizophrenic episode distortion of perception is common. This is illustrated in the next section. Things may look and sound different, people may be misidentified, colours may seem more lively and the emotional response may be quite disturbed. Varsamis & Adamson

(1971) reported that 24 of 44 schizophrenics had alterations in visual perception at the onset of a florid episode—changes in intensity (17), size (4), colour (2), texture (1) and movement (1). In Freedman & Chapman's (1973) study visual illusions, more acute auditory perception and misidentification of people were the most significant perceptual changes. In Freedman's (1974) analysis of autobiographical reports, the following items were prominent: enhanced sensory awareness, muted sensory awareness, less acute vision, visual illusions, changes in depth perception, changes in perception of own voice and mistaking identities of other people. In my study 50% of schizophrenics had experienced some form of visual distortion in the early stages (compared with 20% of depressives) and 17% had experienced auditory distortions (compared with 7% of depressives, (see p. 181).

Subjective experience of perceptual disorder

McGhie & Chapman (1961) quoted the following accounts:

> During the last while back I have noticed that noises all seem to be louder to me than they were before.
> Colours seem to be brighter now, almost as if they were luminous.
> I have noticed a lot recently that I seem to get a little mixed up about where sounds are coming from.
>
> (McGhie & Chapman 1961)

The following account by a patient in my care, given two weeks after the experiences had subsided, illustrates most of the perceptual disorders which can occur:

> I was in the kitchen. All the walls were pulsating. I felt boxed in. Then it started in the living room. Then I thought I was being poisoned. I kept thinking I was being watched by videocameras ... I had a tremendous feeling of claustrophobia. I felt trapped. Traffic was too loud. There were too many people on the pavement . . . Events sounded clearer. It seemed as if I could hear for miles, as if I could hear people down the street. It was all like a story. Middle of day seemed like night-time. All the bright colours were ones that frightened me most. Orange and red . . . I thought I'd been hypnotised because I met people that knew me and I didn't recognise them . . . I thought my language was wrong. I believed that no-one could understand what I said because I couldn't understand what I said. Just high-pitched noises came out. I could understand other people's language but not mine . . . I lost track of time completely and space, well, I'd panic. When the house was getting too small I'd go outside. But outside the noise was too great. Nowhere I could cope. Not even safe in bed.
>
> (Remitted schizophrenic)

The following accounts illustrate certain features in more detail:

> Colours meant a lot to me. Stood out. No I don't mean that there was a change in meaning, but it was just that they stood out. Especially traffic lights. I couldn't cross the road because of this.
>
> (Remitted schizophrenic)

> Sometimes I looked in the mirror and I looked older and sometimes younger. My wife looked fatter.
>
> (Remitted schizophrenic)
>
> People kept coming up to me in the street and they would say 'I know you' but I didn't know them.
>
> (Remitted schizophrenic)
>
> Most of the students there looked normal but one didn't. Nothing about his appearance but something about him disturbed me. The trousers he wore disturbed me—green, tweedy, loose around the bottom, which annoyed me.
>
> (Remitted schizophrenic)
>
> There was some change in colours. Subjective change. Certain shine which identified, well not really a colour.
>
> (Acute schizophrenic)
>
> One chap's eyes looked watery as if he was upset about looking at me.
>
> (Acute schizophrenic)
>
> Black looked brown sometimes. Brown looked red. [People?] They were different, yes, just the expressions on their faces. Just people in a grumpy state. My father seemed different.
>
> (Acute schizophrenic)
>
> Things were bad. As if I was on the Underground. It was like a dream. All I could see were people in a car. They looked like ghosts, statues, monuments, as if cremated.
>
> (Acute schizophrenic)

Compare the following accounts of depressed subjects:

> Things seemed more miserable, gloomier.
> Strange like I'll never get out there. Everything seemed hazy.
> People all looked evil. I could feel the evil in the air.

EXPERIMENTAL EVIDENCE

Visual perception

Basic processes

1. Sensitivity throughout visual field. Mednick (1955) and Kirschner (1964) claimed that schizophrenics were more likely to respond to stimuli in the periphery of the visual field than normals. They regarded this as evidence of stimulus generalisation, which Mednick used in his general theory of schizophrenia (p. 46). Cegalis & Tegtmeyer (1980) and Cegalis & Deptula (1981), however, showed that chronic schizophrenics had impaired perception both in the periphery *and* in the central field, relative to normals. Acute schizophrenics were not significantly different from neurotic controls.

It would appear, therefore, that there is no marked alteration of sensitivity in different parts of the visual field in schizophrenia.

2. Critical stimulus duration. This is the time that a thing has to be exposed for correct identification. Collins et al (1978) presented stimuli for 2 ms, 4 ms and 6 ms and then measured reaction time. Schizophrenics had similar reaction times to those of psychiatric controls. They were, in fact, nonsignificantly faster. Brody et al (1980) presented the letters T or A to

elderly normals, acute schizophrenics and depressives. The mean exposure time for correct recognition was respectively 210 ms, 26 ms and 13 ms, the latter difference being nonsignificant. Magaro & Page (1982) also found no difference between chronic schizophrenics, acute schizophrenics and normals in what they called 'icon threshold'.

It appears, therefore, that critical stimulus duration is also normal in acute schizophrenia.

3. Hemispheric integration. Spaulding et al (1980) presented different patterns of dots to each hemisphere simultaneously. Viewed separately they appeared random, but superimposed they made a recognisable number (e.g. 29). Acute schizophrenics saw numbers as often as normals did. The authors concluded that 'icon-processing abnormalities, as represented by visual pattern integration deficits, cannot account for posticonic abnormalities in schizophrenia'.

4. Visual search, span of apprehension. Several investigators have examined whether schizophrenics are differentially affected by having to identify one item in an array of several.

The usual procedure is to present a letter, or other symbol, in a matrix which is varied in size from 0 to as many as 200 other letters or symbols. Whether subjects are asked to report all the items (Cash et al 1972), only the target item (Davidson & Neale 1974, Russell et al 1980), or whether their reaction time is measured (Russell & Page 1976), the results have clearly indicated that schizophrenics are not *differentially* affected by increases in display size, although chronic schizophrenics are generally slower on all display sizes (Russell & Knight 1977).

5. Critical interstimulus interval. So far, it is clear that neither visual acuity, critical stimulus duration nor span or apprehension is specifically impaired. The next issue is whether the critical interstimulus interval, the time taken to adequately encode the stimulus, is abnormal. This is measured by presenting a stimulus for the critical duration and then masking it with another stimulus at various intervals after this. The critical interstimulus interval is the period during which masking interferes with recognition, and its duration is recorded by noting the time at which masking no longer causes this interference. Saccuzzo and Braff, in a number of experiments, demonstrated that schizophrenics, both acute and chronic, have a longer critical interstimulus duration than depressives or even manics (Saccuzzo & Braff 1981, Saccuzzo et al 1982). Schwartz & Winstead (1982) demonstrated that the reason for this was different in acute and chronic schizophrenics. In the former it appeared to be a genuine perceptual deficit because it varied with the experimental conditions. In chronic schizophrenics it appeared to be secondary to an attentional and motivational deficit because it remained at the same level of abnormality across all experimental conditions.

6. In conclusion, the only abnormality to have been demonstrated in basic visual perception is slowness in encoding the icon.

Form perception

1. Illusions. Some investigators have claimed that schizophrenics are less prone to see formal illusions than normals. Kelm (1968) reported that the figural after-effect was less marked in schizophrenia. The figural after-effect is elicited by asking a subject to fixate on one figure for a period of time, and then replacing it with another. The second figure will appear to be displaced in space. Kline (1971) claimed that the autokinetic effect, experiencing a pinpoint of light in a dark room as in motion, was absent in 51% of schizophrenics, but present in 100% of his normal controls.

Philip (1953), however, could find no difference between depressives and schizophrenics in the number of reversals of Lissajou figures (similar to the Necker cube); and Le Tourneau (1974) demonstrated that chronic schizophrenics could see the Oppel-Kundt and Muller-Lyer illusions (Fig. 14.1).

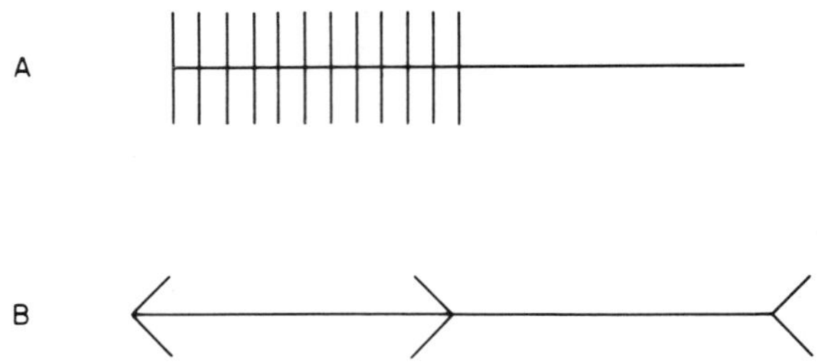

Fig. 14.1 Oppel-Kundt and Müller-Lyer illusions.
A: Oppel-Kundt illusion (scored segment of line looks longer than bare segment, though each is in fact the same length). **B**: Müller-Lyer illusion (second segment of line bounded by convex arrows looks longer than first, though both are the same).

2. General facial perception. Neufeld (1976) gave schematic faces, varying in four dimensions (e.g. length of nose), and demonstrated a deficit in judgements of intelligence in both paranoid and nonparanoid schizophrenics compared with normals. The two groups of schizophrenics differed, however, in the reasons for their deficit. Paranoid schizophrenics were less systematic in the way their judgements related to the dimensions, whereas the nonparanoid group assigned idiosyncratic weights to the dimensions. Levin & Benton (1977) demonstrated that chronic schizophrenics were, as a group, worse than neurotics in their facial recognition scores (matching presented face to sample face). Frith et al (1983) gave 21 acute Catego schizophrenics and 26 neurotics sets of schematic faces, nonsense objects and geometrical forms (histograms). Each of the three sets varied in five ways and subjects had to sort them. Neurotics were better in sorting faces than in sorting the geometrical forms, whereas this was not the case for schizophrenics. The authors concluded that in schizophrenics, unlike normals, 'the integrated gestalt of the face was not dominant over its components'.

3. Perception of facial expression. This has been investigated by asking

subjects to rank order expressions, to comment on them, to identify particular emotions, to classify them, to judge which of two faces shows a particular emotion more strongly and to compare two faces.

Izard (1959) asked 30 paranoid schizophrenics and 30 normals to comment on 16 photographs of normal people, and then rank them in order of preference. Judges rated the schizophrenics' comments as more unfavourable or more ambiguous than those of the normals, but their rank orders were similar. Iscoe & Veldman (1963) asked schizophrenics, children and normal adults to rank order 9 line drawings of faces from happy to unhappy. The normal adults and children ranked them in approximately the same order as the artist had intended, but the schizophrenics deviated from this pattern. Spiegel et al (1962) asked chronic schizophrenics and normals to rank faces (angry to happy), circles (flat oval to upright oval) and shapes (from triangular to circular). Schizophrenics carried out the first two rankings with the same accuracy as normals, but were incorrect on the last.

Pilowsky & Bassett (1980) simply asked schizophrenics and neurotics to comment on photographs of six faces. They found that schizophrenics were less likely to remark on the 'internal state of mind', more likely to relate their comments to aspects of themselves, and were, in general, more verbose.

Grodin & Brown (1967) prepared 81 schematic faces, varying linearly in critical features such as nose length, chin length, distance between eyes and height of forehead. Thirty-two subacute schizophrenics and 32 normals were then asked to identify which was friendly and which unfriendly. The object of the experiment was to see whether individual judgements were a linear function of facial variables. Of the 64 subjects, only 23 had linear regression equations above chance, but 16 of these were normals and only 7 schizophrenics, a proportion which the authors found was significant. Dougherty et al (1974) asked 31 chronic schizophrenics and 23 controls to identify the emotions in 32 faces, 4 of each of 8 types. Schizophrenics were correct 44% of the time, and normals 78%. Muzekari and Bates (1977) asked 32 chronic schizophrenics and 32 student controls to identify happiness, sadness, joy and anger from photos and videotapes. Schizophrenics were significantly less accurate. Walker et al (1980) gave photographs of faces displaying 8 emotions to 48 schizophrenics and 48 nonschizophrenic patients. The former were worse on all emotional types. La Russo (1978) asked 24 schizophrenics and 24 normals to decide whether actors on videotape were expecting an electric shock or merely simulating the expectancy. She found that the schizophrenics were *more* accurate than normals in guessing the genuine but worse in the simulated instances. (She concluded that normals were more adept at appreciating social stereotypes.)

Bespalko (1976), a Russian, and Harizuka (1977), a Japanese, both showed that schizophrenics classified facial expressions in an abnormal way. In Harizuka's experiment, this was only evident when subjects could choose their own categories.

I carried out a study (Cutting 1981) in which acute and chronic schizophrenics, depressives and neurotic controls had to judge whether one of a pair of faces was more friendly than the other. (The pairs had been previously judged by normals to be distinguishable and an accompanying task, judgement of colour of two similar hues, provided a control.) Acute but not chronic schizophrenics were markedly impaired in judging friendliness, relative to the controls, and relative to their judgements about colour (Fig. 14.2). In another experiment I then showed that in a more appropriate control task, judgement of age, acute schizophrenics were unimpaired relative to depressives.

Experiment

20 pairs of faces (all middle-aged men); 20 pairs of colours (similar hues) — to judge which is more friendly (faces) or more typical (colour).

All pairs previously rated by 20 normals so that at least 16 of the 20 agreed that one was more friendly/typical

Subjects

	IQ	*Age*	*Sex* m:f
40 neurotics	101	41	20:20
20 depressives	101	45	6:14
20 acute schizophrenics	100	33	11:9
20 chronic schizophrenics	96	39	17:3

Results

	Neurotics	*Depressives*	*Acute schizophrenics*	*Chronic schizophrenics*
Number of pairs in which subject's choice agreed with standardiser				
Typical colour	15.7	15.7	15.5	15.1
Friendlier face	16.6	16.4	*11.7*	15.3

Fig. 14.2 Experiment on judgement of facial expression by schizophrenics (Cutting).

Finally, there are several experiments in which pairs of photographs are presented and subjects are asked to compare them. The best of these was devised by Dixon (1968). She presented pairs of photographs of different people, displaying the same or a different facial expression. Subjects were asked to 'list all the differences between the people in the pictures', and their responses were then rated for content under 12 headings (activity, background, clothes, emotion, age, nationality, occupation, physique, stance, photographic detail, denial that there were any differences and irrelevant comments). Schizophrenics made more remarks about the background, more often denied any differences and made more irrelevant comments than did normals. The latter made more remarks about emotion, age, occupation or physique. When schizophrenics were divided into those with flattening of affect and those without, the main difference between these two groups was a tendency for those with flattened affect to make fewer comments about emotion. This last finding was confirmed by McPherson et al (1970), who then demonstrated correlations between a reluctance to note emotional differences and an abnormal score on the Bannister grid (see p. 337, McPherson et al 1971). Williams & Quirke (1972) reduced Dixon's categories to two: psychological and nonpsychological. They then found that schizophrenics used fewer psychological words than controls, and this correlated with affective flattening, thought disorder and withdrawal. Bodlakova et al (1974) confirmed the general association between schizophrenia and nonpsychological descriptions, but found it less marked when the comparison was between people that they had nominated than photographs of faces.

4. Perception of ambiguous pictures. Several Russian investigators (Polyakov 1969; Feigenberg 1969) have claimed that if photographs of common objects are presented out-of-focus and then the focussing is gradually improved, schizophrenics recognise them at a later stage (i.e. require more focussing) than normals. (The same investigators claimed that the reverse was true in the case of unusual images, e.g. man writing with foot. This has a bearing on the probabilistic theory of schizophrenia, p. 370.) Ebner & Ritzler (1969), however, found no differences between acute schizophrenics and normals on blurred pictures, but did confirm the Russian findings in the case of chronic schizophrenics.

The reputation of the Rorschach as a diagnostic tool relied on the schizophrenics' tendency to perceive ambiguous forms in an idiosyncratic way. Beck (1944) argued that this was not due to the more fantastic imagination of schizophrenics, because nonpsychotics gave even more fantastic interpretations. What characterised the schizophrenics' responses, according to Beck, were two types of perceptual errors: failure to recognise the presenting stimulus and distortion on the basis of personal needs (e.g. woman's face for man's whilst preoccupied with masturbation).

Crookes & Hutt (1970) demonstrated that schizophrenics were worse than neurotics in perceiving Gottschaldt's embedded figures (one form embedded in another). Straube (1975) reported that both acute and chronic schizophrenics did badly on Gestalt-influenced tests designed to elicit whether subjects could distinguish figure from background.

5. Perceptual strategy. Several investigators have reported that schizophrenics, particularly paranoid and deluded subjects, tend to jump to conclusions more readily than other subjects. McReynolds et al (1964) gave paranoid and nonparanoid schizophrenics the McGill closure test (44 incomplete pictures to identify). The paranoid subjects attempted more than the nonparanoid, from which the authors concluded that 'delusional schizophrenics have a stronger tendency to organise ambiguous stimuli in a meaningful way'. Abroms et al (1966) reported that incorrect recognition of ambiguous pictures correlated with the strength of paranoid delusions, and that despite their incorrect score paranoid subjects made more overall

guesses than nonparanoid or mildly paranoid subjects. The authors concluded that the former tended to 'assimilate information' more readily. Ross & Magaro (1976) reported that paranoid schizophrenics were more influenced by contextual cues under these experimental conditions than nonparanoid schizophrenics or psychiatric controls. Presented with an ambiguous picture they readily accepted the cue in an accompanying sentence (e.g. 'Sam listened to the news on the . . .'.). McCormick & Broekema (1978), presenting blurred pictures of zoo animals, found that paranoid schizophrenics gave more responses than either nonparanoid schizophrenics or alcoholics, and with a greater degree of confidence. They concluded that 'paranoid subjects show a unique jump-to-conclusion response strategy'.

Bemporad (1967), Schwartz Place & Gilmore (1980) and Reich & Cutting (1982) examined a different strategy. In the first study acute, chronic and

Subjects 10 subacute schizophrenics
10 drug addicts (controls)

Material 3 types of cards

1) 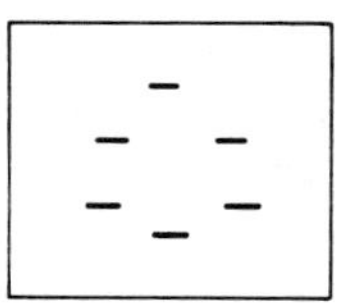 Homogeneous — 3, 4, 5, or 6 lines in same direction

2) 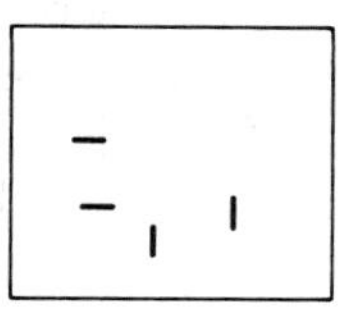 Adjacent heterogeneous — 3, 4, 5, or 6 lines in different directions but in pairs with the same direction

3) 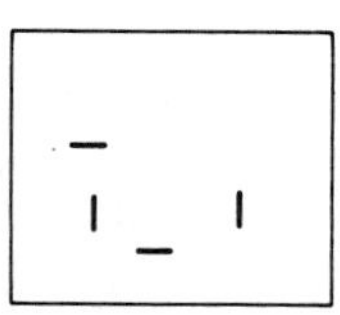 Nonadjacent heterogeneous — 3, 4, 5, or 6 lines in different directions, not paired

Method Cards presented tachistoscopically for 20 milliseconds. Subjects to report how many lines they saw.

Results (% correct)

	Schizophrenics lines				*Controls* lines			
	3	*4*	*5*	*6*	*3*	*4*	*5*	*6*
Homogeneous (1)	62	48	36	24	70	60	41	29
Adjacent heterogeneous (2)	54	42	32	21	44	24	16	5
Nonadjacent heterogeneous (3)	59	47	30	25	48	18	10	0

Fig. 14.3 Experiment on perceptual organisation (Schwartz Place and Gilmore).

remitted schizophrenics and normals were shown cards on which were displayed numbers made up of dots camouflaged in a hazy background. All three schizophrenic groups perceived these less well than normals, but the most striking finding was that they tended to see the dots first and then the number ('bottom-up strategy'), whereas the normals did the reverse ('top-down strategy'). The experiment of Schwartz Place and Gilmore is summarised in Figure 14.3. The chief finding was that, whereas controls found a disorderly configuration more difficult to perceive than an orderly, this was not true of schizophrenics. Most striking of all was the fact that schizophrenics were significantly *better* on the disorderly patterns than were controls. The authors concluded that schizophrenics do not respond to organisational factors in the way normals do, and that they generally adopt an analytic approach to perceptual tasks. Often this is a disadvantage, but in this particular task it was an advantage. The normals' search for some structure in the heterogeneous configurations was an inefficient strategy in this instance. As in Bemporad's study, schizophrenics appeared to favour a piecemeal strategy. In the third study, acute schizophrenics, depressives and normals had to identify the theme of a complex picture (a family packing to go on holiday, Fig. 14.4). Although schizophrenics were not substantially impaired in arriving at the correct theme, they approached the task differently: beginning with detail rather than, as the controls, reaching the conclusion straight away.

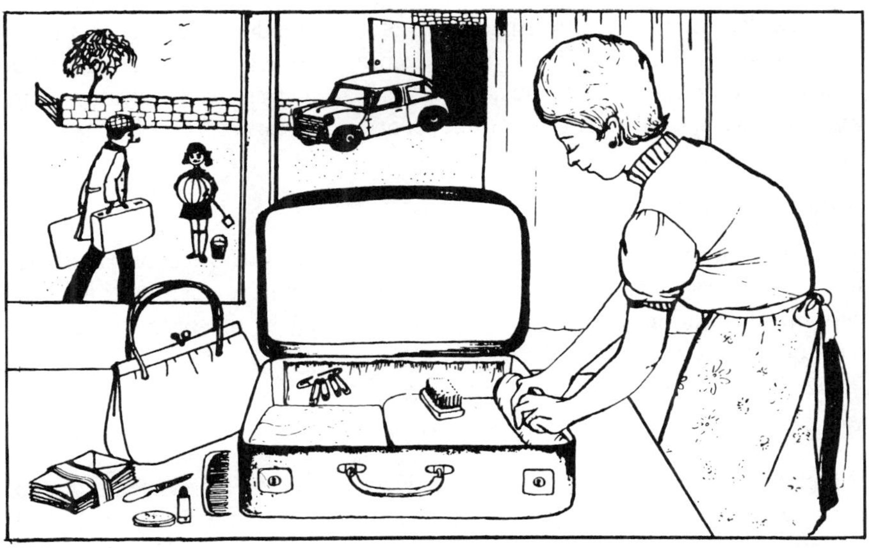

Fig. 14.4 Complex picture used to compare perceptual strategy in acute schizophrenics, depressives and normals.

Space perception

Weckowicz (1957) investigated size constancy by asking subjects to estimate the length of a rod several feet away by adjusting a rod in front of them to the same length. He claimed that schizophrenics tended to underestimate the length of the rod relative to other subjects, and that this was more marked the further away the rod was, implying that they were more influenced by the size of the retinal image than were other subjects.

Since Weckowicz' experiment, there have been a number of other experiments on the matter, with conflicting results. Neale et al (1969b), reviewing the issue, concluded that acute and paranoid schizophrenics tend to underestimate size, and that chronic and nonparanoid schizophrenics tend to overestimate it. In my view, the precise pattern of their size estimation is less important than whether their overall spatial perception is different from appropriate controls. Unfortunately, this is not clear from the numerous experiments.

Summary

Visual perception in schizophrenia has attracted considerable attention from investigators. Basic processes, such as visual acuity in the peripheral field, critical stimulus duration and ability to apprehend items in arrays of different sizes, are probably normal in acute schizophrenia, although there may be some delay in processing this information. Spatial perception may or may not be disturbed. Most experiments on form perception, however, *have* revealed some abnormality. Although some studies have been methodologically unsound, altogether they provide moderate evidence for an abnormality in this sphere. Even more impressive are claims that schizophrenics adopt an unusual, or at least an inappropriate, strategy during such tasks, concentrating on details at the expense of theme.

Auditory perception

Studies of auditory perception fall into three groups: those concerned with basic processes in all schizophrenics, those which have examined the perception of emotion and those which have looked at the predisposition to auditory hallucinations.

Basic processes

Rappaport et al (1972) and Gruzelier & Hammond (1979) reported impaired tone perception, and Balogh (Balogh et al 1979, Balogh & Leventhal 1982) impaired sound localisation in schizophrenics. Bruder et al (1975), however, found a normal auditory threshold for click, and Hemsley & Zawada (1976) no difference from depressives in speech perception. The issue has already been considered on page 254, in the context of language perception. It was concluded then that any differences must be minor in order to explain the normal perception of grammatical and semantical components of language.

It should also be noted that the incidence of schizophrenia in normally hearing and deaf siblings of schizophrenics is equal (Altshuler 1971). If a hearing deficit were important, the deaf sibling would be more susceptible.

Kugler et al (1982) demonstrated a lateralised audiometric impairment in 20 chronic Catego schizophrenics: their hearing was better in the right than in the left ear. (They considered that this favoured a left hemisphere deficit, a mystifying conclusion as to me it signifies right hemisphere dysfunction.)

Perception of emotion

Experiments on the perception of emotion in speech were considered on page 254. There are only two experiments, to my knowledge, on the perception of emotion in music. Simon et al (1951) asked schizophrenics, manics, depressives and normals to identify the dominant mood of eight pieces of music (sad, happy, neither). Schizophrenics were worse than normals or depressives, but equal to manics, in their identification of sad music; and they were worse than normals, but equal to manics and depressives, in identifying happy music. From this one might conclude that schizophrenics are generally anhedonic, whilst depressives merely have a jaundiced view of the world. This is not supported, however, in the other study by Nielzen & Cesarec (1982), who found that depressives found seven pieces of music less cheerful and less attractive than normals or schizophrenics did, but schizophrenics found them more attractive than normals.

Predisposition to auditory hallucinations

Suggested psychological factors predisposing to auditory hallucinations are: hyperactivity of the vocal musculature, altered auditory imagery, impaired auditory perception, inattention and sensory isolation, impaired recognition of own thoughts, poor reality testing, emotional disturbance and a certain personality type.

1. Hyperactivity of the vocal musculature. Gould (1948) carried out electromyograms on the throat of 100 schizophrenics, 48 of whom had hallucinations, and 100 normals. He reported increased potential in only 28% of normals but 83% of those with auditory hallucinations. He proposed that hallucinations were the involuntary intensification of the psychomotor mechanism of speech. In a subsequent article (Gould 1949) he found, in one hallucinating subject, a 'marked correspondence between subvocal speech as heard by an investigator and the voices heard by the subject'. McGuigan (1966) also found that 'covert oral behaviour' (just audible whispering) increased just prior to the subject's report of an auditory hallucination, and that action potentials in the chin muscles and breathing amplitude increased at the same time. Since then, the topic has not attracted any interest, and the findings must remain unproven.

2. Altered auditory imagery. Seitz & Molholm (1947) reported that hallucinating schizophrenics had less vivid auditory imagery to a series of words than nonhallucinating schizophrenics. Mintz & Alpert (1972) found the reverse: hallucinating schizophrenics reported more vivid imagery when asked to imagine, for example, the song *White Christmas* being played. Slade (1976) also found that hallucinating and nonhallucinating schizophrenics had more vivid auditory imagery than normals, but they did not differ between themselves The most recent studies (Brett & Starker 1977, Starker & Jolin 1982, Heilbrun et al 1983) have supported the conclusions of Seitz and Molholm that auditory hallucinations are more common in those with *diminished* capacity for auditory imagery.

3. Impaired auditory perception. Bazhin et al (1975) reported that hallucinating schizophrenics had impaired auditory perception in their right ear, indicated by a raised auditory threshold. Collicutt & Hemsley (1981), however, found that the magnitude of 'just noticeable differences' in hallucinating schizophrenics, old people and neurotics were comparable, and Alpert et al (1976) that nonhallucinating schizophrenics were actually worse than hallucinators on several measures of language perception. It is doubtful, therefore, if a hearing impediment is very important. This is borne out by Altshuler's (1971) report that auditory hallucinations occurred in 22 out of 57 completely deaf schizophrenics (close to the 50% incidence in schizophrenics with normal hearing). Even prelingually profoundly deaf schizophrenics (Critchley et al 1981) report experiences which resemble auditory hallucinations (e.g. 'a voice like a bell', experiencing the deaf and dumb sign for 'talk').

4. Inattention and sensory isolation. Margo et al (1981) demonstrated that hallucinating schizophrenics experienced most hallucinations when presented with white noise over headphones and when visual information was restricted by goggles. Few hallucinations occurred while reading prose or listening to an interesting conversation. Strauss et al (1981) illustrated this with a quote from one of their patients:

> Isn't it funny. When I'm shovelling snow I don't hear voices.
>
> (Strauss et al 1981)

5. Impaired recognition of own thoughts. Heilbrun (1980) claimed that hallucinating schizophrenics were less adept than nonhallucinators at recognising whether an answer to a proverb given earlier was theirs or someone else's.

6. Poor reality testing. Mintz & Alpert (1972) found that, in addition to having more vivid auditory imagery, hallucinators were more confident than nonhallucinators about their performance on a sentence repetition task. This overconfidence, which was accompanied by a substantial error rate, the authors regarded as evidence of poor reality testing. Slade (1976) also came to this conclusion when he demonstrated that hallucinators had a more pronounced 'verbal transformation effect'. A word such as 'tress' is continually

repeated, and subjects have to report how many different words with a phonetic relationship to it (e.g. stress, truss) they hear. The greater the number of words, the greater the verbal transformation effect and the worse the reality testing.

7. Emotional disturbance. Slade (1976) included anxiety in his 'model of hallucinations' (the other components being vivid imagery, poor reality testing, restricted external stimulation and positive reinforcement). His evidence for an emotional component came from the diary he asked one of his patients to keep (Slade 1972). This man experienced an increased number of auditory hallucinations when tense, miserable or angry. Cooklin et al (1983) also found an association between heightened emotion (increase in number of spontaneous GSR fluctuations) and observer ratings of the presence of hallucinations.

8. Personality type. Judkins & Slade (1981) found that persistent hallucinators gave higher scores on a hostility questionnaire than nonhallucinators, though whether this was due to a transient, angry state or an enduring personality trait is not clear. Zigler & Levine (1983) found that hallucinators had less developed social competence (based on Phillips scale, see p. 99) than deluded schizophrenics. In accordance with Strauss' notion (see p. 289) that hallucinations and delusions were points on the same continuum, they believed that personality determined the precise position on this continuum.

Summary

Sensory isolation and heightened arousal are the two most well-established factors predisposing to auditory hallucinations. Impaired hearing is unimportant and diminished rather than enhanced auditory imagery may play a part. Personality, impaired reality testing and hyperactive voice muscles are not researched enough to be sure of their status. There is some evidence that all schizophrenics have impaired hearing, possibly with a lateral bias and possibly affecting perception of emotion more than neutral topics.

Other modes of perception

Proprioception

Ebner et al (1971) asked chronic schizophrenics and normals to move their hand to a predetermined position while observing it through a prism. The schizophrenics were less proficient than normals, which the authors interpreted as evidence for impaired proprioception. (They claimed that normals, under these circumstances, could ignore the unreliable visual information and make use of the reliable proprioceptive channel, but schizophrenics could not.) Ritzler (1977) found that although schizophrenics as a group were worse than nonschizophrenic patients on weight discrimination and arm flexion judgement, this only occurred in chronic patients, and applied equally to chronic nonschizophrenic patients. Erwin & Rosenbaum (1979) demonstrated impaired weight discrimination, but not tactile size estimation or finger gnosis, in chronic schizophrenics. They claimed that proprioception but not tactile perception was deficient.

Pain perception

Marchand et al (1959) reported the incidence of reports of pain in 79 psychotic inpatients who had required a surgical operation (fractured femur, appendicitis, perforated peptic ulcer) over 12 years. In 29 cases there had been no complaint of pain, the proportion being the same amongst schizophrenics as nonschizophrenics. They concluded that 'in a sizeable minority, the meaning of pain' had been lost. Watson et al (1981a) studied the incidence of complaints of pain in 78 Schneiderian schizophrenics. Twenty-nine complained of pain, of whom 16 had no physical cause for it. Although this would appear to contradict the previous report, as schizophrenics had certainly not lost 'the meaning of pain', the authors still considered that the incidence of pain was lower than in other psychiatric illnesses.

Tactile form perception

If a normal person is asked to judge blindfold the length of a bar, they will adjust their estimate after having their hand rubbed along it. This is known as the kinaesthetic after-effect. Houpt et al (1972) demonstrated that schizophrenics tended to reduce their estimate under these circumstances, whilst Ritzler (1977) found no significant differences from controls.

Body image perception

The body image is a loose term for the way one represents one's body. It requires the integration of a number of perceptual modalities. Chapman et al (1978) devised a body image questionnaire which they then gave to schizophrenics, and obtained reports of abnormal bodily experiences. Cleveland et al (1962) and Weckowicz & Sommer (1960) demonstrated abnormal estimates of body parts in schizophrenics asked to judge whether their own body part was the same size as a corresponding picture in front of them.

Vestibular perception

Ornitz (1970), reviewing the evidence for vestibular dysfunction in schizophrenia, concluded that:

> studies of schizophrenic patients in 11 different laboratories during the last 5 decades have found reduced nystagmus in response to galvanic, caloric and

> rotational stimulation of the vestibular system . . . and that central vestibular mechanisms play a fundamental role in the pathogenesis.
>
> (Ornitz 1970)

This must remain speculative, because several authors, including Jones & Pivik (1983), have reported that the usual indices of vestibular reactivity were normal.

Summary

Of the other modes of perception studied, there is a small amount of evidence for a disorder of body image perception in some patients. Whether this arises from an impairment in proprioception, in visual perception or in the integration of the two is not clear.

CONCLUSIONS

Is perception impaired in schizophrenia?

Kraepelin and Bleuler were wrong in their claim that perception is normal. There is overwhelming evidence that complex perception in at least the visual modality is abnormal in acute schizophrenics.

What is the nature of the perceptual disorder?

Basic processes are probably normal, although there may be some slowness in encoding the visual stimulus and possibly a lateralised deficit in auditory perception. The most compelling claim is for a disorder of form perception, affecting the way faces, ambiguous objects, pictures and patterns are seen. The common theme underlying these abnormalities appears to be a disorder of strategy rather than a failure of one aspect of perception. Schizophrenics, in general, appear to be overanalytic and too preoccupied with detail at the expense of forming a gestalt or seeing order in things. Sometimes this is an advantage for them, but usually it is a disadvantage. Shakow (1950) wrote about 'an inability to keep a major set . . . a primary need to establish minor sets' and the fact that a schizophrenic 'can't see the wood for the trees . . . and examines each tree with meticulous care'. Arieti (1966) used the terms 'awholism' and 'perceptual and apperceptual fragmentation'.

What is the cause of the perceptual disorder?

As discussed in the introduction to this chapter, thought disorder, emotional disturbance and attentional deficit have been the most frequent explanations. Bleuler favoured a combination of thought and emotional disorder. Psychoanalysts have usually singled out a disorder of emotion. (Le Roux, 1980, for example, wrote that, 'the function of hallucinatory states often appears to make up for successive frustration, sexual and affective insufficiency'.) Behaviourists also placed great emphasis on emotional disorder. (Claridge, 1972, for example, considered that 'marked changes in arousal in either direction could result in disproportionate alterations in perceptual sensitivity'.) In addition to these main suggestions, disorders of consciousness and memory have also been suggested. (Frith, 1979, wrote that, 'when a speech sound is heard a number of hypotheses are made . . . only the final results of this very rapid process normally arrives into consciousness but clearly a number of incorrect interpretations will be present in the preconscious . . . the awareness of these incorrect early interpretations is the basis of auditory hallucinations'. Hebb, 1968, and Jarvik, 1970, both believed that hallucinations came about through an impairment in memory and learning, which caused a subject to misidentify the contents of memory as the contents of perception.)

In my view perceptual disorder cannot be relegated to a secondary deficit in this way. If it were, then there would be no particular pattern to the disorder, which is not the case. Even more telling, the overanalytic approach to perceptual tasks and the neglect of the gestalt indicates that the perceptual disorder cannot be secondary to another simple functional deficit but must be a consequence of a much wider cognitive disturbance. In my view, the pattern of perceptual disorder provides the strongest evidence yet for a hemispheric imbalance in schizophrenia, and in particular right hemisphere dysfunction in conjuction with left hemisphere functional exaggeration. The argument mainly rests on recent advances in knowledge about hemispheric contributions to perception.

In general, the right hemisphere is more concerned than the left in the perception of meaningless shapes (Warrington & James 1967), particularly if they are complex (Umilta et al 1978). It is generally more efficient at facial perception, but only for upright faces (Yin 1970) and only if global judgements (e.g. emotion) rather than physical details (e.g. size of chin) are asked for (Proudfoot 1982). There is a right hemisphere advantage for perceiving musical chords (Gordon 1970) and meaningless noises (e.g. radio crackling, Faglioni et al 1969). This effect disappears when sounds become meaningful (e.g. dog barking, Faglioni et al 1969, melodies, particularly to a musician, Johnson 1977). The right hemisphere is especially concerned in the perception of extrapersonal space (Semmes et al 1963).

The right hemisphere superiority in perceiving these stimuli is not absolute. Sex, handedness and instructions all modify the effect, though the details are still unclear. Males have been generally found to have a more pronounced right hemisphere advantage in nonverbal tasks (McGlone & Kertesz 1973); left-handedness diminishes the effect (McKeever & van Deventer 1977); and hemispheric differences are magnified when perceptual strategy rather than stimulus is manipulated. When parallel rather than serial (Cohen 1973), holistic rather than analytic (Bradshaw et al 1976) or global rather than detailed (Martin 1979) processing is required, the right hemisphere advantage becomes most marked. Levy (1974) concluded:

> The left hemisphere is almost obsessed with parts . . . patients with an intact left hemisphere but lesions in the right always drew pictures piecemeal, item by item and detail by detail without any grasp of the object as a whole. Patients with an intact right hemisphere but lesions in the left showed the reverse: oversimplified pictures with good gestalt but lacking detail.
>
> (Levy 1974)

This picture of the hemispheric control of perception is borne out if one examines the consequences of right hemisphere dysfunction. Right posterior quadrant damage is responsible for the occurrence of simple, visual hallucinations (Feldman & Bender 1970, Lance 1976), impaired visual position discrimination (Taylor & Warrington 1973) and a variety of visual distortions (Critchley 1953). Abnormal perceptual classification (Warrington & Taylor 1973) and impaired appreciation of the spatial aspects of things (Paterson & Zangwill 1944) also occur. Baldwin (1970) obtained reports of visual hallucinations when he stimulated the right hemisphere of epileptics but rarely when he stimulated the left.

In the light of this neuropsychological evidence it is reasonable to conclude that the visual distortions in the early stages of schizophrenia, the visual hallucinations in the later stages and the overanalysis and underuse of gestalt all point to a right hemisphere dysfunction in the condition.

The cause of auditory hallucinations has always been a mystery, and there are very few plausible explanations. In my view, the fact that in schizophrenia they are invariably verbal and that if anything auditory imagery is diminished points again to exaggerated left hemisphere functions.

SUMMARY

Perception is both the act of representing the world to consciousness, and the contents of that act. The posterior half of the right hemisphere is the main region involved in higher-order perception, but the more familiar, meaningful or easily formulated in words the item, the more the left hemisphere plays a part.

Disorders of visual perception include blindness and simple visual impairment, disturbances of form perception (distortion, object agnosia, prosopagnosia, simultanagnosia), abnormal space and colour perception, alterations in the temporal (palinopsia) and emotional (dysaesthesia) components, synaesthesia (sensation in one modality triggering perception in another) and hallucinations. Auditory disorders include deafness and hearing impairment, distortions of sound, agnosia, neglect and hallucinations. Tactile and kinaesthetic disorders comprise anaesthesia, higher order tactile and proprioceptive loss, neglect, phantom limb and loosely named 'body image disorders'. Olfactory, gustatory, visceral and vestibular disorders also occur.

In schizophrenia, the two chief clinical considerations are the frequency of perceptual changes amongst the early subjective experiences and the form of the hallucinations in subsequent stages.

Investigators have studied basic visual processes (acuity, critical stimulus duration, span of apprehension and critical interstimulus interval), all of which, except for a mild prolongation of the last, have been normal. Form perception, however, is almost certainly abnormal. The most convincing evidence comes from examination of the strategy employed rather than the standard of performance achieved. Schizophrenics tend to adopt a piecemeal, analytic, intellectual approach. An abnormal response to illusion, deficient perception of ambiguous and out-of-focus pictures and impaired facial perception may all be secondary to an inefficient strategy. Deficient space perception may also exist. Studies of auditory perception have addressed three issues: the evaluation of basic hearing processes, evidence of specific impairment in perceiving emotion in sound and the search for any factors which might predispose to hallucinations. Sensory isolation and heightened arousal are the only two definite factors predisposing to hallucinations. There is insufficient evidence to say whether basic processes and perception of nonverbal emotion are normal or not. There are not enough studies of other perceptual modes to say if these are intact.

Theoretical considerations, as in other types of psychological dysfunction, concern the direction of cause and effect. There are attractive explanations of how the perceptual disorder could be secondary to an abnormality of some other function, but these do not give a satisfactory account of the pattern of the disorder. For this reason, I favour an explanation which attributes all abnormalities to an inefficient cognitive strategy rather than to abasic abnormality of some other function or even perception itself. It is this theory which in my view provides the best account of the facts. The general theory promoted in this book, of right hemisphere dysfunction and left hemisphere overactivation, is consistent with this strategic impairment.

15

Thought

INTRODUCTION

Kraepelin gave many examples of disturbed thought in dementia praecox. According to him, the 'train of thought suffered considerably . . . judgement suffered without exception . . . mental efficiency was diminished . . . delusions occurred . . . thought was constrained . . . and there could be stereotypies—persistence of a single idea'. Two other disturbances which he mentioned—'paralogia' and 'derailment in the expression of a thought'—attracted most attention subsequently. Paralogia was a disorder in which 'an idea next in the chain of thought is suppressed and replaced by another related to it'. As an example of derailment he quoted a patient who had said, 'I have a voluntary disease of the eyes'. Kraepelin, however, did not give thought disorder a key role in his concept of dementia praecox, regarding it as secondary to the 'weakening or annihilation of . . . higher emotion and trend of volition'.

Bleuler did regard thought disorder as the most important psychological dysfunction is schizophrenia. For him, it was a direct consequence of the loosening of associations which he considered the basis of the condition. He illustrated the disturbed thinking with a short story written by a schizophrenic. It was called 'The Blossoming-Time of Horticulture' and began as follows:

> At the time of the new moon venuss stands in the Augutsky of Egypt and lights up with its light rays the merchant-travel-harbours of Suez, Cairo and Alexandria. In this historically famous Caliphcity is the museum of Assyrian statues from Macedonia. Besides pisang, also corn, oats, clover and barley grow there. Bananas, figs, lemons, oranges and olives. Olive oil is an Arabian liqueur sauce which the Afghans, Blackamoors and Moslemites use for ostrich breeding . . .
>
> (Bleuler 1911)

Bleuler believed that in schizophrenia:

> The innumerable actual and latent ideas which determine associations in normal trains of ideas may be rendered singly or in any combination ineffective . . . In turn ideas may come into play that have little or no connection to the

> main idea and should have been excluded from the train of thought. Thereby thinking is rendered incoherent, bizarre, incorrect and inept.
>
> (Bleuler 1911)

Freud and Jung saw in schizophrenic thinking a dramatic and living illustration of the workings of the unconscious. In fact Jung later admitted that:

> It was this frequent reversion to archaic forms of association found in schizophrenia that first gave me the idea of an unconscious not consisting only of originally conscious contents that have got lost but having a deeper layer of the same universal character as the mythological motifs which typify human fantasy in general.
>
> (Jung 1958)

Freud wrote:

> In schizophrenia words are subjected to the same process as that which makes the dream-images out of latent dream-thoughts, to what we have called the primary psychical processes.
>
> (Freud 1915)

In the 1920s the distinction between a disorder in the form of thinking—formal thought disorder—and a disorder in its content—delusion—was first emphasised (Schilder 1920). Jaspers and his pupils Gruhle and Schneider concentrated on the nature of the latter, while other psychiatrists suggested explanations of the former. The most popular of these was the notion of regression. Storch, (1924), in a monograph entitled *The primitive archaic forms of inner experience and thought in schizophrenia*, wrote:

> Schizophrenics sink back entirely into a primitive world of feeling and thought, into a world of the percept-images, the magic wish fulfillment, metamorphoses and mystical participants.
>
> (Storch 1924)

Throughout the next three decades thought disorder remained the most investigated psychological dysfunction. Vygotsky (1934) believed that it represented a reactivation of adolescent thinking (see p. 36). Goldstein (1939) attributed it to a loss of the abstract attitude (see p. 38). Cameron (1938) regarded it as an aspect of social maladjustment (see p. 38). It was also an important diagnostic aid. Proverb interpretation and object sorting were widely used for this purpose.

By the 1960s the term schizophrenic thought disorder had acquired so many meanings that many writers on the subject were recommending that it be disbanded. To psychiatrists it generally meant formal thought disorder—a clinically observed disorder of the form of thought confined to a minority of schizophrenics—for which there were many vivid but overlapping descriptions (e.g. derailment, knight's move thinking, etc., see p. 320). It was being ignored as a diagnostic aid in favour of certain types of delusions and hallucinations, as recommended by Schneider. To psychologists it generally meant the overall psychological dysfunction, but as this was conceived differently according to the theoretical orientation of the psychologist (behaviourist, cognitive, psychoanalytic), and as psychologists generally had a broader view of schizophrenia than psychiatrists, thought disorder had become virtually synonymous with mental disorder. Attempts to measure the disorder or to identify a specific pattern were unsatisfactory. One of the most promising measures, Bannister's repertory grid (see p. 337), failed because subjects were so inconsistent in their responses that no pattern could be reliably demonstrated. For these reasons investigators turned to other explanations of psychological dysfunction (e.g. attentional deficit, perceptual disorder, communication breakdown) and tended to regard thought disorder as a nonspecific disturbance with multiple causes.

Whilst acknowledging that much of the thought disorder in schizophrenia *is* heterogeneous in nature, the purpose of this chapter is to discover whether some forms are characteristic of the condition.

CLINICAL CONSIDERATIONS

General disorders of thinking

Thinking and thought have a number of meanings and components, and these are reflected in the various terms used to describe disordered thought. Wittgenstein asked:

> What is thinking? . . . What has one learnt to use this word for? . . . When I think in language, there aren't meanings going through my mind in addition to the verbal expressions: the language is itself the vehicle of thought . . . It isn't true that thinking is a kind of speaking, as I once said. The concept 'thinking' is categorically different from the concept 'speaking' . . . The word 'thinking' can be used to signify, roughly speaking, a talking for a purpose . . . a speaking in the imagination, a 'speaking in the head' as it were.
>
> (Wittgenstein 1980)

According to Johnson (1972) thought denotes four things: a topic (a subset of psychological data), a mental experience (what one is attending to), a means of solving problems (reasoning and judgement) and a process (involving concepts and categories). Psychologists tend to interpret the meaning more strictly than philosophers, as Cohen put it:

> For the psychologist, studies of thinking tend to be restricted to goal-directed reasoning, problem solving and categorisation processes, and many kinds of mental activity which take place without identifiable input and output, such as believing, reflecting, considering, musing and imagining, are excluded.
>
> (Cohen 1977)

A classification of thought disorders is presented in Table 15.1. They will be briefly summarised so that any pattern to schizophrenic thought can be placed in perspective.

Table 15.1 Classification of thought disorders

Abnormality of:	Example	Characteristic of:
Flow and control		
speed	Bradyphrenia, racing	Parkinson's, mania
resistance to unwelcome thoughts	Obsessional thinking	Obsessional neurosis
sense of ownership	Thought interference	Schizophrenia
impulse to start or change	Perseveration	Frontal lesions
General quality	Confusion, muzzy thinking	Acute organic reaction
Specific varieties		
concept attainment	Paralogia, formal thought disorder	Schizophrenia, acute organic states
categorisation	Overinclusive thinking	Acute schizophrenia
abstract thinking	Concrete thinking	Chronic organic states
belief	Delusion	Organic and functional psychosis
spatial thought	Topographical disorientation	Right parietal lesions
temporal thought	Disorientation for time	Organic states
thought about psychological and social topics	Autism	Asperger's syndrome, schizophrenia
imagery	Loss of imagery	Head injury
metaphor	Inadequate, uncreative thinking, poverty of content	Chronic organic states, schizophrenia

Disorders of flow and control

Slowing of thoughts or bradyphrenia characteristically occurs in Parkinson's disease and other types of subcortical dementia (Wilson et al 1980). Speeding up of thoughts is seen in mania (Braden & Ho 1981). Unwelcome thinking, where certain thoughts intrude into consciousness against the wish of the subject, occurs in temporal lobe epilepsy ('forced thinking', Penfield & Jasper 1954), in postencephalitic Parkinsonism (Schwab et al 1951) and as a condition in itself—obsessive-compulsive neurosis (e.g. Stern & Cobb 1978). In these conditions the thoughts are recognised as belonging to oneself, unlike schizophrenia where subjects may experience their thoughts as alien, inserted, known to others or extracted from their minds by an outside agency. Perseveration—continuing inappropriately along an established train of thought—and lack of initiative are both examples of an abnormality in the impulses governing thought. They are characteristic of frontal lesions (Brickner 1936).

Disorders of the general quality

The terms 'confusion' and 'muddled thinking' are nonspecific descriptions of disturbed thought.

Disorders of concept attainment

A concept exists 'whenever two or more distinguishable objects or events are set aside from other objects on the basis of some common feature' (Bourne 1966). Many terms have been used for a deviation from standard, logical verbal thinking. Illogicality, paralogia, the Ganser state (approximate answers, Vorbeireden) and dereistic thinking are some of them. Illogicality is the most general term. Paralogia (von Domarus 1944, Brown 1977) is a type in which two nouns are considered identical because they have one property in common (e.g. because stags and Indians are both swift it is concluded that stags are the same as Indians). Von Domarus regarded it as 'an adjective processing fault', and Brown as 'describing one thing through the semantic field of another'. In the Ganser state a subject gives an answer to a simple question which is false, but so close to the correct answer that one has to assume that they are aware of the correct answer. (How many legs has a cow? Three. What do 4 and 2 add up to? 5.) It was originally described by Ganser (1898) in three prisoners awaiting trial, all of whom were psychotic and all of whom had a history of organic factors—head injury, typhoid. For these reasons, it has never been clear if it is a form of hysteria, malingering, a functional psychotic phenomenon or a consequence of cerebral dysfunction.

Dream-like thinking (or dereistic thinking, Oswald 1962) is also a deviation from standard concept attainment. Freud gave the most comprehensive account in *The Interpretation of Dreams*:

> Dreams think predominantly in visual images . . . they make use of auditory images . . . they replace thoughts by hallucinations . . . Dreams construct a situation out of these images . . . they dramatise an idea . . . We appear not to think but to experience; that is, we attach complete belief to the hallucination.
>
> (Freud 1900)

It occurs in hypnagogic states and, when awake, in mescaline intoxication (Ardis & McKellar 1956) and following various subcortical and limbic lesions (e.g. temporal lobe epilepsy, cingulectomy, Kleine-Levin syndrome).

Impaired categorisation

Categorisation is similar to conceptual thinking but is more concerned with the order of things. Foucault (1970) argued that human categorisation is arbitrary, and quoted a fable by the writer Borges, with approval:

> Animals are divided into a) belonging to the emperor, b) embalmed, c) tame, d) sucking pigs, e) sirens, f) fabulous, g) stray dogs, h) included in the present classification, i) frenzied, j) innumerable, k) drawn with a very fine camelhair brush, l) et cetera, m) having just broken the water pitcher, and n) that from a long way off look like flies.

Rosch (1977) took the opposite view:

> A theory of the psychological principles underlying the formation of categories was previously inhibited by the assumption that categories were arbitrary . . . Category cuts in the environment should be those which follow the structure of co-occurrence of attributes in the real world.
>
> (Rosch 1977)

Overinclusive and underinclusive thinking are the most studied abnormalities of categorisation. Cameron's (1939) original definition of overinclusive thinking was:

> an inability to select and to restrict and to eliminate the less closely related elements from the conceptual structure (which) means that the psychological boundaries are functionally insufficient.
>
> (Cameron 1939)

It denotes a widening of the category limits so as to include items which normal people would reject. For example, if the category were birds, it would be overinclusive to select bat, claw, feather or cage. Underinclusive thinking, abnormally narrow categorisation (e.g. exclusing ostriches, ducks and penguins from the category of birds), also occurs.

Impaired abstract thinking

According to Goldstein (Goldstein & Scheerer 1941) there were eight 'aspects of the abstract attitude': detaching the ego from the outer world or inner experience, assuming a mental set, accounting for acts to oneself or others, shifting from one aspect of a situation to another, holding several aspects of a thing in one's mind at the same time, grasping the essential of a whole, appreciating common properties or forming hierarchical concepts and planning ahead. This is a rather heterogeneous collection of mental activities, and some psychologists (e.g. Kammann & Streeter 1971) restrict the meaning to only two: the extent to which something is accessible to the senses (imageability) and the position of a thing in a hierarchy (e.g. animal–dog–poodle). Goldstein emphasised concrete thinking as typical of organic states and schizophrenia, but overly abstract thinking is regarded as more characteristic of schizophrenia by some investigators (Shimkunas 1972).

Abnormal beliefs

According to Jaspers:

> A delusion is a false judgement; it is held with extraordinary conviction with an incomparable subjective certainty; there is an imperviousness to other experiences and to compelling counter-argument; the content is impossible.
>
> (Jaspers 1913)

Fish (1967) gave a shorter definition, but along the same lines:

> A delusion is a false unshakeable belief out of keeping with the patient's social and cultural background.
>
> (Fish 1967)

There is a tendency to regard both these definitions as too strict nowadays and to acknowledge, as Wittgenstein did, that there must be some indefiniteness in the concept of belief:

> Where do we get the concept thinking from . . . From everyday language . . . But the use of this word is tangled. Nor can we expect anything else. And that can be said of all psychological verbs . . . Man thinks, feels, wishes, believes, intends . . . an enumeration of all those things man does with his mind . . . I have said that hope, belief, etc. were embedded in human life, in all of the situations and reactions which constitute human life . . . (and that) if a concept depends on a pattern of life, there must be some indefiniteness in it.
>
> (Wittgenstein 1980)

Moor & Tucker (1979) gave a more lenient definition of delusion:

> . . . a belief held when there is considerable evidence against . . . and comparatively little or no evidence for it . . . when the ability to evaluate this evidence is preserved . . . but when the subject would maintain the belief even if given ample opportunity and incentives to evaluate it.
>
> (Moor & Tucker 1979)

Delusions are sometimes distinguished from 'overvalued ideas', because of preserved insight or lack of insistence in the latter. They are also divided into primary (or autochthonous) and secondary (with a basis in recognisable psychological dysfunction, e.g. intellectual impairment, perceptual disorder). Neither distinction is generally accepted amongst psychologists, because they were introduced by the early phenomenological psychiatrists who believed that schizophrenia was by nature ununderstandable and inexplicable by any known psychological dysfunction and their concept of delusion reflected this in a rather circular manner. Those psychologists who have proposed a perceptual or attentional basis to schizophrenia naturally regard all their delusions as secondary.

Impaired spatial thought

Abnormal thought about spatial matters can take a number of forms. The simplest is disorientation for place. This is considered one of the best indices of an organic mental state, regardless of site of lesion. Disorientation for place, however, can occur as a relatively isolated phenomenon. Environmental reduplication (Ruff & Volpe 1981), where a subject maintains that a particular place (e.g. hospital room) has an identical duplicate in some other location, is a complex example of a disturbance in spatial thought. It has many similarities with reduplicative paramnesia (p. 267) and Capgras syndrome (p.344). In some cases, a patient entertains a series of delusions, all with a spatial component. Vighetto et al (1980), for example, reported a man with a right parietotemporal infarct who believed wrongly that his cousin had moved from Lyons, that his wife had changed flats, that he himself resided at the town of his birth (200 miles from the hospital where he in fact was), and that he regularly made the journey to the hospital in 30 minutes (despite attempts to prove to him that this was impossible).

Impaired temporal thought

As in the case of spatial disorientation, disorientation for time can be both a reliable indicator of general brain damage and a relatively isolated phenomenon. Losing track of time is pronounced in sleep deprivation (Williams et al 1962) and drug intoxication (particularly cannabis, Melges 1982). According to Spiegel et al (1976), thalamotomy induces a marked 'confusion in time' without disorientation in space.

Impaired thinking about psychological and social topics

There are a number of conditions in which it is claimed there is a relative inability or unwillingness to understand psychological or social aspects of life, with often a compensatory preoccupation with abstract or mechanical topics. These conditions include early infantile autism (Kanner 1943), Asperger's syndrome (autistic psychopathy, Asperger 1944), schizoid personality and schizophrenia itself.

The clinical distinction between the first three is hazy and disputed. (Lorna Wing, 1981, gives the best account.) According to Kanner (1943), the pathognomonic feature of infantile autism was an:

> inability to relate themselves in the ordinary way to situations and people from the beginning of life.
>
> (Kanner 1943)

According to Asperger (1944), it was impossible for a subject with autistic psychopathy to:

> feel with others, to put himself into somebody else's emotional position, to achieve empathy . . . they had become an emotional imbecile . . . the basic disturbance was a lack of intuition.
>
> (Asperger 1944)

In schizoid personalities, according to Chick et al (1979), there is an impairment in 'psychological construing', measured by a tendency to identify nonpsychological rather than psychological differences between people on Dixon's test. In schizophrenia, psychological constructs (sociable, carefree, kind, honest), according to McPherson et al (1975) in their version of the Bannister grid, are selectively impaired, both with respect to nonpsychological (strong, well-built, healthy, tall) and with respect to other subjects (neurotics, normals). There are also claims that social concepts are differentially impaired with respect to formal, abstract concepts (Senf et al 1956, Bernstein 1960).

Subjects with Asperger's syndrome, in particular, have the additional disorder of unusual or circumscribed interests. Van Krevelen & Kuipers (1962) defined this as a 'sphere of interests which goes beyond the limits of the field of ordinary children's thoughts'. One of Wing's (1981) patients amassed a large collection of toy buses, cars and trains, and would notice at once if an item were missing. Another was particularly interested in time, and would wear two watches, one set at Greenwich Mean Time and one at local time, even when these were the same. Robinson & Vitale (1954) reported three children with 'circumscribed interest patterns' without the other features of Asperger's syndrome. A preoccupation with philosophy, the meaning of life and bizarre enterprises may dominate the schizophrenic's world. A patient of mine spent years trying to construct an eternal motion machine, another in perfecting a guillotine with which he eventually amputated his penis.

Deficient imagery

According to Richardson (1969) this comprises:

> All those quasisensory or quasiperceptual experiences of which we are self-consciously aware and exist for us in the absence of those stimulus conditions that produce genuine perceptual or sensory counterparts.
>
> (Richardson 1969)

He recognises after-imagery, eidetic imagery, memory imagery and imagination imagery. Only the last two can be regarded as varieties of thought. Paivio (1975) believes imagery of this kind is separate from verbal logical thinking, with its own internal representation and mode of operation. Humphrey & Zangwill (1951) reported three patients who noticed that their visual imagey was worse after a head injury, and Gazzaniga & Le Doux (1978) that frontal lobe damage impaired the ability to fantasise.

Impaired metaphorical thinking

Some psychologists regard metaphor as a special form of thinking. Ortony (1979), for example, wrote:

> The approach seems to entail a role for metaphors in both language and thought . . . in the use of language as essentially creative activity . . . Metaphors seem to play an important role in scientific discovery . . . in the communication of new theories . . . and they permit the articulation of new ideas.
>
> (Ortony 1979)

To Collins & Quillian (1972) metaphor was merely a measure of:

> semantic distance, due to a subject learning the normal case first . . . one man's metaphor is another man's anaphor.
>
> (Collins & Quillian 1972)

Creative and divergent thinking refer to a similar pattern. According to Suler (1980):

> Creativity has been operationally defined in terms of one's talent in constructing narratives, drawing or painting ... Creative thinking requires the ability to tolerate cognitive complexity . . . the ability to generate ideas that are truly novel and often unconventional and illogical, and the ability to synthesise these ideational complexities into a meaningful context.
>
> (Suler 1980)

In chronic schizophrenia (Wing et al 1974), right hemisphere lesions (Critchley 1962b) and frontal lobe damage (Tow 1955, Petrie 1952) there is an impairment in creativity, proverb interpretation and adequacy. For severe forms of this the term poverty of content is used; in mild forms thinking is vague, redundant and lacking in richness. (Not all of the inadequacy of thinking in these conditions can be attributed to reduced use of metaphor, but it is probably a significant component.)

Typical schizophrenic phenomena

Delusions

These are the most characteristic feature of schizophrenia in most modern accounts of the condition.

According to Schneider the most characteristic of all was *delusional perception*:

> It is as if some loftier reality spoke through the perception. Perception itself is not altered, but the meaning of it . . . A schizophrenic described it as follows: 'A dog lay in wait for me as he sat on the steps of a Catholic convent. He got up on his hindlegs and looked at me seriously. He then saluted with his front paw as I approached him. Another man was a little way in front of me. I caught up to him hurriedly and asked if the dog had saluted him too. An astonished 'no' told me I had to deal with a revelation addressed to me'.
>
> (Schneider 1959)

Four more examples from patients in my care illustrate it further:

> A young man was sitting on a rocking chair. It broke, and at the same moment he realised that he had won £1 million on the Football Pools.
>
> A middle-aged man was sitting in a bus and observed that the conductor was handing out coloured sweets to some of the other passengers. He immediately inferred that the recipients of the sweets were in the same state as he was.
>
> A young woman received what she called a divine message on 2nd May 1974. Her watch hand turned black and she knew her father was dying.
>
> A young man noticed that other passengers in the train would occasionally cross their legs. Whenever this happened he knew that the whole scene around him was a play performed for his benefit.

The next most characteristic, according to Schneider, was *delusional intuition*. This is sometimes called delusional idea or delusional notion. It was harder to identify than delusional perception and was less likely to indicate schizophrenia because, according to Schneider, it could always turn out to be true and not a delusion after all. It was an unaccountable false belief, which was irrational and emotionally incomprehensible. The problem for the phenomenologist was not whether people had such beliefs: Schneider, like Jaspers, had no doubt that this was so. The problem lay in excluding all other explanations in any individual case: real, emotional, or in terms of some other psychological deficit (e.g. intellectual impairment). If one could find any reasonable explanation it was regarded as a 'delusion-like reaction'. Examples of delusional intuition are the following:

> A young woman conceived the idea that she was an intermediary in an IRA plot. She believed that she was pregnant, that Canadians were indulging in 'sex games' in the garden and that the electric sockets in her house were transmitting coded messages in rhyme.
>
> A middle-aged woman developed the idea over a number of days that she had bilharziasis, that it was affecting her mouth and that her husband had some role in causing this.
>
> A menopausal woman conceived the notion that her sister might be her daughter, that she was pregnant, that people wanted information from her because she knew something important and that she might have died in the past.

Both delusional perception and intuition are called primary delusions by phenomenologists and each may be heralded by a *delusional mood*, an uncanny and sometimes terrifying atmosphere in which aspects of the outside world are invested with new meaning.

> A young man felt that the whole of London was uncertain and strange. He could only be sure of the date if he bought a newspaper that had been printed outside London, and only sure of the year if he visited a well-known beauty spot to the south of London where there was a fallen tree whose age he knew by the number of rings on the trunk.

The other characteristic schizophrenic delusions are beliefs about *control* or influence of body, will, mind or mood, and beliefs about *thought interference*: withdrawal, insertion or broadcasting.

> A man reported: 'I keep being thrown against the wall. It's not me who's doing it.'
>
> A woman believed that someone was putting pigeon droppings in her flat to make her feel ill, and stretching her legs.
>
> A man said: 'People are torturing my mind. Spirits are jumping into my mind. There's telepathy going on.'
>
> A woman believed that neighbours could read her mind, make her take the wrong turning in the street to prevent her seeing men and make her think violent thoughts because they sensed she liked men.
>
> A man reported: 'Other patients' talkings go through my brain, evaporate like a magnet and seem to glue to my thinking power.'

Other types of delusion—paranoid, reference—are more common than those characteristic ones, but occur in all psychotic conditions. Yet others—

grandiose, poverty, guilt, bodily change, disease—also occur but are more characteristic of affective psychosis. In general, the more bizarre or implausible the delusion, the more characteristic it is of schizophrenia.

> One woman was convinced that she had swallowed a duck.
> A man thought that his stomach had fallen down, that there were weeds in his gullet and that his bowels had slipped.

Several authors have examined pathoplastic factors in schizophrenic delusions. With increasing age, paranoid delusions are more common (Albee 1950, Lucas et al 1962). Women and married people are more likely than men and single people to have delusions with a sexual content; foreign-born people are more likely than natives to have paranoid delusions; and higher social classes have religious and grandiose delusions, whereas lower social classes have more delusions of inferiority (Lucas et al 1962). Subjects with a higher intelligence are more likely to have extensive, coherent and passivity delusions than the less intelligent (Heilburn & Madison 1978).

Some schizophrenic delusions are lateralised. Taylor & Fleminger (1981) found that 24 of 60 schizophrenics had lateralised hypochondriacal delusions—15 on the left, 9 on the right.

Formal thought disorder

Various authorities have suggested descriptions or classifications of the disorder of the form of thinking. Some of these have become enshrined as independent phenomena, almost on the same level as delusions and hallucinations. In fact, they are really shrewd observations or apt metaphors for a variety of thought and language disorders. Kraepelin suggested derailment (p. 249) and Bleuler a loosening of associations. Schilder (1920) recognised condensation (fragments from various spheres of experience inappropriately fused), symbol-like substitution (meaning distorted by sexual and other symbolic images), duplication (one thing becoming manifold and increasingly bizarre, e.g. symbolic distortions of the sexual act) and overidentification (several things becoming one, e.g. characteristics of various relatives all fused into one person). Cameron (1944) suggested asyndetic thinking (paucity of genuinely causal links, e.g. wind blows . . . 'due to velocity'); metonyms (imprecise approximations, e.g. menu is . . . 'something that happens three times a day'); interpenetration of themes (elements derived from some personal preoccupation are inappropriately inserted, e.g. My hair is brown because . . . 'it is a sort of hydraulic evening', in a man preoccupied with engineering); and overinclusion (p. 38). Mayer Gross et al (1960) wrote about 'pseudoscientific ideas' (idiosyncratic technical vocabulary built up around some bizarre enterprise).

Andreasen (1979a) gathered together all such clinical descriptions and tried to rationalise them, combining synonymous terms and excluding unreliable ones. She arrived at 18 mutually exclusive 'thought, language and

Table 15.2 The thinking dysfunction rating scale of Karasu

Item	Definition (his definition)
Flight of ideas	High speed flow . . . leaps from one idea to another
Slowing of ideas	Flow retarded and effortful
Impoverished thought	Shallow, inadequate
Loose associations	Disjointed, disconnected, obscure
Confusion	Inability to think or understand clearly
Circumstantiality	Encumbered with unnecessary detail
Word salad	Meaningless discourse in which grammatical structure lost
Neologisms	Invention of new words
Metonyms and personal idioms	Real words used incorrectly or with private reference
Delusions	False beliefs not influenced by logical arguments and not shared by culture
Paleological thought	Misconceptions on basis of irrelevant or superficial similarities
Stereotypy	Repetition of words or phrases
Perseveration	Repeating same answer to a different question
Forced thought	Involuntary intrusion of specific words or ideas into thought
Preoccupation	Repetitive reference to one major idea
Concrete thinking	Excessive literal thinking
Blocking	Sudden stops in flow
Impaired memory	Not defined
Impaired judgement	Not defined
Impaired orientation	Disorientation
Mutism	Lack of speech
Echolalia	Repetition of words addressed to patient

communication disorders' (listed on p. 249), which can be rated using her definitions and examples. Those most commonly seen in schizophrenia were poverty of content, derailment, loss of goal, tangentiality and illogicality. Illustrations are given on pages 249 to 250. Karasu et al (1979) carried out a similar procedure, extracting 37 terms from 8 major textbooks and 4 review articles, reducing them to 15, and adding on another 7 to make the scale applicable to depression and organic states (Table 15.2). Delusions, blocking, impaired judgement, loose associations, slowing of ideas, preoccupation and confusion characterised schizophrenics, though none of these singly to any significant degree.

In general what clinicians call formal thought disorder is not only difficult to separate from language disorder, but is probably made up of several non-specific and specific types of thinking disturbance. It is impossible to identify a specific pattern from clinical observation alone. In the section on experimental evidence it will be seen that a psychological approach sheds a little more light.

Subjective experience of thought disorder

In the study by Varsamis & Adamson (1971), impaired flow of thought ('foggy mind', 'slowed thinking') occurred in 58% of patients in the early stage. In answer to Freedman & Chapman's (1973) questionnaire, only thought block, amongst items relating to thought disturbance, distinguished schizophrenic from non-schizophrenic patients. But in Freedman's (1974) analysis of schizophrenic autobiographies the following were prominent: 'racing thoughts, slowed thoughts, increased yielding to associative connections between ideas, mental exhaustion, subjective loss of control of thoughts, thought block, confusion, disturbances in judgement and reasoning, thinking in images, and thought replaced by emotion'. McGhie & Chapman (1961) quoted the following accounts:

> My thoughts get all jumbled up. I start thinking or talking about something but I never get there . . . People listening to me get more lost than I do.
>
> My trouble is that I've got too many thoughts. You might think about something, let's say that ashtray and just think, oh! yes, that's for putting my cigarette in, but I would think of it and then I would think of a dozen different things connected with it at the same time.
>
> It's not that I can't concentrate right, it's just that I can't concentrate on the major issues. I get fogged up with all the different bits and lose the important things in the picture.
>
> (McGhie & Chapman 1961)

Rosser (1979) quoted the following from a patient who was seeing her regularly for psychotherapy:

> Nothing has any meaning . . . All my thoughts are rushing. I can't find words . . . Sometimes I am high on a thought, holding it up in my head, then it collapses in the emptiness inside . . . None of my words have any meaning so what can I tell you.
>
> (Rosser 1979)

EXPERIMENTAL EVIDENCE

Introduction

It is difficult to present the large literature on this topic in a systematic way, because of the different interpretations sometimes placed on the same term (e.g. abstraction), and the fact that many experiments are bound to an outdated theory. I shall follow the classification of thought disorder presented earlier, and consider the most theory-bound experiments in the section on nonspecific disorders.

Disorders of flow and control?

Of these disorders only slowness of thinking has been experimentally investigated. Babcock (1933) gave a battery of psychological tests and found that slowness on all of them was more characteristic than specific failure on any one. More recently Foulds et al (1968) showed that three of Babcock's tests (time taken to write one's name, the phrase 'United States of America' and the sentence 'I'm going to leave here shortly') correlated negatively, but not to a significant degree, with delusions. This implies that slowness of thinking is not important in the genesis of delusions. Romney & Leblanc (1975) found that slowness to complete the digit symbol subtest of the WAIS correlated negatively and to a significant degree with thought disorder as measured by the Bannister grid. This implies that slowness does not play a significant part in formal thought disorder either.

Nonspecific disorders?

Random thinking?

Fishkin et al (1979) administered the Whitaker Index of Schizophrenic Thinking (see p. 326) to 36 schizophrenics and found two distinct patterns amongst those who performed poorly. One group gave random responses throughout; the other, whom they designated 'streakers', gave an error-free performance for a while followed by random responses. (The authors attributed the latter pattern to episodic imbalance of attention, but randomness, whether continuous or intermittent, could occur for a number of reasons.)

Vacillating thought?

Kasanin (1944) noted that schizophrenics approached Vygotsky's conceptual task with:

> endless hesitancy and vacillation between various aspects of the material . . . taking into simultaneous consideration all the possibilities.
>
> (Kasanin 1944)

He considered that such ambivalence was quite characteristic, and distinguished schizophrenics from patients with organic brain disease, who seemed cheerfully unaware of their errors. Goldstone (1975) also emphasised this aspect, regarding it as the main distinguishing feature between several groups of schizophrenics and several groups of patients with affective illness examined on seven tasks. This is reflected statistically in many experiments as an unusual degree of 'intrasubject response variance', attributable, in Goldstone's view, to the fact that the schizophrenic 'keeps changing his mind'. The same ambivalence was observed during a perceptual task (Reich & Cutting 1982), and inconsistency on tests of thinking (e.g. sorting, Calev et al 1980) is sometimes regarded as more characteristic than any specific pattern.

Poor motivation?

Hunt & Cofer (1944) and Shakow (1946) attributed great importance to motivational factors in the overall psychological deficit. This became a common element in the behavioural formulations of the late 1950s. Cavanaugh

(1958), for example, demonstrated that concept attainment was impaired relative to normals under usual experimental conditions, but improved considerably, and more so than in normals, when an irritating noise was introduced which only stopped when the right concept was attained. Frith (1977) showed that poor motivation during a card-sorting task was prominent in some schizophrenics (chiefly those with negative symptoms), but was not a feature of deluded or hallucinated subjects, who would persist at the task despite numerous errors. Higgins & Sherman (1978) asked 40 schizophrenics to carry out the Bannister grid and a card-sorting task. Half were rewarded with money for good performance. Those rewarded did better than the others on card sorting but worse on the Bannister grid. The authors concluded that poor motivation was not an adequate explanation for all forms of thought disorder.

Undue sensitivity to certain feedback?

Garmezy (1952) believed that schizophrenic thought disorder only appeared when a subject was exposed to social censure. Johannsen (1961) reported a more general sensitivity to social feedback. Nonparanoid and paranoid schizophrenics were compared with normals on their ability to learn a sequence of button pressings (e.g. right, left, left, right, right, right) under conditions of social (experimenter's comments) and nonsocial feedback (green or red lights for correct or incorrect performance). Normals did better with social feedback, nonparanoid schizophrenics did better with nonsocial feedback, and paranoid subjects were the same with both. Sullivan et al (1980), however, obtained the opposite pattern: chronic schizophrenics gave better proverb interpretations when 'socially censured' (told that the previous response was 'poor') than when praised.

Cognitive disorganisation arising from high drive (anxiety)?

Broen & Storms (1961) proposed that schizophrenics were unduly susceptible to high drive or anxiety and that this led to the 'collapse' of normal response patterns (see p. 366). Watson et al (1981b) tested this notion by asking 100 schizophrenic and 100 nonschizophrenic patients to remember paired associates with or without an electric shock each time they were wrong. They argued that if Broen and Storms were correct, schizophrenics should be disproportionately worse when shocked because the pain would induce disproportionately high drive which would then disrupt their responses. The results were against this hypothesis, because although both subject groups did worse when shocked, this effect was only significant in the case of the nonschizophrenics.

Disorder only manifest on complex tasks?

A theory, put forward by Yates (1966), is that thought disorder is only evident on complex or hard tasks of any kind. In four studies, using different tasks (single and multiple choice reaction time, Court & Garwoli 1968, easy and difficult vocabulary items, Hamsher & Arnold 1976, eight types of card sorting, Hirt et al 1977, and four types of card sorting, Caudrey et al 1980) there was no real support for this proposal. Complex tasks were carried out more poorly than simple in three of these studies, but this was not confined to schizophrenics (Court and Garwoli), was a feature of nonparanoid but not paranoid subjects (Hirt et al) and was seen in some tasks but not others of equivalent complexity (Caudrey et al).

Thought disorder as an excess yielding to normal bias?

Originally suggested by Chapman in 1958 (see p. 461), this proposal is not now given serious attention. Even the Chapmans now regard it as a 'low level explanatory principle' (Chapman et al 1977). In two studies (Miller & Chapman 1968, Naficy & Willerman 1980) a small effect was demonstrated. In the first study, schizophrenics and normals were asked to rank order seven sets of nine things (e.g. foods, ethnic groups) along three dimensions: general evaluative (things I like best), specific evaluative (most healthy) and neutral (weighs most). According to the response bias hypothesis there should be higher correlations between general and specific evaluations in schizophrenics than in normals. The correlation coefficients were 0.82 for schizophrenics and 0.7 for normals. In the second study schizophrenics chose the commonest meaning (e.g. 'financial establishment' rather than 'side of river' as the preferred meaning of 'bank') slightly more often than normals even when the context suggested the latter; manics, however, showed the same tendency.

Thought disorder manifest in response selection rather than stimulus apprehension?

Several studies have used decks of cards where the degree of stimulus uncertainty (e.g. one or more colours, one or more shapes) and response uncertainty (e.g. sort by colour, sort by colour and shape) can be systematically varied. Marshall (1973) and Hemsley (1976) concluded that response uncertainty was more influential in distinguishing schizophrenics from controls than stimulus uncertainty. Neufeld (1977) claimed that this applied to paranoid but not nonparanoid subjects, and Manschreck et al (1981a) demonstrated that thought disorder (SADS clinical rating, Type–Token Ratio) correlated with motor disorder (voluntary motor disturbance, see p. 280).

Conclusions

Judged from their performance on a variety of tasks, some schizophrenics tackle some problems in a *random* or *inconsistent* fashion. Others *vacillate* between one solution and another. Poor motivation, undue susceptibility to negative feedback and anxiety are probably not important. Particular difficulties with complex tasks and a tendency to select the most likely solution regardless of context may account for some of the disorder, but cannot entirely explain it. Using an information processing model, response selection is more impaired than stimulus apprehension.

Impaired concept attainment?

Tests of concept attainment

The similarities subtest of the WAIS, Vygotsky's test (differently shaped blocks with meaningless words inscribed on the back, see p. 36, standardised by Hanfmann & Kasanin 1942), nonverbal tasks (e.g. Feldman & Drasgow 1951, p. 329) and tests of social concept attainment based on an odd-man-out design (e.g. Whiteman 1954, p. 338) have all been tried. None has established itself as the test of choice in schizophrenia. The Whitaker Index of Schizophrenic Thinking (Whitaker 1973) is becoming the most widely used, although it is not entirely clear what aspect of thought it is measuring. It comprises 25 multiple choice questions arranged in 3 sections: 9 'similarities', 9 'word pairs' and 7 'new inventions'. In the first two sections, the subject has to select from several alternatives the one which is most similar in meaning to the stimulus item. An example of 'similarities' is: kill—cause me to die (correct), stab (loose), bloody me (reference), mill (clang) and bapple (nonsense). An example of 'word pairs' is: mother and father—family, boss me, other and father, for nice and float. In the 'new inventions' the subject is given a strange proposal, e.g. 'Houses painted with a new kind of paint will never need repainting', and asked to select one of several suggested consequences—'this paint will cost more to buy, this paint will be used on some houses, it will be my paint, complaint paint, out the into'.

Vygotsky's approach

Vygotsky (1934) was one of the first to examine concept attainment in schizophrenia. He designed blocks varying in size, shape and colour, and inscribed meaningless syllables on them corresponding to artificial concepts (e.g. cev on flat and small, bik on flat and large blocks). He claimed that schizophrenics behaved like adolescents in not achieving adequate concepts. Kasanin & Hanfmann (1938) confirmed Vygotsky's results, but disagreed about the notion of regression. The essence of Vygotsky's approach was whether a subject could attain a concept that the experimenter had selected by being exposed to positive and negative instances of it. He complicated the matter, however, by then asking subjects to sort the blocks. Any deficit in categorisation would thus obscure the issue of whether concept attainment was intact. The two are not always easy to distinguish, but it is worth doing so because some investigators have claimed that impairment of categorisation but not concept attainment is one of the fundamental deficits in schizophrenia. Angyal (1944), for example, argued that schizophrenics were not impaired as far as 'apprehending relationships' (i.e. attaining a concept) but were abnormal in 'system connections' (appreciating category membership).

Simple concept attainment

This is probably normal. Nathan (1964) prepared 120 multiple choice items, divided equally into verbal and nonverbal, formal and social, abstract (identify likeness in unlike) and 'subsumption' (identify unlikeness in alike). (One of the verbal, formal, abstract items was: red, blue, green, yellow—all are book colours, all are colours, all can describe something, all are natural hair colours. One of the nonverbal, social, subsumption items was: pictures of man conducting orchestra, man playing drums, man blowing horn and man playing banjo—which is the drummer?) He gave these items to chronic schizophrenics, acute schizophrenics and normals, and found no significant differences in their performance. Gillis (1969) invited chronic schizophrenics and normals to guess the number (1–15) on the back of a card portraying 1 of 15 geometrical designs or schematic faces. Schizophrenics only did badly on faces and complex designs but not on simple designs. Jerome & Young (1971) designed a panel of buttons which operated a green or red light. The experimenter then selected a problem (e.g. find which button will make light turn red when it is not pressed), and noted how long a subject took to solve it. Schizophrenics were no slower than normals in this.

Complex concept attainment

The performance of chronic schizophrenics on complex tasks is however impaired. Pishkin & Bourne (1981) separated what they called attribute identification from rule learning. They prepared 81 cards showing one to three items, which could be one of three shapes, three colours and three sizes. In the attribute identification task, subjects (chronic schizophrenics and normals) were told the rule, e.g. all small or hexagonal items are positive instances, and asked to sort all the cards into positive and negative instances of the concept. In the rule-learning part they were told the relevant attributes, e.g. red and square, but not the rule. Again they were asked to sort the 81 cards into positive and negative instances of the concept, but this time it was unknown as yet, and they had to discover it by noting which of their choices the experimenter designated as correct and which incorrect. The results were highly significant. Schizophrenics were as good as normals on the first task, but markedly impaired on the second. Normals actually found the second task easier than the first. The authors concluded that schizophrenics could follow a rule provided for them, but could not work it out for themselves. The second task, however, was quite complicated and involved categorisation and the simple formulation suggested earlier, of intact concept attainment but faulty categorisation, may still be true.

Identification of pictorial anomalies

Feinberg & Garman (1961) modified the Progressive Matrices test of nonverbal intelligence: subjects had to choose a correct alternative, an incorrect but plausible answer, or an implausible one. The task is illustrated in Figure 15.1. Acute and chronic schizophrenics and brain-damaged subjects all made more errors than normals, but only acute schizophrenics made more implausible errors. Rudzinski & Auld (1980) presented pairs of pictures, one of which showed a plausible grouping, e.g. cake, glass, cup; the other an implausible grouping, e.g. cake, glass, snake. Clinically thought-disordered acute schizophrenics chose significantly more implausible groupings than normals or nonthought-disordered subjects. Impaired performance on such tasks may reflect perceptual deficit more than thought disorder, but illustrates the point that in acute schizophrenia, nonverbal concept attainment may be disturbed for different reasons than in the case of chronic schizophrenia.

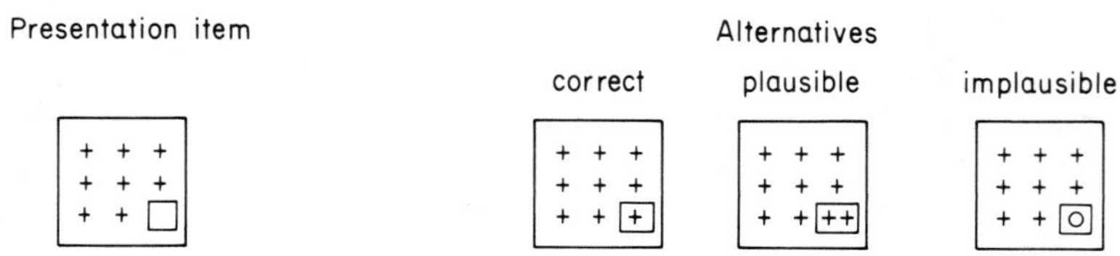

Fig. 15.1 Feinberg and Garman's test of thought disorder

Appreciation of verbal similarities

Performance on the similarities subtest of the WAIS is not impaired in acute (Schmolling & Lapidus 1977) or reactive schizophrenics (Watson 1974), but is impaired in chronic (Albott & Gilbert 1973) and process schizophrenics (Watson 1974).

Recognising nonverbal similarities

Appreciation of complex nonverbal similarities probably is impaired in acute schizophrenics (Feldman & Drasgow 1951). These authors prepared cards

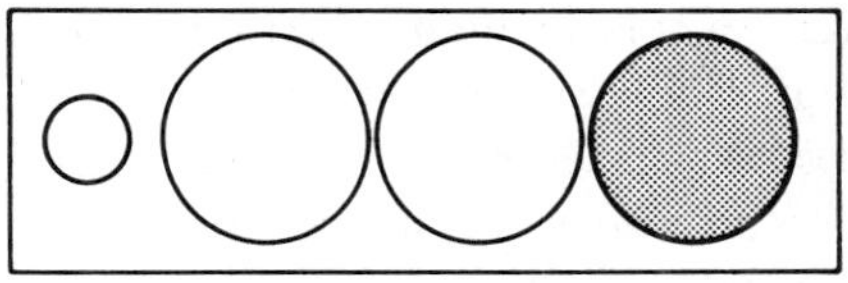

QU: In what two ways are the circles alike?
Results (for 43 cards)

	Mean no of. single misses	*Mean no. of double misses*
40 normals	1.2	0
37 acute schizophrenics	18.0	2.6

Fig. 15.2 Feldman and Drasgow's test

with four circles on, representing two concepts (Fig. 15.2). Subjects had to identify the two concepts in each. Acute schizophrenics were slightly worse than normals in finding one concept per card, but much worse at finding two. Piaget's test of conservation of physical quantities can be regarded as the appreciation of nonverbal similarity. Chronic but not acute schizophrenics were poor on this in a study by Sollod & Lapidus (1977), and hebephrenic but not paranoid schizophrenics in a study by Tissot & Burnand (1980).

Everyday logic

Cameron (1938) was one of the first to systematically describe distortions in everyday logic. He asked simple questions, such as, 'The man fell off the bicycle because . . .', and recorded the answers. He derived 'a geography of schizophrenic reasoning' from these, different aspects of which he named 'asyndetic thinking', 'metonymic distortion' and 'interpenetration of themes' (p. 320). When, however, Biles & Heckel (1968) asked chronic schizophrenics and normals to suggest the cause of 11 recent events (e.g. Senator Johnson died recently: what was the cause?) no subject gave bizarre, illogical or personal answers. Harrow & Prosen (1978) also confirmed that disordered logic was not prominent in the everyday speech of schizophrenics.

Formal logic

Von Domarus (1944) was one of the first to suggest that formal logic might be awry. His example, of what he called paralogical thinking, is well known. Normals regard stags and Indians as possessing one common property—swiftness—but do not consider the two things identical because of this. Schizophrenics, he claimed, attribute other common properties to stags and

Indians, because of this single link, and may generalise their 'adjective processing fault' into the conviction that both things are identical. Blanco (1976) agreed with von Domarus 'that a classical logical system is not available', and that 'primitive unconscious processes' take its place. They saw 'the converse of a relationship as the same as the relation' (e.g. My cat is a mother = my mother is a cat); and 'all members of a class as the same as one another and the same as the class' (e.g. cat = dog = animal), because 'the unconscious does not know individuals but only classes or propositional functions'.

Experiments on these matters have yielded moderately significant findings. Braatz (1970) examined what he called 'preference intransitivity'. If A is preferred to B, and B preferred to C, then A should be preferred to C. If not, then this was referred to as preference intransitivity. He found that schizophrenics had significantly more abnormalities than appropriate controls. Ho (1974) designed a 'deductive inference test': 14 neutral and 14 emotional items. (Neutral: if the radio is on, then there is music; if the radio is not on there is no music—Yes? No? Emotional: if people are plotting against me then my mind is possessed; if people are plotting against me then they would poison me—Yes? No?) Schizophrenics were significantly worse than normals on this test, but not differentially worse on emotional items. Watson & Wold (1981) distinguished four types of syllogistic error: von Domarus type (e.g. All alligators are reptiles; all lizards are reptiles; therefore all alligators are lizards); overexpansive type (e.g. Jimmy is overweight; Jimmy's mother is overweight; therefore Jimmy eats too many sweets); restrictive type (conclusion less general than could be inferred accurately from premises); and contradictions (one conclusion directly contradicted the premises). One hundred schizophrenics made more errors, mainly of the overexpansive type, than 50 normals, but fewer than 50 brain-damaged subjects. The authors concluded that a tendency to make syllogistic errors was not an essential feature of schizophrenia. In an earlier study, however, Watson et al (1976) had given five tests of thinking to 21 schizophrenic and 21 nonschizophrenic patients, and only a test of formal logic differentiated the two subject groups. (The other four were word series—escape, scape, cape . . .; letter series—abab . . .; odd man out—red, green, heavy, blue; and relationships—president is to nation as mayor is to . . .) Tissot & Burnand (1980) gave Piagetian developmental tests to schizophrenics and normals, and claimed that hebephrenics did badly on logical whilst paranoid patients were poor on mathematical reasoning.

Conclusions

The following conclusions can be drawn about concept attainment in schizophrenia, with, however, more than the usual reservations, because of the complexity of the issue. Neither acute nor chronic schizophrenics are intrinsically impaired in their ability to attain simple concepts. Both groups of subjects appear inefficient in complex tasks, but this may be partly attributable to perceptual deficit in the case of acute, and categorisation problems in the case of chronic subjects. There is mild to moderate distortion of everyday and formal logic in some schizophrenics, but the extent of this is unlikely to account for the major phenomena of the condition.

Categorisation disorder?

Tests of categorisation

Although Goldstein meant his various sorting tests (Goldstein & Scheerer 1941) to be measures of the abstract attitude, they were adopted by subsequent investigators as conceptual or categorisation tests. Rapaport (1945) standardised the object-sorting test. There are two parts. First, the experimenter offers subjects 33 objects and asks them to put them in 7 successive groups (the first chosen by the subject, the remainder chosen by the experimenter and illustrated with a standard object). Next, the experimenter asks the subjects why the last 6 groupings go together, and records their comments. McGaughran & Moran (1956) modified it yet further so that responses which were not conventionally abstract could be further subdivided. Their four divisions were public open (e.g. 'they're red'), public closed (e.g. 'you need a hammer to knock in a nail'), private open (e.g. 'they're things that please me') and private closed (e.g. 'I have them on my desk at home'). Overinclusive thinking is usually measured by noting the number of unusual items included in a category during an object sorting test. Payne & Friedlander (1962) recommended the average of the scores on three tests: their own object classification task (12 small objects to be arranged in 10 ways), yet another modification of Goldstein's test, and the number of words used during proverb interpretation.

Overinclusion

This has been the chief topic to be investigated. It is estimated to occur in 50% of all schizophrenics (Payne & Friedlander 1962). This figure, however, was based on a concept of overinclusion which was wider than the usual one. (Payne pooled three measures—number of objects included in Goldstein's test, number of sortings tried in his own object sorting test, and number of words used in proverb interpretation.) Epstein (1953) estimated that 63% of schizophrenics compared with 22% of normals were overinclusive on a test which required subjects to select items which were essential to the designated concept (e.g. *man*—arms, shoes, hat, toes, head, none). According to Payne and Friedlander, overinclusion is characteristic of acute schizophrenia in relapse, and is not a feature of either chronic schizophrenia or other psychiatric disorders. This statement has since had to be modified because overinclusion occurs in mania (Andreasen & Powers 1974), and correlates with how florid the psychosis is (Davis & Blaney 1976). It is more common in unmedicated patients than those on phenothiazines (Chapman & Knowles 1964). What it represents is unclear. Payne (1966) concluded that it was not a disturbance of thinking at all, but the manifestation of an incompetent sensory filter, but his concept was itself overinclusive! Sims-Knight & Knight (1978) regarded even the narrow concept as heterogeneous, comprising four entities—nonlogical classification, logical approximation, impaired reclassification and overextensiveness.

It is probable that overextensiveness is the core deficit, but why this occurs is open to speculation. Angyal (1944) believed that schizophrenics 'drifted from one semantic stratum into another'. McGaughran & Moran (1956) considered that it was secondary to a disorder of social communication (because sorting tended to be of the open, private variety, e.g. 'things that please me', suggesting an autistic tendency). Polyakov (1969) and other Russian investigators incorporated it in their general theory of 'impaired probabilistic prognosis' (see p. 370), where past experience no longer determines current thinking.

Underinclusion

Less investigated, but, according to Epstein (1953), at least half as common, is underinclusion, abnormally restrictive category membership. It is characteristic of a heterogeneous group of brain-damaged patients (Tutko & Spence 1962), and process (Tutko & Spence 1962) or chronic schizophrenics (Daut & Chapman 1974).

Nonverbal categorisation

Zaslow (1950) demonstrated abnormal categorisation of geometrical shapes in schizophrenia. Subjects were given 14 cards which, arranged in order, made a systematic progression from triangle to circle. Schizophrenics differed from normals in two major ways, when asked to indicate the card which formed the boundary between circle and triangle. Whereas 94% of 16 normals chose cards 3, 4 or 5 as the boundary, and 88% of them maintained the same card on four trials, only 17% of 24 schizophrenics chose cards 3 to 5, and only 8% maintained the card they had selected. Griffith et al (1980) invited schizophrenics and other psychiatric patients to sort 30 abstract shapes and 30 schematic faces, matched so that the number of dimensions of the former were the same as the number of features of the latter. Subjects had to sort them into two or more groups and four measures of their performance were made: time taken, number of groupings, and number of features and dimensions strongly distinguishing the groups. On a general sorting factor (derived from factor analysis) schizophrenics were worse overall, but the most striking finding was their relatively good performance on shapes and relatively bad one on faces.

Table 15.3 Study of categorisation using Rosch's model (Cutting)

	Psychiatric controls	Depressives	Acute schizophrenics	Chronic schizophrenics with thought disorder	Chronic schizophrenics without thought disorder
No.	20	20	20	9	11
Age	42.3	44.6	33.1	37.8	42.9
Sex—m:f	12:8	6:14	11:9	9:0	8:3
IQ (Nelson Adult Reading Test)	101.1	100.8	99.7	91.8	99.4
Agreement with standardisers/15					
Colours	12.5	12.0	11.6	10.8	12.2
Verbal categories	12.4	12.0	11.3	8.8	10.6
Pictorial categories	12.4	11.3	11.1	9.7	11.0

Other disorders of categorisation

I carried out an unpublished study applying Rosch's (1977) model of categorisation. She proposes that normal real-world categories do reflect the order of things 'out there', and all categories have a definite and predictable structure. They comprise a prototype (e.g. robin for birds, football for sports, in the western world at least) reflecting the essence of that category. And all other category members can be represented in terms of their deviation from this prototype (e.g. birds—robin, owl, penguin, dodo; sports—football, cycling, dancing, bridge). I prepared a set of 45 cards each portraying 2 members of the same category (e.g. bird—sparrow and owl), and asked subjects to indicate which was the more typical. The object was not, as in studies of overinclusion or underinclusion, to examine the boundaries of the category, but to study the internal structure with regard to a protypical instance. The final 45 cards were selected from a much larger pool shown to normals, and represented those where 80% of the normal standardisers had agreed that one was more typical than the other. There were 15 colours, 15 verbal and 15 pictorial categories. The results are shown in Table 15.3 and Figure 15.3. Only chronic schizophrenics with clinical thought disorder (rating of at least 2 on one of Andreasen's items in her TLC scale, p. 249) were significantly worse than psychiatric controls (neurotics).

Conclusions

There is good evidence that both acute and chronic schizophrenics have a disorder of categorisation. Acute subjects tend to overinclude—have abnormally wide categories—and chronic subjects tend to underinclude—have abnormally narrow categories.

Score	Psychiatric controls	Depressives	Acute schizophrenics	Chronic schizophrenics with thought disorder	Chronic schizophrenics without thought disorder
45					
44					
43	x		x		
42	x				
41	x				
40	xx	xxx	xx		x
39	xx	x			
38	xxx	xxx			
37		xxx	x		
36	xxx	xx	xx	x	x
35	xxx	xxx	xxxx		xxx
34	xx	x	xx	x	x
33	xx			x	xx
32	2 s.d. from mean of psychiatric controls		xxxx		xxx
31				x	
30		xx			
29				x	
28			xxx		
27		x	x		
26				x	
25				x	
24		x		x	
23					
22					
21					
20					
19					
18				x	

Fig. 15.3 Individual scores on combined tasks of category judgement—application of Rosch's model (Cutting)

Abstract thinking impairment?

Tests of abstraction

Proverb interpretation, introduced by Benjamin (1944) and developed by Gorham (1956), is still widely used. In Gorham's free-response version the interpretations of 12 well-known proverbs are rated for abstractness. The Shipley-Hartford Scale (Shipley 1940) is also regarded as a measure of abstracting ability. It consists of 20 series (e.g. AZBYCXD. . . ., mist is, wasp as, pint in, tone. . . .) for a subject to complete. Multiple choice vocabulary tests are another measure, whilst Goldstein's own tests are less used for this purpose.

Concrete thinking

Goldstein first proposed that schizophrenics think more concretely than normals. His ideas were rather ambiguous and were heavily criticised from the outset. Few careful studies have ever confirmed them. Andreasen (1977), for example, tested 14 RDC schizophrenics, 15 manics and 15 depressives. She gave 10 proverbs and asked 24 normals to rate each interpretation on a three-point scale on each of five dimensions (abstract, correct, concrete, bizarre and personalised). Schizophrenics gave responses which were significantly less correct, less abstract, more bizarre and more personalised (but not more concrete) than depressives, but manics were actually worse than schizophrenics. A second measure, multiple choice vocabulary, has proved equally unrewarding. Although schizophrenics are less likely than normals to choose the abstract of two alternative meanings of a word (Flavell 1956) this tendency is observed in depressed (Braff & Beck 1974) and brain-damaged subjects (Hamlin & Folsom 1977). Further, it does not generalise to all abstract words. In Flavell's study, for example, schizophrenics chose significantly more homonyms and this tendency (noted by Chaika, see p. 69) may have secondarily affected their selections. I examined three separate aspects of abstractness (Cutting & Ryan 1982): memory for high and low imageable words, imagery value of spontaneously produced words, and relative imageability of two words assessed by how easily the things represented could be drawn. None of these three measures significantly distinguished schizophrenics from appropriate controls.

Overly abstract thinking

Despite their ambiguity and lack of experimental confirmation, Goldstein's ideas continue to attract investigators. In this sense they have proved fertile ground for a variety of ideas on the psychology of schizophrenia. Weiner (1966) and Shimkunas (1972) even turned them on their head and made the paradoxical suggestion that schizophrenics did not think in a *less* abstract manner but in a *more* abstract way. For example, on the similarities subtest of the WAIS, Weiner quoted the following schizophrenic responses: orange and banana—'nature's produce'; coat and dress—'maintain human modesty'; axe and saw—'building blocks of modern society'; and dog and lion—'creatures of God'. In answer to the question, 'In what way are a table and a chair alike', Shimkunas noted that a concrete response would be, 'You can sit on the chair and write on the table', whereas an overgeneralised response would be, 'They are objects in the universe'. Shimkunas regards abstraction as a 'modal or normal conceptual response category', with deviations in either direction—concrete (excessive discrimination) and over-abstract (excessive generalisation)—both possible in schizophrenia. He believed that the latter was more common.

Conclusions

Schizophrenia is not characterised by concrete thinking, whether measured by proverb interpretation, choice of vocabulary or other means. Under some circumstances schizophrenics are less likely to give a conventionally abstract response but this may reflect a preoccupation with other aspects of words (e.g. sound rather than meaning). Paradoxically, the most interesting finding to emerge is the very opposite of what Goldstein suggested, namely that schizophrenics have a bias towards *more* abstract thinking than normals.

Belief?

There are only a handful of experimental studies on delusions. Southard (1916) examined the number, sex and type of person involved. Heilbrun & Heilbrun (1977) looked at the language in which they were recounted: number of clauses, number of references to external environment. Sacks et al (1974) and Heilbrun & Madison (1978) rated the strength of the belief. The most informative study is that of Kendler et al (1983) who analysed five 'dimensions of delusional experience': degree of conviction, extent of subject's life affected, bizarreness (extent to which the belief departed from cultural norms), disorganisation (internal inconsistency) and degree of preoccupation. The authors claimed that ratings on the five dimensions correlated poorly with one another and this suggested to them that schizophrenic delusions were multifactorial in origin.

Further studies of this topic are clearly essential to understand what is the most striking feature of schizophrenia.

Spatial thinking?

Hartlage & Garber (1976) devised spatial and nonspatial syllogisms (e.g. John is in front of Mary; Mary is in front of Bill; Is Bill in front of John? Fred is smarter than Jane: Jane is smarter than Mick; Is Mick smarter than

Fred?). Chronic schizophrenics were significantly worse on the spatial relative to the nonspatial questions, and with respect to normal subjects. To my knowledge there are no other studies on spatial thought in schizophrenia.

Temporal thinking?

There are no experimental studies on this, if one excludes the small literature on the ability to judge the passage of time, which I have regarded as an aspect of memory (p. 270). There are speculations on the matter by Minkowski (p. 33) and Melges (1982).

Thinking about psychological and social topics?

The impetus for experiments on psychologically-oriented thinking came from Bleuler, influenced by Freud and Jung, and for those on socially-oriented thinking from Cameron. There have been three main experimental approaches: Bannister's grid (repertory grid, personal constructs); assessment of empathic ability; and concept attainment, comparing formal and social concepts.

Bannister's grid

Bannister first applied Kelly's notion of personal constructs to thought disordered schizophrenics. In his first study (Bannister 1960), subjects were asked to write down the names of 36 adults and then rank them according to 10 different constructs (e.g. likeable, serious . . .). He subsequently changed to photos (Bannister 1962) and by 1966 (Bannister & Fransella 1966) had developed a standard procedure: offering 8 photos, each to be ranked on 6 qualities (kindness, stupidity, selfishness, honesty, meanness, sincerity), the whole procedure to be repeated. He derived two scores—intensity (correlation between contrasting qualities, e.g. whether subjects rated the same photo as very kind and not mean) and consistency (test-retest correlation). He claimed that thought-disordered schizophrenics showed low intensity (looser constructs, evident in their rating the same photo as very kind and very mean) and low consistency (their selection the second time differed from the first). The important point was that the low intensity, according to Bannister, was not entirely explained by low consistency, otherwise it would be meaningless to talk about loosening of constructs.

Since that time the test has fallen into disrepute because the crucial point—low intensity not attributable to low consistency—has not been confirmed by several investigators (e.g. Harrison & Phillips 1979). Allon et al (1981) also failed to demonstrate any correlations between an abnormal score and a clinical rating of thought disorder. A third criticism, made by Harrison & Phillips (1979), is that there is no difference in scores if a grid comprising objects is compared with the usual one of photos. This criticism is not so well founded as the other two because several investigators including Bannister (Bannister & Salmon 1966, McPherson & Buckley 1970, Heather 1976) have demonstrated a 'specific' effect for psychological constructs.

Empathic ability

Jackson & Carr (1955) asked 20 schizophrenics and 20 normals to describe themselves using a restricted repertoire of adjectives (e.g. I am a 'merry' person), and then rate the truth of this (1–5 scale) for themselves and for the other normals and schizophrenics in the experiment. Empathic ability was measured as the deviation between a subject's rating of another person and that other person's own rating. Schizophrenics were more deviant than normals. Milgram (1960) invited 32 schizophrenics, 30 brain-damaged subjects and 20 normals to select word associations which would be given by someone of the opposite sex to themselves. Both schizophrenic and organic patients were poor on this task, but the latter alone were additionally impaired on straightforward concept attainment. Milgram concluded that schizophrenics had impaired empathic skills out of proportion to any cognitive impairment.

Differential impairment in concept attainment involving social issues

Whiteman (1954) devised three reasoning tests: formal (e.g. hand has fingers, foot has . . .); pictorial (five designs to place in order); and social (three cards out of four portraying different instances of the same social concept, e.g. rescue, and one showing a different concept). Schizophrenics differed significantly from normals on all three tasks, but were most impaired on the social task. Senf et al (1956) presented 10 cartoons to acute and chronic schizophrenics, depressives and neurotics. (One of them showed penguins on an ice floe, one of whom was wearing sports clothes and saying, 'I get fed up with being formal all the time'.) Chronic schizophrenics were inferior to the other three patient groups, who were all equally proficient, in appreciating the humour of the cartoons. Davis & Harrington (1957) gave schizophrenics and normals 32 pictures portraying people and 32 showing different types of print. Schizophrenics were inferior to normals when they had to identify from clues one of the cards showing people, but were normal at choosing the right print. Bernstein (1960) designed an experiment similar to that of Whiteman, involving verbal, pictorial and social concepts. Schizophrenics were worse than normals on verbal and social concepts, and worse than brain damaged patients only on social concepts.

Conclusions

Although most of the experiments on this issue date back to the 1950s and

1960s, before diagnostic criteria were refined, there is considerable evidence that chronic schizophrenics, at least, are differentially impaired in attaining social concepts, in empathic skills, and possibly in structuring psychological characteristics of others (though in this last case, their performance is inconsistent rather than consistently deficient).

Imagery?

In my study (Cutting & Ryan 1982), there was no evidence for abnormal imaging in schizophrenia, as measured by memory for words varying in imageability, the imagery value of words in speech, or the selection of the more imageable of a pair of words (assessed by ease of drawing the thing represented).

Metaphorical and creative thinking?

Two experimental approaches have a bearing on whether schizophrenics are unusually creative or impoverished in their thinking. Word association responses, although used for a variety of purposes during the century, are one measure. A tendency to give unusual responses would suggest that thought processes were divergent, and the opposite, an excess of common responses, that thinking was inadequate or impoverished. Despite different scoring techniques, most recent studies, including my own (see p. 257), have found a comparable number of unusual responses relative to appropriate controls (Moran et al 1964, Dokecki et al 1965, Fuller & Kates 1969). On this measure, therefore, schizophrenics are neither overly creative nor overly inadequate thinkers. A better measure is the unusual uses test (e.g. Wallach & Kogan 1965). Shimkunas (1972) reported that schizophrenics were significantly less imaginative than nonpsychotic patients in their suggestions for unusual uses for an item, such as a brick. Keefe & Magaro (1980), however, found nonparanoid schizophrenics more imaginative on the same test than paranoid schizophrenics, nonpsychotic patients or normals.

In conclusion, popular attempts to link madness and creativity and clinical observations that schizophrenics show poverty of thought content (e.g. Wing et al 1974, Andreasen 1979a) have not been confirmed by the experiments to date.

CONCLUSIONS

Do schizophrenics have thought disorder?

The answer is undoubtedly yes. Acute schizophrenics almost invariably have delusions or formal thought disorder, and about half have overinclusive categorisation and a tendency to think inefficiently about psychological topics.

Chronic schizophrenics tend to show poverty of content of thought clinically, and on psychological testing underinclusive categorisation and faulty concept attainment.

What is the nature of the thought disorder?

Despite the large number of studies, more than on any other psychological dysfunction, it is still unclear whether there is a specific pattern or not. False beliefs, particularly concerning the independence of their own psychological functioning from outside influences, are the most characteristic feature. An impoverishment in the content of their thoughts (poverty of content) and an unconventional way of expressing them (derailment, tangentiality, loosening of associations) occur in a substantial minority, but the former is true of organic dements and the latter occurs in manics, so neither can be regarded as specific. Further, both are probably better regarded as disorders of the intended meaning of language (pragmatic disorder). Of all the experimental findings, the most consistently present is a disorder of categorisation: overinclusion in the acute stage and underinclusion in the chronic, but the former also occurs in mania and the latter in organic dementia. The next most well-established finding is a selective deficiency in thinking about psychological and social matters with a compensatory tendency to be more abstract. Impaired concept attainment probably occurs, but only if the concept is a complex one. What is almost certainly not true is that acute schizophrenics are more concrete in their thinking.

These are the most specific findings. There are other nonspecific features, such as inconsistency and a tendency to vacillate between solutions to a problem, but these apply to other psychological functions as well and probably occur in other conditions. The general conclusion must be that in many schizophrenics thought processes are little different from normal and that there is no single route for the development and maintenance of a false belief.

What is the cause of delusions?

Any discussion of this topic is beset by two problems. First, most psychological explanations of delusion have not taken into account the distinction between schizophrenia and other conditions (e.g. paranoid psychosis). Secondly, Jaspers and his pupils believed that schizophrenic delusions were primary and therefore neither reducible to any simple psychological dysfunction nor attributable to psychogenic conflict or personality disorder. For these reasons most of the literature is either inappropriate or, if one follows Jaspers, entirely irrelevant. Some of it is presented in the account of the various theoretical schools (Ch. 16). However, because I believe that Jaspers is too strict in his view and because I think that delusions probably have multiple causes in schizophrenia, I shall briefly summarise the main theories. They fall into the two categories which Jaspers rejected.

Is the cause personality disorder or emotional conflict?

Gaupp (1914) and Kretschmer (1927) were keen advocates of the role of personality in the genesis of certain delusions. Gaupp described at length the psychosis of one man whose premorbid personality was marked by sexual guilt and in whom the psychosis began immediately after a homosexual incident. Gaupp believed that the main mechanism of delusional formation was 'projection'. In the man's own words, 'The things which fill one's head, one is only too ready to place into the heads of others'. Although Gaupp accepted that the man had a paranoid and not a schizophrenic condition, he tried to identify similar mechanisms in schizophrenia. Kretschmer identified three personality types with a predisposition to delusional formation: the 'sensitive', the 'fighter' and the 'wishful'. The sensitive person was exquisitely aware of their inadequacy, usually in sexual matters, and at certain times of stress their sense of shame would be turned into a 'perceptible symbol', the observation that the environment was privy to their inner world. This explained the development of delusions of reference. In the second case a 'fighter', someone with an expansive, irritable and litiginous personality, would develop frank paranoid delusions as an escalation of these traits. The 'wishful' person, a naively euphoric dreamer, could develop erotomania—the delusion that a famous or important person was in love with them—also through an escalation of premorbid traits. Like Gaupp, he regarded these conditions as distinct from schizophrenia, but considered that the same principles of delusional formation could apply in the latter.

According to Bleuler (1906) delusions could develop in two distinct ways, either through a weakening of logical association, as in schizophrenia, or through an exaggeration of the emotional attachment to an idea, as in paranoia. An imbalance between the formal qualities of thought and its associated affect was the general mechanism. Most proposals on how paranoid delusions develop conform to Bleuler's second mechanism—emotional overattachment to an idea which is then thwarted by social pressure. Freud (1932) believed that delusions could arise 'either by the unconscious repressed becoming excessively strong . . . or because reality has become so intolerably distressing'. Kehrer (1928), a prolific writer on paranoia, emphasised a 'disordered arrangement of drives' which were incompatible with social norms and hence gave rise to conflict. Behaviourists, such as Dollard & Miller (1950), had a similar conception. People who felt shame over an incident in their lives, they argued, might construct a gradient of reasons for this. This would run from the true reason (which produced most guilt) to more and more incorrect ones (but less and less guilt-provoking). The delusion was the learned explanation along this gradient which was closest to the truth but produced no feelings of guilt. Schulte (1924), like Janet (see p. 230), held a particularly strong social position. He believed that the conflict was between an individual's desire for company and their real condition of social isolation. The isolation might be genuine (deafness, in prison) or adopted by preference (a feeling that one can no longer 'play the game' or 'go through the motions'). The inner thoughts in such cases were, it was assumed, along the lines: 'To be lonely is impossible, but to be persecuted is possible'.

In my view these mechanisms are quite plausible in the case of some delusional developments, and, although they were not formulated specifically to explain schizophrenic delusions, it may be that the psychological dysfunction in schizophrenia merely provides a substrate which renders a subject more susceptible to these mechanisms. (This was essentially what Bleuler believed.)

Is the cause a particular kind of psychological dysfunction?

Primary disorders of perception, attention and consciousness have all been proposed.

Maher (1974) suggested the following sequence based on an initial perceptual deficit:

> The patient's initial beliefs may have a considerable sensory element. . . . Distal perception may be involved . . . increased vividness of colours . . . difficulty in attending selectively to an auditory stimulus against background noise because of the increased prominence of the latter. We should note here that the patient is not presenting a delusion in any technical sense. He is describing an experience . . . Something unusual is happening to the individual in a manner that pervades large areas of his experience. . . . Strange events, felt to be significant, demand explanation. It is the core of the present hypothesis that the explanations, i.e. the delusions, of the patient are derived by cognitive activity that is essentially indistinguishable from that employed by nonpatients, by scientists, and by people generally. . . . A miniature version of the whole sequence may sometimes be seen in elderly people who are becoming hard of hearing. Phenomenologically the person experiences a gradual diminution in the loudness with which other people are speaking, and this readily lends itself to an interpretation that they are whispering. . . . Why. . . . It is perfectly natural to conclude that an attempt is being made to conceal something from the listener. Thus a delusion of conspiracy is not only possible but eminently reasonable.
>
> (Maher 1974)

Support for Maher's position comes from reports of patients with auditory agnosia who developed delusions (Reinhold 1950, Vignolo 1982) and from hypnotically-induced partial deafness in normals who then scored higher on the paranoia scale of the MMPI (Zimbardo et al 1981). Some delusions may be secondary to hallucinations, a possibility discussed by Arthur (1964) in his comprehensive review of the explanations of delusions.

Payne (1966) formulated an attentional theory:

> Overinclusion . . . is first experienced as a feeling, difficult to verbalise, that things look different . . . and these are interpreted as having some special

> significance which cannot be specified . . . gradually delusions develop as a complex interaction between the resulting attention defect and errors of thought which tend to produce unjustified generalisations . . . this receives reinforcement from a hostile reaction from the environment and from doctors who by their 'ums' and 'ahs' may well encourage a patient to talk about his false beliefs.
>
> (Payne 1966)

Frith (1979) believed that delusions were the application of *normal* reasoning on the part of a subject to explain an *abnormal* increase in information arriving in consciousness:

> Delusions can be seen essentially as attempts to explain and understand, using entirely normal principles of reasoning . . . the arrival of a percept. . . . The abnormality lies in the fact that normally we would not bother to interpret such an event. . . . The very arrival means that it is important and needs to be explained. This hyperawareness, noting and remembering for example the colours of the ties of all the guests at a party, is frequently observed in deluded patients.
>
> (Frith 1979)

In my view all these are plausible accounts of delusional formation and may singly or together contribute to the development and maintenance of delusions in schizophrenia.

Can the cause be formulated in neuropsychological terms?

Generalised brain damage can undoubtedly aid the formation of delusions (Cutting 1980). Certain sites of brain damage are probably more significant in this respect than others. The two most pathogenic areas of cerebral dysfunction, in my view, are left temporal and right parietal, probably through different mechanisms.

According to Bear (1979), temporal lobe epileptics, particularly those with left-sided lesions, undergo a progressive physiological modification of limbic function which:

> enhance affective associations to previously neutral stimuli, events or concepts . . . causing objects and events to be shot through with affective colouration which might then be incorporated into a mystical or religious view of the world . . . thus allowing for paranoid interpretation or the conviction that the patient is a pawn in the hands of powerful forces.
>
> (Bear 1979)

There is certainly a statistical association between left temporal lesions and hallucinatory-delusional states (Parnas et al 1982c) and between temporal lesions and schizophrenia with prominent paranoid delusions and delusions of reference (Toone et al 1982a). This would also fit in with Bleuler's view that enhanced emotional attachment to an idea predisposes to delusion.

Right parietal damage, on the other hand, probably encourages delusional formation through its effect on perception. Two types of abnormal belief—the Capgras phenomenon and anosognosia—are vivid illustrations of this.

Capgras & Rebould-Lachaux (1923) first drew attention to what they called the 'illusion des sosies'. (Sosia was the servant of Amphytreon, in Greek mythology, and Mercury assumed his appearance at the request of Jupiter to help the latter seduce Amphytreon's wife.) The essence of the belief, according to Christodoulou (1977), is:

> a delusional negation of identity of a familiar person. The patient believes that a person closely related to him has been replaced by a double, and although he does not dispute the misidentified person's extreme resemblance to the familiar person, he nevertheless believes that they are in fact different.
>
> (Christodoulou 1977)

Most instances meet diagnostic criteria for schizophrenia (Kiriakos & Ananth 1980), although about 25% occur in the context of depression or organic psychosis (Christodoulou 1978). The most compelling explanation is antecedent organic brain damage (Christodoulou 1977), affecting the right hemisphere in particular (Hayman & Abrams 1977, Malliaras et al 1978) and producing its effect through prosopagnosia (Hayman & Abrams 1977, Luauté & Bidault 1983). Links with reduplicative paramnesia (in one of the patients of Christodoulou, 1977) and environmental duplication (Thompson et al 1980) strengthen the case for the Capgras phenomenon being a consequence of right hemisphere dysfunction, as both these other disorders have a more established connection with this focus of damage. The evidence therefore suggests, as Capgras observed, that the phenomenon is an 'illusion', a perceptual deficit, rather than an autochthonous belief. Anosognosia, a term coined by Babinski (1914), is the belief that a physical disability does not exist. It is usually confined to denial of a hemiplegia as in Babinksi's original case, but is sometimes applied to denial of cortical blindness or aphasia. The two most striking features are its almost invariable link with a left hemiplegia, and its frequent occurrence in patients who are well orientated in time and place. In two series of hemiplegia of recent onset, it occurred in 30% of 95 left and none of 129 right hemiplegics (Gross & Kaltenbäck 1955), and in 58% of 47 left and 6% of 52 right hemiplegics (Cutting 1978b). Although disorientation may be absent, and peripheral sensory loss or neglect is not an adequate explanation, most patients have an associated attention defect, a fluctuating clouding of consciousness, a disorder of pragmatic language, visuospatial agnosia and object agnosia. The kind of beliefs which patients entertain are illustrated by the following statements made by my patients: 'Nothing wrong. Sometimes it's a bit stiff. It needs exercise.' 'I thought it was a stroke once, but not now I've seen chaps in the ward with them.' 'I felt it could have been a nurse's hand, a neighbour's, my wife's, a doctor's.' Some patients hold more bizarre beliefs. Nightingale's (1982) patient felt that another person was on his left side and asked for a chair to be placed there. His own left side seemed to be evil and controlled by external agents, his right side was recognised as his own and good, and both sides were in constant conflict. As with the Capgras phenomenon, the most plausible explanations have been organic (e.g. incongruence of visual and kinaesthetic body images, Pötzl 1924; loss of connection between left and right hemispheres, von Angyal & Frick 1941). And in particular, there is strong evidence that the belief, like the Capgras phenomenon, has a strong link with visual agnosia, implicating an underlying perceptual disorder.

In my view both left temporal and right parietal dysfunction could be responsible for some schizophrenic delusions, as it has already been argued (p. 100) that DSM-III schizophrenia is a heterogeneous group of sporadic organically-based psychoses (some of whom have left temporal damage) and familial genetically-based psychoses with a pattern of psychological dysfunction resembling that seen in right hemisphere damage.

What is the cause of formal thought disorder?

There are far fewer plausible suggestions for the origin of formal thought disorder than for delusions. Regression was the commonest one in the first half of the century and still appeals to psychoanalysts. After Cameron's neat experiment in 1938 (see p. 37) it was abandoned as a realistic explanation by most authorities. Freud's (1915) suggestion that it was the substitution of everyday thinking by latent forms (normally active in dreams or the unconscious) has never been experimentally tested, although there are good grounds (see p. 366) for regarding dreams and schizophrenic thinking as quite different: highly image-based in the former and highly abstract in the latter. Social explanations such as those of Cameron (1938), Lidz et al (1958, see p. 58) and Wynne et al (1958, see p. 57) are unsatisfactory in my view because they assume too readily that people will indulge in quite extreme forms of thought disorder because of their current social position in life. Cameron's suggestion is in my view quite implausible:

> In asyndesis (loose association of words with general theme) the patient finds it inconvenient to put himself in another's place, in metonymic thinking (approximate phrases) he does not feel that it is necessary, and in interpenetration (interpolation of personal themes) he is no longer able to effect it.
>
> (Cameron 1938)

The only way of confirming these sorts of views would be to reproduce the social conditions which are claimed to be causative and observe whether extreme thought disorder follows this.

The explanations which I favour are those which regard most 'formal thought disorder' as pragmatic language disorder (e.g. Rochester & Martin 1979, Wykes 1980) and those which attempt a neuropsychological formulation of its origin. The role of pragmatic language disorder was discussed on page 259, where it was argued that a neuropsychological explanation in terms of right hemisphere dysfunction and exaggerated left hemisphere functions was quite likely. Some aspects of thought disorder (e.g. overinclusive categorisation) cannot be reduced to pragmatic language disorder, but even here there is evidence that hemisphere imbalance might play a

Table 15.4 Contrasting hemispheric strategies and Minkowski's contrasting modes of thought in schizophrenia

Left hemisphere functions	Minkowski's 'hypertrophied' aspects	Right hemisphere functions	Minkowski's 'atrophied' aspects
Analysis	Analytic ability	Synthesis	Synthetic ability
Serial processing		Parallel processing	
Sequencing		Nonsequencing	
Propositions	Demand for proof	Appositional aspects of things	Reliance on impressions
Logic	Brain, plan	Creation	Instinct, life
Preoccupation with particular		Holistic approach	
Ideation	Thought, representation	Imagery	Feeling, realisation
Concern with familiar		Concern with novelty	
Concern with similar	Base, objects, immobility, space, extension	Concern with difference	Goal, people and events, movement, succession, time

part. The contrasting cognitive strategies of the two hemisphere are presented in Table 15.4. The right is mainly concerned with imageable, holistic, synthetic and spatial aspects of things; the left with abstract, detailed, analytic and temporal aspects. Right hemisphere damage leads to a loss of creativity (Critchley 1962b), diminished use and appreciation of metaphor (Winner & Gardner 1977), a tendency to be overanalytic and less representative in categorisation (Grossman 1981) and denial of the social consequences of behaviour (Bear 1979). Left hemisphere damage characteristically leaves metaphorical thinking intact (Wapner et al 1981), causes subjects to include only the most representative items in categorisation tasks (Grossman 1981) and is associated with 'a tendency to overemphasise the social aspects of behaviour' (Bear & Fedio 1977). On balance, therefore, the loss of creativity, the impaired metaphor, the overinclusive categorisation and relative preoccupation with abstract as opposed to social concerns seen in schizophrenia is more consistent with right than with left hemisphere dysfunction. It must be admitted, however, that the parallel between schizophrenic thought disorder and the effect of right hemisphere dysfunction is only approximate. (Grossman's findings, for example, in right hemisphere damaged patients do not correspond exactly to overinclusion but they have some similarity. He found that, in response to the category 'bird', such patients 'produce many clusters of related items consisting of *less central*, basic object level words whose referents hold less obvious features in common, e.g. albatross, crane, gull'. Anterior left hemisphere damage resulted in examples 'anchored to the central portions of a superordinate's referential field, e.g. robin, sparrow'.)

If one does compare the general schizophrenic pattern of thought disorder (e.g. the one suggested by Minkowski, p. 34) with the characteristic strategies of each hemisphere (Table 15.4) it is apparent that there is some correspondence with a diminution of right and an exaggeration of left hemisphere contributions.

SUMMARY

There are several varieties of normal adult thinking: conceptual attainment, categorisation, 'inner speech', abstract thinking, metaphorical thinking, belief, imagery, calculation, dreaming, creative thinking and primary process thinking.

Neuropsychological issues mainly concern the contribution of the different parts of the brain. The frontal lobe probably directs the flow, the parietal lobe is involved with spatial thought and imagery, and the temporal lobe may add emotional themes. Each hemisphere contributes its own particular strategy, and subcortical areas are concerned with activation and timing.

There are numerous psychological tests of thinking. The most useful in assessing schizophrenic thinking are Babcock's speed tests, the Whitaker Index of Schizophrenic Thinking, overinclusion on an object-sorting test, the relative proportions of psychological and nonpsychological differences noted between two people in photographs, and the relative proportion of abstract to concrete responses on a verbal similarities test.

Abnormalities of thought comprise retardation, flight of ideas, obsessional thoughts, thought interference, perseveration, confusion, paralogia, concrete thinking, dereistic thinking, poverty of content, overinclusive thinking, abnormalities of dreaming, loss of imagery, acalculia, topographical disorientation, disorientation in time, autism and delusions.

In early schizophrenia, subjects may experience their thoughts and their thinking as different in a number of ways. The abnormalities which clinicians observe in the speech of schizophrenics are referred to as formal thought disorder, and have been given various names, some of which are now incorporated into standard rating scales. The most striking abnormality of thought in schizophrenia is the delusion, about which there is little experimental work. Certain clinical aspects of formal thought disorder and some psychological tests have gained a reputation for being diagnostically useful. There is little evidence to justify these claims, and most clinicians rely more on the content of delusions than on the formal qualities of thought.

Some nonspecific disorders of thinking are prominent in schizophrenia, particularly inconsistency, intermittent random responding and a tendency to vacillate between alternatives. Schizophrenics find complex tasks disproportionately difficult, and in tackling them they often fail to take heed of context.

There is considerable doubt as to whether schizophrenics have either a specific disorder of all varieties of thinking or a disorder of a specific aspect of thinking. The stage of their illness and the presence or absence of identifiable brain damage have an overriding influence on the pattern of their thinking. When one takes this into consideration (i.e. florid illness, chronicity, brain damage) and adds general factors, such as intelligence, prolonged medication, other therapies and lengthy hospitalisation, one is left with the distinct impression that being schizophrenic is a minor variable in this welter of influences.

On the basis of experimental work, there is little support for a breakdown in the formal rules of logical thinking, although occasional patients may make glaring errors (paralogia). There is no support at all for Goldstein's idea that they are more concrete in thinking; if anything, schizophrenics are more preoccupied with abstract topics. The literature on concept attainment is particularly difficult to evaluate, but suggests that simple concepts are well attained. There may be an impairment of complex conceptual attainment, but this could be due to perceptual deficit or institutionalisation. Inefficient categorisation in the form of overinclusion is probably the most well-established deficit, but it is neither universal nor specific to schizophrenia. There is evidence that thinking about psychological or social issues is more affected than thinking about neutral topics, although experiments in which this has been tested have been confounded by many of the non-specific aspects of schizophrenic thought disorder such as inconsistency.

Schizophrenic thought disorder has, at various times, been attributed to perceptual disorder, language dysfunction, attentional deficit and emotional disturbance. It has also been formulated in terms of regression, substitution by latent forms of thinking, disruption of a crucial process (e.g. perceptual accommodation, response selection), lack of social awareness and personality disorder.

It is probable that both delusions and formal thought disorder have multiple causes. The former may arise from a disorder in one of the other functions which are affected in schizophrenia, particularly attention, consciousness, emotion and perception, as well as thinking itself. The premorbid personality and emotional or social conflict may also play a part, although these are probably more important in other forms of psychosis. The underlying hemisphere imbalance, which I am claiming is the chief determinant of all the features of the condition, may also predispose to delusions by affecting the way emotion and perception are integrated with thinking. What clinicians regard as formal thought disorder is partly language disorder, but true thought disorder, such as impaired metaphorical thinking, preoccupation with abstract as opposed to psychosocial aspects of things and overinclusive categorisation is more typical of right than left hemisphere dysfunction.

16

Systematic review of psychological theories of schizophrenia

INTRODUCTION

The purpose of this chapter is to attempt a critical account of the various schools of thought about schizophrenia. Some of the opinions were discussed in Chapter 2 and in Chapters 8–15, but by grouping similar ideas together I hope to show the strengths and weaknesses of the various theoretical approaches. I have presented them in increasing order, in my opinion, of their comprehensiveness and plausibility.

EXISTENTIAL THEORIES

Introduction

The only way to understand this group of theories is to appreciate that they are a logical outcome of Jaspers' phenomenological approach to psychiatry but are yet radically different in emphasis. Phenomenologists merely described the psychic life of schizophrenia, regarding it as secondary to whatever was the cause of the condition. Existentialists, however, considered this psychic life itself the cause of schizophrenia. How this inversion arose is made clearer if one studies the writings of a group of neglected European psychiatrists who represent an intermediate position between the sensible but sterile phenomenologists and the fanciful but fertile existentialists.

Phenomenologists

Jaspers was of the opinion (p. 29) that the psychological nature of schizophrenia was by definition ununderstandable and he could therefore see no point in searching for its origin in the patient's personality, life circumstances or amongst disordered individual mental functions. His phenomenological analysis was purely descriptive. He wrote freely about schizophrenic psychic life but this was merely to stress its uniqueness in each individually affected patient and to emphasise that it was a consequence of whatever caused schizophrenia, which Jaspers assumed must be biological.

Jaspers' pupils in Heidelberg, of whom Gruhle and Kurt Schneider were the most talented, continued this pure phenomenological tradition, although Schneider turned it to diagnostic use. Gruhle's analysis of delusional perception illustrated the approach:

> In delusional perception . . . the patient is not disturbed in the so-called elementary components of his perceptual experience—colour, etc. . . . nor their shape and form—the object has this particular shape—nor in its functional meaning—this is a table—nor in its intelligent eleboration—this is a rococco table—but only in the compulsion of its symbolic experience—this table means that the whole world is as twisted as its legs.
>
> (Gruhle 1915)

Gruhle considered that in delusional perception (which to Kurt Schneider was pathognomonic of schizophrenia) something totally banal in the patient's environment was suddenly imbued with significance but,

> this *something* was never definable as it was hidden between and behind objects and their interrelationships, that is in their symbolism.
>
> (Schmidt, 1940, interpreting Gruhle)

The dilemma facing the phenomenologists was this: they had defined schizophrenia as a psychological state which was inexplicable in terms of personality, life experience or any other mental function. They assumed that the cause must be organic, but all the known types of organic brain disease (of which neurosyphilis was the commonest) produced an entirely different picture, well contrasted with schizophrenia by Jaspers (see p. 30). (They were not of course aware of the curious effects of right hemisphere lesions nor of callosal section.) They also knew that organic brain damage caused impairment of consciousness and basic perception, functions which, as Jaspers appreciated (p. 29), were by definition intact in schizophrenia. They had reached an impasse, where all they could implicate was symbolism. The position they had reached was almost metaphysical.

Theories of symbolic transformation

The first solution was to suppose that the faulty use of symbols was a consequence of a particular kind of mental transformation which affected all functions, but was particularly noticeable in the formal aspects of thinking. A number of psychiatrists subscribed to this position. They were all German, with the exception of Minkowski who was French, and they represented the majority view on the matter in the 1920s and 1930s. In essence they regarded schizophrenia as a disorder of thinking, but not in its elementary components, as suggested by Bleuler, but in the way it reflected some vital and fundamental process. What this consisted of was never altogether clear, despite the lengthy treatises that were devoted to the subject. Suggestions included complex emotional states and personality disorder.

Minkowski's (1923) views are the simplest to grasp:

> The individual life impetus weakens and the synthesis of the human personality disintegrates; those elements which go to make up the personality acquire more independence and act as entities; the feeling of time breaks up and is reduced to a feeling of a succession of similar days; there remains only the person face-to-face with a hostile universe; the objects found in the environment insert themselves between the person and the hostile universe . . . Thus delusions should not be considered only as the products of a morbid imagination or distortions of judgements; on the contrary they represent an attempt to translate the new and unusual situation of the disintegrating personality in terms of prior psychic mechanisms.
>
> (Minkowski 1923)

Wetzel's (1922) analysis of the end-of-the-world experience in schizophrenia emphasised the emotional basis, whereas Zutt (1929) stressed the personality component. Wetzel noted that some patients still experienced the impending end of the world 'as if' it were about to happen; others, however, were convinced it was happening. According to Wetzel, the latter group had merely moved on a step from the former, and both had originally experienced altered feelings which had changed their world view without their knowing why. (Wetzel called this a 'Good Friday atmosphere'). Kronfeld (1930) introduced the term 'delusional feelings' to emphasise that delusions sprang from such mood states and were not primarily disorders of thinking or neutral perception. Zutt (1929) proposed the following sequence. First there was a personality change, but the subject was not aware of this. He was aware, however, that the world looked different than hitherto, and assumed that this was because people were plotting against him or that the end of the world was nigh (etc.). Next, even this awareness of alteration disappeared as the new world view became permanent and settled.

Carl Schneider (1930) gave probably the most opaque account in his book *Die Psychologie der Schizophrenen*. In it he recommended what he called a 'functional analysis', although the disturbed functions bore little resemblance to conventional mental functions:

> Primary delusion is a special aspect of the schizophrenic experience of significance, of the floating interrelationship of objects . . . meaningful connections are created between temporally coincident external impressions, external impressions with the patient's present condition, or perceptions with thoughts which happen to be present, or events and recollections happening to occur in consciousness about the same time.
>
> (C. Schneider 1930)

His explanation for such haphazard and chaotic mental life is unfortunately difficult to grasp. Shorn of its metaphysical component he could not improve much on the phenomenologists' conclusion that:

> delusion is a byproduct of the schizophrenic experience of significance.
>
> (Schneider 1930)

Existential psychiatry

The intermediate group of theories (designated existentio-psychological by Schmidt 1940) had, however, shown a way out of the phenomenological impasse. Either one had to explain the disturbance of symbolism in terms of emotion or personality which merged with the psychodynamic approach, to be discussed in the next section; or one concentrated on the disorder of thinking and other cognitive functions and disputed the phenomenological view that these were intact; this led to cognitive theories. Alternatively one ignored the whole phenomenological exercise and searched for organic causes; this characterised the neuropsychological and psychophysiological approaches. A fourth solution was also available. This was to regard the 'schizophrenic experience of significance' as primary and causal in its own right. This is in essence the existential view (or existentio-ontological according to Schmidt 1940).

Jaspers himself in his first philosophical work *The Psychology of World Views* (1919) had laid the theoretical foundations for existentialism. He had pointed out that there are two boundaries at which we pass beyond the limits of knowledge, limits of what can be expressed in words or have questions asked about it. These are the boundary of *transcendence* and the boundary of *existence*. Philosophers had traditionally dealt with the former—ideas, knowledge and generalities. Jaspers appreciated that one could equally well talk about existence, if one was going to talk about the 'unknowable'. This had been expressed in a literary form during the 19th century by Kierkegaard, a Danish theologian, and Nietzsche, a German moralist. Each had decried the artificial nature of abstract, impersonal thinking. Instead, they made passionate pleas for commitment to life rather than logic, emotions rather than thought. The next step was taken by Heidegger with the publication of his book *Sein und Zeit* (Being and Time) in 1927. Critics have described it as 'untranslatable, even into German'! He labelled the concern with existence as 'Dasein', usually translated as 'being-in the world'. Its literal meaning is 'to be there'. There were two modes of 'being-in-the world': inauthentic and authentic. Most people were most of the time in the inauthentic mode. They were wrapped up in their everyday life, and, according to Heidegger, 'prattled' and 'showed a curiosity in trivia'. At some point in their lives, however, some people would become aware of the futility of this way of life, a discovery which was accompanied by disgust and anguish. Such moments were usually at times of real suffering, in particular the contemplation of one's own death. One then moved into the authentic mode of existence and appreciated for the first time one's future, one's real self and one's true relationship with the rest of the world.

Binswanger, a Swiss psychiatrist, was the first to apply these ideas to mental illness. He did this in the form of commentaries on a series of case histories, the most important being *The case of Ellen West* (Binswanger 1944) and *The case of Ilse* (Binswanger 1945).

Ellen West was a married Jewish woman who first sought psychiatric help in her 30s. She was seen by Kraepelin, who diagnosed melancholia, by Bleuler, who diagnosed schizophrenia, received psychoanalysis from a pupil of Freud, and was regarded as a psychopathic personality by another eminent psychiatrist. Her main symptom was a preoccupation with her weight (and from the case-description many modern psychiatrists would diagnose anorexia nervosa); she finally committed suicide. Binswanger regarded her as a case of what he called 'polymorphous schizophrenia'. Despite the diagnostic uncertainty, he concluded:

> Precisely in this case we were able to trace and display step by step through the tangle and vagueness of the symptomatology the progressive narrowing, loss of power and ... emptying of the personality as observed in the schizophrenic process.
>
> (Binswanger 1944)

The case of Ilse illustrates his notions on cause. Ilse was a 39-year-old married woman whose father was a tyrant and her mother an 'angelic slave'. In an attempt to change her father's attitude towards her mother she put her arm in a fire and this was followed by a psychosis lasting 13 months. The chief phenomena were elated mood and a variety of mood-congruent and incongruent delusions. She believed that other people chose their seats to be close to her, at other times that she was being persecuted. This case too is far from being typical of schizophrenia. Nevertheless, Binswanger interpreted her psychosis:

> as a disorder of existence . . . brought about by her decision to do something to be rid of the torturing atmosphere . . . her entire existence is now limited to the motions of unrest, of being attracted, and rejected.
>
> (Binswanger 1945)

Later (Binswanger 1963), he proposed four stages in the unfolding of schizophrenia:

> 1) Whereas natural experience moves unreflectively, unproblematically, unobtrusively as a natural chain of events, in schizophrenia there is a breakdown in consistency of natural experience, an inability to let things be . . . What makes thier lives such a torment is that they are not able to come to terms with inconsistency and disorder in their own experience, and so seek a way out so that order can be re-established. . . . 2) There is now a splitting off of experiential consistency into a rigid either/or, producing extravagant ideals . . . (accompanied by) 3) a Sisyphus-like effort to conceal that side of the alternative that is unbearable . . . and finally 4) Existence is worn away as though through fiction.
>
> (Binswanger 1963)

Binswanger's ideas were taken up by a handful of psychiatrists in several countries. Most accounts are turgid, and the best are mere elaborations of the phenomenological position, conveying no fresh insight into how schizophrenic psychic life comes about. Straus in Germany, Laing in Britain, Ellenberger in North America and Lopez-Ibor in Spain provide the most illuminating accounts.

Straus (1958) stressed the inadequacy of traditional terms such as hallucinations and delusions, because:

> The schizophrenic patient does not live in a space or a world in common with us and that therefore his behaviour should not be understood as an eccentric mode of activity still related to the structure of space familiar to us, but as corresponding to the structure of the peculiar world in which he lives.
>
> (Straus 1958)

For this reason Straus believed that:

> many of the delusional experiences and the so-called ideas of reference have a much more elemental sensory content than indicated by our current terminology [and conversely] the hearing of voices stands midway between hallucinations and the realm of such phenomena as automatic thinking, ideas-snatched-away or thoughts being heard.
>
> (Straus 1958)

Also he cautioned against simplistic notions such as comparing schizophrenic thought with dreaming:

> The schizophrenic does not withdraw from reality into a land of dreams; he is immersed in an alien reality with physiognomies (his experience of the real world) which in the severest cases paralyse all action and cut off all communication.
>
> (Straus 1958)

These observations provide a counterbalance to some of the more naive cognitive and behavioural theories to be discussed later, but do not in themselves constitute causal notions.

Ellenberger (1958) stressed the fact that an understanding of the schizophrenic's appreciation of space and time is crucial:

> hallucination and delusion cannot be understood without the knowledge of the patient's spatial experience.
>
> (Ellenberger 1958)

Laing's (1959) views were discussed on page 52. His main contribution was the introduction of social and psychodynamic components to make the origin of the existential position more plausible, and his interpretation of the critical element as one of ontological insecurity:

> a basically ontologically secure person will encounter all the hazards of life—social, ethical, spiritual, biological—from a centrally firm sense of his own and other people's reality and identity . . . for the ontologically insecure person . . . the ordinary circumstances of everyday life constitute a continual and deadly threat.
>
> (Laing 1959)

Lopez-Ibor (1982) suggested a difference between neurotic anxiety and the anxiety or anguish which existentialists assumed underlay schizophrenia:

> The essential form of the fundamental schizophrenic disorder consists of a state of mood in which the patient is sensitive to everything . . . superficially this state of mood is similar to anxiety, but its internal structure is different.

> In a state of anxiety anything can happen, whereas in delusional moods something strange, enigmatic and incomprehensible is already happening. . . . Existential philosophy is based upon and starts with the analysis of mood. However the anxiety that is the starting point in the existential analysis is not an experience, but a structure that throbs deep in the core of the experience.
> (Lopez-Ibor 1982)

De Koning (1982) noted a similar difference between suspicion and delusion:

> Losing one's stance, losing one's boundaries and being overpowered is much more pronounced and extreme . . . in delusion.
> (De Koning 1982)

Conclusion

Existential accounts of schizophrenia are the most vivid, the most compassionate and, as descriptions of psychosis (though not always typically schizophrenic), the most accurate. They also provide a reminder, largely unheeded, of the danger of assuming that if a person makes an unusual statement, for example that they are hearing voices, this is a false perception in the way a normal person understands this. As plausible and comprehensive explanations of schizophrenia, however, they are inadequate, in my view, for the following reasons. There is no experimental work, whatsoever, to support the notion that ontologically insecure people (if these could be identified) are at greater risk than others to develop schizophrenia. Conversely, there is no evidence that schizophrenics are more likely than others to have been ontologically insecure prior to their psychosis. Further, the mechanism whereby such insecurity or sensitivity or feelings of being threatened are transformed into delusions, hallucinations and thought disorder is not specified.

PSYCHODYNAMIC THEORIES

Introduction

Psychodynamic theories of schizophrenia were first and most comprehensively set out by Freud in a number of publications during his lifetime. Subsequent writers on the subject have done little more than discuss the relative merits of his two main proposals (usually known as the 'conflict' and 'deficit' theories), modify them slightly in the light of changes in basic psychoanalytic teachings, question Freud's observations on the efficacy of psychoanalytic treatment, and incorporate such organic and genetic facts as the basic theory would allow.

Freud

Freud's initial remarks on psychosis were made between 1894 and 1896 and are presented on page 25. This was before Kraepelin had separated dementia praecox from other psychoses, and his use of terms such as hallucinatory psychosis, paraphrenia and paranoia is idiosyncratic by current diagnostic schemes. Ogden (1980) gives a concise summary of his general views at this time, which have become known as the 'conflict theory'. A psychotic patient, according to Freud, was subject to an extreme form of conflict involving unacceptable wishes and defences against these. The difference between neurosis and psychosis lay in the different types of defence mustered and the degree to which the unacceptable idea and its associated affects could be disowned.

As early as 1896, according to Ogden, Freud had a nagging doubt that the first theory was wrong, but in his celebrated psychoanalysis of Schreber (Freud 1911) this first theory was still adhered to. Although he called Schreber a case of paranoia, he added 'dementia paranoides' (Kraepelin's term) in parenthesis, and the man would undoubtedly be diagnosed as schizophrenic today, in view of the length of the illness and the bizarre nature of the delusions. (Schreber believed, for example, that he had no lungs, a torn oesophagus and, whenever he swallowed, part of his larynx went down with his food.) Freud concluded:

> The relation between the patient and his persecutor can be reduced to a simple formula—the person is either identical with someone who played an equally important part in the patient's emotional life before his illness or is easily recognisable as a substitute for him . . . the intensity of emotion is projected while its quality is changed into the opposite . . . at the core of the conflict in cases of paranoia among males is a homosexual wishful phantasy of loving a man.
>
> (Freud 1911)

From 1911 onwards, Freud began to regard psychosis as more and more distinct from neurosis. There was still an element of conflict, but this became less important than a disturbance in the relation with the outside world:

> Neurotics turn away from reality because they find it unbearable, either the whole or parts of it. The most extreme type of this turning away from reality is shown by certain cases of hallucinatory psychosis which seek to deny the particular event that occasioned the outbreak of their insanity.
>
> (Freud 1911)
>
> Neurosis is the result of a conflict between the ego and its id, whereas psychosis is the analogous outcome of a similar disturbance in the relations between the ego and the external world . . . a delusion is found applied like a patch over the place where originally a rent had appeared in the ego's relation with the external world.
>
> (Freud 1924)
>
> In psychoses, however, the turning away from reality is brought about in two kinds of way: either by the unconscious repressed becoming excessively strong so that it overwhelms the conscious, which is attached to reality, or because reality has become so intolerably distressing that the threatened ego throws itself into the arms of the unconscious instinctual forces in a desperate revolt.
>
> (Freud 1932)

What is known as the 'deficit theory' is best illustrated by this passage:

> In schizophrenia words are subjected to the same process as that which makes the dream-images out of latent dream-thoughts—to what we have called the primary psychological processes. . . . If we ask ourselves what it is that gives the character of strangeness to the . . . symptom in schizophrenia, we eventually come to realise that it is the predominance of what has to do with words over what has to do with things. . . . If now we put this finding alongside the hypothesis that in schizophrenia object-cathexes (vital energy or psychological effort applied to appreciation of objects) are given up, we shall be obliged to modify the hypothesis by adding that the cathexis of the word-presentations of objects is retained.
>
> (Freud 1915)

What this last passage means to me, in current psychological terms, is that the physical qualities of objects in the real world are ignored in favour of their abstract, linguistic representations. (This, as I shall argue in the last chapter, was a remarkable insight into the nature of schizophrenia.)

In summary, it seems to me that Freud never really abandoned the notion that psychosis was a consequence of severe emotional conflict. In later years, however, he became more aware of the need to specify the psychological mechanisms, and adapted some of his early neuropsychological views on the nature of aphasia and agnosia to this end.

Jung, Abraham and Adler

Freud's original circle of colleagues were reluctant to espouse a wholly psychodynamic explanation for schizophrenia.

Jung (1907), as discussed on page 26, considered hysteria and dementia praecox to be similar in the abnormal fixation of complexes, but whereas he regarded these as causal in hysteria, in dementia praecox they were only secondary and influenced the form of the symptoms. Later (Jung 1939) he adopted a more committed psychodynamic position, but never seemed entirely confident of this.

Abraham (1907) in a paper entitled *On the significance of sexual trauma in childhood for the symptomatology of dementia praecox* concluded:

> It remains an open question whether such pathological phantasies . . . are in themselves an early manifestation of dementia praecox or whether a dementia praecox which develops at a later age merely makes use of infantile sexual phantasies and experiences.
>
> (Abraham 1907)

Adler wrote about paranoia and hallucinations but not about schizophrenia, and by then he had broken completely from Freud to develop a theory of 'individual psychology' based on compensation for feelings of inferiority:

> Paranoia attacks people whose attitude toward society is characterised by the fact that after a fairly mild upward tendency of their activity or life-line they

> come to a halt at some distance from their goal and . . . obtain an unconscious excuse for either covering up or justifying or indefinitely postponing their possible or anticipated defeat in life.
>
> (Adler 1924)

Sullivan and early North American psychotherapy

In North America Freud's ideas were received with enthusiasm, and, contrary to Freud's advice, optimism about the therapeutic possibilities. Sullivan (1924) is the key figure in this movement (p. 188). His theoretical position has also been presented (p. 36), less orthodox than Freud's, and incorporating regression, dream-like thinking, dissociation, deficit, conflict and social disruption into one unwieldy formulation. Fromm-Reichmann (1948), who also coined the term 'schizophrenogenic mother', and Searles (1965), who gave a very personal account of psychotherapy with schizophrenics, took up Sullivan's enthusiasm for psychoanalytic treatment.

French psychoanalysis

Lacan is the most well-known French psychoanalyst. He recorded his views on the nature of psychosis in 1932. Influenced by Janet (see p. 230) as well as Freud, he believed that psychosis originated in 'an anomaly of the personality', more specifically an arrested development leading to immature handling of sexual feelings. This produced a state of 'autopunition' (self-punishment) out of which the clinical picture emerged. Sechehaye (1954) had a similar conception: unsatisfied needs and frustrations which had been building up since infancy.

German psychoanalysis

Freud had surprisingly little influence amongst German-speaking psychiatrists, although there was a psychodynamic component to many of the existential proposals. Schultz-Hencke (1952) is the most well-known of those who formulated schizophrenia in terms of inner conflict. He believed that schizophrenia was a neurosis, and that the development of delusions was neither bizarre nor sudden, but entirely comprehensible if one studied the unconscious mental life of the patient. Other German psychodynamic formulations refer to paranoia rather than schizophrenia. The main theme of these is the inversion of the original feeling: *I do not belong to them* or *I should not love him* becomes *they hate me* or *he hates me*.

British psychoanalysis

Melanie Klein (1946), in one of the most radical alterations to orthodox Freudian theory, chose the words 'schizoid' and 'paranoid' to refer to a normal stage of infant development. Her choice of the word schizoid reflected her view that the characteristic psychological processes at that age—splitting—bore some resemblance to those seen in schizophrenics and also that schizophrenia itself involved a regression to the thought patterns of an infant in that stage:

> In the first few months of life anxiety is predominantly experienced as a fear of persecution and this contributes to certain mechanisms and defences which characterise the paranoid and schizoid positions . . . Outstanding among these defences is the mechanism of splitting internal and external objects, emotions and the ego. These mechanisms and defences are part of normal development and at the same time form the basis for later schizophrenic illness.
>
> (Klein 1946)

Segal (1964) interpreted this to mean that the cause of schizophrenia, according to Klein, was a regression to a phase of development which already possessed the potential for pathological thinking. This phase was 'a fixation point' for the psychosis. Normal infants negotiated the 'schizoid-paranoid stage' normally by splitting 'good' and 'bad objects' by means of projection and introjection. This resulted in 'good objects' predominating over 'bad'. Infants who did not achieve this were left with 'bad' predominating over 'good objects' and with pathological thought processes characterised by 'splintering' and 'disintegration'. Segal's interpretation of Klein clarifies the original, but it still not certain whether either of them regards schizophrenia as a regression to an abnormal or a normal schizoid position, nor whether they regard schizophrenia as more likely in those who had an abnormal passage through the schizoid position at the time.

Bion (1955), another psychoanalyst noted for his theoretical writings, is no clearer. Rosenfeld (1965), however, sheds some light on these issues. He believes that in those who subsequently develop schizophrenia there is a predisposition from birth. This takes the form of a destructive instinct which dominates the rudimentary ego so that during the paranoid-schizoid stage the fragmentation, splitting and projection which are normal at this time become greatly exaggerated, leaving a residue of 'psychotic parts' which may break through in adulthood and cause schizophrenia.

North American eclecticism

Some North American psychoanalysts tried to incorporate genetic, organic, social and other psychological elements into the basic theory. Rado's (Rado et al 1956) concept of inherited 'anhedonia—weakness of the motivating power of pleasure' and 'proprioceptive diathesis—distortion of awareness of bodily self' was the most novel, and has been the most influential. Bychowski (1952) attempted a rather naive reconciliation of some organic and psychological facts:

> I could show that the waves of energy originating in the brain of schizophrenics have special characteristics. They are incomplete and imperfect as regards

> their tempo as well as the degree of their delimitation . . . The waves become easily independent and are unable to reach their goal. The inhibition of the stream of cerebral energy seems to be closely connected with the pathologic process itself . . . The disturbance of the categoric function is a symptom of final regression indicative of dynamic elimination of the superior cortical apparatus.'
>
> (Bychowski 1952)

Arieti (1974) had a large social component in his picture of an infancy exposed to terrifying and bizarre parents, an adolescence ruined by social awkwardness, an early adulthood marked by low self-esteem and finally the psychosis when a bleak future could no longer be faced. Space & Cromwell (1978) brought in personal construct theory and repertory grids in support of their view that schizophrenics develop such 'an antihedonic position' that punishment and dissatisfaction become the dominant themes in their beliefs. This then led to the psychosis, though why it should is not at all clear to me.

Conflict, deficit, regression and developmental failure

These terms comprise the main elements of all psychodynamic theories of schizophrenia. Some psychoanalysts base their theory wholly around one, most give some consideration to all four.

Arlow & Brenner (1969) favoured *intrapsychic conflict* as the dominant cause, and followed Freud's early views in considering psychosis merely a severe form of neurosis. Ogden (1980) also favoured the conflict theory but interpreted this very loosely. In neurotic conflict, he argued, there was a tension between the perception of two sets of incompatible meanings (e.g. sexual wishes and prohibitions against them), whilst in psychosis the conflict was:

> between wishes to maintain a psychological state in which meaning can exist, and wishes to destroy meaning and thought.
>
> (Ogden 1980)

This is stretching the meaning of the term psychological conflict to unreasonable lengths, and most psychoanalysts accept that there *is* cognitive disorganisation of a type not seen in neurosis.

This *psychological deficit* has been formulated in various ways. In orthodox Freudian terms (Federn 1943):

> The primary schizophrenic process appears to be a functional deficiency or even exhaustion of ego-cathexis.
>
> (Federn 1943)

Or echoing the last of Freud's remarks quoted above (Hoffer 1946):

> There is a fundamental impairment of certain ego functions which manifest themselves for instance in the separation of concrete and verbal manifestations. Words lose much of or even all their objective content and are used as if they were things in themselves.
>
> (Hoffer 1946)

Wexler (1971) is clear on the matter:

> It needs to be spelled out explicitly that schizophrenia involves a progressive disintegration and disappearance of object representations ... sharply differentiated from neurosis ... where such representations are retained in the unconscious.
>
> (Wexler 1971)

Regression was emphasised by Fenichel (1945):

> ... there is a return to the time when the ego was not yet established or had just begun to be established.
>
> (Fenichel 1945)

Developmental failure is illustrated by the conclusions of Blatt & Wild (1976):

> 'Various disturbances in schizophrenia can be considered at least in part as the expression of the impairment of early developmental processes and specifically as impairment in the capacity to experience, perceive and represent boundaries.
>
> (Blatt & Wild 1976)

Conclusion

Psychodynamic theories show a justifiable concern with the early childhood of the future schizophrenic and with the psychological processes during the actual psychosis. My main criticism is that the developmental abnormality is not plausibly linked with the proposed psychological mechanism, and neither of these is unique to schizophrenia. For this reason, I reject their claim to be a comprehensive explanation of the condition.

SOCIAL THEORIES

Introduction

There are two sorts of social theory of schizophrenia. The first denies any specific psychological status at all to the condition, regarding it as an artefact of social forces to label people as mad. The second admits the fact that some individuals do have an abnormal psychological state, but attributes this entirely to the social conditions in which they live.

Schizophrenia as an artefact

These theories were fully described on pages 52–54. The essence of the argument is that society licenses certain professional groups (lawyers, doctors) to label certain social misfits as mad, and this absolves society from the unpleasant role of punishing them for their contravention of its rules. Szasz (1961) emphasises the advantage to the doctor of this, Laing (1971) the benefit to the family and Scheff (1966) the role of society.

The most one can say in favour of these theories, in my view, is that they point out the social consequences of one's diagnostic actions. They do not begin to tackle, however, the reasons why schizophrenia has been separated from other mental disorders, and ignore the fact that, on the whole, schizophrenics are more law-abiding than other classes of mental patients, for example, alcoholics or psychopaths.

Social origins of schizophrenia

The essence of this group of theories is that the future schizophrenic is born with a normal brain and psychological potential but develops the condition because of unfortunate contact with adverse social conditions entirely outside his control. This is a strict requirement, but a necessary one in view of the fact that social skills, emotional rapport and shared beliefs are particularly vulnerable once the condition has developed, and cause and effect are especially difficult to disentangle.

These theories were discussed on pages 57 and 58. Three groups can be discerned, roughly corresponding to the stage of life when the adverse social circumstances were at a maximum. First are proposals which implicate abnormal child-rearing patterns. Secondly, there are loose formulations linking abnormal personality development and social disarticulation during late adolescence. Finally there are theories which attribute schizophrenia to events or social circumstances in adulthood.

Bateson's double-bind theory (Bateson et al 1956, see p. 57), Lidz et al's (1958, see p. 58) 'transmission of irrationality' and Wynne et al's (1958, see p. 57) account of familial thought disorder all claim to show how an otherwise normal child can become thought disordered through exposure to the odd patterns of communication of its parents. In Bateson's proposal the mechanism is one of conflicting double messages which the child cannot resolve. In the theory of Lidz, it is submersion in the paranoid and illogical reasoning of the parents. In Wynne's account the child is constantly drawn into the inconsequential and deviant conversation of its parents and receives no 'normal' model to compensate this.

Meyer and Cameron came to the conclusion that schizophrenia had a social origin by a process of exclusion. Having rejected both organic and psychodynamic explanations they adopted a social framework for its origin. Meyer's actual proposal was poorly formulated and lacking in substance, but Cameron's is one of the most detailed social accounts:

> Schizophrenic disorders are syndromes of disorganisation and desocialisation . . . the socially immature person who develops a schizophrenic disorder has entered adolescence or adulthood inadequately socialised. He lacks the degree of role-taking skill necessary for ease in shifting perspectives under stress. . . . When, through altered social interaction or private preoccupation, he encounters severe conflict and develops marked anxiety he is almost sure to show disorganisation.
>
> (Cameron & Margaret 1951)

Murphy (1968) and Brody (1976) put forward explanations in terms of adverse life circumstances in adulthood. Murphy, having concluded that there was a higher rate of schizophrenia amongst certain communities (see p. 128), identified 'role conflict' as a common pattern in these instances. He claimed that there was a problem of choice affecting an individual, pressure by the community to make the choice but contradiction in the guidance given. If these conditions were fulfilled then schizophrenia was likely to occur. He was particularly struck by the high rate in Western Yugoslavia (see p. 126), a society which, he claimed, typified these conditions as it was at the junction of Eastern and Western Europe. The members of this society, according to him, were torn between two cultures and the resulting turmoil predisposed to schizophrenia. Brody listed three types of 'psychosocial events' which he regarded as pathogenic:

> 1) labelling—reinforcing a person's mistrust of himself or permitting the release of otherwise restrained behaviour; 2) crossing social system boundaries, as by migration, resulting in strangeness, isolation and loss of accustomed support systems; and 3) repeated stressful experiences as bereavements.
>
> (Brody 1976)

Both Kellett (1973) and Wing (1978) discerned a general pattern in the way in which social factors affected the condition, but neither claimed that these were primary. Wing regarded the common denominator as 'social overstimulation', which explained for him facts such as the effectiveness of neuroleptics in patients living with overinvolved relatives and the better prognosis of schizophrenia in underdeveloped countries. Kellett explained the distribution of schizophrenia in a community as an attempt by patients to avoid 'undue proximity and an excess of social interaction'.

Conclusion

Social theories deserve to be taken more seriously than either existential or psychodynamic because they have been evaluated in a scientific way. In some cases too the sequence of events—social → psychological → psychosis—is more detailed and more plausible. Unfortunately, for the reputation of social theories, such epidemiological and experimental studies as have been carried out have not found social factors to be of pre-eminent importance. The evidence was presented in Chapter 5. (Despite an unexpectedly high incidence in some communities of the world it is not certain that this is due to psychosocial factors. Experimental confirmation of the pathogenic effect of anomalous child-rearing patterns or deviant family communication is lacking. Large surveys of the aftermath of harrowing events such as war and migration have been inconclusive. The only real support comes from a handful of studies demonstrating a small increased risk after a life event in the preceding weeks or months.) My main criticisms of the best of this evidence is that the magnitude of the social effect is small; its significance diminishes further if one confines one's study to first episodes;

its complete independence from personality, genetic and organic factors is not definite; and the most convincing accounts of psychosis following a life event rarely take the form of typical schizophrenia, but consist of delusions alone (paranoia), perplexity (reactive psychosis) or mood-congruent phenomena (reactive depressive psychosis). For these reasons I am not convinced that typical schizophrenia can be attributed to social causes alone.

SCHIZOPHRENIA AS AN ANOMALOUS EXPERIENCE

Introduction

Anomalous experiences are those which occur in normal people under certain unusual or exceptional circumstances. They range from those encountered by virtually all people at some stage of their lives (e.g. hypnagogic imagery when falling asleep) to those reported by only the few who journey to the limits of human endurance (e.g. hallucinations when crossing the Atlantic on a raft). It is frequently suggested that schizophrenia is an anomalous rather than an abnormal psychological state, because its major phenomena appear in normals under such extraordinary conditions. The question then becomes not, What causes schizophrenia? but, Why do such experiences occur during ordinary,waking conditions?

Situations which give rise to anomalous experience

The list of situations in which anomalous experiences occur is long. It includes sleep deprivation (Kleitman 1939, Tyler 1955), sensory deprivation (Heron 1957, Leff 1968), the hypnagogic and hypnapompic states (Oswald 1962), hypnosis (King 1957), mystical states (Buckley 1981), forced introspection (Hunt & Chefurka 1976), sensory overload (Miller 1960), time pressure (Usdansky & Chapman 1960), social isolation (Lewis et al 1964) and 'near death' (Gabbard et al 1981).

Varieties of anomalous experience

Most of these situations produce a remarkably similar clinical picture, illustrated by Tyler's study of 350 men exposed to 40 hours of sleep deprivation. Anxiety, gastro-intestinal upset and irritability appeared in 15%; visual or auditory illusions appeared in 70%, but only 2% had true hallucinations, mainly visual; thinking was disturbed in the majority, as judged from rambling, garrulous speech, inappropriate answers and mistakes on naming, but only 1% developed paranoid delusions; silly laughter, elation and depression were not uncommon. This transient affective state with non-specific disturbances of thinking and perceptual distortions can be considered the typical anomalous experiential syndrome.

Some authors emphasise one of these components more than the others (e.g. elation in mystical states, Buckley 1981; thought disorder in hypnagogic states, Oswald 1962; the double, Todd & Dewhurst 1955, and out-of-body experiences, Twemlow et al 1982, in sensory and social isolation). It is probable, however, that they are all part of the same typical syndrome.

Relationship of anomalous experience to schizophrenia

Virtually all of the conditions listed above have been proposed at some time as a model of schizophrenia—sensory deprivation (Rosenzweig 1959), sleep deprivation (Bliss et al 1959), hypnosis (King 1957), hypnagogic state (Oswald 1962), time pressure (Usdansky & Chapman 1960), sensory overload (Hemsley 1977) and mystical states (Watson 1982). Reed (1972) put forward the most comprehensive case , and one can also include the numerous writers, even before Freud, who saw a resemblance between dreams and psychosis.

Other proposals, emphasising anomalous thinking rather than anomalous experiences, also belong in this group of theories. Boisen (1947) saw a connection between schizophrenia and dramatic attempts at problem-solving. Epstein (1979) expressed this ungrammatically but vividly in his claim that schizophrenia is a natural healing process of the mind involving a Kuhnian paradigm shift:

> Some patients have a mental illness and then get well and then they get weller. I mean they get better than they ever were.
>
> (Epstein 1979)

Conclusion

A transient psychosis can undoubtedly occur if the customary pattern of perceptual input is disrupted for a period, or if a severe state of physiological distress is induced. Delusions, hallucinations, emotional changes and thought disorder may occur in varying proportions and to a different extent in a number of exposed subjects. Those who propose this as a model of schizophrenia fail to appreciate two points. First, as Leff (1968) demonstrated in the case of sensory deprivation, those subjects who report the most vivid experiences are often the most schizoid individuals, and the unusual condition may be no more than a precipitant in a predisposed individual. Secondly, and more important, in my view, is the fact that the typical mental state of schizophrenia bears very little resemblance to the typical anomalous experiential syndrome. Although delusions, hallucinations, emotional change and thought disorder are common to both, the specific pattern of each of these differs in the two conditions. No subject in a typical anomalous experiential state would fulfil criteria for schizophrenia by current diagnostic schemes; and delusions of control, bizarre delusions, thought interference, third person hallucinations and emotional blunting are not a part of the anomalous experiential syndrome. For these reasons I reject the notion that anomalous experience is a good model of schizophrenia. (I also consider that dreams and schizophrenic thinking are qualitatively different—marked imagery in the former and marked abstractness in the latter—but the evidence for this is less compelling.)

PSYCHOPHYSIOLOGICAL (BEHAVIOURAL) THEORIES

Introduction

The common element in this group of theories is a physiological disturbance (anxiety or arousal deficit) which disrupts the subject's perceptions and thoughts. The way in which the physiological disturbance effects the disruption is usually described in behavioural terms.

Anxiety

Underlying these theories is the assumption that schizophrenia is a consequence of anxiety. They differ on how this gives rise to the psychotic phenomena. Mednick (1958) believed that anxiety had two main consequences (see p. 46). First it led to what he called stimulus generalisation—the tendency to attribute the source of one's anxiety to incorrect and often trivial objects and events in the environment (e.g. barman's smile—delusion). Secondly, it eventually led to the learning that anxiety was reduced if one maintained certain postures for long periods (catatonia) or indulged in irrelevant thoughts (thought disorder). Broen & Storms (1966) supposed that the chief consequence was a 'collapse of response hierarchies', with the result that improbable or illogical responses were as likely as sensible ones. Delusions were the improbable responses in the sphere of thinking, and hallucinations those in the field of perception. The following example should clarify their argument. A person might normally have an 80% chance of saying black, a 10% chance of saying snow and a 4% chance of saying red, whenever he hears the word white. When he is very anxious this ranking, and the likelihood ratios will not be the same, according to Broen and Storms. This is what they mean by a 'collapse of response hierarchies'. In fact, at very high levels of anxiety or drive the chance of saying black or snow or red will be equal. More important for their argument, the chances of saying something ridiculous like banana or ostrich will be the same as saying black, snow or red. McReynolds (1960) also thought that anxiety had a crucial role. According to him it caused a failure to 'assimilate percepts'. Delusions, hallucinations and thought disorder were then the byproducts of a person's continual attempts to assimilate these percepts.

There are three problems with these theories. One is the questionable status of the experimental findings on which they draw. For example, several investigators have tried to confirm Mednick's claim that schizophrenics tend to overgeneralise and Broen and Storms' claim that their response hierarchies collapse, all without success. It is also questionable if other groups of anxious people give indiscriminate sources for their anxiety (as was once maintained by Schachter & Singer 1962) or say and do ridiculous things in order to reduce it. The second problem is that there is no awareness on the part of the authors of the massive differences between an anxious subject and a schizophrenic. The latter are often anxious in the acute stage, but an association does not constitute a cause. Thirdly, there is no account of the reason why schizophrenics should be more prone to anxiety.

Arousal deficit

Other psychophysiological theories go some way towards resolving these problems. The most plausible are those which incorporate some deficit of arousal. Venables (1964, 1977a) considered that acute schizophrenics were underaroused due to an overactive parasympathetic system, and chronic schizophrenics overaroused through their active sympathetic system. This affected the span of their attention and hence their entire perceptual and thought processes. Although the association of low arousal and acute schizophrenia is surprising, the general form of the proposal was more sophisticated than the pure anxiety theories. Epstein (Epstein & Coleman, 1970) appreciated that one had to introduce an additional element to explain why schizophrenia and anxiety neurosis were different. He suggested that as normals became more anxious and excited there was a compensatory increase in inhibition to prevent cognitive disorganisation; in schizophrenia, he claimed, this was not true as they had an 'inadequately modulated inhibitory system'. Lapidus & Schmolling (1975) proposed a similar mechanism in the form of 'a divergence among arousal systems which were formerly in equilibrium'.

The cause of the physiological disturbance is never made clear in most of these theories. Eysenck (1972) and Claridge (1972) favoured an explanation in terms of personality. Rodnick & Garmezy (1957) believed that schizophrenics were unduly sensitive to criticism, a characteristic which could be traced back to the 'more formative periods of personality development'.

Cortical theories

The previous group of theories linked schizophrenia with predominantly subcortical disturbance. It is worth distinguishing another set of theories which propose a *cortical* origin for the neurophysiological changes. Pavlov wrote:

> One can hardly doubt that schizophrenia in certain of its variations and phases is actually a chronic hypnosis . . . this hypnosis is profoundly based on the weak nervous system, and especially the weakness of the cortical cells . . . chronic hypnosis is inhibition in different degrees of extremity and intensity.
>
> (Pavlov 1930)

Fish (1961) combined Hebb's neuropsychological ideas on normal function with Conrad's gestalt approach to produce what he called a 'neurophysiological theory of schizophrenia':

> the trema (acute stage) is due to overactivity of the reticular system which results in undue diversion and disruption of the central process (physiological correlate of attention) by the sensory input. Internal apophany (established delusions and hallucinations) and catatonic symptoms are explained as due to disruption of the central processes with the formation of shortlived parallel central processes.
>
> (Fish 1961)

Sleep disturbance

Analogies with the effect of sleep deprivation were discussed in the previous section, where it was argued that neither the usual clinical picture (anomalous experiential syndrome) nor dreaming itself bore much resemblance to schizophrenia. Several authors, however, have proposed that some physiological disturbance might cause dreaming to become dissociated from sleep and appear in the waking state. Evarts (1962), Hernandez-Peon (1966) and Dement et al (1970) were all of the opinion that hallucinations might arise in this way, and Fischman (1983) produces the same argument for schizophrenia as a whole.

Conclusion

Psychophysiological theories of schizophrenia are usually plausible, comprehensive and backed up by experiment. Even the best, however, fail on four counts. There is no satisfactory explanation for why habitually anxious people or normal people who suddenly encounter something terrible should be immune from schizophrenia nor why some schizophrenics even in their first episode should feel calm. Secondly, they ignore the body of evidence which shows that disorders of arousal, drive and attention are not confined to schizophrenia, may be absent in that condition, and are probably more common and more marked in other psychiatric disorders such as depression. Thirdly, although the link between anxiety or arousal deficit and some of the clinical phenomena such as paranoid delusions is plausible, the link with others, such as hallucinations, formal thought disorder, bizarre delusions, thought interference, delusional perception and emotional incongruence, is not so well formulated. Fourthly, the original cause of the psychophysiological disturbance is not usually specified. For these reasons I reject the psychophysiological approach as incomplete and probably incorrect in many of its assumptions.

COGNITIVE THEORIES

Introduction

Common to all cognitive theories is the proposal of a deficit in or between the main cognitive functions—attention, perception, thinking, memory—

without involving emotion or personality and without specifying a physiological or organic substrate. Theories suggesting a disturbance of consciousness can also be included here, although there is some doubt about whether consciousness is best regarded as a cognitive 'function' like the others. Most cognitive theories do not propose a straightforward disturbance in one traditional function, but refer more broadly to a disorder of strategy or integration between several functions.

Attentional disorder

This was a popular suggestion in the first two decades of the century and again in the 1960s. Weygandt (1907) called it 'apperceptive deterioration' and Berze (1914) 'primary insufficiency of psychic activation'. Payne et al (1959), McGhie & Chapman (1961) and Silverman (1964) revived the concept. More precisely, they suggested a 'breakdown of a filter mechanism' (Payne), 'that the spotlight of attention which picks up unconscious processes gets out of control' (McGhie & Chapman, p. 60) and 'a deficit of sensory input processing—ideational gating' (Silverman, p. 61).

As discussed in Chapters 2 and 8, such theories were undermined and then virtually abandoned when it became clear that all the usual ways of measuring attention failed to uncover a fundamental deficit which was specific to schizophrenia and occurred in the large majority of cases.

Perceptual deficit

There are suggestions as to how a perceptual deficit could provide the basis for delusions (Maher 1974, see p. 342) and hallucinations (Bazhin et al 1975, see p. 302) but there has been a reluctance to explain the entire condition in this way. Kirk (1968), however, concluded that:

> the association between defective perception and schizophrenia emerges as the strongest, most consistent, most generally agreed upon association.
>
> (Kirk 1968)

She then proposed that an unrecognised perceptual deficit in childhood could become a learning handicap for the child and then a role handicap for the parent, a sequence of events adequate, in her view, to explain the clinical course of the whole condition. Corbett (1976) also considered that perceptual disorder was the primary abnormality, concluding that 'minor changes in perception . . . beyond our capacity to quantify . . . may be the building blocks of psychosis'. Thomas (1968) drew an analogy with computer failure, noting that:

> the most dangerous sites for malfunction are in the higher levels of the sensing and pattern recognition system, for here a malfunction may distort the whole behaviour and be much harder for the monitoring system to recognise.
>
> (Thomas 1968)

Kline (1971) made the radical claim that 'the reason why schizophrenics are schizophrenics is that they see the world the way it really is'. He based this proposal on his finding that 80% of a group of schizophrenics did *not* see an illusion recognised by virtually 100% of normals.

Although I do not dispute the fact that perceptual deficit is a critical determinant of many of the phenomena of schizophrenia, these accounts do not explain how this comes about and must be regarded as incomplete.

Disorders of thinking and memory

It is surprising how little attention has been given to a disorder of memory, considering its importance in determining the content of conscious experience and providing a standard by which to judge perceptual events. The few theories which mention it (Jarvik 1970, Sengel & Lovallo 1980) consider that there is some disturbance in the way items are retrieved, with the result that inappropriate matching of perceptual event and memory element takes place.

A primary disorder of thinking is, however, a common suggestion. Regression (Storch 1924, Vygotsky 1934, see p. 36) was a widely held explanation in the first half of the century. Substitution of ordinary logical thinking by latent forms was one of Freud's theories, recently revived by Blanco (1976). Behavioural and cognitive psychologists have preferred to break down thinking into several components, and examine which is most at fault. Broen & Storms (1966) selected the 'response hierarchy' as the site of the deficit, collapse of which would produce a relatively uniform response to a number of stimuli. This explained, for him, the tendency for deluded people to interpret all sorts of incidents around them (car headlights flashing, people whispering, smiles) in a single-minded way (paranoid delusion). Hemsley (1977) proposed a similar mechanism, which he called 'approximation' (a handful of responses having to accommodate a host of situations). Schilder (1920) had emphasised an impairment in the 'driving force . . . insufficient for tying together the preparatory phases of thought'. (He was much influenced by the Gestalt school of psychology.) Polyakov (1969), and other Russian investigators, believed that current thinking was no longer influenced by the events of the past through which one had learnt the probability of certain events occurring (e.g. being struck by lightning). The result was that unlikely and likely events were treated in the same way. (This might turn out to be an advantage under some circumstances, as in one experiment, where schizophrenics were quicker than normals at solving an unusual problem—how to unequalise balanced scales using a handful of objects, one of which was a candle. They realised more quickly than normals that a burning candle would lose weight.) Magaro (1980) formulated another common theory, which crops up in various forms in a number of articles. The essence of it is that perception and thinking are no longer integrated, and each loses the modifying influence of the other.

Disorder of consciousness

This was a favourite theory at the turn of the century (e.g. sejunction—splitting—of consciousness, Wernicke 1900) and was recently revived by Jaynes (1976) and Frith (1979). The form which it takes is disputed. Jaynes, for example, claims that schizophrenics have a reduced awareness of their perceptions, actions and thoughts, and tend to behave automatically, as if anything that a normal person would reflect upon is for them an immediate reality. Frith (1979) suggests the opposite, a view more in keeping with experiments showing that schizophrenics vacillate in problem solving because they are more than usually aware of a vast number of possibilities. Their consciousness, according to Frith, is flooded with the byproducts of cognitive processing which a normal person is unaware of. The misperceptions which ensue are not therefore abnormal in themselves, but become so by virtue of their arrival in consciousness. The schizophrenic assumes that only important percepts will be let through, and assigns meaning accordingly. He is wrong in this, because he is not aware that the threshold of importance has been lowered. Thought and movement disorder are explained in a similar way. Both result, according to Frith, from the premature entry into consciousness of normally preconscious processes—alternative meanings in the case of thought disorder, preoccupation with previously automatic motor sequences in the case of catatonia.

Frith's suggestion is, in my view, quite plausible, but as with other cognitive theories it is limited in its scope and has no biological correlate.

Failure of functional integration

Most acute observers of schizophrenia have usually pointed out that the hallmark of the condition is not a disturbance of one function by itself but a lack of cohesion amongst several relatively normal functions. The very name schizophrenia (Bleuler) is an acknowledgement of this, to which can be added the 'discordance' of Chaslin, the 'loss of inner unity' of Kraepelin and the 'intrapsychic ataxia' of Stransky.

The modern equivalent of such proposals is an 'inability to integrate perceptual and cognitive processes' (Magaro 1980). Carini (1973) noted the consequences of such dissociation:

> . . . experiencings are totally determined by the proximal stimulation if there are no symbolic representations to transform it . . . [and] totally determined by symbolic representations if there are no proximal stimuli to constrain them.
> (Carini 1973)

Salzinger et al (1978) emphasised the first possibility, the perceptual side of the equation: schizophrenic functioning was controlled by stimuli 'immediate in the environment'.

These theories are plausible, but too general to be of much value.

Strategic imbalance

Investigators with very different psychological orientations have converged on the idea that schizophrenia may represent an inappropriate cognitive strategy rather than any specific functional deficit. Minkowski, an existentialist, noted the 'atrophy' and 'hypertrophy' of contrasting modes of thought (p. 34). Conrad (1958), an advocate of Gestalt psychology, considered that subjects could no longer form a gestalt, and therefore:

> The clouds of essential properties, which every object holds confined within itself, have been set free.
>
> (Conrad 1958)

Shakow (1950), a behaviourist, observed how subjects could not keep a major set, 'could not see the wood for the trees' and had 'a primary need to establish minor sets . . . to examine each tree with meticulous care'. Schwartz Place & Gilmore (1980), cognitive psychologists, concluded that schizophrenics did not respond in a global, gestalt way to pictures, but in an analytic, serial way. Callaway & Naghdi (1982) offered an 'information processing model for schizophrenia', in which the vulnerable processes were those which were 'conscious, serial and limited in channel capacity', whilst 'automatic, unconscious, parallel processes' were 'unlimited in capacity and normal or *supernormal*'.

Conclusion

Cognitive models specify the psychological mechanism of schizophrenia more precisely than any other set of theories, in my view. On the other hand, they lack, more than any other set of theories, a biological, social or developmental component which can account for the psychological proposal. Of the theories in this section, I am inclined to favour those which recognise that the fundamental problem is a lack of cohesion or, more compelling, an inappropriate strategy, rather than a simple failure of one traditional function.

NEUROPSYCHOLOGICAL THEORIES

Introduction

Neuropsychological theories share the assumption that schizophrenia is a consequence of cerebral dysfunction and that it is possible to link the psychological deficit to the site of brain involved. They differ in what they regard as the critical site. Some mention, in addition, an agent, exogenous or endogenous.

Kraepelin, Bleuler

The originators of the concept of schizophrenia put forward what was essentially a neuropsychological theory of its nature (pp. 23–24), in which the site of brain damage was unspecified but its psychological sequelae described in great detail.

Generalised brain damage and its consequences

Since that time several authors have followed this approach, but given less detail than Bleuler, at least, about the psychological mechanism. Buscaino (1978) found 'nonspecific structural brain pathology . . . clods of disintegration in clusters' at autopsy which he claimed were caused by toxic substances in the gut and which resulted in dissociation of function and hence disruption of cognitive activity. Richter (1978) suggested that a neurotropic virus caused partial disorganisation of synaptic transmission which in turn disrupted 'the processing of sensory data'. Fish (1977) proposed an inherited 'pandevelopmental retardation' which affected arousal, visuomotor coordination and cognitive development; these deficits were eventually the cause of the psychotic phenomena. Parnas et al (1982b) had a similar conception, but some of 'the premorbid cognitive and emotional deviations' were organic in origin (birth trauma) and some genetic. Bellak (1979) believed in the malign effect of 'minimal brain damage', and Walker & Green (1982) in its ability to cause 'neuromotor dysfunction'.

Different sites of brain damage leading to different clinical conditions

Kleist's (1960) was the most radical neuropsychological approach. He described subtypes, each linked to a different site of brain damage, e.g. catatonia and brain stem disorder, hebephrenia and mid-brain disturbance. Mirsky (1969) produced a complex formulation in which a fundamental 'hyperfunction of the central mesodiencephalic core' was modified by additional cortical lesions (e.g. frontal, temporal) to produce the different clinical pictures.

Focal brain damage

The limbic system has been the most frequently cited pathogenic area. Torrey & Peterson (1974) present the most reasoned account, in which an agent (possibly a virus) with a predilection for this region causes attentional deficit and this provides the basis for the development of schizophrenia. Mesulam & Geschwind (1978) suggested a 'disruption of neural connections between neocortex and limbic system' which results in inattention and emotional disturbance.

Other subcortical structures are the next most commonly implicated. Ingvar (1980) proposed a 'malfunction of subcortico-cortical projection systems involving thalamus as well as basal ganglia'. Chronister & DeFrance (1983) gave most importance to the nucleus accumbens, a neuro-endocrine organ amongst the basal ganglia largely responsible for the distribution of dopamine throughout the brain. Damage at this point might, according to the authors:

> increase dopamine action leading to an increase in the signal/noise ratio . . . or contrast enhancement.
>
> (Chronister & DeFrance 1983)

(Holzman, 1972, took the cause outside the brain completely, attributing the perceptual disorder to muscular damage which interfered with the integrity of proprioception.)

Hemispheric imbalance

The growth of neuropsychological knowledge in the last 20 years, particularly with respect to functional differences between the hemispheres (see p. 151) has led to several suggestions on how hemispheric imbalance might underlie schizophrenia. The evidence for these claims was presented on pages 152–160, and in the conclusions to Chapters 8–15. There are four main proposals: left hemisphere dysfunction, right hemisphere dysfunction, impaired callosal transfer, and differing patterns of imbalance in different subtypes of schizophrenia.

Left hemisphere dysfunction

Flor-Henry (1979) has been the most committed to this theory. According to him, Bleuler's concept of thought disorder was the most characteristic feature of schizophrenia and the left hemisphere the area of the brain with a major role in thinking. (He was unaware of the right hemisphere's contribution to pragmatic language and thought, pp. 263 and 346.) Shimkunas (1978) also favoured left hemisphere dysfunction as the underlying cause. He claimed that the attentional deficits were consistent with this, and that overinclusion, which he regarded as a failure to appreciate similarity, was a breakdown in the left hemisphere's predominant involvement in this. (As pointed out on p. 346, there is more evidence suggesting that right hemisphere dysfunction produces categorisation deficits resembling overinclusion.)

Right hemisphere dysfunction

Gur (1979), although she believed that the left hemisphere was dysfunctional, considered that the effect of this was to make it overactive and dominate the right. This is equivalent to saying that the right hemisphere is actually the one whose contribution to mental life is relatively diminished. This is also the theory that I hold (see Ch. 17).

Callosal transfer deficit

Beaumont & Dimond (1973) first suggested this. They proposed that there was a functional abnormality of the corpus callosum which led to a reduction in the passage of information between the two hemispheres. A schizophrenic, according to them, resembled the split-brain patients described by the Californian neuropsychologists (see p. 148). Nasrallah (1982) proposed the opposite, an increase in the passage of information, with the result that the left hemisphere was unusually aware of the right hemisphere's activities and interpreted these wrongly as alien forces imposing or intruding on its own consciousness, thoughts and will. (Galin, 1976, took the view that a functional dissociation of the two hemispheres could occur through exposure to conflicting parental messages in early childhood. This was his attempt to incorporate Bateson's double-bind theory into a neuropsychological model. A mother, according to him, could be presenting one message verbally, which was perceived and stored by the future schizophrenic's left hemisphere. Meanwhile the right hemisphere was noting the contrary message in the mother's facial expression and storing this. In adulthood such contradictory representations would then present as the functioning of two independent systems of thought and action.)

Different imbalance in different schizophrenic subtypes

Gruzelier (1981) suggested that schizophrenia was made up of two neuropsychological syndromes. In one, there was 'left hemisphere enhancement' with 'exaggerated self-concepts, pressure of speech, flight of ideas and increased motoric arousal'. He claimed that this corresponded to a paranoid picture, in which the patient was 'locked in a left hemisphere processing mode with overly intellectualised orientation'. The other syndrome was due to a reduction in left hemisphere functioning and gave rise to 'loss of self-confidence, reduced speech, slow muddled thinking, motor retardation and blunted affect'. This, he claimed, was typical of the nonparanoid subtype. (Like Flor-Henry, he neglects the contribution of the right hemisphere to normal function, and assumes that the left hemisphere is dominant in all aspects of emotion, thinking and language.) Magaro & Chamrad (1983) also propose a correspondence between the paranoid and nonparanoid subtypes and, respectively, right and left hemisphere impaired function. (Their scheme also ignores the evidence that the features of non-paranoid schizophrenia—blunting of affect and thought disorder—are more likely to result from *right* than left hemisphere impairment, pp. 240 and 346.)

Conclusion

Neuropsychological theories have an advantage over the other sets mentioned in this chapter in that the cause, in this case cerebral dysfunction, is plausibly linked with the psychological deficit, e.g. subcortical dysfunction and attentional disorder, hemisphere imbalance and altered self-concept. The most compelling theory of all, in my view, is hemisphere imbalance, and, in particular, right hemisphere dysfunction. This will be elaborated in the final chapter.

SUMMARY

Seven sets of psychological theories have been examined in this chapter.

Phenomenological and existential accounts are important in that they drew attention to the specific nature of the patient's experiences at a time when schizophrenia was regarded as a manifestation of brain damage. It became clear that such organic conditions as were known at the beginning of the century produced entirely different clinical pictures. Some of the earlier existential theories, implicating strange moods or personality change, were well thought out and carry much truth about the nature of schizophrenia. Later theories crossed the boundary between psychology and metaphysics and brought all phenomenological and existential approaches into disrepute.

Psychodynamic formulations have not changed much since Freud's time. He had first drawn attention to the similarity between neurosis and psychosis ('conflict theory'), but later concentrated on their differences, and in particular how the disturbance in appreciating reality came about ('deficit theory').

Social theories of schizophrenia are of two sorts. In one, schizophrenia is regarded as nothing more than a label for those who disobey society's rules. These can be rejected as mere politics. Another set of theories attributes the condition to adverse life circumstances (incompetent or deviant upbringing, faulty learning in adolescence, unfortunate encounter with unpleasant event as adult).

Some have tried to compare schizophrenia with the effect of some normal but unusual physiological condition (e.g. sleep deprivation, sensory deprivation). It is thus regarded as anomalous rather than abnormal. Such theories are attractive but incorrect, as the two clinical pictures which are brought together (anomalous experiental syndrome and schizophrenia) bear only a superficial resemblance to one another.

Psychophysiological theories, usually described in behavioural terms, contend that either anxiety or arousal deficit is the fundamental problem. Such theories are probably incorrect in their insistence on a primary disturbance of attention or arousal.

Cognitive theories are the most sophisticated in their analysis of the psychological deficit, but ignore the need to explain how this comes about, whether by organic, genetic or psychological means.

Neuropsychological theories, linking cerebral dysfunction and psychological deficit, are the most plausible in my view. Of these, hemispheric imbalance, particularly right hemisphere dysfunction in the acute stage, is the most attractive.

17

Conclusions

ORIGIN OF THE CONDITION

Schizophrenia was separated from other forms of madness at the turn of the century by Kraepelin (who called it dementia praecox) and Bleuler (who gave it its present name). Before this time it is uncertain whether the condition existed or not. One body of opinion (Cooper & Sartorius 1977) contends that it has always existed, and that its 'recognition' by psychiatrists at the end of the 19th century was the consequence of the segregation of mad people in institutions at this time and hence their availability for study. The opposite opinion (Hare 1983) is that the condition appeared for the first time in Western Europe at the beginning of the 19th century. The evidence for this is the lack of reference to insanity of early adulthood prior to this period and the fact that there was a definite increase in new admissions with this sort of insanity throughout the century. It is difficult to decide between these two proposals. On balance, I favour the suggestion of Cooper and Sartorius.

FORMULATIONS OF SCHIZOPHRENIA DURING THE 20TH CENTURY

In Kraepelin's opinion, dementia praecox was a disease of the brain (of unknown origin and with an unspecified site of cerebral dysfunction) which selectively impaired the correct functioning of the will, leading to a loss of cohesion between and within other crucial functions such as emotion and intelligence.

Bleuler also put forward a neuropsychological theory in which the primary cause was again an unknown agent and unspecified cerebral dysfunction. He differed from Kraepelin in proposing that it primarily affected thinking ('broken association'),and secondarily, through the pathological development of emotional complexes (a notion which he owed to Freud and Jung),caused delusions and hallucinations.

Jaspers, in his monumental work *General Psychopathology*, had a profound influence on ideas about schizophrenia. The publication of his book in 1913 ushered in a period of phenomenological analysis, in which the many facets of a schizophrenic's experience were described and classified. In so far as it shed light on the *cause* of schizophrenia, it was essentially sterile. Gruhle, one of his most able pupils, concluded that there was a disturbance in 'the compulsion of an object's symbolic experience'. Kurt Schneider, his other famous pupil, put his ideas to diagnostic use.

The 1920s are a crucial period for an understanding of schizophrenia. Unfortunately, few of the many Germans writing on schizophrenia have been translated into English, and their contributions cannot be properly evaluated. Some of them indulged in too much metaphysical speculation; this paved the way for postwar existential theories but generally gave the whole topic of psychological analysis of schizophrenia a bad name. What is important about this period are the attempts to solve the dilemma posed by the phenomenologists. They had concluded that the chief characteristic of schizophrenia was its 'ununderstandability' in terms of personality or life experience, and the fact that a disorder of perception, language, thinking or emotion could *not* be blamed for its development. For this reason, they believed that it was essentially an organic disorder, but when they compared schizophrenia with the known types of organic brain disease, it was entirely different both in its clinical form and in the fact that perception, thinking and orientation were grossly affected in these organic disorders but intact, according to them, in schizophrenia. This is why the phenomenologists were reduced to suggesting an abnormality of 'symbolic transformation'.

Several German psychiatrists at this period, however, appreciated that, although a relatively simple abnormality of mood (such as anxiety, depression or elation) or a simple disorder of thinking (such as 'broken associations', suggested by Bleuler) were unlikely, complex mood change or complex thought disorder might explain the condition. Those who suggested an intrinsic alteration in mood or personality believed that this would result in a profound change in the way a subject perceived the world, the actual basis of which would remain unknown to the subject. This 'symbolic transformation' was thus 'projected' or 'realised' as altered significance of objects in the world. The other suggestion, that the change originated with a disturbance in thinking, appealed more to the American psychologists who took over the problem in the 1930s and 1940s.

These American psychologists, of whom Cameron, Hunt and Cofer, and Shakow are the most important, tried to understand thought disorder in terms of the psychological concepts current in North America at the time, in particular intelligence and social psychology. Goldstein, who emigrated to North America at this time, offered a third formulation in terms of impaired abstract attitude. The resulting proposals were social disarticulation (Cameron), psychological deficit (a fluctuating intellectual impairment sensitive to motivational factors—Hunt and Cofer, Shakow) and concrete thinking (Goldstein). The first two, but not the last, are correct interpretations of important aspects of schizophrenia, but became separated from the mainstream of psychiatric thought on cause and treatment which was increasingly biological in orientation.

In the 1950s there was a return to the notion of an underlying mood disorder but, unlike the complex existential proposals of the 1920s, it was regarded as simple anxiety both by behaviourists and psychoanalysts. The effect of this on a subject's perception, however, was described in a similar way as it had been by the early existentialists. A subject became anxious, attributed the source of his anxiety to events in the environment, the whole time remaining unaware of the affective cause of the change in his world view.

In the 1960s, another plausible explanation of schizophrenia emerged, in the form of attention deficit. It appeared an ideal explanation for the generally accepted lack of cohesion between mental functions, and received biological support from the newly discovered efficacy of neuroleptics, and suggestions that dopamine and subcortical regions of the brain might be involved in both attention and schizophrenia.

In the early 1970s cognitive psychology and information processing models were the chief source of theories of schizophrenia, and both attentional and emotional proposals diminished in importance. In the late 1970s neuropsychological theories of schizophrenia were revived, as it had become apparent that hemisphere imbalance and interference with callosal transfer could occur in schizophrenia. The phenomenologists' dilemma was now close to resolution. They had assumed that schizophrenia was organic in nature, but knew of no organic condition which produced a comparable clinical picture. Their organic models had been presenile and senile dementia, general paralysis of the insane and Korsakoff's syndrome, none of which resembled schizophrenia. With the appreciation in the 1950s of the sequelae of right hemisphere damage and in the 1960s of the subtle effects of callosal section, an appropriate organic model was finally available to explain the 'symbolic transformation' of Gruhle, the altered modes of thought of Minkowski (see p. 34) and even Freud's 'giving up of object-cathexes' (see p. 357).

CLINICAL CONSIDERATIONS

Diagnosis

Much work was done in the 1960s and 1970s on refining the diagnostic criteria of schizophrenia. Although this was a healthy trend, much of it is, in retrospect, ill-conceived, because the only validating criterion was prognosis, and it is becoming increasingly clear that outcome is mainly determined by social factors extrinsic to the nature of the psychiatric disorder. Summers & Hersh (1983), for example, compared the outcome of 146 schizophrenics and 149 nonschizophrenic patients on various social and psychiatric parameters: there was virtually no difference. Zubin et al (1983) concluded that:

> the view of schizophrenia as an essentially chronic condition reflects not so much the natural history of the disorder as iatrogenic influences, lack of satisfactory extramural care, the accumulation of a relatively small proportion of truly chronic illnesses and the failure to recognise the termination of an episode of illness in patients with poor premorbid personalities.
>
> (Zubin et al 1983)

The most widely used diagnostic scheme for research purposes is DSM-III, prepared by the American Psychiatric Association, which requires six months disability and nonparanoid delusions or hallucinations in the absence of significant disturbance of mood. Clinicians in Britain, however, still rely heavily on Schneider's first-rank symptoms. In my view, neither of these is satisfactory, and cannot be so until a fundamental psychological or biological standard, not outcome, is found.

Phenomena

Schizophrenia is still largely identified by questioning a subject about their subjective experiences and classifying these into phenomena, chiefly abnormal beliefs (delusions) and abnormal perceptual experiences (hallucinations). Certain observed abnormalities in the way in which ideas are expressed (formal thought disorder), inappropriate emotional responses (flattened or inappropriate affect) and unusual movement or posture (catatonic signs) are also regarded as phenomena, but are given less weight in diagnostic schemes. (Disturbances of consciousness, intellect and will can also be considered under the heading of phenomena, but they are peripheral to the traditional concept.)

What these phenomena represent is often misunderstood by psychiatrists and psychologists. For this reason they are overemphasised by the former and neglected by the latter. Originally, they were astute clinical observations. They were then refined by phenomenological analysis and added to by successive schools of opinion. Finally, they were given certain weight by diagnosticians on the basis of reliability and ease of recognition rather than validity. The pressures of clinical practice, particularly the availability of apparently specific treatment, led to their becoming virtually pathognomonic signs of schizophrenia in the minds of many psychiatrists. On the other hand, those psychologists who ignored their importance in their theoretical formulations produced nothing more than a nonspecific explanation of mental disorder, or at best only part of the schizophrenic picture.

Classification

The classification of psychosis is a welter of eponyms, outdated concepts stripped of their original meaning and national prejudices. It is also a muddle of causal, phenomenological and outcome-orientated approaches. Schizophrenia stands in the midst of all these terms. The most well-established nonschizophrenic psychoses are depressive psychosis, mania and paranoia (including all pure delusional disorders).

Schizophrenia itself has been the subject of numerous classifications. The following points seem to be generally true.

1. Catatonia is best removed completely from the concept of schizophrenia. I agree with Magrinat et al (1983) that most cases are better regarded as affective disorders, and with Mahendra (1981) that the remainder are the result of organic brain damage of a kind not responsible for typical schizophrenia. (This does not mean that some forms of movement disorder cannot occur in schizophrenia.)

2. It is possible to separate another group of patients from the main body of schizophrenics. They have the following characteristics: abnormal personality and poor socialisation prior to the actual diagnosable psychosis, poor social outcome and heavy use of psychiatric services when the florid manifestations have abated, radiological evidence of cerebral atrophy and limited response to neuroleptics. This group has been given various labels: poor premorbid (because of their personality disorder), type II (Crow's term to distinguish them from typical type I), early onset (reflecting age of onset) and chronic (reflecting poor prognosis). Although some psychiatrists, following Kraepelin, would regard this as typical schizophrenia, I consider it atypical because I believe it is itself heterogeneous and does not conform to the traditional descriptions of schizophrenia represented by the views of Bleuler, Jaspers and Schneider.

It probably comprises at least two varieties.

First, some of these are essentially typical schizophrenics but various factors exert a malign pathoplastic influence on the form and course of the condition (see p. 136). A marked schizoid nature, low intelligence, inadequate opportunity to socialise and generalised brain damage are among these factors. (Brain damage can be pathoplastic as well as pathogenic as demonstrated in the several C.T. studies which have found a higher incidence of cerebral atrophy in chronic than in acute schizophrenics. It is vividly illustrated in a study by Rieder et al, 1983, who found comparable C.T. scan abnormalities in three separate groups of diagnostic categories of patients—28 schizophrenics, 15 schizoaffectives and 19 bipolar affectives—but who resembled one another in having a chronic form to their illness.)

Secondly, some of these patients have a type of brain damage which *is* pathogenic but produces a different clinical picture from that seen in either typical schizophrenia or typical organic psychosis (delirium, dementia). There are a host of physical illnesses and conditions which produce such a psychosis without the classical organic triad of clouding of consciousness, inattention and amnesia (Davison & Bagley 1969) and they have been shown in several studies (e.g. Slater et al 1963, Toone et al 1982a, Parnas et al 1982c) to differ in the precise pattern of the phenomena despite fulfilling broad criteria for schizophrenia. The link between recognisable causes of brain damage and psychosis has furthered understanding on how delusions and hallucinations can arise. For the purpose of understanding how the majority of schizophrenic illnesses arise, however, they may be misleading because there is evidence (see p. 343) that different sites of brain damage can give rise to psychosis for different psychological reasons (e.g. left temporal through its effect on emotion, right parietal through an effect on perception).

3. Having narrowed the concept of typical schizophrenia by discarding catatonia and schizophrenia with recognised causes of brain damage one has to widen it again, but in another direction, by considering those people who, though not deluded or hallucinated, resemble typical schizophrenia because of their social and emotional responses. Terms such as schizoid personality, pseudoneurotic schizophrenia, borderline schizophrenia and schizotypal personality disorder all refer to such people. It is ironic that they are now considered (by genetically-orientated psychiatrists at least) to be more closely linked with typical schizophrenia than institutionalised chronic schizophrenics which provided Kraepelin with his original inspiration. I agree with this view, that such people share with schizophrenics the basic psychological patterns of thinking and emotional responses without which typical schizophrenia cannot emerge. A similar view is expressed by Siever & Gunderson (1983):

> Social isolation and suspiciousness are better discriminators of individuals with a genetic relatedness to schizophrenia than is psychotic-like ideation or perceptual distortion.
>
> (Siever & Gunderson 1983)

4. The question then arises as to whether there is a typical schizophrenia. The answer in my view is yes. Clinically it largely corresponds to the descriptions of Bleuler (his insistence on thought disorder, emotional disturbance, autism and ambivalence), Jaspers (his notion of 'ununderstandability'), the early existential psychiatrists (their ideas of a primary alteration in the significance of things due to emotional and personality change) and Schneider (delusional perception rather than other first-rank symptoms). It does not owe much to Kraepelin's ideas because of his emphasis on catatonia and poor outcome, nor on the DSM-III concept which gives too much weight to delusions, hallucinations and chronicity.

Prevalence

What is remarkable about the incidence or lifetime prevalence of schizophrenia is its relative invariance across countries and cultures. The few exceptions can be attributed to the pooling of predisposed individuals through social isolation, migration or downward social drift. (There is more variation in point prevalence rates, but these reflect differences in the tendency for the condition to become chronic, for which there is considerable evidence, most clearly demonstrated in the International Pilot Study of Schizophrenia.) The invariance in incidence is not only evidence against psychosocial causes but organic too. If the cause were viral or perinatal brain damage, for example, one would expect marked differences in time and place corresponding to fluctuations in the incidence of viral epidemics or poor obstetric care. There is some evidence for this, but it is not compelling.

Psychological causes

Of possible psychological causes, the least likely is some adverse life event in adulthood in a normal person. Although there are numerous documented instances of people going mad after something dreadful happening, closer inspection of these reveals that affective or catatonic features were prominent (Jung, p. 129; Binswanger, p. 353; Boisen, p. 129). And most psychodynamic accounts of psychosis refer to paranoia and not schizophrenia (Adler, p. 357; Lacan, p. 358). Further, the typical psychological consequence of disaster or prolonged, harrowing experience is nothing like schizophrenia (see Menninger, p. 130). Finally the few studies which have demonstrated a signficant effect of independent life events have not specified whether they applied to people without a schizoid personality.

The next possible psychological cause is personality disorder. It is fairly well established that an abnormal personality precedes a typical schizophrenic episode in about 40% of cases, of whom about 25% are schizoid and 15% have other prominent abnormal traits. However, it is quite likely that the schizoid personality is not in itself a cause of schizophrenia but rather that both schizoid personality and schizophrenia are both manifestations of the same underlying cause. Nonschizoid personality traits are not more common in schizophrenics than others (Cowen & Cutting 1985), a fact which supports the contention that an abnormal personality is not in itself a cause of schizophrenia.

The third possibility is an exposure to a pathogenic life event in early life. Superficially this is quite plausible. It would explain the characteristic age incidence (late teens onwards) *and* the premorbid schizoid personality. Despite many ingenious theoretical suggestions (see pp. 57–58), however, the evidence that this is so is very weak, and in my view early adverse life experience due to anomalous child-rearing patterns or deviant family communication is not a compelling explanation.

Genetic causes

The evidence that schizophrenia is largely inherited is overwhelming. It is probably the 'hardest' fact there is about the condition. Attempts over the years to undermine it and substitute organic or psychological explanations for twin concordance rates are unconvincing.

Organic causes

As discussed on pages 131–134 the issue of organic causes of schizophrenia has a number of facets which must be kept separate.

First, one has to be sure that the organic factor one is putting forward is not an effect of the condition or its treatment, nor a causally insignificant but pathoplastically relevant factor (e.g. generalised cerebral atrophy worsening prognosis).

Secondly, one needs to know whether the psychosis which turns out to have an organic basis is really the same as typical schizophrenia. It was suggested on page 100 that the numerous physical conditions, sites of brain damage and biochemical disturbances that can give rise to a psychosis produce a clinical picture which only superficially resembles typical schizophrenia. As with instances of psychosis after a devastating life event, such schizophreniform psychoses turn out on careful study to be short-lived, to have a pronounced affective component and to consist only of delusions or hallucinations. This was evident in my study (Cutting 1980) of 74 psychoses with acute cerebral dysfunction. Twenty-eight had delusions or hallucinations without clouding of consciousness (i.e. schizophreniform psychosis) but only 1 had first-rank symptoms. (In most studies of typical schizophrenics with no apparent cerebral dysfunction, between 60% and 80% have first-rank symptoms.)

Having excluded patients with causally insignificant cerebral dysfunction and those where it is causing a different type of psychosis, one can now put the question. Is there an organic cause of typical schizophrenia? in a more informed way. The question still has to be elaborated. Is there evidence of cerebral dysfunction at the anatomical level (recognisable at autopsy, radiologically, on neurological examination or by immunological techniques) or at the biochemical, physiological or neuropsychological levels? Is there a regular association with a particular site of cerebral dysfunction, including hemisphere imbalance? And is a specific agent (e.g. virus) or event (e.g. obstetric complications) consistently reported?

Concerning the level of cerebral dysfunction, there is a vast amount of experimental data, reviewed in Chapter 5. The findings which appear most significant to me are, first radiological evidence on C.T. scan of enlarged ventricles in an identical twin who develops schizophrenia compared with the one who does not. Secondly, although the precise neurotransmitter abnormality is unclear, there does seem to be some biochemical dysfunction, possibly of dopamine, during the acute psychosis, which is reversed by neuroleptics. Thirdly, there are changes in evoked potential during the psychosis which point to a central physiological abnormality.

Concerning the site of cerebral dysfunction, I am more impressed with evidence of hemispheric imbalance than dysfunction within a hemisphere or of some subcortical structure. Of the various formulations of the nature of the hemispheric imbalance, the most compelling in my view is a right hemisphere deficit in the acute stage. Earlier suggestions of a left hemisphere dysfunction originated with the study of psychotic epileptics, most of whom were not typical schizophrenics by my definition. Parnas et al (1982c), in support of this view, interviewed 29 epileptic psychotics, of whom 16 had a 'paranoid-hallucinatory psychosis', 5 paranoia alone, 5 Bleulerian schizophrenia, 2 pseudoneurotic schizophrenia and 1 an affective psychosis. Within the two schizophrenic groups, 3 subjects had right-sided lesions, 3 diffuse and only 1 had left-sided. But of the 16 paranoid-hallucinatory states, 7 had left, 7 bilateral or diffuse and only 2 had a right-sided lesion. Some investigators have suggested that right hemisphere dysfunction underlies paranoid but not nonparanoid schizophrenics (Magaro & Chamrad 1983) and overaroused but not underaroused schizophrenics (Gruzelier 1981) but these divisions do not correspond to the present attempt to separate typical schizophrenia from other psychotic forms. Right hemisphere damage acquired in early childhood gives rise to 'chronic emotional difficulties, disturbance of interpersonal skills and poor visuospatial ability' (Weintraub & Mesulam 1983), a syndrome which is remarkably similar to some of the descriptions of schizoid personality.

Concerning possible agents (physical conditions or events) which might be responsible for the cerebral dysfunction, it is particularly difficult to sift the numerous claims. As I believe that the *site* of the cerebral dysfunction is the crucial determinant, not the *level* or the *agent*, I therefore favour agents which can give rise to localised brain damage. All current biochemical explanations assume a generalised cortical or subcortical origin for the condition and are inadequate by my criterion. A study by Caine & Shoulson (1983) illustrates this point clearly, with results which undermine most of the current biochemical theories of schizophrenia. They interviewed 30 patients with Huntington's chorea, a condition with a relatively simple biochemical defect, and found that 24 of them had one or more of 7 different psychiatric disorders by DSM-III criteria, including 3 patients with schizophrenia. The authors concluded:

> When we examine Huntington's chorea, a disorder with a known unitary pathogenetic mechanism we find clinical heterogeneity ... This raises questions about the assumptions underlying the current approach to psychiatric nosology . . . [which consist of] attempts to demarcate homogeneous behavioural syndromes with their implied underlying biological unity.
>
> (Caine & Shoulson 1983)

The point they are making is that, if a single biochemical abnormality can give rise to seven different psychiatric conditions, it is fruitless to search for a single biochemical abnormality in one of these. For this reason, I favour the suggestions of Parnas et al (1982b) and Reveley et al (1984) that perinatal trauma is a likely cause, because this could in theory produce damage in the right hemisphere. It may be, however, that the right hemisphere dysfunction is inherited and brain damage in various sites merely increases the likelihood of this becoming clinically apparent in later life.

Outcome and treatment

The overwhelming impression one receives from studies on outcome is that social factors determine the degree of disability following an episode of schizophrenia. These social factors are partly extrinsic to the condition (e.g. cultural attitudes to rehabilitation) and partly intrinsic (a premorbid schizoid personality which has impaired the ability to cope in a socially acceptable way with a 'breakdown').

The efficacy of neuroleptics in shortening an episode and preventing relapse is the most striking feature in the literature on treatment. In my view, their effectiveness through a blocking of dopamine receptors throughout the brain is not inconsistent with redressing a hemispheric imbalance. If the left hemisphere is relatively overactive it will be more susceptible to the effect of the neuroleptic, the result of which will be less functional imbalance than before.

The efficacy of psychosocial treatments such as family therapy is also consistent with an original neuropsychological basis to the condition, because a right hemisphere dysfunction has led the schizophrenic to prefer an autistic lifestyle but not equipped him with the social skills to achieve this. He therefore dislikes overinvolvement with others but is vulnerable to their criticisms about the way he leads his life. Teaching relatives to desist from overinvolvement and criticism should therefore have a beneficial effect.

PSYCHOLOGICAL DEFICIT

If typical schizophrenia is a consequence of right hemisphere dysfunction and a relatively overactive left hemisphere it should be possible to identify the various psychological deficits claimed for schizophrenia in the neuropsychological literature on right hemisphere damage.

Attention

In general, schizophrenics find it difficult to maintain attention and to shift their attention to a new topic. In the acute phase their span of attention may be widened and in the chronic phase reduced. Impaired selectivity is not characteristic. There is some evidence that their attention fluctuates over time, particularly for information received at the left hemisphere (Niwa et al 1983).

The right hemisphere, according to Dimond (1976), is concerned with maintaining attention at a low but steady level of competence, whilst the left, though more vigilant in the short term, tires easily. Shifting from one topic to another probably requires the active co-operation of both hemispheres (Kinsbourne 1974b).

Thus, impaired maintenance of attention in schizophrenia is consistent with right hemisphere dysfunction, whilst intermittent gaps, particularly for information arriving at the left hemisphere, is consistent with a normally functioning left hemisphere without the benefit of its partner to cover its breaks in vigilance. If one hemisphere is relatively inactive, one would expect shifts of attention to be disturbed too.

Consciousness

In schizophrenia, some of the reported experiences have been attributed to the awareness of cognitive processes which in normal people fail to reach consciousness (Frith 1979). The experience of alien thoughts, emotions and impulses has been attributed to increased awareness of a whole mode of processing not available to the consciousness of a normal person (Nasrallah 1982).

Subjects whose corpus callosum has been cut or damaged may report that actions carried out by the isolated right hemisphere appear alien to them (see p. 279). Information received by the right hemisphere under such circumstances may be denied or confabulated by the 'speaking' left hemisphere.

Although the neuropsychological sequelae of callosal section are not comparable with a dysfunctional right hemisphere, they illustrate the point that if the normal hemispheric relationship is disturbed, consciousness of one set of processes by another can be disrupted and can appear alien.

Movement

Although I have excluded catatonia from the concept of typical schizophrenia, it is probable that some observed and experienced abnormal motor behaviour may form part of the typical picture. Such abnormalities would be consistent with hemisphere imbalance, as the execution of high level motor functions (praxis) is largely controlled by the left hemisphere, overactivation of which might lead to exaggerated movements and unusual posture.

Memory

The only disorders of memory in schizophrenia not attributable to coexistent generalised brain damage are impaired encoding of emotional words (Koh 1978) and incompetent mnemonic strategies (Koh et al 1973).

These disorders are quite consistent with the present hypothesis, as right hemisphere damage impairs the processing of emotional information (see p. 240) and general control strategies (Coughlan & Warrington 1978).

Language

In typical schizophrenia, syntax (grammar) and semantics (formal meaning of words) are not disturbed. (The occurrence of incoherence and neologisms would appear to contradict this view, but both are rare and there may be other explanations—generalised brain damage or thought disorder.) The perception and expression of the prosodic component of phonemes and pragmatic language (the intended rather than the formal meaning) are however, impaired.

In right hemisphere damage it is these two components which are also most affected. Patients with right hemisphere lesions are impaired in recognising the mood of a speaker and in expressing emotions in their own speech on request (Ross 1981). They fail to understand 'the underlying intention of a question or comment' (Wapner et al 1981).

It would appear therefore that, in the case of language, schizophrenics and patients with right hemisphere damage resemble one another very closely.

Emotion

Schizophrenics have a disorder of emotion with the following characteristics. It is *not specifically the experience of an intense mood*, such as depression, anxiety or elation, although they may experience these moods more than normals do and be rated as pathologically depressed or anxious at interview. It is rather a *qualitative change in the way they experience all emotions*. To an observer this may appear as blunting or inappropriate affect. They themselves may report feeling numb, and questioned about a range of topics they may deny pleasurable experiences. This has been called anhedonia. The qualitative change may not be experienced as such but is apparent in impaired expression of facial or speech emotion, in difficulty in recognising other people's emotions in face or speech, in differentially impaired memory for emotional topics and in disorganised thinking about emotive subjects.

In right hemisphere damage there is also a disorder of emotion with very similar characteristics. For example, Bauer (1982) reported a man (with bilateral occipitotemporal damage, but right hemisphere lesions are more often cited in the literature) who failed to be aroused emotionally by visual cues. All natural scenery looked the same, and so he stopped one of his favourite pastimes, that of hiking. He also felt no emotion when he saw a pretty girl, and cancelled his subscription to Playboy. In this case the man's emotional reactions were quite normal to music and to touch.

Qualitative changes in the experience of emotion of this kind could well be the origin of delusional mood and, as suggested by some of the existential psychiatrists (see p. 35), might, if projected on to the environment without awareness of what had happened, be a powerful source of 'symbolic transformation' (see p. 350) and delusions.

Perception

In the early stages of a schizophrenic episode subjects experience a bewildering array of visual, tactile and auditory distortions in their perception. Later they report hallucinations, particularly auditory-verbal. Experimental evaluation has uncovered disturbances in form and spatial perception in the visual modality which are particularly marked if the task involves items which require holistic and Gestalt analysis rather than analytic and piecemeal.

The right hemisphere has a specific role in visual perception of form and space, and right hemiphere damage results in perceptual distortion and various kinds of agnosia. The right hemisphere is generally considered to adopt a holistic and Gestalt-orientated strategy in perception, although its contribution in any task is affected by numerous variables such as the nature of the task, the status of the subject (sex, handedness) and the instructions given.

It would appear, therefore, that many of the schizophrenic abnormalities of perception conform to the pattern of right hemisphere dysfunction or left hemisphere overactivation. (Auditory hallucinations are not so easily explained, but if one elaborates Frith's proposal, in which they are regarded as unusual awareness of preconscious processes, it is possible that an overactive 'verbal' left hemisphere might well compensate for inadequate nonverbal processing in the right hemisphere by confabulating its own explanation for sensory events.)

Thinking

Schizophrenic thought disorder, paradoxically in view of the historical importance of the concept, is the hardest of all functional deficits to evaluate. It is probably inevitable that this is so because of the numerous nonspecific influences which play a part. Of the various claims concerning its nature, I am most impressed with impaired categorisation in the form of thinking and a tendency to be preoccupied with abstract at the expense of psychological and social topics in its content. As an illustration, compare Freud's description and the account given to me by an intelligent patient.

> If we ask ourselves what it is that gives the character of strangeness to . . . the symptom in schizophrenia, we eventually come to realise that it is the predominance of what has to do with words over what has to do with things . . . in schizophrenia object-cathexes [preoccupation with objects] are given up . . . and word-presentations of objects are retained.
>
> (Freud 1915)

> I was lying on my bed and reality somehow passed inwards as if my brain turned round . . . I then became more interested in memory than perceiving reality around me . . . I was interested in doing things and being places which brought out my memory rather than seeking new experiences . . . Perception in itself of new things I was no longer curious of . . . As my illness progressed, I lost sense of my own self and reality changed . . . Reality became rather threatening, separate, boring . . . At the beginning I had a sense of despair almost amounting to terror, later replaced by flattening . . . I became the opposite of spontaneous, as a result of which I became very diffident, very laboured . . . A woman would become a name, she would then become a symbol for all my sexual feelings. Some of these names would become overdetermined, charged with emotion and whereas I would respond to people very flatly, the name would be very emotional.
>
> (Intelligent chronic schizophrenic)

In right hemisphere damage the complementary strategy of the left hemisphere is unopposed (p. 346), and such patients are often humourless, overanalytic and uncreative. Their categorisation, relative to patients with left hemisphere damage, tends to be 'overanalytic . . . and less representative ... of a hierarchically structured semantic field' (Grossman 1981).

The few notable features of schizophrenics' formal thought disorder are consistent with an overactive left and underactive right hemisphere. Their delusions, however, are not attributable, in my view, to a single psychological deficit. In the same way as psychological trauma in a certain personality and brain damage of various sorts can lead to delusions, it is likely that schizophrenic delusions have multiple causes. In some patients the alteration in the emotional quality of perception may give rise to the belief that people look strange and threatening and therefore to be feared (existential explanation). In other patients the change in perception itself, the prominence of parts and the haziness of wholes (Gestalt view), might lead to secondary elaboration of plots, or if the body itself were perceived in this way to bizarre somatic delusions. Overinclusion and a reliance on abstract concepts could result in bizarre notions about the order of things in the world. Changes in the extent to which one is conscious of the various cognitive processes at work at any moment could act as a focus for strange notions about alien forces (Nasrallah's view). There is also the possibility that the unusual way in which ideas are expressed, because of a disorder in pragmatic language, might itself appear bizarre to an observer and be interpreted by them as a false belief.

SUMMARY

Schizophrenia, in its typical form, is attributable to a disturbance in right hemisphere functions. This affects all psychological functions in a relatively specific manner and is responsible for the characteristic phenomena. The actual cause of the hemispheric imbalance is partly genetic and partly organic. Social factors play a prominent role in determining onset and outcome, because the hemisphere dysfunction makes a subject susceptible to social influences which a normal person is barely aware of.

References

Abraham K 1907 On the significance of sexual trauma in childhood for the symptomatology of dementia praecox. Republished 1955 in: Clinical papers and essays on psychoanalysis. Hogarth, London, p 13–20
Abrahamson D 1983 Schizophrenic deterioration. British Journal of Psychiatry 143: 82–83
Abrams R, Taylor M A 1976 Catatonia. Archives of General psychiatry 33: 579–581
Abrams R, Taylor M A 1978 A rating scale for emotional blunting. American Journal of Psychiatry 135: 226–229
Abrams R, Redfield J, Taylor M A 1981 Cognitive dysfunction in schizophrenia, affective disorder and organic brain disease. British Journal of Psychiatry 139: 190–194
Abroms G M, Taintor Z C, Lhamon W T 1966 Percept assimilation and paranoid severity. Archives of General Psychiatry 14: 491–496
Achté K A, Hillbom E, Aalberg V 1969 Psychoses following war brain injuries. Acta Psychiatrica Scandinavica 45: 1–18
Acker W, Toone B 1978 Attention, eye tracking and schizophrenia. British Journal of Social and Clinical Psychology 17: 173–181
Ackner B 1954 Depersonalisation. Journal of Mental Science 100: 838–872
Ackner B, Harris A, Oldham A J 1957 Insulin treatment of schizophrenia—a controlled study. Lancet i: 607–611
Adams H E, Malatesta V, Brantley P J, Turkat I D 1981 Modification of cognitive processes: a case study of schizophrenia. Journal of Consulting and Clinical Psychology 49: 460–464
Adler A (1924) The practice and theory of individual psychology. Kegan Paul, Trench, Trubner & Co, London
Akelaitis A J 1944 A study of gnosis, praxis and language following section of the corpus callosum and anterior commissure. Journal of Neurosurgery 1: 94–102
Alanen Y O 1958 The mothers of schizophrenic patients. Acta Psychiatrica Scandinavica Supplement 124
Alanen Y O 1966 The family in the pathogenesis of schizophrenic and neurotic disorders. Acta Psychiatrica Scandinavica Supplement 189
Albee G W 1950 Delusions in schizophrenia as a function of chronological age. Journal of Consulting Psychology 14: 340–342
Albott W L, Gilbert L G 1973 Comparision of nonbrain-damaged schizophrenic and brain-damaged nonschizophrenic males on the WIST. Psychological Reports 32: 187–194
Allen H A 1982 Dichotic monitoring and focused versus divided attention in schizophrenia. British Journal of Clinical Psychology 21: 205–212
Allison R S, Hurwitz L J 1967 On perseveration in aphasics. Brain 90: 429–448
Allon R, Stewart M F, Lancee W J, Brawley P 1981 Conditional probabilities and the grid test for schizophrenic thought disorder. British Journal of Social and Clinical Psychology 20: 57–66
Alpert M, Martz M J 1977 Cognitive views of schizophrenia in light of recent studies of brain asymmetry. In: Shagass C, Gershon S, Friedhoff A J (eds) Psychopathology and brain dysfunction. Raven Press, New York
Alpert M, Silvers K N 1970 Perceptual characteristics distinguishing auditory hallucinations

in schizophrenia and acute alcoholic psychoses. American Journal of Psychiatry 127: 298–302
Alpert M, Rubinstein H, Kesselman M 1976 Asymmetry of information processing in hallucinators and nonhallucinators. Journal of Nervous and Mental Diseases 162: 258–265
Altshuler K Z 1971 Studies of the deaf: relevance to psychiatric theory. American Journal of Psychiatry 127: 1521–1526
American Psychiatric Association 1980 Diagnostic and statistical manual of mental disorders, 3rd edn. American Psychiatric Association, Washington
Anastasi A 1961 Psychological testing, 2nd edn. Macmillan, New York
Anderson C M, Hogarty G E, Reiss D J 1980 Family treatment of adult schizophrenic patients: a psychoeducational approach. Schizophrenia Bulletin 6: 490–505
Anderson E W 1938 A clinical study of states of ecstasy occurring in affective disorders. Journal of Neurology and Psychiatry 1: 80–99
Andreasen N C 1977 Reliability and validity of proverb interpretation to assess mental status. Comprehensive Psychiatry 18: 465–472
Andreasen N C 1979a Thought, language and communication disorders. Archives of General Psychiatry 36: 1315–1330
Andreasen N C 1979b Affective flattening and the criteria for schizophrenia. American Journal of Psychiatry 136: 944–947
Andreasen N C 1982a Negative symptoms in schizophrenia. Archives of General Psychiatry 39: 784–788
Andreasen N C 1982b The relationship between schizophrenic language and the aphasias. In: Henn F A, Nasrallah H A (eds) Schizophrenia as a brain disease. Oxford University Press, New York, ch 6, p 99–111
Andreasen N C, Grove W 1979 The relationship between schizophrenic language, manic language and aphasia. In: Gruzelier J, Flor-Henry P (eds) Hemisphere asymmetries of function in psychopathology. Elsevier, Amsterdam, p 373–390
Andreasen N C, Olsen S 1982 Negative v positive schizophrenia. Archives of General Psychiatry 39: 789–794
Andreasen N C, Powers P S 1974 Overinclusive thinking in mania and schizophrenia. British Journal of Psychiatry 125: 452–456
Andreasen N C, Alpert M, Martz M J 1981 Acoustic analysis: an objective measure of affective flattening. Archives of General Psychiatry 38: 281–285
Andreasen N C, Smith M R, Jacoby C G, Dennert J W, Olsen S A 1982a Ventricular enlargement in schizophrenia: definition and prevalence. American Journal of Psychiatry 139: 292–296
Andreasen N C, Olsen S A, Dennert J W, Smith M R 1982b Ventricular enlargement in schizophrenia: relationship to positive and negative symptoms. American Journal of Psychiatry 139: 297–301
Andreasen N C, Dennert J W, Olsen S A, Damasio A R 1982c Hemispheric asymmetries and schizophrenia. American Journal of Psychiatry 139: 427–430
Andrews G, Tennant C 1978 Life event stress and psychiatric illness. Psychological Medicine 8: 545–549
Angermeyer M C, Timpe F H 1980 Psychopathology and language behaviour in schizophrenics. Archiv für Psychiatrie und Nervenkrankheiten 228: 151–160
Angyal A 1944 Disturbances of thinking in schizophrenia. In: Kasanin J S (ed) Language and thought in schizophrenia. University of California Press, Berkeley, p 115–123
Anton-Stephens D 1954 Preliminary observations on the psychiatric uses of chlorpromazine. Journal of Mental Science 100: 543–557
Ardis J A, McKellar P 1956 Hypnagogic imagery and mescaline. Journal of Mental Science 102: 22–29
Arieti S 1966 Schizophrenic cognition. In: Hoch P H, Zubin J (eds) Psychopathology of schizophrenia. Grune & Stratton, New York, p 37–48
Arieti S 1974 Interpretation of schizophrenia. Crosby Lockwood Staples, London
Arieti S 1976 The psychotherapeutic approach to schizophrenia. In: Kemali D, Bartholini G, Richter D (eds) Schizophrenia today. Pergamon, Oxford, p 245–257
Arlow J A, Brenner C 1969 The psychopathology of the psychoses: a proposed revision. International Journal of Psychoanalysis 50: 5–14

Arnold O H 1955 Schizophrener Prozess and Schizophrene Symptom-gesetze. Maudrich, Vienna
Arnold T 1782 Observations on the nature of insanity. Ireland: Leicester
Arthur A Z 1964 Theories and explanations of delusions: a review. American Journal of Psychiatry 121: 105–115
Asarnow R F, MacCrimmon D J 1978 Residual performance deficit in clinically remitted schizophrenics: a marker of schizophrenia? Journal of Abnormal Psychology 87: 597–608
Asarnow R F, MacCrimmon D J 1981 Span of apprehension deficits during the postpsychotic stages of schizophrenia. Archives of General Psychiatry 38: 1006–1011
Asperger H 1944 Die 'autistischen Psychopathen' im Kindesalter. Archiv für Psychiatrie und Nervenkrankheiten 117: 76–136
Astrachan B M, Harrow M, Adler D, Brauer L, Schwartz A, Schwartz C, et al 1972 A checklist of the diagnosis of schizophrenia. British Journal of Psychiatry 121: 529–539
Astrup C, Odegaard O 1960 Internal migration and mental disease in Norway. Psychiatric Quarterly Supplement 34: 116–130
Ayllon T, Azrin N H 1965 The measurement and reinforcement of behavior of psychotics. Journal of Experimental Analysis of Behavior 8: 357–383
Ayllon T, Azrin N H 1968 The token economy: a motivational system for therapy and rehabilitation. Appleton-Century-Crofts, New York
Ayllon T, Michael J 1959 The psychiatric nurse as a behavioral engineer. Journal of Experimental Analysis of Behavior 2: 323–334
Babcock H 1933 Dementia praecox: a psychological study. Science Press, New York
Babinski M J 1914 Contribution a l'étude des troubles mentaux dans l'hemiplégie organique cérébrale. Revue Neurologique i: 845–848
Baldwin J A 1979 Schizophrenia and physical disease. Psychological Medicine 9: 611–618
Baldwin J A 1980 Schizophrenia and physical disease: a preliminary análysis of the data from the Oxford Research Linkage Study. In: Hemmings G (ed) Biochemistry of schizophrenia and addiction. MTP, Lancaster, ch 21, p 297–318
Baldwin M 1970 Neurologic syndromes and hallucinations. In: Keup W (ed) Origin and mechanisms of hallucinations. Plenum Press, New York, p 3–12
Balogh D W, Leventhal D B 1982 The use of temporal and amplitude cues by schizophrenics, psychiatric controls and aged normals in auditory lateralisation. Journal of Nervous and Mental Diseases 170: 553–560
Balogh D W, Schuck J R, Leventhal D B 1979 A study of schizophrenics' ability to localise the source of sound. Journal of Nervous and Mental Diseases 167: 484–487
Bannister D 1960 Conceptual structure in thought-disordered schizophrenics. Journal of Mental Science 106: 1230–1249
Bannister D 1962 Nature and measurement of schizophrenic thought disorder. Journal of Mental Science 108: 825–842
Bannister D, Fransella F 1966 A grid test of schizophrenic thought disorder. British Journal of Social and Clinical Psychology 5: 95–102
Bannister D, Salmon P 1966 Schizophrenic thought disorder—specific or diffuse. British Journal of Medical Psychology 39: 215–219
Bär E S 1976 Semiotic studies in schizophrenia and senile psychosis. Semiotica 16: 269–283
Baribeau-Braun J, Picton T W, Gosselin J-Y 1983 Schizophrenia: a neurophysiological evaluation of abnormal information processing. Science 219: 874–876
Barnes T R E, Bridges P K 1980 Disturbed behaviour induced by high-dose antipsychotic drugs. British Medical Journal ii: 274–275
Baron M, Gruen R, Asnis L 1982 Schizophrenia: a comparative study of patients with and without family history. British Journal of Psychiatry 140: 561–517
Baruk H 1959 Les délires passionnels. Translated 1974 in: Hirsch S R, Shepherd M (eds) Themes and variations in European psychiatry. J Wright, Bristol, ch 15, p 375–383
Baruk H 1978 Psychoses from digestive origins. In: Hemmings G, Hemmings W A (eds) The biological basis of schizophrenia. MTP, England, ch 3, p 37–44
Bateson G, Jackson D D, Haley J, Weakland J 1956 Toward a theory of schizophrenia. Behavioral Science 1: 251–264
Battie W 1758 A treatise on madness. Whiston & White, London
Bauer R M 1982 Visual hypoemotionality as a symptom of visual–limbic disconnection in man. Archives of Neurology 39: 702–708

Bauman E 1971a Schizophrenic short-term memory: a deficit in subjective organisation. Canadian Journal of Behavioural Science 3: 55–65
Bauman E 1971b Schizophrenic short-term memory: the role of organisation at input. Journal of Consulting and Clinical Psychology 36: 14–19
Bauman E, Kolisnyk E 1976 Interference effects in schizophrenic short-term memory. Journal of Abnormal Psychology 85: 303–308
Bauman E, Murray D J 1968 Recognition versus recall in schizophrenia. Canadian Journal of Psychology 22: 18–25
Bazhin E F, Wasserman L I, Tonkonogii I M 1975 Auditory hallucinations and left temporal lobe pathology. Neuropsychologia 13: 481–487
Bazhin E F, Korneva T V, Lomachenko A S 1978 The ability of emotional perception in schizophrenic patients. Summarised 1980 in: Studies of language and schizophrenia in the USSR. In: Rieber R W (ed) Applied psycholinguistics and mental health. Plenum Press, New York
Bear D M 1979 The temporal lobes: an approach to the study of organic behavioral changes. In: Gazzaniga M S (ed) Handbook of behavioral neurobiology, vol 2. Plenum Press, New York
Bear D M, Fedio P 1977 Quantitative analysis of interictal behavior in temporal lobe epilepsy. Archives of Neurology 34: 454–467
Beard A W 1959 The association of hepatolenticular degeneration with schizophrenia. Acta Psychiatrica Scandinavica 34: 411–428
Beaumont J G, Dimond S J 1973 Brain disconnection and schizophrenia. British Journal of Psychiatry 123: 661–662
Beck S J 1944 Errors in perception and fantasy in schizophrenia. In: Kasanin J S (ed) Language and thought in schizophrenia. University of California Press, Berkeley, p 91–103
Bellak L 1948 Dementia praecox. Grune & Stratton, New York
Bellak L 1979 Schizophrenic syndrome related to minimal brain dysfunction: a possible neurologic subgroup. Schizophrenia Bulletin 5: 480–489
Bellissimo A, Steffy R A 1972 Redundancy-associated deficit in schizophrenic reaction time performance. Journal of Abnormal Psychology 80: 299–307
Bemporad J R 1967 Perceptual disorders in schizophrenia. American Journal of Psychiatry 123: 971–976
Bender L 1934 Psychoses associated with somatic diseases that distort the body structure. Archives of Neurology and Psychiatry 32: 1000–1029
Bender L 1959 The concept of pseudopsychopathic schizophrenia in adolescents. American Journal of Orthopsychiatry 29: 491–512
Bender M B 1963 Disorders in visual perception. In: Halpern L (ed) Problems of dynamic neurology. Department of Nervous Diseases, University of Hadassah Hospital, Jerusalem, p 319–375
Benedetti G 1952 Die Alkoholhalluzinosen. Thieme, Stuttgart
Benedetti G 1975 Psychological factors in the aetiology of schizophrenia. In: von Praag H M (ed) On the origin of schizophrenic psychoses. De Erven Bohn, Amsterdam
Benedetti G 1980 Individual psychotherapy of schizophrenia. Schizophrenia Bulletin 6: 633–638
Benjamin J D 1944 A method for distinguishing and evaluating formal thinking disorders in schizophrenia. In: Kasanin J S (ed) Language and thought in schizophrenia. University of California Press, Berkeley, p 65–90
Benjamin T B, Watt T F 1969 Psychopathology and semantic interpretation of ambiguous words. Journal of Abnormal Psychology 74: 706–714
Bennett D 1978 Community psychiatry. British Journal of Psychiatry 132: 209–220
Berg P A, Leventhal D B 1977 The effect of distractor strength versus rate of item presentation on retention in schizophrenics. British Journal of Social and Clinical Psychology 16: 147–152
Berger P A, Rexroth K 1980 Tardive dyskinesia: clinical, biological and pharmacological properties. Schizophrenia Bulletin 6: 102–116
Berkowitz R 1981 The distinction between paranoid and non-paranoid forms of schizophrenia. British Journal of Social and Clinical Psychology 20: 15–23
Berlyne N 1972 Confabulation. British Journal of Psychiatry 120: 31–39

Bernstein L 1960 The interaction of process and content on thought disorders of schizophrenic and brain-damaged patients. Journal of General Psychology 62: 53–68
Berze J 1914 Primary insufficiency of psychic activation. Translated 1986 in: Cutting J C, Shepherd M (eds) Schizophrenia: the origin and development of its study in Europe. Cambridge University Press, Cambridge
Bespalko I G 1976 Peculiarities in the perception of mimicry in schizophrenic patients connected with the disturbance of probable evaluations. Summarised 1980 in: Studies of language and schizophrenia in the USSR. In: Rieber R W (ed) Applied psycholinguistics and mental health. Plenum Press, New York
Bienenfeld D, Hartford J T 1982 Pseudodementia in an elderly woman with schizophrenia. American Journal of Psychiatry 139: 114–115
Bigelow L B, Nasrallah H A, Rauscher F P 1983 Corpus callosum thickness in chronic schizophrenia. British Journal of Psychiatry 142: 284–287
Biles P E, Heckel R V 1968 'Awareness' in chronic schizophrenics: II awareness of causal factors in recent events. Psychological Reports 22: 255–258
Bingley T 1958 Mental symptoms in temporal lobe epilepsy and glioma. Acta Psychiatrica et Neurologica Scandinavica Supplement 120
Binswanger L 1944 Der Fall Ellen West. Translated 1958 as The case of Ellen West. In: May R, Angel E, Ellenberger H F (eds) Existence. Basic Books, New York, p 237–364
Binswanger L 1945 Insanity as life-historical phenomenon and as mental disease: the case of Ilse. Translated 1958 in: May R, Angel E, Ellenberger H F (eds) Existence. Basic Books, New York, p 214–236
Binswanger L 1963 Being-in-the-world, selected papers of Ludwig Binswanger. Basic Books, New York
Bion W R 1955 Language and the schizophrenic. In: Klein M, Heimann P, Money-Kyrle R E (eds) New directions in psychoanalysis. Tavistock, London, ch 9, p 220–239
Birley J L T, Brown G W 1970 Crises and life changes preceding the onset or relapse of acute schizophrenia: clinical aspects. British Journal of Psychiatry 116: 327–333
Birnbaum K 1923 The making of a psychosis: the principles of structural analysis in psychiatry. Translated 1974 in: Hirsch S R, Shepherd M S (eds) Themes and variations in European psychiatry. J Wright, Bristol, ch 9, p 199–238
Black F W 1975 Unilateral brain lesions and MMPI performance. Perceptual and Motor Skills 40: 87–93
Blanco I M 1976 Basic logicomathematical structures in schizophrenia. In: Kemali D, Bartholini G, Richter D (eds) Schizophrenia today. Pergamon, Oxford, p 211–233
Bland R C, Orn H 1978 14-year outcome in early schizophrenia. Acta Psychiatrica Scandinavica 58: 327–338
Blaney P H 1974 Two studies on the language behavior of schizophrenics. Journal of Abnormal Psychology 83: 23–31
Blatt S J, Wild C M 1976 Schizophrenia: a development analysis. Academic Press, New York
Blau J N, Hinton J M 1960 Hypopituitary coma and psychosis. Lancet i: 408–409
Blau T H 1977 Torque and schizophrenic vulnerability. American Psychologist 32: 997–1005
Bleuler E 1906 Affektivität, Suggestibilität, Paranoia. Marhold, Halle
Bleuler E 1908 The prognosis of dementia praecox (the group of schizophrenias). Translated 1986 in: Cutting J C, Shepherd M (eds) Schizophrenia: the origin and development of its study in Europe. Cambridge University Press, Cambridge
Bleuler E 1911 Dementia praecox or the group of schizophrenias. Translated 1950. International University Press, New York
Bleuler M 1951 Psychiatry of cerebral diseases. British Medical Journal ii: 1233–1238
Bleuler M 1972 The schizophrenic disorders. Translated 1978. Yale University Press, New Haven
Bleuler M 1983 Schizophrenic deterioration. British Journal of Psychiatry 143: 78–79
Bliss E L, Clark L D, West C D 1959 Studies of sleep deprivation: relationship to schizophrenia. Archives of Neurology and Psychiatry 81: 348–359
Blum R A Livingston P B, Shader R I 1969 Changes in cognition, attention and language in acute schizophrenia. Diseases of the Nervous System 30: 31–36
Bodlakova V, Hemsley D R, Mumford S J 1974 Psychological variables and flattening of affect. British Journal of Medical Psychology 47: 227–234

Boeringa J A, Castellani S 1982 Reliability and validity of emotional blunting as a criterion for diagnosis of schizophrenia. American Journal of Psychiatry 139: 1131–1135
Bogen J E 1979 The callosal syndrome. In: Heilman K M, Valenstein E (eds) Clinical neuropsychology. Oxford University Press, New York, ch 11, p 308–359
Boisen A T 1947 Onset in acute schizophrenia. Psychiatry 10: 159–166
Boklage C E, Elston R C, Potter R H 1979 Cellular origins of functional asymmetries. In: Gruzelier J, Flor-Henry P (eds) Hemisphere asymmetries of function in psychopathology. Elsevier, Amsterdam, p 79–104
Bolles M, Goldstein K 1938 A study of the impairment of 'abstract behavior' in schizophrenic patients. Psychiatric Quarterly 12: 42–65
Bolton D 1984 Philosophy and psychiatry. In: McGuffin P, Shanks M F, Hodgson R (eds) The scientific principles of psychopathology. Academic Press, London
Bond E D, Abbot E S 1912 A comparison of personal characteristics in dementia praecox and manic-depressive psychosis. American Journal of Insanity 68: 359–370
Bonhoeffer K 1909 Exogenous psychoses. Translated 1974 in: Hirsch S R, Shepherd M (eds) Themes and variations in European psychiatry. J Wright, Bristol, ch 3, p 47–64
Böök J A 1953 Schizophrenia as a gene mutation. Acta Genetica et Statistica Medica 4: 133–139
Bornstein B 1963 Prosopagnosia. In: Halpern L (ed) Problems of dynamic neurology. Department of Nervous Diseases, Hadassah University Hospital, Jerusalem, p 283–318
Bourne L E 1966 Human conceptual behaviour. Allyn & Bacon, Boston
Braatz G A 1970 Preference intransitivity as an indicator of cognitive slippage in schizophrenia. Journal of Abnormal Psychology 75: 1–6
Braden W, Ho C K 1981 Racing thoughts in psychiatric inpatients. Archives of General Psychiatry 38: 71–75
Bradshaw J L, Gates A, Patterson K 1976 Hemispheric differences in processing visual patterns. Quarterly Journal of Experimental Psychology 28: 667–681
Braff D L, Beck A T 1974 Thinking disorder in depression. Archives of General Psychiatry 31: 456–459
Braff D L, Callaway E, Naylor H 1977 Very short-term memory dysfunction in schizophrenia. Archives of General Psychiatry 34: 25–30
Bransford J D, Franks J J 1971 The abstraction of linguistic ideas. Cognitive Psychology 2: 331–350
Brauchi J T, West L J 1959 Sleep deprivation. Journal of the American Medical Association 171: 97–100
Brecher M, Begleiter H 1983 Event-related brain potentials to high-incentive stimuli in unmedicated schizophrenic patients. Biological Psychiatry 18: 661–674
Bresnihan B, Hohmeister R, Cutting J, Travers R L, Waldburger M, Black C, et al 1979 The neuropsychiatric disorder in systemic lupus erythematosus. Annals of the Rheumatic Diseases 38: 301–306
Brett E A, Starker S 1977 Auditory imagery and hallucinations. Journal of Nervous and Mental Diseases 164: 394–400
Brezinova V, Kendell R E 1977 Smooth pursuit eye movements of schizophrenics and normal people under stress. British Journal of Psychiatry 130: 59–63
Brickner R M 1936 The intellectual functions of the frontal lobes. MacMillan, New York
Brion S, Jedrynak C-P 1972 Troubles du transfert interhémisphérique a propos de trois observations de tumeurs du corps calleux. Le sign de la main étrangère. Revue Neurologique 126: 257–266
Broadbent D E 1958 Perception and communication. Pergamon, London
Brockington I F, Leff J P 1979 Schizoaffective psychosis: definitions and incidence. Psychological Medicine 9: 91–99
Brockington I F, Kendell R E, Leff J P 1978a Definitions of schizophrenia: concordance and prediction of outcome. Psychological Medicine 8: 387–398
Brockington I F, Kendell R E, Kellett J M, Curry S H, Wainwright S 1978b Trials of lithium, chlorpromazine and amitriptyline in schizoaffective patients. British Journal of Psychiatry 133: 162–166
Brockington I F, Perris C, Kendell R E, Hillier V E, Wainwright S 1982a The course and outcome of cycloid psychosis. Psychological Medicine 12: 97–105
Brockington I F, Helzer J E, Hillier V F, Francis A F 1982b Definitions of depression: concordance and prediction of outcome. American Journal of Psychiatry 139: 1022–1027

Brodsky M 1963 Interpersonal stimuli as interference in a sorting task. Journal of Personality 31: 517–533
Brody D, Saccuzzo D P, Braff D L 1980 Information processing for masked and unmasked stimuli in schizophrenia and old age. Journal of Abnormal Psychology 89: 617–622
Brody E B 1976 Societal determinants of schizophrenic behavior. In: Kemali D, Bartholini G, Richter D (eds) Schizophrenia today. Pergamon, Oxford, p 23–48
Broen W E, Storms L H 1961 A reaction potential ceiling and response decrements in complex situations. Psychological Review 68: 405–415
Broen W E, Storms L H 1966 Lawful disorganisation: the process underlying a schizophrenic syndrome. Psychological Review 73: 265–279
Brooks G W, Deane W N, Hugel R W 1968 Some aspects of the subjective experience of schizophrenia. Diseases of the Nervous System 29: Supply 5, 78–82
Brown G W, Birley J L T 1968 Crises and life changes and the onset of schizophrenia. Journal of Health and Social Behaviour 9: 203–214
Brown G W, Monck E M, Carstairs G M, Wing J K 1962 Influence of family life on the course of schizophrenic illness. British Journal of Preventative and Social Medicine 16: 55–68
Brown G W, Bone M, Dalison B, Wing J K 1966 Schizophrenia and social care. Institute of Psychiatry, Maudsley Monographs No 17. Oxford University Press, London
Brown G W, Birley J L T, Wing J K 1972 Influence of family life on the course of schizophrenic disorders: a replication. British Journal of Psychiatry 121: 241–258
Brown G W, Harris T D, Peto J 1973 Life events and psychiatric disorders, Part 2: nature of causal link. Psychological Medicine 3: 159–176
Brown J 1977 Mind, brain and consciousness: the neuropsychology of cognition. Academic Press, New York
Brown R 1973 Schizophrenia, language and reality. American Psychologist 28: 395–403
Brown S-L 1981 Dissociation of pleasure in psychopathology. Journal of Nervous and Mental Diseases 169: 3–17
Bruder G E, Sutton S, Babkoff H, Gurland B J, Yozawitz A, Fleiss J L 1975 Auditory signal detectability and facilitation of simple reaction time in psychiatric patients and nonpatients. Psychological Medicine 5: 260–272
Bruens J H 1971 Psychoses in epilepsy. Psychiatria, Neurologia, Neurochirurgia 74: 174–192
Bryden M P, Ley R G, Sugarman J H 1982 A left-ear advantage for identifying the emotional quality of tonal sentences. Neuropsychologia 20: 83–87
Buchsbaum M 1975 Average evoked response augmenting/reducing in schizophrenia and affective disorders. In: Freedman D X (ed) Biology of the major psychoses. Association for Research in Nervous and Mental Disease, vol 54, Raven Press, New York, p 129–142
Buchsbaum M S 1979 Neurophysiological aspects of the schizophrenic syndrome. In: Bellak L (ed) Disorders of the schizophrenic syndrome. Basic Books, New York
Buchsbaum M S, Ingvar D H, Kessler R, Waters R N, Cappelletti J, van Kammen D P et al 1982 Cerebral glucography with positron tomography. Archives of General Psychiatry 39: 251–259
Buckley P 1981 Mystical experience and schizophrenia. Schizophrenia Bulletin 7: 516–521
Buckley P 1982 Identifying schizophrenic patients who should not receive medication. Schizophrenia Bulletin 8: 429–432
Bucknill J C, Tuke D H 1879 A manual of psychological medicine, 4th edn. Churchill, London
Bull H C, Venables P H 1974 Speech perception in schizophrenia. British Journal of Psychiatry 125: 350–354
Burrows G M 1828 Commentaries on insanity. T & G Underwood, London
Bursten B 1961 Psychoses associated with thyrotoxicosis. Archives of General Psychiatry 4: 267–273
Buscaino G A 1978 The amino-hepato-entero-toxic theory of schizophrenia. In: Hemmings G, Hemmings W A (eds) The biological basis of schizophrenia. MTP Press, England, ch 4, p 45–54
Bychowski G 1952 Psychotherapy of psychosis. Grune & Stratton, New York
Bynum W F 1981 Rationales of therapy in British psychiatry. In: Scull A (ed) Madhouses, Mad-doctors and Madmen. Athlone Press, London, ch 2, p 35–57
Caine E D 1981 Pseudodementia. Archives of General Psychiatry 38: 1359–1364

Caine E D, Shoulson I 1983 Psychiatric syndromes in Huntington's disease. American Journal of Psychiatry 140: 728–733
Calev A, Monk A F, Venables P H 1980 Sorting consistency as a diagnostic tool for schizophrenics and normals. Psychiatry Research 2: 231–239
Callaway E, Naghdi S 1982 An information processing model for schizophrenia. Archives of General Psychiatry 39: 339–347
Cameron N 1938 Reasoning, regression and communication in schizophrenics. Psychological Monographs 50
Cameron N 1939 Schizophrenic thinking in a problem-solving situation. Journal of Mental Science 85: 1012–1035
Cameron N 1944 Experimental analysis of schizophrenic thinking. In: Kasanin J S (ed) Language and thought in schizophrenia. University of California Press, Berkeley, p 50–64
Cameron N, Margaret A 1951 Behavior pathology. Houghton Mifflin & Co, Boston
Cantor N, Smith E E, French R de S, Mezzich J 1980 Psychiatric diagnosis as prototype categorisation. Journal of Abnormal Psychology 89: 181–193
Capgras J, Rebould-Lachaux A 1923 Illusions des sosies dans un délire systematisé chronique. Bulletin Société Clinique de Médecine Mentale 11: 6
Carini L 1973 Explanation of percepts and concepts in schizophrenia. Psychiatria, Neurologia, Neurochirurgia 76: 129–138
Carlsson A, Lindquist M 1963 Effect of chlorpromazine or haloperidal on formation of 3 methoxytyramine and normetanephrine in mouse brain. Acta Pharmacologia 20: 140–144
Carmon A 1970 Impaired utilization of kinaesthetic feedback in right hemispheric lesions. Neurology 20: 1033–1037
Carmon A, Nachson I 1973 Ear asymmetry in perception of emotional nonverbal stimuli. Acta Psychologica 37: 351–357
Carnap R 1964 Foundation of logic and mathematics. In: Fodor J A, Katz J J (eds) The structure of language—readings in the philosophy of language. Prentice Hall, New Jersey
Carpenter M D 1976 Sensitivity to syntactic strucutre: good versus poor premorbid schizophrenics. Journal of Abnormal Psychology 85: 41–50
Carpenter W T, Strauss J S, Bartko J J 1973 Flexible system for the diagnosis of schizophrenia. Science 182: 1275–1278
Carpenter W T, McGlashan T H, Strauss J S 1977 The treatment of acute schizophrenia without drugs: an investigation of some current assumptions. American Journal of Psychiatry 134: 14–20
Carpenter W T, Bartko J J, Strauss J S, Hawk A B 1978 Signs and symptoms as predictors of outcome: a report from the International Pilot Study of Schizophrenia. American Journal of Psychiatry 135: 940–945
Carr S A 1980 Interhemispheric transfer of stereognostic information of chronic schizophrenics. British Journal of Psychiatry 136: 53–58
Cash T F, Neale J M, Cromwell R L 1972 Span of apprehension in acute schizophrenics. Journal of Abnormal Psychology 79: 322–326
Cattell R B 1970 The integration of functional and psychometric requirements in a quantitative and computerised diagnostic system. In: Mahrer A R (ed) New approaches to personality classification. Columbia University Press, New York, ch 1, p 9–52
Caudrey D J, Kirk K 1979 The perception of speech in schizophrenia and affective disorders. In: Gruzelier J, Flor-Henry P (eds) Hemisphere asymmetries of function in psychopathology. Elsevier, Amsterdam, p 581–602
Caudrey D J, Kirk K, Thomas P C, Ng K O 1980 Perceptual deficit in schizophrenia: a defect in redundancy utilization, filtering or scanning? British Journal of Psychiatry 137: 352–360
Cavanaugh D K 1958 Improvement in the performance of schizophrenics on concept formation tasks as a function of motivational change. Journal of Abnormal Psychology 57: 8–12
Cegalis J A, Deptula D 1981 Attention in schizophrenia: signal detection in the visual periphery. Journal of Nervous and Mental Diseases 169: 751–760
Cegalis J A, Tegtmeyer P F 1980 Visual selectivity in schizophrenia. Journal of Nervous and Mental Diseases 168: 229–235
Cegalis J A, Leen D, Solomon E J 1977 Attention in schizophrenia: an analysis of selectivity in functional visual field. Journal of Abnormal Psychology 86: 470–482
Chaika E 1974 A linguist looks at 'schizophrenic' language. Brain and Language 1: 257–276

Chang Chui H, Damasio A R 1980 Human cerebral asymmetries evaluated by computed tomography. Journal of Neurology, Neurosurgery and Psychiatry 43: 873–878
Chapman J, McGhie A 1964 Echopraxia in schizophrenia. British Journal of Psychiatry 110: 365–374
Chapman L J 1958 Intrusion of associative responses into schizophrenic conceptual performance. Journal of Abnormal Psychology 56: 374–379
Chapman L J 1960 Confusion of figurative and literal usages of words by schizophrenics and brain-damaged patients. Journal of Abnormal Psychology 60: 412–416
Chapman L J 1961 Emotional factors in schizophrenic deficit. Psychological Reports 9: 564
Chapman L J, Chapman J P 1973 Disordered thought in schizophrenia. Appleton-Century-Crofts, New York
Chapman L J, Chapman J P 1980 Scales for rating psychotic and psychotic-like experiences as continua. Schizophrenia Bulletin 6: 476–489
Chapman L J, Knowles R R 1964 The effects of phenothiazine on disordered thought in schizophrenia. Journal of Consulting Psychology 28: 165–169
Chapman L J, Chapman J P, Miller G A 1977 A theory of verbal behavior in schizophrenia. In: Maher B A (ed) Contributions to the psychopathology of schizophrenia. Academic Press, New York. p 135–167
Chapman L J, Chapman J P, Raulin M L 1978 Body-image aberration in schizophrenia. Journal of Abnormal Psychology 87: 399–407
Chapman L J, Chapman J P, Raulin M L 1980 Scales for physical and social anhedonia. Journal of Abnormal Psychology 85: 374–382
Chaslin P 1912 The discordant form of insanity. Translated 1986 in: Cutting J C, Shepherd M (eds) Schizophrenia: the origin and development of its study in Europe. Cambridge University Press, Cambridge
Chaugule V B, Master R S 1981 Impaired cerebral dominance and schizophrenia. British Journal of Psychiatry 139: 23–24
Cheadle A J, Freeman H L, Korer J 1978 Chronic schizophrenic patients in the community. British Journal of Psychiatry 132: 221–227
Chick J, Waterhouse, L, Wolff S 1979 Psychological construing in schizoid children grown up. British Journal of Psychiatry 135: 425–430
Chodorkoff B, Mussen P 1952 Qualitative aspects of the vocabulary responses of normals and schizophrenics. Journal of Consulting Psychology 16: 43–48
Chomsky N 1957 Syntactic structures. Mouton & Co, The Hague
Christie Brown J R W, Ebringer L, Freedman L S 1977 A survey of a long-stay psychiatric population. Psychological Medicine 7: 113–126
Christodoulou G N 1977 The syndrome of Capgras. British Journal of Psychiatry 130: 556–564
Christodoulou G N 1978 Course and prognosis of the syndrome of doubles. Journal of Nervous and Mental Diseases 166: 68–72
Chronister R B, De France J F 1982 Implications from studies of the nucleus accumbens: towards a multifactor theory of schizophrenia. Medical Hypotheses 9: 115–123
Cicone M, Wapner W, Gardner H 1980 Sensitivity to emotional expressions and situations in organic patients. Cortex 16: 145–158
Ciompi L 1980 Catamnestic long-term study on the course of life and aging of schizophrenics. Schizophrenia Bulletin 6: 606–618
Ciompi L 1983 Schizophrenic deterioration. British Journal of Psychiatry 143: 79–80
Claridge G 1972 The schizophrenias as nervous types. British Journal of Psychiatry 121: 1–17
Clemmer E J 1980 Psycholinguistic aspects of pauses and temporal patterns in schizophrenic speech. Journal of Psycholinguistic Research 9: 161–185
Cleveland S E, Fisher S, Reitman E E, Rothaus P 1962 Perception of body size in schizophrenia. Archives of General Psychiatry 7: 277–285
Clooney J L, Murray D J 1977 Same-different judgements in paranoid and schizophrenic patients: a laterality study. Journal of Abnormal Psychology 86: 655–658
Cohen B D 1978 Referent communication disturbances in schizophrenia. In: Schwartz S (ed) Language and cognition in schizophrenia. Lawrence Erlbaum, Hillsdale N J, ch 1, p 1–34
Cohen G 1973 Hemispheric differences in serial versus parallel processing. Journal of Experimental Psychology 97: 349–356

Cohen G 1977 The psychology of cognition. Academic Press, London
Cohen R, Engel D, Kelter S, List G, Strohner H 1976 Restricted associations in aphasics and schizophrenics. Archiv für Psychiatrie und Nervenkrankheiten 222: 325–338
Colbourn C J 1979 Laterality measurement and theory. In: Gruzelier J, Flor-Henry P (eds) Hemisphere asymmetries of function in psychopathology. Elsevier, Amsterdam, p 65–76
Colbourn C J, Lishman W A 1979 Lateralisation of function and psychotic illness: a left hemisphere deficit? In: Gruzelier J, Flor-Henry P (eds) Hemisphere asymmetries of function in psychopathology. Elsevier, Amsterdam, p 539–560
Colby K M, Faught W S, Parkinson R C 1979 Cognitive therapy of paranoid conditions. Cognitive Therapy and Research 3: 55–60
Cole J O, Klerman C L, Goldberg S C 1964 Phenothiazine treatment of acute schizophrenia. Archives of General Psychiatry 10: 246–261
Cole M, Zangwill O L 1963 Deja vu in temporal lobe epilepsy. Journal of Neurology, Neurosurgery and Psychiatry 26: 37–38
Collicutt J R, Hemsley D R 1981 A psychophysical investigation of auditory functioning in schizophrenia. British Journal of Social and Clinical Psychology 20: 199–204
Collins A M, Quillian M R 1972 How to make a language user. In: Tulving E, Donaldson W (eds) Organisation of memory. Academic Press, New York, ch 8, p 310–351
Collins P J, Kietzman M L, Sutton S, Shapiro E 1978 Visual temporal integration in psychiatric patients. Journal of Psychiatric Research 14: 203–213
Connell P H 1958 Amphetamine psychosis. Institute of Psychiatry Maudsley Monographs No 5, Chapman & Hall, London
Connolly J F, Gruzelier J H, Kleinman K M, Hirsch S R 1979 Lateralised abnormalities in hemisphere-specific tachistoscopic tasks in psychiatric patients and controls. In: Gruzelier J, Flor-Henry P (eds) Hemisphere asymmetries of function in psychopathology. Elsevier, Amsterdam, p 491–510
Connolly J F, Gruzelier J H, Manchanda R, Hirsch S R 1983 Visual evoked potentials in schizophrenia. British Journal of Psychiatry 142: 152–155
Conrad K 1952 Gestalt analysis in psychiatry. Translated 1974 in: Hirsch S R, Shepherd M (eds) Themes and variations in European psychiatry. J Wright, Bristol, ch 10, p 241–260
Conrad K 1958 The early stages of schizophrenia. Die beginnende schizophrenie. G. Thieme, Stuttgart
Cook M, Simukonda F 1981 Anhedonia and schizophrenia. British Journal of Psychiatry 139: 523–525
Cooklin R, Sturgeon D, Leff J 1983 The relationship between auditory hallucinations and spontaneous fluctuations of skin conductance in schizophrenia. British Journal of Psychiatry 142: 47–52
Cooper J, Sartorius N 1977 Cultural and temporal variations in schizophrenia: a speculation on the importance of industrialization. British Journal of Psychiatry 130: 50–55
Corbett L 1976 Perceptual dyscontrol: a possible organising principle for schizophrenia research. Schizophrenia Bulletin 2: 249–265
Coughlan A K, Warrington E K 1978 Word-comprehension and word-retrieval in patients with localized cerebral lesions. Brain 101: 163–185
Court J H, Garwoli E 1968 Schizophrenic performance on a reaction-time task with increasing levels of complexity. British Journal of Social and Clinical Psychology 7: 216–223
Cowen P, Cutting J 1985 Personality and psychosis. Psychological Medicine (in press)
Cox S M, Ludwig A M 1979 Neurological soft signs and psychopathology. Journal of Nervous and Mental Diseases 167: 161–165
Crain P, Goldstone S, Lhamon W T 1975 Temporal information processing and psychopathology. Perceptual and Motor Skills 41: 219–224
Critchley E M R, Denmark J C, Warren F, Wilson K A 1981 Hallucinatory experiences of prelingually profoundly deaf schizophrenics. British Journal of Psychiatry 138: 30–32
Critchley M 1951 Types of visual perseveration: 'palinopsia' and 'illusory visual spread'. Brain 74: 267–279
Critchley M 1953 The parietal lobes. Hafner, New York
Critchley M 1962a Periodic hypersomnia and megaphagia in adolescent males. Brain 85: 627–656
Critchley M 1962b Speech and speech loss in relation to the duality of the brain. In:

Mountcastle V (ed) Interhemispheric relations and cerebral dominance. Johns Hopkins University Press, Baltimore, p 208–213
Crookes T G, Hutt S J 1970 Perception of hidden figures by neurotic and schizophrenic patients. British Journal of Psychiatry 116: 335–336
Crow T J 1978 An evaluation of the dopamine hypothesis of schizophrenia. In: Hemmings G, Hemmings W A (eds) The biological basis of schizophrenia. MTP Press, England, ch 6, p 63–78
Crow T J 1980 Molecular pathology of schizophrenia: more than one disease process? British Medical Journal i: 66–68
Crow T J 1983 Is schizophrenia an infectious disease? Lancet i: 173–175
Crow T J, Johnstone E C 1977 Cerebral atrophy and cognitive impairment in chronic schizophrenia. Lancet i: 357
Crow T J, Mitchell W S 1975 Subjective age in chronic schizophrenia: evidence for a subgroup of patients with defective learning capacity? British Journal of Psychiatry 126: 360–363
Crow T J, Johnstone E C, McClelland H A 1976 The coincidence of schizophrenia and Parkinsonism: some neurochemical implications. Psychological Medicine 6: 227–233
Crow T J, Ferrier I N, Johnstone E C, MacMillan J F, Owens D G C, Parry R D et al 1979 Characteristics of patients with schizophrenia or neurological disorder and virus-like agent in cerebrospinal fluid. Lancet i: 842–844
Cunningham Owens D G, Johnstone E C, Frith C D 1982 Spontaneous involuntary disorders of movement. Archives of General Psychiatry 39: 452–461
Cutting J C 1976 Chronic mania in childhood: case report of a possible association with a radiological picture of cerebellar disease. Psychological Medicine 6: 635–642
Cutting J 1978a A reappraisal of alcoholic psychoses. Psychological Medicine 8: 285–295
Cutting J 1978b Study of anosognosia. Journal of Neurology, Neurosurgery and Psychiatry 41: 548–555
Cutting J 1979 Memory in functional psychosis. Journal of Neurology, Neurosurgery and Psychiatry 42: 1031–1037
Cutting J 1980 Physical illness and psychosis. British Journal of Psychiatry 136: 109–119
Cutting J 1981 Judgement of emotional expression in schizophrenics. British Journal of Psychiatry 139: 1–6
Cutting J, Ryan K 1982 The appreciation of imagery by schizophrenics: an interpretation of Goldstein's impairment of the abstract attitude. Psychological Medicine 12: 585–590
Cutting J C, Clare A W, Mann A H 1978 Cycloid psychosis: an investigation of the diagnostic concept. Psychological Medicine 8: 637–648
Daut R L, Chapman L J 1974 Object sorting and the heterogeneity of schizophrenia. Journal of Abnormal Psychology 83: 581–584
Davidson G S, Neale J M 1974 The effects of signal-noise similarity on visual information processing of schizophrenics. Journal of Abnormal Psychology 83: 683–686
Davies-Osterkamp S, Rist F, Bangert A 1977 Selective attention, breadth of attention and shifting attention in chronic nonparanoid schizophrenics. Journal of Abnormal Psychology 86: 461–469
Davis J M, Garver D L 1978 Neuroleptics: clinical use in psychiatry. In: Iversen L L, Iversen S D, Snyder S H (eds) Handbook of psychopharmacology, vol 10. Plenum Press, New York, ch 4, p 129–164
Davis J M, Schaffer C B, Killian G A, Kinard C, Chan C 1980 Important issues in the drug treatment of schizophrenia. Schizophrenia Bulletin 6: 70–87
Davis K M, Blaney P H 1976 Overinclusion and self-editing in schizophrenia. Journal of Abnormal Psychology 85: 51–60
Davis R H, Harrington R W 1957 The effect of stimulus class on the problem-solving behavior of schizophrenics and normals. Journal of Abnormal Psychology 54: 126–128
Davison K 1976 Drug-induced psychoses and their relationship to schizophrenia. In: Kemali D, Bartholini G, Richter D (eds) Schizophrenia today. Pergamon, Oxford, p 105–133
Davison K, Bagley C R 1969 Schizophrenia-like psychoses associated with organic disorders of the central nervous system: a review of the literature. In: Herrington R N (ed) Current problems in neuropsychiatry. Headley, Ashford, p 113–194
Dawson D F L, Bartolucci G, Blum H M 1980 Language and schizophrenia: towards a synthesis. Comprehensive Psychiatry 21: 81–90

De Clérambault G 1942 Oeuvre psychiatrique. Le Francois, Paris
Deering G 1963 Affective stimuli and disturbance of thought processes. Journal of Consulting Psychology 27: 338–343
Deese J 1970 Psycholinguistics. Allyn & Bacon, Boston
De Koning A 1982 Suspicion and delusion. In: De Koning A J J, Jenner F A (eds) Phenomenology and psychiatry. Academic Press, London
De Kosky S T, Heilman K M, Bowers D, Valenstein E 1980 Recognition and discrimination of emotional faces and pictures. Brain and Language 9: 206–214
Delay J, Deniker P 1952 Le traitement des psychoses par une méthode neurolytique dérivée de l'hibernothérapie. In: Ossa P C (ed) Congrès de médecins aliénistes et neurologistes de France. Maisson, Paris, p 497–502
Dement W, Halper C, Pivik T, Ferguson J, Cohen H, Henriksen S et al 1970 Hallucinations and dreaming. In: Perception and its disorders. Association for Research in Nervous and Mental Disease No 48. Williams & Wilkins, Baltimore, p 335–359
De Morsier G 1938 Les hallucinations. Revue d'Oto-neuro-ophtalmologie 16: 241–352
Denford J, Schachter J, Temple N, Kind P, Rosser R 1983 Selection and outcome in inpatient psychotherapy. British Journal of Medical Psychology 56: 225–243
Dennis M 1981 Language in a congenitally acallosal brain. Brain and Language 12: 33–53
De Renzi E 1968 Nonverbal memory and hemispheric side of lesion. Neuropsychologia 6: 181–189
De Silva W P, Hemsley D R 1977 The influence of context on language perception in schizophrenia. British Journal of Social and Clinical Psychology 16: 337–345
Dewhurst K 1969 The neurosyphilitic psychoses today. British Journal of Psychiatry 115: 31–38
Diefendorf A R, Dodge R 1908 An experimental study of the ocular reactions of the insane from photographic records. Brain 31: 451–489
Diem O 1903 The simple dementing form of dementia praecox. Translated 1986 in: Cutting J C, Shepherd M (eds) Schizophrenia: the origin and development of its study in Europe. Cambridge University Press, Cambridge
Dimond S J 1976 Depletion of attentional capacity after total commissurotomy in man. Brain 99: 347–356
Dimond S J 1979 Disconnection and psychopathology. In: Gruzelier P, Flor-Henry P (eds) Hemisphere asymmetries of function in psychopathology. Elsevier, Amsterdam, p 35–46
Dimond S J, Beaumont J G 1973 Difference in the vigilance performance of the right and left hemispheres. Cortex 9: 259–265
Dimond S J, Beaumont J G 1974 Experimental studies of hemisphere function in the human brain. In: Dimond S J, Beaumont J G (eds) Hemisphere function in the human brain. Elek Science, London, ch 4, p 48–88
Dimond S J, Farrington L, Johnson P 1976 Differing emotional response from right and left hemispheres. Nature 261: 690–692
Dimond S J, Scammell R E, Pryce I G, Huws D, Gray C 1979 Callosal transfer and left-hand anomia in schizophrenia. Biological Psychiatry 14: 735–739
Di Simoni G G, Darley F L, Aronson A E 1977 Patterns of dysfunction in schizophrenic patients on an aphasia test battery. Journal of Speech and Hearing Disorders 42: 498–513
Dixon N F, Lear T E 1962 Perceptual regulation and mental disorder. Journal of Mental Science 108: 356–361
Dixon P M 1968 Reduced emotional responsiveness in schizophrenia. University of London Ph D thesis.
Docherty J P, van Kammen D P, Siris S G, Marder S R 1978 Stages of onset of schizophrenic psychosis. American Journal of Psychiatry 135: 420–426
Doerner K 1981 Madmen and the bourgeoisie. Blackwell, Oxford
Dohan F C 1966 Wartime changes in hospital admissions for schizophrenia. Acta Psychiatrica Scandinavica 42: 1–23
Dohrenwend B P, Egri G 1981 Recent stressful life events and episodes of schizophrenia. Schizophrenia Bulletin 7: 12–23
Dokecki P R, Polidoro L G, Cromwell R L 1965 Commonality and stability of word association responses in good and poor premorbid schizophrenics. Journal of Abnormal Psychology 70: 312–316
Dollard J, Miller N E 1950 Personality and psychotherapy. McGraw Hill, New York

Dongier M, Dubrovsky B, Garcia-Rill E 1974 Les potentiels cérébraux lents en psychiatrie. Canadian Psychiatric Association Journal 19: 177–183
Dongier M, Dubrovsky B, Engelsmann F 1977 Event-related slow potentials in psychiatry. In: Shagass C, Gershon S, Friedhoff A J (eds) Psychopathology and brain dysfunction. Raven Press, New York
Donlon P T, Rada R T, Arora K K 1976 Depression and the reintegration phase of acute schizophrrenia. American Journal of Psychiatry 133: 1265–1268
Donnelly E F, Weinberger D R, Waldman I N, Wyatt R J 1980 Cognitive impairment associated with morphological brain abnormalities on computed tomography in chronic schizophrenic patients. Journal of Nervous and Mental Diseases 168: 305–308
Dougherty F E, Bartlett E S, Izard C E 1974 Responses of schizophrenics to expressions of the fundamental emotions. Journal of Clinical Psychology 30: 243–246
Dunham H W 1965 Community and schizophrenia: an epidemiological analysis. Wayne State University Press, Detroit
Dunham H W 1976 Society, culture and mental disorder. Archives of General Psychiatry 33: 147–156
Dunn W L 1954 Visual discrimination of schizophrenic subjects as a function of stimulus meaning. Journal of Personality 23: 48–64
Dupré E 1913 Coenestopathic states. Translated 1974 In: Hirsch S R, Shepherd M (eds) Themes and variations in European psychiatry. J Wright, Bristol, ch 16, p 385–394
Dupré E, Logre J 1911 Delusional states of the imagination. Translated 1986 in: Cutting J C, Shepherd M (eds) Schizophrenia: the origin and development of its study in Europe. Cambridge University Press, Cambridge
Durbin M, Martin R L 1977 Speech in mania: syntactic aspects. Brain and Language 4: 208–218
Dussik K T 1968 Schizophrenia as a disorder of neuropsychological control mechanisms. Diseases of the Nervous System Suppl 5: 68–77
Eaton E M 1979 Hemisphere-related visual information processing in acute schizophrenia before and after neuroleptic treatment. In: Gruzelier J, Flor-Henry P (eds) Hemisphere asymmetries of function in psychopathology. Elsevier, Amsterdam, p 511–526
Ebner E, Ritzler B 1969 Perceptual recognition in chronic and acute schizophrenics. Journal of Consulting and Clinical Psychology 33: 200–206
Ebner E, Broekema V, Ritzler B 1971 Adaptation to altered visual-proprioceptive input in normals and schizophrenics. Archives of General Psychiatry 24: 367–371
Eccles J C 1977 Evolution of the brain in relation to the development of the self conscious mind. Annals of the New York Academy of Science 299: 161–179
Eisenson J 1961 Language dysfunction associated with right brain damage. Excerpta Medica International Congress Series 38: 29–30
Eitinger L 1965 Schizophrenia and persecution. Acta Psychiatrica Scandinavica Supplement 180: 141–145
Ekman P, Sorenson E R, Friesen W V 1969 Pancultural elements in facial displays of emotion. Science 164: 86–88
Eliseo T S 1968 Figurative and literal misinterpretations of words by process and reactive schizophrenics. In: Vetter H J (ed) Language behavior in schizophrenia. Charles C Thomas, Springfield
Ellenberger H F 1958 A clinical introduction to psychiatric phenomenology and existential analysis. In: May R, Angel E, Ellenberger H F (eds) Existence. Basic Books, New York, p 92–124
Endicott J, Nee J, Fleiss J, Cohen J, Williams J B W, Simon R 1982 Diagnostic criteria for schizophrenia. Archives of General Psychiatry 39: 884–889
Epstein S 1953 Overinclusive thinking in a schizophrenic and a control group. Journal of Consulting Psychology 17: 384–388
Epstein S 1979 Natural healing processes of the mind. Schizophrenia Bulletin 5: 313–321
Epstein S, Coleman M 1970 Drive theories of schizophrenia. Psychosomatic Medicine 32: 113–140
Erlenmeyer-Kimling L, Cornblatt B, Friedman D, Marcuse Y, Rutschmann J, Simmens S et al 1982 Neurological, electrophysiological, and attentional deviations in children at risk for schizophrenia. In: Henn F A, Nasrallah H A (eds) Schizophrenia as a brain disease. Oxford University Press, New York, ch 5, p 61–98

Erwin B J, Rosenbaum G 1979 Parietal lobe syndrome and schizophrenia: comparison of neuropsychological deficits. Journal of Abnormal Psychology 88: 234–241
Escobar J I, Chandel V 1977 Nuclear symptoms of schizophrenia after cingulotomy: a case report. American Journal of Psychiatry 134: 1304–1305
Esquirol J E D 1838 Mental maladies: a treatise on insanity. Translated 1965. Hafner, New York
Essen-Möller E, Wohlfahrt S 1947 Suggestions for the amendment of the official Swedish classification of mental disorders. Acta Psychiatrica et Neurologica Scandinavica Supplement 47: 551–555
Evarts E V 1962 A neurophysiologic theory of hallucinations. In : West L J (ed) Hallucinations. Grune & Stratton, New York
Everitt B S, Gourlay A J, Kendell R E 1971 An attempt at validation of traditional psychiatric syndromes by cluster analysis. British Journal of Psychiatry 119: 399–412
Ey H 1950 Etudes psychiatriques. Desclée de Brouwer & Cie, Paris
Eysenck H J 1951 Schizothymia-cyclothymia as a dimension of personality. Journal of Personality 20: 345–384
Eysenck H J 1972 An experimental and genetic model of schizophrenia. In: Kaplan A R (ed) Genetic factors in schizophrenia. Charles C Thomas, Springfield, ch 28, p 504–515
Eysenck S B G, Eysenck H J 1970 Crime and personality. British Journal of Criminology 10: 225–239
Faber R, Reichstein M B 1981 Language dysfunction in schizophrenia. British Journal of Psychiatry 139: 519–522
Faergeman P M 1963 Psychogenic psychoses. Butterworths, London
Faglioni P, Spinnler H, Vignolo L A 1969 Contrasting behaviour of right and left hemisphere damaged patients on a discrimination and semantic task of auditory recognition. Cortex 5: 366–389
Fairbanks H 1944 The quantitative differentiation of samples of spoken language. Psychological Monographs 56: 19–38
Fairweather D S 1947 Psychiatric aspects of the postencephalitic syndrome. Journal of Mental Science 93: 201–254
Falloon I R H, Boyd J L, McGill C W, Razani J, Moss H B, Gilderman A M 1982 Family management in the prevention of exacerbations of schizophrenia. New England Journal of Medicine 306: 1437–1440
Falret J 1854 Leçons cliniques de médecine mentale. Bailliere, Paris
Farina A, Holzberg J D 1967 Attitudes and behaviors of fathers and mothers of male schizophrenic patients. Journal of Abnormal Psychology 72: 381–387
Faris R E L, Dunham H W 1939 Mental disorders in urban areas. Hafner, New York
Farmer A E, McGuffin P, Spitznagel E L 1983 Heterogeneity in schizophrenia: a cluster-analytic approach. Psychiatry Research 8: 1–12
Feder R 1982 Auditory hallucinations treated by radio headphones. American Journal of Psychiatry 139: 1188–1190
Federn P 1943 Psychoanalysis of psychoses. Psychiatric Quarterly 17: 1–19
Feffer M H 1961 The influence of affective factors on conceptualization in schizophrenia. Journal of Abnormal Psychology 63: 588–596
Feigenberg I M 1969 Probabilistic prognosis and its significance in normal and pathological subjects. In: Cole M, Maltzman I (eds) A handbook of contemporary Soviet psychology. Basic Books, New York
Feighner J P, Robins E, Guze S B, Woodruff R A, Winokur G, Munoz R 1972 Diagnostic criteria for use in psychiatric research. Archives of General Psychiatry 26: 57–63
Feinberg I 1962 A comparison of the visual hallucinations in schizophrenia with those induced by mescaline and LSD-25. In: West L J (ed) Hallucinations. Grune & Stratton, New York
Feinberg I, Garman E M 1961 Studies of thought disorder in schizophrenia. Archives of General Psychiatry 4: 191–201
Feldman M, Bender M B 1970 Visual illusions and hallucinations in parieto-occipital lesions of the brain. In: Keup W (ed) Origin and mechanisms of hallucinations. Plenum, New York, p 23–36
Feldman M J, Drasgow J 1951 A visual–verbal test for schizophrenia. Psychiatric Quarterly Supplement 25: 55–64

Feldstein S 1962 The relationship of interpersonal involvement and affectiveness of content to the verbal communication of schizophrenic patients. Journal of Abnormal Psychology 64: 39–45
Feldstein S, Jaffe J 1962 Vocabulary diversity of schizophrenics and normals. Journal of Speech and Hearing Research 5: 76–78
Fenichel O 1945 The psychoanalytic theory of neurosis. W W Norton & Co, New York
Fey E T 1951 The performance of young schizophrenics and young normals on the Wisconsin card-sorting test. Journal of Consulting Psychology 15: 311–319
Fischman L G 1983 Dreams, hallucinogenic drug states and schizophrenia: a psychological and biological comparison. Schizophrenia Bulletin 9: 73–94
Fish B 1977 Neurobiological antecedents of schizophrenia in children. Archives of General Psychiatry 34: 1297–1313
Fish F 1961 A neurophysiological theory of schizophrenia. Journal of Mental Science 107: 828–838
Fish F 1967 Clinical psychopathology. J Wright, Bristol
Fisher M 1956 Left hemiplegia and motor impersistence. Journal of Nervous and Mental Diseases 123: 201–218
Fishkin S M, Lovallo W R, Whitaker L C, Pishkin V 1979 Randomness and the 'streaking' phenomenon: attentional anomalies in performance on the Whitaker index of schizophrenic thinking. Journal of Clinical Psychology 35: 289–295
Flavell J H 1956 Abstract thinking and social behaviour in schizophrenia. Journal of Abnormal Psychology 52: 208–211
Fleminger J J, Dalton R, Standage K F 1977 Handedness in psychiatric patients. British Journal of Psychiatry 131: 448–452
Flor-Henry P 1969 Psychosis and temporal lobe epilepsy: a controlled investigation. Epilepsia 10: 363–395
Flor-Henry P 1976 Lateralized temporal-limbic dysfunction and psychopathology. Annals of the New York Academy of Sciences 280: 777–797
Flor-Henry P 1979 Laterality, shifts of cerebral dominance, sinistrality and psychosis. In: Gruzelier J, Flor-Henry P (eds) Hemisphere asymmetries of function in psychopathology. Elsevier, Amsterdam, p 3–19
Flor-Henry P, Yeudall L T 1979 Neuropsychological investigation of schizophrenia and manic-depressive psychoses. In: Gruzelier J, Flor-Henry P (eds) Hemisphere asymmetries of function in psychopathology. Elsevier, Amsterdam, p 341–362
Flor-Henry P, Koles Z J, Howarth B G, Burton L 1979 Neurophysiological studies of schizophrenia, mania and depression. In: Gruzelier J, Flor-Henry P (eds) Hemisphere asymmetries of function in psychopathology. Elsevier, Amsterdam, p 189–222
Fodor J A, Bever T G 1965 The psychological reality of linguistic segments. Journal of Verbal Learning and Verbal Behavior 4: 414–420
Fonseca J S, Gil M T, Figueira M L, Barata J G, Peto F, Pacheco M F 1978 How do normal subjects learn a simple adaptative task: how and why do paranoid schizophrenics fail? Archiv für Psychiatrie und Nervenkrankheiten 225: 31–53
Forrest D V 1969 New words and neologisms. Psychiatry 32: 44–73
Foucault M 1965 Madness and civilisation: a history of insanity in the Age of Reason. Pantheon, New York
Foucault M 1970 The order of things: an archaeology of the human sciences. Pantheon, New York
Foulds G A 1965 Personality and personal illness. Tavistock, London
Foulds G A, Hope K, McPherson F M, Mayo P R 1968 Paranoid delusions, retardation and overinclusive thinking. Journal of Clinical Psychology 24: 177–178
Fowler R C, McCabe M S, Cadoret R J, Winokur G 1972 The validity of good prognosis schizophrenia. Archives of General Psychiatry 26: 182–185
Fowler R C, Liskow B I, Tanna V L, Lytle L, Mezzich J 1980 Schizophrenia—primary affective disorder discrimination. Archives of General Psychiatry 37: 811–817
Francis A F 1979 Familial basal ganglia calcification and schizophreniform psychosis. British Journal of Psychiatry 135: 360–362
Freedman B J 1974 The subjective experience of perceptual and cognitive disturbances in schizophrenia: a review of autobiographical accounts. Archives of General Psychiatry 30: 333–340

Freedman B, Chapman L J 1973 Early subjective experience in schizophrenic episodes. Journal of Abnormal Psychology 82: 46–54
Freeman T, Gathercole C E 1966 Perseveration—the clinical symptom—in chronic schizophrenia and organic dementia. British Journal of Psychiatry 112: 27–32
Freud S 1894 The neuropsychoses of defence. Republished 1962 in: The standard edition of the complete psychological works of Sigmund Freud, vol 3. Hogarth, London, p 45–61
Freud S 1896 Further remarks on the neuro-psychoses of defence. Republished 1962 in: The standard edition of the complete psychological works of Sigmund Freud, vol 3. Hogarth, London p 174–185
Freud S 1900 The interpretation of dreams. Translated 1954. Allen & Unwin, London.
Freud S 1911 Psychoanalytic notes on an autobiographical account of a case of paranoia. Republished 1958 in: The standard edition of the complete psychological works of Sigmund Freud, vol 12. Hogarth, London, p 9–82
Freud S 1915 Assessment of the unconscious. Republished 1957 in: The standard edition of the complete psychological works of Sigmund Freud, vol 14. Hogarth, London, p 203
Freud S 1924 Neurosis and psychosis. Republished 1961 in: The standard edition of the complete psychological works of Sigmund Freud, vol 19. Hogarth, London, p 149–153
Freud S 1932 Revision of the theory of dreams. Republished 1964 in: The standard edition of the complete psychological works of Sigmund Freud, vol 22. Hogarth, London, p 16
Freud S 1938 The technique of psychoanalysis. Republished 1964 in: The standard edition of the complete psychological works of Sigmund Freud, vol 23. Hogarth, London, p 173
Frey T S, Hambert G 1972 Neuropsychiatric aspects of logorrhoea. Särtryck ur Nordisk psykiatrisk Tidsskrift 26: 158–173 (English summary)
Frieske D A, Wilson W P 1966 Formal qualities of hallucinations in patients with schizophrenic, organic and affective psychoses. In: Hoch P H, Zubin J (eds) Psychopathology of schizophrenia. Grune & Stratton, New York, p 49–62
Frith C D 1977 Two kinds of cognitive deficit associated with chronic schizophrenia. Psychological Medicine 7: 171–173
Frith C D 1979 Consciousness, information processing and schizophrenia. British Journal of Psychiatry 134: 225–235
Frith C D, Stevens M, Johnstone E C, Crow T J 1979 Skin conductance responsivity during acute episodes of schizophrenia as a predictor of symptomatic improvement. Psychological Medicine 9: 101–106
Frith C D, Stevens M, Johnstone E C, Crow T J 1982 Skin conductance habituation during acute episodes of schizophrenia: qualitative differences from anxious and depressed patients. Psychological Medicine 12: 575–583
Frith C D, Stevens M, Johnstone E C, Owens D C, Crow T J 1983 Integration of schematic faces and other complex objects in schizophrenia. Journal of Nervous and Mental Diseases 171: 34–39
Froeschels E 1946 A peculiar intermediary state between waking and sleep. Journal of Clinical Psychopathology 7: 825–833
Fromkin V A 1975 A linguist looks at a 'a linguist looks at schizophrenic language'. Brain and Language 2: 498–503
Fromm-Reichmann F 1939 Transference problems in schizophrenics. Psychoanalytic Quarterly 8: 412–426
Fromm-Reichmann F 1948 Notes on the development of treatment of schizophrenics by psychoanalytic psychotherapy. Psychiatry 11: 263–273
Fuller G D, Kates S L 1969 Word association repertoires of schizophrenics and normals. Journal of Consulting and Clinical Psychology 33: 497–500
Gabbard G D, Twemlow S W, Jones F C 1981 Do 'near death experiences' occur only near death? Journal of Nervous and Mental Diseases 169: 374–377
Gainotti G 1972 Emotional behaviour and hemisphere side of lesion. Cortex 8: 41–55
Galdi J 1983 The causality of depression in schizophrenia. British Journal of Psychiatry 142: 621–625
Galdston I 1967 Psyche and soul: psychiatry in the Middle Ages. In: Galdston I (ed) Historic derivations of modern psychiatry. McGraw Hill, New York, ch 2, p 19–40
Galin D 1976 Hemispheric specialization: implications for psychiatry. In: Grenell R G, Gabay S (eds) Biological foundations of psychiatry, vol 1. Raven Press, New York, p 145–176

Gall F J 1818 Anatomie et physiologie du système nerveux. Librairie Greque-Latine-Allemande, Paris
Ganser S J M 1898 A peculiar hysterical state. Translated 1974 in: Hirsch S R, Shepherd M (eds) Themes and variations in European psychiatry. J Wright, Bristol, ch 4, p 67–77
Garmezy N 1952 Stimulus differentiation by schizophrenic and normal subjects under conditions of reward and punishment. Journal of Personality 20: 253–276
Garmezy N 1970 Process and reactive schizophrenia: some conceptions and issues. Schizophrenia Bulletin 1 (2): 30–74
Garmezy N 1978 Attentional processes in adult schizophrenia and in children at risk. Journal of Psychiatric Research 14: 3–34
Gaspar D 1980 Hollymoor hospital dementia service. Lancet i: 1402–1405
Gaupp R 1914 The scientific importance of the case of Wagner. Translated 1974 in: Hirsch S R, Shepherd M (eds) Themes and variations in European psychiatry. J Wright, Bristol, ch 7, p 121–133
Gazzaniga M S 1970 The bisected brain. Appleton-Century-Crofts, New York
Gazzaniga M S, Le Doux J E 1978 The integrated mind. Plenum Press, New York
Gelder M, Kolakowska T 1979 Variability of response to neuroleptics in schizophrenia. Comprehensive Psychiatry 5: 397–408
Gelenberg A J 1976 The catatonic syndrome. Lancet i: 1339–1341
Gerson S N, Benson D F, Frazier S H 1977 Diagnosis: schizophrenia versus posterior aphasia. American Journal of Psychiatry 134: 966–969
Gerver D 1967 Linguistic rules and the perception and recall of speech by schizophrenic patients. British Journal of Social and Clinical Psychology 6: 204–211
Gerver D, Lawson J S, Gerver M E 1976 Schizophrenic speech: a factor-analytic approach. Language and Speech 19: 46–56
Geschwind N 1964 Nonaphasic disorders of speech. International Journal of Neurology 4: 207–214
Gibbs F A 1951 Ictal and nonictal psychiatric disorders in temporal lobe epilepsy. Journal of Nervous and Mental Diseases 113: 522–528
Giliarovsky V A 1957 Speech and thinking of schizophrenic patients. Summarised 1982 in: Zavarin V, Tonkonogy J, Ostwald P Cognitive processes in schizophrenia and related disorders: experimental studies in the USSR. Pavlovian Journal of Biological Sciences 17: 188–203
Gillis J S 1969 Schizophrenic thinking in a probabilistic situation. Psychological Record 19: 211–224
Gjerde P F 1983 Attentional capacity dysfunction and arousal in schizophrenia. Psychological Bulletin 93: 57–72
Gjessing R 1938 Disturbances of somatic functions in catatonia with a periodic course and their compensation. Journal of Mental Science 84: 608–621
Glazer W, Prusoff B, John K, Williams D 1981 Depression and social adjustment among chronic schizophrenic outpatients. Journal of Nervous and Mental Diseases 169: 712–717
Goffman E 1961 Asylums. Anchor Books, New York
Goldberg E M, Morrison S L 1963 Schizophrenia and social class. British Journal of Psychiatry 109: 785–802
Goldberg G, Mayer N H, Toglia J U 1981 Medial frontal cortex infarction and the alien hand sign. Archives of Neurology 38: 683–686
Goldberg S C, Klerman G L, Cole J O 1965 Changes in schizophrenic psychopathology and ward behavior after phenothiazines. British Journal of Psychiatry 111: 120–133
Golden C J, Graber B, Coffman J, Berg R A, Newlin D B, Bloch S 1981 Structural brain deficits in schizophrenia: identification by computed tomographic scan density measurements. Archives of General Psychiatry 38: 1014–1017
Golden C J, MacInnes W D, Ariel R N, Ruedrich S L, Chu C-C, Coffman J A et al 1982 Cross-validation of the ability of the Luria-Nebraska neuropsychological battery to differentiate chronic schizophrenics with and without ventricular enlargement. Journal of Consulting and Clinical Psychology 50: 87–95
Goldhamer H, Marshall A W 1953 Psychosis and civilisation. The Free Press, Glencoe
Goldstein A L, Rossio J, Kolyaskina G I, Emory L E, Overall J E, Thurman G B et al 1980 Immunological components in schizophrenia. In: Baxter C, Melnechuk T (eds) Perspectives in schizophrenia research. Raven Press, New York, p 249–262

Goldstein A P, Martens J, Hubben J, van Belle H A, Schaaf W, Wiersma H et al 1973 The use of modeling to increase independent behavior. Behaviour Research and Therapy 11: 31–42
Goldstein G, Halperin K M 1977 Neuropsychological differences among subtypes of schizophrenia. Journal of Abnormal Psychology 86: 34–40
Goldstein K 1936 The modification of behavior consequent to cerebral lesions. Psychiatric Quarterly 10: 586–610
Goldstein K 1939 The significance of special mental tests for diagnosis and prognosis in schizophrenia. American Journal of Psychiatry 96: 575–588
Goldstein K 1944 Methodological approach to the study of schizophrenic thought disorder. In: Kasanin J S (ed) Language and thought in schizophrenia. University of California Press, Berkeley, p 17–40
Goldstein K 1959 Concerning the concreteness in schizophrenia. Journal of Abnormal Psychology 59: 146–148
Goldstein K, Scheerer M 1941 Abstract and concrete behaviour. Psychological Monographs 53: 1–151
Goldstein M J, Rodnick E H, Evans J R, May P R A, Steinberg M R 1978 Drug and family therapy in the aftercare of acute schizophrenics. Archives of General Psychiatry 35: 1169–1177
Goldstone S 1975 The variability of temporal judgement in psychopathology. In: Kietzman M L, Sutton S, Zubin J (eds) Experimental approaches to psychopathology. Academic Press, New York
Goodman A B, Siegel C, Craig T J, Lin S P 1983 The relationship between socioeconomic class and prevalence of schizophrenia, alcoholism and affective disorders treated by inpatient care in a suburban area. American Journal of Psychiatry 140: 166–170
Gordon H W 1970 Hemispheric asymmetries in the perception of musical chords. Cortex 6: 387–398
Gorham D R 1956 A proverbs test for clinical and experimental use. Psychological Reports 2: 1–12
Gottesman I I, Shields J 1982 Schizophrenia: the epigenetic puzzle. Cambridge University Press, Cambridge
Gottheil E, Thornton C C, Exline R V 1976 Appropriate and background affect in facial displays of emotion. Archives of General Psychiatry 33: 565–568
Gottheil E, Exline R V, Winkelmayer R 1979 Judging emotions of normal and schizophrenic subjects. American Journal of Psychiatry 136: 1049–1054
Gottschalk L A, Gleser G C 1964 Distinguishing characteristics of the verbal communication of schizophrenic patients. Association for Research into Nervous and Mental Disease 42: 400–407
Gottschalk L A, Gleser G C 1969 The measurement of psychological states through the content analysis of verbal behavior. University of California Press, Berkeley
Gould L N 1948 Verbal hallucinations and activity of vocal musculature. American Journal of Psychiatry 105: 367–372
Gould L N 1949 Auditory hallucinations and subvocal speech. Journal of Nervous and Mental Diseases 109: 418–427
Granville-Grossman K L 1966 Birth order and schizophrenia. British Journal of Psychiatry 112: 1119–1126
Greden J F, Carroll B J 1981 Psychomotor function in affective disorders: an overview of new monitoring techniques. American Journal of Psychiatry 138: 1441–1448
Green P 1978 Interhemispheric transfer in schizophrenia. Behavioural Psychotherapy 6: 105–110
Green P, Kotenko V 1980 Superior speech comprehension in schizophrenics under monaural versus binaural listening conditions. Journal of Abnormal Psychology 89: 399–408
Green P, Preston M 1981 Reinforcement of vocal correlates of auditory hallucinations by auditory feedback. British Journal of Psychiatry 139: 204–208
Griesinger W 1845 Mental pathology and therapeutics. Translated 1867. New Sydenham Society, London
Griffith J H, Frith C D, Eysenck S B G 1980 Psychoticism and thought disorder in psychiatric patients. British Journal of Social and Clinical Psychology 19: 65–71

Griffiths D 1981 Psychological aspects of rehabilitation. In: Wing J K, Morris B (eds) Handbook of psychiatric rehabilitation. Oxford University Press, Oxford, ch 5, p 49–55
Grinspoon L, Ewalt J R, Shader R I 1972 Schizophrenia: pharmacotherapy and psychotherapy. Williams & Wilkins, Baltimore
Gripp R F, Magaro P A 1974 The token economy program in the psychiatric hospital: a review and analysis. Behavioural Research and Therapy 12: 205–228
Grodin M, Brown D R 1967 Multivariate stimulus processing by normal and paranoid schizophrenic subjects. Psychonomic Science 8: 525–526
Gross G, Huber G, Schüttler R 1981 Computer tomographic and psychopathological investigations on schizophrenic diseases. Abstracts of the 3rd World Congress of Biological Psychiatry, vol 2. Stockholm, F172
Gross H, Kaltenbäck E 1955 Die Anosognosie. Wiener Zeitschrift für Nervenheilkunde 11: 374–418
Gross O 1904 On the meaning of the term 'dementia sejunctiva'. Translated 1986 in: Cutting J C, Shepherd M (eds) Schizophrenia: the origin and development of its study in Europe. Cambridge University Press, Cambridge
Grossman M 1981 A bird is a bird is a bird: making reference within and without superordinate categories. Brain and Language 12: 313–331
Gruhle H W 1915 Selbstschilderung and Einfühlung. Zeitschrift für die gesamte Neurologie und Psychiatrie 28: 148–231
Gruhle H W 1924 Die ursprüngliche Persönlichkeit schizophren Erkrankter. Allgemeine Zeitschrift für Psychiatrie 80: 269–273
Gruzelier J 1973 Bilateral asymmetry of skin conductance orienting activity and levels in schizophrenics. Biological Psychology 1: 21–41
Gruzelier J 1981 Hemispheric imbalances masquerading as paranoid and nonparanoid syndromes? Schizophrenia Bulletin 7: 662–673
Gruzelier J, Hammond N 1979 Lateralized auditory processing in medicated and unmedicated schizophrenic patients. In: Gruzelier J, Flor-Henry P (eds) Hemisphere asymmetries of function in psychopathology. Elsevier, Amsterdam, p 603–636
Gruzelier J, Manchanda R 1982 The syndrome of schizophrenia: relations between electrodermal response, lateral asymmetries and clinical ratings. British Journal of Psychiatry 141: 488–495
Guggenheim F G, Barbigian H M 1974 Catatonic schizophrenia: epidemiology and clinical course. Journal of Nervous and Mental Diseases 158: 291–305
Guiraud P 1950 Pathogénie-étiologie des délires. Proceedings of the First International Congress of Psychiatry, Paris. Psychopathologie des délires, Hermann & Co, Paris, p 1–57
Gulman N C, Wildschiodtz G, Orbaek K 1982 Alterations of interhemispheric conduction through corpus callosum in chronic schizophrenia. Biological Psychiatry 17: 585–594
Gunderson J G 1980 A re-evaluation of milieu therapy for nonchronic schizophrenic patients. Schizophrenia Bulletin 6: 64–69
Gunderson J 1983 Recent advances in psychotherapeutic approaches to schizophrenic disorders. In: Zales M R (ed) Affective and schizophrenic disorders. Brunner/Mazel, New York, ch 9, p 207–221
Gur R E 1977 Motor laterality imbalance in schizophrenia. Archives of General Psychiatry 34: 33–37
Gur R E 1978 Left hemisphere dysfunction and left hemisphere overactivation in schizophrenia. Journal of Abnormal Psychology 87: 226–238
Gur R E 1979 Cognitive concomitants of hemispheric dysfunction in schizophrenia. Archives of General Psychiatry 36: 269–274
Hall R C W, Gardner E R, Stickney S K, Lecann A F, Popkin M K 1980 Physical illness manifesting as psychiatric disease. Archives of General Psychiatry 37: 989–995
Halpern H, Darley F L, Brown J R 1973 Differential language and neurological characteristics in cerebral involvement. Journal of Speech and Hearing Disorders 38: 162–173
Hamlin R M, Folsom A T 1977 Impairment in abstract responses of schizophrenics, neurotics and brain-damaged patients. Journal of Abnormal Psychology 86: 483–491
Hammond N V, Gruzelier J H 1978 Laterality, attention and rate effects in the auditory temporal discrimination of chronic schizophrenics: the effect of treatment with chlorpromazine. Quarterly Journal of Experimental Psychology 30: 91–103

Hamsher K de S, Arnold K O 1976 A test of Chapman's theory of schizophrenic thought disorder. Journal of Abnormal Psychology 85: 296–302
Hanfmann E, Kasanin J 1942 Conceptual thinking in schizophrenia. Nervous and Mental Disease Monographs 67
Hanson D R, Gottesman I I, Heston L L 1976 Some possible childhood indicators of adult schizophrenia inferred from children of schizophrenics. British Journal of Psychiatry 129: 142–154
Harder D W, Gift T E, Strauss J S, Ritzler B A, Kokes R F 1981 Life events and two-year outcome in schizophrenia. Journal of Consulting and Clinical Psychology 49: 619–626
Hare E H 1956 Family setting and the urban distribution of schizophrenia. Journal of Mental Science 102: 753–760
Hare E H 1973 A short note on pseudohallucinations. British Journal of Psychiatry 122: 469–476
Hare E H 1975 Season of birth in schizophrenia and neurosis. American Journal of Psychiatry 132: 1168–1171
Hare E H 1983 Was insanity on the increase? British Journal of Psychiatry 142: 439–455
Hare E H, Price J S 1970 Birth rank in schizophrenia: with a consideration of the bias due to changes in birth-rate. British Journal of Psychiatry 116: 409–420
Hare E H, Walter S D 1978 Seasonal variation in admissions of psychiatric patients and its relation to seasonal variation in their birth. Journal of Epidemiology and Community Health 32: 47–52
Harizuka S 1977 Perception of schizophrenic patients in classifying pictures of facial expresion. Japanese Journal of Psychology 48: 231–238
Harris A, Metcalfe M 1956 Inappropriate affect. Journal of Neurology, Neurosurgery and Psychiatry 19: 308–313
Harris A, Norris V 1954 Clinical signs, diagnosis and prognosis in the functional psychoses. Journal of Mental Science 100: 727–731
Harris A, Linker I, Norris V, Shepherd M 1956 Schizophrenia: a social and prognostic study. British Journal of Preventative and Social Medicine 10: 107–114
Harrison A, Phillips J P N 1979 The specificity of schizophrenic thought disorder. British Journal of Medical Psychology 52: 105–117
Harrow M, Prosen M 1978 Intermingling and disordered logic as influences on schizophrenic 'thought disorders'. Archives of General Psychiatry 35: 1213–1218
Harrow M, Grinker R R, Holzman P S, Kayton L 1977 Anhedonia and schizophrenia. American Journal of Psychiatry 134: 794–797
Hartlage L C, Garber J 1976 Spatial vs nonspatial reasoning ability in chronic schizophrenics. Journal of Clinical Psychology 32: 235–237
Hartman L M, Cushman F E 1983 Cognitive-behavioral and psychopharmacological treatment of delusional symptoms: a preliminary report. Behavioural Psychotherapy 11: 50–61
Hartmann E, Russ D, van der Kolk B, Falke R, Oldfield M 1981 A preliminary study of the personality of the nightmare sufferer: relationship to schizophrenia and creativity? American Journal of Psychiatry 138: 794–797
Hathaway S R, McKinley J C 1943 Manual for the Minnesota Multiphasic Personality Inventory. The Psychological Corporation. New York
Haug J O 1962 Pneumoencephalographic studies in mental disease. Acta Psychiatrica Scandinavica Supplement 165
Hayman M A, Abrams R 1977 Capgras' syndrome and cerebral dysfunction. British Journal of Psychiatry 130: 68–71
Haywood H C, Moelis I 1963 Effect of symptom change on intellectual function in schizophrenia. Journal of Abnormal Psychology 67: 76–78
Heath R G 1954 Studies in schizophrenia. Harvard University Press, Mass.
Heather N 1976 The specificity of schizophrenic thought disorder. British Journal of Social and Clinical Psychology 15: 131–137
Heathfield K W G 1967 Huntington's chorea. Brain 90: 203–232
Heaton R K, Baade L E, Johnson K L 1978 Neuropsychological test results associated with psychiatric disorders in adults. Psychological Bulletin 85: 141–162
Hebb D O 1968 Concerning imagery. Psychological Review 75: 466–477
Hecker E 1871 Die Hebephrenie. Virchows Archiv für pathologische Anatomie 52: 392–449.

Translated 1976 in part in: Altschule M D The development of traditional psychopathology. Hemisphere Publishing, Washington, p 234–240
Heilbrun A B 1977 An analogue study of disattentional strategies in schizophrenia. Journal of Abnormal Psychology 86: 135–144
Heilbrun A B 1980 Impaired recognition of self-expressed thought in patients with auditory hallucinations. Journal of Abnormal Psychology 89: 728–736
Heilbrun A B, Heilbrun K S 1977 Content analysis of delusions in reactive and process schizophrenics. Journal of Abnormal Psychology 86: 597–608
Heilburn A B, Madison J K 1978 An analysis of structural factors in schizophrenic delusions. Journal of Clinical Psychology 34: 326–329
Heilbrun A B, Blum N, Haas M 1983 Cognitive vulnerability to auditory hallucinations. British Journal of Psychiatry 143: 294–299
Heilman K M, Scholes R, Watson R T 1975 Auditory affective agnosia. Journal of Neurology, Neurosurgery and Psychiatry 38: 69–72
Heinroth J C 1818 Textbook of disturbances of mental life or disturbances of the soul and their treatment, vol 1, theory. Translated 1975. Johns Hopkins University Press, Baltimore
Helmchen H 1975 Schizophrenia: diagnostic concepts in the ICD-8. In: Lader M H (ed) Studies in schizophrenia. Headley, Ashford, ch 1, p 10–18
Hemsley D R 1976 Attention and information processing in schizophrenia. British Journal of Social and Clinical Psychology 15: 199–209
Hemsley D R 1977 What have cognitive deficits to do with schizophrenic symptoms? British Journal of Psychiatry 130: 167–173
Hemsley D R, Zawada S L 1976 Filtering and the cognitive deficit in schizophrenia. British Journal of Psychiatry 128: 456–461
Henn F A 1982 Dopamine: a role in psychosis or schizophrenia. In: Henn F A, Nasrallah H A (eds) Schizophrenia as a brain disease. Oxford University Press, New York, ch 9, p 176–195
Hernandez-Peon R 1966 A neurophysiological model of dreams and hallucinations. Journal of Nervous and Mental Diseases 141: 623–650
Herodotus 500 B.C. The histories. Translated 1954. Penguin, London
Heron W 1957 The pathology of boredom. Scientific American 196: 52–56
Hersen M 1976 Token economies in institutional settings. Journal of Nervous and Mental Diseases 162: 206–211
Hersen M, Bellack A S 1976 Social skills training for chronic psychiatric patients. Comprehensive Psychiatry 17: 559–580
Hersen M, Turner S M, Edelstein B A, Pinkston S G 1975 Effects of phenothiazines and social skills training in a withdrawn schizophrenic. Journal of Clinical Psychology 31: 588–594
Herz M I, Melville C 1980 Relapse in schizophrenia. American Journal of Psychiatry 137: 801–805
Heston L L 1966 Psychiatric disorders in foster home reared children of schizophrenic mothers. British Journal of Psychiatry 112: 819–825
Heston L L 1970 The genetics of schizophrenic and schizoid disease. Science 167: 249–256
Higgins K, Sherman M 1978 The effect of motivation on loose thinking in schizophrenics as measured by the Bannister-Fransella grid test. Journal of Clinical Psychology 34: 624–628
Hill D 1952 E.E.G. in episodic psychotic and psychopathic behaviour. Electroencephalography and Clinical Neurophysiology 4: 419–442
Hill D 1953 Psychiatric disorders of epilepsy. Medical Press 229: 473–475
Hill D 1976 Cerebral atrophy and cognitive impairment in chronic schizophrenia. Lancet ii: 1132
Hill J 1982 Reasons and causes: the nature of explanations in psychology and psychiatry. Psychological Medicine 12: 501–514
Hillbom E 1951 Schizophrenia-like psychoses after brain trauma. Acta Psychiatrica et Neurologica Scandinavica Supplement 60: 36–47
Hillsberg B 1979 A comparison of visual discrimination performance of the dominant and the nondominant hemispheres in schizophrenia. In: Gruzelier J, Flor-Henry P (eds) Hemisphere asymmetries of function in psychopatholgy. Elsevier, Amsterdam, p 527–538

Himmelhoch J, Pincus J, Tucker G, Detre T 1970 Subacute encephalitis: behavioural and neurological aspects. British Journal of Psychiatry 116: 531–538
Hinton J, Withers E 1971 The usefulness of clinical tests of the sensorium. British Journal of Psychiatry 119: 9–18
Hirsch S R 1982 Depression 'revealed' in schizophrenia. British Journal of Psychiatry 140: 421–424
Hirsch S R, Leff J P 1975 Abnormalities in parents of schizophrenics. Institute of Psychiatry Maudsley Monogrpahs No 22, Oxford University Press, London
Hirst W 1982 The amnesic syndrome: descriptions and explanations. Psychological Bulletin 91: 435–460
Hirt M, Cutler M, Genshaft J 1977 Information processing by schizophrenics when task complexity increases. Journal of Abnormal Psychology 86: 256–260
Ho D Y F 1974 Modern logic and schizophrenic thinking. Genetic Psychology Monographs 89: 145–165
Hoch A 1910 Constitutional factors in the dementia praecox group. Review of Neurology and Psychiatry 8: 463–473
Hoch A, Kirby G H 1919 A clinical study of psychoses characterised by distressed perplexity. Archives of Neurology and Psychiatry 1: 415–418
Hoch P, Polatin P 1949 Pseudoneurotic forms of schizophrenia. Psychiatric Quarterly 23: 248–276
Hoffer W 1946 Diaries of adolescent schizophrenics. The Psychoanalytic Study of the Child 2: 293–312
Hogan T P, Awad A G, Eastwood R 1983 A self-report scale predictive of drug compliance in schizophrenics. Psychological Medicine 13: 177–183
Hogarty G E, Goldberg S C, Schooler N R, Ulrich R F 1974 Drug and sociotherapy in the aftercare of schizophrenic patients. Archives of General Psychiatry 31: 603–608
Hogarty G E, Schooler N R, Ulrich R, Mussare F, Ferro P, Herron E 1979 Fluphenazine and social therapy in the aftercare of schizophrenic patients. Archives of General Psychiatry 36: 1283–1294
Hogben G L, Jacobs I A 1972 Two verbal aspects of language and thought in schizophrenia. Journal of Consulting and Clinical Psychology 38: 296–298
Hollingshead A B, Redlich F C 1958 Social class and mental illness. J Wiley, New York
Holmboe R, Astrup C 1957 A follow-up study of 255 patients with acute schizophrenia and schizoprehniform psychoses. Acta Psychiatrica et Neurologica Scandinavica Supplement 115
Holzman P S 1972 Assessment of perceptual functioning in schizophrenia. Psychopharmacologia (Berlin) 24: 29–41
Holzman P S, Proctor L R, Levy D L, Yasillo N J, Meltzer H Y, Hurt S W 1974 Eye-tracking dysfunction in schizophrenic patients and their relatives. Archives of General Psychiatry 31: 143–151
Holzman P S, Levy D L, Proctor L R 1976 Smooth pursuit eye movements, attention and schizophrenia. Archives of General Psychiatry 33: 1415–1420
Holzman P S, Levy D L, Proctor L R 1978 The several qualities of attention in schizophrenia. In: Wynne L C, Cromwell R L, Matthysse S (eds) The nature of schizophrenia. J Wiley, New York, ch 29, p 295–310
Horowitz M J, Adams J E 1970 Hallucinations on brain stimulation. In: Keup W (ed) Origin and mechanisms of hallucinations. Plenum Press, New York
Houpt J L, Tucker G J, Harrow M 1972 Disordered cognition and stimulus processing. American Journal of Psychiatry 128: 1505–1510
Huber G, Gross G, Schüttler R, Linz M 1980 Longitudinal studies of schizophrenic patients. Schizophrenia Bulletin 6: 592–605
Hudgens R W 1974 Personal catastrophe and depression. In: Dohrenwend B S, Dohrenwend B P (eds) Stressful life events. J Wiley, New York
Humphrey M E, Zangwill O L 1951 Cessation of dreaming after brain injury. Journal of Neurology, Neurosurgery and Psychiatry 14: 322–325
Hunt H T, Chefurka C M 1976 A test of the psychedelic model of altered states of consciousness. Archives of General Psychiatry 33: 867–876
Hunt J McV, Cofer C N 1944 Psychological deficit. In: Hunt J McV (ed) Personality and the behavior disorders, vol 2. Ronald Press, New York, ch 32, p 971–1032

Hwu H-G, Chen C-C, Tsuang M T, Tseng W-S 1981 Derealization syndrome and the outcome of schizophrenia. British Journal of Psychiatry 139: 313–318
Ingvar D H 1980 Abnormal distribution of cerebral activity in chronic schizophrenia: a neurophysiological interpretation. In: Baxter C, Melnechuk T (eds) Perspectives in schizophrenia research. Raven Press, New York, p 107–125
Irigary L 1973 Le langage des dements. Mouton, The Hague
Isaacs W, Thomas J, Goldiamond I 1960 Application of operant conditioning to reinstate verbal behavior in psychotics. Journal of Speech and Hearing Disorders 25: 8–12
Iscoe I, Veldman D J 1963 Perception of an emotional continuum by schizophrenics, normal adults and children. Journal of Clinical Psychology 19: 272–276
Itil T M 1977 Qualitative and quantitative E.E.G. findings in schizophrenia. Schizophrenia Bulletin 3: 61–79
Izard C E 1959 Paranoid schizophrenic and normal subjects' perceptions of photographs of human faces. Journal of Consulting Psychology 23: 119–124
Izard C E, Buechler S 1980 Aspects of consciousness and personality in terms of differential emotions theory. In: Plutchik R, Kellerman H (eds) Emotion: theory, research and experience, vol 1. Academic Press, New York, ch 7, p 165–187
Jablensky A, Sartorius N 1975 Culture and schizophrenia. In: van Praag H M (ed) On the origin of schizophrenic psychoses. De Erven Bohn, Amsterdam
Jackson D D 1960 A critique of the literature on the genetics of schizophrenia. In: Jackson D D (ed) Etiology of schizophrenia. Basic Books, New York, p 37–87
Jackson J H 1932 On the nature of the duality of the brain. In: Taylor J (ed) Selected writings of John Hughlings Jackson, vol 2. Hodder & Stoughton, p 129–145
Jackson W, Carr A C 1955 Empathic ability in normals and schizophrenics. Journal of Abnormal Psychology 51: 79–82
Jacobs S, Myers J 1976 Recent life events and acute schizophrenic psychosis. Journal of Nervous and Mental Diseases 162: 75–87
James W 1891 The principles of psychology, vol 1. McMillan, London
Janet P 1932 Les sentiments dans le délire de persécution. Journal de Psychologie 29: 161–240
Jarvik M 1970 Drugs, hallucinations and memory. In: Keup W (ed) Origin and mechanisms of hallucinations. Plenum Press, New York, p 277–302
Jaspers K 1913 General psychopathology. Translated 1963. Manchester University Press, Manchester
Jaspers K 1919 Psychologie der Weltanschauungen. Springer, Berlin
Jaynes J 1976 The origin of consciousness in the breakdown of the bicameral mind. Houghton Mifflin, Boston
Jenkins J J 1970 The 1952 Minnesota word association norms. In: Postman L, Keppel G (eds) Norms of word association. Academic Press, New York, ch 1, p 1–38
Jernigan T L, Zatz L M, Moses J A, Cardellins J P 1982 Computed tomography in schizophrenics and normal volunteers:ii cranial asymmetry. Archives of General Psychiatry 39: 771–773
Jerome E A, Young M L 1971 Means-end thinking of schizophrenics. Psychological Reports 29: 855–862
Johannsen W J 1961 Responsiveness of chronic schizophrenics and normals to social and nonsocial feedback. Journal of Abnormal Psychology 62: 106–113
Johanson E 1958 A study of schizophrenia in the male. Acta Psychiatrica et Neurologica Scandinavica Supplement 125
John R S, Mednick S A, Schulsinger F 1982 Teacher reports as a predictor of schizophrenia and borderline schizophrenia. Journal of Abnormal Psychology 91: 399–413
Johnson D A W 1981 Studies of depressive symptoms in schizophrenia. British Journal of Psychiatry 139: 89–101
Johnson D M 1972 Systematic introduction to the psychology of thinking. Harper & Row, New York
Johnson J H, Klingler D E, Williams T A 1977 Recognition in episodic long-term memory in schizophrenia. Journal of Clinical Psychology 33: 643–647
Johnson O, Crockett D 1982 Changes in perceptual asymmetries with clinical improvement of depresssion and schizophrenia. Journal of Abnormal Psychology 91: 45–54
Johnson P R 1977 Dichotically-stimulated ear differences in musicians and nonmusicians. Cortex 13: 385–389

Johnstone E, Crow T J, Frith C D, Husband J, Kreel L 1976 Cerebral ventricular size and cognitive impairment in chronic schizophrenia. Lancet ii: 924–926
Johnstone E C, Frith C D, Crow T J, Carney M W P, Price J S 1978 Mechanism of the antipsychotic effect in the treatment of acute schizophrenia. Lancet i: 848–850
Johnstone E C, Cunningham Owens D G, Gold A, Crow T J, MacMillan J F 1981 Institutionalization and the defects of schizophrenia. British Journal of Psychiatry 139: 195–203
Johnstone E C, Crow T J, Ferrier I N, Frith C D, Owens D G C, Bourne D C et al 1983 Adverse effects of anticholinergic medication on positive schizophrenic symptoms. Psychological Medicine 13: 513–527
Jones A M, Pivik R T 1983 Abnormal visual-vestibular interactions in psychosis. Biological Psychiatry 18: 45–61
Jones G H, Miller J J 1981 Functional tests of the corpus callosum in schizophrenia. British Journal of Psychiatry 139: 553–557
Jones H G 1978 Psychological aspects of treatment of inpatients. In: Wing J K (ed) Schizophrenia: towards a new synthesis. Academic Press, London
Jones I H 1965 Observations on schizophrenic stereotypies. Comprehensive Psychiatry 6: 323–335
Jones J E 1977 Patterns of transactional style deviance in the TATs of parents of schizophrenics. Family Process 16: 327–337
Jones M 1952 Social psychiatry: a study of therapeutic communities. Tavistock, London
Jones-Gotman M 1979 Incidental learning of image-mediated or pronounced words after right temporal lobectomy. Cortex 15: 187–197
Jones-Gotman M, Milner B 1978 Right temporal lobe contribution to image-mediated verbal learning. Neuropsychologia 16: 61–71
Jonsson C-O, Sjöstedt A 1973 Auditory perception in schizophrenia: a second study of the intonation test. Acta Psychiatrica Scandinavica 49: 588–600
Joyston-Bechal N P 1966 The clinical features and outcome of stupor. British Journal of Psychiatry 112: 967–981
Judkins M, Slade P 1981 A questionnaire study of hostility in persistent auditory hallucinators. British Journal of Medical Psychology 54: 243–250
Jung C G 1907 The psychology of dementia praecox. Translated 1960 in: The collected works of C G Jung, vol 3. Routledge and Kegan Paul, London, p 1–152
Jung C G 1939 On the psychogenesis of schizophrenia. Journal of Mental Science 85: 999–1011
Jung C G 1958 Schizophrenia. Translated 1960 in: The collected works of C G Jung, vol 3. Routledge and Kegan Paul, London, p 256–271
Kahlbaum K L 1874 Catatonia. Translated 1973. Johns Hopkins University Press, Baltimore
Kales A, Cadieux R J, Soldatos C R, Bixler E O, Schweitzer P K, Prey W T et al 1982 Narcolepsy-cataplexy. Archives of Neurology 39: 164–171
Kallmann F J 1938 The genetics of schizophrenia. Augustin, New York
Kallmann F J 1946 The genetic theory of schizophrenia: an analysis of 691 schizophrenic twin index families. American Journal of Psychiatry 103: 309–322
Kammann R, Streeter L 1971 Two meanings of word abstractness. Journal of Verbal Learning and Verbal Behavior 10: 303–306
Kanner L 1943 Autistic disturbances of affective contact. Nervous Child 2: 217–250
Kant I 1798 Anthropology from a pragmatic point of view. Translated 1974. Martinus Nijhoff, The Hague
Kant O 1941 A comparative study of recovered and deteriorated schizophrenic patients. Journal of Nervous and Mental Diseases 93: 616–624
Kantor R E, Wallner J M, Winder C L 1953 Process and reactive schizophrenia. Journal of Consulting Psychology 17: 157–162
Kapur N, Coughlan A K 1980 Confabulation and frontal lobe dysfunction. Journal of Neurology, Neurosurgery and Psychiatry 43: 461–463
Karasu T B, Plutchik R, Nemetz P, Cont H R 1979 Measurement of thinking dysfunction. Journal of Nervous and Mental Diseases 167: 696–703
Kasanin J 1933 The acute schizoaffective psychoses. American Journal of Psychiatry 90: 97–126
Kasanin J S 1944 The disturbance of conceptual thinking in schizophrenia. In: Kasanin J S

(ed) Language and thought in schizophrenia. University of California Press, Berkeley, p 41–49
Kasanin J, Hanfmann E 1938 An experimental study of concept formation in schizophrenia. American Journal of Psychiatry 95: 35–52
Kasanin J, Knight E, Sage P 1934 The parent-child relationship in schizophrenia. Journal of Nervous and Mental Diseases 79: 249–263
Kay D W K, Roth M 1961 Factors in schizophrenia of old age. Journal of Mental Science 107: 649–686
Kay S R 1982 Conceptual disorder in schizophrenia as a function of encoding orientation. Journal of Nervous and Mental Diseases 170: 154–163
Kay S R, Singh M M 1979 Cognitive abnormality in schizophrenia: a dual-process model. Biological Psychiatry 14: 155–176
Kazdin A E 1977 The token economy. Plenum Press, New York
Keefe J A, Magaro P A 1980 Creativity and schizophrenia: an equivalence of cognitive processing. Journal of Abnormal Psychology 89: 390–398
Kehrer F 1928 Paranoische Zustände. In: Bumke O (ed) Handbuch der Geisteskrankheiten, Band 6, Teil 2. Springer, Berlin, p 232–364
Kelleher M J, Copeland J R M, Smith A J 1974 High first admission rates for schizophrenia in the west of Ireland. Psychological Medicine 4: 460–462
Kellett J M 1973 Evolutionary theory for the dichotomy of the functional psychoses. Lancet i: 860–863
Kelm H 1968 Visual figural aftereffect in schizophrenic and nonschizophrenic patients. Journal of Abnormal Psychology 73: 273–275
Kendell R E 1975 The role of diagnosis in psychiatry. Blackwells, Oxford
Kendell R E, Gourlay J 1970 The clinical distinction between the affective psychoses and schizophrenia. British Journal of Psychiatry 117: 261–266
Kendell R E, Brockington I F, Leff J P 1979 Prognostic implications of six alternative definitions of schizophrenia. Archives of General Psychiatry 36: 25–31
Kendler K S, Hays P 1982a Familial and sporadic schizophrenia: a symptomatic, prognostic and e.e.g. comparison. American Journal of Psychiatry 139: 1557–1562
Kendler K S, Hays P 1982b Schizophrenia with premorbid inferiority feelings. Archives of General Psychiatry 39: 643–647
Kendler K S, Glazer W M, Morgenstern H 1983 Dimensions of delusional experience. American Journal of Psychiatry 140: 466–469
Kennedy A, Neville J 1957 Sudden loss of memory. British Medical Journal ii: 428–433
Kent G H, Rosanoff A J 1910 A study of association in insanity. American Journal of Insanity 67: 317–390
Kety S S, Woodford R B, Harmel M H, Freyhan F A, Appel K E, Schmidt C F 1948 Cerebral blood flow and metabolism in schizophrenia. American Journal of Psychiatry 104: 765–770
Kety S S, Rosenthal D, Wender P H, Schulsinger F 1968 The types and prevalence of mental illness in the biological and adoptive families of adopted schizophrenics. In: Rosenthal D, Kety S S (eds) The transmission of schizophrenia. Pergamon, Oxford, p 345–362
Kimura D 1963 Right temporal-lobe damage. Archives of Neurology 8: 264–271
Kimura D 1977 Acquisition of a motor skill after left-hemisphere damage. Brain 100: 527–542
King P D 1957 Hypnosis and schizophrenia. Journal of Nervous and Mental Diseases 125: 481–486
Kinsbourne M 1974a Direction of gaze and distribution of cerebral thought processes. Neuropsychologia 12: 279–281
Kinsbourne M 1974b Mechanisms of hemisphere interaction in man. In: Kinsbourne M, Smith W L (eds) Hemispheric disconnection and cerebral function. Charles C Thomas, Springfield, ch 13, p 260–285
Kirby G H 1913 The catatonic syndrome and its relation to manic-depressive insanity. Journal of Nervous and Mental Diseases 40: 694–704
Kiriakos R, Ananth J 1980 Review of 13 cases of Capgras syndrome. American Journal of Psychiatry 137 1605–1607
Kirk R V 1968 Perceptual defect and role handicap: missing links in explaining the aetiology of schizophrenia. British Journal of Psychiatry 114: 1509–1521

Kirschner D 1964 Differences in gradients of stimulus generalization as a function of 'abstract' and 'concrete' attitude. Journal of Consulting Psychology 28: 160–164
Klein D F 1980 Psychosocial treatment of schizophrenia or psychosocial help for people with schizophrenia? Schizophrenia Bulletin 6: 122–130
Klein D N 1982 Relation between current diagnostic criteria for schizophrenia and the dimensions of the premorbid adjustment, paranoid symptomatology and chronicity. Journal of Abnormal Psychology 91: 319–325
Klein D N, Williamson P 1981 Premorbid adjustment and affective symptomatology in schizophrenia. Journal of Nervous and Mental Diseases 169: 497–502
Klein M 1946 Notes on some schizoid mechanisms. International Journal of Psychoanalysis 27: 99–110
Kleinman J E, Gillin J C, Wyatt R J 1977 A comparison of the phenomenonology of hallucinogens and schizophrenia from some autobiographical accounts. Schizophrenia Bulletin 3: 560–586
Kleist K 1914 Aphasia und Geisteskrankheit. Münchener Medizinische Wochenschrift 61: 8–12
Kleist K 1928 Cycloid, paranoid and epileptoid psychoses and the problem of degeneration psychoses. Translated 1974 in: Hirsch S R, Shepherd M (eds) Themes and variations in European psychiatry. J Wright, Bristol, ch 12, p 297–331
Kleist K 1960 Schizophrenic symptoms and cerebral pathology. Journal of Mental Science 106: 246–255
Kleitman N 1939 Sleep and wakefulness as alternating phases in the cycle of existence. University of Chicago Press, Chicago
Kline N S 1971 The autokinetic phenomenon. American Journal of Psychiatry 128: 784
Knight R A, Sims-Knight J E 1979 Integration of linguistic ideas in schizophrenics. Journal of Abnormal Psychology 88: 191–202
Knight R A, Sims-Knight J E 1980 Integration of visual patterns in schizophrenics. Journal of Abnormal Psychology 89: 623–634
Knight R, Sherer M, Shapiro J 1977 Iconic imagery in overinclusive and nonoverinclusive schizophrenics. Journal of Abnormal Psychology 86: 242–255
Knight R, Sherer M, Putchat C, Carter G 1978 A picture integration task for measuring iconic memory in schizophrenics. Journal of Abnormal Psychology 87: 314–321
Knight R A, Roff J D, Barrnett J, Moss J L 1979 Concurrent and predictive validity of thought disorder and affectivity: a 22-year follow-up of acute schizophrenics. Journal of Abnormal Psychology 88: 1–12
Knights A, Hirsch S R 1981 'Revealed' depression and drug treatment of schizophrenia. Archives of General Psychiatry 38: 806–811
Knox S J 1961 Severe psychiatric disturbances in the postoperative period. Journal of Mental Science 107: 1078–1096
Koh S D 1978 Remembering of verbal materials by schizophrenic young adults. In: Schwartz S (ed) Language and cognition in schizophrenia. Lawrence Erlbaum, Hillsdale, ch 3, p 55–99
Koh S D, Kayton L 1974 Memorisation of unrelated word strings by young nonpsychotic schizophrenics. Journal of Abnormal Psychology 81: 299–310
Koh S D, Kayton L, Berry R 1973 Mnemonic organisation in young nonpsychotic schizophrenics. Journal of Abnormal Psychology 81: 299–310
Koh S D, Kayton L, Schwartz C 1974 The structure of word-storage in the permanent memory of nonpsychotic schizophrenics. Journal of Consulting and Clinical Psychology 42: 879–887
Koh S D, Kayton L, Peterson R A 1976 Affective encoding and consequent remembering in schizophrenic young aduults. Journal of Abnormal Psychology 85: 156–166
Koh S D, Grinker R R, Marusarz T Z, Forman P L 1981 Affective memory and schizophrenic anhedonia. Schizophrenia Bulletin 7: 292–307
Kolb B, Whishaw I Q 1983 Performance of schizophrenic patients on tests sensitive to left or right frontal, temporal or parietal function in neurological patients. Journal of Nervous and Mental Diseases 171: 435–443
Kopstein J H, Neale J M 1972 A multivariate study of attention dysfunction in schizophrenia. Journal of Abnormal Psychology 80: 294–298
Korboot P J, Damiani N 1976 Auditory processing speed and signal detection in schizophrenia. Journal of Abnormal Psychology 85: 287–295

Kornetsky C, Orzack M H 1978 Physiological and behavioral correlates of attention dysfunction in schizophrenic patients. Journal of Psychiatric Research 14: 69–79
Kostandov E A 1980 Asymmetry of visual perception and interhemispheric interaction. Neuroscience and Behavioral Physiology 10: 36–47
Koukkou M 1982 E.E.G. states of the brain, information processing and schizophrenic primary symptoms. Psychiatry Research 6: 235–244
Kraepelin E 1896 Psychiatrie, 5th edn. Translated in part 1986 in: Cutting J C, Shepherd M (eds) Schizophrenia: the origin and development of its study in Europe. Cambridge University Press, Cambridge
Kraepelin E 1904 Comparative psychiatry. Translated 1974 in: Hirsch S R, Shepherd M (eds) Themes and variations in European psychiatry. J Wright, Bristol, ch 1, p 3–30
Kraepelin E 1913 Psychiatrie, Vol 3, Pt 2, 8th edn. Translated 1919 as: Dementia praecox and paraphrenia. Livingstone, Edinburgh.
Kräupl Taylor F 1971 A logical analysis of the medicopsychological concept of disease. Psychological Medicine 1: 356–364
Kräupl Taylor F 1981 On pseudohallucinations. Psychological Medicine 11: 265–271
Kreitman N, Sainsbury P, Morrissey J, Towers J, Scrivener J 1961 The reliability of psychiatric assessment. Journal of Mental Science 107: 887–908
Kretschmer E 1921 Physique and character. Translated 1936. Kegan Paul, Trench Trubner & Co, London
Kretschmer E 1922 A textbook of medical psychology. Translated 1952. The Hogarth Press, London
Kretschmer E 1927 The sensitive delusion of reference. Translated 1974 in: Hirsch S R, Shepherd M (eds) Themes and variations in European psychiatry. J Wright, Bristol, ch 8, p 153–195
Kringlen E 1968 An epidemiological-clinical twin study on schizophrenia. In: Rosenthal D, Kety S S (eds) The transmission of schizophrenia. Pergamon, Oxford, p 49–64
Kritskaia V P 1971 Characteristics in perception of speech in schizophrenic patients. Summarised 1982 in: Zavarin V, Tonkonogy J, Ostwald P Cognitive processes in schizophrenia and related disorders: experimental studies in the USSR. Pavlovian Journal of Biological Sciences 17: 188–203
Kroll J, Bachrach B 1982 Medieval visions and contemporary hallucinations. Psychological Medicine 12: 709–721
Kronfeld A 1930 Perspektiven der Seelenheilkunde. Thieme, Leipzig
Kugler B T, Caudrey D J, Gruzelier J H 1982 Bilateral auditory acuity of schizophrenic patients: effects of repeated testing, time of day and medication. Psychological Medicine 12: 775–781
Kupfer D J, Gordon Foster F 1975 The sleep of psychotic patients: does it all look alike? In: Freedman D X (ed) Biology of the major psychoses. Association for Research in Nervous and Mental Disease, vol 54, Raven Press, New York, p 143–164
Kutty I N, Prendes J L 1980 Psychosis and cerebellar degeneration. Journal of Nervous and Mental Diseases 169: 390–391
Lacan J 1932 The relationship between paranoid psychosis and personality. Translated 1986 in part in: Cutting J C, Shepherd M (eds) Schizophrenia: the origin and development of its study in Europe. Cambridge University Press, Cambridge
Laffal J 1965 Pathological and normal language. Atherton Press, New York
Laing R D 1959 The divided self. Tavistock, London
Laing R D 1971 The politics of the family. Tavistock, London
Laing R D, Esterson A 1964 Sanity, madness and the family, pt 1. Basic Books, New York
Lamb H R 1982 Treating the mentally ill. Jossey-Bass, San Francisco
Lance J W 1976 Simple formed hallucinations confined to the area of a specific visual field defect. Brain 99: 719–734
Landis T, Assal G, Perret E 1979 Opposite cerebral hemispheric superiorities for visual associative processing of emotional facial expressions and objects. Nature 278: 739–740
Landis T, Graves R, Goodglass H 1981 Dissociated awareness of manual performance on two different visual associative tasks: a 'split-brain' phenomenon in normal subjects? Cortex 17: 435–440
Landolt H 1958 Serial E.E.G. investigations during psychotic episodes in epileptic patients and during schizophrenic attacks. In: de Hass L (ed) Lectures on epilepsy. Elsevier, Amsterdam, p 91–133

Langfeldt G 1937 The prognosis in schizophrenia and the factors influencing the course of the disease. Levin & Munksgaard, Copenhagen
Langfeldt G 1939 The schizophrenic states. Munksgaard, Copenhagen
Langfeldt G 1960 Diagnosis and prognosis of schizophrenia. Proceedings of the Royal Society of Medicine 53: 1047–1052
Langsley D G, Pittman F S, Swank G E 1969 Family crises in schizophrenics and other mental patients. Journal of Nervous and Mental Diseases 149: 270–276
Lapidus L B, Schmolling P 1975 Anxiety, arousal and schizophrenia. Psychological Bulletin 82: 689–710
Larsen S F, Fromholt P 1976 Mnemonic organisation and free recall in schizophrenia. Journal of Abnormal Psychology 85: 61–65
La Russo L 1978 Sensitivity of paranoid patients to nonverbal cues. Journal of Abnormal Psychology 87: 463–471
Lawson J S, McGhie A, Chapman J 1964 Perception of speech in schizophrenia. British Journal of Psychiatry 110: 375–380
Lecours A R, Vanier-Clément M 1976 Schizophasia and jargonaphasia. Brain and Language 3: 516–565
Leff J P 1968 Perceptual phenomena and personality in sensory deprivation. British Journal of Psychiatry 114: 1499–1508
Leff J P 1981 Psychiatry around the globe: a transcultural view. Marcel Dekker, New York
Leff J P 1983 Papers presented at Quarterly meeting of Royal College of Psychiatrists (February) and one-day conference on schizophrenia at Institute of Psychiatry (November)
Leff J P, Wing J K 1971 Trial of maintenance therapy in schizophrenia. British Medical Journal iii: 599–604
Leff J P, Abberton E 1981 Voice pitch measurements in schizophrenia and depression. Psychological Medicine 11: 849–852
Leff J, Kuipers L, Berkowitz R, Eberlein-Vries R, Sturgeon D 1982 A controlled trial of social intervention in the families of schizophrenic patients. British Journal of Psychiatry 141: 121–134
Lehman A F, Ward N C, Linn L S 1982 Chronic mental patients: the quality of life issue. American Journal of Psychiatry 139: 1271–1276
Leonhard K 1957 The classification of endogenous psychoses. Translated 1979. Irvington, New York
Leonhard K 1961 Cycloid psychoses—endogenous psychoses which are neither schizophrenic nor manic–depressive. Journal of Mental Science 107: 633–638
Le Roux A 1980 Formes actuelles de la persistance de la psychose hallucinatoire chronique. Annales médicopsychologiques 138: 1199–1212
Le Tourneau J E 1974 The Oppel-Kundt and the Müller-Lyer illusions among schizophrenics. Perceptual and Motor Skills 39: 775–778
Levin H S, Benton A L 1977 Facial recognition in 'pseudoneurological' patients. Journal of Nervous and Mental Diseases 164: 135–138
Levine D N, Finklestein S 1982 Delayed psychosis after right temporoparietal stroke or trauma. Neurology 32: 267–273
Levy J 1974 Cerebral asymmetries as manifested in split-brain man. In; Kinsbourne M, Smith W L (eds) Hemispheric disconnection and cerebral function. Charles C Thomas, Springfield, ch 9, p 165–183
Levy J 1978 Lateral differences in the human brain in cognition and behavioral control. In: Buser P A, Rougeul-Buser A (eds) Cerebral correlates of conscious experience. Elsevier, Amsterdam
Levy R, Maxwell A E 1968 The effect of verbal context on the recall of schizophrenics and other psychiatric patients. British Journal of Psychiatry 114: 311–316
Lewine R R J, Strauss J S, Gift T E 1981 Sex differences in age at first hospital admission for schizophrenia: fact or artifact? American Journal of Psychiatry 138: 440–444
Lewinsohn P M, Elwood D L 1961 The role of contextual constraint in the learning of language samples in schizophrenia. Journal of Nervous and Mental Diseases 133: 79–81
Lewis A 1934 The psychopathology of insight. British Journal of Medical Psychology 14: 332–348
Lewis A 1970 Paranoia and paranoid: a historical perspective. Psychological Medicine 1: 2–12
Lewis A 1972 Psychogenic: a word and its mutations. Psychological Medicine 2: 209–215

Lewis D J 1961 Lilliputian hallucinations in the functional psychoses. Canadian Psychiatric Association Journal 6: 177–201
Lewis H E, Harries J M, Lewis D H, Monchaux C de 1964 Voluntary solitude: studies of men in a singlehanded transatlantic sailing race. Lancet i: 1431–1435
Lewis N 1949 Criteria for early differential diagnosis of psychoneurosis and schizophrenia. American Journal of Psychotherapy 3: 4–18
Ley R G, Bryden M P 1979 Hemispheric differences in processing emotions and faces. Brain and Language 7: 127–138
Ley R G, Bryden M P 1981 Consciousness, emotion and the right hemisphere. In: Underwood G, Stevens R (eds) Aspects of consciousness, vol 2. Academic Press, London
Liberman R P 1970 Behavior modification with chronic mental patients. Journal of Chronic Diseases 23: 803–812
Lidsky T I, Weinhold P M, Levine F M 1979 Implications of basal ganglionic dysfunction for schizophrenia. Biological Psychiatry 14: 3–12
Lidsky T I, Labuszewski T, Levine F M 1981 Are movement disorders the most serious side effects of maintenance therapy with anti-psychotic drugs? Biological Psychiatry 16: 1189–1194
Lidz R W, Lidz T 1949 The family environment of schizophrenic patients. American Journal of Psychiatry 106: 332–345
Lidz T, Cornelison A R, Fleck S, Terry D 1957 The intrafamilial environment of schizophrenic patients: II marital schism and marital skew. American Journal of Psychiatry 114: 241–248
Lidz T, Cornelison A, Terry D, Fleck S 1958 Intrafamilial environment of the schizophrenic patient: vi the transmission of irrationality. Archives of Neurology and Psychiatry 79: 305–316
Liem J H 1974 Effects of verbal communications of parents and children. Journal of Consulting and Clinical Psychology 42: 438–450
Lin I F, Spiga R, Fortsch W 1979 Insight and adherence to medication in chronic schizophrenia. Journal of Clinical Psychiatry 40: 430–432
Linder R 1965 Diagnosis: description or prescription? Perceptual and Motor Skills 20: 1081–1092
Lindsay W R 1982 The effects of labeling: blind and nonblind ratings of social skills in schizophrenic and nonschizophrenic control subjects. American Journal of Psychiatry 139: 216–219
Lindsley O R, Skinner B F 1954 A method for the experimental analysis of psychotic patients. American Psychologist 9: 419–420
Lipton F R, Cohen C I, Fischer E, Katz S E 1981 Schizophrenia: a network crisis. Schizophrenia Bulletin 7: 144–151
Lipton R B, Levy D L, Holzman P S, Levin J 1983 Eye movement dysfunctions in psychiatric patients: a review. Schizophrenia Bulletin 9: 13–32
Lishman W A 1968 Brain damage in relation to psychiatric disability after head injury. British Journal of Psychiatry 114: 373–410
Lishman W A 1978 Organic psychiatry. Blackwell, Oxford
Lishman W A, McMeekan E R L 1976 Hand preference patterns in psychiatric patients. British Journal of Psychiatry 129: 158–166
Lishman W A, Toone B K, Colbourn C J, McMeekan E R L, Mance R M 1978 Dichotic listening in psychotic patients. British Journal of Psychiatry 132: 333–341
Littlewood R, Lipsedge M 1981 Acute psychotic reactions in Caribbean-born patients. Psychological Medicine 11: 303–318
Lloyd G G 1977 Psychological reactions to physical illness. British Journal of Hospital Medicine 18: 352–358
Locke J 1690 An essay concerning human understanding. Republished 1924, Oxford University Press, New York
Lopez-Ibor J 1982 Delusional perception and delusional mood: a phenomenological and existential analysis. In: de Koning A J J, Jenner F A (eds) Phenomenology and psychiatry. Academic Press, London
Lorenz M, Cobb S 1954 Language patterns in psychotic and psychoneurotic subjects. Archives of Neurology and Psychiatry 72: 665–673
Luauté J P, Bidault E 1983 Prosopagnosia and delusional misidentification. Abstracts of the 7th World Congress of Psychiatry, Vienna, p 194

Lucas C J, Sainsbury P, Collins J G 1962 A social and clinical study of delusions in schizophrenia. Journal of Mental Science 108: 747–758
Luchins D J, Weinberger D R, Wyatt R J 1979 Schizophrenia: evidence of a subgroup with reversed cerebral asymmetry. Archives of General Psychiatry 36: 1309–1311
Luchins D, Pollin W, Wyatt R J 1980 Laterality in monozygotic schizophrenic twins. Biological Psychiatry 15: 87–93
Luchins D J, Morihisa J M, Weinberger D R, Wyatt R J 1981 Cerebral asymmetry and cerebellar atrophy in schizophrenia: a controlled postmortem study. American Journal of Psychiatry 138: 1501–1503
Lukianowicz N 1958 Autoscopic phenomena. Archives of Neurology and Psychiatry 80: 199–220
Lukianowicz N 1967 Body image disturbances in psychiatric disorders. British Journal of Psychiatry 113: 31–47
Luria A R, Homaskaya E D 1963 The human brain and psychic processes. Academy of Psychological Sciences of the RSFSR, Moscow
Lutz J, Marsh T K 1981 The effect of a dual level word list on schizophrenic free recall. Schizophrenia Bulletin 7: 509–515
Luxenburger H 1928 Vorläufiger Bericht über psychiatrische Serienuntersuchungen an Zwillingen. Zeitschrift für die gesamte Neurologie und Psychiatrie 116: 297–326
Luxon L, Lees A J, Greenwood R J 1979 Neurosyphilis today. Lancet i: 90–93
Lyon K, Wilson J, Golden C J, Graber B, Coffman J A, Bloch S 1981 Effects of long-term neuroleptic use on brain density. Psychiatry Research 5: 33–37
Maack L H, Mullen P E 1983 The Doppelgänger, disintegration and death: a case report. Psychological Medicine 13: 651–654
Machon R A, Mednick S A, Schulsinger F 1983 The interaction of seasonality, place of birth, genetic risk and subsequent schizophrenia in a high-risk sample. British Journal of Psychiatry 143: 383–388
Magaro P A 1980 Cognition in schizophrenia and paranoia. Lawrence Erlbaum, Hillsdale
Magaro P A, Chamrad D L 1983 Information processing and lateralization in schizophrenia. Biological Psychiatry 18: 29–44
Magaro P A, Page J 1982 Icon thresholds in paranoid and nonparanoid schizophrenics. British Journal of Clinical Psychology 21: 213–219
Magaro P A, Page J 1983 Brain disconnection, schizophrenia and paranoia. Journal of Nervous and Mental Diseases 171: 133–140
Magnan V 1893 Leçons cliniques sur les maladies mentales. Progrès Medical, Paris
Magrinat G, Danziger J A, Lorenzo I C, Flemenbaum A 1983 A reassessment of catatonia. Comprehensive Psychiatry 24: 216–228
Maguire G P, Granville-Grossman K L 1968 Physical illness in psychiatric patients. British Journal of Psychiatry 114: 1365–1367
Mahendra B 1981 Where have all the catatonics gone? Psychological Medicine 11: 669–671
Maher B 1972 The language of schizophrenia. British Journal of Psychiatry 120: 3–17
Maher B A 1974 Delusional thinking and perceptual disorder. Journal of Individual Psychology 30: 98–113
Maher B A, McKean K O, McLaughlin B 1966 Studies in psychotic language. In: Stone P J, Dunphy D C, Smith M S, Ogilvie D M (eds) The general inquirer: a computer approach to content analysis. MIT, Cambridge, Mass, p 469–503
Maher B A, Manschreck T C, Rucklos M E 1980 Contextual constraint and the recall of verbal material in schizophrenia: the effect of thought disorder. British Journal of Psychiatry 137: 69–73
Malamud N 1967 Psychiatric disorders with intracranial tumours of limbic system. Archives of Neurology 17: 113–123
Malenka R C, Angel R W, Hampton B, Berger P A 1982 Impaired central error-correcting behavior in schizophrenia. Archives of General Psychiatry 39: 101–107
Malitz S, Kanzler M 1970 Effects of drugs on perception in man. Association for Research in Nervous and Mental Disease, vol 48. Williams & Wilkins, Baltimore, p 35–53
Malitz S, Wilkens B, Esecover H 1962 A comparison of drug-induced hallucinations with those seen in spontaneously occurring psychoses. In: West L J (ed) Hallucinations. Grune & Stratton, New York
Malliaras D E, Kossovitsa Y T, Christodoulou G N 1978 Organic contributions to the intermetamorphosis syndrome. American Journal of Psychiatry 135: 985–987

Maloney M P, Sloane R B, Whipple K, Razani J, Eaton E M 1976 Auditory attention in process and reactive schizophrenia. Biological Psychiatry 11: 325–332
Mann M B 1944 The quantitative differentiation of samples of written language. Psychological Monographs 56: 41–74
Mann S A 1971 A study of factors leading to prolonged stay in a mental hospital. M Phil thesis, University of London.
Manschreck T C, Maher B A, Rucklos M E, White M T 1979 The predictability of thought disordered speech in schizophrenic patients. British Journal of Psychiatry 134: 595–601
Manschreck T C, Maher B A, Ader D N 1981a Formal thought disorder, the type-token ratio, and disturbed voluntary motor movement in schizophrenia. British Journal of Psychiatry 139: 7–15
Manschreck T C, Maher B A, Rucklos M E, Vereen D R, Ader D N 1981b Deficient motor synchrony in schizophrenia. Journal of Abnormal Psychology 90: 321–328
Manschreck T C, Maher B A, Rucklos M E, Vereen D R 1982 Disturbed voluntary motor activity in schizophrenic disorder. Psychological Medicine 12: 73–84
Marchand W E, Sarota B, Marble H C, Leary T M, Burbank C B, Bellinger M J 1959 Occurrence of painless acute surgical disorders in psychotic patients. New England Journal of Medicine 260: 580–585
Margo A, Hemsley D R, Slade P D 1981 The effects of varying auditory input on schizophrenic hallucinations. British Journal of Psychiatry 139: 122–127
Mark J C 1953 The attitudes of the mothers of male schizophrenics toward child behavior. Journal of Abnormal Psychology 48: 185–189
Marsden C D 1976 Cerebral atrophy and cognitive impairment in chronic schizophrenia. Lancet ii: 1079
Marsden C D, Jenner P 1980 The pathophysiology of extrapyramidal side-effects of neuroleptic drugs. Psychological Medicine 10: 55–72
Marshall W L 1973 Cognitive functioning in schizophrenia. British Journal of Psychiatry 123: 413–433
Martin M 1979 Hemisphere specialization for local and global processing. Neuropsychologia 17: 33–40
Mathew R J, Meyer J S, Francis D J, Schoolan J C, Weinman M, Mortell K F 1981 Regional cerebral blood flow in schizophrenia: a preliminary report. American Journal of Psychiatry 138: 112–113
Matthysse S, Williams R 1982 Neurohistological studies in schizophrenia. In: Henn F A, Nasrallah H A (eds) Schizophrenia as a brain disease. Oxford University Press, New York, ch 12, p 253–272
Maudsley H 1899 The pathology of mind, 3rd edn. Appleton & Co, New York
May P R A 1968 Treatment of schizophrenia: a comparative study of five treatment methods. Science House, New York
May P R A, Ebaugh F G 1953 Pathological intoxication, alcoholic hallucinosis and other reactions to alcohol. Quarterly Journal of Studies on Alcohol 14: 200–227
Mayer W 1950 Remarks on abortive cases of schizophrenia. Journal of Nervous and Mental Diseases 112: 539–542
Mayer-Gross W 1924 Selbstschilderungen der Verwirrtheit: die oneiroide Erlebnisform. Springer Verlag, Berlin
Mayer-Gross W 1935 On depersonalisation. British Journal of Medical Psychology 15: 103–126
Mayer Gross W, Slater E, Roth M 1960 Clinical psychiatry, 2nd edn. Cassel & Co, London, p 258
McCabe M S 1975 Reactive psychoses. Acta Psychiatrica Scandinavica Supplement 259
McConaghy N 1959 The use of an object sorting test in elucidating the hereditary factor in schizophrenia. Journal of Neurology, Neurosurgery and Psychiatry 22: 243–246
McCormick D J, Broekema V J 1978 Size estimation, perceptual recognition, and cardiac rate response in acute paranoid and nonparanoid schizophrenics. Journal of Abnormal Psychology 87: 385–398
McEvoy J P, Aland J, Wilson W H, Guy W, Hawkins L 1981 Measuring chronic schizophrenic patients' attitudes towards their illness and treatment. Hospital and Community Psychiatry 32: 856–858
McGaughran L S, Moran L J 1956 Conceptual level vs conceptual area analysis of object-

sorting behavior of schizophrenic and nonpsychiatric groups. Journal of Abnormal Psychology 52: 43–50
McGhie A 1969 Pathology of attention. Penguin, Harmondsworth
McGhie A, Chapman J 1961 Disorders of attention and perception in early schizophrenia. British Journal of Medical Psychology 34: 103–115
McGlashan T H 1982 Aphanisis: the syndrome of pseudodepression in chronic schizophrenia. Schizophrenia Bulletin 8: 118–134
McGlashan T H, Carpenter W T 1976 Postpsychotic depression in schizophrenia. Archives of General Psychiatry 33: 231–239
McGlashan T H, Carpenter W T 1981 Does attitude toward psychosis relate to outcome? American Journal of Psychiatry 138: 797–801
McGlone J, Kertesz A 1973 Sex differences in cerebral processing of visuospatial tasks. Cortex 9: 313–319
McGuffin P, Farmer A E, Rajah S M 1978 Histocompatibility antigens and schizophrenia. British Journal of Psychiatry 132: 149–151
McGuffin P, Festenstein H, Murray R 1983 A family study of HLA antigens and other genetic markers in schizophrenia. Psychological Medicine 13: 31–43
McGuigan F J 1966 Covert oral behavior and auditory hallucinations. Psychophysiology 3: 73–80
McKeever W F, Van Deventer A D 1977 Visual and auditory language processing asymmetries. Cortex 13: 225–241
McNeil T F, Kaij L 1978 Obstetric factors in the development of schizophrenia: complications in the births of preschizophrenics and in reproduction by schizophrenic parents. In: Wynne L C, Cromwell R L, Matthysse S (eds) The nature of schizophrenia. J Wiley, New York, p 401–429
McPherson F M, Buckley F 1970 Thought-process disorder and personal construct subsystems. British Journal of Social and Clinical Psychology 9: 380–381
McPherson F M, Barden V, Buckley F 1970 The use of 'psychological' constructs by affectively flattened schizophrenics. British Journal of Medical Psychology 43: 291–293
McPherson F M, Buckley F, Draffan J 1971 'Psychological' constructs, thought-process disorder and flattening of affect. British Journal of Social and Clinical Psychology 10: 267–270
McPherson F M, Armstrong J, Heather B B 1975 Psychological construing, 'difficulty' and thought disorder. British Journal of Medical Psychology 48: 303–315
McReynolds P 1960 Anxiety, perception and schizophrenia. In: Jackson D D (ed) The etiology of schizophrenia. Basic Books, New York, p 248–292
McReynolds P, Collins B, Acker M 1964 Delusional thinking and cognitive organization in schizophrenia. Journal of Abnormal Psychology 69: 210–212
Mednick S A 1955 Distortions in the gradient of stimulus generalization related to cortical brain damage and schizophrenia. Journal of Abnormal and Social Psychology 51: 536–542
Mednick S A 1958 A learning theory approach to research in schizophrenia. Psychological Bulletin 55: 316–327
Mednick S A, Schulsinger F 1968 Some premorbid characteristics related to breakdown in children with schizophrenic mothers. In: Rosenthal D, Kety S S (eds) The transmission of schizophrenia. Pergamon, London, p 267–291
Meduna L von 1937 Die Konvulsiontherapie der Schizophrenie. Marhold, Halle
Meduna L J 1950 Oneirophrenia—the confusional state. University of Illinois Press, Urbana
Meehl P E 1962 Schizotaxia, schizotypy, schizophrenia. American Psychologist 17: 827–838
Meehl P E 1975 Hedonic capacity: some conjectures. Bulletin of the Menninger Clinic 39: 295–307
Mefferd R B 1979 Word association: capacity of chronic schizophrenics to follow formal semantic, syntactic and instructional rules. Psychological Reports 45: 431–442
Meichenbaum D, Cameron R 1973 Training schizophrenics to talk to themselves. Behavior Therapy 4: 515–534
Melges F T 1982 Time and the inner future. J Wiley, New York
Mellor C S 1970 First-rank symptoms of schizophrenia. British Journal of Psychiatry 117: 15–23
Mellor C S, Sims A C P, Cope R V 1981 Change of disgnosis in schizophrenia and first rank symptoms: an eight-year follow-up. Comprehensive Psychiatry 22: 184–188

Menninger K A 1926 Influenza and schizophrenia. American Journal of Psychiatry 82: 469–529
Menninger K 1967 The vital balance. Viking, New York
Mentzos S, Lyrakos A, Tsidis A 1971 Akute Verwirrtheitszustände bei endogenen Psychosen. Der Nervenarzt 42: 10–17
Mesulam M M, Geschwind N 1978 On the possible role of neocortex and its limbic connections in attention and schizophrenia. In: Wynne L C, Cromwell R L, Matthysse S (eds) The nature of schizophrenia. J Wiley, New York, ch 14, p 161–166
Mesulam M M, Waxman S G, Geschwind N, Sabin T D 1976 Acute confusional states with right middle cerebral artery infarction. Journal of Neurology, Neurosurgery and Psychiatry 39: 84–89
Meyer A 1910 The nature and conception of dementia praecox. Journal of Abnormal Psychology 5: 274–298
Meyer A 1957 Psychobiology: a science of man. Charles C Thomas, Springfield
Mezey A G 1960 Personal background, emigration and mental disorder in Hungarian refugees. Journal of Mental Science 106: 618–627
Michael R P, Gibbons J L 1963 Interrelationships between the endocrine system and neuropsychiatry. International Review of Neurobiology 5: 243–302
Milgram N A 1959 Preference for abstract versus concrete word meanings in schizophrenic and brain-damaged patients. Journal of Clinical Psychology 15: 207–212
Milgram N A 1960 Cognitive and empathic factors in role-taking by schizophrenic and brain-damaged patients. Journal of Abnormal Psychology 60: 219–224
Miller B 1974 Semantic misinterpretation of ambiguous communication in schizophrenia. Archives of General Psychiatry 30: 435–440
Miller G A, Chapman L J 1968 Response bias and schizophrenic beliefs. Journal of Abnormal Psychology 73: 252–255
Miller G A, Selfridge J A 1950 Verbal context and the recall of meaningful material. American Journal of Psychology 63: 176–185
Miller J G 1960 Information input overload and psychopathology. American Journal of Psychiatry 116: 695–704
Miller W K, Phelan J G 1980 Comparison of adult schizophrenics with matched normal native speakers of English as to 'acceptability' of English sentences. Journal of Psycholinguistic Research 9: 579–593
Milner B 1958 Psychological defects produced by temporal lobe excision. Research Publication of the Association for Research into Nervous and Mental Disease 36: 244–257
Milton F, Patwa V K, Hafner R J 1978 Confrontation vs belief modification in persistently deluded patients. British Journal of Medical Psychology 51: 127–130
Minkowski E 1923 Findings in a case of schizophrenic depression. Translated 1958 in: May R, Angel E, Ellenberger H F (eds) Existence. Basic Books, New York, p 127–138
Minkowski E 1927 The essential problem of schizophrenia. Translated 1986 in part in: Cutting J C, Shepherd M (eds) Schizophrenia: the origin and development of its study in Europe. Cambridge University Press, Cambridge
Minkowski E 1950 Psychopathologie des délires. Proceedings of the International Congress on Psychiatry, Paris. Hermann & Co, Paris
Mintz S, Alpert M 1972 Imagery vividness, reality testing and schizophrenic hallucinations. Journal of Abnormal Psychology 79: 310–316
Mirsky A F 1969 Neuropsychological bases of schizophrenia. Annual Review of Psychology 20: 321–348
Mishler E G, Waxler N E 1975 The sequential patterning of interaction in normal and schizophrenic families. Family Process 14: 17–50
Monro J 1758 Remarks on Dr Battie's treatise on madness. John Clarke, London
Moon A F, Mefferd R B, Wieland B A, Pokorny A D, Falconer G A 1968 Perceptual dysfunction as a determinant of schizophrenic word associations. Journal of Nervous and Mental Diseases 146: 80–84
Moor J H, Tucker G J 1979 Delusions: analysis and criteria. Comprehensive Psychiatry 20: 388–393
Mora G 1967 From demonology to the Narrenturm. In: Galdston I (ed) Historic derivations of modern psychiatry. McGraw Hill, New York, ch 3, p 41–74

Moran L J, Mefferd R B, Kimble J P 1964 Idiodynamic sets in word association. Psychological Monographs 78: 1–22

Morel B A 1857 Traité des dégénerescences de l'espèce humaine. Baillière, Paris

Morel B A 1860 Traité des maladies mentales. Masson, Paris

Morrison J R 1973 Catatonia: retarded and excited types. Archives of General Psychiatry 28: 39–41

Morstyn R, Duffy F H, McCarley R W 1983 Altered P_{300} topography in schizophrenia. Archives of General Psychiatry 40: 729–734

Moses J A, Golden C J 1980 Discrimination between schizophrenic and brain-damaged patients with the Luria Nebraska neuropsychological test battery. International Journal of Neuroscience 10: 121–128

Mosher L R, Keith S J 1980 Psychosocial treatment: individual, group, family, and community support approaches. Schizophrenia Bulletin 6: 10–41

Mosher L R, Menn A K 1976 Dinosaur or astronaut? One-year follow-up data from the Soteria project. American Journal of Psychiatry 133: 919–920

Mullen P 1979 The phenomenology of disordered mental function. In: Hill P, Murray R, Thorley A (eds) Essentials of postgraduate psychiatry. Academic Press, London, ch 2, p 25–54

Munro A 1980 Monosymptomatic hypochondriacal psychosis. British Journal of Hospital Medicine 24: 34–38

Murphy D L, Wyatt R J 1972 Reduced monoamine oxidase activity in blood platelets from schizophrenic patients. Nature 238: 225–226

Murphy G 1923 Type of word-association in dementia praecox, manic-depressives and normal persons. American Journal of Psychiatry 79: 539–571

Murphy H B M 1968 Cultural factors in the genesis of schizophrenia. In: Rosenthal D, Kety S S (eds) The transmission of schizophrenia. Pergamon, Oxford, p 137–154

Murphy H B M 1977 Migration, culture and mental health. Psychological Medicine 7: 677–684

Muzekari L H, Bates M E 1977 Judgement of emotion among chronic schizophrenics. Journal of Clinical Psychology 33: 662–666

Nachmani G, Cohen B D 1969 Recall and recognition free learning in schizophrenics. Journal of Abnormal Psychology 74: 511–516

Naficy A, Willerman L 1980 Excessive yielding to normal biases is not a distinctive sign of schizophrenia. Journal of Abnormal Psychology 89: 697–703

Nameche G, Waring M, Ricks D 1964 Early indicators of outcome in schizophrenia. Journal of Nervous and Mental Diseases 139: 232–240

Namyslowska I 1975 Thought disorders in schizophrenia before and after pharmacological treatment. Comprehensive Psychiatry 16: 37–42

Nasrallah H A 1982 Laterality and hemispheric dysfunction in schizophrenia. In: Henn F A, Nasrallah H A (eds) Schizophrenia as a brain disease. Oxford University Press, New York, ch 13, p 273–294

Nasrallah H A, McChesney C M 1981 Psychopathology of corpus callosum tumours. Biological Psychiatry 16: 663–669

Nasrallah H A, McCalley-Whitters M, Kuperman S 1982 Neurological differences between paranoid and nonparanoid schizophrenia: pt 1 sensory-motor lateralisation. Journal of Clinical Psychiatry 43: 305–306

Nathan P E 1964 A comparative investigation of schizophrenic and normal conceptual performance. Journal of Nervous and Mental Diseases 138: 443–451

Neale J M, McIntyre C W, Fox R, Cromwell R L 1969a Span of apprehension in acute schizophrenics. Journal of Abnormal Psychology 74: 593–596

Neale J M, Held J M, Cromwell R L 1969b Size estimation in schizophrenics: a review and reanalysis. Psychological Bulletin 71: 210–221

Neufeld R W J 1976 Relationship between conceptual judgements and stimulus dimensions among schizophrenics and normals. British Journal of Social and Clinical Psychology 15: 85–91

Neufeld R W J 1977 Response-selection process in paranoid and nonparanoid schizophrenia. Perceptual and Motor Skills 44: 499–505

Neufeld R W J 1978 The nature of deficit among paranoid and nonparanoid schizophrenics in the interpretation of sentences. Journal of Clinical Psychology 34: 333–339

Neuringer C, Goldstein G, Fiske J P 1969 Schizophrenic adherence to strong meaning associations. Perceptual and Motor Skills 29: 394
Nielsen J M 1958 Cerebral localization and the psychoses. Research Publication of the Association for Research in Nervous and Mental Diseases 36: 467–477
Nielzen S, Cesarec Z 1982 Emotional experience of music by psychiatric patients compared with normal subjects. Acta Psychiatrica Scandinavica 65: 450–460
Nightingale S 1982 Somatoparaphrenia: a case report. Cortex 18: 463–467
NIMH 1974 Abnormal involuntary movements scale. Public Health Service, Bethesda
Nissen H A, Spencer K A 1936 The psychogenic problem in chronic arthritis. New England Journal of Medicine 214: 576–581
Niwa S-I, Hiramatsu K-I, Kameyama T, Saitoh O, Utena K, Utena I 1983 Left hemisphere's inability to sustain attention over extended time periods in schizophrenics. British Journal of Psychiatry 142: 477–481
Norman D A 1981 Categorization of action slips. Psychological Review 88: 1–15
Norris V 1959 Mental illness in London. Institute of Psychiatry Maudsley Monograph No 6, Chapman & Hall, London
Nuechterlein K H 1983 Signal detection in vigilance tasks and behavioral attributes among offspring of schizophrenic mothers and among hyperactive children. Journal of Abnormal Psychology 92: 4–28
Nuller Y L 1982 Depersonalisation—symptoms, meaning, therapy. Acta Psychiatrica Scandinavica 66: 451–458
Obler L 1981 Review of Le langage des dements. Brain and Language 12: 375–386
O'Brian J P, Weingartner H 1970 Associative structure in chronic schizophrenia. Archives of General Psychiatry 22: 136–142
Oddy H C, Lobstein T J 1972 Hand and eye dominance in schizophrenia. British Journal of Psychiatry 120: 331–332
Odegaard O 1932 Emigration and insanity. Acta Psychiatrica et Neurologica Supplement 4
Ogden T H 1980 On the nature of schizophrenic conflict. International Journal of Psychoanalysis 61: 513–533
Oltmanns T F 1978 Selective attention in schizophrenic and manic psychoses: the effect of distraction on information processing. Journal of Abnormal Psychology 87: 212–225
Oltmanns T F, Neale J M 1978 Distractibility in relation to other aspects of schizophrenic disorder. In: Schwartz S (ed) Language and cognition in schizophrenia. Lawrence Erlbaum, Hillsdale, ch 5, p 117–143
Orme J E 1966 Time estimation and the nosology of schizophrenia. British Journal of Psychiatry 112: 37–39
Ornitz E M 1970 Vestibular dysfunction in schizophrenia and childhood autism. Comprehensive Psychiatry 11: 159–173
Ortony A 1979 Metaphor: a multidimensional problem. In: Ortony A (ed) Metaphor and thought. Cambridge University Press, Cambridge, p 1–16
Orzack M H, Kornetsky C 1966 Attention dysfunction in chronic schizophrenia. Archives of General Psychiatry 14: 323–326
Orzack M H, Kornetsky C, Freeman H 1967 The effects of daily administration of carphenazine on attention in the schizophrenic patient. Psychopharmacologia (Berlin) 11: 31–38
Osmond H, Smythies J 1952 Schizophrenia: a new approach. Journal of Mental Science 98: 309–315
Oswald I 1962 Sleeping and waking. Elsevier, Amsterdam
Owens D G C, Johnstone E C 1980 The disabilities of chronic schizophrenia—their nature and the factors contributing to their development. British Journal of Psychiatry 136: 384–395
Paivio A 1975 Imagery and long-term memory. In: Kennedy A, Wilkes A (eds) Studies in long-term memory. J Wiley, London
Pandey R S, Gupta A K, Chaturvedi V C 1981 Autoimmune model of schizophrenia with special reference to antibrain antibodies. Biological Psychiatry 16: 1123–1136
Parker S, Schilder P 1935 Acoustic imagination and acoustic hallucinations. Archives of Neurology and Psychiatry 34: 744–757
Parnas J, Schulsinger F, Schulsinger H, Mednick S A, Teasdale T T 1982a Behavioral precursors of schizophrenia spectrum. Archives of General Psychiatry 39: 658–664
Parnas J, Schulsinger F, Teasdale T W, Schulsinger H, Feldman P M, Mednick S A 1982b

Perinatal complications and clinical outcome within the schizophrenia spectrum. British Journal of Psychiatry 140: 416–420
Parnas J, Korsgaard S, Krautwald O, Jensen P S 1982c Chronic psychosis in epilepsy. Acta Psychiatrica Scandinavica 66: 282–293
Paster S 1948 Psychotic reactions among soldiers of World War II. Journal of Nervous and Mental Diseases 108: 54–66
Paterson A, Zangwill O L 1944 Disorders of visual space perception associated with lesions of the right cerebral hemisphere. Brain 67: 331–358
Pattison E M, Pattison M L 1981 Analysis of a schizophrenic psychosocial network. Schizophrenia Bulletin 7: 135–143
Paul G L, Lentz R J 1977 Psychosocial treatment of chronic mental patients. Harvard University Press, Cambridge
Pauleikhoff B 1957 Atypische Psychosen. Bibliotheca Psychiatrica et Neurologica 99
Pavlov I P 1930 An attempt of a physiologist to digress into the domain of psychiatry. Translated 1955 in: Selected works of I P Pavlov. Foreign Language Publishing House, Moscow
Pavlov I P 1932 Pavlov's theory of schizophrenia. Archives of Neurology and Psychiatry 28: 210–218
Pavy D, Grinspoon L, Shador R I 1969 Word frequency measure of verbal disorder in schizophrenia. Diseases of the Nervous System 30: 553–556
Paykel E S 1978 Contribution of life events to causation of psychiatric illness. Psychological Medicine 8: 245–253
Payne R W 1966 The measurement and significance of overinclusive thinking and retardation in schizophrenic patients. In: Hoch P H, Zubin J (eds) Psychopathology of schizophrenia. Grune & Stratton, New York, p 77–97
Payne R W, Friedlander D 1962 A short battery of simple tests for measuring overinclusive thinking. Journal of Mental Science 108: 362–367
Payne R W, Mattussek P, George E I 1959 An experimental study of schizophrenic thought disorder. Journal of Mental Science 105: 627–652
Peck R E 1962 Circumstantial schizophrenia. Psychiatric Quarterly 36: 655–664
Penfield W, Jasper H 1954 Epilepsy and the functional anatomy of the human brain. Churchill, London
Perez M M, Trimble M R 1980 Epileptic psychosis—diagnostic comparison with process schizophrenia. British Journal of Psychiatry 137: 245–249
Perris C 1974 A study of cycloid psychosis. Acta Psychiatrica Scandinavica Supplement 253
Petrie A 1952 Personality and the frontal lobe. Routledge and Kegan Paul, London
Philip B R 1953 Reversals in the perception of Lissajou figures by psychotics. Canadian Journal of Psychology 7: 115–125
Phillips L 1953 Case history data and prognosis in schizophrenia. Journal of Nervous and Mental Diseases 117: 515–525
Pick A 1891 Uber primäre chronische Demenz im jugendlichen Alter. Prager medizinische Wochenschrift 16: 312–315
Pick A 1903 On reduplicative paramnesia. Brain 26: 260–267
Pic'l A K, Magaro P A, Wade E A 1979 Hemispheric functioning in paranoid and nonparanoid schizophrenia. Biological Psychiatry 14: 891–903
Pilowsky I, Bassett D 1980 Schizophrenia and the response to facial emotions. Comprehensive Psychiatry 21: 236–244
Pinel P 1801 A treatise on insanity. Translated 1962. Hafner, New York
Pishkin V, Bourne L E 1981 Abstraction and the use of available information by schizophrenic and normal individuals. Journal of Abnormal Psychology 90: 197–203
Pogue-Geile M F, Oltmanns T F 1980 Sentence perception and distractibility in schizophrenic, manic and depressed patients. Journal of Abnormal Psychology 89: 115–124
Pokorny A D 1964 Suicide rates in various psychiatric disorders. Journal of Nervous and Mental Diseases 139: 499–506
Polyakov V F 1969 The experimental investigation of cognitive functioning in schizophrenia. In: Cole M, Maltzman I (eds) A handbook of contemporary Soviet psychology. Basic Books, New York
Pond D A 1957 Psychiatric aspects of epilepsy. Journal of the Indian Medical Profession 3: 1441–1451

Porteus S D 1957 Maze test reactions after chlorpromazine. Journal of Consulting Psychology 21: 15–21
Porteus S D, Barclay J E 1957 A further note on chlorpromazine: maze reactions. Journal of Consulting Psychology 21: 297–299
Posner M I, Boies S J 1971 Components of attention. Psychological Review 78: 391–408
Potkin S G, Weinberger D, Kleinman J, Nasrallah H, Luchins D, Bigelow L et al 1981 Wheat gluten challenge in schizophrenic patients. American Journal of Psychiatry 138: 1208–1211
Pötzl O 1924 Uber störungen der Selbstwahrnehmung bei linkseitiger Hemiplegie. Zeitschrift für die gesamte Neurologie und Psychiatrie 93: 117–168
Powdermaker F B, Frank J D 1953 Group psychotherapy. Harvard University Press, Cambridge
Pribram K H 1976 Problems concerning the structure of consciousness. In: Globus G G, Maxwell G, Savodnik I (eds) Consciousness and the brain. Plenum Press, New York
Prichard J C 1835 A treatise on insanity and other disorders affecting the mind. Sherwood, London
Proudfoot R E 1982 Hemispheric asymmetry for face recognition. Neuropsychologia 20: 129–144
Puente A E, Heidelberg-Sanders C, Lund N 1982 Detection of brain damage in schizophrenics as measured by the Whitaker index of schizophrenic thinking and the Luria-Nebraska neuropsychological battery. Perceptual and Motor Skills 54: 495–499
Pylyshyn Z W 1970 Clinical correlates of some syntactic features of patients' speech. Journal of Nervous and Mental Diseases 150: 307–316
Quitkin F, Rifkin A, Klein D F 1976 Neurological soft signs in schizophrenia and character disorders. Archives of General Psychiatry 33: 845–853
Rabin A I 1944 Fluctuations in the mental level of schizophrenic patients. Psychiatric Quarterly 18: 78–91
Rabin A I 1957 Time estimation of schizophrenics and nonpsychotics. Journal of Clinical Psychology 13: 88–90
Rabin A I, King G F, Ehrmann J C 1955 Vocabulary performance of short-term and long-term schizophrenics. Journal of Abnormal Psychology 50: 255–258
Rado S, Buchenholz B, Dunton H, Karlen S H, Senescu R 1956 Schizotypal organization. In: Rado S, Daniels G E (eds) Changing concepts of psychoanalytical medicine. Grune &Stratton, New York, ch 15, p 225–235
Raeburn J M, Tony J E 1968 Experiments on contextual contraint in schizophrenia. British Journal of Psychiatry 114: 43–52
Rail D, Scholtz C, Swash M 1981 Postencephalitic Parkinsonism: current experience. Journal of Neurology, Neurosurgery and Psychiatry 44: 670–676
Ramani S V 1981 Psychosis associated with frontal lobe lesions in Schilder's cerebral sclerosis: a case report with C.T. scan evidence. Journal of Clinical Psychiatry 42: 250–252
Rao D C, Morton N E, Gottesman I I, Lew R 1981 Path analysis of qualitative data on pairs of relatives: application to schizophrenia. Human Heredity 31: 325–333
Rapaport D 1945 Diagnostic psychological testing, vol 1. The Year Book Publishers, Chicago
Rappaport M, Hopkins H K, Silverman J, Hall K 1972 Auditory signal detection in schizophrenics. Psychopharmacologia (Berlin) 24: 6–28
Rappaport M, Hopkins H K, Hall K, Belleza T, Silverman J 1978 Are there schizophrenics for whom drugs may be unnecessary or contraindicated? International Pharmacopsychiatry 13: 100–110
Rappaport S R, Webb W B 1950 An attempt to study intellectual deterioration by premorbid and psychotic testing. Journal of Consulting Psychology 14: 95–98
Rausch M A, Prescott T E, De Wolfe A S 1980 Schizophrenic and aphasic language: discriminable or not? Journal of Consulting and Clinical Psychology 48: 63–70
Raven J C 1958 Verbal dysfunction in mental illness. Language and Speech 1: 218–225
Reed G 1972 The psychology of anomalous experience. Hutchinson, London
Rees W D 1971 The hallucinations of widowhood. British Medical Journal iv: 37–41
Reich S S, Cutting J 1982 Picture perception and abstract thought in schizophrenia. Psychological Medicine 12: 91–96
Reil J C 1803 Rhapsodieen über die Anwendung der psychischen Curmethode auf Geisteszerrüttungen. Curtschen, Halle

Reilly F E, Harrow M, Tucker G J 1973 Language and thought content in acute psychosis. American Journal of Psychiatry 130: 411–417
Reinhold A 1950 A case of auditory agnosia. Brain 73: 203–223
Retterstol N 1981 Somatic disorders as disposing of precipitating factor in paranoid psychoses. Abstracts of the 3rd World Congress of Biological Psychiatry, vol 1, Stockholm, S 321
Reveley A M, Reveley M A, Clifford C A, Murray R M 1982 Cerebral ventricular size in twins discordant for schizophrenia. Lancet i: 540–541
Reveley A M, Reveley M A, Murray R M 1984 Cerebral ventricular enlargement to nongenetic schizophrenia: a controlled twin study. British Journal of Psychiatry 144: 89–93
Reynolds E H 1968 Epilepsy and schizophrenia. Lancet i: 398–401
Richardson A 1969 Mental imagery. Routledge and Kegan Paul, London
Richter D 1978 Clues to the causation of schizophrenia. In: Hemmings G, Hemmings W A (eds) The biological basis of schizophrenia. MTP Press, England, ch 5, p 55–61
Ricks D F, Nameche G 1966 Symbiosis, sacrifice and schizophrenia. Mental Hygiene 50: 541–551
Ridley R M, Baker H F 1982 Stereotypy in monkeys and humans. Psychological Medicine 12: 61–72
Rieder R O, Mann L S, Weinberger D R, van Kammen D P, Post R M 1983 Computed tomographic scans in patients with schizophrenia, schizoaffective and bipolar affective disorder. Archives of General Psychiatry 40: 735–739
Rieger W, Friedman H 1970 Memory organization in schizophrenia. Journal of Genetic Psychology 116: 15–20
Rin H, Lin T 1962 Mental illness among Formosan aboriginies as compared with the Chinese in Taiwan. Journal of Mental Science 108: 134–146
Rinkel M, De Shon H J, Hyde R W, Solomon H C 1952 Experimental schizophrenia-like symptoms. American Journal of Psychiatry 108: 572–578
Rippon G 1979 Bilateral differences in skin conductance level in schizophrenic patients. In: Gruzelier J, Flor-Henry P (eds) Hemisphere asymmetries of function in psychopathology. Elsevier, Amsterdam, p 169–187
Ritzler B A 1977 Proprioception and schizophrenia. Journal of Abnormal Psychology 86: 501–509
Robins L N 1966 Deviant children grow up. Williams & Wilkins, Baltimore
Robins L N, Helzer J E, Croughan J, Ratcliff I C S 1981 The NIMH Diagnostic Interview Schedule: its history, characteristics and validity. Archives of General Psychiatry 38: 381–389
Robinson J F, Vitale L J 1954 Children with circumscribed interest patterns. American Journal of Orthopsychiatry 24: 755–764
Rochester S R 1978 Are language disorders in acute schizophrenia actually information processing problems? Journal of Psychiatric Research 14: 275–283
Rochester S R, Martin J R 1979 Crazy talk. Plenum Press, New York
Rochford J M, Detre T, Tucker G J, Harrow M 1970 Neuropsychological impairments in functional psychiatric diseases. Archives of General Psychiatry 22: 114–119
Rodnick E H, Garmezy N 1957 An experimental approach to the study of motivation in schizophrenia. In: Nebraska symposium on motivation. University of Nebraska Press, Lincoln, p 109–184
Rodnick E, Shakow D 1940 Set in the schizophrenic as measured by a composite reaction time index. American Journal of Psychiatry 97: 214–225
Rogers C R, Gendlin E T, Kiesler D J, Truax C B 1967 The therapeutic relationship and its impact: a study of psychotherapy with schizophrenia. University of Wisconsin Press, Madison
Romney D, Leblanc E 1975 Relationship between formal thought disorder and retardation in schizophrenia. Journal of Consulting and Clinical Psychology 43: 217–222
Rorschach H 1921 Psychodiagnostics. Translated 1942. Verlag Hans Huber, Berne
Rosch E 1977 Human categorisation. In: Warren N (ed) Studies in crosscultural psychology. Academic Press, London, ch 1, p 1–49
Rosen G 1968 Madness in society. Routledge & Kegan Paul, London
Rosen J N 1947 The treatment of schizophrenic psychosis by direct analytic therapy. Psychiatric Quarterly 21: 3–37

Rosenberg S D, Tucker G J 1979 Verbal behavior and schizophrenia: the semantic dimension. Archives of General Psychiatry 36: 1331–1337
Rosenfeld H A 1965 Psychotic states: a psychoanalytic approach. Hogarth, London
Rosenfeld H 1976 The treatment of psychotic states, particularly schizophrenia, by psychoanalysis. In: Kamali D, Bartholini G, Richter D (eds) Schizophrenia today. Pergamon, Oxford, p 259–270
Rosenthal D, Wender P H, Kety S S, Schulsinger F, Welner J, Ostergaard L 1968 Schizophrenics' offspring reared in adoptive homes. In: Rosenthal D, Kety S S (eds) The transmission of schizophrenia. Pergamon, Oxford, p 377–392
Rosenthal R, Bigelow L B 1972 Quantitative brain measurements in chronic schizophrenia. British Journal of Psychiatry 121: 259–264
Rosenzweig N 1959 Sensory deprivation and schizophrenia. American Journal of Psychiatry 116: 326–329
Ross E D 1981 The aprosodias: functional-anatomic organization of the affective components of language in the right hemisphere. Archives of Neurology 38: 561–569
Ross E D, Mesulam M-M 1979 Dominant language functions of the right hemisphere? Prosody and emotional gesturing. Archives of Neurology 36: 144–148
Ross E D, Rush A J 1981 Diagnosis and neuroanatomical correlates of depression in brain-damaged patients. Archives of General Psychiatry 38: 1344–1354
Ross M B, Magaro P A 1976 Cognitive differentiation between paranoid and nonparanoid schizophrenics. Psychological Reports 38: 991–994
Rosser R 1979 The psychopathology of feeling and thinking in a schizophrenic. International Journal of Psychoanalysis 60: 177–188
Rosvold H E, Mirsky A F, Sarason I, Bransome E D, Beck L H 1956 A continuous performance test of brain damage. Journal of Consulting Psychology 20: 343–350
Roth M 1963 Neurosis, psychosis and the concept of disease in psychiatry. Acta Psychiatrica Scandinavica 39: 128–145
Roy A 1976 Psychiatric aspects of narcolepsy. British Journal of Psychiatry 128: 562–565
Roy A 1982 Suicide in chronic schizophrenia. British Journal of Psychiatry 141: 171–177
Royer F L, Friedman S 1973 Scanning time of schizophrenics and normals for visual designs. Journal of Abnormal Psychology 82: 212–219
Rubert S L, Hollender M H, Mehrhof E G 1961 Olfactory hallucinations. Archives of General Psychiatry 5: 313–318
Rubin R L 1978 Adolescent infectious mononucleosis with psychosis. Journal of Clinical Psychiatry 39: 773–775
Rudden M, Gilmore M, Frances A 1982 Delusions: when to confront the facts of life. American Journal of Psychiatry 139: 929–932
Rudin D O 1981 The choroid plexus and system disease in mental illness. II Systemic lupus erythematosus: a combined transport dysfunction model for schizophrenia. Biological Psychiatry 16: 373–397
Rüdin E 1916 Zur Vererbung und Neuentstehung der Dementia Praecox. Springer, Berlin
Rudzinski D, Auld F 1980 Development of a picture-preference measure of thought disorder. British Journal of Social and Clinical Psychology 19: 369–376
Ruff R L, Volpe B T 1981 Environmental reduplication associated with right frontal and parietal lobe injury. Journal of Neurology, Neurosurgery and Psychiatry 44: 382–386
Russell P N, Beekhuis M E 1976 Organization in memory: a comparison of psychotics and normals. Journal of Abnormal Psychology 85: 527–534
Russell P N, Knight R G 1977 Performance of process schizophrenics on tasks involving visual search. Journal of Abnormal Psychology 86: 16–26
Russell P N, Page A E 1976 Comparison of schizophrenics and normals on a visual search task. Perceptual and Motor Skills 42: 399–402
Russell P N, Bannatyne P A, Smith J F 1975 Associative strength as a mode of organization in recall and recognition: a comparison of schizophrenics and normals. Journal of Abnormal Psychology 84: 122–128
Russell P N, Consedine C E, Knight R G 1980 Visual and memory search by process schizophrenics. Journal of Abnormal Psychology 89: 109–114
Rutner I T, Bugle C 1969 An experimental procedure for the modification of psychotic behavior. Journal of Consulting and Clinical Psychology 33: 651–653
Rutter D R 1977 Speech patterning in recently admitted and chronic long-stay schizophrenic patients. British Journal of Social and Clinical Psychology 16: 47–55

Rutter D R 1979 The reconstruction of schizophrenic speech. British Journal of Psychiatry 134: 356–359
Rutter D R, Wishner J, Callaghan B A 1975 The prediction and predictability of speech in schizophrenic patients. British Journal of Psychiatry 126: 571–576
Ryle G 1949 The concept of mind. Penguin, England
Rylander G 1939 Personality changes after operations on the frontal lobes. Acta Psychiatrica et Neurologica Scandinavica Supplement 20
Saccuzzo D P, Braff D L 1981 Early information processing deficit in schizophrenia. Archives of General Psychiatry 38: 175–179
Saccuzzo D P, Hirt M, Spencer T J 1974 Backward masking as a measure of attention in schizophrenia. Journal of Abnormal Psychology 83: 512–522
Saccuzzo D P, Braff D L, Sprock J 1982 The effect of mental retardation and schizophrenia on information processing. Journal of Nervous and Mental Diseases 170: 102–106
Sackeim H A, Gur R C 1978 Lateral asymmetry in intensity of emotional expression. Neuropsychologia 16: 473–481
Sackeim H A, Greenberg M S, Weiman A L, Gur R C, Hungerbuhler J P, Geschwind N 1982 Hemisphere asymmetry in the expression of positive and negative emotions. Archives of Neurology 39: 210–218
Sacks M H, Carpenter W T, Strauss J S 1974 Recovery from delusions. Archives of General Psychiatry 30: 117–120
Sakai A 1983 The verbal expressions of auditory hallucinations of schizophrenia. Abstracts of the 7th World Congress of Psychiatry, Vienna, p 507
Salmon P, Bramley J, Presley A S 1967 The word-in-context test as a measure of conceptualisation in schizophrenia with and without thought disorder. British Journal of Medical Psychology 40: 253–259
Salzinger K, Portnoy S, Feldman R S 1964 Verbal behaviour of schizophrenic and normal subjects. Annals of the New York Academy of Sciences 105: 845–860
Salzinger K, Portnoy S, Feldman R S 1978 Communicability deficit in schizophrenics resulting from a more general deficit. In: Schwartz S (ed) Language and cognition in schizophrenia. Lawrence Erlbaum, Hillsdale, ch 2, p 35–53
Sartorius N, Jablensky A, Shapiro R 1977 Two-year follow-up of the patients included in the WHO International Pilot Study of Schizophrenia. Psychological Medicine 7: 529–541
Sattler J M, Normark T 1971 Verbal learning in schizophrenics and normals. Psychological Record 21: 241–246
Savodnik I 1976 Mind, brain and the symbolic consciousness. In: Globus G G, Maxwell G, Savodnik I (eds) Consciousness and the brain. Plenum Press, New York
Scadding J G 1967 Diagnosis: the clinician and the computer. Lancet ii: 877–882
Scarone S, Pieri E, Gambini O, Massironi R, Cazzullo C L 1982 The asymmetric lateralization of tactile extinction in schizophrenia. British Journal of Psychiatry 141: 350–353
Schachter S, Singer J E 1962 Cognitive, social and physiological determinants of emotional state. Psychological Review 69: 379–399
Scharfetter C 1980 General psychopathology: an introduction. Cambridge University Press, Cambridge
Scheff T J 1966 Being mentally ill. Aldine, Chicago
Scherer M, Storms L 1981 Attention and visual reaction time in schizophrenia. Journal of Nervous and Mental Diseases 169: 348–356
Schilder P 1920 On the development of thoughts. Translated 1951 in: Rapaport D (ed) Organization and pathology of thought. Columbia University Press, New York, p 497–518
Schilder P 1924 Medical psychology. Translated 1953. International Universities Press, New York
Schilder P 1935 The image and appearance of the human body. Kegan Paul, Trench, Trubner & Co, London
Schlesinger B 1950 Mental changes in intracranial tumours. Confinia Neurologia 10: 225–263
Schmidt G 1940 A review of the German literature on delusional states over the last 25 years. Translated 1986 in: Cutting J C, Shepherd M (eds) Schizophrenia: the origin and development of its study in Europe. Cambridge University Press, Cambridge
Schmolling P, Lapidus L B 1977 Effect of enriched stimulus and instructional conditions on verbal abstracting ability in acute schizophrenics. Psychological Reports 41: 1203–1210

Schneider C 1930 Die Psychologie der Schizophrenen. G Thieme, Leipzig
Schneider K 1957 Primary and secondary symptoms in schizophrenia. Translated 1974 in: Hirsch S R, Shepherd M (eds) Themes and variations in European psychiatry. J Wright, Bristol, ch 2, p 40–44
Schneider K 1959 Clinical psychopathology. Translated Grune & Stratton, New York
Schneider S J 1976 Selective attention in schizophrenia. Journal of Abnormal Psychology 85: 167–173
Schneider S J 1982 Electrodermal activity and therapeutic response to neuroleptic treatment in chronic schizophrenic inpatients. Psychological Medicine 12: 607–613
Schneider S J 1983 Multiple measures of hemisphere dysfunction in schizophrenia and depression. Psychological Medicine 13: 287–297
Schofield W, Balian L 1959 A comparative study of the personal histories of schizophrenic and nonpsychiatric patients. Journal of Abnormal Psychology 59: 216–225
Schulte H 1924 Versuch einer Theorie der paranoischen Eigenbeziehung und Wahnbildung. Psychologische Forschung 5: 1–23
Schultz-Hencke H 1952 Das Problem der Schizophrenie. G Thieme, Stuttgart
Schwab R S, Fabing H D, Prichard J S 1951 Psychiatric symptoms and syndromes in Parkinson's disease. American Journal of Psychiatry 107: 901–907
Schwartz B D, Winstead D K 1982 Visual processing deficits in acute and chronic schizophrenics. Biological Psychiatry 17: 1377–1387
Schwartzman A E, Douglas V I 1962 Intellectual loss in schizophrenia. Canadian Journal of Psychology 16: 1–10
Schwartz Place E J, Gilmore G C 1980 Perceptual organization in schizophrenia. Journal of Abnormal Psychology 89: 409–418
Schweitzer L 1979 Differences of cerebral lateralization among schizophrenic and depressed patients. Biological Psychiatry 14: 721–733
Schweitzer L 1982 Evidence of right cerebral hemisphere dysfunction in schizophrenic patients with left hemisphere overactivation. Biological Psychiatry 17: 655–673
Schweitzer L, Chacko R 1980 Cerebral lateralization: relation to subject's sex. Cortex 16: 559–566
Schweitzer L, Becker E, Welsh H 1978 Abnormalities of cerebral lateralisation in schizophrenic patients. Archives of General Psychiatry 35: 982–985
Searle J R 1969 Speech acts: an essay in the philosophy of language. Cambridge University Press, Cambridge
Searles H F 1965 Collected papers on schizophrenia and related subjects. The Hogarth Press, London
Sechehaye M A 1954 Introduction à une psychotherapie des schizophrènes. Presses Universitaires de France, Paris
Seeman M V 1982 Gender differences in schizophrenia. Canadian Journal of Psychiatry 27: 107–112
Segal H 1950 Some aspects of the analysis of a schizophrenic. International Journal of Psychoanalysis 31: 268–278
Segal H 1964 Introduction to the works of Melanie Klein. Basic Books, New York
Segarra J M 1970 Cerebral vascular disease and behaviour: the syndrome of the mesencephalic artery. Archives of Neurology 22: 408–418
Seitz P F D, Molholm H B 1947 Relation of mental imagery to hallucinations. Archives of Neurology and Psychiatry 57: 469–480
Semmes J, Weinstein S, Ghent L, Teuber H-L 1963 Correlates of impaired orientation in personal and extrapersonal space. Brain 86: 747–772
Senf R, Huston P E, Cohen B D 1956 The use of comic cartoons for the study of social comprehension in schizophrenia. American Journal of Psychiatry 113: 45–51
Sengel R A, Lovallo W R 1980 A random process model of cognitive deficit in schizophrenia. Schizophrenia Bulletin 6: 526–535
Serban G, Gidynski C B 1975 Differentiating criteria for acute-chronic distinction in schizophrenia. Archives of General Psychiatry 32: 705–712
Sérieux P, Capgras J 1909 Forms of insanity due to false reasoning and interpretation. Translated 1986 in: Cutting J C, Shepherd M (eds) Schizophrenia: the origin and development of its study in Europe. Cambridge University Press, Cambridge
Shagass C 1975 E.E.G. and evoked potentials in the psychoses. In: Freedman D X (ed)

Biology of the major psychoses. Association for Research in Nervous and Mental Disease, Vol 54, Raven Press, New York, p 101–128
Shagass C, Roemer R A, Straumanis J J, Amadeo M 1979 Evoked potential evidence of lateralized hemispheric dysfunction in the psychoses. In: Gruzelier J, Flor-Henry P (eds) Hemisphere asymmetries of function in psychopathology. Elsevier, Amsterdam, p 293–316
Shagass C, Josiassen R C, Roemer R A, Straumanis J J, Slepner S M 1983 Failure to replicate evoked potential observations suggesting corpus callosum dysfunction in schizophrenia. British Journal of Psychiatry 142: 471–476
Shakow D 1946 The nature of deterioration in schizophrenic conditions. Nervous and Mental Disease Monographs 70
Shakow D 1950 Some psychological features of schizophrenia. In: Reymert M L (ed) Feelings and emotions. McGraw Hill, New York, ch 31, p 383–390
Shakow D 1963 Psychological deficit in schizophrenia. Behavioral Science 8: 275–305
Shallice T 1972 Dual functions of consciousness. Psychological Review 79: 383–393
Shapiro S A 1981 Contemporary theories of schizophrenia. McGraw Hill, New York
Shattan S P, Dcamp L, Fujii E, Fross G G, Wolff R J 1966 Group treatment of conditionally discharged patients in a mental health clinic. American Journal of Psychiatry 122: 798–805
Sheldrick C, Jablensky A, Sartorius N, Shepherd M 1977 Schizophrenia succeeded by affective illness: catamnestic and statistical enquiry. Psychological Medicine 7: 619–624
Shen W W 1981 Akathisia: an overlooked, distressing, but treatable condition. Journal of Nervous and Mental Diseases 169: 599–600
Sheppard G, Manchanda R, Gruzelier J, Connolly J, Hirsch S R, Frackowiak R et al 1981 Positron emission tomography in acute schizophrenia. Abstracts of the 3rd World Congress of Biological Psychiatry, Stockholm, Vol 2, F 446
Sherwin I 1981 Psychosis associated with epilepsy: significance of the laterality of the epileptogenic lesion. Journal of Neurology, Neurosurgery and Psychiatry 44: 83–85
Shimkunas A M 1972 Conceptual deficit in schizophrenia: a reappraisal. British Journal of Medical Psychology 45: 149–157
Shimkunas A 1978 Hemisphere asymmetry and schizophrenic thought disorder. In: Schwartz S (ed) Language and cognition in schizophrenia. Lawrence Erlbaum, Hillsdale, ch 7, p 193–235
Shipley W C 1940 A self-administering scale for measuring intellectual impairment and deterioration. Journal of Psychology 9: 371–377
Shur E 1982 Season of birth in high and low genetic risk schizophrenics. British Journal of Psychiatry 140: 410–415
Siever L J, Gunderson J G 1983 The search for a schizotypal personality: historical origins and current status. Comprehensive Psychiatry 24: 199–212
Silverberg-Shalev R, Gordon H W, Bentin S, Aranson A 1981 Selective language deterioration in chronic schizophrenia. Journal of Neurology, Neurosurgery and Psychiatry 44: 547–551
Silverman G 1973 Redundancy, repetition and pausing in schizophrenic speech. British Journal of Psychiatry 122: 407–413
Silverman J 1964 The problem of attention in research and theory in schizophrenia. Psychological Review 71: 352–379
Silverstein M L, Harrow M 1980 Auditory misperceptions of word-association stimuli in schizophrenia. Perceptual and Motor Skills 50: 1192–1194
Simon B, Holzberg J D, Alessi S L, Garrity D A 1951 The recognition and acceptance of mood in music by psychotic patients. Journal of Nervous and Mental Diseases 114: 66–78
Simpson L, McKellar P 1955 Types of synaesthesia. Journal of Mental Science 101: 141–147
Sims-Knight J E, Knight R A 1978 Logical and nonlogical classification systems: a look at the underlying complexity of overinclusion in schizophrenics. Journal of Clinical Psychology 34: 857–865
Sims-Knight J E, Petchers-Cassell M 1977 Overinclusion, broad scanning and picture recognition in schizophrenics. Journal of Clinical Psychology 33: 635–642
Singer M T, Wynne L C 1963 Differentiating characteristics of parents of childhood

schizophrenics, childhood neurotics and young adult schizophrenics. American Journal of Psychiatry 120: 234–243
Singer M T, Wynne L C 1966 Principles for scoring communication defects and deviances in parents of schizophrenics: Rorschach and TAT scoring manuals. Psychiatry 29: 260–288
Singh M M, Kay S R 1976 Wheat gluten as a pathogenic factor in schizophrenia. Science 191: 401–402
Slade P D 1972 The effects of systematic densensitisation on auditory hallucinations. Behaviour Research and Therapy 10: 85–91
Slade P D 1976 Towards a theory of auditory hallucinations: outline of an hypothetical four-factor model. British Journal of Social and Clinical Psychology 15: 415–423
Slater E 1953 Psychotic and neurotic illness in twins. MRC Special Publication 278, H M S O, London
Slater E, Beard A W, Glithero E 1963 The schizophrenia-like illnesses of epilepsy. British Journal of Psychiatry 109: 95–150
Small I F, Small J G, Milstein V, Moore J E 1972 Neuropsychological observations with psychosis and somatic treatment. Journal of Nervous and Mental Diseases 155: 6–13
Smith E E 1969 Short-term memory impairment in chronic schizophrenics. Canadian Journal of Psychology 23: 114–126
Smith E E 1970 Associative and editing processes in schizophrenic communication. Journal of Abnormal Psychology 75: 182–186
Snezhnevsky A V 1968 The symptomatology, clinical forms and nosology of schizophrenia. In: Howells J G (ed) Modern perspectives in world psychiatry, vol 2. Oliver & Boyd, Edinburgh, p 425–447
Sollod R, Lapidus L B 1977 Concrete operational thinking, diagnosis and psychopathology in hospitalized schizophrenics. Journal of Abnormal Psychology 86: 199–202
Solvberg H A, Blakar R M 1975 Communication efficiency in couples with and without a schizophrenic offspring. Family Process 14: 515–534
Sommer R 1894 Diagnostik der Geisteskrankheiten. Urban & Schwarzenburg, Wein
Sours J A 1963 Narcolepsy and other disturbances in the sleep-waking rhythm. Journal of Nervous and Mental Diseases 137: 525–542
Southard E E 1916 On descriptive analysis of manifest delusions from the subject's point of view. Journal of Abnormal Psychology 11: 189–202
Space L G, Cromwell R L 1978 Personal constructs among schizophrenic patients. In: Schwartz S (ed) Language and cognition in schizophrenia. Lawrence Erlbaum, Hillsdale, ch 6, p 145–191
Spaulding W, Rosenzweig L, Huntzinger R, Cromwell R L, Briggs D, Hayes T 1980 Visual pattern integration in psychiatric patients. Journal of Abnormal Psychology 89: 635–643
Sperry R W 1976 Mental phenomena as causal determinants in brain function. In: Globus G G, Maxwell G, Savodnik I (eds) Consciousness and the brain. Plenum Press, New York
Spiegel D E, Gerard R M, Grayson H M, Gengerelli J A 1962 Reactions of chronic schizophrenic patients and college students to facial expressions and geometric forms. Journal of Clinical Psychology 18: 396–402
Spiegel E A, Wycis H T, Orchnik C, Freed H 1976 Thalamic chronotaraxis. American Journal of Psychiatry 113: 97–105
Spitzer R L, Endicott J 1978 Schedule for affective disorders and schizophrenia. New York State Psychiatric Institute, New York
Spitzer R L, Endicott J, Robins E 1975 Research diagnostic criteria. New York State Psychiatric Institute, New York
Spohn H E, Thetford P E, Woodham F L 1970 Span of apprehension and arousal in schizophrenia. Journal of Abnormal Psychology 75: 113–123
Spohn H E, Lacoursiere R B, Thompson K, Coyne L 1977 Phenothiazine effects on psychological and psychophysiological dysfunction in chronic schizoprenics. Archives of General Psychiatry 34: 633–644
Spurzheim J G 1817 Observations on the deranged manifestations of the mind or insanity. Baldwin, Cradock & Jay, London
Stabenau J R, Pollin W 1967 Early characteristics of monozygotic twins discordant for schizophrenia. Archives of General Psychiatry 17: 723–734

Starker S, Jolin A 1982 Imagery and hallucinations in schizophrenic patients. Journal of Nervous and Mental Diseases 170: 448–451
Stengel E 1947 A clinical and psychological study of echo-reactions. Journal of Mental Science 93: 598–612
Stengel E 1964 Speech disorders and mental disorders. In: De Reuck A V S, O'Connor M (eds) Disorders of language. CIBA Foundation, J & A Churchill, London, p 285–292
Stengel E, Zeitlyn B B, Rayner E H 1958 Postoperative psychoses. Journal of Mental Science 104: 389–402
Stephens D A, Atkinson M W, Kay D W K, Roth M, Garside R F 1975 Psychiatric morbidity in parents and sibs of schizophrenics and nonschizophrenics. British Journal of Psychiatry 127: 97–108
Stern R S, Cobb J P 1978 Phenomenology of obsessive-compulsive neurosis. British Journal of Psychiatry 132: 233–239
Stevens F M, Lloyd R S, Gerachty S M J, Reynolds M T G, Sarsfield M J, McNicholl B et al 1977 Schizophrenia and coeliac disease—the nature of the relationship. Psychological Medicine 7: 259–263
Stevens J R 1982 Neurology and neuropathology of schizophrenia. In: Henn F A, Nasrallah H A (eds) Schizophrenia as a brain disease. Oxford University Press, New York, ch 7, p 112–147
Stoll W A 1947 Lysergsäure-diäthylamid, ein Phantastikum aus der Mutterkorngruppe. Schweizer Archiv für Neurologie und Psychiatrie 60: 279–323
Stone A A, Eldred S H 1959 Delusion formation during the activation of chronic schizophrenic patients. Archives of General Psychiatry 1: 177–179
Storch A 1924 The primitive archaic forms of inner experiences and thought in schizophrenia. Nervous and Mental Diseases Monographs 36
Storey P B 1970 Brain damage and personality change after subarachnoid haemorrhage. British Journal of Psychiatry 117: 129–142
Störring G E 1939 The nature and significance of perplexity as a symptom in psychiatric illnesses. Translated 1986 in part in: Cutting J C, Shepherd M (eds) Schizophrenia: the origin and development of its study in Europe. Cambridge University Press, Cambridge
Stransky E 1904 How to understand certain symptoms of dementia praecox. Translated 1986 in: Cutting J C, Shepherd M (eds) Schizophrenia: the origin and development of its study in Europe. Cambridge University Press, Cambridge
Straube E 1975 Experimente zur Wahrnehmung Schizophrener. Archiv für Psychiatrie und Nervenkrankheiten 220: 139–158
Straube E R, Germer C K 1979 Dichotic shadowing and selective attention to word meaning in schizophrenia. Journal of Abnormal Psychology 88: 346–353
Straube E, Barth U, König B 1979 Do schizophrenics use linguistic rules in speech recall? British Journal of Social and Clinical Psychology 18: 407–415
Straus E W 1958 Aesthesiology and hallucinations. In: May R, Angel E, Ellenberger H F (eds) Existence. Basic Books, New York, p 139–169
Strauss J S 1969 Hallucinations and delusions as points on continua function. Archives of General Psychiatry 21: 581–586
Strauss J S 1983 The evolution of psychotherapeutic approaches for affective and schizophrenic disorders. In: Zales M R (ed) Affective and schizophrenic disorders. Brunner/Mazel, New York, ch 7, p 163–177
Strauss J S, Carpenter W T 1981 Schizophrenia. Plenum Press, New York
Strauss J S, Gift T E 1977 Choosing an approach for diagnosing schizophrenia. Archives of General Psychiatry 34: 1248–1253
Strauss J S, Harder D W, Chandler M 1979 Egocentrism in children of parents with a history of psychotic disorders. Archives of General Psychiatry 36: 191–200
Strauss J S, Bartko J J, Carpenter W T 1981 New directions in diagnosis: the longitudinal processes of schizophrenia. American Journal of Psychiatry 138: 954–958
Strohner H, Cohen R, Kelter S, Woll G 1978 'Semantic' and 'acoustic' errors of aphasic and schizophrenic patients in a sound-picture matching task. Cortex 14: 391–403
Struve F A, Willner A E 1983 Cognitive dysfunction and tardive dyskinesia. British Journal of Psychiatry 143: 597–600
Stuss D T, Benson D F, Kaplan E F, Weir W S, Malva C D 1981 Leucotomized and

nonleucotomized schizophrenics: comparison on tests of attention. Biological Psychiatry 16: 1085–1100
Suberi M, McKeever W F 1977 Differential right hemispheric memory storage of emotional and nonemotional faces. Neuropsychologia 15: 757–768
Suler J R 1980 Primary process thinking and creativity. Psychological Bulletin 88: 144–165
Sullivan H S 1924 Schizophrenia: its conservative and malignant features. American Journal of Psychiatry 81: 77–91
Sullivan H S 1931 The modified psychoanalytic treatment of schizophrenia. American Journal of Psychiatry 88: 519–540
Sullivan H S 1944 The language of schizophrenia. In: Kasanin J S (ed) Language and thought in schizophrenia. University of California Press, Berkeley, p 4–16
Sullivan H S, Acosta F X, Storms L H 1980 Modification of chronic schizophrenics' abstractions through enriched stimuli and social censure. Journal of Clinical Psychology 36: 852–858
Summers F, Hersh S 1983 Psychiatric chronicity and diagnosis. Schizophrenia Bulletin 9: 122–132
Summers F, Walsh F 1977 The nature of the symbiotic bond between mother and schizophrenic. American Journal of Orthopsychiatry 47: 484–494
Summers F, Walsh F 1979 Symbiosis and confirmation between father and schizophrenic. American Journal of Orthopsychiatry 49: 136–148
Summerskill W H J, Davidson E A, Sherlock S, Steiner R E 1956 The neuropsychiatric syndrome associated with hepatic cirrhosis and an extensive portal collateral circulation. Quarterly Journal of Medicine 25: 245–266
Symonds C 1921 Encephalitis lethargica: a critical review. Quarterly Journal of Medicine 14: 283–308
Szasz T S 1961 The myth of mental illness. Hoeber Harper, New York
Takahashi R, Fuji I, Akiyama A, Kadota K 1981 CT scanning and the investigation of schizophrenia. Abstracts of the 3rd World Congress on Biological Psychiatry, vol 1, Stockholm S 371
Tanaka Y, Hazama, H, Kawahara R, Kobayashi K 1981 Computerized tomography of the brain in schizophrenic patients. Acta Psychiatrica Scandinavica 63: 191–197
Tarrier N, Vaughn C, Lader M H, Leff J P 1979 Bodily reactions to people and events in schizophrenics. Archives of General Psychiatry 36: 311–315
Taylor A M, Warrington E K 1973 Visual discrimination in patients with localised cerebral lesions. Cortex 9: 82–93
Taylor D C 1975 Factors influencing the occurrence of schizophrenia-like psychosis in patients with temporal lobe epilepsy. Psychological Medicine 5: 249–254
Taylor E 1980 Developmental aspects of attention. In: Rutter M (ed) Scientific foundations of developmental psychiatry. Heinemann, London, ch 17, p 185–197
Taylor M A, Abrams R 1975 A critique of the St Louis psychiatric research criteria for schizophrenia. American Journal of Psychiatry 132: 1276–1280
Taylor M A, Greenspan B, Abrams R 1979 Lateralized neuropsychological dysfunction in affective disorder and schizophrenia. American Journal of Psychiatry 136: 1031–1034
Taylor M A, Redfield J, Abrams R 1981 Neuropsychological dysfunction in schizophrenia and affective disease. Biological Psychiatry 16: 467–478
Taylor P, Fleminger J J 1980 E.C.T. for schizophrenia. Lancet i: 1380–1382
Taylor P, Fleminger J J 1981 The lateralization of symptoms in schizophrenia. British Journal of Medical Psychology 54: 59–65
Taylor W L 1953 Cloze procedure: a new tool for measuring readability. Journalism Quarterly 30: 415–433
Terzian H, Ore G D 1955 Syndrome of Klüver and Bucy. Neurology 5: 373–380
Thacore V R, Shukla S R P 1976 Cannabis psychosis and paranoid schizophrenia. Archives of General Psychiatry 33: 383–386
Thomas E L 1968 Abnormal behavior in nonliving systems. Diseases of the Nervous System 29, Supplement 5: 53–67
Thompson C 1982 Anwesenheit: psychopathology and clinical associations. British Journal of Psychiatry 141: 628–630
Thompson M I, Silk K R, Hover G L 1980 Misidentification of a city: delimiting criteria for Capgras syndrome. American Journal of Psychiatry 137: 1270–1272

Tissot R, Burnand Y 1980 Aspects of cognitive activity in schizophrenia. Psychological Medicine 10: 657–663
Todd J, Dewhurst K 1955 The double: its psychopathology and psychophysiology. Journal of Nervous and Mental Diseases 122: 47–55
Todt E H, Howell R J 1980 Vocal cues as indices of schizophrenia. Journal of Speech and Hearing Research 23: 517–526
Tolor A 1981 Torque behavior in schizophrenics, elderly persons and other special groups. Journal of Nervous and Mental Diseases 169: 357–363
Tonks C M 1964 Mental illness in hypothyroid patients. British Journal of Psychiatry 110: 706–710
Toone B K 1981 Psychoses of epilepsy. In: Reynolds E H, Trimble M R (eds) Epilepsy and psychiatry. Churchill Livingstone, Edinburgh, ch 10, p 113–137
Toone B K, Cooke E, Lader M H 1979 The effect of temporal lobe surgery on electrodermal activity. Psychological Medicine 9: 281–285
Toone B K, Cooke E, Lader M H 1981 Electrodermal activity in the affective disorders and schizophrenia. Psychological Medicine 11: 497–508
Toone B K, Garralda M E, Ron M A 1982a The psychoses of epilepsy and the functional psychoses. British Journal of Psychiatry 141: 256–261
Toone B K, Dawson J, Driver M V 1982b Psychoses of epilepsy: a radiological evaluation. British Journal of Psychiatry 140: 244–248
Torrey E F 1980 Neurological abnormalities in schizophrenic patients. Biological Psychiatry 15: 381–388
Torrey E F, Peterson M R 1974 Schizophrenia and the limbic system. Lancet ii: 942–946
Torrey E F, Torrey B B, Burton-Bradley B G 1974 The epidemiology of schizophrenia in Papua New Guinea. American Journal of Psychiatry 131: 567–573
Tow P M 1955 Personality changes following frontal leucotomy. Oxford University Press, London
Trapp C E, James E B 1937 Comparative intelligence ratings on the four types of dementia praexoc. Journal of Nervous and Mental Diseases 86: 399–404
Traupmann K L 1975 Effects of categorization and imagery on recognition and recall by process and reactive schizophrenics. Journal of Abnormal Psychology 84: 307–314
Traupmann K L 1980 Encoding processes and memory for categorically related words by schizophrenic patients. Journal of Abnormal Psychology 89: 704–716
Traupmann K L, Berzofsky M, Kesselman M 1976 Encoding of taxonomic word categories by schizophrenics. Journal of Abnormal Psychology 85: 350–355
Tress K H, Kugler B T, Caudrey D J 1979 Interhemispheric integration in schizophrenia. In: Gruzelier J, Flor-Henry P (eds) Hemisphere asymmetries of function in psychopathology. Elsevier, Amsterdam, p 449–462
Tress K H, Caudrey D J, Mehta B 1983 Tactile-evoked potentials in schizophrenia. British Journal of Psychiatry 143: 156–164
Trevarthen C 1974 Functional relations of disconnected hemispheres with the brain stem and with each other: monkey and man. In: Kinsbourne M, Smith W L (eds) Hemispheric disconnection and cerebral function. Charles C Thomas, Springfield, p 187–207
Trimble M R 1982 The interictal psychoses of epilepsy. In: Benson D F, Blumer D (eds) Psychiatric aspects of neurologic disease, vol 2. Grune & Stratton, New York, ch 4, p 75–88
Truscott I P 1970 Contextual constraint and schizophrenic language. Journal of Consulting and Clinical Psychology 35: 189–194
Tsuang M T 1982 Memory deficit and long-term outcome in schizophrenia: a preliminary study. Psychiatry Research 6: 355–360
Tsuang M T, Woolson R F, Fleming J A 1980 Cause of death in schizophrenia and manic-depression. British Journal of Psychiatry 136: 239–242
Tucker D M, Watson R T, Heilman K M 1977 Discrimination and evocation of affectively intoned speech in patients with right parietal disease. Neurology 27: 947–950
Tucker G J, Campion E W, Silberfarb P M 1975 Sensorimotor functions and cognitive disturbance in psychiatric patients. American Journal of Psychiatry 132: 17–21
Tune L E, Strauss M E, Lew M F, Breitlinger E, Coyle J T 1982 Serum levels of

anticholinergic drugs and impaired recent memory in chronic schizophrenic patients. American Journal of Psychiatry 139: 1460–1462
Turbiner M 1961 Choice discrimination in schizophrenic and normal subjects for positive, negative and neutral affective stimuli. Journal of Consulting Psychology 25: 92
Turner J B 1964 Schizophrenics as judges of vocal expressions of emotional meaning. In: Davitz J R (ed) The communication of emotional meaning. McGraw Hill, New York, ch 10, p 129–142
Tutko T A, Spence J T 1962 The performance of process and reactive schizophrenics and brain-injured subjects on a conceptual task. Journal of Abnormal Psychology 65: 387–394
Twemlow S W, Gabbard G O, Jones F C 1982 The out-of-body experience: a phenomenological typology based on questionnaire response. American Journal of psychiatry 139 450–455
Tyler D B 1955 Psychological changes during experimental sleep deprivation. Diseases of the Nervous System 16: 293–299
Tyrrell D A J, Parry R P, Crow T J, Johnstone E, Ferrier I N 1979 Possible virus in schizophrenia and some neurological disorders. Lancet i: 839–841
Ullman M 1962 Behavioural changes in patients following strokes. Charles C Thomas, USA
Umilta C, Bagnara S, Simion F 1978 Laterality effects for simple and complex geometrical figures and nonsense patterns. Neuropsychologia 16: 43–49
Usdansky G, Chapman L J 1960 Schizophrenia-like responses in normal subjects under time pressure. Journal of Abnormal Psychology 60: 143–146
Vaillant G E 1964a Prospective prediction of schizophrenic remission. Archives of General Psychiatry 11: 509–518
Vaillant G E 1964b An historical review of the remitting schizophrenias. Journal of Nervous and Mental Diseases 138: 48–56
Van den Bosch R J 1982 Attentional correlates of schizophrenia and related disorders. Swets & Zeitlinger, Lisse
Van Krevelen A, Kuipers C 1962 The psychopathology of autistic psychopathy. Acta Paedopsychiatrica 29: 22–31
Van Putten T, May P R A 1978 Akinetic depression in schizophrenia. Archives of General Psychiatry 35: 1101–1107
Vardy M M, Kay S R 1983 LSD psychosis or LSD-induced schizophrenia? Archives of General Psychiatry 40: 877–883
Varsamis J, Adamson J D 1971 Early schizophrenia. Canadian Psychiatric Association Journal 16: 487–497
Vaughn C E, Leff J P 1976 The influence of family and social factors on the course of psychiatric illness. British Journal of Psychiatry 129: 125–137
Venables P H 1964 Input dysfunction in schizophrenia. In: Maher B A (ed) Progress in experimental personality research, vol 1. Academic Press, New York, p 1–47
Venables P H 1977a Input dysfunction in schizophrenia. In: Maher B (ed) Contributions to the psychopathology of schizophrenia. Academic Press, New York, p 1–56
Venables P H 1977b The electrodermal psychophysiology of schizophrenics and children at risk for schizophrenia. Schizophrenia Bulletin 3: 28–48
Vetter H J 1969 Language behavior and psychopathology. Rand McNully, Chicago
Victor M, Hope J M 1958 The phenomenon of auditory hallucinations in chronic alcoholics. Journal of Nervous and Mental Diseases 126: 451–481
Vighetto A, Aimard G, Confaureux C, Devic M 1980 Une observation anatomo-clinique de fabulation (ou délire) topografique. Cortex 16: 501–507
Vignolo L A 1982 Auditory agnosia. In: Broadbent D E, Weiskrantz L (eds) The neuropsychology of cognitive function. Royal Society, London
Virchow R 1847 Standpoints in scientific medicine. Translated 1958 in: Disease, life and man, selected essays by Rudolf Virchow. Stanford University Press, Stanford, p 26–39
Von Angyal L, Frick F 1941 Beiträge zur Anosognosie und zu der Regression des Phantomgliedes. Zeitschrift für die gesamte Neurologie und Psychiatrie 173: 440–447
Von Domarus E 1944 The specific laws of logic in schizophrenia. In: Kasanin J S (ed) Language and thought in schizophrenia. University of California Press, Berkeley, p 104–114
Vygotsky L S 1934 Thought in schizophrenia. Archives of Neurology and Psychiatry 31: 1063–1077

Wagner P S 1946 Psychiatric activities during the Normandy Offensive June 20-August 20 1944. Psychiatry 9: 341–364

Wahl C W 1956 Some antecedent factors in the family histories of 568 male schizophrenics of the United States Navy. American Journal of Psychiatry 113: 201–210

Wahl O F 1976 Monozygotic twins discordant for schizophrenia. Psychological Bulletin 83: 91–106

Wahl O F, Sieg D 1980 Time estimation among schizophrenics. Perceptual and Motor Skills 50: 535–541

Walker E 1981 Attentional and neuromotor functions of schizophrenics, schizoaffectives and patients with other affective disorders. Archives of General Psychiatry 38: 1355–1358

Walker E, Green M 1982 Motor proficiency and attentional task performance by psychotic patients. Journal of Abnormal Psychology 91: 261–268

Walker E, Marwit S J, Emory E 1980 A cross-sectional study of emotion recognition in schizophrenics. Journal of Abnormal Psychology 89: 428–436

Wallace C J, Nelson C J, Liberman R P, Aitchison R A, Lukoff D, Elder J P et al 1980 A review and critique of social skills training with schizophrenic patients. Schizophrenia Bulletin 6: 42–63

Wallach M A, Kogan N 1965 Models of thinking in young children: a study of the creativity-intelligence distinction. Holt, Rinehart & Winston, New York

Wallis G G 1972 Stress as a predictor in schizophrenia. British Journal of Psychiatry 120: 375–384

Walsh F W 1979 Breaching of family generation boundaries by schizophrenics, disturbed nonschizophrenics and normals. International Journal of Family Therapy 1: 254–275

Wansborough S N 1981 The place of work in rehabilitation. In: Wing J K, Morris B (eds) Handbook of psychiatric rehabilitation practice. Oxford University Press, London, ch 8, p 79–94

Wapner W, Hamby S, Gardner H 1981 The role of the right hemisphere in the apprehension of complex linguistic materials. Brain and Language 14: 15–33

Warrington E K, James M 1967 Disorders of visual perception in patients with localised cerebral lesions. Neuropsychologia 5: 253–266

Warrington E K, Taylor A M 1973 The contribution of the right parietal lobe to object recognition. Cortex 9: 152–164

Warrington E K, Weiskrantz L 1982 Amnesia: a disconnection syndrome? Neuropsychologia 20: 233–248

Watson C G 1974 Effects of content verbalness and intangibility on schizophrenics' deficits in abstract thinking. Psychological Reports 34: 1115–1118

Watson C G, Jacobs L 1980 Interrelationships and correlates of four measures of pleasure deficit. Journal of Clinical Psychology 36: 142–147

Watson C G, Plemel D 1981 A test of the interference and normal associate bias theories of schizophrenic cognitive deficit. Journal of Nervous and Mental Diseases 169: 185–190

Watson C G, Wold J 1981 Logical reasoning deficits in schizophrenia and brain damage. Journal of Clinical Psychology 37: 466–471

Watson C G, Wold J, Kucala T 1976 A comparison of abstractive and nonabstractive deficits in schizophrenics and psychiatric controls. Journal of Nervous and Mental Diseases 163: 193–199

Watson C G, Jacobs L, Kucala T 1979 A note on the pathology of anhedonia. Journal of Clinical Psychology 35: 740–743

Watson C G, Wold J, Anderson R, Schulte D, Jacobs L 1981b A test of the Broen-Storms theory of cognitive deficit in schizophrenia. Journal of Clinical Psychology 37: 698–705

Watson G D, Chandarana P C, Merskey H 1981a Relationships between pain and schizophrenia. British Journal of Psychiatry 138: 33–36

Watson J P 1982 Aspects of personal meaning in schizophrenia. In: Shepherd E, Watson J P (eds) Personal meanings. J Wiley, New York, p 175–189

Watt N F 1972 Longitudinal changes in the social behavior of children hospitalized for schizophrenia as adults. Journal of Nervous and Mental Diseases 155: 42–54

Watts F N, Bennett D H 1984 Theory and practice of psychiatric rehabilitation. J Wiley, London

Watts F N, Powell G E, Austin S V 1973 The modification of abnormal beliefs. British Journal of Medical Psychology 46: 359–363

Wechsler A F 1973 The effect of organic brain disease on recall of emotionally charged versus neutral narrative texts. Neurology 23: 130–135
Weckowicz T E 1957 Size constancy in schizophrenic patients. Journal of Mental Science 103: 475–486
Weckowicz T E, Sommer R 1960 Body image and self-concept in schizophrenia. Journal of Mental Science 106: 17–39
Weinberger D R, Wyatt R J 1982 Brain morphology in schizophrenia: in vivo studies. In: Henn F A, Nasrallah H A (eds) Schizophrenia as a brain disease. Oxford University Press, New York, ch 8, p 148–175
Weinberger D R, Torrey E F, Neophytides A N, Wyatt R J 1979a Lateral cerebral ventricular enlargement in chronic schizophrenia. Archives of General Psychiatry 36: 735–739
Weinberger D R, Torrey E F, Neophytides A N, Wyatt R J 1979b Structural abnormalities in the cerebral cortex of chronic schizophrenic patients. Archives of General Psychiatry 36: 935–939
Weinberger D R, Bigelow L B, Kleinman J E, Klein S T, Rosenblatt J E, Wyatt R J 1980a Cerebral ventricular enlargement in chronic schizophrenia. An association with poor response to treatment. Archives of General Psychiatry 37: 11–13
Weinberger D R, Cannon-Spoor E, Potkin S G, Wyatt R J 1980b Poor premorbid adjustment and C.T. scan abnormalities in chronic schizophrenia. American Journal of Psychiatry 137: 1410–1413
Weinberger D R, Delisi L E, Neophytides A N, Wyatt R J 1981 Familial aspects of C.T. scan abnormalities in chronic schizophrenic patients. Psychiatry Research 4: 65–71
Weiner I B 1966 Psychodiagnostics in schizophrenia. J Wiley, New York
Weinstein E A, Kahn R L 1952 Nonaphasic misnaming in organic brain disease. Archives of Neurology and Psychiatry 67: 72–79
Weintraub S, Mesulam M-M 1983 Developmental learning disabilities of the right hemisphere: emotional, interpersonal and cognitive components. Archives of Neurology 40: 463–468
Weintraub S, Mesulam M-M, Kramer L 1981 Disturbances in prosody: a right hemisphere contribution to language. Archives of Neurology 38: 742–744
Weller M, Kugler B 1979 Tactile discrimination in schizophrenic and affective psychoses. In: Gruzelier J, Flor-Henry P (eds) Hemisphere asymmetries of function in psychopathology Elsevier, Amsterdam, p 463–474
Weller M, Montagu J D 1979 Electroencephalographic coherence in schizophrenia. In: Gruzelier J, Flor-Henry P (eds) Hemisphere asymmetries of function in psychopathology. Elsevier, Amsterdam, p 285–292
Wender P H, Rosenthal D, Kety S S, Schulsinger F, Welner J 1974 Crossfostering. Archives of General Psychiatry 30: 121–128
Werner H, Kaplan B 1963 Symbol formation. J Wiley, New York
Wernicke C 1900 Grundriss der Psychiatrie. G Thieme, Leipzig
Wetzel A 1922 Das Weltuntergangserlebnis in der Schizophrenie. Zeitschrift für die gesamte Neurologie und Psychiatrie 78: 403–428
Wexler B E, Heninger G R 1979 Alterations in cerebral laterality during acute psychotic illness. Archives of General Psychiatry 36: 278–284
Wexler M 1951 The structural problem in schizophrenia: therapeutic implications. International Journal of Psychoanalysis 32: 157–166
Wexler M 1971 Schizophrenia: conflict and deficiency. Psychoanalytic Quarterly 40: 83–99
Weygandt W 1907 Critical remarks on the psychology of dementia praecox. Translated 1986 in: Cutting J C, Shepherd M (eds) Schizophrenia: the origin and development of its study in Europe. Cambridge University Press, Cambridge
Whitaker L C 1973 The Whitaker index of schizophrenic thinking. Western Psychological Services, Los Angeles
Whitehorn J C, Zipf G K 1943 Schizophrenic language. Archives of Neurology and Psychiatry 49: 831–851
Whiteman M 1954 The performance of schizophrenics on social concepts. Journal of Abnormal Psychology 49: 266–271
Whitman J R 1969 Impairment in serial learning of visually presented spatial patterns. Perceptual and Motor Skills 28: 443–449

Whitwell J R 1936 Historical notes on psychiatry. H K Lewis, London
Wieck H H 1979 Psychological explanations of function psychoses. In: Fukuda T, Mitsuda H (eds) World issues in the problems of schizophrenic psychoses. Igaku-Shoin, Tokyo
Wild C M, Shapiro L N, Goldenberg L 1975 Transactional communication disturbances in families of male schizophrenics. Family Process 14: 131–160
Wild C M, Shapiro L N, Abelin T 1977 Communication patterns and role structure in families of male schizophrenics. Archives of General Psychiatry 34: 58–70
Williams D 1968 Man's temporal lobe. Brain 91: 639–654
Williams E, Quirke C 1972 Psychological construing in schizophrenics. British Journal of Medical Psychology 45: 79–84
Williams H L, Morris G O, Lubin A 1962 Illusions, hallucinations and sleep loss. In: West L J (ed) Hallucinations. Grune & Stratton, New York
Williams R M, Hemsley D R, Denning-Duke C 1976 Language behaviour in acute and chronic schizophrenia. British Journal of Social and Clinical Psychology 15: 73–83
Wilson G, Rupp C, Wilson W W 1950 Amnesia. American Journal of Psychiatry 106: 481–485
Wilson L G 1976 Viral encephalopathy mimicking functional psychosis. American Journal of Psychiatry 133: 165–170
Wilson R S, Kasniak A W, Klawans H L, Garron D C 1980 High speed memory scanning in Parkinsonism. Cortex 16: 67–72
Wing J K 1961 A simple and reliable subclassification of chronic schizophrenia. Journal of Mental Science 107: 862–875
Wing J K 1978 The social context of schizophrenia. American Journal of Psychiatry 135: 1333–1339
Wing J K 1982 Course and prognosis of schizophrenia. In: Wing J K, Wing L (eds) Handbook of psychiatry, vol 3. Cambridge University Press, Cambridge, ch 7, p 33–41
Wing J K, Brown D W 1970 Institutionalism and schizophrenia. Cambridge University Press, Cambridge
Wing J K, Morris B 1981 Clinical basis of rehabilitation. In: Wing J K, Morris B (eds) Handbook of psychiatric rehabilitation practice. Oxford University Press, Oxford, ch 1, p 3–16
Wing J K, Birley J L T, Cooper J E, Graham P, Isaacs A D 1967 Reliability of a procedure for measuring and classifying Present Psychiatric State. British Journal of Psychiatry 113: 499–515
Wing J K, Cooper J E, Sartorius N 1974 Measurement and classification of psychiatric symptoms. Cambridge University Press, Cambridge.
Wing L 1981 Asperger's syndrome. Psychological Medicine 11: 115–130
Winner E, Gardner H 1977 The comprehension of metaphor in brain-damaged patients. Brain 100: 717–729
Winokur G 1977 Delusional disorder (paranoia). Comprehensive Psychiatry 18: 511–521
Winokur G, Morrison J, Clancy J, Crowe R 1974 Iowa 500: the clinical and genetic distinction of hebephrenic and paranoid schizophrenia. Journal of Nervous and Mental Diseases 159: 12–19
Wittgenstein L 1980 Remarks on the philosophy of psychology. Blackwell, Oxford
Wittgenstein L 1982 Last writings on the philosophy of psychology. Blackwell, Oxford
Woerner M G, Pollack M, Klein D F 1973 Pregnancy and birth complications in psychiatirc patients: a comparison of schizophrenic and personality disorder patients with their siblings. Acta Psychiatrica Scandinavica 49: 712–721
Wohlberg G W, Kornetsky C 1973 Sustained attention in remitted schizophrenics. Archives of General Psychiatry 28: 533–537
Wolf A, Cowen D 1952 Histopathology of schizophrenia and other psychoses of unknown origin. In: The biology of mental health and disease. Milbank Memorial Fund, P B Hoebner, New York, ch 28, p 469–485
Wolff H G, Curran D 1935 Nature of delirium and allied states. Archives of Neurology and Psychiatry 33: 1175–1215
Wolff S, Chick J 1980 Schizoid personality in childhood: a controlled follow-up study. Psychological Medicine 10: 85–100
Wolpe J 1969 The practice of behavior therapy. Pergamon, New York

Woolley D W, Shaw E N 1957 Evidence for the participation of serotonin in mental processes. Annals of the New York Academy of Sciences 66: 649–667
World Health Organisation 1973 Report of the International Pilot Study of Schizophrenia. vol 1. WHO, Geneva
World Health Organisation 1977 ICD Ninth Revision, vol 1. WHO, Geneva
World Health Organisation 1979 Schizophrenia: an international follow-up study. J Wiley, Chichester
Wundt W 1911 Grundriss der Psychologie, 10th edn. Wilhelm Engelmann, Leipzig
Wyatt R J, Potkin S G, Bridge T P, Phelps B H, Wise C D 1980 Monoamine oxidase in schizophrenia: an overview. Schizophrenia Bulletin 6: 199–207
Wyke M 1971 The effects of brain lesions on the learning of a bimanual co-ordination task. Cortex 7: 59–72
Wykes T 1980 Language and schizophrenia. Psychological Medicine 10: 403–406
Wynne L C 1968 Methodologic and conceptual issues in the study of schizophrenics and their families. In: Rosenthal D, Kety S S (eds) The transmission of schizophrenia. Pergamon, Oxford, p 185–200
Wynne L C, Singer M T 1963 Thought disorder and family relations of schizophrenics. Archives of General Psychiatry 9: 191–206
Wynne L C, Ryckoff I M, Day J, Hirsch S 1958 Pseudomutuality in the family relations of schizophrenics. Psychiatry 21: 205–220
Wyrsch J 1956 La personne du schizophrene. Presses Universitaires de France, Paris
Yarden P E, Raps C S 1981 Identity alterations and prognosis in schizophrenia. British Journal of Psychiatry 138: 495–497
Yates A J 1966 Psychological deficit. Annual Review of Psychology 17: 111–144
Yin R K 1970 Face recognition by brain-injured patients: a dissociable entity. Neuropsychologia 8: 395–402
Yu H K, Johnson J H 1979 Imagery in the associative learning of schizophrenics. Journal of Clinical Psychology 35: 265–269
Zahn T P 1980 Predicting outcome from measures of attention and autonomic functioning. In: Baxter C, Melnechuk T (eds) Perspectives in schizophrenia research. Raven Press, New York, p 81–104
Zaidel D, Sperry R W 1974 Memory impairment after commissurotomy. Brain 97: 263–272
Zaidel D W, Rausch R 1981 Effects of semantic organization on the recognition of pictures following temporal lobectomy. Neuropsychologia 19: 813–817
Zaidel E 1978 Lexical organization in the right hemisphere. In: Buser P A, Rougeul-Buser A (eds) Cerebral correlates of conscious experience. Elsevier, Amsterdam
Zaslow R W 1950 A new approach to the problem of conceptual thinking in schizophrenia. Journal of Consulting Psychology 14: 335–339
Zigler E, Levine J 1981 Age on first hospitalisation of schizophrenics: a developmental approach. Journal of Abnormal Psychology 90: 458–467
Zigler E, Levine J 1983 Hallucinations vs delusions: a developmental approach. Journal of Nervous and Mental Diseases 171: 141–146
Zilboorg G 1941 A history of medical psychology. W W Norton, New York
Zimbardo P G, Andersen S M, Kabat L G 1981 Induced hearing deficit generates experimental paranoia. Science 212: 1529–1531
Ziskind E, Somerfield E, Jens R 1971 Can schizophrenia change to affective psychosis? American Journal of Psychiatry 128: 331–335
Zubin J 1975 Problem of attention in schizophrenia. In: Kietzman M L, Sutton S, Zubin J (eds) Experimental approaches to psychopathology. Academic Press, New York
Zubin J, Magaziner J, Steinhauer S R 1983 The metamorphosis of schizophrenia: from chronicity to vulnerability. Psychological Medicine 13: 511–571
Zucker D K, Livingston R L, Nakra R, Clayton P J 1981 B12 deficiency and psychiatric disorders: case report and literature review. Biological Psychiatry 16: 197–205
Zutt J 1929 Die innere Haltung: eine psychologische Untersuchung und ihre Bedeutung für die Psychopathologie insbessondere im Bereich schizophrener Erkrankungen. Monatsschrift für Psychiatrie und Neurologie 73: 330–383

Author Index

Subject Index